OPERATING
SYSTEM
CONCEPTS
with
JAVA

OPERATING SYSTEM CONCEPTS

with
JAVA

SIXTH EDITION

ABRAHAM SILBERSCHATZ
Yale University

PETER BAER GALVIN
Corporate Technologies, Inc.

GREG GAGNE
Westminster College

WILEY

JOHN WILEY & SONS, INC.

ACQUISITIONS EDITOR	Paul Crockett
MARKETING MANAGER	Ilse Wolfe
SENIOR PRODUCTION EDITOR	Ken Santor
COVER DESIGNER	Madelyn Lesure
COVER ART	Susan E. Cyr

This book was set in Palatino by Abraham Silberschatz and printed and bound by Courier-Westford. The cover was printed by Phoenix Color Corporation.

This book is printed on acid-free paper.

ISBN 0-471-48905-0

Printed in the United States of America

10 9 8 7 6 5 4 3 2 1

In memory of my parents, Wira and Joseph,
   and my grandparents, Stepha and Aaron Rosenblum

   Avi Silberschatz

To my wife, Carla,
   and my children, Gwendolyn, Owen, and Madelyn

   Peter Baer Galvin

To my parents, Marlene and Roland,
   my wife, Pat, and my sons, Tom and Jay

   Greg Gagne

PREFACE

Operating systems are an essential part of any computer system. Similarly, a course on operating systems is an essential part of any computer-science education. This field is undergoing change at a rapid rate, as computers are now prevalent in virtually every application, from games for children through the most sophisticated planning tools for governments and multinational firms. Yet the fundamental concepts remain fairly clear, and it is on these that we base this book.

We wrote this book as a text for an introductory course in operating systems at the junior or senior undergraduate level or at the first-year graduate level. We hope that practitioners will also find it to be of use. It provides a clear description of the *concepts* that underlie operating systems. As prerequisites, we assume that the reader is familiar with basic data structures, computer organization, and a high-level language, such as C. The hardware topics required for an understanding of operating systems are included in Chapter 2. For code examples, we use predominantly Java, with some C, but the reader can still understand the algorithms without a thorough knowledge of these languages.

Concepts are presented using intuitive descriptions. Important theoretical results are covered, but formal proofs are omitted. The bibliographical notes contain pointers to research papers in which results were first presented and proved, as well as references to material for further reading. In place of proofs, figures and examples are used to suggest why we should expect the result in question to be true.

The fundamental concepts and algorithms covered in the book are often based on those used in existing commercial operating systems. Our aim is to present these concepts and algorithms in a general setting that is not tied to one particular operating system. We present a large number of examples that pertain to the most popular operating systems, including Sun Microsystems' Solaris; Linux; Mach; Microsoft MS-DOS, Windows NT, Windows 2000 and Windows XP; DEC VMS and TOPS-20; IBM OS/2; and the Apple Macintosh and Mac OS X operating systems.

In this text, when we refer to Windows XP as an example operating system, we are implying both Windows XP and Windows 2000. If a feature exists in Windows XP that is not available in Windows 2000, we will state this explicitly. If a feature exists in Windows 2000 but not in Windows XP, then we will refer to that system as Windows 2000.

Content of this Book

The text is organized in seven major parts:

- **Overview:** Chapters 1 through 3 explain what operating systems *are,* what they *do,* and how they are *designed* and *constructed.* They explain how the concept of an operating system has developed, what the common features of an operating system are, what an operating system does for the user, and what it does for the computer-system operator. The presentation is motivational, historical, and explanatory in nature. We have avoided a discussion of how things are done internally in these chapters. Therefore, they are suitable for individuals or for students in lower-level classes who want to learn what an operating system is, without getting into the details of the internal algorithms. Chapter 2 covers the hardware topics that are important to an understanding of operating systems. Readers well versed in hardware topics, including I/O, DMA, and hard-disk operation, may choose to skim or skip this chapter.

- **Process management:** Chapters 4 through 8 describe the process concept and concurrency as the heart of modern operating systems. A *process* is the unit of work in a system. Such a system consists of a collection of *concurrently* executing processes, some of which are operating-system processes (those that execute system code), and the rest of which are user processes (those that execute user code). These chapters cover methods for process scheduling, interprocess communication, process synchronization, and deadlock handling. Also included under this topic is a discussion of threads.

- **Storage management:** Chapters 9 through 12 deal with a process in main memory during execution. To improve both the utilization of the CPU and the speed of its response to its users, the computer must keep several processes in memory. There are many different memory-management schemes reflecting various approaches to memory management, and the effectiveness of the different algorithms depends on the situation. Since main memory is usually too small to accommodate all data and programs, and since it cannot store data permanently, the computer system must provide secondary storage to back up main memory. Most modern computer systems use disks as the primary on-line storage medium for information, both programs and data. The file system provides the mechanism for on-line storage of and access to both data and programs residing on the disks. These chapters describe the classic internal algorithms and structures of storage management. They provide a firm practical understanding of the algorithms used—the properties, advantages, and disadvantages.

- **I/O systems:** Chapters 13 and 14 describe the devices that attach to a computer and the multiple dimensions on which they vary. Because these devices differ so widely, the operating system needs to provide a wide range of functionality to applications to allow them to control all aspects of the devices. This section discusses system I/O in depth, including I/O system design, interfaces, and internal system structures and functions. In many ways, I/O devices are also the slowest major components of the computer. Because they are a performance bottleneck, performance issues are examined. Matters related to secondary and tertiary storage are explained as well.

- **Distributed systems:** Chapters 15 through 17 deal with a collection of processors that do not share memory or a clock—a *distributed system*. By providing the user with access to the various resources that it maintains, a distributed system can improve computation speed and data availability and reliability. Such a system also provides the user with a distributed file system, which is a file-service system whose users, servers, and storage devices are dispersed among the sites of a distributed system. A distributed system must provide various mechanisms for process synchronization and communication and for dealing with the deadlock problem and the variety of failures that are not encountered in a centralized system.

- **Protection and security:** Chapters 18 and 19 discuss the processes in an operating system that must be protected from one another's activities. For the purposes of protection and security, we use mechanisms that ensure that only processes that have gained proper authorization from the operating system can operate on the files, memory segments, CPU, and other resources. Protection is a mechanism for controlling the access of programs, processes, or users to the resources defined by a computer system. This mechanism must provide a means of specifying the controls to be imposed, as well as a means of enforcement. Security protects the information stored in the system (both data and code), as well as the physical resources of the computer system, from unauthorized access, malicious destruction or alteration, and accidental introduction of inconsistency.

- **Case studies:** Chapters 20 through 22 in the book, and Appendices A through C on the website, integrate the concepts described in this book by describing real operating systems. These systems include Linux, Windows XP, Windows 2000, FreeBSD, and Mach. We chose Linux and FreeBSD because UNIX—at one time—was almost small enough to understand yet was not a "toy" operating system. Most of its internal algorithms were selected for *simplicity,* rather than for speed or sophistication. Both Linux and FreeBSD are readily available to computer-science departments, so many students have access to these systems. We chose Windows XP and Windows 2000 because they provide an opportunity for us to study a modern operating system with a design and implementation drastically different from those of UNIX. Chapter 22 briefly describes a few other influential operating systems.

The Sixth Edition with Java

This text blends the material from the Sixth Edition of *Operating System Concepts* (OSC) and the First Edition of *Applied Operating System Concepts* (AOSC). Much of the material in the text was derived from OSC, which presents concepts fundamental to all operating systems, rather than particular implementations of systems. The text illustrates specific algorithms using Java and provides detailed descriptions of the Java code. Thus, it can be considered a more applied text than OSC.

In addition, the treatment of Java in this text updates the coverage in AOSC. Almost all Java code has been revised to use a more object-oriented approach, including interfaces. Java is used extensively to illustrate threads, interprocess communication, thread scheduling and synchronization, and deadlock. There are several new Java programs illustrating TCP and UDP socket programming, remote method invocation (RMI), memory-mapped I/O, and file locking. Several extra Java code examples are found in on-line Appendix A, Distributed Communication, which is based on the chapter of the same name from AOSC. Finally, the Java Primer, available on-line as Appendix E, should be of aid to students not yet familiar with the details of the language.

As we wrote this Java version of OSC, we were guided by the many comments and suggestions we received from readers of our previous editions, as well as by our own observations about the rapidly changing fields of operating systems and networking. We rewrote the material in most of the chapters by bringing older material up to date and removing material that was no longer of interest.

The following list describes the specific differences between AOSC and this new text.

- **Chapter 1, Introduction,** offers new coverage of multiprocessor and distributed systems, including clusters and hand-held systems. Also new are the discussions of client–server and peer-to-peer computing and of computing environments, including traditional, web-based, and embedded computing.

- **Chapter 2, Computer-System Structures,** now covers network structures, including local-area networks (small LANs), wide-area networks (small WANs), and wireless LANs.

- **Chapter 3, Operating-System Structures,** features updated coverage of system structures, including microkernels and loadable modules, as well as updated coverage of virtual machines and the Java virtual machine (JVM).

- **Chapter 4, Processes,** now discusses communication in client–server systems, including sockets, remote procedure calls (RPCs), and Java's remote method invocation (RMI). It also has updated coverage of message passing in Windows XP.

- **Chapter 5, Threads,** offers new material on Pthreads; threading issues, including cancellation, thread pools, thread-specific data and scheduler activations, and threading in Windows XP and Linux. In addition, new Java programs illustrate thread cancellation and thread-specific data.

- **Chapter 6, CPU Scheduling,** has new coverage of the scheduling API in Pthreads and scheduling in Solaris, Windows XP, and Linux.

- **Chapter 7, Process Synchronization,** now covers atomic transactions and describes synchronization in Windows XP, Linux, and Pthreads.

- **Chapter 8, Deadlocks,** has expanded coverage of deadlock avoidance, including the banker's algorithm.

- **Chapter 9, Memory Management,** has updated coverage of paging, including hierarchical and hashed page tables. Also updated is coverage of segmentation on Pentium systems.

- **Chapter 10, Virtual Memory,** features new material motivating the use of virtual memory, including copy-on-write, shared memory, and shared libraries. It also has new coverage of memory-mapped files and updated coverage of memory management in Windows XP and Solaris.

- **Chapters 11 and 12, File-System Interface** and **File-System Implementation,** are based on the previous Chapter 11. Coverage of most topics is expanded, and coverage of NFS has been brought forward from the Distributed File System chapter (Chapter 16).

- **Chapter 13, I/O,** has a new STREAMS section.

- **Chapter 14, Mass Storage Structure,** is based on the previous Chapter 13 but includes new discussions of RAID and disk attachment.

- **Chapter 15, Distributed System Structures,** is the previous Chapter 14, with an expanded discussion of topology.

- **Chapter 16, Distributed File Systems,** is the previous Chapter 17, with the NFS example replaced by AFS. NFS is now covered in Chapter 12.

- **Chapter 17, Distributed Coordination,** is the previous Chapter 16, with added sections on atomicity and concurrency control.

- **Chapter 18, Security,** has new coverage of Java security.

- **Chapter 19, Security,** features a new section on securing systems and facilities.

- **Case Studies** have been reorganized.   Older operating systems have been moved to on-line appendices, and the discussion of the Nachos system has been removed from the appendices.   For more information on Nachos, please refer to the project web site at http://www.cs.washington.edu/homes/tom/nachos.

- **Java Primer** is now an on-line appendix.

Java

This book uses Java to illustrate many operating-system concepts, such as multitasking, CPU scheduling, process synchronization, deadlock, security, and distributed systems. Java is more a technology than a programming language, so it is an excellent vehicle for demonstrations.

Java was originally developed as a language to program microprocessors in consumer devices such as cellular telephones and set-top boxes. The advent of the Web in the mid-1990s showed the Java team at Sun Microsystems the language's potential usefulness across the Internet: Programmers can use Java to write applications and *applets*—programs that run on web pages. Java also provides support for development of database applications, graphical user interfaces (GUIs), reusable objects, and two-dimensional and three-dimensional modeling, to name a few. All such programs can run on a single computer or on a distributed system across the Internet.

We provide an overview of Java technology in Chapter 3 and illustrate the creation and coordination of multithreaded Java programs in Chapters 5 and 7. In Chapter 4, we use Java to demonstrate how different processes can communicate using shared memory and message passing. In Chapter 6, we use Java to demonstrate CPU-scheduling algorithms; in Chapter 8, we illustrate deadlock and deadlock-recovery methods using Java. Chapters 10 and 11 use Java to demonstrate memory-mapped I/O and file locking, respectively. Java programs are used in Chapter 4 to illustrate distributed systems issues, such as remote-method invocation (RMI) and TCP sockets. In the on-line appendix Distributed Communication, we show additional distributed systems features, such as UDP sockets and scalable servers using nonblocking I/O. To a lesser extent, we also use Java to illustrate a virtual machine, as well as memory management and computer security.

Much of the Java-related material in this text has been developed and class-tested in undergraduate operating-systems classes. From our experience, students entering these classes lacking knowledge of Java—but with experience using C++ and basic object-oriented principles—generally have little trouble with Java. Rather, most difficulties lie in understanding such concepts as multithreading and data sharing by multiple, concurrently running threads. These concepts are systematic rather than being specific to Java; even students with a sound knowledge of Java are likely to have difficulty with them. We thus emphasize concurrency and passing of object references to several threads rather than concentrating on syntax.

Java is an especially fast-moving technology; however, we use Java examples that are core to the language and are unlikely to change in the near future. All the Java programs in this text compile with the Java Development Kit (JDK), Release 1.4. Although you do not need a thorough knowledge of Java to understand the examples in the text, if you do not know Java, you should read the Java Primer, which you can find on the web page for this book, described below.

Organization of This Book

The organization of this text reflects our many years of teaching about operating systems. Consideration was also given to the feedback provided by the reviewers of the text, as well as comments submitted by readers of earlier editions. In addition, the content of the text corresponds to the suggestions from *Computing Curricula 2001* for teaching operating systems, published by the Joint Task Force of the IEEE Computing Society and the Association for Computing Machinery (ACM).

On the supporting web page for this text, we provide several sample syllabi that suggest various approaches for using the text in both introductory and advanced operating systems courses. As a general rule, we encourage readers to progress sequentially through the chapters, as this strategy provides the most thorough study of operating systems. However, by using the sample syllabi, a reader can select a different ordering of chapters (or subsections of chapters).

Teaching Supplements and Web Page

The web page for the book contains such material as a set of slides to accompany the book, model course syllabi, Java source code, and up-to-date errata. The web page also contains the book's three case study appendices, the Java Primer appendix, and the Distributed Communication appendix (Chapter 15 from AOSC. The URL is:

> http://www.os-book.com

To obtain restricted supplements, contact your local John Wiley & Sons sales representative. You can find your representative at the "Find a Rep?" web page: http://www.jsw-edcv.wiley.com/college/findarep.

Mailing List

We have switched to the mailman system for communication among the users of *Operating System Concepts*. If you wish to use this facility, please visit the following URL and follow the instructions there to subscribe:

> http://mailman.cs.yale.edu/mailman/listinfo/os-book-list

The mailman mailing list system provides many benefits, such as an archive of postings, and several subscription options, including digest and Web only. To send messages to the list, send e-mail to:

> os-book-list@cs.yale.edu

Depending on the message, we will either reply to you personally or forward the message to everyone on the mailing list. The list is moderated, so you will receive no inappropriate mail.

Students who are using this book as a text for class should not use the list to ask for answers to the exercises. They will not be provided.

Suggestions

We have attempted to clean up every error in this new edition, but—as happens with operating systems—a few obscure bugs may remain. We would appreciate hearing from you about any textual errors or omissions that you identify.

If you would like to suggest improvements or to contribute exercises, we would also be glad to hear from you. Please send correspondence to os-book@cs.yale.edu.

Acknowledgments

This book is derived from the previous editions, the first three of which were coauthored by James Peterson. Others who helped us with previous editions include Hamid Arabnia, Rida Bazzi, Randy Bentson, David Black, Joseph Boykin, Jeff Brumfield, Gael Buckley, Roy Campbell, P. C. Capon, John Carpenter, Gil Carrick, Thomas Casavant, Ajoy Kumar Datta, Joe Deck, Sudarshan K. Dhall, Thomas Doeppner, Caleb Drake, M. Raşit Eskicioğlu, Hans Flack, Robert Fowler, G. Scott Graham, Richard Guy, Max Hailperin, Rebecca Hartman, Wayne Hathaway, Christopher Haynes, Mark Holliday, Ahmed Kamel, Richard Kieburtz, Carol Kroll, Morty Kwestel, Thomas LeBlanc, John Leggett, Jerrold Leichter, Ted Leung, Gary Lippman, Carolyn Miller, Michael Molloy, Yoichi Muraoka, Jim M. Ng, Banu Özden, Ed Posnak, Boris Putanec, Charles Qualline, John Quarterman, Gustavo Rodriguez-Rivera, Carolyn J. C. Schauble, Thomas P. Skinner, Yannis Smaragdakis, Jesse St. Laurent, John Stankovic, Adam Stauffer, Steven Stepanek, Hal Stern, Louis Stevens, Pete Thomas, David Umbaugh, Steve Vinoski, Tommy Wagner, Larry L. Wear, John Werth, James M. Westall, J. S. Weston, and Yang Xiang

We thank the following people who contributed to this edition of the book: Bruce Hillyer reviewed and helped with the rewrite of Chapters 2, 12, 13, and 14. Mike Reiter reviewed and helped with the rewrite of Chapter 18. Parts of Chapter 14 were derived from a paper by Hillyer and Silberschatz [1996]. Parts of Chapter 17 were derived from a paper by Levy and Silberschatz [1990]. Chapter 20 was derived from an unpublished manuscript by Stephen Tweedie. Chapter 21 was derived from an unpublished manuscript by Dave Probert, Cliff Martin, and Avi Silberschatz. Appendix C was derived from an unpublished manuscript by Cliff Martin. Cliff Martin also helped with updating the UNIX appendix to cover FreeBSD. Mike Shapiro reviewed the Solaris information, and Jim Mauro answered several Solaris-related questions.

We thank the following people who reviewed this version of the book: Djamel Bouchaffra, Tom Boyd, Daren Che, Robert Chun, John Collins, Douglas Jones, Ben Miller, Paul Lu, Gustavo Rodriguez-Rivera, Carolyn Schauble, Charles Shub, Dan Stanzione, Paul Stelling

Our Acquisitions Editor, Paul Crockett, provided expert guidance as we prepared this edition. Paul was assisted by Simon Durkin, who managed many details of this project smoothly. The Senior Production Editor was Ken Santor. The cover illustrator was Susan Cyr, and the cover designer was Madelyn Lesure. Barbara Heaney was in charge of overseeing the copy editing, and Beverly Peavler copy-edited the manuscript. The freelance proofreader was Katrina Avery; the freelance indexer was Rosemary Simpson. The Senior Illustration Coordinator was Anna Melhorn. Marilyn Turnamian helped generate figures and presentation slides.

Finally, we would like to add some personal notes. Avi is starting a new chapter in his life, returning to academia and partnering with Valerie. This combination has given him the peace of mind to focus on the writing of this text. Pete would like to acknowledge the birth of Madelyn, his third child, during this project. Greg would like to acknowledge two friends—Bob Frey and Peter Ormsby—for their interest and encouragement in this and other writing projects.

Abraham Silberschatz, New Haven, CT, 2004
Peter Baer Galvin, Burlington, MA, 2004
Greg Gagne, Salt Lake City, UT, 2004

CONTENTS

PART ONE ■ OVERVIEW

Chapter 1   Introduction

Chapter 2   Computer-System Structures

Chapter 3   Operating-System Structures

PART TWO   ■   PROCESS MANAGEMENT

Chapter 4   Processes

Chapter 5   Threads

Chapter 6   CPU Scheduling

Chapter 7   Process Synchronization

Chapter 8   Deadlocks

PART THREE   ■   STORAGE MANAGEMENT

Chapter 9   Memory Management

Chapter 10   Virtual Memory

Chapter 11   File-System Interface

Chapter 12   File-System Implementation

PART FOUR   ■   I/O SYSTEMS

Chapter 13   I/O Systems

Chapter 14   Mass-Storage Structure

PART FIVE ■ DISTRIBUTED SYSTEMS

PART SIX ■ PROTECTION AND SECURITY

Chapter 19   Security

PART SEVEN ■ CASE STUDIES

Chapter 20   The Linux System

Chapter 21   Windows XP

Chapter 22   Influential Operating Systems

Appendix A   The FreeBSD System (contents online)

Appendix B   The Mach System (contents online)

Appendix C   Windows 2000 (contents online)

Appendix D   Distributed Communication (contents online)

Appendix E   Java Primer (contents online)

Part One

OVERVIEW

An *operating system* is a program that acts as an intermediary between the user of a computer and the computer hardware. The purpose of an operating system is to provide an environment in which a user can execute programs in a *convenient* and *efficient* manner.

Understanding the evolution of operating systems gives us an appreciation for what an operating system does and how it does it. We trace the development of operating systems from the first hands-on systems, through multiprogrammed and time-shared systems, to current handheld and real-time systems.

The operating system must ensure the correct operation of the computer system. The hardware must provide appropriate mechanisms to prevent user programs from interfering with the proper operation of the system. We describe the basic computer architecture that makes it possible to write a correct operating system.

The operating system provides certain services to programs and to the users of those programs in order to make their tasks easier. The services differ from one operating system to another, but we identify and explore some common classes of these services.

Chapter 1

INTRODUCTION

An **operating system** is a program that manages the computer hardware. It also provides a basis for application programs and acts as an intermediary between the computer user and the computer hardware. An amazing aspect of operating systems is how varied they are in accomplishing these tasks. Mainframe operating systems are designed primarily to optimize utilization of hardware. Personal computer (PC) operating systems support complex games, business applications, and everything in between. Operating systems for handheld computers are designed to provide an environment in which a user can easily interface with the computer to execute programs. Thus, some operating systems are designed to be *convenient,* others to be *efficient,* and others some combination of the two.

To truly understand what operating systems are, we must first understand how they have developed. In this chapter, after offering a general description of what operating systems do, we trace the development of operating systems from the first hands-on systems through multiprogrammed and time-shared systems to PCs and handheld computers. We also discuss operating system variations, such as parallel, real-time, and embedded systems. As we move through the various stages, we see how the components of operating systems evolved as natural solutions to problems in early computer systems.

1.1 ■ What Operating Systems Do

We begin our discussions by looking at the operating system's role in the overall computer system. A computer system can be divided roughly into four

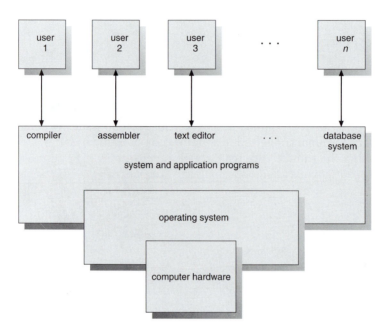

Figure 1.1   Abstract view of the components of a computer system.

components: the *hardware,* the *operating system,* the *application programs,* and the *users* (Figure 1.1).

The **hardware**—the **central processing unit (CPU)**, the **memory**, and the **input/output (I/O) devices**—provides the basic computing resources for the system. The **application programs**—such as word processors, spreadsheets, compilers, and web browsers—define the ways in which these resources are used to solve users' computing problems. The operating system controls and coordinates the use of the hardware among the various application programs for the various users.

We can also look at a computer system as consisting of hardware, software, and data. The operating system provides the means for proper use of these resources in the operation of the computer system. An operating system is similar to a *government.* Like a government, it performs no useful function by itself. It simply provides an *environment* within which other programs can do useful work.

To understand more fully the operating systems role, we next explore operating systems from two viewpoints: that of the user and that of the system.

1.1.1 User View

The user's view of the computer varies according to the interface being used. Most computer users sit in front of a PC, consisting of a monitor, keyboard, mouse, and system unit. Such a system is designed for one user to monopolize its resources. The goal is to maximize the work (or play) that the user is performing. In this case, the operating system is designed mostly for **ease of use**, with some attention paid to performance and none paid to **resource utilization** —how various hardware and software resources are shared. Performance is, of course, important to the user; but the demands placed on the system by a single user are too low to make resource utilization an issue. In some cases, a user sits at a terminal connected to a **mainframe** or **minicomputer**. Other users are accessing the same computer through other terminals. These users share resources and may exchange information. The operating system in such cases is designed to maximize resource utilization—to assure that all available CPU time, memory, and I/O are used efficiently and that no individual user takes more than her fair share.

In still other cases, users sit at **workstations** connected to networks of other workstations and servers. These users have dedicated resources at their disposal, but they also share resources such as networking and servers—file, compute and print servers. Therefore, their operating system is designed to compromise between individual usability and resource utilization.

Recently, many varieties of handheld computers have come into fashion. These devices are mostly standalone units used singly by individual users. Some are connected to networks, either directly by wire or (more often) through wireless modems. Because of power and interface limitations, they perform relatively few remote operations. Their operating systems are designed mostly for individual usability, but performance per amount of battery life is important as well.

Some computers have little or no user view. For example, embedded computers in home devices and automobiles may have numeric keypads and may turn indicator lights on or off to show status, but mostly they and their operating systems are designed to run without user intervention.

1.1.2 System View

From the computer's point of view, the operating system is the program most intimately involved with the hardware. In this context, we can view an operating system as a **resource allocator**. A computer system has many resources— hardware and software—that may be required to solve a problem: CPU time, memory space, file-storage space, I/O devices, and so on. The operating system acts as the manager of these resources. Facing numerous and possibly conflicting requests for resources, the operating system must decide how to allocate them to specific programs and users so that it can operate the computer system efficiently and fairly. As we have seen, resource allocation is especially important where many users access the same mainframe or minicomputer.

A slightly different view of an operating system emphasizes the need to control the various I/O devices and user programs. An operating system is a control program. A **control program** manages the execution of user programs to prevent errors and improper use of the computer. It is especially concerned with the operation and control of I/O devices.

1.1.3 Defining Operating Systems

We have looked at the operating system's role from the views of the user and of the system. How, though, can we define what an operating system is? In general, we have no completely adequate definition of an operating system. Operating systems exist because they offer a reasonable way to solve the problem of creating a usable computing system. The fundamental goal of computer systems is to execute user programs and to make solving user problems easier. Toward this goal, computer hardware is constructed. Since bare hardware alone is not particularly easy to use, application programs are developed. These programs require certain common operations, such as those controlling the I/O devices. The common functions of controlling and allocating resources are then brought together into one piece of software: the operating system.

In addition, we have no universally accepted definition of what is part of the operating system. A simple viewpoint is that it includes everything a vendor ships when you order "the operating system." The features included, however, vary greatly across systems. Some systems take up less than 1 megabyte of space and lack even a full-screen editor, whereas others require gigabytes of space and are entirely based on graphical windowing systems. (A kilobyte, or KB, is 1,024 bytes; a megabyte, or MB, is $1,024^2$ bytes; and a gigabyte, or GB, is $1,024^3$ bytes. Computer manufacturers often round off these numbers and say that a megabyte is 1 million bytes and a gigabyte is 1 billion bytes.) A more common definition is that the operating system is the one program running at all times on the computer (usually called the **kernel**), with all else being systems programs and application programs. This last definition is the one that we generally follow.

The matter of what constitutes an operating system has become increasingly important. In 1998, the United States Department of Justice filed suit against Microsoft, in essence claiming that Microsoft included too much functionality in its operating systems and thus prevented application vendors from competing. For example, a web browser was an integral part of the operating system. As a result, Microsoft was found guilty of using its operating system monopoly to limit competition.

1.1.4 System Goals

It is easier to define an operating system by what it *does* than by what it *is*, but even this can be tricky. The primary goal of some operating systems is *convenience for the user*. Operating systems exist because computing with them is supposedly easier than computing without them. As we have seen, this view is particularly clear when you look at operating systems for small PCs. The primary goal of other operating systems is *efficient* operation of the computer system. This is the case for large, shared, multiuser systems. These systems are expensive, so it is desirable to make them as efficient as possible. These two goals—convenience and efficiency—are sometimes contradictory. In the past, efficiency was often more important than convenience (Section 1.2.1). Thus, much of operating-system theory concentrates on optimal use of computing resources.

Operating systems have also evolved over time in ways that have affected system goals. For example, UNIX started with a keyboard and printer as its interface, limiting its convenience for users. Over time, hardware changed, and UNIX was ported to new hardware with more user-friendly interfaces. Many **graphic user interfaces (GUIs)** were added, allowing UNIX to be more convenient to use while still concentrating on efficiency.

Designing any operating system is a complex task. Designers face many tradeoffs, and many people are involved not only in bringing the operating system to fruition but also in constantly revising and updating it. How well any given operating system meets its design goals is open to debate and involves subjective judgments on the part of different users.

To examine more closely what operating systems are and what they do, we next consider how they have developed over the past 50 years. By tracing that evolution, we can identify the common elements of operating systems and see how and why these systems have developed as they have.

Operating systems and computer architecture have influenced each other a great deal. To facilitate the use of the hardware, researchers developed operating systems. Users of the operating systems then proposed changes in hardware design to simplify them. In this short historical review, notice how identification of operating-system problems led to the introduction of new hardware features.

1.2 ■ Mainframe Systems

Mainframe computer systems were the first computers used to tackle many commercial and scientific applications. In this section, we trace the growth of mainframe systems from simple **batch systems**, in which the computer runs one—and only one—application, to **time-shared systems**, which allow user interaction with the computer system.

1.2.1 Batch Systems

Early computers were physically enormous machines run from consoles. The common input devices were card readers and tape drives. The common output

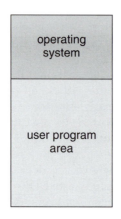

Figure 1.2   Memory layout for a simple batch system.

devices were line printers, tape drives, and card punches. The user did not interact directly with the computer system. Rather, the user prepared a job —which consisted of the program, the data, and some control information about the nature of the job (control cards)—and submitted it to the computer operator. The job was usually in the form of punch cards. At some later time (after minutes, hours, or days), the output appeared. The output consisted of the result of the program, as well as a dump of the final memory and register contents for debugging.

The operating system in these early computers was fairly simple. Its major task was to transfer control automatically from one job to the next. The operating system was always resident in memory (Figure 1.2).

To speed up processing, operators **batched** together jobs with similar needs and ran them through the computer as a group. Thus, the programmers would leave their programs with the operator. The operator would sort programs into batches with similar requirements and, as the computer became available, would run each batch. The output from each job would be sent back to the appropriate programmer.

In this execution environment, the CPU is often idle, because it works so much faster than the mechanical I/O devices. Even a slow CPU works in the microsecond range, executing thousands of instructions per second. A fast card reader, in contrast, might read 1200 cards per minute (or 20 cards per second). Thus, the difference in speed between the CPU and its I/O devices may be three orders of magnitude or more. Over time, of course, improvements in technology and the introduction of disks resulted in faster I/O devices. However, CPU speeds increased even more, so the problem was not only unresolved but exacerbated.

The introduction of disk technology allowed the operating system to keep all jobs on a disk, rather than in a serial card reader. With direct access to several jobs, the operating system could perform **job scheduling** to use resources and perform tasks more efficiently. We discuss a few important aspects of job and CPU scheduling here; we discuss them in detail in Chapter 6.

1.2.2 Multiprogrammed Systems

The most important aspect of job scheduling is the ability to multiprogram. A single user cannot, in general, keep either the CPU or the I/O devices busy at all times. **Multiprogramming** increases CPU utilization by organizing jobs so that the CPU always has one to execute.

The idea is as follows: The operating system keeps several jobs in memory simultaneously (Figure 1.3). This set of jobs is a subset of the jobs kept in the job pool—which contains all jobs that enter the system—since the number of jobs that can be kept simultaneously in memory is usually much smaller than the number of jobs that can be kept in the job pool. The operating system picks and begins to execute one of the jobs in the memory. Eventually, the job may have to wait for some task, such as an I/O operation, to complete. In a nonmultiprogrammed system, the CPU would sit idle. In a multiprogrammed system, the operating system simply switches to, and executes, another job. When *that* job needs to wait, the CPU is switched to *another* job, and so on. Eventually, the first job finishes waiting and gets the CPU back. As long as at least one job needs to execute, the CPU is never idle.

This idea is common in other life situations. A lawyer does not work for only one client at a time, for example. While one case is waiting to go to trial or have papers typed, the lawyer can work on another case. If he has enough clients, the lawyer will never be idle for lack of work. (Idle lawyers tend to become politicians, so there is a certain social value in keeping lawyers busy.)

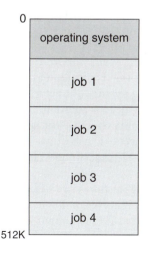

Figure 1.3   Memory layout for a multiprogramming system.

Multiprogramming represents the first instance in which the operating system was required to make decisions for the users. Multiprogrammed operating systems are therefore fairly sophisticated. As mentioned, all the jobs that enter the system are kept in the job pool. This pool consists of all processes residing on disk awaiting allocation of main memory. If several jobs are ready to be brought into memory, and if there is not enough room for all of them, then the system must choose among them. Making this decision is *job scheduling*, which is discussed in Chapter 6. When the operating system selects a job from the job pool, it loads that job into memory for execution. Having several programs in memory at the same time requires some form of memory management, which is covered in Chapters 9 and 10. In addition, if several jobs are ready to run at the same time, the system must choose among them. Making this decision is *CPU scheduling*, which is discussed in Chapter 6. Finally, running multiple jobs concurrently requires that their ability to affect one another be limited in all phases of the operating system, including process scheduling, disk storage, and memory management. These considerations are discussed throughout the text.

1.2.3 Time-Sharing Systems

Multiprogrammed batched systems provided an environment in which the various system resources (for example, CPU, memory, peripheral devices) were utilized effectively, but it did not provide for user interaction with the computer system. **Time sharing** (or **multitasking**) is a logical extension of multiprogramming. In time-sharing systems, the CPU executes multiple jobs by switching among them, but the switches occur so frequently that the users can interact with each program while it is running.

Time sharing requires an **interactive** (or **hands-on**) **computer system**, which provides direct communication between the user and the system. The user gives instructions to the operating system or to a program directly, using a keyboard or a mouse, and waits for immediate results. Accordingly, the **response time** should be short—typically less than one second.

A time-shared operating system allows many users to share the computer simultaneously. Since each action or command in a time-shared system tends to be short, only a little CPU time is needed for each user. As the system switches rapidly from one user to the next, each user is given the impression that the entire computer system is dedicated to her use, even though it is being shared among many users.

A time-shared operating system uses CPU scheduling and multiprogramming to provide each user with a small portion of a time-shared computer. Each user has at least one separate program in memory. A program loaded into memory and executing is commonly referred to as a **process**. When a process executes, it typically executes for only a short time before it either finishes or needs to perform I/O. I/O may be interactive; that is, output goes to a display for the user and input comes from a user keyboard, mouse, or other device. Since interactive I/O typically runs at "people speeds," it may take a long time to complete. Input, for example, may be bounded by the user's typing speed; seven characters per second is fast for people, but incredibly slow for computers. Rather than let the CPU sit idle as this interactive input takes place, the operating system will rapidly switch the CPU to the program of some other user.

Time-sharing operating systems are even more complex than multiprogrammed operating systems. In both, several jobs must be kept simultaneously in memory, so the system must have memory management and protection (Chapter 9). To obtain a reasonable response time, the system may have to swap jobs in and out of main memory to the disk that now serves as a backing store for main memory. A common method for achieving this goal is **virtual memory**, a technique that allows the execution of a job that is not completely in memory (Chapter 10). The main advantage of the virtual-memory scheme is that it enables users to run programs that are larger than actual **physical memory**. Further, it abstracts main memory into a large, uniform array of storage, separating **logical memory** as viewed by the user from physical memory. This arrangement frees programmers from concern over memory-storage limitations.

Time-sharing systems must also provide a file system (Chapters 11 and 12). The file system resides on a collection of disks; hence, disk management must be provided (Chapter 14). Also, time-sharing systems provide a mechanism for concurrent execution, which requires sophisticated CPU-scheduling schemes (Chapter 6). To ensure orderly execution, the system must provide mechanisms for job synchronization and communication (Chapter 7), and it may ensure that jobs do not get stuck in a deadlock, forever waiting for one another (Chapter 8).

The idea of time sharing was demonstrated as early as 1960; but since time-shared systems are difficult and expensive to build, they did not become common until the early 1970s. Although some batch processing is still done, most systems today, including personal computers, use time sharing. Accordingly, multiprogramming and time sharing are the central themes of modern operating systems, and they are the central themes of this book.

1.3 ■ Desktop Systems

Personal computers (PCs) appeared in the 1970s. During their first decade, the CPUs in PCs lacked the features needed to protect an operating system from user programs. PC operating systems therefore were neither multiuser nor multitasking. Contemporary CPUs in PCs typically now provide such features. However, unlike multiprogrammed and time-shared systems whose primary goals are maximizing CPU and peripheral utilization, PC operating systems must also maximize user convenience and responsiveness. These systems include PCs running Microsoft Windows and the Apple Macintosh. The MS-DOS operating system from Microsoft has been superseded by multiple flavors of Microsoft Windows. The Apple Macintosh operating system has been ported to more advanced hardware and now includes features such as virtual memory and multitasking. With the release of Mac OS X, the core of the operating system is now based on Mach and FreeBSD UNIX for scalability, performance, and features, but it retains the same rich GUI. Linux, an open-source UNIX operating system available for PCs, has all of these features as well and has become quite popular.

Operating systems for these computers have benefited in several ways from the development of operating systems for mainframes. Of course, some of the design decisions made for mainframe operating systems are not appropriate for smaller systems. Because hardware costs for microcomputers are relatively low, one individual generally has sole use of a microcomputer. Thus, whereas efficient CPU utilization is a primary concern for mainframes, it is no longer so important for systems supporting a single user. Other design decisions still apply, however. For example, file protection was, at first, not necessary on personal machines. However, these computers are now often connected to other computers over local-area networks or other Internet connections. When other computers and other users can access the files on a PC, file protection again becomes a necessary feature of the operating system. Indeed, the lack of such protection has made it easy for malicious programs to destroy data on systems such as MS-DOS. These programs may be self-replicating and may spread rapidly via **worm** or **virus** mechanisms and disrupt entire companies or even worldwide networks. Advanced time-sharing features such as protected memory and file permissions are not enough, on their own, to safeguard a system from attack. Recent security breaches have shown that time and again. These topics are discussed in Chapters 18 and 19.

1.4 ▪ Multiprocessor Systems

Most systems to date have been single-processor systems; that is, they have had only one main CPU. However, **multiprocessor systems** (also known as **parallel systems** or **tightly coupled systems**) are growing in importance. Such systems have more than one processor in close communication, sharing the computer bus, the clock, and sometimes memory and peripheral devices.

Multiprocessor systems have three main advantages.

1. **Increased throughput**. By increasing the number of processors, we hope to get more work done in less time. The speed-up ratio with N processors is not N; rather, it is less than N. When multiple processors cooperate on a task, a certain amount of overhead is incurred in keeping all the parts working correctly. This overhead, plus contention for shared resources,

lowers the expected gain from additional processors. Similarly, a group of N programmers working closely together does not produce N times the amount of work a single programmer would produce.

2. **Economy of scale**. Multiprocessor systems can cost less than equivalent multiple single-processor systems, because they can share peripherals, mass storage, and power supplies. If several programs operate on the same set of data, it is cheaper to store those data on one disk and to have all the processors share them than to have many computers with local disks and many copies of the data. Blade servers are a recent development in which multiple processor boards, I/O boards, and networking boards can be placed in the same chassis. The difference between these and traditional multiprocessor systems is that each blade processor board boots independently and runs its own operating system.

3. **Increased reliability**. If functions can be distributed properly among several processors, then the failure of one processor will not halt the system, only slow it down. If we have ten processors and one fails, then each of the remaining nine processors must pick up a share of the work of the failed processor. Thus, the entire system runs only 10 percent slower, rather than failing altogether. This ability to continue providing service proportional to the level of surviving hardware is called **graceful degradation**. Systems designed for graceful degradation are also called **fault tolerant**.

Note that the third advantage, continued operation in the presence of failures, requires a mechanism to allow the failure to be detected, diagnosed, and, if possible, corrected. The Tandem system uses both hardware and software duplication to ensure continued operation despite faults. The system consists of two identical processors, each with its own local memory. The processors are connected by a bus. One processor is the primary and the other is the backup. Two copies are kept of each process: one on the primary processor and the other on the backup. At fixed checkpoints in the execution of the system, the state information of each job—including a copy of the memory image—is copied from the primary machine to the backup. If a failure is detected, the backup copy is activated and is restarted from the most recent checkpoint. This solution is expensive, since it involves considerable hardware duplication.

Two types of multiple-processor systems are in use today. The most common use **symmetric multiprocessing (SMP)**, in which each processor runs a copy of the operating system and these copies communicate with one another as needed. Some systems use **asymmetric multiprocessing**, in which each processor is assigned a specific task. A master processor controls the system; the other processors either look to the master for instruction or have predefined tasks. This scheme defines a master–slave relationship. The master processor schedules and allocates work to the slave processors.

SMP means that all processors are peers; no master–slave relationship exists between processors. Each processor, as mentioned, concurrently runs a copy of the operating system. Figure 1.4 illustrates a typical SMP architecture. An example of the SMP system is Solaris, a commercial version of UNIX designed by Sun Microsystems. A Solaris system can be configured to employ dozens of processors, all running copies of UNIX. The benefit of this model is that many processes can run simultaneously—N processes can run if there are N CPUs—without causing a significant deterioration of performance. However, we must carefully control I/O to ensure that the data reach the appropriate processor. Also, since the CPUs are separate, one may be sitting idle while another is overloaded, resulting in inefficiencies. These inefficiencies can be avoided if the processors share certain data structures. A multiprocessor system of this form will allow processes and resources—such as memory—to be shared dynamically among the various processors and can lower the variance among the processors. Such a system must be written carefully, as we shall see in Chapter 7. Virtually all modern operating systems—including Windows 2000, Windows XP, Mac OS X, and Linux—now provide support for SMP.

The difference between symmetric and asymmetric multiprocessing may result from either hardware or software. Special hardware can differentiate the multiple processors, or the software can be written to allow only one master and multiple slaves. For instance, Sun's operating system SunOS Version 4 provides asymmetric multiprocessing, whereas Version 5 (Solaris) is symmetric on the same hardware.

As microprocessors become less expensive and more powerful, additional operating-system functions are off-loaded to slave processors (or **back-ends**). For example, it is fairly easy to add a microprocessor with its own memory to manage a disk system. The microprocessor could receive a sequence of requests from the main CPU and implement its own disk queue and scheduling algorithm. This arrangement relieves the main CPU of the overhead of disk scheduling. PCs contain a microprocessor in the keyboard to convert the keystrokes into codes to be sent to the CPU. In fact, this use of microprocessors has become so common that it is no longer considered multiprocessing.

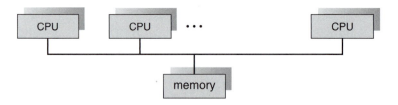

Figure 1.4   Symmetric multiprocessing architecture.

1.5 ■ Distributed Systems

The growth of computer networks—especially the Internet and World Wide Web (WWW)—has had a profound influence on the recent development of operating systems. When PCs were introduced in the 1970s, they were designed for "personal" use and were generally considered standalone computers. With the beginning of widespread public use of the Internet in the 1980s for e-mail, ftp, and gopher, many PCs became connected to computer networks. With the introduction of the Web in the mid-1990s, network connectivity became an essential component of a computer system.

Virtually all modern PCs and workstations are capable of running a web browser for accessing **hypertext** documents on the Web. Operating systems (such as Windows, Mac OS X, and UNIX) now also include the system software (such as TCP/IP and PPP) that enables a computer to access the Internet via a local-area network or telephone connection. Several include the web browser itself, as well as electronic mail, remote login, and file-transfer clients and servers.

In contrast to the tightly coupled systems discussed in Section 1.4, the computer networks used in these applications consist of a collection of processors that do not share memory or a clock. Instead, each processor has its own local memory. The processors communicate with one another through various communication lines, such as high-speed buses or telephone lines. These systems are usually referred to as **distributed systems** (or **loosely coupled systems**).

Because they are able to communicate, distributed systems can share computational tasks and provide a rich set of features to users. In this section, we look at computer networks and how they can be structured to form distributed systems. We also explore the client–server and peer-to-peer strategies for providing services in a distributed system. Finally, we look at how distributed systems have affected the design of operating systems.

1.5.1 Computer Networks

A **network**, in the simplest terms, is a communication path between two or more systems. Distributed systems depend on networking for their functionality. Networks vary by the protocols used, the distances between nodes, and the transport media. TCP/IP is the most common network protocol, although ATM and other protocols are in widespread use. Likewise, operating-system support of protocols varies. Most operating systems support TCP/IP, including the Windows and UNIX operating systems. Some systems support proprietary protocols to suit their needs. To an operating system, a network protocol simply needs an interface device—a network adapter, for example—with a device driver to manage it, as well as software to handle data. These concepts are discussed throughout the book.

Networks are characterized based on the distances between their nodes. A **local-area network (LAN)** connects computers within a room, a floor, or a building. A **wide-area network (WAN)** usually links buildings, cities, or countries. A global company may have a WAN to connect its offices worldwide. These networks may run one protocol or several protocols. The continuing advent of new technologies brings about new forms of networks. For example, a **metropolitan-area network (MAN)** could link buildings within a city. BlueTooth and 802.11b devices use wireless technology to communicate over a distance of several feet, in essence creating a **small-area network** such as might be found in a home.

The media to carry networks are equally varied. They include copper wires, fiber strands, and wireless transmissions between satellites, microwave dishes, and radios. When computing devices are connected to cellular phones, they create a network. Even very short-range infrared communication can be used for networking. At a rudimentary level, whenever computers communicate, they use or create a network. These networks also vary in their performance and reliability.

1.5.2 Client-Server Systems

As PCs have become faster, more powerful, and cheaper, designers have shifted away from centralized system architecture. Terminals connected to centralized systems are now being supplanted by PCs. Correspondingly, user-interface functionality once handled directly by the centralized systems is increasingly being handled by the PCs. As a result, centralized systems today act as **server systems** to satisfy requests generated by **client systems**. The general structure of a client–server system is depicted in Figure 1.5.

Server systems can be broadly categorized as compute servers and file servers:

- The **compute-server system** provides an interface to which a client can send requests to perform an action; in response, the server executes the action and sends back results to the client. A server running a database that responds to client requests for data is an example of such a system.

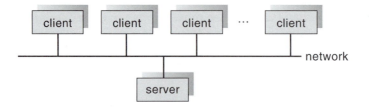

Figure 1.5   General structure of a client–server system.

- The **file-server system** provides a file-system interface where clients can create, update, read, and delete files. An example of such a system is a web server that delivers files to clients running web browsers.

1.5.3 Peer-to-Peer Systems

Another structure for a distributed system is the peer-to-peer (P2P) system model. In this model, clients and servers are not distinguished from one another; instead, all nodes within the system are considered peers, and each may act as either a client or a server, depending on whether it is requesting or providing a service. Peer-to-peer systems offer an advantage over traditional client-server systems. In a client-server system, the server is a bottleneck; but in a peer-to-peer system, services can be provided by several nodes distributed throughout the network.

To participate in a peer-to-peer system, a node must first join the network of peers. Once a node has joined the network, it can begin providing services to—and requesting services from—other nodes in the network. Determining what services are available is accomplished in one of two general ways:

- When a node joins a network, it registers its service with a centralized lookup service on the network. Any node desiring a specific service first contacts this centralized lookup service to determine which node provides the service. The remainder of the communication takes place between the client and the service provider.

- A peer acting as a client must first discover what node provides a desired service by broadcasting a request for the service to all other nodes in the network. The node (or nodes) providing that service responds to the peer making the request. To support this approach, a *discovery protocol* must be provided that allows peers to discover services provided by other peers in the network.

Peer-to-peer networks gained widespread popularity in the late 1990s with several music-sharing services, such as *Napster* and *Gnutella*, that enable peers to exchange files with one another. The Napster system uses an approach similar to the first type described above; a centralized server maintains an index of all files stored on peer nodes in the Napster network, and the actual exchanging of files takes place between the peer nodes. The Gnutella system uses a technique similar to the second type; a client broadcasts file requests to other nodes in the system, and nodes that can service the request respond directly to the client. The future of exchanging music files remains uncertain because of laws governing the distribution of copyrighted material. In any case, though, peer-to-peer technology undoubtedly will play a role in the future of many services, such as searching, file exchange, and e-mail.

1.5.4 Distributed Operating Systems

Some operating systems have taken the concept of networks and distributed systems further than the notion of providing network connectivity. A **network operating system** is an operating system that provides features such as file sharing across the network and that includes a communication scheme that allows different processes on different computers to exchange messages. A computer running a network operating system acts autonomously from all other computers on the network, although it is aware of the network and is able to communicate with other networked computers. A distributed operating system provides a less autonomous environment: The different operating systems communicate closely enough to provide the illusion that only a single operating system controls the network. We cover computer networks and distributed systems in Chapters 15 through 17.

1.6 ■ Clustered Systems

Yet another development in operating systems involves clustered systems. Like parallel systems, **clustered systems** gather together multiple CPUs to accomplish computational work. Clustered systems differ from parallel systems, however, in that they are composed of two or more individual systems coupled together. The definition of the term *clustered* is not concrete; many commercial packages wrestle with what a clustered system is and why one form is better than another. The generally accepted definition is that clustered computers share storage and are closely linked via LAN networking.

Clustering is usually used to provide **high-availability** service; that is, service will continue to be provided even if one or more systems in the cluster fail. High availability is generally obtained by adding a level of redundancy in the system. A layer of cluster software runs on the cluster nodes. Each node can monitor one or more of the others (over the LAN). If the monitored machine fails, the monitoring machine can take ownership of its storage and restart the applications that were running on the failed machine. The users and clients of the applications would see only a brief interruption of service.

Clustering can be structured asymmetrically or symmetrically. In **asymmetric clustering**, one machine is in **hot-standby mode** while the other is running the applications. The hot-standby host machine does nothing but monitor the active server. If that server fails, the hot-standby host becomes the active server. In **symmetric mode**, two or more hosts are running applications, and they are monitoring each other. This mode is obviously more efficient, as it uses all of the available hardware. It does require that more than one application be available to run.

Other forms of clusters include parallel clusters and clustering over a WAN. Parallel clusters allow multiple hosts to access the same data on the shared storage. Because most operating systems lack support for simultaneous data access by multiple hosts, parallel clusters are usually accomplished by use of special versions of software and special releases of applications. For example, Oracle Parallel Server is a version of Oracle's database that has been designed to run on a parallel cluster. Each machine runs Oracle, and a layer of software tracks access to the shared disk. Each machine has full access to all data in the database. To provide this shared access to data, the system must also supply access control and locking to ensure that no conflicting operations occur. This function, commonly known as a **distributed lock manager (DLM)**, is included in some cluster technology.

Cluster technology is changing rapidly. Directions for the future include clusters of dozens of nodes and global clusters, in which the machines could be anywhere in the world (or anywhere a WAN reaches). Such projects are still the subject of research and development. Many of these improvements are made possible by **storage-area networks (SANs)**, as described in Section 14.6.3, which allow many systems to attach to a pool of storage. SANs allow easy attachment of multiple hosts to multiple storage units. In contrast, current clusters are usually limited to two or four hosts owing to the complexity of connecting the hosts to shared storage.

1.7 ■ Real-Time Systems

Another form of special-purpose operating system is the **real-time system**. A real-time system is used when rigid time requirements have been placed on the operation of a processor or the flow of data; thus, it is often used as a control device in a dedicated application. Sensors bring data to the computer. The computer must analyze the data and possibly adjust controls to modify the sensor inputs. Systems that control scientific experiments, medical imaging systems, industrial control systems, and certain display systems are real-time systems. Some automobile-engine fuel-injection systems, home-appliance controllers, and weapon systems are also real-time systems.

A real-time system has well-defined, fixed time constraints. Processing *must* be done within the defined constraints, or the system will fail. For instance, it would not do for a robot arm to be instructed to halt *after* it had smashed into the car it was building. A real-time system functions correctly only if it returns the correct result within its time constraints. Contrast this system with a time-sharing system, where it is desirable (but not mandatory) to respond quickly, or a batch system, which may have no time constraints at all.

Real-time systems come in two flavors: hard and soft. A **hard real-time system** guarantees that critical tasks are completed on time. This goal requires that all delays in the system be bounded, from the retrieval of stored data to the time it takes the operating system to perform any request made of it. Such time constraints dictate the facilities that are available in hard real-time systems. Secondary storage of any sort is usually limited or absent, with data instead being stored in short-term memory or in read-only memory (ROM). ROM is located on nonvolatile storage devices that retain their contents even in the case of electric outage; most other types of memory are volatile. Most advanced operating-system features are absent too, since they tend to separate the user from the hardware, and that separation results in uncertainty about the amount of time an operation will take. For instance, virtual memory (Chapter 10) is almost never found on real-time systems. Therefore, hard real-time systems conflict with the operation of time-sharing systems, and the two cannot be mixed. Since none of the existing general-purpose operating systems support hard real-time functionality, we do not concern ourselves with this type of system in this text.

A less restrictive type of real-time system is a **soft real-time system**, where a critical real-time task gets priority over other tasks and retains that priority until its execution has been completed. As in hard real-time systems, the operating-system kernel delays must be bounded: A real-time task cannot be kept waiting indefinitely.

Soft real time is an achievable goal that can be mixed with other types of systems. Soft real-time systems, however, have more limited utility than hard real-time systems. Given their lack of deadline support, they are risky to use for industrial control and robotics. They are useful, however in several areas, including multimedia, virtual reality, and advanced scientific projects—such as undersea exploration and planetary rovers. These systems need advanced operating-system features that cannot be supported by hard real-time systems. Because of the expanded uses for soft real-time functionality, it is finding its way into most current operating systems, including major versions of UNIX.

In Chapter 6, we consider the scheduling facility needed to implement soft real-time functionality in an operating system. In Chapter 10, we describe the design of memory management for real-time computing. Finally, in Chapter 21, we describe the real-time components of the Windows 2000 operating system.

1.8 ■ Handheld Systems

Handheld systems include **personal digital assistants (PDAs)**, such as *Palm*, Pocket-PCs or cellular telephones. Developers of handheld systems and applications face many challenges, most of which are due to the limited size of such devices. For example, a PDA is typically about 5 inches in height and 3 inches in width, and it weighs less than one-half pound. Because of their size, most handheld devices have a small amount of memory, slow processors, and small display screens. We will take a look now at each of these limitations.

Many handheld devices have between 512 KB and 128 MB of memory. (Contrast this with a typical PC or workstation, which may have several gigabytes of memory!) As a result, the operating system and applications must manage memory efficiently. This includes returning all allocated memory back to the memory manager when the memory is not being used. In Chapter 10, we will explore virtual memory, which allows developers to write programs that behave as if the system has more memory than is physically available. Currently, not many handheld devices use virtual memory techniques, so program developers must work within the confines of limited physical memory.

A second issue of concern to developers of handheld devices is the speed of the processor used in the devices. Processors for most handheld devices run at a fraction of the speed of a processor in a PC. Faster processors require more power. To include a faster processor in a handheld device would require a larger battery, which would have to be replaced (or recharged) more frequently. To minimize the size of most handheld devices, smaller, slower processors that consume less power are typically used. Therefore, the operating system and applications must be designed not to tax the processor.

The last issue confronting program designers for handheld devices is the small display screens typically available. Whereas a monitor for a home computer may measure up to 23 inches, the display for a handheld device is often no more than 3 inches square. Familiar tasks, such as reading e-mail or browsing web pages, must be condensed onto smaller displays. One approach for displaying the content in web pages is **web clipping**, where only a small subset of a web page is delivered and displayed on the handheld device.

Some handheld devices use wireless technology, such as BlueTooth (Section 1.5), allowing remote access to e-mail and web browsing. Cellular telephones with connectivity to the Internet fall into this category. However, for PDAs that do not provide wireless access, downloading data typically requires the user to first download the data to a PC or workstation and then download the data to the PDA. Some PDAs allow data to be directly copied from one device to another using an infrared link.

Generally, the limitations in the functionality of PDAs are balanced by their convenience and portability. Their use continues to expand as network connections become more available and other options, such as digital cameras and MP3 players, expand their utility.

1.9 ◼ Feature Migration

Overall, an examination of operating systems for mainframes and microcomputers shows that features once available only on mainframes have been adopted for microcomputers. The same operating-system concepts are appropriate for the various classes of computers: mainframes, minicomputers, microcomputers, and handhelds. Many of the concepts and features depicted in Figure 1.6 will be covered later in this book. However, to start understanding modern operating systems, you need to recognize the theme of feature migration and the long history of many operating-system features.

A good example of this movement occurred with the MULTiplexed Information and Computing Services (MULTICS) operating system. MULTICS

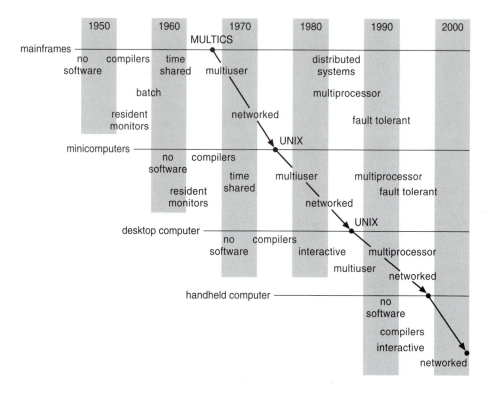

Figure 1.6   Migration of operating-system concepts and features.

was developed from 1965 to 1970 at the Massachusetts Institute of Technology (MIT) as a computing **utility**. It ran on a large, complex mainframe computer (the GE 645).   Many of the ideas that were developed for MULTICS were subsequently used at Bell Laboratories (one of the original partners in the development of MULTICS) in the design of UNIX. The UNIX operating system was designed around 1970 for a PDP-11 minicomputer. Around 1980, the features of UNIX became the basis for UNIX-like operating systems on microcomputer systems; and these features are being included in more recent operating systems, such as Microsoft Windows 2000 and Windows XP, and the Mac OS X operating system. Thus, features developed for a large mainframe system have moved to microcomputers over time. Linux includes some of these same features and can now be found on PDAs.

1.10 ■ Computing Environments

We have traced the development of operating systems from the first hands-on systems through multiprogrammed and time-shared systems to PCs and handheld computers. We conclude with a brief overview of how such systems are used in a variety of computing environments.

1.10.1 Traditional Computing

As computing matures, the lines separating many of the traditional computing environments are blurring. Consider the "typical office environment." Just a few years ago, this environment consisted of PCs connected to a network, with servers providing file and print services. Remote access was awkward, and portability was achieved by use of laptop computers. Terminals attached to mainframes were prevalent at many companies as well, with even fewer remote access and portability options.

The current trend is toward providing more ways to access these environments. Web technologies are stretching the boundaries of traditional computing. Companies establish **portals**, which provide web accessibility to their internal servers. **Network computers** are essentially terminals that understand web-based computing. Handheld computers can synchronize with PCs to allow very portable use of company information. Handheld PDAs can also connect to **wireless networks** to use the company's web portal (as well as the myriad other web resources).

At home, most users had a single computer with a slow modem connection to the office, the Internet, or both. Today, network-connection speeds once available only at great cost are relatively inexpensive, giving home users more access to more data. These fast data connections are allowing home computers to serve up web pages and to run networks that include printers, client PCs, and servers. Some homes even have **firewalls** to protect these home environments from security breaches. Those firewalls cost thousands of dollars a few years ago and did not even exist a decade ago.

1.10.2 Web-Based Computing

The Web has become ubiquitous, leading to more access by a wider variety of devices than was dreamt of a few years ago. PCs are still the most prevalent access devices, with workstations, handheld PDAs, and even cell phones also providing access.

Web computing has increased the emphasis on networking. Devices that were not previously networked now include wired or wireless access. Devices that were networked now have faster network connectivity, provided by either improved networking technology, optimized network implementation code, or both.

The implementation of web-based computing has given rise to new categories of devices, such as **load balancers**, which distribute network connections among a pool of similar servers. Operating systems like Windows 95, which acted as web clients, have evolved into Windows 2000 and Windows XP, which can act as web servers as well as clients. Generally, the Web has increased the complexity of devices, because their users require them to be web-enabled.

1.10.3 Embedded Computing

Embedded computers, which run embedded real-time operating systems, are the most prevalent form of computers in existence. These devices are found everywhere, from car engines and manufacturing robots to VCRs and microwave ovens. They tend to have very specific tasks. The systems they run on are usually primitive, and so the operating systems provide limited features. Usually, for example, they have little or no user interface, preferring to spend their time monitoring and managing hardware devices, such as automobile engines and robotic arms.

As an example, consider the aforementioned firewalls and load balancers. Some are general-purpose computers, running standard operating systems— such as UNIX—with special-purpose applications to implement the functionality. Others are hardware devices with a special-purpose embedded operating system providing just the functionality desired.

The use of embedded systems continues to expand. The power of those devices, both as standalone units and as members of networks and the Web, is sure to increase as well. Even now, entire houses can be computerized, so that a central computer—either a general-purpose computer or an embedded system —can control heating and lighting, alarm systems, and even coffee makers. Web access can enable a home owner to tell the house to heat up before she arrives home. Someday, the refrigerator may call the grocery store when it notices the milk is gone.

1.11 ▪ Summary

Operating systems have been developed over the past 50 years for two main purposes. First, the operating system attempts to schedule computational activities to ensure good performance of the computing system. Second, it provides a convenient environment for the development and execution of programs.

Initially, computer systems were used from the front console. Software such as assemblers, loaders, linkers, and compilers improved the convenience of programming the system but also required substantial set-up time.

Batch systems allowed automatic job sequencing by a resident operating system and greatly improved the overall utilization of the computer. The computer no longer had to wait for human operation. CPU utilization was still low, however, because of the slow speed of the I/O devices relative to that of the CPU.

To improve the overall performance of the computer system, developers introduced the concept of multiprogramming, so that several jobs could be kept in memory at one time. The CPU is switched back and forth among them to increase CPU utilization and to decrease the total time needed to execute the jobs.

Multiprogramming not only improves performance but also allows for time sharing. Time-shared operating systems enable many users (from one to several hundred) to use a computer system interactively at the same time.

PCs are microcomputers that are considerably smaller and less expensive than mainframe systems. Operating systems for these computers have benefited from the development of operating systems for mainframes in several ways. Since an individual has sole use of the computer, CPU utilization is not a prime concern. Hence, some of the design decisions made for mainframe operating systems may not be appropriate for these smaller systems. Other design decisions, such as those for security, are appropriate for both small and large systems, as PCs can now be connected to other computers and users through networks and the Web.

Multiprocessor systems, or parallel systems, are made up of two or more CPUs in close communication. The CPUs share the computer bus and sometimes share memory and peripheral devices. Such systems can provide increased throughput and enhanced reliability.

Distributed systems allow users to share resources on geographically dispersed hosts connected via a computer network. Services may be provided through either the client-server model or the peer-to-peer model. In a clustered system, multiple machines can perform computations on data residing on shared storage, and computing can continue even when some subset of cluster members fails.

A hard real-time system is often used as a control device in a dedicated application. A hard real-time operating system has well-defined, fixed time constraints. Processing *must* be done within the defined constraints, or the system will fail. Soft real-time systems have less stringent timing constraints and do not support deadline scheduling.

Handheld systems are increasingly popular and present several challenges for application developers due to less memory and slower processors than desktop PCs.

Recently, the influence of the Internet and the World Wide Web has encouraged the development of modern operating systems that include web browsers and networking and communication software as integral features.

We have shown the logical progression of operating-system development, driven by inclusion of features in the CPU hardware needed for advanced functionality. This trend can be seen today in the evolution of PCs, with inexpensive hardware being improved sufficiently to allow, in turn, improved characteristics.

■ Exercises

1.1 What are the two main purposes of an operating system?

1.2 List the four steps necessary to run a program on a completely dedicated machine.

1.3 What is the main advantage of multiprogramming?

1.4 What are the main differences between operating systems for mainframe computers and PCs?

1.5 In a multiprogramming and time-sharing environment, several users share the system simultaneously. This situation can result in various security problems.

  a. What are two such problems?

  b. Can we ensure the same degree of security in a time-shared machine as we have in a dedicated machine? Explain your answer.

1.6 Define the essential properties of the following types of operating systems:

  a. Batch

  b. Interactive

  c. Time sharing

  d. Real time

  e. Network

  f. Parallel

  g. Distributed

  h. Clustered

  i. Handheld

1.7 We have stressed the need for an operating system to make efficient use of the computing hardware. When is it appropriate for the operating system to forsake this principle and to "waste" resources? Why is such a system not really wasteful?

1.8 Under what circumstances would a user be better off using a time-sharing system rather than a PC or single-user workstation?

1.9 Describe the differences between symmetric and asymmetric multiprocessing. What are three advantages and one disadvantage of multiprocessor systems?

1.10 What is the main difficulty that a programmer must overcome in writing an operating system for a real-time environment?

1.11 Distinguish between the client-server and peer-to-peer models of distributed systems.

1.12 Consider the various definitions of *operating system*. Consider whether the operating system should include applications such as web browsers and mail programs. Argue both pro and con positions, and support your answers.

1.13 What are the tradeoffs inherent in handheld computers?

1.14 Consider a computing cluster consisting of two nodes running a database. Describe two ways in which the cluster software can manage access to the data on the disk. Discuss the benefits and disadvantages of each.

Bibliographical Notes

Time-sharing systems were proposed first by Strachey [1959]. The earliest time-sharing systems were the Compatible Time-Sharing System (CTSS) developed at MIT (Corbato et al. [1962]) and the SDC Q-32 system, built by the System Development Corporation (Schwartz et al. [1964], Schwartz and Weissman [1967]). Other early, but more sophisticated, systems include the MULTiplexed Information and Computing Services (MULTICS) system developed at MIT (Corbato and Vyssotsky [1965]), the XDS-940 system developed at the University of California at Berkeley (Lichtenberger and Pirtle [1965]), and the IBM TSS/360 system (Lett and Konigsford [1968]).

An overview of the Linux operating system is presented in Bovet and Cesati [2002]. Solomon and Russinovich [2000] give an overview of Microsoft Windows 2000 and considerable technical detail about the system internals and components. Mauro and McDougall [2001] cover the Solaris operating system. Mac OS X is presented at http://www.apple.com/macosx.

Coverage of peer-to-peer systems includes Parameswaran et al. [2001], Gong [2002], and Ripeanu et al. [2002]. A good coverage of cluster computing is presented by Buyya [1999]. Recent advances in cluster computing are described by Ahmed [2000].

Discussions concerning handheld devices are offered by Murray [1998] and Rhodes and McKeehan [1999].

Many general textbooks cover operating systems, including Stallings [2000b], Nutt [2000] and Tanenbaum [2001].

Chapter 2

COMPUTER-SYSTEM STRUCTURES

Before we can explore the details of computer system operation, we need to know something about system structure. In this chapter, we look at several parts of this structure. The chapter is mostly concerned with computer-system architecture, so you can skim or skip it if you already understand the concepts.

We begin by discussing the basic functions of system startup, I/O, and storage. Later in the chapter, we describe the basic computer architecture that makes it possible to write a functional operating system. We conclude with an overview of network architecture.

2.1 ■ Computer-System Operation

A modern, general-purpose computer system consists of a CPU and a number of device controllers and adapters that are connected through a common bus that provides access to shared memory (Figure 2.1). Each device controller is in charge of a specific type of device (for example, disk drives, input devices, I/O bus, and video displays). The CPU and the device controllers can execute concurrently, competing for memory cycles. To ensure orderly access to the shared memory, a memory controller is provided whose function is to synchronize access to the memory. There certainly are variations on this basic structure, including multiple CPUs and dedicated CPU-memory busses, but the concepts in this chapter apply regardless.

For a computer to start running—for instance, when it is powered up or rebooted—it needs to have an initial program to run. This initial program,

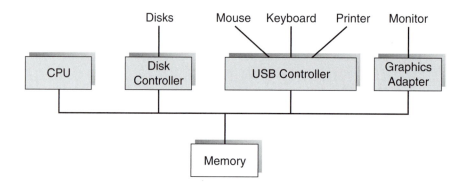

Figure 2.1   A modern computer system.

or **bootstrap program**, tends to be simple. Typically, it is stored in read-only memory (ROM) such as firmware or EEPROM within the computer hardware. It initializes all aspects of the system, from CPU registers to device controllers to memory contents. The bootstrap program must know how to load the operating system and how to start executing that system. To accomplish this goal, the bootstrap program must locate and load into memory the operating-system kernel. The operating system then starts executing the first process, such as "init," and waits for some event to occur.

The occurrence of an event is usually signaled by an **interrupt** from either the hardware or the software. Hardware may trigger an interrupt at any time by sending a signal to the CPU, usually by way of the system bus. Software may trigger an interrupt by executing a special operation called a **system call** (also called a **monitor call**).

Modern operating systems are **interrupt driven**. If there are no processes to execute, no I/O devices to service, and no users to whom to respond, an operating system will sit quietly, waiting for something to happen. Events are almost always signaled by the occurrence of an interrupt or a trap. A **trap** (or an **exception**) is a software-generated interrupt caused either by an error (for example, division by zero or invalid memory access) or by a specific request from a user program that an operating-system service be performed. The interrupt-driven nature of an operating system defines that system's general structure. For each type of interrupt, separate segments of code in the operating system determine what action should be taken, and an interrupt service routine is provided to deal with the interrupt.

When the CPU is interrupted, it stops what it is doing and immediately transfers execution to a fixed location. The fixed location usually contains the starting address where the service routine for the interrupt is located. The interrupt service routine executes; on completion, the CPU resumes the interrupted computation. A time line of this operation is shown in Figure 2.2.

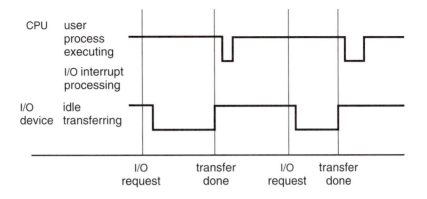

Figure 2.2   Interrupt time line for a single process doing output.

Interrupts are an important part of a computer architecture. Each computer design has its own interrupt mechanism, but several functions are common. For one thing, the interrupt must transfer control to the appropriate interrupt service routine. The straightforward method for handling this transfer would be to invoke a generic routine to examine the interrupt information and then call the interrupt-specific handler. However, because only a predefined number of interrupts is possible, a table of pointers to interrupt routines can be used instead. The interrupt routine is then called indirectly through the table, with no intermediate routine needed, speeding up the handling of interrupts. Generally, the table of pointers is stored in low memory (the first hundred or so locations). These locations hold the addresses of the interrupt service routines for the various devices. This array, or **interrupt vector**, of addresses is indexed by a unique device number, which is given with the interrupt request, to provide the address of the interrupt service routine for the interrupting device. Operating systems as different as MS-DOS and UNIX dispatch interrupts in this manner.

The interrupt architecture must also save the address of the interrupted instruction. Many old designs simply stored the interrupt address in a fixed location or in a location indexed by the device number. More recent architectures store the return address on the system stack. If the interrupt routine needs to modify the processor state—for instance, by modifying register values—it must explicitly save the current state and then restore that state before returning. After the interrupt is serviced, the saved return address is loaded into the program counter, and the interrupted computation resumes as though the interrupt had not occurred.

A system call is invoked in a variety of ways, depending on the functionality provided by the underlying processor. In all forms, it is the method used by a process to request action by the operating system. A system call usually takes the form of a trap to a specific location in the interrupt vector. This trap can be executed by a generic `trap` instruction, although some systems (such as the MIPS R2000 family) have a specific `syscall` instruction.

2.2 ■ I/O Structure

As mentioned in Section 2.1, a general-purpose computer system consists of a CPU and multiple device controllers that are connected through a common bus. Each device controller is in charge of a specific type of device. Depending on the controller, there may be more than one attached device. For instance, seven or more devices can be attached to the **small computer-systems interface (SCSI)** controller. A device controller maintains some local buffer storage and a set of special-purpose registers. The device controller is responsible for moving the data between the peripheral devices that it controls and its local buffer storage. The size of the local buffer within a device controller varies from one controller to another, depending on the particular device being controlled. For example, the size of the buffer of a disk controller is the same as or a multiple of the size of the smallest addressable portion of a disk, called a **sector**, which is usually 512 bytes. Currently, 2MB to 8MB disk controller buffers are common.

2.2.1 I/O Interrupts

To start an I/O operation, the CPU loads the appropriate registers within the device controller. The device controller, in turn, examines the contents of these registers to determine what action to take. For example, if it finds a read request, the controller will start the transfer of data from the device to its local buffer. Once the transfer of data is complete, the device controller informs the CPU that it has finished its operation. It accomplishes this communication by triggering an interrupt.

This situation will occur, in general, as the result of a user process requesting I/O. Once the I/O is started, two courses of action are possible. In the simplest case, the I/O is started; then, at I/O completion, control is returned to the user process. This case is known as **synchronous** I/O. The other possibility, called **asynchronous** I/O, returns control to the user program without waiting for the I/O to complete. The I/O then can continue while other system operations are occurring (Figure 2.3).

Whichever approach is used, waiting for I/O completion is accomplished in one of two ways. Some computers have a special `wait` instruction that idles the CPU until the next interrupt. Machines that do not have such an instruction may have a wait loop:

Loop: `jmp` *Loop*

This tight loop simply continues until an interrupt occurs, transferring control to another part of the operating system. Such a loop might also need to poll any I/O devices that do not support the interrupt structure but that instead simply set a flag in one of their registers and expect the operating system to notice that flag.

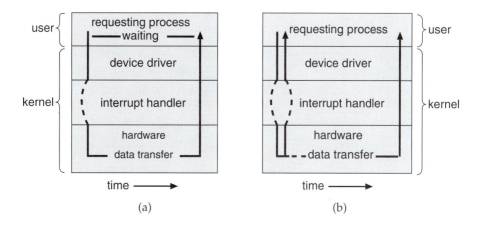

Figure 2.3   Two I/O methods: (a) synchronous, and (b) asynchronous.

If the CPU always waits for I/O completion, as it does when the synchronous approach is used, only one I/O request can be outstanding at a time. Thus, whenever an I/O interrupt occurs, the operating system knows exactly which device is interrupting. However, this approach makes it impossible to operate several I/O devices concurrently or to perform useful computation at the same time as I/O.

A better alternative is to start the I/O and then continue processing other operating-system or user program code—the asynchronous approach. A system call is then needed to allow the user program to wait for I/O completion, if desired. If no user programs are ready to run, and the operating system has no other work to do, we still require the `wait` instruction or idle loop, as before. We also need to be able to keep track of many I/O requests at the same time. For this purpose, the operating system uses a table containing an entry for each I/O device: the **device-status table** (Figure 2.4). Each table entry indicates the device's type, address, and state (not functioning, idle, or busy). If the device is busy with a request, the type of request and other parameters will be stored in the table entry for that device. Since it is possible for other processes to issue requests to the same device, the operating system will also maintain a **wait queue**—a list of waiting requests—for each I/O device.

An I/O device interrupts when it needs service. When an interrupt occurs, the operating system first determines which I/O device caused the interrupt. It then indexes into the I/O device table to determine the status of that device and modifies the table entry to reflect the occurrence of the interrupt. For most devices, an interrupt signals completion of an I/O request. If there are additional requests waiting in the queue for this device, the operating system starts processing the next request.

Finally, control is returned from the I/O interrupt. If a process was waiting for this request to complete (as recorded in the device-status table), we can now

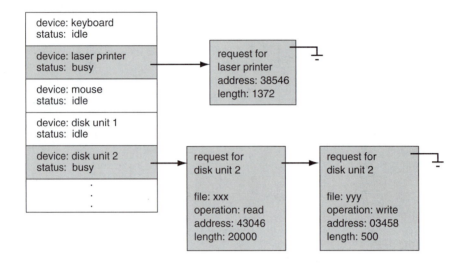

Figure 2.4   Device-status table.

return control to it. Otherwise, we return to whatever we were doing before the I/O interrupt: to the execution of the user program or to the wait loop. In a time-sharing system, the operating system could switch to another ready-to-run process.

The schemes used by specific input devices may vary from this one. Many interactive systems allow users to type ahead—to enter data before the data are requested—on the keyboard. In this case, interrupts may occur, signaling the arrival of characters from the terminal, while the device-status block indicates that no program has requested input from this device. If typeahead is to be allowed, then a buffer must be provided to store the typeahead characters until some program wants them. In general, we keep a kernel buffer for each device, just as each device has its own buffer.

In a simple terminal-input driver, when a line is to be read from the terminal, the first character typed is sent to the computer. When that character is received, the asynchronous-communication (or serial-port) device to which the terminal line is connected interrupts the CPU. When the interrupt request from the terminal arrives, the CPU is about to execute some instruction. (If the CPU is in the middle of executing an instruction, the interrupt is normally held pending the completion of instruction execution.) The address of this interrupted instruction is saved, and control is transferred to the interrupt service routine for the appropriate device.

The interrupt service routine saves the contents of any CPU registers that it will need to use. It checks for any error conditions that might have resulted from the most recent input operation. It then takes the character from the device and stores that character in a buffer. The interrupt routine must also adjust pointer and counter variables, to be sure that the next input character will be stored at the next location in the buffer. The interrupt routine next sets a flag in memory indicating to the other parts of the operating system that new input has been received. The other parts are responsible for processing the data in the buffer and for transferring the characters to the program that is requesting input. Then, the interrupt service routine restores the contents of any saved registers and transfers control back to the interrupted instruction.

It should be clear that the main advantage of asynchronous I/O is increased system efficiency. While I/O is taking place, the system CPU can be used for processing or starting I/Os to other devices. Because I/O can be slow compared to processor speed, the system makes efficient use of its facilities. In Section 2.2.2, we describe another mechanism for improving system performance.

2.2.2 DMA Transfers

Consider characters being typed on a keyboard. The keyboard can accept and transfer one character approximately every 1 millisecond, or 1,000 microseconds. A well-written interrupt service routine to input characters into a buffer may require 2 microseconds per character, leaving 998 microseconds out of every 1000 for CPU computation (and for servicing of other interrupts). Because of this disparity, asynchronous I/O is usually assigned a low interrupt priority, allowing other, more important interrupts to be processed first or even to pre-empt the current interrupt. A high-speed device, however—such as a tape, disk, or communications network—may be able to transmit information at speeds close to memory speeds; if the CPU needs 2 microseconds to respond to each interrupt and interrupts arrive, say, every 4 microseconds, that does not leave much time for process execution.

To solve this problem, **direct memory access** (**DMA**) is used for high-speed I/O devices. After setting up buffers, pointers, and counters for the I/O device, the device controller transfers an entire block of data directly to or from its own buffer storage to memory, with no intervention by the CPU. Only one interrupt is generated per block, rather than the one interrupt per byte generated for low-speed devices.

The basic operation of the CPU is the same. A user program, or the operating system itself, may request data transfer. The operating system finds a buffer (an empty buffer for input or a full buffer for output) from a pool of buffers for the transfer. (The buffers in a buffer pool may have a fixed size or may vary with the kind of I/O being performed.) Next, a portion of the operating system called a **device driver** sets the DMA controller registers to use appropriate source and destination addresses and transfer length. The DMA controller is then instructed to start the I/O operation. While the DMA controller is performing the data transfer, the CPU is free to perform other tasks. Since the memory generally can transfer only one word at a time, the DMA controller "steals" memory cycles from the CPU. This cycle stealing can slow down the CPU execution while a DMA transfer is in progress.

Some high-end systems use switch rather than bus architecture within. On these systems, multiple components can talk to other components concurrently, rather than competing for cycles on a shared bus. In this case, DMA is even more effective, as no cycle stealing need occur during I/O-to-memory transfers. The DMA controller interrupts the CPU when the transfer has been completed. The CPU can then free the output buffer or signal the process waiting for the input buffer that I/O is waiting.

2.3 ■ Storage Structure

Computer programs must be in main memory (also called **random-access memory** or **RAM**) to be executed. Main memory is the only large storage area (millions to billions of bytes) that the processor can access directly. It is implemented in a semiconductor technology called **dynamic random-access memory** (**DRAM**), which forms an array of memory words. Each word has its own address. Interaction is achieved through a sequence of load or store instructions to specific memory addresses. The load instruction moves a word from main memory to an internal register within the CPU, whereas the store instruction moves the content of a register to main memory. In addition to explicit loads and stores, the CPU automatically loads instructions from main memory for execution.

A typical instruction–execution cycle, as executed on a system with a **von Neumann** architecture, will first fetch an instruction from memory and store that instruction in the **instruction register**. The instruction is then decoded and may cause operands to be fetched from memory and stored in some internal register. After the instruction on the operands has been executed, the result may be stored back in memory. Notice that the memory unit sees only a stream of memory addresses; it does not know how they are generated (by the instruction counter, indexing, indirection, literal addresses, and so on) or what they are for (instructions or data). Accordingly, we can ignore *how* a memory address is generated by a program. We are interested only in the sequence of memory addresses generated by the running program.

Ideally, we want the programs and the data to reside in main memory permanently. This arrangement, however, is not possible for the following two reasons:

1. Main memory is usually too small to store all needed programs and data permanently.

2. Main memory is a *volatile* storage device that loses its contents when power is rebooted or otherwise lost.

Thus, most computer systems provide **secondary storage** as an extension of main memory. The main requirement for secondary storage is that it be able to hold large quantities of data permanently.

The most common secondary storage device is a **magnetic disk,** which provides storage for both programs and data. Most programs (web browsers, compilers, word processors, spreadsheets, and so on) are stored on a disk until they are loaded into memory. Many programs then use the disk as both a source and a destination of information for processing. Hence, the proper management of disk storage is of central importance to a computer system, as we discuss in Chapter 14.

In a larger sense, however, the storage structure that we have described— consisting of registers, main memory, and magnetic disks—is only one of many possible storage systems. Other possibilities include cache memory, CD-ROM, magnetic tapes, and so on. Each storage system provides the basic functions of storing a datum and of holding that datum until it is retrieved. The main differences among the various storage systems lie in speed, cost, size, and volatility. In Sections 2.3.1 through 2.3.3, we describe main memory, magnetic disks, and magnetic tapes, because they illustrate the general properties of all important, commercially available storage devices. In Chapter 14, we discuss the properties of many specific devices, such as floppy disks, hard disks, CD-ROMs, and DVDs.

2.3.1 Main Memory

As suggested earlier, main memory and the registers built into the processor itself are the only storage that the CPU can access directly. There are machine instructions that take memory addresses as arguments, but none that take disk addresses. Therefore, any instructions in execution, and any data being used by the instructions, must be in one of these direct-access storage devices. If the data are not in memory, they must be moved there before the CPU can operate on them.

In the case of I/O, as mentioned in Section 2.1, each I/O controller includes registers to hold commands and the data being transferred. Usually, special I/O instructions allow data transfers between these registers and system memory. To provide more convenient access to I/O devices, many computer architectures use **memory-mapped I/O**. In this case, ranges of memory addresses are set aside and mapped to the device registers. Reads and writes to these memory addresses cause the data to be transferred to and from the device registers. This method is appropriate for devices that have fast response times, such as video controllers. In the IBM PC, each location on the screen is mapped to a memory location. Displaying text on the screen is almost as easy as writing the text into the appropriate memory-mapped locations.

Memory-mapped I/O is also convenient for other devices, such as the serial and parallel ports used to connect modems and printers to a computer. The

CPU transfers data through these kinds of devices by reading and writing a few device registers, called I/O **ports**. To send out a long string of bytes through a memory-mapped serial port, the CPU writes one data byte to the data register, then sets a bit in the control register to signal that the byte is available. The device takes the data byte and then clears the bit in the control register to signal that it is ready for the next byte. Then the CPU can transfer the next byte. The CPU may use polling to watch the control bit, constantly looping to see whether the device is ready; this method of operation is called **programmed I/O (PIO)**. If the CPU does not poll the control bit, but instead receives an interrupt when the device is ready for the next byte, the data transfer is **interrupt driven**.

Registers that are built into the CPU are generally accessible within one cycle of the CPU clock. Most CPUs can decode instructions and perform simple operations on register contents at the rate of one or more operations per clock tick. The same cannot be said of main memory, which is accessed via a transaction on the memory bus. Accessing memory may take many cycles of the CPU clock, in which case the processor normally needs to **stall**, since it does not have the data required to complete the instruction that it is executing. Because memory is accessed so frequently, this situation is intolerable. The remedy is to add fast memory between the CPU and main memory. A memory buffer used to accommodate a speed differential, called a **cache**, is described in Section 2.4.1.

2.3.2 Magnetic Disks

Magnetic disks provide the bulk of secondary storage for modern computer systems. Conceptually, disks are relatively simple (Figure 2.5). Each disk **platter** has a flat circular shape, like a CD. Common platter diameters range from 1.8 to 5.25 inches. The two surfaces of a platter are covered with a magnetic material. We store information by recording it magnetically on the platters.

A read–write head "flies" just above each surface of every platter. The heads are attached to a **disk arm**, which moves all the heads as a unit. The surface of a platter is logically divided into circular **tracks**, which are subdivided into **sectors**. The set of tracks that are at one arm position forms a **cylinder**. A disk drive may have thousands of concentric cylinders, and each track may contain hundreds of sectors. The storage capacity of common disk drives is measured in gigabytes.

When the disk is in use, a drive motor spins it at high speed. Most drives rotate 60 to 250 times per second. Disk speed has two parts. The **transfer rate** is the rate at which data flow between the drive and the computer. The **positioning time**, sometimes called the **random-access time**, consists of the time required to move the disk arm to the desired cylinder, called the **seek time**, plus the time required for the desired sector to rotate to the disk head, called the **rotational latency**. Typical disks can transfer several megabytes of data per second, and they have seek times and rotational latencies of several milliseconds.

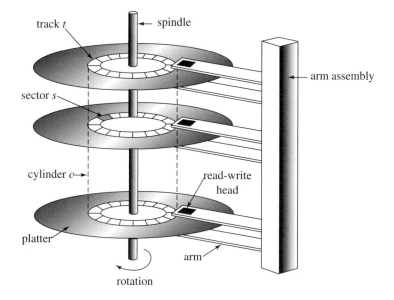

Figure 2.5   Moving-head disk mechanism.

Because the disk head flies on an extremely thin cushion of air (measured in microns) the head can sometimes make contact with the disk surface. When that happens, even though the disk platters are coated with a thin protective layer, the magnetic surface can be damaged. This accident is called a **head crash**. A head crash normally cannot be repaired; the entire disk must be replaced.

Disks can be **removable**, allowing different disks to be mounted as needed. A removable magnetic disk generally consists of one platter, which is held in a plastic case to protect it from damage while it is not in the disk drive. A **floppy disk** is an inexpensive removable magnetic disk consisting of a flexible platter in a soft plastic case. The head of a floppy-disk drive generally sits directly on the disk surface, so the drive is designed to rotate more slowly than a hard-disk drive to reduce the wear on the disk surface. The storage capacity of a floppy disk is typically only 1 MB or so. However, removable disks are available that work much like normal hard disks and have capacities measured in gigabytes. Other removable media include CD-ROMs and DVD-ROMs, which are read by a laser beam that detects pits on the media. CD-ROMs and DVD-ROMs are generally read-only, but read–write versions exist as well. Almost all removable media are slower than fixed media.

A disk drive is attached to a computer by a set of wires called an **I/O bus**. Several kinds of buses are available, including **enhanced integrated drive electronics (EIDE)**, **advanced technology attachment (ATA)**, **fibre channel (FC)**, and **small computer system interface (SCSI)** buses. The data transfers on a bus are carried out by special electronic processors called **controllers**. The

host controller (or host bus adapter, HBA) is the controller at the computer end of the bus. A **disk controller** is built into each disk drive. To perform a disk I/O operation, the computer places a command into the host controller, typically using memory-mapped I/O ports, as described in Section 2.3.1. The host controller then sends the command via messages to the disk controller, and the disk controller operates the disk-drive hardware to carry out the command. Disk controllers usually have a built-in cache. Data transfer at the disk drive happens between the cache and the disk surface, and data transfer to the host, at fast electronic speeds, occurs between the cache and the host controller.

2.3.3 Magnetic Tapes

Magnetic tape was used early as a secondary storage medium. Although it is relatively permanent and can hold large quantities of data, its access time is slow compared with that of main memory. In addition, random access to magnetic tape is about a thousand times slower than random access to magnetic disk. Because of these problems with speed, tapes are not very useful for secondary storage. They are used mainly for backup, for storage of infrequently used information, and as a medium for transferring information from one system to another.

A tape is kept in a spool and is wound or rewound past a read–write head. Moving to the correct spot on a tape can take minutes; but once positioned, tape drives can write data at speeds comparable to those of disk drives. Tapes and their drivers are usually categorized by width, including 4, 8, and 19 millimeters and 1/4 and 1/2 inch. Tape capacities vary greatly, depending on the kind of tape drive. Today, tapes and disks are generally comparable in terms of capacity.

2.4 ■ Storage Hierarchy

The wide variety of storage systems available for computer systems can be organized in a hierarchy (Figure 2.6) according to speed and cost. The higher levels are expensive, but they are fast. As we move down the hierarchy, the cost per bit generally decreases, whereas the access time generally increases. This tradeoff is reasonable; if a given storage system were both faster and less expensive than another—other properties being the same—then there would be no reason to use the slower, more expensive memory. In fact, many early storage devices, including paper tape and core memories, are relegated to museums now that magnetic tape and **semiconductor memory** have become faster and cheaper. The top four levels of memory in Figure 2.6 may be constructed using semiconductor memory.

In addition to having differing speeds and costs, the various storage systems are either volatile or nonvolatile. **Volatile storage** loses its contents when

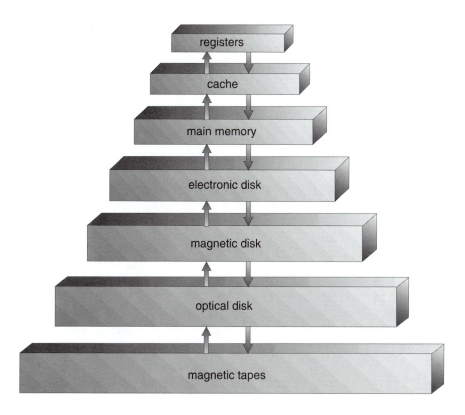

Figure 2.6   Storage-device hierarchy.

the power to the device is removed. In the absence of expensive battery and generator backup systems, data must be written to **nonvolatile storage** for safe-keeping. In the hierarchy shown in Figure 2.6, the storage systems above the electronic disk are volatile, whereas those below are nonvolatile. An **electronic disk** can be designed to be either volatile or nonvolatile. During normal operation, the electronic disk stores data in a large DRAM array, which is volatile. But many electronic-disk devices contain a hidden magnetic hard disk and a battery for backup power. If external power is interrupted, the electronic-disk controller copies the data from RAM to the magnetic disk. When external power is restored, the controller copies the data back into the RAM.

The design of a complete memory system must balance all these factors: It uses only as much expensive memory as necessary while providing as much inexpensive, nonvolatile memory as possible. Where a large access-time or transfer-rate disparity exists between two components, caches can be installed to improve performance.

2.4.1 Caching

Caching, which we have already referred to several times in this chapter, is an important principle of computer systems. Information is normally kept in some storage system (such as main memory). As it is used, it is copied into a faster storage system—the cache—on a temporary basis. When we need a particular piece of information, we first check whether it is in the cache. If it is, we use the information directly from the cache; if it is not, we read the information from the slower source, putting a copy in the cache under the assumption that we will need it again soon.

In addition, internal programmable registers, such as index registers, provide a high-speed cache for main memory. The programmer (or compiler) implements the register-allocation and register-replacement algorithms to decide which information to keep in registers and which to keep in main memory.

There are also caches that are implemented totally in hardware. For instance, most systems have an instruction cache to hold the next instructions expected to be executed. Without this cache, the CPU would have to wait several cycles while an instruction was fetched from main memory. For similar reasons, most systems have one or more high-speed data caches in the memory hierarchy. We are not concerned with these hardware-only caches in this text, since they are outside of the control of the operating system.

Because caches have limited size, **cache management** is an important design issue. Careful selection of the cache size and of a replacement policy can result in a system in which 80 to 99 percent of all accesses take place in the cache, greatly increasing performance. Various replacement algorithms for software-controlled caches are discussed in Chapter 10.

Main memory can be viewed as a fast cache for secondary storage, since data in secondary storage must be copied into main memory for use and data must be in main memory before being moved to secondary storage for safekeeping. The file-system data, which resides permanently on secondary storage, may appear on several levels in the storage hierarchy. At the highest level, the operating system may maintain a cache of file-system data in main memory. Also, electronic RAM disks (also known as **solid-state disks**) may be used for high-speed storage that is accessed through the file-system interface. The bulk of secondary storage is on magnetic disks. The magnetic-disk storage, in turn, is often backed up onto magnetic tapes or removable disks to protect against data loss in case of a hard-disk failure. Some systems automatically archive old file data from secondary storage to tertiary storage, such as tape jukeboxes, to lower the storage cost (see Chapter 14).

The movement of information between levels of a storage hierarchy may be either explicit or implicit, depending on the hardware design and the controlling operating-system software. For instance, data transfer from cache to CPU and registers is usually a hardware function, with no operating-system intervention. In contrast, transfer of data from disk to memory is usually controlled by the operating system.

2.4.2 Coherency and Consistency

In a hierarchical storage structure, the same data may appear in different levels. For example, suppose that integer A is located in file B, which resides on magnetic disk. Integer A is to be incremented by 1. The increment operation proceeds by first issuing an I/O operation to copy the disk block on which A resides to main memory. Next, A is copied to the cache and to an internal register. Thus, the copy of A appears in several places: on the magnetic disk, in main memory, in the cache, and in an internal register (see Figure 2.7). Once the increment takes place in the internal register, the values of A in the various storage systems differ. The values become the same only after the new value of A is written from the internal register back to the magnetic disk.

In a computing environment where only one process executes at a time, this arrangement poses no difficulties, since an access to the integer A will always be to the copy at the highest level of the hierarchy. However, in a multitasking environment, where the CPU is switched back and forth among various processes, extreme care must be taken to ensure that, if several processes wish to access A, then each of these processes will obtain the most recently updated value of A.

The situation becomes still more complicated in a multiprocessor environment, where, in addition to maintaining internal registers, each of the CPUs also contains a local cache. In such an environment, a copy of A may exist simultaneously in several caches. Since the various CPUs can all execute concurrently, we must make sure that an update to the value of A in one cache is immediately reflected in all other caches where A resides. This situation is called **cache coherency**, and it is usually a hardware problem (handled below the operating-system level).

In a distributed environment, the situation becomes even more complex. In such an environment, several copies (or replicas) of the same file can be kept on different computers that are distributed in space. Since the various replicas may be accessed and updated concurrently, we must ensure that, when a replica is updated in one place, all other replicas are brought up to date as soon as

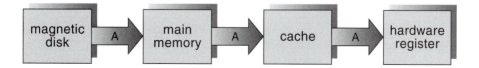

Figure 2.7   Migration of integer A from disk to register.

possible. There are various ways to achieve this guarantee, as we discuss in Chapter 16.

2.5 ■ Hardware Protection

As we have seen, early computer systems were single-user programmer-operated systems. When programmers operated the computer from the console, they had complete control over the system. As operating systems developed, however, this control shifted. Early operating systems were called **resident monitors**; and starting with resident monitors, operating systems began to perform many of the functions, especially I/O, for which the programmer had previously been responsible.

In addition, to improve system utilization, the operating system began to *share* system resources among several programs simultaneously. With *spooling*, for example, one program might have been executing while I/O occurred for other processes; the disk simultaneously held data for many processes. With multiprogramming, several programs might be in memory at the same time.

This sharing both improved utilization and increased problems. When the system was run without sharing, an error in a program could cause problems only for the one program that was running. With sharing, many processes could be adversely affected by a bug in one program.

For example, consider the simple batch operating system (Section 1.2.1), which provides nothing more than automatic job sequencing. If a program gets stuck in a loop reading input cards, the program will read through all its data and, unless something stops it, will continue reading the cards of the next job, and the next, and so on. This loop could prevent the correct operation of many jobs.

More subtle errors can occur in a multiprogramming system, where one erroneous program might modify another program, the data of another program, or even the resident monitor itself. MS-DOS and the Macintosh OS both allow this kind of error.

Without protection against these sorts of errors, either the computer must execute only one process at a time or all output must be suspect. A properly designed operating system must ensure that an incorrect (or malicious) program cannot cause other programs to execute incorrectly.

2.5.1 Dual-Mode Operation

To ensure proper operation, we must protect the operating system and all other programs and their data from any malfunctioning program. Protection is needed for any shared resource. The approach taken by many operating systems provides hardware support that allows us to differentiate among various modes of execution.

At the very least, we need two separate **modes** of operation: **user mode** and **monitor mode** (also called **supervisor mode**, **system mode**, or **privileged mode**). A bit, called the **mode bit**, is added to the hardware of the computer to indicate the current mode: monitor (0) or user (1). With the mode bit, we are able to distinguish between a task that is executed on behalf of the operating system and one that is executed on behalf of the user. As we shall see, this architectural enhancement is useful for many other aspects of system operation as well.

At system boot time, the hardware starts in monitor mode. The operating system is then loaded and starts user processes in user mode. Whenever a trap or interrupt occurs, the hardware switches from user mode to monitor mode (that is, changes the state of the mode bit to 0). Thus, whenever the operating system gains control of the computer, it is in monitor mode. The system always switches to user mode (by setting the mode bit to 1) before passing control to a user program.

The dual mode of operation provides us with the means for protecting the operating system from errant users—and errant users from one another. We accomplish this protection by designating some of the machine instructions that may cause harm as **privileged instructions**. The hardware allows privileged instructions to be executed only in monitor mode. If an attempt is made to execute a privileged instruction in user mode, the hardware does not execute the instruction but rather treats it as illegal and traps it to the operating system.

The concept of privileged instructions also provides the means for a user program to ask the operating system to perform tasks that are reserved to the operating system on the user program's behalf. Each such request is invoked by the user executing a privileged instruction. Such a request is known as a *system call* (also called a *monitor call* or an *operating-system function call*)—as described in Section 2.1.

When a system call is executed, it is treated by the hardware as a software interrupt. Control passes through the interrupt vector to a service routine in the operating system, and the mode bit is set to monitor mode. The system-call service routine is a part of the operating system. The monitor examines the interrupting instruction to determine what system call has occurred; a parameter indicates what type of service the user program is requesting. Additional information needed for the request may be passed in registers, on the stack, or in memory (with pointers to the memory locations passed in registers). The monitor verifies that the parameters are correct and legal, executes the request, and returns control to the instruction following the system call.

The lack of a hardware-supported dual mode can cause serious shortcomings in an operating system. For instance, MS-DOS was written for the Intel 8088 architecture, which has no mode bit and, therefore, no dual mode. A user program running awry can wipe out the operating system by writing over it with data; and multiple programs are able to write to a device at the same time, with possibly disastrous results. More recent and advanced versions of the

Intel CPU, such as the Pentium, do provide dual-mode operation. Accordingly, more recent operating systems, such as Microsoft Windows 2000 and XP, IBM OS/2, and Linux and Solaris for x86 systems, take advantage of this feature and provide greater protection for the operating system.

Once hardware protection is in place, errors violating modes are detected by the hardware. These errors are normally handled by the operating system. If a user program fails in some way—such as by making an attempt either to execute an illegal instruction or to access memory that is not in the user's address space—then the hardware will trap to the operating system. The trap transfers control through the interrupt vector to the operating system, just as an interrupt does. When a program error occurs, the operating system must terminate the program abnormally. This situation is handled by the same code as is a user-requested abnormal termination. An appropriate error message is given, and the memory of the program may be dumped. The memory dump is usually written to a file so that the user or programmer can examine it and perhaps correct it and restart the program.

2.5.2 I/O Protection

A user program may disrupt the normal operation of the system by issuing illegal I/O instructions, by accessing memory locations within the operating system itself, or by refusing to relinquish the CPU. We can use various mechanisms to ensure that such disruptions cannot take place in the system.

To prevent users from performing illegal I/O, we define all I/O instructions to be privileged instructions. Thus, users cannot issue I/O instructions directly; they must do it through the operating system by means of a system call (Figure 2.8). The operating system, executing in monitor mode, checks to make sure that the request is valid and (if it is valid) performs the I/O requested. The operating system then returns to the user.

For I/O protection to be complete, we must be sure that a user program can never gain control of the computer in monitor mode. If it could, I/O protection could be compromised. Consider a computer executing in user mode. It will switch to monitor mode whenever an interrupt or trap occurs, jumping to the address determined from the interrupt vector. If a user program, as part of its execution, stores a new address in the interrupt vector, this new address could overwrite the previous address with an address in the user program. Then, when a corresponding trap or interrupt occurred, the hardware would switch to monitor mode and would transfer control through the (modified) interrupt vector to the user program! The user program could gain control of the computer in monitor mode. User programs could gain control of the computer in monitor mode in many other ways as well. In addition, new bugs are discovered every day that can be exploited to bypass system protections. These topics are discussed in Chapters 18 and 19.

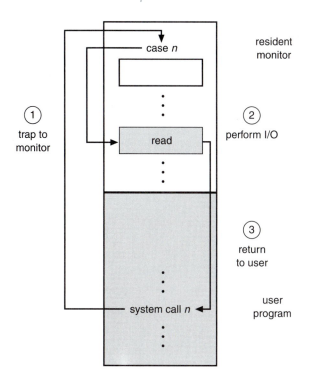

Figure 2.8   Use of a system call to perform I/O.

2.5.3 Memory Protection

To ensure correct operation, we must protect the interrupt vector from modification by a user program. In addition, we must protect the interrupt-service routines in the operating system from modification. Even if the user did not gain unauthorized control of the computer, modifying the interrupt service routines would probably disrupt the proper operation of the computer system and of its spooling and buffering.

We see, then, that we must provide memory protection at least for the interrupt vector and the interrupt-service routines of the operating system. In general, we want to protect the operating system from access by user programs and, in addition, to protect user programs from one another. This protection must be provided by the hardware. It can be implemented in several ways, as we describe in Chapter 9. Here, we outline one possible implementation.

To separate each program's memory space from the others', we need the ability to determine the range of legal addresses that the program may access and to protect the memory outside that space. We can provide this protection by using two registers, usually a base and a limit, as illustrated in Figure 2.9. The **base register** holds the smallest legal physical memory address; the **limit register** contains the size of the range. For example, if the base register holds

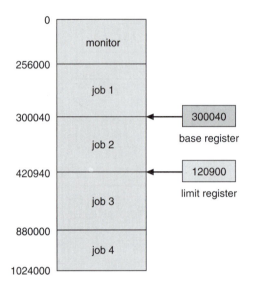

Figure 2.9   A base and a limit register define a logical address space.

300040 and the limit register is 120900, then the program can legally access all addresses from 300040 through 420940 inclusive.

The CPU hardware compares *every* address generated in user mode with the registers. Any attempt by a program executing in user mode to access monitor memory or other users' memory results in a trap to the monitor, which treats the attempt as a fatal error (Figure 2.10). This scheme prevents the user program from (accidentally or deliberately) modifying the code or data structures of either the operating system or other users.

The base and limit registers can be loaded only by the operating system, which uses a special privileged instruction. Since privileged instructions can be executed only in monitor mode, and since only the operating system executes in monitor mode, only the operating system can load the base and limit registers. This scheme allows the monitor to change the value of the registers but prevents user programs from changing the registers' contents.

The operating system, executing in monitor mode, is given unrestricted access to both the monitor and users' memory. This provision allows the operating system to load users' programs into users' memory, to dump out those programs in case of errors, to access and modify parameters of system calls, and so on.

2.5.4 CPU Protection

In addition to protecting I/O and memory, we must ensure that the operating system maintains control. We must prevent a user program from, for example,

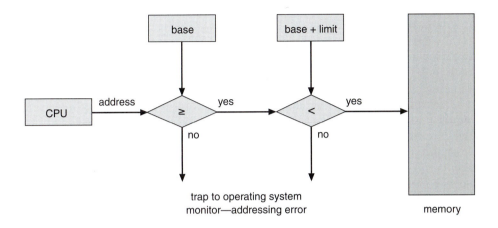

Figure 2.10   Hardware address protection with base and limit registers.

getting stuck in an infinite loop and never returning control to the operating system. To accomplish this goal, we can use a **timer**. A timer can be set to interrupt the computer after a specified period. The period may be fixed (for example, 1/60 second) or variable (for example, from 1 millisecond to 1 second). A **variable timer** is generally implemented by a fixed-rate clock and a counter. The operating system sets the counter. Every time the clock ticks, the counter is decremented. When the counter reaches 0, an interrupt occurs. For instance, a 10-bit counter with a 1-millisecond clock allows interrupts at intervals from 1 millisecond to 1,024 milliseconds, in steps of 1 millisecond.

Before turning over control to the user, the operating system ensures that the timer is set to interrupt. If the timer interrupts, control transfers automatically to the operating system, which may treat the interrupt as a fatal error or may give the program more time. Clearly, instructions that modify the operation of the timer are privileged.

Thus, we can use the timer to prevent a user program from running too long. A simple technique is to initialize a counter with the amount of time that a program is allowed to run. A program with a 7-minute time limit, for example, would have its counter initialized to 420. Every second, the timer interrupts, and the counter is decremented by 1. As long as the counter is positive, control is returned to the user program. When the counter becomes negative, the operating system terminates the program for exceeding the assigned time limit.

A more common use of a timer is to implement time sharing. In the most straightforward case, the timer could be set to interrupt every N milliseconds, where N is the **time slice** that each user is allowed to execute before the next user gets control of the CPU. The operating system is invoked at the end of each time slice to perform various housekeeping tasks, such as adding the value N to the record that specifies (for accounting purposes) the amount of time the user program has executed thus far. The operating system also saves registers, internal variables, and buffers and changes several other parameters to prepare for the next program to run. This procedure is known as a **context switch**; it is explored in Chapter 4. Following a context switch, the next program continues with its execution from the point at which it left off (when its previous time slice ran out).

Another use of the timer is to compute the current time. A timer interrupt signals the passage of some period, allowing the operating system to compute the current time in reference to some initial time. If we have interrupts every 1 second, for example, and we have had 1,427 interrupts since we were told that it was 1:00 P.M., then we can compute that the current time is 1:23:47 P.M. Some computers determine the current time in this manner, but the calculations must be done carefully for the time to be kept accurately, since the interrupt-processing time (and other times when interrupts are disabled) tends to cause the software clock to slow down. Most computers have a separate hardware time-of-day clock that is independent of the operating system.

2.6 ■ Network Structure

Our discussions thus far have covered single, stand-alone computer systems. However, by connecting two—or more—computer systems to a network, a distributed system can be formed. Such a system can provide a rich set of services to users as outlined in Section 1.5. In this section we explore two techniques for constructing computer networks.

As discussed in Chapter 1, there are basically two types of networks: local-area networks (LAN) and wide-area networks (WAN). The main difference between the two is the way in which they are geographically distributed. Local-area networks are composed of processors that are distributed over small geographical areas (such as a single building or a number of adjacent buildings). Wide-area networks, in contrast, are composed of a number of autonomous processors that are distributed over a large geographical area (such as the United States). These differences imply major variations in the speed and reliability of the communications network, and they are reflected in the distributed operating-system design.

2.6.1 Local-Area Networks

Local-area networks emerged in the early 1970s as a substitute for large mainframe computer systems. For many enterprises, it is more economical to have a number of small computers, each with its own self-contained applications, than a single large system. Because each small computer is likely to need a full complement of peripheral devices (such as disks and printers), and because some form of data sharing is likely to occur in a single enterprise, it was a natural step to connect these small systems into a network.

LANs are generally used in an office environment (and even a home environment). All the sites in such systems are close to one another, so the communication links tend to have a higher speed and lower error rate than do their counterparts in wide-area networks. High-quality (expensive) cables are needed to attain this higher speed and reliability. Generally, LAN cables are used exclusively for data network traffic. Over longer distances, the cost of using high-quality cable is enormous, and exclusive use of the cable tends to be prohibitively expensive.

The most common links in a local-area network are twisted-pair (copper) and fiber-optic cabling. The most common configurations are multiaccess bus, star, and ring networks. Communication speeds range from 1 megabit per second, for networks such as AppleTalk and Bluetooth local radio network, to 10 gigabits per second for 10 gigabit Ethernet. Ten megabits per second is common and is the speed of **10BaseT Ethernet**. 100BaseT Ethernet, which runs at 100 megabits per second, requires a higher-quality cable but is becoming common. Also growing is the use of optical-fiber-based FDDI networking. The FDDI network is token-based and runs at over 100 megabits per second. The use of gigabit Ethernet (1000BaseT) to link servers within a data center is spreading, as is the use of wireless access, which involves no physical cabling. The two most common schemes for wireless systems are 802.11b and 802.11g, which run at 11 Mbps and 54 Mbps respectively.

A typical LAN may consist of a number of computers (from mainframes to laptops or PDAs), various shared peripheral devices (such as laser printers and magnetic-tape drives), and one or more gateways (specialized processors) that provide access to other networks (Figure 2.11). An Ethernet scheme is commonly used to construct LANs. An Ethernet network has no central controller, because it is a multiaccess bus, so new hosts can be added easily to the network.

2.6.2 Wide-Area Networks

Wide-area networks emerged in the late 1960s, mainly as an academic research project to provide efficient communication among sites, allowing hardware and software to be shared conveniently and economically by a wide community of users. The first WAN to be designed and developed was the *Arpanet*. Begun in 1968, the Arpanet has grown from a four-site experimental network to a worldwide network of networks—the Internet—comprising millions of computer systems.

Because the sites in a WAN are physically distributed over a large geographical area, the communication links are, by default, relatively slow (transmission rates range from 56K bits per second to over 1 megabit per second) and sometimes unreliable. Typical links are telephone lines, leased (dedicated data) lines, microwave links, and satellite channels. These communication links are controlled by special **communication processors** (Figure 2.12), which are

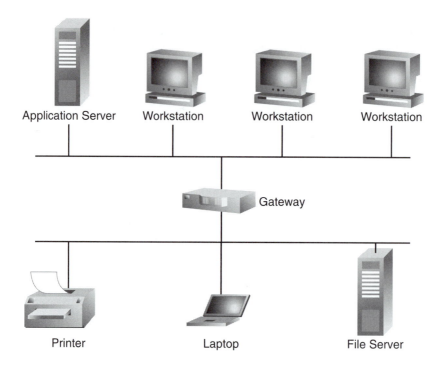

Figure 2.11   Local-area network.

responsible for defining the interface through which the sites communicate over the network, as well as for transferring information among the various sites.

Consider the Internet as an example. The host computers that communicate via the Internet typically differ from one another in type, speed, word length, operating system, and so on. Hosts are generally on LANs, which are, in turn, connected to the Internet via regional networks. The regional networks, such as NSFnet in the northeast United States, are interlinked with **routers** (Section 15.3.2) to form the worldwide network. Connections between networks frequently use a telephone-system service called T1, which provides a transfer rate of 1.544 megabits per second over a leased line. For sites requiring faster Internet access, T1s are collected into multiple-T1 units that work in parallel to provide more throughput. For instance, a T3 is composed of 28 T1 connections and has a transfer rate of 45 megabits per second. The routers control the path each message takes through the net. This routing may be either dynamic, to increase communications efficiency, or static, to reduce security risks or to allow communications charges to be computed.

Other WANs use standard telephone lines as their primary means of communication. **Modems** are devices that accept digital data from the computer side and convert it to the analog signals that the telephone system uses. A modem at the destination site converts the analog signal back to digital, and the

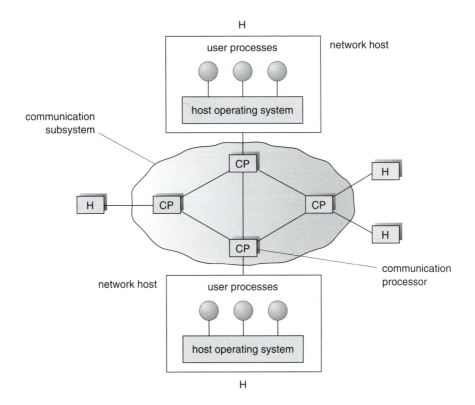

Figure 2.12   Communication processors in a wide-area network.

destination receives the data. The UNIX news network, UUCP, allows systems to communicate with each other at predetermined times, via modems, to exchange messages. The messages are then routed to other nearby systems and in this way either are propagated to all hosts on the network (public messages) or are transferred to their destination (private messages). UUCP has been superseded by PPP, the point-to-point protocol. PPP functions over modem connections, allowing home computers to be fully connected to the Internet. Many other connection methods are available, including DSL and cable modem. Access varies depending on physical location and service provider offerings, cost, and speed.

2.7 ▪ Summary

Multiprogramming and time-sharing systems improve performance by over-lapping CPU and I/O operations on a single machine. Such an overlap requires that data transfer between the CPU and an I/O device be handled either by polled or interrupt-driven access to an I/O port or by a DMA data transfer.

For a computer to do its job of executing programs, the programs must be in main memory. Main memory is the only large storage area that the processor can access directly. It is an array of words or bytes, ranging in size from millions to billions. Each word has its own address. The main memory is a volatile storage device that loses its contents when power is turned off or lost. Most computer systems provide secondary storage as an extension of main memory. The main requirement of secondary storage is the ability to hold large quantities of data permanently. The most common secondary storage device is a magnetic disk, which provides storage of both programs and data. A magnetic disk is a nonvolatile storage device that also provides random access. Magnetic tapes are used mainly for backup, for storage of infrequently used information, and as a medium for transferring information from one system to another.

The wide variety of storage systems in a computer system can be organized in a hierarchy according to their speed and cost. The higher levels are expensive, but they are fast. As we move down the hierarchy, the cost per bit generally decreases, whereas the access time generally increases.

The operating system ensures correct operation of the computer system in a number of ways. To prevent user programs from interfering with the proper operation of the system, the hardware has two modes: user mode and monitor mode. Various instructions (such as I/O instructions and halt instructions) are privileged and can be executed only in monitor mode. The memory in which the operating system resides is protected from modification by the user. A timer prevents infinite loops. These facilities—dual mode, privileged instructions, memory protection, and timer interrupt—are basic building blocks used by operating systems to achieve correct operation. Chapter 3 continues this discussion with details of the facilities that operating systems provide.

LANs and WANs are the two basic types of networks. LANs, usually connected by expensive twisted-pair or fiber-optic cabling, enable processors distributed over a small geographical area to communicate. WANs, connected by telephone lines, leased lines, microwave links, or satellite channels, allow processors distributed over a larger geographical area to communicate. LANs typically transmit more than 100 megabits per second, whereas slower WANs transmit from 56K bits per second to more than 1 megabit per second.

■ Exercises

2.1 *Prefetching* is a method of overlapping the I/O of a job with that job's own computation. The idea is simple. After a read operation completes and the job is about to start operating on the data, the input device is instructed to begin the next read immediately. The CPU and input device are then both busy. With luck, by the time the job is ready for the next data item, the input device will have finished reading that data item. The CPU can then begin processing the newly read data, while the input device starts to read the following data. A similar idea can be used for output. In this case, the job creates data that are put into a buffer until an output device can accept them.

Compare the prefetching scheme with *spooling*, where the CPU overlaps the input of one job with the computation and output of other jobs.

2.2 How does the distinction between monitor mode and user mode function as a rudimentary form of protection (security) system?

2.3 What are the differences between a trap and an interrupt? What is the use of each function?

2.4 For what types of operations is DMA useful? Explain your answer.

2.5 Which of the following instructions should be privileged?

    a. Set value of timer.

    b. Read the clock.

    c. Clear memory.

    d. Turn off interrupts.

    e. Switch from user to monitor mode.

2.6 Some computer systems do not provide a privileged mode of operation in hardware. Is it possible to construct a secure operating system for these computers? Give arguments both that it is and that it is not possible.

2.7 Some early computers protected the operating system by placing it in a memory partition that could not be modified by either the user job or the operating system itself. Describe two difficulties that you think could arise with such a scheme.

2.8 Protecting the operating system is crucial to ensuring that the computer system operates correctly. Provision of this protection is the reason for dual-mode operation, memory protection, and the timer. To allow maximum flexibility, however, you should also place minimal constraints on the user.

The following is a list of instructions that are normally protected. What is the *minimal* set of instructions that must be protected?

    a. Change to user mode.

    b. Change to monitor mode.

    c. Read from monitor memory.

    d. Write into monitor memory.

    e. Fetch an instruction from monitor memory.

      f. Turn on timer interrupt.

      g. Turn off timer interrupt.

2.9 Give two reasons why caches are useful. What problems do they solve? What problems do they cause? If a cache can be made as large as the device for which it is caching (for instance, a cache as large as a disk), why not make it that large and eliminate the device?

2.10 Writing an operating system that can operate without interference from malicious or undebugged user programs requires hardware assistance. Name three hardware aids for writing an operating system, and describe how they could be used together to protect the operating system.

2.11 Some CPUs provide for more than two modes of operation. What are two possible uses of these multiple modes?

2.12 What are the main differences between a WAN and a LAN?

2.13 What network configuration would best suit the following environments?

      a. A dormitory floor.

      b. A university campus.

      c. A state.

      d. A nation.

Bibliographical Notes

Hennessy and Patterson [2002] provide coverage of I/O systems and buses and of system architecture in general. Tanenbaum [1990] describes the architecture of microcomputers, starting at a detailed hardware level.

Discussions concerning magnetic-disk technology are presented by Freedman [1983] and by Harker et al. [1981]. Optical disks are covered by Kenville [1982], Fujitani [1984], O'Leary and Kitts [1985], Gait [1988], and Olsen and Kenley [1989]. Discussions of floppy disks are offered by Pechura and Schoeffler [1983] and by Sarisky [1983].

Cache memories, including associative memory, are described and analyzed by Smith [1982]. That paper also includes an extensive bibliography on the subject.

General discussions concerning mass-storage technology are offered by Chi [1982] and by Hoagland [1985].

Tanenbaum [2003] and Halsall [1992] provide general overviews of computer networks. Fortier [1989] presents a detailed discussion of networking hardware and software.

Chapter 3

OPERATING-SYSTEM STRUCTURES

An operating system provides the environment within which programs are executed. Internally, operating systems vary greatly in their makeup, since they are organized along many different lines. The design of a new operating system is a major task. It is important that the goals of the system be well defined before the design begins. These goals form the basis for choices among various algorithms and strategies.

We can view an operating system from several vantage points. One view focuses on the services that the system provides; another, on the interface that it makes available to users and programmers; and a third, on its components and their interconnections. In this chapter, we explore all three aspects of operating systems, showing the viewpoints of users, programmers, and operating-system designers. We consider what services an operating system provides, how they are provided, and what the various methodologies are for designing such systems. Finally, we describe how operating systems are created and how a computer starts its operating system.

3.1 ■ System Components

We can create a system as large and complex as an operating system only by partitioning it into smaller pieces. Each of these pieces should be a well-delineated portion of the system, with carefully defined inputs, outputs, and functions. Obviously, not all systems have the same structure. However, many modern systems share the goal of supporting the system components outlined in Sections 3.1.1 through 3.1.8.

3.1.1 Process Management

A program does nothing unless its instructions are executed by a CPU. A program in execution can be thought of as a **process**. A time-shared user program such as a compiler is a process. A word-processing program being run by an individual user on a PC is a process. A system task, such as sending output to a printer, also is a process. For now, you can consider a process to be a job or a time-shared program, but later you will learn that the concept is more general. As we shall see in Chapter 4, it is possible to provide system calls that allow processes to create subprocesses to execute concurrently.

A process needs certain resources—including CPU time, memory, files, and I/O devices—to accomplish its task. These resources are either given to the process when it is created or allocated to it while it is running. In addition to the various physical and logical resources that a process obtains when it is created, various initialization data (input) may be passed along. For example, consider a process whose function is to display the status of a file on the screen of a terminal. The process will be given as an input the name of the file and will execute the appropriate instructions and system calls to obtain and display on the terminal the desired information. When the process terminates, the operating system will reclaim any reusable resources.

We emphasize that a program by itself is not a process; a program is a *passive* entity, such as the contents of a file stored on disk, whereas a process is an *active* entity. A single-threaded process has one **program counter** specifying the next instruction to execute. (Threads will be covered in Chapter 5.) The execution of such a process must be sequential. The CPU executes one instruction of the process after another, until the process completes. Further, at any time, one instruction at most is executed on behalf of the process. Thus, although two processes may be associated with the same program, they are nevertheless considered two separate execution sequences. It is common to have a program that spawns many processes as it runs. A multithreaded process has multiple program counters, each pointing to the next instruction to execute for a given thread.

A process is the unit of work in a system. Such a system consists of a collection of processes, some of which are operating-system processes (those that execute system code) and the rest of which are user processes (those that execute user code). All these processes can potentially execute concurrently—by multiplexing the CPU among them on a single CPU, for example.

The operating system is responsible for the following activities in connection with process management:

- Creating and deleting both user and system processes

- Suspending and resuming processes

- Providing mechanisms for process synchronization

- Providing mechanisms for process communication

- Providing mechanisms for deadlock handling

We discuss process-management techniques in Chapters 4 through 7.

3.1.2 Main-Memory Management

As we discussed in Chapter 1, the main memory is central to the operation of a modern computer system. Main memory is a large array of words or bytes, ranging in size from hundreds of thousands to billions. Each word or byte has its own address. Main memory is a repository of quickly accessible data shared by the CPU and I/O devices. The central processor reads instructions from main memory during the instruction-fetch cycle and both reads and writes data from main memory during the data-fetch cycle (at least on a Von Neumann architecture). The I/O operations implemented via DMA also read and write data in main memory. The main memory is generally the only large storage device that the CPU is able to address and access directly. For example, for the CPU to process data from disk, those data must first be transferred to main memory by CPU-generated I/O calls. In the same way, instructions must be in memory for the CPU to execute them.

For a program to be executed, it must be mapped to absolute addresses and loaded into memory. As the program executes, it accesses program instructions and data from memory by generating these absolute addresses. Eventually, the program terminates, its memory space is declared available, and the next program can be loaded and executed.

To improve both the utilization of the CPU and the speed of the computer's response to its users, we must keep several programs in memory, creating a need for memory management. Many different memory-management schemes are used. These schemes reflect various approaches, and the effectiveness of the different algorithms depends on the particular situation. Selection of a memory-management scheme for a specific system depends on many factors —especially on the *hardware* design of the system. Each algorithm requires its own hardware support.

The operating system is responsible for the following activities in connection with memory management:

- Keeping track of which parts of memory are currently being used and by whom

- Deciding which processes are to be loaded into memory when memory space becomes available

- Allocating and deallocating memory space as needed

Memory-management techniques will be discussed in Chapters 9 and 10.

3.1.3 File Management

File management is one of the most visible components of an operating system. Computers can store information on several different types of physical media. Magnetic disk, optical disk, and magnetic tape are the most common. Each of these media has its own characteristics and physical organization. Each medium is controlled by a device, such as a disk drive or tape drive, that also has its own unique characteristics. These properties include access speed, capacity, data-transfer rate, and access method (sequential or random).

For convenient use of the computer system, the operating system provides a uniform logical view of information storage. The operating system abstracts from the physical properties of its storage devices to define a logical storage unit, the file. The operating system maps files onto physical media and accesses these files via the storage devices.

A **file** is a collection of related information defined by its creator. Commonly, files represent programs (both source and object forms) and data. Data files may be numeric, alphabetic, alphanumeric, or binary. Files may be free-form (for example, text files), or they may be formatted rigidly (for example, fixed fields). Clearly, the concept of a file is an extremely general one.

The operating system implements the abstract concept of a file by managing mass storage media, such as tapes and disks, and the devices that control them. Also, files are normally organized into directories to make them easier to use. Finally, when multiple users have access to files, it may be desirable to control by whom and in what ways (for example, read, write, append) files may be accessed.

The operating system is responsible for the following activities in connection with file management:

- Creating and deleting files

- Creating and deleting directories

- Supporting primitives for manipulating files and directories

- Mapping files onto secondary storage

- Backing up files on stable (nonvolatile) storage media

File-management techniques will be discussed in Chapters 11 and 12.

3.1.4 I/O-System Management

One of the purposes of an operating system is to hide the peculiarities of specific hardware devices from the user. For example, in UNIX, the peculiarities of I/O devices are hidden from the bulk of the operating system itself by the **I/O subsystem**. The I/O subsystem consists of

- A memory-management component that includes buffering, caching, and spooling

- A general device-driver interface

- Drivers for specific hardware devices

Only the device driver knows the peculiarities of the specific device to which it is assigned.

We discussed in Chapter 2 how interrupt handlers and device drivers are used in the construction of efficient I/O subsystems. In Chapter 13, we discuss how the I/O subsystem interfaces to the other system components, manages devices, transfers data, and detects I/O completion.

3.1.5 Secondary-Storage Management

The main purpose of a computer system is to execute programs. These programs, with the data they access, must be in main memory, or **primary storage**, during execution. Because main memory is too small to accommodate all data and programs, and because the data that it holds are lost when power is lost, the computer system must provide **secondary storage** to back up main memory. Most modern computer systems use disks as the principal on-line storage medium for both programs and data. Most programs—including compilers, assemblers, word processors, editors, and formatters—are stored on a disk until loaded into memory and then use the disk as both the source and destination of their processing. Hence, the proper management of disk storage is of central importance to a computer system. The operating system is responsible for the following activities in connection with disk management:

- Free-space management

- Storage allocation

- Disk scheduling

Because secondary storage is used frequently, it must be used efficiently. The entire speed of operation of a computer may hinge on the speeds of the disk subsystem and of the algorithms that manipulate that subsystem. Techniques for secondary-storage management will be discussed in Chapter 14.

3.1.6 Networking

A **distributed system** is a collection of processors that do not share memory, peripheral devices, or a clock. Instead, each processor has its own local memory and clock, and the processors communicate with one another through various communication lines, such as high-speed buses or networks. The processors in a distributed system vary in size and function. They may include small microprocessors, workstations, minicomputers, and large, general-purpose computer systems.

The processors in the system are connected through a **communication network**, which can be configured in a number of different ways. The network may be fully or partially connected. The communication-network design must consider message routing and connection strategies, as well as the problems of contention and security.

A distributed system collects physically separate, possibly heterogeneous, systems into a single coherent system, providing the user with access to the various resources that the system maintains.   Access to a shared resource increases computation speed, functionality, data availability, and reliability. Operating systems usually generalize network access as a form of file access, with the details of networking contained in the network interface's device driver. The protocols that create a distributed system can greatly affect that system's utility and popularity. The innovation of the World Wide Web was to create a new access method for information sharing. It improved on the existing file-transfer protocol (FTP) and network file-system (NFS) protocol by removing the need for a user to log in before gaining access to a remote resource. It defined a new protocol, **http**, for use in communication between a web server and a web browser. A web browser need only send a request for information to a remote machine's web server, and the information (text, graphics, links to other information) is returned. This increase in convenience fostered huge growth in the use of http and of the Web in general.

We discuss networks and distributed systems, with particular focus on distributed computing using Java, in Chapters 15 and 16.

3.1.7 Protection System

If a computer system has multiple users and allows the concurrent execution of multiple processes, then the various processes must be protected from one another. For that purpose, mechanisms ensure that files, memory segments, CPU, and other resources can be operated on by only those processes that have gained proper authorization from the operating system. For example, memory-addressing hardware ensures that a process can execute only within its own address space. The timer ensures that no process can gain control of the CPU without eventually relinquishing control. Device-control registers are not accessible to users, so the integrity of the various peripheral devices is protected.

Protection, then, is any mechanism for controlling the access of programs, processes, or users to the resources defined by a computer system.   This mechanism must provide means for specification of the controls to be imposed and means for enforcement.

Protection can improve reliability by detecting latent errors at the interfaces between component subsystems. Early detection of interface errors can often prevent contamination of a healthy subsystem by another subsystem that is malfunctioning. An unprotected resource cannot defend against use (or misuse) by an unauthorized or incompetent user. A protection-oriented system provides a means to distinguish between authorized and unauthorized usage, as we discuss in Chapter 18.

3.1.8 Command-Interpreter System

One of the most important systems programs for an operating system is the **command interpreter**, which is the interface between the user and the operating system. Some operating systems include the command interpreter in the kernel. Others, such as MS-DOS and UNIX, treat the command interpreter as a special program that is running when a job is initiated or when a user first logs on (on time-sharing systems).

Many commands are given to the operating system by **control statements**. When a new job is started in a batch system, or when a user logs onto a time-shared system, a program that reads and interprets control statements is executed automatically. This program is sometimes called the **control-card interpreter**, or **shell**. Its function is simple: to get the next command statement and execute it.

Operating systems are frequently differentiated in the area of the shell, with a user-friendly command interpreter making the system more agreeable to some users. One style of user-friendly interface is the mouse-based window and menu system used in the Macintosh and in Microsoft Windows. The mouse is moved to position the mouse pointer on images, or **icons**, on the screen that represent programs, files, and system functions. Depending on the mouse pointer's location, clicking a button on the mouse can invoke a program, select a file or directory—known as a **folder**—or pull down a menu that contains commands. More powerful, complex, and difficult-to-learn shells are appreciated by other users. In some of these shells, commands are typed on a keyboard and displayed on a screen or printing terminal, with the enter (or return) key signaling that a command is complete and is ready to be executed. The MS-DOS and UNIX shells operate in this way.

The command statements themselves deal with process creation and management, I/O handling, secondary-storage management, main-memory management, file-system access, protection, and networking.

3.2 ■ Operating-System Services

An operating system provides an environment for the execution of programs. It provides certain services to programs and to the users of those programs. The specific services provided, of course, differ from one operating system to another, but we can identify common classes. These operating-system services are provided for the convenience of the programmer, to make the programming task easier.

One set of operating-system services provides functions that are helpful to the user.

- *Program execution:* The system must be able to load a program into memory and to run that program. The program must be able to end its execution, either normally or abnormally (indicating error).

- *I/O operations:* A running program may require I/O, which may involve a file or an I/O device. For specific devices, special functions may be desired (such as rewinding a tape drive or blanking a CRT screen). For efficiency and protection, users usually cannot control I/O devices directly. Therefore, the operating system must provide a means to do I/O.

- *File-system manipulation:* The file system is of particular interest. Obviously, programs need to read and write files and directories. They also need to create and delete them by name, search for a given file, and list file information.

- *Communications:* There are many circumstances in which one process needs to exchange information with another process. Such communication may occur between processes that are executing on the same computer or between processes that are executing on different computer systems tied together by a computer network. Communications may be implemented via *shared memory* or through *message passing,* in which packets of information are moved between processes by the operating system.

- *Error detection:* The operating system constantly needs to be aware of possible errors. Errors may occur in the CPU and memory hardware (such as a memory error or a power failure), in I/O devices (such as a parity error on tape, a connection failure on a network, or lack of paper in the printer), and in the user program (such as an arithmetic overflow, an attempt to access an illegal memory location, or a too-great use of CPU time). For each type of error, the operating system should take the appropriate action to ensure correct and consistent computing.

Another set of operating-system functions exists not for helping the user but rather for ensuring the efficient operation of the system itself. Systems with multiple users can gain efficiency by sharing the computer resources among the users.

- *Resource allocation:* When there are multiple users or multiple jobs running at the same time, resources must be allocated to each of them. Many different types of resources are managed by the operating system. Some (such as CPU cycles, main memory, and file storage) may have special allocation code, whereas others (such as I/O devices) may have much more general request and release code. For instance, in determining how best to use the CPU, operating systems have CPU-scheduling routines that take into account the speed of the CPU, the jobs that must be executed, the number of registers available, and other factors. There might also be routines to allocate a tape drive for use by a job. One such routine locates an unused tape drive and marks an internal table to record the drive's new user. Another routine is used to clear that table. These routines may also allocate printers, modems, and other peripheral devices.

- *Accounting:* We want to keep track of which users use how much and what kinds of computer resources. This record keeping may be used for accounting (so that users can be billed) or simply for accumulating usage statistics. Usage statistics may be a valuable tool for researchers who wish to reconfigure the system to improve computing services.

- *Protection and security:* The owners of information stored in a multiuser computer system may want to control use of that information. When several disjoint processes execute concurrently, it should not be possible for one process to interfere with the others or with the operating system itself. Protection involves ensuring that all access to system resources is controlled. *Security* of the system from outsiders is also important. Such security starts with requiring each user to authenticate himself or herself to the system, usually by means of a password, to gain access to system resources. It extends to defending external I/O devices, including modems and network adapters, from invalid access attempts and to recording all such connections for detection of break-ins. If a system is to be protected and secure, precautions must be instituted throughout it. A chain is only as strong as its weakest link.

3.3 ■ System Calls

System calls provide the interface between a process and the operating system. These calls are generally available as assembly-language instructions and are usually listed in the manuals used by assembly-language programmers.

Certain systems allow system calls to be made directly from a higher-level language program, in which case the calls normally resemble predefined function or subroutine calls. They may generate a call to a special run-time routine that makes the system call, or the system call may be generated directly in-line.

Several languages—notably C and C++—have been defined to replace assembly language for systems programming. These languages allow system calls to be made directly. For example, UNIX system calls may be invoked directly from a C or C++ program. System calls for modern Microsoft Windows platforms are part of the Win32 API, which is available for use by all the compilers written for Microsoft Windows.

Java does not allow system calls to be made directly, because a system call is specific to an operating system and results in platform-specific code. However, if an application requires system-specific features, a Java program can call a method that has been written in another language—typically C or C++—that can make the system call. Such methods are known as "native" methods.

As an example of how system calls are used, consider writing a simple program to read data from one file and copy them to another file. The first input that the program will need is the names of the two files: the input file and the output file. These names can be specified in many ways, depending on the operating-system design. One approach is for the program to ask the user for the names of the two files. In an interactive system, this approach will require a sequence of system calls, first to write a prompting message on the screen and then to read from the keyboard the characters that define the two files. On mouse-based and icon-based systems, a menu of file names is usually displayed in a window. The user can then use the mouse to select the source name, and a window can be opened for the destination name to be specified. This sequence would require many I/O system calls.

Once the two file names are obtained, the program must open the input file and create the output file. Each of these operations requires another system call. There are also possible error conditions for each operation. When the program tries to open the input file, it may find that there is no file of that name or that the file is protected against access. In these cases, the program should print a message on the console (another sequence of system calls) and then terminate abnormally (another system call). If the input file exists, then we must create a new output file. We may find that there is already an output file with the same name. This situation may cause the program to abort (a system call), or we may delete the existing file (another system call) and create a new one (another system call). Another option, in an interactive system, is to ask the user (via a sequence of system calls to output the prompting message and to read the response from the terminal) whether to replace the existing file or to abort the program.

Now that both files are set up, we enter a loop that reads from the input file (a system call) and writes to the output file (another system call). Each read and write must return status information regarding various possible error conditions. On input, the program may find that the end of the file has been reached or that there was a hardware failure in the read (such as a parity error). The write operation may encounter various errors, depending on the output device (no more disk space, physical end of tape, printer out of paper, and so on).

Finally, after the entire file is copied, the program may close both files (another system call), write a message to the console or window (more system calls), and finally terminate normally (the final system call). As we can see, programs may make heavy use of the operating system. Frequently, systems execute thousands of system calls per second.

Most programmers never see this level of detail, however. The run-time support system (the set of functions built into libraries included with a compiler) for most programming languages provides a much simpler interface. For example, the cout() statement in C++ is probably compiled into a call to a run-time support routine that issues the necessary system calls, checks for errors, and finally returns to the user program. Thus, most of the details of the operating-system interface are hidden from the programmer by the compiler and by the run-time support package.

System calls occur in different ways, depending on the computer in use. Often, more information is required than simply the identity of the desired system call. The exact type and amount of information vary according to the particular operating system and call. For example, to get input, we may need to specify the file or device to use as the source, as well as the address and length of the memory buffer into which the input should be read. Of course, the device or file and length may be implicit in the call.

Three general methods are used to pass parameters to the operating system. The simplest approach is to pass the parameters in *registers*. In some cases, however, there may be more parameters than registers. In these cases, the parameters are generally stored in a *block*, or table, in memory, and the address of the block is passed as a parameter in a register (Figure 3.1). This is the approach taken by Linux. Parameters also can be placed, or *pushed*, onto the *stack* by the program and *popped* off the stack by the operating system. Some operating systems prefer the block or stack methods, because those approaches do not limit the number or length of parameters being passed.

System calls can be grouped roughly into five major categories: **process control**, **file manipulation**, **device manipulation**, **information maintenance**, and **communications**. In Sections 3.3.1 through 3.3.5, we discuss briefly the types of system calls that may be provided by an operating system. Most of

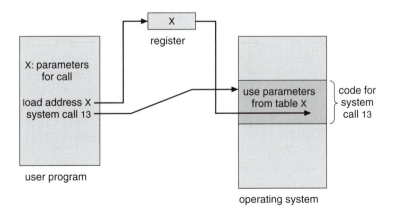

Figure 3.1   Passing of parameters as a table.

these system calls support, or are supported by, concepts and functions that are discussed in later chapters. Figure 3.2 summarizes the types of system calls normally provided by an operating system.

3.3.1 Process Control

A running program needs to be able to halt its execution either normally (end) or abnormally (abort). If a system call is made to terminate the currently running program abnormally, or if the program runs into a problem and causes an error trap, a dump of memory is sometimes taken and an error message generated. The dump is written to disk and may be examined by a *debugger*—a system program designed to aid the programmer in finding and correcting bugs—to determine the cause of the problem. Under either normal or abnormal circumstances, the operating system must transfer control to the invoking command interpreter. The command interpreter then reads the next command. In an interactive system, the command interpreter simply continues with the next command; it is assumed that the user will issue an appropriate command to respond to any error. In a batch system, the command interpreter usually terminates the entire job and continues with the next job. Some systems allow control cards to indicate special recovery actions in case an error occurs. If the program discovers an error in its input and wants to terminate abnormally, it may also want to define an error level. More severe errors can be indicated by a higher-level error parameter. It is then possible to combine normal and abnormal termination by defining a normal termination as error at level 0. The command interpreter or a following program can use this error level to determine the next action automatically.

A process or job executing one program may want to load and execute another program. This feature allows the command interpreter to execute a program as directed by, for example, a user command, the click of a mouse, or a batch command. An interesting question is where to return control when the loaded program terminates. This question is related to the problem of whether the existing program is lost, saved, or allowed to continue execution concurrently with the new program.

If control returns to the existing program when the new program terminates, we must save the memory image of the existing program; thus, we have effectively created a mechanism for one program to call another program. If both programs continue concurrently, we have created a new job or process to be multiprogrammed. Often, there is a system call specifically for this purpose (create process or submit job).

If we create a new job or process, or perhaps even a set of jobs or processes, we should be able to control its execution. This control requires the ability to determine and reset the attributes of a job or process, including the job's priority, its maximum allowable execution time, and so on (get process attributes and set process attributes). We may also want to termi-

- Process control
  - end, abort
  - load, execute
  - create process, terminate process
  - get process attributes, set process attributes
  - wait for time
  - wait event, signal event
  - allocate and free memory
- File management
  - create file, delete file
  - open, close
  - read, write, reposition
  - get file attributes, set file attributes
- Device management
  - request device, release device
  - read, write, reposition
  - get device attributes, set device attributes
  - logically attach or detach devices
- Information maintenance
  - get time or date, set time or date
  - get system data, set system data
  - get process, file, or device attributes
  - set process, file, or device attributes
- Communications
  - create, delete communication connection
  - send, receive messages
  - transfer status information
  - attach or detach remote devices

Figure 3.2   Types of system calls.

nate a job or process that we created (`terminate process`) if we find that it is incorrect or is no longer needed.

Having created new jobs or processes, we may need to wait for them to finish their execution. We may want to wait for a certain amount of time (`wait time`); more probably, we will want to wait for a specific event to occur (`wait event`). The jobs or processes should then signal when that event has occurred (`signal event`). System calls of this type, dealing with the coordination of concurrent processes, are discussed in great detail in Chapter 7.

Another set of system calls is helpful in debugging a program. Many systems provide system calls to dump memory. This provision is useful for debugging. A program `trace` lists each instruction as it is executed; it is provided by fewer systems. Even microprocessors provide a CPU mode known as *single step*, in which a trap is executed by the CPU after every instruction. The trap is usually caught by a debugger.

Many operating systems provide a time profile of a program. It indicates the amount of time that the program executes at a particular location or set of locations. A time profile requires either a tracing facility or regular timer interrupts. At every occurrence of the timer interrupt, the value of the program counter is recorded. With sufficiently frequent timer interrupts, a statistical picture of the time spent on various parts of the program can be obtained.

There are so many facets of and variations in process and job control that we next use two examples—one involving a single-tasking system and the other a multitasking system—to clarify these concepts. The MS-DOS operating system is an example of a single-tasking system, which has a command interpreter that is invoked when the computer is started (Figure 3.3(a)). Because MS-DOS is single-tasking, it uses a simple method to run a program and does not create a

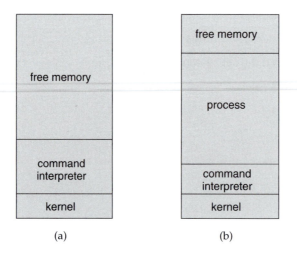

(a)   (b)

Figure 3.3   MS-DOS execution. (a) At system startup. (b) Running a program.

new process. It loads the program into memory, writing over most of itself to give the program as much memory as possible (Figure 3.3(b)). Next, it sets the instruction pointer to the first instruction of the program. The program then runs, and either an error causes a trap, or the program executes a system call to terminate. In either case, the error code is saved in the system memory for later use. Following this action, the small portion of the command interpreter that was not overwritten resumes execution. Its first task is to reload the rest of the command interpreter from disk. Then the command interpreter makes the previous error code available to the user or to the next program.

Although the MS-DOS operating system does not have general multitasking capabilities, it does provide a method for limited concurrent execution. A TSR program is a program that "hooks an interrupt" and then exits with the terminate and stay resident system call. For instance, it can hook the clock interrupt by placing the address of one of its subroutines into the list of interrupt routines to be called when the system timer is triggered. This way, the TSR routine will be executed several times per second, at each clock tick. The terminate and stay resident system call causes MS-DOS to reserve the space occupied by the TSR, so it will not be overwritten when the command interpreter is reloaded.

FreeBSD (derived from Berkeley UNIX) is an example of a multitasking system. When a user logs on to the system, the shell of the user's choice is run. This shell is similar to the MS-DOS shell in that it accepts commands and executes programs that the user requests. However, since FreeBSD is a multitasking system, the command interpreter may continue running while another program is executed (Figure 3.4). To start a new process, the shell

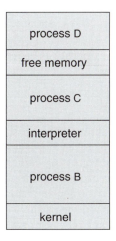

Figure 3.4   Free BSD running multiple programs.

executes a `fork()` system call. Then, the selected program is loaded into memory via an `exec()` system call, and the program is executed. Depending on the way the command was issued, the shell then either waits for the process to finish or runs the process "in the background." In the latter case, the shell immediately requests another command. When a process is running in the background, it cannot receive input directly from the keyboard, because the shell is using this resource. I/O is therefore done through files or through a mouse and windows interface. Meanwhile, the user is free to ask the shell to run other programs, to monitor the progress of the running process, to change that program's priority, and so on. When the process is done, it executes an `exit()` system call to terminate, returning to the invoking process a status code of 0 or a nonzero error code. This status or error code is then available to the shell or other programs. Processes are discussed in Chapter 4 with an program example using the `fork()` and `exec()` system calls.

3.3.2 File Management

The file system will be discussed in more detail in Chapters 11 and 12. We can identify several common system calls dealing with files, however.

We first need to be able to `create` and `delete` files. Either system call requires the name of the file and perhaps some of the file's attributes. Once the file is created, we need to `open` it and to use it. We may also `read`, `write`, or `reposition` (rewinding or skipping to the end of the file, for example). Finally, we need to `close` the file, indicating that we are no longer using it.

We may need these same sets of operations for directories if we have a directory structure for organizing files in the file system. In addition, for either files or directories, we need to be able to determine the values of various attributes and perhaps to reset them if necessary. File attributes include the file name, a file type, protection codes, accounting information, and so on. At least two system calls, `get file attribute` and `set file attribute`, are required for this function. Some operating systems provide many more calls.

3.3.3 Device Management

A program, as it is running, may need additional resources to proceed— more memory, tape drives, access to files, and so on. If the resources are available, they can be granted, and control can be returned to the user program. Otherwise, the program will have to wait until sufficient resources are available.

Files can be thought of as abstract or virtual devices. Thus, many of the system calls for files are also needed for devices. If there are multiple users of the system, however, we must first `request` the device, to ensure exclusive use of it. After we are finished with the device, we must `release` it. These functions are similar to the `open` and `close` system calls for files.

Once the device has been requested (and allocated to us), we can `read`, `write`, and (possibly) `reposition` the device, just as we can with ordinary files. In fact, the similarity between I/O devices and files is so great that many operating systems, including UNIX and MS-DOS, merge the two into a combined file–device structure. In this case, a set of system calls is used on files and devices. Sometimes, I/O devices are identified by special file names, directory placement, or file attributes.

3.3.4 Information Maintenance

Many system calls exist simply for the purpose of transferring information between the user program and the operating system. For example, most systems have a system call to return the current `time` and `date`. Other system calls may return information about the system, such as the number of current users, the version number of the operating system, the amount of free memory or disk space, and so on.

In addition, the operating system keeps information about all its processes, and there are system calls to access this information. Generally, there are also calls to reset the process information (`get process attributes` and `set process attributes`). In Section 4.1.3, we discuss what information is normally kept.

3.3.5 Communication

There are two common models of communication: the message-passing model and the shared-memory model. In the **message-passing model**, information is exchanged through an interprocess-communication facility provided by the operating system. Before communication can take place, a connection must be opened. The name of the other communicator must be known, be it another process on the same system or a process on another computer connected by a communications network. Each computer in a network has a *host name*, such as an IP name, by which it is commonly known. Similarly, each process has a *process name*, which is translated into an identifier by which the operating system can refer to it. The `get hostid` and `get processid` system calls do this translation. These identifiers are then passed to the general-purpose `open` and `close` calls provided by the file system or to specific `open connection` and `close connection` system calls, depending on the system's model of communications. The recipient process usually must give its permission for communication to take place with an `accept connection` call. Most processes that will be receiving connections are special-purpose *daemons*, which are systems programs provided for that purpose. They execute a `wait for connection` call and are awakened when a connection is made. The source of the communication, known as the *client*, and the receiving daemon, known as a *server*, then exchange messages by `read message` and `write message` system calls. The `close connection` call terminates the communication.

In the **shared-memory model**, processes use `map memory` system calls to gain access to regions of memory owned by other processes. Recall that, normally, the operating system tries to prevent one process from accessing another process's memory. Shared memory requires that two or more processes agree to remove this restriction. They may then exchange information by reading and writing data in the shared areas. The form of the data and the location are determined by these processes and are not under the operating system's control. The processes are also responsible for ensuring that they are not writing to the same location simultaneously. Such mechanisms are discussed in Chapter 7. In Chapter 5, we look at a variation of the process model—threads—in which memory is shared by default.

Both of the models just discussed are common in operating systems, and some systems even implement both. Message passing is useful for exchanging smaller amount of data, because no conflicts need to be avoided. It is also easier to implement than is shared memory for intercomputer communication. Shared memory allows maximum speed and convenience of communication, as it can be done at memory speeds when within a computer. Problems exist, however, in the areas of protection and synchronization. The two communications models are contrasted in Figure 3.5. In Chapter 4, we look at a Java implementation of each model.

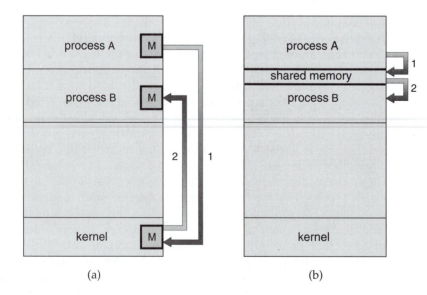

(a)   (b)

Figure 3.5   Communications models. (a) Msg passing. (b) Shared memory.

3.4 ■ System Programs

Another aspect of a modern system is the collection of system programs. Recall Figure 1.1, which depicted the logical computer hierarchy. At the lowest level is hardware. Next is the operating system, then the system programs, and finally the application programs. System programs provide a convenient environment for program development and execution. Some of them are simply user interfaces to system calls; others are considerably more complex. They can be divided into these categories:

- *File management:* These programs create, delete, copy, rename, print, dump, list, and generally manipulate files and directories.

- *Status information:* Some programs simply ask the system for the date, time, amount of available memory or disk space, number of users, or similar status information. That information is then formatted and printed to the terminal or other output device or file.

- *File modification:* Several text editors may be available to create and modify the content of files stored on disk or tape.

- *Programming-language support:* Compilers, assemblers, and interpreters for common programming languages (such as C, C++, Java, Visual Basic, and PERL) are often provided to the user with the operating system, although some of these programs are now priced and provided separately.

- *Program loading and execution:* Once a program is assembled or compiled, it must be loaded into memory to be executed. The system may provide absolute loaders, relocatable loaders, linkage editors, and overlay loaders. Debugging systems for either higher-level languages or machine language are needed also.

- *Communications:* These programs provide the mechanism for creating virtual connections among processes, users, and computer systems. They allow users to send messages to one another's screens, to browse web pages, to send electronic-mail messages, to log in remotely, or to transfer files from one machine to another.

In addition to systems programs, most operating systems are supplied with programs that are useful in solving common problems or performing common operations. Such programs include web browsers, word processors and text formatters, spreadsheets, database systems, compilers, plotting and statistical-analysis packages, and games. These programs are known as **system utilities** or **application programs**.

Perhaps the most important system program for an operating system is the **command interpreter**. The main function of this program is to get and execute the next user-specified command. Many of the commands given at this level manipulate files: create, delete, list, print, copy, execute, and so on. There are two general ways in which these commands can be implemented.

In one approach, the command interpreter itself contains the code to execute the command. For example, a command to delete a file may cause the command interpreter to jump to a section of its code that sets up the parameters and makes the appropriate system call. In this case, the number of commands that can be given determines the size of the command interpreter, since each command requires its own implementing code.

An alternative approach—used by UNIX, among other operating systems —implements most commands through system programs. In this case, the command interpreter does not understand the command in any way; it merely uses the command to identify a file to be loaded into memory and executed. Thus, the UNIX command to delete a file

rm G

would search for a file called *rm*, load the file into memory, and execute it with the parameter G. The function associated with the rm command would be defined completely by the code in the file *rm*. In this way, programmers can add new commands to the system easily by creating new files with the proper names. The command-interpreter program, which can be small, does not have to be changed for new commands to be added.

Although this second approach to command-interpreter design offers advantages, it also has problems. Notice first that, because the code to execute a command is a separate system program, the operating system must provide a mechanism for passing parameters from the command interpreter to the system program. This task can often be clumsy, because the command interpreter and the system program may not be in memory at the same time, and the parameter list can be extensive. Also, it is slower to load a program and to execute it than simply to jump to another section of code within the current program.

Another problem is that the interpretation of the parameters is left up to the programmer of the system program. Thus, parameters may be provided inconsistently across programs that appear similar to the user but that were written at different times by different programmers.

The view of the operating system seen by most users is thus defined by the system programs, rather than by the actual system calls. Consider PCs. When her computer is running the Microsoft Windows operating system, a user might see a command-line MS-DOS shell or the graphical mouse and windows interface. Both use the same set of system calls, but the system calls look different and act in different ways. Consequently, this user view may be substantially removed from the actual system structure. The design of a useful and friendly user interface is therefore not a direct function of the operating system. In this book, we concentrate on the fundamental problems of providing adequate service to user programs. From the point of view of the operating system, we do not distinguish between user programs and system programs.

3.5 ■ System Structure

A system as large and complex as a modern operating system must be engineered carefully if it is to function properly and be modified easily. A common approach is to partition the task into small components rather than have one monolithic system. Each of these modules should be a well-defined portion of the system, with carefully defined inputs, outputs, and functions. We have already discussed briefly the common components of operating systems (Section 3.1). In this section, we discuss how these components are interconnected and melded into a kernel.

3.5.1 Simple Structure

Many commercial systems do not have well-defined structures. Frequently, such operating systems started as small, simple, and limited systems and then grew beyond their original scope. MS-DOS is an example of such a system. It was originally designed and implemented by a few people who had no idea that it would become so popular. It was written to provide the most functionality in the least space (because of the limited hardware on which it ran), so it was not divided into modules carefully. Figure 3.6 shows its structure.

In MS-DOS, the interfaces and levels of functionality are not well separated. For instance, application programs are able to access the basic I/O routines to

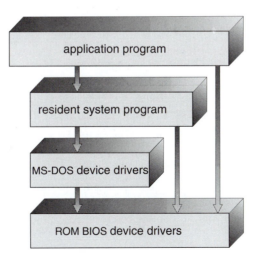

Figure 3.6   MS-DOS layer structure.

write directly to the display and disk drives. Such freedom leaves MS-DOS vulnerable to errant (or malicious) programs, causing entire system crashes when user programs fail. Of course, MS-DOS was also limited by the hardware of its era. Because the Intel 8088 for which it was written provides no dual mode and no hardware protection, the designers of MS-DOS had no choice but to leave the base hardware accessible.

Another example of limited structuring is the original UNIX operating system. UNIX is another system that initially was limited by hardware functionality. It consists of two separable parts: the kernel and the system programs. The kernel is further separated into a series of interfaces and device drivers, which have been added and expanded over the years as UNIX has evolved. We can view the traditional UNIX operating system as being layered, as shown in Figure 3.7. Everything below the system-call interface and above the physical hardware is the kernel. The kernel provides the file system, CPU scheduling, memory management, and other operating-system functions through system calls. Taken in sum, that is an enormous amount of functionality to be combined into one level. This monolithic structure was difficult to implement and maintain. System programs use the kernel-supported system calls to provide useful functions, such as compilation and file manipulation.

System calls define the **application programmer interface** (**API**) to UNIX; the set of system programs commonly available defines the **user interface**. The programmer and user interfaces define the context that the kernel must support.

New versions of UNIX are designed to use more advanced hardware. Given proper hardware support, operating systems may be broken into pieces that are smaller and more appropriate than those allowed by the original MS-

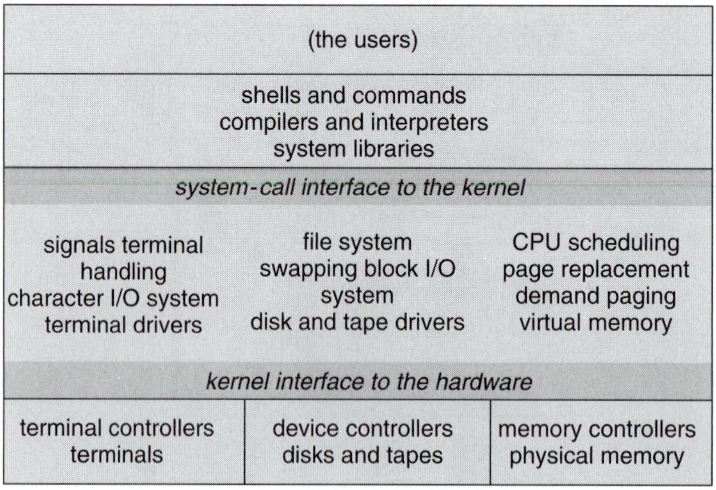

(the users)		
shells and commands compilers and interpreters system libraries		
system-call interface to the kernel		
signals terminal handling character I/O system terminal drivers	file system swapping block I/O system disk and tape drivers	CPU scheduling page replacement demand paging virtual memory
kernel interface to the hardware		
terminal controllers terminals	device controllers disks and tapes	memory controllers physical memory

Figure 3.7   UNIX system structure.

DOS or UNIX systems. The operating system can then retain much greater control over the computer and over the applications that make use of that computer. Implementors have more freedom in changing the inner workings of the system and in creating modular operating systems. Under the top-down approach, the overall functionality and features are determined and are separated into components. Information hiding is also important, because it leaves programmers free to implement the low-level routines as they see fit, provided that the external interface of the routine stays unchanged and that the routine itself performs the advertised task.

3.5.2 Layered Approach

A system can be made modular in many ways. One method is the **layered approach**, in which the operating system is broken up into a number of layers (levels). The bottom layer (layer 0) is the hardware; the highest (layer N) is the user interface.

An operating-system layer is an implementation of an abstract object made up of data and the operations that can manipulate those data. A typical operating-system layer—say, layer M—is depicted in Figure 3.8. It consists of data structures and a set of routines that can be invoked by higher-level layers. Layer M, in turn, can invoke operations on lower-level layers.

The main advantage of the layered approach is **modularity**. The layers are selected so that each uses functions (operations) and services of only lower-level layers. This approach simplifies debugging and system verification. The first layer can be debugged without any concern for the rest of the system, because, by definition, it uses only the basic hardware (which is assumed correct) to implement its functions. Once the first layer is debugged, its correct functioning

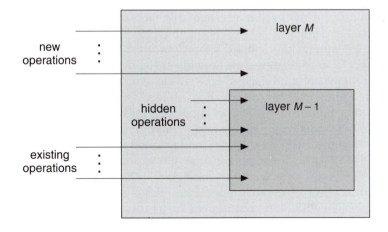

Figure 3.8   An operating-system layer.

can be assumed while the second layer is debugged, and so on. If an error is found during the debugging of a particular layer, the error must be on that layer, because the layers below it are already debugged. Thus, the design and implementation of the system is simplified when the system is broken down into layers.

Each layer is implemented with only those operations provided by lower-level layers. A layer does not need to know how these operations are implemented; it needs to know only what these operations do. Hence, each layer hides the existence of certain data structures, operations, and hardware from higher-level layers.

The major difficulty with the layered approach involves appropriately defining the various layers. Because a layer can use only lower-level layers, careful planning is necessary. For example, the device driver for the backing store (disk space used by virtual-memory algorithms) must be at a level lower than that of the memory-management routines, because memory management requires the ability to use the backing store.

Other requirements may not be so obvious. The backing-store driver would normally be above the CPU scheduler, because the driver may need to wait for I/O and the CPU can be rescheduled during this time. However, on a large system, the CPU scheduler may have more information about all the active processes than can fit in memory. Therefore, this information may need to be swapped in and out of memory, requiring the backing-store driver routine to be below the CPU scheduler.

A final problem with layered implementations is that they tend to be less efficient than other types. For instance, when a user program executes an I/O operation, it executes a system call that is trapped to the I/O layer, which calls the memory-management layer, which in turn calls the CPU-scheduling layer, which is then passed to the hardware. At each layer, the parameters may be modified, data may need to be passed, and so on. Each layer adds overhead to the system call; the net result is a system call that takes longer than does one on a nonlayered system.

These limitations have caused a small backlash against layering in recent years. Fewer layers with more functionality are being designed, providing most of the advantages of modularized code while avoiding the difficult problems of layer definition and interaction. For instance, OS/2 is a descendant of MS-DOS that adds multitasking and dual-mode operation, as well as other features. Because of this added complexity and the more powerful hardware for which OS/2 was designed, the system was implemented in a more layered fashion. Contrast the MS-DOS structure with that shown in Figure 3.9; from both the system-design and implementation standpoints, OS/2 has the advantage. For instance, direct user access to low-level facilities is not allowed, providing the operating system with more control over the hardware and more knowledge of which resources each user program is using.

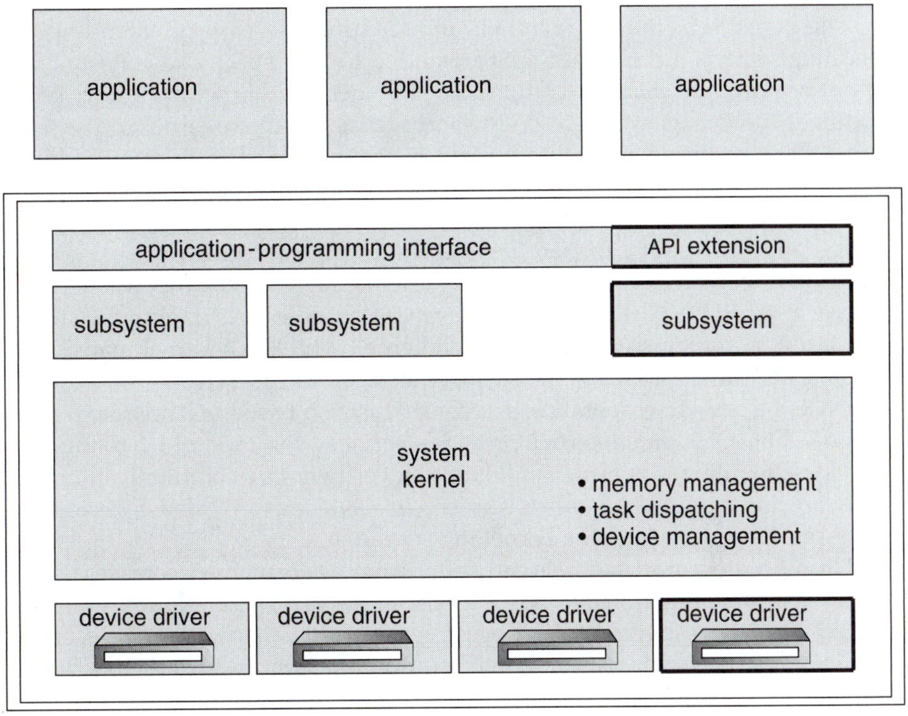

Figure 3.9   OS/2 layer structure.

3.5.3 Microkernels

As UNIX expanded, the kernel became large and difficult to manage. In the mid-1980s, researchers at Carnegie Mellon University developed an operating system called **Mach** that modularized the kernel using the **microkernel** approach. This method structures the operating system by removing all nonessential components from the kernel and implementing them as system and user-level programs. The result is a smaller kernel. There is little consensus regarding which services should remain in the kernel and which should be implemented in user space. In general, however, microkernels typically provide minimal process and memory management, in addition to a communication facility.

The main function of the microkernel is to provide a communication facility between the client program and the various services that are also running in user space. Communication is provided by *message passing*, which was described in Section 3.3.5. For example, if the client program wishes to access a file, it must interact with the file server. The client program and service never interact directly. Rather, they communicate indirectly by exchanging messages with the microkernel.

The benefits of the microkernel approach include ease of extending the operating system. All new services are added to user space and consequently do not require modification of the kernel. When the kernel does have to be modified, the changes tend to be fewer, because the microkernel is a smaller kernel. The resulting operating system is easier to port from one hardware design to another. The microkernel also provides more security and reliability, since most services are running as user—rather than kernel—processes. If a service fails, the rest of the operating system remains untouched.

Several contemporary operating systems have used the microkernel approach. Tru64 UNIX (formerly Digital UNIX) provides a UNIX interface to the user, but it is implemented with a Mach kernel. The Mach kernel maps UNIX system calls into messages to the appropriate user-level services.

QNX is a real-time operating system that is also based on the microkernel design. The QNX microkernel provides services for message passing and process scheduling. It also handles low-level network communication and hardware interrupts. All other services in QNX are provided by standard processes that run outside the kernel in user mode.

Unfortunately, microkernels can suffer from performance decreases due to increased system function overhead. Consider the history of Windows NT. The first release had a layered microkernel organization. However, this version delivered low performance compared with that of Windows 95. Windows NT 4.0 partially redressed the performance problem by moving layers from user space to kernel space and more closely integrating them. By the time Windows XP was designed, its architecture was more monolithic than microkernel.

The Apple Macintosh OS X operating system uses a hybrid structure. OS X (also known as *Darwin*) structures the operating system using a layered technique where one layer consists of the Mach microkernel. The structure of OS X appears in Figure 3.10.

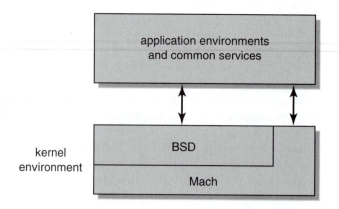

Figure 3.10   The OS X structure.

The top layers include application environments and a set of services providing a graphical interface to applications. Below these layers is the kernel environment, which consists primarily of the Mach microkernel and the BSD kernel. Mach provides memory management; support for remote procedure calls (RPCs) and interprocess communication (IPC) facilities, including message passing, and thread scheduling. The BSD component provides a BSD command line interface, support for networking and file systems, and an implementation of POSIX APIs, including Pthreads. In addition to Mach and BSD, the kernel environment provides an I/O kit for development of device drivers and dynamically loadable modules (which OS X refers to as **kernel extensions**). As shown in the figure, applications and common services can make use of either the Mach or BSD facilities directly.

3.5.4 Modules

Perhaps the best current operating-system-design methodology involves the use of object-oriented programming techniques to create a modular kernel. Here, the kernel has a set of core components and dynamically links in additional services either during boot time or during run time. Such a strategy uses dynamically loadable modules and is common in modern implementations of UNIX such as Solaris, Linux, and Mac OS X. For example, the Solaris operating system structure, shown in Figure 3.11, is organized around a core kernel with seven types of loadable kernel modules:

1. Scheduling classes

2. File systems

3. Loadable system calls

4. Executable formats

5. STREAMS modules

6. Device and bus drivers

7. Miscellaneous

Such a design allows the kernel to provide core services yet also allows certain features to be implemented dynamically. For example, device and bus drivers for specific hardware can be added to the kernel, and support for different file systems can be added as loadable modules. The overall result resembles a layered system in that each kernel section has defined, protected interfaces; but it is more flexible than a layered system in that any module can call any other module. Furthermore, the approach is like the microkernel approach in that the primary module has only core functions and

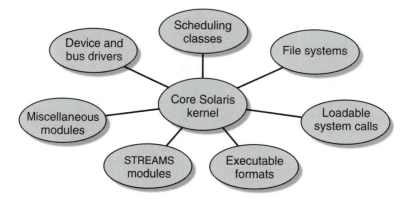

Figure 3.11   Solaris loadable modules.

knowledge of how to load and communicate with other modules; but it is more efficient, because modules do not need to invoke message passing in order to communicate.

3.6 ■ Virtual Machines

The layered approach is taken to its logical conclusion in the concept of a **virtual machine**. The VM operating system for IBM systems is the best example of the virtual-machine concept, because IBM pioneered the work in this area.

By using CPU scheduling (Chapter 6) and virtual-memory techniques (Chapter 10), an operating system can create the illusion that a process has its own processor with its own (virtual) memory. Normally, a process has additional features, such as system calls and a file system, that are not provided by the bare hardware. The virtual-machine approach does not provide any such additional functionality but rather provides an interface that is *identical* to the underlying bare hardware. Each process is provided with a (virtual) copy of the underlying computer (Figure 3.12).

The physical computer shares resources to create the virtual machines. CPU scheduling can share out the CPU to create the appearance that users have their own processors. Spooling and a file system can provide virtual card readers and virtual line printers. A normal user time-sharing terminal provides the function of the virtual-machine operator's console.

A major difficulty with the virtual-machine approach involves disk systems. Suppose that the physical machine has three disk drives but wants to support seven virtual machines. Clearly, it cannot allocate a disk drive to each virtual machine, because the virtual-machine software itself will need substantial disk space to provide virtual memory and spooling. The solution is to provide virtual disks—termed *minidisks* in IBM's VM operating system—which

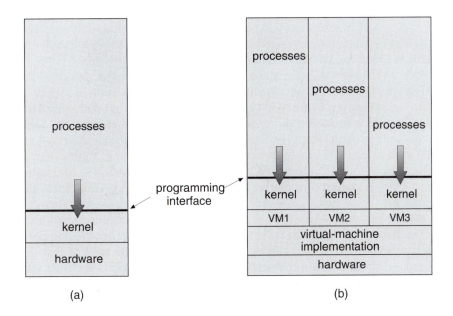

Figure 3.12   System models. (a) Nonvirtual machine. (b) Virtual machine.

are identical in all respects except size. The system implements each minidisk by allocating as many tracks on the physical disks as the minidisk needs. Obviously, the sum of the sizes of all minidisks must be smaller than the size of the physical disk space available.

Users thus are given their own virtual machines. They can then run any of the operating systems or software packages that are available on the underlying machine. For the IBM VM system, a user normally runs CMS—a single-user interactive operating system. The virtual-machine software is concerned with multiprogramming multiple virtual machines onto a physical machine, but it does not need to consider any user-support software. This arrangement may provide a useful way to divide the problem of designing a multiuser interactive system into two smaller pieces.

3.6.1 Implementation

Although the virtual-machine concept is useful, it is difficult to implement. Much work is required to provide an *exact* duplicate of the underlying machine. Remember that the underlying machine has two modes: user mode and monitor mode. The virtual-machine software can run in monitor mode, since it is the operating system. The virtual machine itself can execute in only user mode. Just as the physical machine has two modes, however, so must the virtual machine. Consequently, we must have a virtual user mode and a virtual monitor mode, both of which run in a physical user mode. Those actions that cause a transfer from user mode to monitor mode on a real machine (such as a system call or an attempt to execute a privileged instruction) must also cause a transfer from virtual user mode to virtual monitor mode on a virtual machine.

Such a transfer can be accomplished as follows. When a system call, for example, is made by a program running on a virtual machine in virtual user mode, it will cause a transfer to the virtual-machine monitor in the real machine. When the virtual-machine monitor gains control, it can change the register contents and program counter for the virtual machine to simulate the effect of the system call. It can then restart the virtual machine, noting that it is now in virtual monitor mode. If the virtual machine then tries, for example, to read from its virtual card reader, it will execute a privileged I/O instruction. Because the virtual machine is running in physical user mode, this instruction will trap to the virtual-machine monitor. The virtual-machine monitor must then simulate the effect of the I/O instruction. First, it finds the spooled file that implements the virtual card reader. Then, it translates the read of the virtual card reader into a read on the spooled disk file and transfers the next virtual "card image" into the virtual memory of the virtual machine. Finally, it can restart the virtual machine. The state of the virtual machine has been modified exactly as though the I/O instruction had been executed with a real card reader for a real machine executing in a real monitor mode.

The major difference, of course, is time. Whereas the real I/O might have taken 100 milliseconds, the virtual I/O might take less time (because it is spooled) or more time (because it is interpreted). In addition, the CPU is being multiprogrammed among many virtual machines, further slowing down the virtual machines in unpredictable ways. In the extreme case, it may be necessary to simulate all instructions to provide a true virtual machine. VM works for IBM machines because normal instructions for the virtual machines can execute directly on the hardware. Only the privileged instructions (needed mainly for I/O) must be simulated and hence execute more slowly.

3.6.2 Benefits

The virtual-machine concept has several advantages. Notice that, in this environment, there is complete protection of the various system resources. Each virtual machine is completely isolated from all other virtual machines, so there are no protection problems. At the same time, however, there is no direct sharing of resources. Two approaches to provide sharing have been implemented. First, it is possible to share a minidisk and thus to share files. This scheme is modeled after a physical shared disk but is implemented by software. Second, it is possible to define a network of virtual machines, each of which can send information over the virtual communications network. Again, the network is modeled after physical communication networks but is implemented in software.

Such a virtual-machine system is a perfect vehicle for operating-systems research and development. Normally, changing an operating system is a difficult task. Operating systems are large and complex programs, and it is difficult to be sure that a change in one part will not cause obscure bugs in some other part. The power of the operating system makes changing it particularly dangerous. Because the operating system executes in monitor mode, a wrong change in a pointer could cause an error that would destroy the entire file system. Thus, it is necessary to test all changes to the operating system carefully.

The operating system, however, runs on and controls the entire machine. Therefore, the current system must be stopped and taken out of use while changes are made and tested. This period is commonly called *system-development time*. Since it makes the system unavailable to users, system-development time is often scheduled late at night or on weekends, when system load is low.

A virtual-machine system can eliminate much of this problem. System programmers are given their own virtual machine, and system development is done on the virtual machine instead of on a physical machine. Normal system operation seldom needs to be disrupted for system development.

3.6.3 Examples

Despite the advantages of virtual machines, they received little attention for a number of years after they were first developed. Today, however, virtual machines are coming back into fashion as a means of solving system compatibility problems. For instance, there are thousands of programs available for Microsoft Windows on Intel CPU-based systems. Computer vendors such as Sun Microsystems use other processors but would like their customers to be able to run these Windows applications. The solution is to create a virtual Intel machine on top of the native processor. A Windows program is run in this environment, and its Intel instructions are translated into the native instruction set. Microsoft Windows is also run in this virtual machine, so the program can make its system calls as usual. The net result is a program that appears to be running on an Intel-based system but is really executing on a different processor. If the processor is sufficiently fast, the Windows program will run quickly, even though every instruction is being translated into several native instructions for execution. Similarly, the PowerPC-based Apple Macintosh includes a Motorola 68000 virtual machine to allow execution of binary codes that were written for the older 68000-based Macintosh. Unfortunately, the more complex the machine being emulated, the more difficult it is to build an accurate virtual machine, and the more slowly that virtual machine runs.

A more recent example has arisen with the growth of the Linux operating system. Virtual machines now exist that allow Windows applications to run on Linux-based computers. The virtual machine runs both the Windows application and the Windows operating system.

As we will see next, the Java platform runs on a virtual machine, typically on top of an operating system of any of the design types discussed earlier. Thus, operating system design methods—simple, layers, microkernel, modules, and virtual machines—are not mutually exclusive.

3.7 ■ Java

Java is a technology introduced by Sun Microsystems in 1995. We refer to it as a *technology* rather than just a programming language because it provides more than a conventional programming language. Java technology consists of three essential components:

1. Programming-language specification

2. Application-programming interface (API)

3. Virtual-machine specification

We provide an overview of these three components in this section.

3.7.1 Programming Language

The Java language can best be characterized as an object-oriented, architecture-neutral, distributed, and multithreaded programming language. Java objects are specified with the class construct; a Java program consists of one or more classes. For each Java class, the Java compiler produces an architecture-neutral *bytecode* output (.class) file that will run on any implementation of the Java virtual machine (JVM). Java was originally favored by the Internet programming community because of its support for **applets**, which are programs with limited resource access that run within a web browser. Java also provides high-level support for networking and distributed objects. It is a multithreaded language, meaning that a Java program may have several different threads, or flows, of control. We cover distributed objects using Java's remote method invocation (RMI) in Chapter 4, and we discuss multithreaded Java programs in Chapter 5.

Java is considered a secure language. This feature is especially important considering that a Java program may be executing across a distributed network. We look at Java security in Chapter 19. Java also automatically manages memory by performing **garbage collection**—the practice of reclaiming memory from objects no longer in use and returning it to the system.

3.7.2 API

The Java API consists of three subsets:

1. A standard API for designing desktop applications and applets with basic language support for graphics, I/O, utilities, and networking

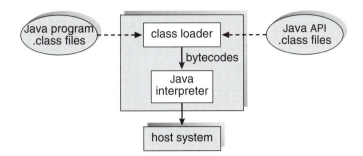

Figure 3.13 The Java virtual machine.

2. An enterprise API for designing server applications with support for databases and server-side applications (known as **servlets**)

3. An API for small devices such as handheld computers, pagers, and cellular telephones

We will focus on the standard API in this text.

3.7.3 Virtual Machine

The JVM is a specification for an abstract computer. It consists of a **class loader** and a Java interpreter that executes the architecture-neutral bytecodes, as diagrammed in Figure 3.13. The class loader loads .class files from both the Java program and the Java API for execution by the Java interpreter. The Java interpreter may be a software interpreter that interprets the bytecodes one at a time, or it may be a **just-in-time** (**JIT**) compiler that turns the architecture-neutral bytecodes into native machine language for the host computer. In other instances, the interpreter may be implemented in a hardware chip that executes Java bytecodes natively.

The **Java platform** consists of the JVM and Java API; it is shown in Figure 3.14. The Java platform may be implemented on top of a host operating system, such as UNIX or Windows; as part of a web browser; or in hardware.

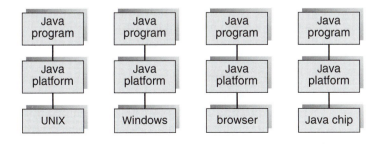

Figure 3.14 The Java platform.

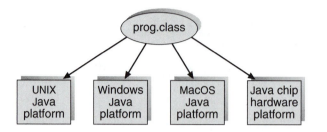

Figure 3.15   Java .`class` file on cross platforms.

An instance of the JVM is created whenever a Java application or applet is run. This instance of the JVM starts running when the `main()` method of a program is invoked. This is also true for applets even though the programmer does not define a `main()`. In this case, the browser executes the `main()` method before creating the applet. If we simultaneously run two Java programs and a Java applet on the same computer, we will have three instances of the JVM.

It is the Java platform that makes it possible to develop programs that are architecture neutral and portable. The platform implementation is system specific, and it abstracts the system in a standard way to the Java program, providing a clean, architecture-neutral interface. This interface allows a .`class` file to run on any system that has implemented the JVM and API; it is shown in Figure 3.15. Implementing the Java platform consists of developing a JVM and Java API for a specific system (such as Windows or UNIX) according to the specification for the JVM.

We use the JVM throughout this text to illustrate operating-system concepts. We refer to the specification of the JVM, rather than to any particular implementation.

3.7.4 Java Development Environment

The Java development environment consists of a compile-time environment and a run-time environment. The compile-time environment turns a Java source file into a bytecode (.`class` file). The Java source file may be either a Java program or applet. The run-time environment is the Java platform for the host system. The development environment is portrayed in Figure 3.16.

3.7.5 Java Operating Systems

Most operating systems are written in a combination of C and assembly-language code, primarily because of the performance benefits of these languages and the ease of interfacing with hardware. However, recent efforts have been made to write operating systems in Java. Such a system, known as a **language-based extensible systems** runs in a single address space.

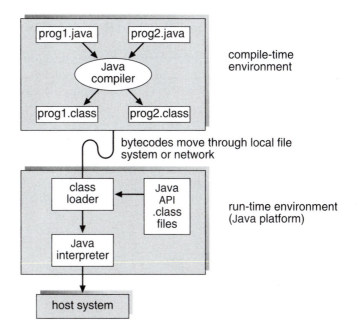

Figure 3.16   Java development environment.

One of the difficulties in designing language-based systems concerns memory protection—protecting the operating system from malicious user programs as well as protecting user programs from one another. Traditional operating systems rely on hardware features to provide memory protection (Section 2.5.3). Language-based systems instead rely on type-safety features of the language to implement memory protection. As a result, language-based systems are desirable on small hardware devices, which may lack hardware features that provide memory protection.

The JX operating system is written almost entirely in Java and provides a run-time system for Java applications as well. JX organizes its system according to **domains**. Each domain contains its own set of classes and threads. Additionally, each domain is responsible for allocating memory for object creation and threads within itself, as well as for garbage collection. Domain zero is a microkernel (Section 3.5.3) responsible for low-level details such as system initialization and saving and restoring the state of the CPU. Domain zero is written in C and assembly language; all other domains are written entirely in Java. Communication between domains occurs through **portals**, communication mechanisms similar to the remote procedure calls (RPCs) used by the Mach microkernel. Protection within and between domains relies on the type safety of the Java language for security. Since domain zero is not written in Java, it must be considered **trusted**.

3.8 ■ System Design and Implementation

In this section, we discuss problems we face when designing and implementing an operating system. There are, of course, no complete solutions to the design problems, but there are approaches that have been successful.

3.8.1 Design Goals

The first problem in designing a system is to define goals and specifications. At the highest level, the design of the system will be affected by the choice of hardware and type of system: batch, time shared, single user, multiuser, distributed, real time, or general purpose.

Beyond this highest design level, the requirements may be much harder to specify. The requirements can, however, be divided into two basic groups: *user* goals and *system* goals.

Users desire certain obvious properties in a system: The system should be convenient to use, easy to learn and to use, reliable, safe, and fast. Of course, these specifications are not particularly useful in the system design, since there is no general agreement on how to achieve them.

A similar set of requirements can be defined by those people who must design, create, maintain, and operate the system: The system should be easy to design, implement, and maintain; it should be flexible, reliable, error free, and efficient. Again, these requirements are vague and may be interpreted in various ways.

There is, in short, no unique solution to the problem of defining the requirements for an operating system. The wide range of systems in existence shows that different requirements can result in a large variety of solutions for different environments. For example, the requirements for VxWorks, a real-time operating system for embedded systems, must have been substantially different from those for MVS, the large multiuser, multiaccess operating system for IBM mainframes.

Specifying and designing an operating system is a highly creative task. Although no textbook can tell you how to do it, general principles have been developed in the field of **software engineering**, and we turn now to a discussion of some of these principles.

3.8.2 Mechanisms and Policies

One important principle is the separation of **policy** from **mechanism**. Mechanisms determine *how* to do something; policies determine *what* will be done. For example, the timer construct (see Section 2.5) is a mechanism for ensuring CPU protection, but deciding how long the timer is to be set for a particular user is a policy decision.

The separation of policy and mechanism is important for flexibility. Policies are likely to change across places or over time. In the worst case, each change in policy would require a change in the underlying mechanism. A general mechanism insensitive to changes in policy would be more desirable. A change in policy would then require redefinition of only certain parameters of the system. For instance, consider a mechanism for giving priority to certain types of programs over others. If the mechanism is properly separated and policy independent, it can be used to support a policy decision that I/O-intensive programs should have priority over CPU-intensive ones or to support the opposite policy.

Microkernel-based operating systems take the separation of mechanism and policy to one extreme by implementing a basic set of primitive building blocks. These blocks are almost policy free, allowing more advanced mechanisms and policies to be added via user-created kernel modules or via user programs themselves. As an example, consider the history of UNIX. At first, it had a time-sharing scheduler. In the latest version of Solaris, scheduling is controlled by loadable tables. Depending on the table currently loaded, the system can be time shared, batch processing, real time, fair share, or any combination. Making the scheduling mechanism general purpose allows vast policy changes to be made with a single `load-new-table` command. At the other extreme is a system such as Windows, in which both mechanism and policy are encoded in the system to enforce a global look and feel. All applications have similar interfaces, because the interface itself is built into the kernel.

Policy decisions are important for all resource allocation. Whenever it is necessary to decide whether or not to allocate a resource, a policy decision must be made. Whenever the question is *how* rather than *what*, it is a mechanism that must be determined.

3.8.3 Implementation

Once an operating system is designed, it must be implemented. Traditionally, operating systems have been written in assembly language. Now, however, they are most commonly written in higher-level languages such as C or C++. In Section 3.7.5 we saw recent efforts at writing systems in Java.

The first system that was not written in assembly language was probably the Master Control Program (MCP) for Burroughs computers. MCP was written in a variant of ALGOL. MULTICS, developed at MIT, was written mainly in PL/1. The Linux and Windows XP operating systems are written mostly in C, although there are some small sections of assembly code for device drivers and saving and restoring the state of registers during context switches.

The advantages of using a higher-level language, or at least a systems-implementation language, for implementing operating systems are the same as those accrued when the language is used for application programs: The code can be written faster, is more compact, and is easier to understand and debug. In addition, improvements in compiler technology will improve the generated code for the entire operating system by simple recompilation. Finally, an operating system is far easier to *port*—to move to some other hardware—if it is written in a high-level language. For example, MS-DOS was written in Intel 8088 assembly language. Consequently, it is available on only the Intel family of CPUs. The Linux operating system, in contrast, which is written mostly in C, is available on a number of different CPUs, including Intel 80X86, Motorola 680X0, SPARC, and MIPS RX000.

The major claimed disadvantages of implementing an operating system in a higher-level language are reduced speed and increased storage requirements. Although an expert assembly-language programmer can produce efficient small routines, for large programs a modern compiler can perform complex analysis and apply sophisticated optimizations that produce excellent code. Modern processors have deep pipelining and multiple functional units, which can handle complex dependencies that can overwhelm the limited ability of the human mind to keep track of details.

As is true in other systems, major performance improvements in operating systems are more likely to be the result of better data structures and algorithms than of excellent assembly-language code. In addition, although operating systems are large, only a small amount of the code is critical to high performance; the memory manager and the CPU scheduler are probably the most critical routines. After the system is written and is working correctly, bottleneck routines can be identified and can be replaced with assembly-language equivalents.

To identify bottlenecks, we must be able to monitor system performance. Code must be added to compute and display measures of system behavior. In a number of systems, the operating system does this task by producing trace listings of system behavior. All interesting events are logged with their time and important parameters and are written to a file. Later, an analysis program can process the log file to determine system performance and to identify bottlenecks and inefficiencies. These same traces can be run as input for a simulation of a suggested improved system. Traces also can help people to find errors in operating-system behavior.

An alternative is to compute and display the performance measures in real time. For example, a timer can trigger a routine to store the current instruction pointer value. The result is a statistical picture of the program locations most frequently used within the program. This approach may allow system operators to become familiar with system behavior and to modify system operation in real time.

3.9 ■ System Generation

It is possible to design, code, and implement an operating system specifically for one machine at one site. More commonly, however, operating systems are designed to run on any of a class of machines at a variety of sites with a variety of peripheral configurations. The system must then be configured or generated for each specific computer site, a process sometimes known as **system generation (SYSGEN)**.

The operating system is normally distributed on disk or CD-ROM. To generate a system, we use a special program. The SYSGEN program reads from a given file, or asks the operator of the system for information concerning the specific configuration of the hardware system, or probes the hardware directly to determine what components are there. The following kinds of information must be determined.

- What CPU is to be used? What options (extended instruction sets, floating-point arithmetic, and so on) are installed? For multiple CPU systems, each CPU must be described.

- How much memory is available? Some systems will determine this value themselves by referencing memory location after memory location until an "illegal address" fault is generated. This procedure defines the final legal address and hence the amount of available memory.

- What devices are available? The system will need to know how to address each device (the device number), the device interrupt number, the device's type and model, and any special device characteristics.

- What operating-system options are desired, or what parameter values are to be used? These options or values might include how many buffers of which sizes should be used, what type of CPU-scheduling algorithm is desired, what the maximum number of processes to be supported is, and so on.

Once this information is determined, it can be used in several ways. At one extreme, a system administrator can use it to modify a copy of the source code of the operating system. The operating system then is completely compiled. Data declarations, initializations, and constants, along with conditional compilation, produce an output object version of the operating system that is tailored to the system described.

At a slightly less tailored level, the system description can cause the creation of tables and the selection of modules from a precompiled library. These modules are linked together to form the generated operating system. Selection allows the library to contain the device drivers for all supported I/O devices, but only those needed are linked into the operating system. Because the system is not recompiled, system generation is faster, but the resulting system may be overly general.

At the other extreme, it is possible to construct a system that is completely table driven. All the code is always part of the system, and selection occurs at execution time, rather than at compile or link time. System generation involves simply creating the appropriate tables to describe the system.

The major differences among these approaches are the size and generality of the generated system and the ease of modification as the hardware configuration changes. Consider the cost of modifying the system to support a newly acquired graphics terminal or another disk drive. Balanced against that cost, of course, is the frequency (or infrequency) of such changes.

After an operating system is generated, it must be made available for use by the hardware. But how does the hardware know where the kernel is, or how to load that kernel? The procedure of starting a computer by loading the kernel is known as *booting* the system. On most computer systems, there is a small piece of code, stored in ROM, known as the *bootstrap program* or *bootstrap loader*. This code is able to locate the kernel, load it into main memory, and start its execution. Some computer systems, such as PCs, use a two-step process in which a simple bootstrap loader fetches a more complex boot program from disk, which in turn loads the kernel. Booting a system is discussed in Section 14.3.2 and in Appendix A.

3.10 ▪ System Boot

When a CPU receives a reset event—for instance, when it is powered up or rebooted—the instruction register is loaded with a predefined memory location, and execution starts there. At that location is the initial **bootstrap** program. This program is in the form of **read-only memory** (**ROM**), because the RAM is at an unknown state at system startup. ROM is convenient because it needs no initialization and cannot be infected by a computer virus.

This bootstrap program can perform a variety of tasks. Usually, one task is to run diagnostics to determine the state of the machine. If the diagnostics pass, the program can continue with the booting steps. It can also initialize all aspects of the system, from CPU registers to device controllers and the contents of main memory. Sooner or later, it starts the operating system.

Some systems—such as cellular phones, PDAs, and game consoles—store the entire operating system in ROM. Storing the operating system in ROM is suitable for small operating systems, simple supporting hardware, and rugged operation. A problem with this approach is that changing the bootstrap code requires changing the ROM hardware chips. Some systems resolve this problem by using **erasable programmable read-only memory** (**EPROM**), which is read-only except when explicitly given a command to become writeable. All forms of ROM are also known as **firmware**, since their characteristics fall somewhere between those of hardware and those of software. A problem with firmware in general is that executing code there is slower than executing code in RAM. Some systems store the operating system in firmware and copy it to RAM for fast execution. A final issue with firmware is that it is relatively expensive, so usually only small amounts are available.

For large operating systems (including most general-purpose operating systems like Windows, Mac OS X, and UNIX) or for systems that change frequently, the bootstrap loader is stored in firmware, and the operating system is on disk. In this case, the bootstrap runs diagnostics and has a bit of code that can read in a single block at a fixed location (say block zero) from disk into memory and execute the code from that **boot block**. The program stored in the boot block may be sophisticated enough to load the entire operating system into memory and begin its execution. More typically, it is simple code (as it fits in a single disk block) and only knows the address on disk and length of the remainder of the bootstrap program. All of the disk-bound bootstrap, and the operating system itself, can be easily changed by writing new versions to disk. A disk that has a boot partition (more on that in section 14.3.1) is called a **boot disk** or **system disk**.

Now that the full bootstrap program has been loaded, it knows how to traverse the file system to find the operating system kernel, load it into memory, and start its execution. It is only at this point that the system is said to be **running**.

3.11 ■ Summary

Operating systems provide a number of services. At the lowest level, system calls allow a running program to make requests from the operating system directly. At a higher level, the command interpreter or shell provides a mechanism for a user to issue a request without writing a program. Commands may come from files during batch-mode execution or directly from a terminal when in an interactive or time-shared mode. System programs are provided to satisfy many common user requests.

The types of requests vary according to the level of the request. The system-call level must provide the basic functions, such as process control and file and device manipulation. Higher-level requests, satisfied by the command interpreter or system programs, are translated into a sequence of system calls. System services can be classified into several categories: program control, status requests, and I/O requests. Program errors can be considered implicit requests for service.

Once the system services are defined, the structure of the operating system can be developed. Various tables are needed to record the information that defines the state of the computer system and the status of the system's jobs.

The design of a new operating system is a major task. It is important that the goals of the system be well defined before the design begins. The type of system desired is the foundation for choices among various algorithms and strategies that will be needed.

Since an operating system is large, modularity is important. Designing a system as a sequence of layers or using a microkernel is considered a good technique. The virtual-machine concept takes the layered approach and treats both the kernel of the operating system and the hardware as though they were all hardware. Even other operating systems may be loaded on top of this virtual machine.

Any operating system that has implemented the JVM is able to run all Java programs, because the JVM abstracts the underlying system to the Java program, providing an architecture-neutral interface.

Throughout the entire operating-system design cycle, we must be careful to separate policy decisions from implementation details (mechanisms). This separation allows maximum flexibility if policy decisions are to be changed later.

Operating systems are now almost always written in a systems-implementation language or in a higher-level language. This feature improves their implementation, maintenance, and portability. To create an operating system for a particular machine configuration, we must perform system generation.

For a system to begin running, the CPU must initialize and start executing the bootstrap program in firmware. The bootstrap can execute the operating system directly if the operating system is also in the firmware, or it can complete a sequence in which it loads progressively smarter programs from firmware and disk until the operating system itself is loaded into memory and executed.

■ Exercises

3.1 What are the five major activities of an operating system in regard to process management?

3.2 What are the three major activities of an operating system in regard to memory management?

3.3 What are the three major activities of an operating system in regard to secondary-storage management?

3.4 What are the five major activities of an operating system in regard to file management?

3.5 What is the purpose of the command interpreter? Why is it usually separate from the kernel?

3.6 List five services provided by an operating system. Explain how each provides convenience to the users. In what cases it would be impossible for user-level programs to provide these services? Explain.

3.7 What is the purpose of system calls?

3.8 Using system calls, write a program in either C or C++ that reads data from one file and copies it to another file. Such a program was described in Section 3.3.

3.9 Why does Java provide the ability to call from a Java program native methods that are written in, say, C or C++? Provide an example where a native method is useful.

3.10 What is the purpose of system programs?

3.11 What is the main advantage of the layered approach to system design?

3.12 What is the main advantage of the microkernel approach to system design?

3.13 What is the main advantage for an operating-system designer of using a virtual-machine architecture? What is the main advantage for a user?

3.14 Why is a just-in-time compiler useful for executing Java programs?

3.15 Why is the separation of mechanism and policy desirable?

3.16 The experimental Synthesis operating system has an assembler incorporated within the kernel. To optimize system-call performance, the kernel assembles routines within kernel space to minimize the path that the system call must take through the kernel. This approach is the antithesis of the layered approach, in which the path through the kernel is extended to make building the operating system easier. Discuss the pros and cons of the Synthesis approach to kernel design and system-performance optimization.

3.17 Why do some systems store the operating system in firmware and others on disk?

3.18 How could a system be designed to allow a choice of operating systems to boot from? What would the bootstrap program need to do?

Bibliographical Notes

Dijkstra [1968] advocated the layered approach to operating-system design. Brinch-Hansen [1970] was an early proponent of the construction of an operating system as a kernel (or nucleus) on which can be built more complete systems.

The first operating system to provide a virtual machine was the CP/67 on an IBM 360/67. The commercially available IBM VM/370 operating system was derived from CP/67. Cheung and Loong [1995] explored issues of operating systems structuring from microkernel to extensible systems.

MS-DOS, Version 3.1, is described in Microsoft [1986]. Windows NT and Windows 2000 are described by Solomon [1998] and Solomon and Russinovich [2000]. BSD UNIX is described in McKusick et al. [1996]. A good description of OS/2 is given by Iacobucci [1988]. Bovet and Cesati [2002] covers the Linux kernel in detail. Several UNIX systems—including Mach—are covered in detail in Vahalia [1996]. Mac OS X is presented at http://www.apple.com/macosx. The experimental Synthesis operating system is discussed by Massalin and Pu [1989]. Solaris is fully described in Mauro and McDougall [2001].

The specification for the Java language and the Java virtual machine is presented by Gosling et al. [1996] and by Lindholm and Yellin [1999], respectively. The internal workings of the Java virtual machine is fully described by Venners [1998]. Golm et al. [2002] highlight the JX operating system; Back et al. [2000] cover several issues in the design of Java operating systems. More information on Java is available on the Web at http://www.javasoft.com.

Part Two

PROCESS
MANAGEMENT

A *process* can be thought of as a program in execution. A process will need certain resources—such as CPU time, memory, files, and I/O devices—to accomplish its task. These resources are allocated to the process either when it is created or while it is executing.

A process is the unit of work in most systems. Such a system consists of a collection of processes: Operating-system processes execute system code, and user processes execute user code. All these processes may execute concurrently.

Although traditionally a process contained only a single *thread* of control as it ran, most modern operating systems now support processes that have multiple threads.

The operating system is responsible for the following activities in connection with process and thread management: the creation and deletion of both user and system processes; the scheduling of processes; and the provision of mechanisms for synchronization, communication, and deadlock handling for processes.

Chapter 4

PROCESSES

Early computer systems allowed only one program to be executed at a time. This program had complete control of the system and had access to all the system's resources. In contrast, current-day computer systems allow multiple programs to be loaded into memory and executed concurrently. This evolution required firmer control and more compartmentalization of the various programs; and these needs resulted in the notion of a **process**, which is a program in execution. A process is the unit of work in a modern time-sharing system.

The more complex the operating system is, the more it is expected to do on behalf of its users. Although its main concern is the execution of user programs, it also needs to take care of various system tasks that are better left outside the kernel itself. A system therefore consists of a collection of processes: operating-system processes executing system code and user processes executing user code. Potentially, all these processes can execute concurrently, with the CPU (or CPUs) multiplexed among them. By switching the CPU between processes, the operating system can make the computer more productive.

In this chapter, we look more closely at processes. We begin by discussing the process concept and go on to describe various features of processes, including scheduling, creation and termination, and communication. We end the chapter by describing communication in client–server systems.

4.1 ■ Process Concept

A question that arises in discussing operating systems involves what to call all the CPU activities. A batch system executes *jobs*, whereas a time-shared system has *user programs*, or *tasks*. Even on a single-user system such as Microsoft Windows, a user may be able to run several programs at one time: a word processor, a web browser, and an e-mail package. Even if the user can execute only one program at a time, the operating system may need to support its own internal programmed activities, such as memory management. In many respects, all these activities are similar, so we call all of them *processes*.

The terms *job* and *process* are used almost interchangeably in this text. Although we personally prefer the term *process*, much of operating-system theory and terminology was developed during a time when the major activity of operating systems was job processing. It would be misleading to avoid the use of commonly accepted terms that include the word *job* (such as *job scheduling*) simply because *process* has superseded *job*.

4.1.1 The Process

Informally, as mentioned earlier, a process is a program in execution. A process is more than the program code, which is sometimes known as the **text section**. It also includes the current activity, as represented by the value of the **program counter** and the contents of the processor's registers. A process generally also includes the process **stack**, which contains temporary data (such as method parameters, return addresses, and local variables), and a **data section**, which contains global variables. A process may also include a **heap**, which is memory that is dynamically allocated during process run time.

We emphasize that a program by itself is not a process; a program is a *passive* entity, such as a file containing a list of instructions stored on disk, whereas a process is an *active* entity, with a program counter specifying the next instruction to execute and a set of associated resources.

Although two processes may be associated with the same program, they are nevertheless considered two separate execution sequences. For instance, several users may be running different copies of the mail program, or the same user may invoke many copies of the editor program. Each of these is a separate process; and although the text sections are equivalent, the data sections vary. It is also common to have a process that spawns many processes as it runs. We discuss such matters in Section 4.4.

4.1.2 Process State

As a process executes, it changes **state**. The state of a process is defined in part by the current activity of that process. Each process may be in one of the following states:

- **New:** The process is being created.

- **Running:** Instructions are being executed.

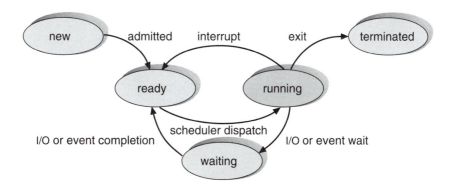

Figure 4.1   Diagram of process state.

- **Waiting:** The process is waiting for some event to occur (such as an I/O completion or reception of a signal).

- **Ready:** The process is waiting to be assigned to a processor.

- **Terminated:** The process has finished execution.

These names are arbitrary, and they vary across operating systems. The states that they represent are found on all systems, however. Certain operating systems also more finely delineate process states. It is important to realize that only one process can be *running* on any processor at any instant. Many processes may be *ready* and *waiting,* however. The state diagram corresponding to these states is presented in Figure 4.1.

4.1.3 Process Control Block

Each process is represented in the operating system by a **process control block** (**PCB**)—also called a *task control block.* A PCB is shown in Figure 4.2. It contains many pieces of information associated with a specific process, including these:

- *Process state:* The state may be new, ready, running, waiting, halted, and so on.

- *Program counter:* The counter indicates the address of the next instruction to be executed for this process.

- *CPU registers:* The registers vary in number and type, depending on the computer architecture. They include accumulators, index registers, stack pointers, and general-purpose registers, plus any condition-code information. Along with the program counter, this state information must be saved when an interrupt occurs, to allow the process to be continued correctly afterward (Figure 4.3).

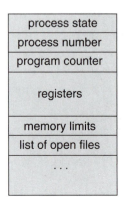

Figure 4.2   Process control block ((PCB).

- *CPU-scheduling information:* This information includes a process priority, pointers to scheduling queues, and any other scheduling parameters.
  (Chapter 6 describes process scheduling.)

- *Memory-management information:* This information may include such information as the value of the base and limit registers, the page tables, or the
  segment tables, depending on the memory system used by the operating
  system (Chapter 9).

- *Accounting information:* This information includes the amount of CPU and
  real time used, time limits, account numbers, job or process numbers, and
  so on.

- *I/O status information:* This information includes the list of I/O devices
  allocated to the process, a list of open files, and so on.

In brief, the PCB simply serves as the repository for any information that may
vary from process to process.

4.1.4 Threads

The process model discussed so far has implied that a process is a program that
performs a single **thread** of execution. For example, when a process is running a
word processor program, a single thread of instructions is being executed. This
single thread of control allows the process to perform only one task at one time.
The user cannot simultaneously type in characters and run the spell checker
within the same process, for example. Many modern operating systems have
extended the process concept to allow a process to have multiple threads of
execution and thus to perform more than one task at a time. Chapter 5 explores
multithreaded processes in detail.

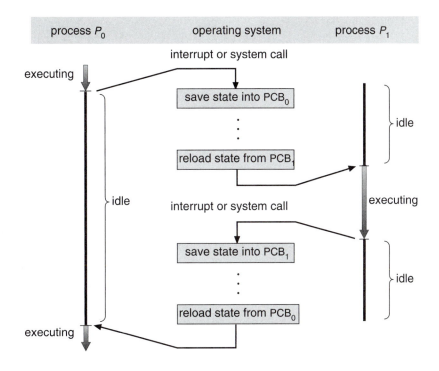

Figure 4.3   Diagram showing CPU switch from process to process.

4.2 ■ Process Scheduling

The objective of multiprogramming is to have some process running at all times, to maximize CPU utilization. The objective of time sharing is to switch the CPU among processes so frequently that users can interact with each program while it is running. To meet these objectives, the **process scheduler** selects an available process (possibly from a set of several available processes) for program execution on the CPU. For a uniprocessor system, there will never be more than one running process. If there are more processes, the rest will have to wait until the CPU is free and can be rescheduled.

4.2.1 Scheduling Queues

As processes enter the system, they are put into a **job queue**, which consists of all processes in the system. The processes that are residing in main memory and are ready and waiting to execute are kept on a list called the **ready queue**. This queue is generally stored as a linked list. A ready-queue header contains pointers to the first and final PCBs in the list. Each PCB includes a pointer field that points to the next PCB in the ready queue.

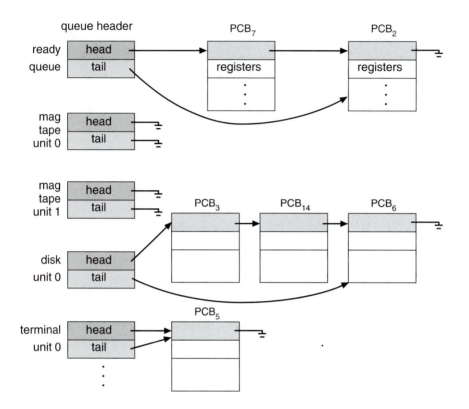

Figure 4.4   The ready queue and various I/O device queues.

The system also includes other queues. When a process is allocated the CPU, it executes for a while and eventually quits, is interrupted, or waits for the occurrence of a particular event, such as the completion of an I/O request. Suppose the process makes an I/O request to a shared device, such as a disk. Since there are many processes in the system, the disk may be busy with the I/O request of some other process. The process therefore may have to wait for the disk. The list of processes waiting for a particular I/O device is called a **device queue**. Each device has its own device queue (Figure 4.4).

A common representation for a discussion of process scheduling is a **queueing diagram**, such as that in Figure 4.5. Each rectangular box represents a queue. Two types of queues are present: the ready queue and a set of device queues. The circles represent the resources that serve the queues, and the arrows indicate the flow of processes in the system.

A new process is initially put in the ready queue. It waits there until it is selected for execution, or is **dispatched**. Once the process is allocated the CPU and is executing, one of several events could occur:

- The process could issue an I/O request and then be placed in an I/O queue.

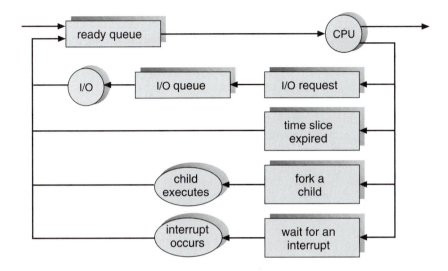

Figure 4.5   Queueing-diagram representation of process scheduling.

- The process could create a new subprocess and wait for the subprocess's termination.

- The process could be removed forcibly from the CPU, as a result of an interrupt, and be put back in the ready queue.

In the first two cases, the process eventually switches from the waiting state to the ready state and is then put back in the ready queue. A process continues this cycle until it terminates, at which time it is removed from all queues and has its PCB and resources deallocated.

4.2.2 Schedulers

A process migrates among the various scheduling queues throughout its lifetime. The operating system must select, for scheduling purposes, processes from these queues in some fashion. The selection process is carried out by the appropriate **scheduler**.

Often, in a batch system, more processes are submitted than can be executed immediately. These processes are spooled to a mass-storage device (typically a disk), where they are kept for later execution. The **long-term scheduler**, or **job scheduler**, selects processes from this pool and loads them into memory for execution. The **short-term scheduler**, or **CPU scheduler**, selects from among the processes that are ready to execute and allocates the CPU to one of them.

The primary distinction between these two schedulers lies in frequency of execution. The short-term scheduler must select a new process for the CPU frequently. A process may execute for only a few milliseconds before waiting for an I/O request. Often, the short-term scheduler executes at least once every 100 milliseconds. Because of the short time between executions, the short-term scheduler must be fast. If it takes 10 milliseconds to decide to execute a process for 100 milliseconds, then $10/(100 + 10) = 9$ percent of the CPU is being used (wasted) simply for scheduling the work.

The long-term scheduler executes much less frequently; minutes may separate the creation of one new process and the next. The long-term scheduler controls the **degree of multiprogramming** (the number of processes in memory). If the degree of multiprogramming is stable, then the average rate of process creation must be equal to the average departure rate of processes leaving the system. Thus, the long-term scheduler may need to be invoked only when a process leaves the system. Because of the longer interval between executions, the long-term scheduler can afford to take more time to decide which process should be selected for execution.

It is important that the long-term scheduler make a careful selection. In general, most processes can be described as either I/O bound or CPU bound. An **I/O-bound process** is one that spends more of its time doing I/O than it spends doing computations. A **CPU-bound process**, in contrast, generates I/O requests infrequently, using more of its time doing computations. It is important that the long-term scheduler select a good **process mix** of I/O-bound and CPU-bound processes. If all processes are I/O bound, the ready queue will almost always be empty, and the short-term scheduler will have little to do. If all processes are CPU bound, the I/O waiting queue will almost always be empty, devices will go unused, and again the system will be unbalanced. The system with the best performance will thus have a combination of CPU-bound and I/O-bound processes.

On some systems, the long-term scheduler may be absent or minimal. For example, time-sharing systems such as UNIX and Microsoft Windows systems often have no long-term scheduler but simply put every new process in memory for the short-term scheduler. The stability of these systems depends

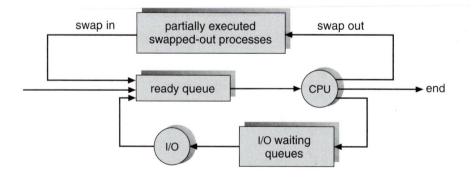

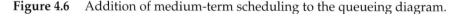

Figure 4.6   Addition of medium-term scheduling to the queueing diagram.

either on a physical limitation (such as the number of available terminals) or on the self-adjusting nature of human users. If the performance declines to unacceptable levels on a multiuser system, some users will simply quit.

Some operating systems, such as time-sharing systems, may introduce an additional, intermediate level of scheduling. This **medium-term scheduler** is diagrammed in Figure 4.6. The key idea behind a medium-term scheduler is that sometimes it can be advantageous to remove processes from memory (and from active contention for the CPU) and thus reduce the degree of multiprogramming. Later, the process can be reintroduced into memory, and its execution can be continued where it left off. This scheme is called **swapping**. The process is swapped out, and is later swapped in, by the medium-term scheduler. Swapping may be necessary to improve the process mix or because a change in memory requirements has overcommitted available memory, requiring memory to be freed up. Swapping is discussed in Chapter 9.

4.2.3 Context Switch

Switching the CPU to another process requires saving the state of the old process and loading the saved state of the new process. This task is known as a **context switch**. The **context** of a process is represented in the PCB of the process; it includes the value of the CPU registers, the process state (see Figure 4.1), and memory-management information. When a context switch occurs, the kernel saves the context of the old process in its PCB and loads the saved context of the new process scheduled to run. Context-switch time is pure overhead, because the system does no useful work while switching. Its speed varies from machine to machine, depending on the memory speed, the number of registers that must be copied, and the existence of special instructions (such as a single instruction to load or store all registers). Typical speeds are less than 10 milliseconds.

Context-switch times are highly dependent on hardware support. For instance, some processors (such as the Sun UltraSPARC) provide multiple sets of registers. A context switch here simply requires changing the pointer to the current register set. Of course, if there are more active processes than there are register sets, the system resorts to copying register data to and from memory, as before. Also, the more complex the operating system, the more work must be done during a context switch. As we will see in Chapter 9, advanced memory-management techniques may require extra data to be switched with each context. For instance, the address space of the current process must be preserved as the space of the next task is prepared for use. How the address space is preserved, and what amount of work is needed to preserve it, depend on the memory-management method of the operating system. As we will see in Chapter 5, context switching has become such a performance bottleneck that programmers are using alternative structures (threads) to speed it up—and possibly even avoid it—whenever possible.

4.3 ■ Operations on Processes

The processes in most systems can execute concurrently, and they may be created and deleted dynamically. Thus, these operating systems must provide a mechanism for process creation and termination.

4.3.1 Process Creation

A process may create several new processes, via a create-process system call, during the course of execution. The creating process is called a **parent** process, and the new processes are called the **children** of that process. Each of these new processes may in turn create other processes, forming a **tree** of processes (Figure 4.7).

In general, a process will need certain resources (CPU time, memory, files, I/O devices) to accomplish its task. When a process creates a subprocess, that subprocess may be able to obtain its resources directly from the operating system, or it may be constrained to a subset of the resources of the parent process. The parent may have to partition its resources among its children, or it may be able to share some resources (such as memory or files) among several of its children. Restricting a child process to a subset of the parent's resources prevents any process from overloading the system by creating too many subprocesses.

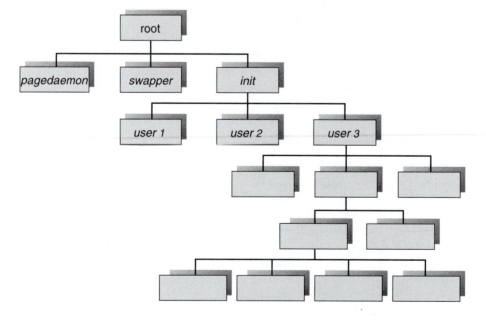

Figure 4.7   A tree of processes on a typical UNIX system.

In addition to the various physical and logical resources that a process obtains when it is created, initialization data (input) may be passed along by the parent process to the child process. For example, consider a process whose function is to display the contents of a file—say, *F1*—on the screen of a terminal. When it is created, it will get, as an input from its parent process, the name of the file *F1*, and it will use that file name, open the file, and write the contents out. It may also get the name of the output device. Some operating systems pass resources to child processes. On such a system, the new process may get two open files, *F1* and the terminal device, and may simply transfer the datum between the two.

When a process creates a new process, two possibilities exist in terms of execution:

1. The parent continues to execute concurrently with its children.

2. The parent waits until some or all of its children have terminated.

There are also two possibilities in terms of the address space of the new process:

1. The child process is a duplicate of the parent process (it has the same program and data as the parent).

2. The child process has a new program loaded into it.

To illustrate these differences, let us consider the UNIX operating system. In UNIX, each process is identified by its **process identifier**, which is a unique integer. A new process is created by the fork() system call. The new process consists of a copy of the address space of the original process. This mechanism allows the parent process to communicate easily with its child process. Both processes (the parent and the child) continue execution at the instruction after the fork(), with one difference: The return code for the fork() is zero for the new (child) process, whereas the (nonzero) process identifier of the child is returned to the parent.

Typically, the exec() system call is used after a fork() system call by one of the two processes to replace the process's memory space with a new program. The exec() system call loads a binary file into memory (destroying the memory image of the program containing the exec() system call) and starts its execution. In this manner, the two processes are able to communicate and then go their separate ways. The parent can then create more children; or, if it has nothing else to do while the child runs, it can issue a wait() system call to move itself off the ready queue until the termination of the child.

The C program shown in Figure 4.8 illustrates the UNIX system calls previously described. We now have two different processes running a copy of the same program. The value of *pid* for the child process is zero; that for the parent is an integer value greater than zero. The child process overlays its address

```
#include <stdio.h>
#include <unistd.h>

int main(int argc, char *argv[])
{
int pid;

    /* fork another process */
    pid = fork();

    if (pid < 0) { /* error occurred */
        fprintf(stderr, "Fork Failed");
        exit(-1);
    }
    else if (pid == 0) { /* child process */
        execlp("/bin/ls","ls",NULL);
    }
    else { /* parent process */
        /* parent will wait for the child to complete */
        wait(NULL);
        printf("Child Complete");
        exit(0);
    }
}
```

Figure 4.8   C program forking a separate process.

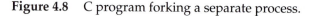

space with the UNIX command /bin/ls (used to get a directory listing) using
the execlp() system call (execlp() is a version of the exec() system call).
The parent waits for the child process to complete with the wait() system call.
When the child process completes, the parent process resumes from the call to
wait(), where it completes using the exit() system call.

The DEC VMS operating system, in contrast, creates a new process, loads
a specified program into that process, and starts it running. The Microsoft
Windows NT operating system supports both models: The parent's address
space may be duplicated, or the parent may specify the name of a program
for the operating system to load into the address space of the new process.

4.3.2 Process Termination

A process terminates when it finishes executing its final statement and asks the
operating system to delete it by using the exit() system call. At that point, the
process may return a status value (typically an integer) to its parent process (via
the wait() system call). All the resources of the process—including physical and

virtual memory, open files, and I/O buffers—are deallocated by the operating system.

Termination can occur in other circumstances as well. A process can cause the termination of another process via an appropriate system call (for example, abort()). Usually, such a system call can be invoked by only the parent of the process that is to be terminated. Otherwise, users could arbitrarily kill each other's jobs. Note that a parent needs to know the identities of its children. Thus, when one process creates a new process, the identity of the newly created process is passed to the parent.

A parent may terminate the execution of one of its children for a variety of reasons, such as these:

- The child has exceeded its usage of some of the resources that it has been allocated. (To determine whether this has occurred, the parent must have a mechanism to inspect the state of its children.)

- The task assigned to the child is no longer required.

- The parent is exiting, and the operating system does not allow a child to continue if its parent terminates.

Many systems, including VMS, do not allow a child to exist if its parent has terminated. In such systems, if a process terminates (either normally or abnormally), then all its children must also be terminated. This phenomenon, referred to as **cascading termination**, is normally initiated by the operating system.

To illustrate process execution and termination, we consider that, in UNIX, we can terminate a process by using the exit() system call; its parent process may wait for the termination of a child process by using the wait() system call. The wait() system call returns the process identifier of a terminated child, so that the parent can tell which of its possibly many children has terminated. If the parent terminates, however, all its children have assigned as their new parent the *init* process. Thus, the children still have a parent to collect their status and execution statistics.

4.4   ▪ Cooperating Processes

The concurrent processes executing in the operating system may be either independent processes or cooperating processes. A process is **independent** if it cannot affect or be affected by the other processes executing in the system. Any process that does not share data (temporary or persistent) with any other process is independent. A process is **cooperating** if it can affect or be affected by the other processes executing in the system. Clearly, any process that shares data with other processes is a cooperating process.

There are several reasons for providing an environment that allows process cooperation:

- *Information sharing:* Since several users may be interested in the same piece of information (for instance, a shared file), we must provide an environment to allow concurrent access to these types of resources.

- *Computation speedup:* If we want a particular task to run faster, we must break it into subtasks, each of which will be executing in parallel with the others. Notice that such a speedup can be achieved only if the computer has multiple processing elements (such as CPUs or I/O channels).

- *Modularity:* We may want to construct the system in a modular fashion, dividing the system functions into separate processes or threads, as we discussed in Chapter 3.

- *Convenience:* Even an individual user may work on many tasks at the same time. For instance, a user may be editing, printing, and compiling in parallel.

Concurrent execution that requires cooperation among the processes requires mechanisms to allow processes to communicate with one another (Section 4.5) and to synchronize their actions (Chapter 7).

To illustrate the concept of cooperating processes, let us consider the producer–consumer problem, which is a common paradigm for cooperating processes. A **producer** process produces information that is consumed by a **consumer** process. For example, a compiler may produce assembly code, which is consumed by an assembler. The assembler, in turn, may produce object modules, which are consumed by the loader. The producer–consumer problem also provides a useful metaphor for the client–server paradigm. We generally think of a server as a producer and a client as a consumer. For example, a file server produces (that is, provides) a file which is consumed (that is, read) by the client requesting the file.

To allow producer and consumer processes to run concurrently, we must have available a buffer of items that can be filled by the producer and emptied

```
public interface Buffer
{
   // producers call this method
   public abstract void insert(Object item);

   // consumers call this method
   public abstract Object remove();
}
```

Figure 4.9   Interface for buffer implementations.

by the consumer. A producer can produce one item while the consumer is consuming another item. The producer and consumer must be synchronized, so that the consumer does not try to consume an item that has not yet been produced. In this situation, the consumer must wait until an item is produced.

Solutions to the producer–consumer problem may implement the Buffer interface shown in Figure 4.9. The producer process invokes the insert() method when it wishes to enter an item in the buffer, and the consumer calls the remove() method when it wants to consume an item from the buffer.

The nature of the buffer—unbounded or bounded—provides a way to further describe the producer–consumer problem. The **unbounded-buffer** producer–consumer problem places no practical limit on the size of the buffer. The

```
import java.util.*;

public class BoundedBuffer implements Buffer
{
    private static final int BUFFER_SIZE = 5;
    private int count; // number of items in the buffer
    private int in; // points to the next free position
    private int out; // points to the next full position
    private Object[] buffer;

    public BoundedBuffer() {
        // buffer is initially empty
        count = 0;
        in = 0;
        out = 0;

        buffer = new Object[BUFFER_SIZE];
    }

    // producers calls this method
    public void insert(Object item) {
        // Figure 4.11
    }

    // consumers calls this method
    public Object remove() {
        // Figure 4.12
    }

}
```

Figure 4.10 Shared-memory solution to the producer–consumer problem.

```
public void insert(Object item) {
   while (count == BUFFER_SIZE)
         ; // do nothing -- no free buffers

   // add an item to the buffer
   ++count;
   buffer[in] = item;
   in = (in + 1) % BUFFER_SIZE;
}
```

Figure 4.11   The insert() method.

consumer may have to wait for new items, but the producer can always produce new items. The **bounded-buffer** producer–consumer problem assumes that the buffer size is fixed. In this case, the consumer must wait if the buffer is empty, and the producer must wait if the buffer is full.

The buffer may be either provided by the operating system through the use of an interprocess-communication (IPC) facility (Section 4.5) or explicitly coded by the application programmer with the use of shared memory. Although Java does not provide support for shared memory, we can design a solution to the bounded-buffer problem in Java that emulates shared memory by allowing the producer and consumer processes to share an instance of the BoundedBuffer class (Figure 4.10), which implements the Buffer interface. Such sharing involves passing a reference to an instance of the BoundedBuffer class to the producer and consumer processes.

The shared buffer is implemented as a circular array with two logical pointers: in and out. The variable in points to the next free position in the buffer; out points to the first full position in the buffer. count is the number

```
public Object remove() {
   Object item;

   while (count == 0)
         ; // do nothing -- nothing to consume

   // remove an item from the buffer
   --count;
   item = buffer[out];
   out = (out + 1) % BUFFER_SIZE;

   return item;
}
```

Figure 4.12   The remove() method.

of items currently in the buffer. The buffer is empty when `count == 0` and is full when `count == BUFFER_SIZE`. Note that both the producer and the consumer will block in the `while` loop if the buffer is not usable to them. In Chapter 7, we discuss how synchronization among cooperating processes can be implemented effectively in a shared-memory environment.

4.5 ▪ Interprocess Communication

In Section 4.4, we showed how cooperating processes can communicate in a shared-memory environment. The scheme requires that these processes share a common buffer pool and that the code for implementing the buffer be written explicitly by the application programmer. Another way to achieve the same effect is for the operating system to provide the means for cooperating processes to communicate with each other via an **interprocess communication** (IPC) facility.

IPC provides a mechanism to allow processes to communicate and to synchronize their actions without sharing the same address space. IPC is particularly useful in a distributed environment, where the communicating processes may reside on different computers connected with a network. An example is a **chat** program used on the World Wide Web.

IPC is best provided by a message-passing system, and message systems can be defined in many different ways. Here, we look at different design issues and present a Java solution to the producer–consumer problem that uses message passing.

4.5.1 Message-Passing System

The function of a message system is to allow processes to communicate with one another without the need to resort to shared data. An IPC facility provides at least the two operations `send`(message) and `receive`(message).

Messages sent by a process can be of either fixed or variable size. If only fixed-sized messages can be sent, the system-level implementation is straightforward. This restriction, however, makes the task of programming more difficult. Conversely, variable-sized messages require a more complex system-level implementation, but the programming task becomes simpler. This is a common kind of tradeoff seen through operating system design.

If processes *P* and *Q* want to communicate, they must send messages to and receive messages from each other; a **communication link** must exist between them. This link can be implemented in a variety of ways. We are concerned here not with the link's physical implementation (such as shared memory, hardware bus, or network, which are covered in Chapter 15), but rather with its logical implementation. Here are several methods for logically implementing a link and the `send()`/`receive()` operations:

- Direct or indirect communication

- Synchronous or asynchronous communication

- Automatic or explicit buffering

We look at issues related to each of these features next.

4.5.2 Naming

Processes that want to communicate must have a way to refer to each other. They can use either direct or indirect communication.

4.5.2.1 Direct Communication

Under **direct communication**, each process that wants to communicate must explicitly name the recipient or sender of the communication. In this scheme, the send() and receive() primitives are defined as:

- send(P, message) — Send a message to process P.

- receive(Q, message) — Receive a message from process Q.

A communication link in this scheme has the following properties:

- A link is established automatically between every pair of processes that want to communicate. The processes need to know only each other's identity to communicate.

- A link is associated with exactly two processes.

- Between each pair of processes, there exists exactly one link.

This scheme exhibits *symmetry* in addressing; that is, both the sender and the receiver processes have to name the other to communicate. A variant of this scheme employs *asymmetry* in addressing. Only the sender names the recipient; the recipient is not required to name the sender. In this scheme, the send() and receive() primitives are defined as follows:

- send(P, message) – Send a message to process P.

- receive(id, message) – Receive a message from any process; the variable *id* is set to the name of the process with which communication has taken place.

The disadvantage in both of these schemes (symmetric and asymmetric) is the limited modularity of the resulting process definitions. Changing the identifier of a process may necessitate examining all other process definitions. All references to the old identifier must be found, so that they can be modified to the new identifier. In general, any such **hard-coding** techniques where identifiers must be explicitly stated are less desirable than those involving a level of indirection, as described next.

4.5.2.2 Indirect Communication

With **indirect communication**, the messages are sent to and received from **mailboxes**, or **ports**. A mailbox can be viewed abstractly as an object into which messages can be placed by processes and from which messages can be removed. Each mailbox has a unique identification. In this scheme, a process can communicate with some other process via a number of different mailboxes. Two processes can communicate only if the processes have a shared mailbox, however. The send() and receive() primitives are defined as follows:

- send(A, message) —Send a message to mailbox A.

- receive(A, message) — Receive a message from mailbox A.

In this scheme, a communication link has the following properties:

- A link is established between a pair of processes only if both members of the pair have a shared mailbox.

- A link may be associated with more than two processes.

- Between each pair of communicating processes, there may be a number of different links, with each link corresponding to one mailbox.

Now suppose that processes P_1, P_2, and P_3 all share mailbox A. Process P_1 sends a message to A, while P_2 and P_3 each execute a receive() from A. Which process will receive the message sent by P_1? The answer depends on the scheme that we choose:

- Allow a link to be associated with at most two processes.

- Allow at most one process at a time to execute a receive() operation.

- Allow the system to select arbitrarily which process will receive the message (that is, either P_2 or P_3, but not both, will receive the message). The system also may define an algorithm for selecting which process will receive the message (that is, round robin). The system may identify the receiver to the sender.

A mailbox may be owned either by a process or by the operating system. If the mailbox is owned by a process (that is, the mailbox is part of the address space of the process), then we distinguish between the owner (who can only receive messages through this mailbox) and the user of the mailbox (who can only send messages to the mailbox). Since each mailbox has a unique owner, there can be no confusion about who should receive a message sent to this mailbox. When a process that owns a mailbox terminates, the mailbox disappears. Any process that subsequently sends a message to this mailbox must be notified that the mailbox no longer exists.

In contrast, a mailbox that is owned by the operating system has an existence of its own. It is independent and is not attached to any particular process. The operating system then must provide a mechanism that allows a process to do the following:

- Create a new mailbox

- Send and receive messages through the mailbox

- Delete a mailbox

The process that creates a new mailbox is that mailbox's owner by default. Initially, the owner is the only process that can receive messages through this mailbox. However, the ownership and receiving privilege may be passed to other processes through appropriate system calls. Of course, this provision could result in multiple receivers for each mailbox.

4.5.3 Synchronization

Communication between processes takes place by calls to send() and receive() primitives. There are different design options for implementing each primitive. Message passing may be either **blocking** or **nonblocking**— also known as **synchronous** and **asynchronous**.

- **Blocking send:** The sending process is blocked until the message is received by the receiving process or by the mailbox.

- **Nonblocking send:** The sending process sends the message and resumes operation.

- **Blocking receive:** The receiver blocks until a message is available.

- **Nonblocking receive:** The receiver retrieves either a valid message or a null.

Different combinations of send() and receive() are possible. When both the send() and receive() are blocking, we have a **rendezvous** between the sender and the receiver.

Note that the concepts of synchronous and asynchronous occur frequently in operating-system I/O algorithms, as will be seen throughout this text.

4.5.4 Buffering

Whether the communication is direct or indirect, messages exchanged by communicating processes reside in a temporary queue. Basically, there are three ways to implement such a queue:

- **Zero capacity:** The queue has maximum length 0; thus, the link cannot have any messages waiting in it. In this case, the sender must block until the recipient receives the message.

- **Bounded capacity:** The queue has finite length n; thus, at most n messages can reside in it. If the queue is not full when a new message is sent, the latter is placed in the queue (either the message is copied or a pointer to the message is kept), and the sender can continue execution without waiting. The link has a finite capacity, however. If the link is full, the sender must block until space is available in the queue.

- **Unbounded capacity:** The queue has potentially infinite length; thus, any number of messages can wait in it. The sender never blocks.

The zero-capacity case is sometimes referred to as a message system with no buffering; the other cases are referred to as automatic buffering.

4.5.5 Producer–Consumer Example

We can now present a solution to the producer–consumer problem that uses message passing. Our solution will implement the Channel interface shown in Figure 4.13. The producer and consumer will communicate indirectly using the shared mailbox illustrated in Figure 4.14.

The buffer is implemented using the java.util.Vector class, meaning that it will be a buffer of unbounded capacity. Also note that both the send() and receive() methods are nonblocking.

When the producer generates an item, it places that item in the mailbox via the send() method. The code for the producer is shown in Figure 4.15.

```
public interface Channel
{
    // Send a message to the channel
    public abstract void send(Object item);

    // Receive a message from the channel
    public abstract Object receive();
}
```

Figure 4.13   Interface for message passing.

```
import java.util.Vector;

public class MessageQueue implements Channel
{
    private Vector queue;

    public MessageQueue() {
        queue = new Vector();
    }

    // This implements a nonblocking send
    public void send(Object item) {
        queue.addElement(item);
    }

    // This implements a nonblocking receive
    public Object receive() {
        if (queue.size() == 0)
            return null;
        else
            return queue.remove(0);
    }
}
```

Figure 4.14   Mailbox for message passing.

The consumer obtains an item from the mailbox using the `receive()` method. Because `receive()` is nonblocking, the consumer must evaluate the value of the `Object` returned from `receive()`. If it is `null`, the mailbox is empty. The code for the consumer is shown in Figure 4.16.

Chapter 5 shows how to implement the producer and consumer as separate threads of control and how to allow the mailbox to be shared between the threads.

```
Channel mailBox;

while (true) {
    Date message = new Date();
    mailBox.send(message);
}
```

Figure 4.15   The producer process.

```
Channel mailBox;

while (true) {
   Date message = (Date) mailBox.receive();
   if (message != null)
      // consume the message
}
```

Figure 4.16   The consumer process.

4.5.6 An Example: Mach

As an example of a message-based operating system, we next consider the Mach operating system, developed at Carnegie Mellon University. We introduced Mach in Chapter 3 as part of the Mac OS X operating system. The Mach kernel supports the creation and destruction of multiple tasks, which are similar to processes but have multiple threads of control. Most communication in Mach —including most of the system calls and all intertask information—is carried out by *messages*. Messages are sent to and received from mailboxes, called *ports* in Mach.

Even system calls are made by messages. When a task is created, two special mailboxes—the Kernel mailbox and the Notify mailbox—are also created. The Kernel mailbox is used by the kernel to communicate with the task. The kernel sends notification of event occurrences to the Notify port. Only three system calls are needed for message transfer. The msg_send call sends a message to a mailbox. A message is received via msg_receive. Remote procedure calls (RPCs) are executed via msg_rpc, which sends a message and waits for exactly one return message from the sender. In this way, RPC models a typical subroutine procedure call but can work between systems.

The port_allocate system call creates a new mailbox and allocates space for its queue of messages. The maximum size of the message queue defaults to eight messages. The task that creates the mailbox is that mailbox's owner. The owner also is given receive access to the mailbox. Only one task at a time can either own or receive from a mailbox, but these rights can be sent to other tasks if desired.

The mailbox has an initially empty queue of messages. As messages are sent to the mailbox, the messages are copied into the mailbox. All messages have the same priority. Mach guarantees that multiple messages from the same sender are queued in first-in, first-out (FIFO) order but does not guarantee an absolute ordering. For instance, messages from two senders may be queued in any order.

The messages themselves consist of a fixed-length header, followed by a variable-length data portion. The header includes the length of the message and two mailbox names. When a message is sent, one mailbox name is the mailbox to which the message is being sent. Commonly, the sending thread expects a reply; the mailbox name of the sender is passed on to the receiving task, which may use it as a "return address" to send messages back.

The variable part of a message is a list of typed data items. Each entry in the list has a type, size, and value. The type of the objects specified in the message is important, since operating-system–defined objects—such as the ownership or receive access rights, task states, and memory segments—may be sent in messages.

The send and receive operations themselves are flexible. For instance, when a message is sent to a mailbox, the mailbox may be full. If the mailbox is not full, the message is copied to the mailbox and the sending thread continues. If the mailbox is full, the sending thread has four options:

1. Wait indefinitely until there is room in the mailbox.

2. Wait at most n milliseconds.

3. Do not wait at all, but rather return immediately.

4. Temporarily cache a message. One message can be given to the operating system to keep, even though the mailbox to which it is being sent is full. When the message can be put in the mailbox, a message is sent back to the sender; only one such message to a full mailbox can be pending at any time for a given sending thread.

The final option is meant for server tasks, such as a line-printer driver. After finishing a request, these tasks may need to send a one-time reply to the task that had requested service; but they must also continue with other service requests, even if the reply mailbox for a client is full.

The receive operation must specify from which mailbox or mailbox set to receive a message. A **mailbox set** is a collection of mailboxes, as declared by the task, which can be grouped together and treated as one mailbox for the purposes of the task. Threads in a task can receive from only a mailbox or mailbox set for which that task has receive access. A port_status system call returns the number of messages in a given mailbox. The receive operation attempts to receive from (1) any mailbox in a mailbox set or (2) a specific (named) mailbox. If no message is waiting to be received, the receiving thread may either wait at most n milliseconds, or not wait at all.

The Mach system was especially designed for distributed systems, which we discuss in Chapters 15 through 17, but Mach is also suitable for single-processor systems. The major problem with message systems has generally been poor performance caused by double copying of messages; the message is copied first from the sender to the mailbox and then from the mailbox to the receiver. The Mach message system attempts to avoid double-copy operations by using virtual-memory-management techniques (Chapter 10). Essentially, Mach maps the address space containing the sender's message into the receiver's address space. The message itself is never actually copied. This message-management technique provides a large performance boost but works for only intrasystem messages. The Mach operating system is discussed in the extra chapter that is posted on our web site.

4.5.7 An Example: Windows XP

The Windows XP operating system is an example of modern design that employs modularity to increase functionality and decrease the time needed to implement new features. Windows XP provides support for multiple operating environments, or *subsystems,* with which application programs communicate via a message-passing mechanism. The application programs can be considered to be clients of the Windows XP subsystem server.

The message-passing facility in Windows XP is called the **local procedure-call (LPC)** facility. The LPC in Windows XP communicates between two processes that are on the same machine. It is similar to the standard RPC mechanism that is widely used, but it is optimized for and specific to Windows XP. Like Mach, Windows XP uses a port object to establish and maintain a connection between two processes. Every client that calls a subsystem needs a communication channel, which is provided by a port object and is never inherited. Windows XP uses two types of ports: connection ports and communication ports. They are really the same but are given different names according to how they are used. Connection ports are named *objects* and are visible to all processes; they give applications a way to set up a communication channel (Chapter 21). This communication works as follows:

- The client opens a handle to the subsystem's connection port object.

- The client sends a connection request.

- The server creates two private communication ports and returns the handle to one of them to the client.

- The client and server use the corresponding port handle to send messages or callbacks and to listen for replies.

Windows XP uses two types of message-passing techniques over a port that the client specifies when it establishes the channel. The simplest, which is used for small messages, uses the port's message queue as intermediate storage and copies the message from one process to the other. Under this method, messages of up to 256 bytes can be sent.

If a client needs to send a larger message, it passes the message through a section object (or shared memory). The client has to decide, when it sets up the channel, whether or not it will need to send a large message. If the client determines that it does want to send large messages, it asks for a section object to be created. Likewise, if the server decides that replies will be large, it creates a section object. So that the section object can be used, a small message is sent that contains a pointer and size information about that section object. This method is more complicated than the first method, but it avoids the data copying. In both cases, a callback mechanism can be used when either the client or the server cannot respond immediately to a request. The callback mechanism allows them to perform asynchronous message handling.

4.6 ■ Communication in Client-Server Systems

In Sections 4.4 and 4.5, we described how processes can communicate using shared memory and message passing. These techniques can be used for communication in client–server systems (1.5.2) as well. In this section, we explore three other strategies for communication in client–server systems: sockets, remote procedure calls (RPCs), and Java's remote method invocation (RMI).

4.6.1 Sockets

A **socket** is defined as an endpoint for communication. A pair of processes communicating over a network employs a pair of sockets—one for each process. A socket is identified by an IP address concatenated with a port number. In general, sockets use a client–server architecture. The server waits for incoming client requests by listening to a specified port. Once a request is received, the server accepts a connection from the client socket to complete the connection.

Servers implementing specific services (such as telnet, ftp, and http) listen to well-known ports (a telnet server listens to port 23, an ftp server listens to port 21, and a web, or http, server listens to port 80). All ports below 1024 are considered *well known*; we can use them to implement standard services.

When a client process initiates a request for a connection, it is assigned a port by the host computer. This port is some arbitrary number greater than 1024. For example, if a client on host X with IP address 146.86.5.20 wishes to establish a connection with a web server (which is listening on port 80) at address 161.25.19.8, host X may be assigned port 1625. The connection will consist of a pair of sockets: (146.86.5.20:1625) on host X and (161.25.19.8:80) on the web server. This situation is illustrated in Figure 4.17. The packets traveling between the hosts are delivered to the appropriate process, based on the destination port number.

All connections must be unique. Therefore, if another process also on host X wished to establish another connection with the same web server, it would be assigned a port number greater than 1024 and not equal to 1625. This ensures that all connections consist of a unique pair of sockets.

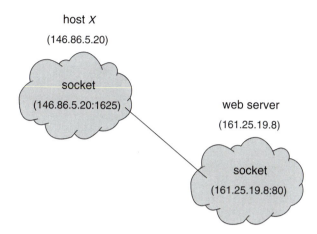

Figure 4.17   Communication using sockets.

To further explore socket programming, we turn next to an illustration using Java. Java provides an easy interface for socket programming and has a rich library for additional networking utilities. Those interested in socket programming in C or C++ should consult the Bibliographical Notes.

Java provides three different types of sockets. **Connection-oriented (TCP) sockets** are implemented with the Socket class. **Connectionless (UDP) sockets** use the DatagramSocket class. Finally, the MulticastSocket class is a subclass of the DatagramSocket class. A multicast socket allows data to be sent to multiple recipients.

Our example describes a date server that uses connection-oriented TCP sockets. The operation allows clients to request the current date and time from the server. The server listens to port 6013, although the port could be any arbitrary number greater than 1024. When a connection is received, the server returns the date and time to the client.

The date server is shown in Figure 4.18. The server creates a ServerSocket that specifies it will listen to port 6013. The server then begins listening to the port with the accept() method. The server blocks on the accept() method waiting for a client to request a connection. When a connection request is received, accept() returns a socket that the server can use to communicate with the client.

The details illustrating how the server communicates with the socket are as follows. The server first establishes a PrintWriter object that it will use to communicate with the client. A PrintWriter object allows the server to write to the socket using the routine print() and println() methods for output. The server process sends the date to the client, calling the method println(). Once it has written the date to the socket, the server closes the socket to the client and resumes listening for more requests.

```java
import java.net.*;
import java.io.*;

public class DateServer
{
    public static void main(String[] args) throws IOException {
        try {
            ServerSocket sock = new ServerSocket(6013);

            // now listen for connections
            while (true) {
                Socket client = sock.accept();

                PrintWriter pout = new
                  PrintWriter(client.getOutputStream(), true);

                // write the Date to the socket
                pout.println(new java.util.Date().toString());

                // close the socket and resume
                // listening for connections
                client.close();
            }
        }
        catch (IOException ioe) {
            System.err.println(ioe);
        }
    }
}
```

Figure 4.18   Date server.

A client communicates with the server by creating a socket and connecting to the port the server is listening on. We implement such a client in the Java program shown in Figure 4.19. The client creates a Socket and requests a connection with the server at IP address 127.0.0.1 on port 6013. Once the connection is made, the client can read from the socket using normal stream I/O statements. After it has received the date from the server, the client closes the socket and exits. The IP address 127.0.0.1 is a special IP address known as the **loopback**. When a computer refers to IP address 127.0.0.1, it is referring to itself. This mechanism allows a client and server on the same host to communicate using the TCP/IP protocol. The IP address 127.0.0.1 could be replaced with the IP address of another host running the date server. In addition to using an IP address, an actual host name, such as **www.westminstercollege.edu**, can be used as well.

```java
import java.net.*;
import java.io.*;

public class DateClient
{
    public static void main(String[] args) throws IOException {
        try {
            //make connection to server socket
            Socket sock = new Socket("127.0.0.1",6013);

            InputStream in = sock.getInputStream();
            BufferedReader bin = new
                BufferedReader(new InputStreamReader(in));

            // read the date from the socket
            String line;
            while ( (line = bin.readLine()) != null)
                System.out.println(line);

            // close the socket connection
            sock.close();
        }
        catch (IOException ioe) {
            System.err.println(ioe);
        }
    }
}
```

Figure 4.19   Date client.

Communication using sockets—although common and efficient—is considered a low-level form of communication between distributed processes. One reason is that sockets allow only an unstructured stream of bytes to be exchanged between the communicating threads. It is the responsibility of the client or server application to impose a structure on the data. We will cover sockets in more detail in Appendix D. In the next two subsections, we look at two alternative higher-level methods of communication: remote procedure calls (RPCs) and remote method invocation (RMI).

4.6.2 Remote Procedure Calls

One of the most common forms of remote service is the RPC paradigm, which we discussed briefly in Section 4.5.4. The RPC was designed as a way to abstract the procedure-call mechanism for use between systems with network connections. It is similar in many respects to the IPC mechanism described in Section 4.5, and it is usually built on top of such a system. Here, however, because we are dealing with an environment in which the processes are executing on separate systems, we must use a message-based communication scheme to provide remote service. In contrast to the IPC facility, the messages exchanged for RPC communication are well structured and are thus no longer just packets of data. Each message is addressed to an RPC daemon listening to a port on the remote system and contains an identifier of the function to execute and the parameters to pass to that function. The function is then executed as requested, and any output is sent back to the requester in a separate message.

A *port* is simply a number included at the start of a message packet. Whereas a system normally has one network address, it can have many ports within that address to differentiate the many network services it supports. If a remote process needs a service, it addresses a message to the proper port. For instance, if a system wished to allow other systems to be able to list the current users on it, it would have a daemon supporting such an RPC attached to a port —say, port 3027. Any remote system could obtain the needed information (that is, the list of current users) by sending an RPC message to port 3027 on the server; the data would be received in a reply message.

The semantics of RPCs allow a client to invoke a procedure on a remote host as it would invoke a procedure locally. The RPC system hides the details that allow communication to take place by providing a **stub** on the client side. Typically, a separate stub exists for each separate remote procedure. When the client invokes a remote procedure, the RPC system calls the appropriate stub, passing it the parameters provided to the remote procedure. This stub locates the port on the server and *marshalls* the parameters. Parameter marshalling involves packaging the parameters into a form that can be transmitted over a network. The stub then transmits a message to the server using message passing. A similar stub on the server side receives this message and invokes the procedure on the server. If necessary, return values are passed back to the client using the same technique.

One issue that must be dealt with concerns differences in data representation on the client and server machines. Consider the representation of 32-bit integers. Some systems use the high memory address to store the most significant byte (known as *big-endian*), while other systems store the least significant byte at the high memory address (known as *little-endian*). To resolve differences like this, many RPC systems define a machine-independent representation of data. One such representation is known as **external data representation (XDR)**. On the client side, parameter marshalling involves converting the machine-dependent data into XDR before being sent to the server. On the server side, the XDR data is unmarshalled and converted into the machine-dependent representation for the server.

Another important issue is the semantics of a call. Whereas local procedure calls fail only under extreme circumstances, RPCs can fail, or be duplicated and executed more than once, as a result of common network errors. One way to address this problem is for the operating system to ensure that messages are acted on *exactly once*, rather than *at most once*. Most local procedure calls have this functionality, but it is more difficult to implement.

First, we consider "at most once". This semantic can be assured by attaching to each message a timestamp. The server must keep a history of all the timestamps of messages it has already processed or a history large enough to ensure that repeated messages are detected. Incoming messages that have a timestamp already in the history are ignored. The client can then send a message one or more times and be assured that it only executed once. (Generation of these timestamps is discussed in Section 17.1.)

For "exactly once," we need to remove the risk that the server never received the request. To accomplish this, the server must implement the "at most once" protocol described above, as well as acknowledge to the client that the RPC call was received and executed. These "ACK" messages are common throughout networking. The client must resend each RPC call periodically until it receives the "ACK" for that call.

Another important issue concerns the communication between a server and a client. With standard procedure calls, some form of binding takes place during link, load, or execution time (Chapter 9), such that a procedure call's name is replaced by the memory address of the procedure call. The RPC scheme requires a similar binding of the client and the server port, but how does a client know the port numbers on the server? Neither system has full information about the other because they do not share memory.

Two approaches are common. First, the binding information may be predetermined, in the form of fixed port addresses. At compile time, an RPC call has a fixed port number associated with it. Once a program is compiled, the server cannot change the port number of the requested service. Second, binding can be done dynamically by a rendezvous mechanism. Typically, an operating system provides a rendezvous (also called a **matchmaker**) daemon on a fixed RPC port. A client then sends a message, containing the name of the RPC, to the rendezvous daemon requesting the port address of the RPC it needs to execute. The port number is returned, and the RPC calls may be sent to that port until the process terminates (or the server crashes). This method requires the extra overhead of the initial request but is more flexible than the first approach. Figure 4.20 shows a sample interaction.

The RPC scheme is useful in implementing a distributed file system (Chapter 16). Such a system can be implemented as a set of RPC daemons and clients. The messages are addressed to the DFS port on a server on which a file operation is to take place. The message contains the disk operation to be performed. Disk operations might be `read`, `write`, `rename`, `delete`, or `status`, corresponding to the usual file-related system calls. The return message contains any data resulting from that call, which is executed by the DFS daemon on behalf of the client. For instance, a message might contain a request to transfer a whole file to a client or be limited to simple block requests. In the latter case, several such requests might be needed if a whole file is to be transferred.

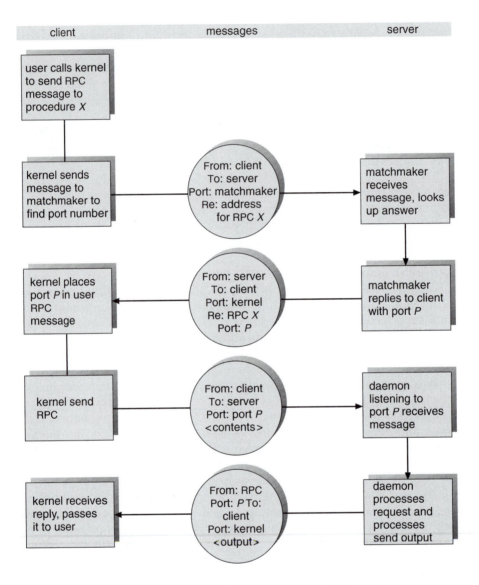

Figure 4.20   Execution of a remote procedure call (RPC).

4.6.3 Remote Method Invocation

Remote method invocation (RMI) is a Java feature similar to RPCs. RMI allows a thread to invoke a method on a remote object. Objects are considered remote if they reside in a different Java virtual machine (JVM). Therefore, the remote object may be in a different JVM on the same computer or on a remote host connected by a network. This situation is illustrated in Figure 4.21.

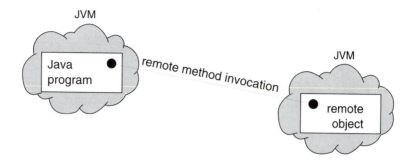

Figure 4.21   Remote method invocation.

RMI and RPCs differ in two fundamental ways. First, RPCs support procedural programming whereby only remote procedures or functions may be called. In contrast, RMI is object-based: It supports invocation of methods on remote objects. Second, the parameters to remote procedures are ordinary data structures in RPC; with RMI, it is possible to pass objects as parameters to remote methods. By allowing a Java program to invoke methods on remote objects, RMI makes it possible for users to develop Java applications that are distributed across a network.

To make remote methods transparent to both the client and the server, RMI implements the remote object using stubs and skeletons. A **stub** is a proxy for the remote object; it resides with the client. When a client invokes a remote method, the stub for the remote object is called. This client-side stub is responsible for creating a **parcel** consisting of the name of the method to be invoked on the server and the marshalled parameters for the method. The stub then sends this parcel to the server, where the skeleton for the remote object receives it. The **skeleton** is responsible for unmarshalling the parameters and invoking the desired method on the server. The skeleton then marshals the return value (or exception, if any) into a parcel and returns this parcel to the client. The stub unmarshals the return value and passes it to the client.

Let us look more closely at how this process works. Assume that a client wishes to invoke a method on a remote object `server` with a signature `someMethod(Object, Object)` that returns a `boolean` value. The client executes the statement

```
boolean val = server.someMethod(A, B);
```

The call to `someMethod()` with the parameters *A* and *B* invokes the stub for the remote object. The stub marshals into a parcel the parameters *A* and *B* and the name of the method that is to be invoked on the server, then sends this parcel to the server. The skeleton on the server unmarshals the parameters and invokes the method `someMethod()`. The actual implementation of `someMethod()` resides on the server. Once the method is completed, the skeleton marshals the `boolean` value returned from `someMethod()` and sends this value back to the client. The stub unmarshals this return value and passes it to the client. The process is shown in Figure 4.22.

Fortunately, the level of abstraction that RMI provides makes the stubs and skeletons transparent, allowing Java developers to write programs that invoke distributed methods just as they would invoke local methods. It is crucial, however, to understand a few rules about the behavior of parameter passing.

- If the marshalled parameters are **local** (or **nonremote**) objects, they are passed by copy using a technique known as **object serialization**. However, if the parameters are also remote objects, they are passed by reference. In our example, if A is a local object and B a remote object, A is serialized and passed by copy, and B is passed by reference. This would in turn allow the server to invoke methods on B remotely.

- If local objects are to be passed as parameters to remote objects, they must implement the interface *java.io.Serializable*. Many objects in the core Java API implement *Serializable*, allowing them to be used with RMI. Object serialization allows the state of an object to be written to a byte stream.

Next, using RMI, we build an application similar to the socket-based program shown in Section 4.6.1 that returns the current date and time. We cover RMI in further detail in Chapter D (available online), where we implement a message-passing solution to the producer-consumer problem using RMI.

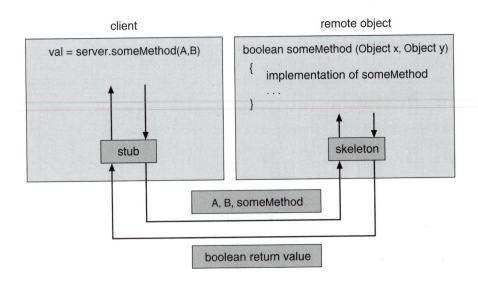

Figure 4.22   Marshalling parameters.

4.6.3.1 Remote Objects

Building a distributed application initially requires defining the necessary remote objects. We define remote objects by first declaring an interface that specifies the methods that can be invoked remotely. In this example of a date server, the remote method will be named `getDate()` and will return a `Date` containing the current date. To provide for remote objects, this interface must also extend the `java.rmi.Remote` interface, which identifies objects implementing this interface as being remote. Further, each method declared in the interface must throw the exception `java.rmi.RemoteException`. For remote objects, we provide the `RemoteDate` interface shown in Figure 4.23.

The class that defines the remote object must implement the `RemoteDate` interface (Figure 4.24). In addition to defining the `getDate()` method, the class must also extend `java.rmi.server.UnicastRemoteObject`. Extending `UnicastRemoteObject` allows the creation of a single remote object that listens for network requests using RMI's default scheme of sockets for network communication. This class also includes a `main()` method. The `main()` method creates an instance of the object and registers with the RMI registry running on the server with the `rebind()` method. In this case, the object instance registers itself with the name "DateServer". Also note that we must create a default constructor for the `RemoteDateImpl` class, and it must throw a `RemoteException` if a communication or network failure prevents RMI from exporting the remote object.

4.6.3.2 Access to the Remote Object

Once an object is registered on the server, a client (as shown in Figure 4.25) can get a proxy reference to this remote object from the RMI registry running on the server by using the static method `lookup()` in the `Naming` class. RMI provides a URL-based lookup scheme using the form `rmi://host/objectName`, where `host` is the IP name (or address) of the server on which the remote object `objectName` resides. `objectName` is the name of the remote object specified by the server in the `rebind()` method (in this case, `DateServer`). Once the client has the proxy reference to the remote object, it invokes the remote method `getDate()`, which returns the current date. Because remote methods—as well

```
import java.rmi.*;
import java.util.Date;

public interface RemoteDate extends Remote
{
    public abstract Date getDate() throws RemoteException;
}
```

Figure 4.23   The `RemoteDate` interface.

```
import java.rmi.*;
import java.rmi.server.UnicastRemoteObject;
import java.util.Date;

public class RemoteDateImpl extends UnicastRemoteObject
        implements RemoteDate
{
   public RemoteDateImpl() throws RemoteException { }

   public Date getDate() throws RemoteException {
      return new Date();
   }

   public static void main(String[] args) {
      try {
         RemoteDate dateServer = new RemoteDateImpl();

         // Bind this object instance to the name "DateServer"
         Naming.rebind("DateServer", dateServer);
      }
      catch (Exception e) {
         System.err.println(e);
      }
   }
}
```

Figure 4.24   Implementation of the RemoteDate interface.

as the Naming.lookup() method—can throw exceptions, they must be placed in try-catch blocks.

4.6.3.3 Running of the Programs

We now demonstrate the steps necessary to run the example programs. For simplicity, we are assuming that all programs are running on the local host— that is, IP address 127.0.0.1. However, communication is still considered remote, because the client and server programs are each running in their own JVM.

1. *Compile all source files.*

2. *Generate the stub and skeleton.* The user generates the stub and skeleton, using the tool rmic, by entering

```
rmic RemoteDateImpl
```

```java
import java.rmi.*;

public class RMIClient
{
   public static void main(String args[]) {
      try {
         String host = "rmi://127.0.0.1/DateServer";

         RemoteDate dateServer = (RemoteDate)Naming.lookup(host);
         System.out.println(dateServer.getDate());
      }
      catch (Exception e) {
         System.err.println(e);
      }
   }
}
```

Figure 4.25   The RMI client.

on the command line; this creates the files RemoteDateImpl_Skel.class and RemoteDateImpl_Stub.class. (If you are running this example on two different computers, make sure that all the class files—including the stub classes—are available on each computer. It is possible to load classes dynamically using RMI, a topic beyond the scope of this text but covered in texts mentioned in the Bibliographical Notes.)

3. *Start the registry and create the remote object.* To start the registry on UNIX platforms, the user can type

   rmiregistry &

   For Windows, the user can type

   start rmiregistry

   This command starts the registry with which the remote object will register. Next, create an instance of the remote object with

   java RemoteDateImpl

   This remote object will register using the name DateServer.

4. *Reference the remote object.* The statement

   java RMIClient

   is entered on the command line to start the client. This program will get a proxy reference to the remote object named DateServer and invokes the remote method getDate().

4.6.3.4 RMI versus Sockets

Contrast the socket-based client program shown in Figure 4.19 with the client using RMI shown in Figure 4.25. The socket-based client must manage the socket connection, including opening and closing the socket and establishing an `InputStream` to read from the socket. The design of the client using RMI is much simpler. All it must do is get a proxy for the remote object, which allows it to invoke the remote method `getDate()` as it would invoke an ordinary local method.

This illustrates the appeal of techniques such as RPCs and RMI: They provide developers of distributed systems a communication mechanism allowing them to design distributed programs without incurring the overhead of socket management.

4.7 ■ Summary

A process is a program in execution. As a process executes, it changes state. The state of a process is defined by that process's current activity. Each process may be in one of the following states: new, ready, running, waiting, or terminated. Each process is represented in the operating system by its own process-control block (PCB).

A process, when it is not executing, is placed in some waiting queue. There are two major classes of queues in an operating system: I/O request queues and the ready queue. The ready queue contains all the processes that are ready to execute and are waiting for the CPU. Each process is represented by a PCB, and the PCBs can be linked together to form a ready queue. Long-term (job) scheduling is the selection of processes to be allowed to contend for the CPU. Normally, long-term scheduling is heavily influenced by resource-allocation considerations, especially memory management. Short-term (CPU) scheduling is the selection of one process from the ready queue.

The processes in most systems can execute concurrently. There are several reasons for allowing concurrent execution: information sharing, computation speedup, modularity, and convenience. Concurrent execution requires a mechanism for process creation and deletion.

The processes executing in the operating system may be either independent processes or cooperating processes. Cooperating processes must have the means to communicate with each other. Principally, communication is achieved through two complementary schemes: shared memory and message systems. The shared-memory method requires communicating processes to share some variables. The processes are expected to exchange information through the use of these shared variables. In a shared-memory system, the responsibility for providing communication rests with the application programmers; the operating system needs to provide only the shared memory. The message-system method allows the processes to exchange messages. The responsibility for providing communication may rest with the operating system itself. These two schemes are not mutually exclusive and can be used simultaneously within a single operating system.

Communication in client-server systems may use (1) sockets, (2) remote procedure calls (RPCs), or (3) Java's remote method invocation (RMI). A socket is defined as an endpoint for communication. A connection between a pair of applications consists of a pair of sockets, one at each end of the communication channel. RPCs are another form of distributed communication. An RPC occurs when a process (or thread) calls a procedure on a remote application. RMI is the Java version of an RPC. RMI allows a thread to invoke a method on a remote object just as it would invoke a method on a local object. The primary distinction between RPCs and RMI is that in RPC data are passed to a remote procedure in the form of an ordinary data structure, whereas RMI allows objects to be passed in remote method calls.

■ Exercises

4.1 Palm OS provides no means of concurrent processing. Discuss three major complications that concurrent processing adds to an operating system.

4.2 Describe the differences among short-term, medium-term, and long-term scheduling.

4.3 The Sun UltraSPARC processor has multiple register sets. Describe the actions of a context switch if the new context is already loaded into one of the register sets. What else must happen if the new context is in memory rather than in a register set and all the register sets are in use?

4.4 Describe the actions taken by a kernel to context-switch between processes.

4.5 What are the benefits and the disadvantages of each of the following? Consider both the system level and the programmer levels.

   a. Synchronous and asynchronous communication

   b. Automatic and explicit buffering

   c. Send by copy and send by reference

   d. Fixed-sized and variable-sized messages

4.6 Consider the RPC mechanism. Describe the undesirable circumstances that could arise from not enforcing either the "at most once" or "exactly once" semantic. Describe possible uses for a mechanism that has neither of these guarantees.

4.7 Again considering the RPC mechanism, consider the "exactly once" semantic. Does the algorithm for implementing this semantic execute correctly even if the "ACK" message back to the client is lost because of a network problem? Describe the sequence of messages and whether "exactly once" is still preserved.

4.8 Modify the date server shown in Figure 4.18 so that it delivers random one-line fortunes rather than the current date.

4.9 Modify the RMI date server shown in Figure 4.24 so that it delivers random one-line fortunes rather than the current date.

Bibliographical Notes

The subject of interprocess communication was discussed by Brinch-Hansen [1970] with respect to the RC 4000 system. Schlichting and Schneider [1982] discussed asynchronous message-passing primitives. The IPC facility implemented at the user level was described by Bershad et al. [1990].

Details of interprocess communication in UNIX systems were presented by Gray [1997]. Barrera [1991] and Vahalia [1996] presented interprocess communication in the Mach system. Solomon and Russinovich [2000] and Stevens [1999] outline interprocess communication in Windows 2000 and UNIX respectively.

Discussions concerning the implementation of RPCs were presented by Birrell and Nelson [1984]. A design of a reliable RPC mechanism was presented by Shrivastava and Panzieri [1982]. A survey of RPCs was presented by Tay and Ananda [1990]. Stankovic [1982] and Staunstrup [1982] discussed procedure calls versus message-passing communication. Grosso [2002] discusses RMI in significant detail. Calvert and Donahoo [2001] provide coverage of socket programming in Java.

Chapter 5

THREADS

The process model introduced in Chapter 4 assumed that a process was an executing program with a single thread of control. Many modern operating systems now provide features enabling a process to contain multiple threads of control. This chapter introduces many concepts associated with multithreaded computer systems, including a discussion of the Pthreads API and Java threads. We look at many issues related to multithreaded programming and how it affects the design of operating systems. Finally, we explore how several modern operating systems support threads at the kernel level.

5.1 ▪ Overview

A thread is a basic unit of CPU utilization; it comprises a thread ID, a program counter, a register set, and a stack. It shares with other threads belonging to the same process its code section, data section, and other operating-system resources, such as open files and signals. A traditional (or **heavyweight**) process has a single thread of control. If the process has multiple threads of control, it can do more than one task at a time. Figure 5.1 illustrates the difference between a traditional single-threaded process and a multithreaded process.

5.1.1 Motivation

Many software packages that run on modern desktop PCs are **multithreaded**. An application typically is implemented as a separate process with several

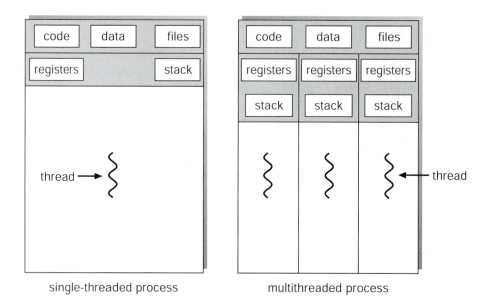

single-threaded process   multithreaded process

Figure 5.1   Single- and multithreaded processes.

threads of control. A web browser might have one thread display images or text while another thread retrieves data from the network, for example. A word processor may have a thread for displaying graphics, another thread for reading keystrokes from the user, and a third thread for performing spelling and grammar checking in the background.

In certain situations, a single application may be required to perform several similar tasks. For example, a web server accepts client requests for web pages, images, sound, and so forth. A busy web server may have several (perhaps thousands) of clients concurrently accessing it. If the web server ran as a traditional **single-threaded** process, it would be able to service only one client at a time. The amount of time that a client might have to wait for its request to be serviced could be enormous.

One solution is to have the server run as a single process that accepts requests. When the server receives a request, it creates a separate process to service that request. In fact, this process-creation method was in common use before threads became popular. Process creation is time-consuming and resource intensive, as was shown in the previous chapter. If the new process will perform the same tasks as the existing process, why incur all that overhead? It is generally more efficient for one process that contains multiple threads to serve the same purpose. This approach would multithread the web-server process. The server would create a separate thread that would listen for client requests; when a request was made, rather than creating another process, it would create another thread to service the request.

Threads also play a vital role in remote procedure call (RPC) systems. Recall from Chapter 4 that RPCs allow interprocess communication by providing a communication mechanism similar to ordinary function or procedure calls. Typically, RPC servers are multithreaded. When a server receives a message, it services the message using a separate thread. This allows the server to service several concurrent requests. RMI systems work similarly.

Finally, many operating system kernels are now multithreaded; several threads operate in the kernel, and each thread performs a specific task, such as managing devices or interrupt handling. For example, Solaris creates a set of threads in the kernel specifically for interrupt handling.

5.1.2 Benefits

The benefits of multithreaded programming can be broken down into four major categories:

1. **Responsiveness:** Multithreading an interactive application may allow a program to continue running even if part of it is blocked or is performing a lengthy operation, thereby increasing responsiveness to the user. For instance, a multithreaded web browser could still allow user interaction in one thread while an image is being loaded in another thread.

2. **Resource sharing:** By default, threads share the memory and the resources of the process to which they belong. The benefit of code sharing is that it allows an application to have several different threads of activity within the same address space.

3. **Economy:** Allocating memory and resources for process creation is costly. Because threads share resources of the process to which they belong, it is more economical to create and context-switch threads. Empirically gauging the difference in overhead can be difficult, but in general it is much more time consuming to create and manage processes than threads. In Solaris, for example, creating a process is about thirty times slower than is creating a thread, and context switching is about five times slower.

4. **Utilization of multiprocessor architectures:** The benefits of multithreading can be greatly increased in a multiprocessor architecture, where threads may be running in parallel on different processors. A single-threaded process can only run on one CPU, no matter how many are available. Multithreading on a multi-CPU machine increases concurrency.

5.1.3 User and Kernel Threads

Our discussion so far has treated threads in a generic sense. However, support for threads may be provided at either the user level, for **user threads**, or by the kernel, for **kernel threads**. User threads are supported above the kernel and are managed without kernel support, whereas kernel threads are supported and managed directly by the operating system. Most contemporary operating systems—including Windows XP, Solaris, and Tru64 UNIX (formerly Digital UNIX)—support kernel threads. In Section 5.2, we will explore the relationship between user and kernel threads in more detail.

5.1.4 Thread Libraries

A **thread library** provides the programmer an API for creating and managing threads. There are two primary ways of implementing a thread library. The first approach is to provide a library entirely in user space with no kernel support. All code and data structures for the library exist in user space. This means that invoking a function in the library results in a local function call in user space and not a system call.

The second approach is to implement a kernel-level library supported directly by the operating system. In this case, code and data structures for the library exist in kernel space. Invoking a function in the API for the library typically results in a system call to the kernel.

Three main thread libraries are in use today: (1) POSIX Pthreads, (2) Java, and (3) Win32. An implementation of the POSIX standard may be of either the first or the second type. The Win32 thread library is a kernel-level library. The Java thread API may be implemented by Pthreads or Win32 or possibly another library. We cover Pthreads and Java in Sections 5.4 and 5.7and explore Win32 in Section 5.5, which covers Windows. Additionally, we will look at thread support in the Linux operating system in Section 5.6, although Linux does not quite refer to them as *threads*.

5.2 ■ Multithreading Models

In Section 5.1.3, we distinguished between threads at the user and kernel levels. Ultimately, there must exist a relationship between these two types of structures. In this section, we look at three common ways of establishing this relationship.

5.2.1 Many-to-One Model

The many-to-one model (Figure 5.2) maps many user-level threads to one kernel thread. Thread management is done by the thread library in user space, so it is efficient; but the entire process will block if a thread makes a blocking system call. Also, because only one thread can access the kernel at a time, multiple threads are unable to run in parallel on multiprocessors. **Green**

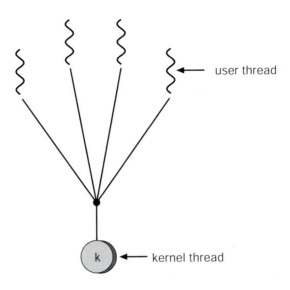

Figure 5.2   Many-to-one model.

threads—a thread library available for Solaris—uses this model, as does **GNU Portable Threads**.

5.2.2 One-to-One Model

The one-to-one model (Figure 5.3) maps each user thread to a kernel thread. It provides more concurrency than the many-to-one model by allowing another thread to run when a thread makes a blocking system call; it also allows multiple threads to run in parallel on multiprocessors. The only drawback to this model is that creating a user thread requires creating the corresponding kernel thread. Because the overhead of creating kernel threads can burden the performance of an application, most implementations of this model restrict the number of threads supported by the system. Linux, along with the fam-

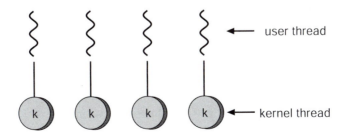

Figure 5.3   One-to-one model.

ily of Windows operating systems—including Windows 95/98/NT/2000/XP—implement the one-to-one model.

5.2.3 Many-to-Many Model

The many-to-many model (Figure 5.4) multiplexes many user-level threads to a smaller or equal number of kernel threads. The number of kernel threads may be specific to either a particular application or a particular machine (an application may be allocated more kernel threads on a multiprocessor than on a uniprocessor). Whereas the many-to-one model allows the developer to create as many user threads as she wishes, true concurrency is not gained because the kernel can schedule only one thread at a time. The one-to-one model allows for greater concurrency, but the developer has to be careful not to create too many threads within an application (and in some instances may be limited in the number of threads she can create). The many-to-many model suffers from neither of these shortcomings: Developers can create as many user threads as necessary, and the corresponding kernel threads can run in parallel on a multiprocessor. Also, when a thread performs a blocking system call, the kernel can schedule another thread for execution.

One popular variation on the many-to-many model still multiplexes many user-level threads to a smaller or equal number of kernel threads but also allows a user-level thread to be bound to a kernel thread. This variation, sometimes referred to as the *two-level model* (Figure 5.5), is supported by operating systems such as IRIX, HP-UX, and Tru64 UNIX. The Solaris operating system supported

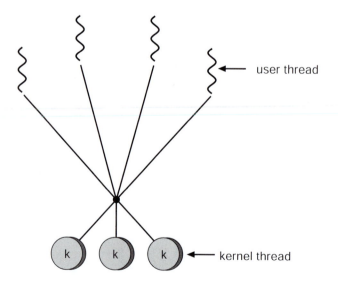

Figure 5.4   Many-to-many model.

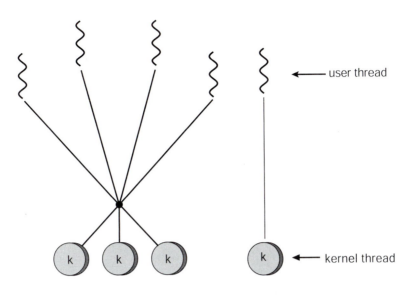

Figure 5.5   Two-level model.

the two-level model in versions older than Solaris 9. However, beginning with Solaris 9, this system uses the one-to-one model.

5.3 ■ Threading Issues

In this section, we discuss some of the issues to consider with multithreaded programs.

5.3.1 The fork() and exec() System Calls

In Chapter 4, we described how the fork() system call is used to create a separate, duplicate process. In a multithreaded program, the semantics of the fork() and exec() system calls change.

If one thread in a program calls fork(), does the new process duplicate all threads, or is the new process single-threaded? Some UNIX systems have chosen to have two versions of fork(), one that duplicates all threads and another that duplicates only the thread that invoked the fork() system call.

The exec() system call typically works in the same way as described in Chapter 4. That is, if a thread invokes the exec() system call, the program specified in the parameter to exec() will replace the entire process—including all threads and LWPs.

Which of the two versions of fork() to use depends on the application. If exec() is called immediately after forking, then duplicating all threads is unnecessary, as the program specified in the parameters to exec() will replace the process. In this instance, duplicating only the calling thread is appropriate. If, however, the separate process does not call exec() after forking, the separate process should duplicate all threads.

5.3.2 Cancellation

Thread cancellation is the task of terminating a thread before it has completed. For example, if multiple threads are concurrently searching through a database and one thread returns the result, the remaining threads might be cancelled. Another situation might occur when a user presses a button on a web browser that stops a web page from loading any further. Often, a web page is loaded using several threads (each image is loaded in a separate thread). When a user presses the *stop* button, all threads loading the page are cancelled.

A thread that is to be cancelled is often referred to as the **target thread**. Cancellation of a target thread may occur in two different scenarios:

1. **Asynchronous cancellation:** One thread immediately terminates the target thread.

2. **Deferred cancellation:** The target thread can periodically check whether it should terminate, allowing the target thread an opportunity to terminate itself in an orderly fashion.

The difficulty with cancellation occurs in situations where resources have been allocated to a cancelled thread or where a thread is cancelled while in the middle of updating data it is sharing with other threads. This becomes especially troublesome with asynchronous cancellation. Often, the operating system will reclaim system resources from a cancelled thread but will not reclaim all resources. Therefore, cancelling a thread asynchronously may not free a necessary systemwide resource.

With deferred cancellation, in contrast, one thread indicates that a target thread is to be cancelled, but cancellation occurs only after the target thread has checked a flag to determine if it should be cancelled or not. This allows a thread to check whether it should be cancelled at a point when it can be cancelled safely. Pthreads refers to such points as **cancellation points**.

5.3.3 Signal Handling

A **signal** is used in UNIX systems to notify a process that a particular event has occurred. A signal may be received either synchronously or asynchronously, depending on the source and the reason for the event being signaled. All signals, whether synchronous or asynchronous, follow the same pattern:

1. A signal is generated by the occurrence of a particular event.

2. A generated signal is delivered to a process.

3. Once delivered, the signal must be handled.

An example of a synchronous signal includes an illegal memory access or division by 0. If a running program performs either of these actions, a signal is generated. Synchronous signals are delivered to the same process that performed the operation causing the signal (that is the reason they are considered synchronous).

When a signal is generated by an event external to a running process, that process receives the signal asynchronously. Examples of such signals include terminating a process with specific keystrokes (such as <control><C>) and having a timer expire. Typically, an asynchronous signal is sent to another process.

Every signal may be *handled* by one of two possible handlers:

1. A default signal handler

2. A user-defined signal handler

Every signal has a **default signal handler** that is run by the kernel when handling that signal. This default action may be overridden by a **user-defined signal handler** function. In this instance, the user-defined function is called to handle the signal rather than the default action. Signals may be handled in different ways. Some signals may be simply ignored (such as changing the size of a window); others may be handled by terminating the program (such as an illegal memory access).

Handling signals in single-threaded programs is straightforward; signals are always delivered to a process. However, delivering signals is more complicated in multithreaded programs, where a process may have several threads. Where then should a signal be delivered?

In general, the following options exist:

1. Deliver the signal to the thread to which the signal applies.

2. Deliver the signal to every thread in the process.

3. Deliver the signal to certain threads in the process.

4. Assign a specific thread to receive all signals for the process.

The method for delivering a signal depends on the type of signal generated. For example, synchronous signals need to be delivered to the thread causing the signal and not to other threads in the process. However, the situation with asynchronous signals is not as clear. Some asynchronous signals—such as a signal that terminates a process (<control><C>, for example)—should be sent to all threads. Most multithreaded versions of UNIX allow a thread to specify which signals it will accept and which it will block. Therefore, in some cases, an asynchronous signal may be delivered to only those threads that are not blocking it. However, because signals need to be handled only once, a signal is typically delivered only to the first thread found that is not blocking it.

Although Windows does not explicitly provide support for signals, they can be emulated using **asynchronous procedure calls (APCs)**. The APC facility allows a user thread to specify a function that is to be called when the user thread receives notification of a particular event. As indicated by its name, an APC is roughly equivalent to an asynchronous signal in UNIX. However, whereas UNIX must contend with how to deal with signals in a multithreaded environment, the APC facility is more straightforward, as an APC is delivered to a particular thread rather than a process.

5.3.4 Thread Pools

In Section 5.1, we mentioned multithreading in a web server. In this situation, whenever the server receives a request, it creates a separate thread to service the request. Whereas creating a separate thread is certainly superior to creating a separate process, a multithreaded server nonetheless has potential problems. The first concerns the amount of time required to create the thread prior to servicing the request, together with the fact that this thread will be discarded once it has completed its work. The second issue is more problematic: If we allow all concurrent requests to be serviced in a new thread, we have not placed a bound on the number of threads concurrently active in the system. Unlimited threads could exhaust system resources, such as CPU time or memory. One solution to this issue is to use **thread pools**.

The general idea behind a thread pool is to create a number of threads at process startup and place them into a *pool*, where they sit and wait for work. When a server receives a request, it awakens a thread from this pool—if one is available—and passes it the request to service. Once the thread completes its service, it returns to the pool and awaits more work. If the pool contains no available thread, the server waits until one becomes free.

Thread pools offer these benefits:

1. Servicing a request with an existing thread is usually faster than waiting to create a thread.

2. A thread pool limits the number of threads that exist at any one point. This is particularly important on systems that cannot support a large number of concurrent threads.

The number of threads in the pool can be set heuristically based on factors such as the number of CPUs in the system, the amount of physical memory, and the expected number of concurrent client requests. More sophisticated thread-pool architectures can dynamically adjust the number of threads in the pool according to usage patterns. Such architectures provide the further benefit of having a smaller pool—thereby consuming less memory—when the load on the system is low.

5.3.5 Thread-Specific Data

Threads belonging to a process share the data of the process. Indeed, this sharing of data provides one of the benefits of multithreaded programming. However, in some circumstances, each thread might need its own copy of certain data. We will call such data **thread-specific data**. For example, in a transaction-processing system, we might service each transaction in a separate thread. Furthermore, each transaction may be assigned a unique identifier. To associate each thread with its unique identifier, we could use thread-specific data. Most thread libraries—including Win32 and Pthreads—provide some form of support for thread-specific data. Java provides support as well, and we will explore this in Section 5.7.5.

5.3.6 Scheduler Activations

A final issue to be considered with multithreaded programs concerns communication between the kernel and the thread library, which may be required by the many-to-many and two-level models discussed in Section 5.2.3. Such coordination allows the number of kernel threads to be dynamically adjusted to help ensure the best performance.

Many systems implementing either the many-to-many or two-level model place an intermediate data structure between the user and kernel threads. This data structure, typically known as a lightweight process or LWP, is shown in Figure 5.6. To the user-thread library, the LWP appears to be a *virtual processor* on which the application can schedule a user thread to run. Each LWP is attached to a kernel thread, and it is kernel threads that the operating system schedules to run on physical processors. If a kernel thread blocks (such as while waiting for an I/O operation to complete), the LWP blocks as well. Up the chain, the user-level thread attached to the LWP also blocks.

An application may require any number of LWPs to run efficiently. Consider a CPU-bound application running on a uniprocessor. In this scenario, only one thread may be running at once, so one LWP is sufficient. An application that is I/O-intensive may require multiple LWPs to execute, however. Typically, an LWP is required for each concurrent blocking system call. Suppose, for example, that five different file-read requests occur simultaneously. Five LWPs are needed, because all could be waiting for I/O completion in the kernel. If a process has only four LWPs, then the fifth request must wait for one of the LWPs to return from the kernel.

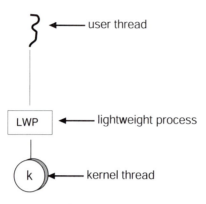

Figure 5.6   Lightweight process (LWP.)

One scheme for communication between the user-thread library and the kernel is known as **scheduler activation**. It works as follows: The kernel provides an application with a set of virtual processors (LWPs), and the application can schedule user threads onto an available virtual processor. Furthermore, the kernel must inform an application about certain events. This procedure is known as an **upcall**. Upcalls are handled by the thread library with an **upcall handler**, and upcall handlers must run on a virtual processor. One event that triggers an upcall occurs when an application thread is about to block. In this scenario, the kernel makes an upcall to the application informing it that a thread is about to block and identifying the specific thread. The kernel then allocates a new virtual processor to the application. The application runs an upcall handler on this new virtual processor, which saves the state of the blocking thread and relinquishes the virtual processor on which the blocking thread is running. The upcall handler then schedules another thread that is eligible to run on this new virtual processor. When the event that the blocking thread was waiting on occurs, the kernel makes another upcall to the thread library informing it that the previously blocked thread is now eligible to run. The upcall handler for this event also requires a virtual processor, and the kernel may allocate a new virtual processor or preempt one of the user threads and run the upcall handler on its virtual processor. After marking the unblocked thread as eligible to run, the application schedules an eligible thread to run on an available virtual processor.

5.4 ■ Pthreads

Pthreads refers to the POSIX standard (IEEE 1003.1c) defining an API for thread creation and synchronization. This is a *specification* for thread behavior, not an *implementation*. Operating system designers may implement the specification in any way they wish. Numerous systems implement the Pthreads specification, including Solaris, Linux, Tru64 UNIX, and Mac OS X. *Shareware* implementations are available in the public domain for the various Windows operating systems as well.

In this section, we introduce some of the Pthreads API as an example of a user-level thread library. We refer to it as a user-level library because no distinct relationship exists between a thread created using the Pthreads API and any associated kernel threads. The C program shown in Figure 5.7 demonstrates the basic Pthreads API for constructing a multithreaded program. If you are interested in more details on programming Pthreads, we encourage you to consult the Bibliographical Notes.

The program shown in Figure 5.7 creates a separate thread for the summation of a non-negative integer. In a Pthreads program, separate threads begin execution in a specified function. In Figure 5.7, this is the `runner()` function. When this program begins, a single thread of control begins in `main()`. After some initialization, `main()` creates a second thread that begins control in the `runner()` function. Both threads share the global data `sum`.

We now provide a more detailed overview of this program. All Pthreads programs must include the `pthread.h` header file. The statement `pthread_t tid` declares the identifier for the thread we will create. Each thread has a set of attributes, including stack size and scheduling information. The `pthread_attr_t attr` declaration represents the attributes for the thread. We will set the attributes in the function call `pthread_attr_init(&attr)`. Because we did not explicitly set any attributes, we will use the default attributes provided. (In Chapter 6, we will discuss some of the scheduling attributes provided by the Pthreads API.) A separate thread is created with the `pthread_create()` function call. In addition to passing the thread identifier and the attributes for the thread, we also pass the name of the function where the new thread will begin execution—in this case, the `runner()` function. Last, we pass the integer parameter that was provided on the command line, `argv[1]`.

At this point, the program has two threads: the initial thread in `main()` and the thread performing the summation in the `runner()` function. After creating the second thread, the `main()` thread will wait for the `runner()` thread to complete by calling the `pthread_join()` function. The `runner()` thread will complete when it calls the function `pthread_exit()`. Once the `runner()` thread has returned, the `main()` thread outputs the value of the shared data `sum`.

5.5 ■ Windows XP Threads

Windows XP implements the Win32 API. The Win32 API is the primary API for the family of Microsoft operating systems (Windows 95/98/NT, Windows 2000 and Windows XP.) Indeed, much of what is mentioned in this section applies to this family of operating systems.

```c
#include <pthread.h>
#include <stdio.h>

int sum; /* this data is shared by the thread(s) */
void *runner(void *param); /* the thread */

int main(int argc, char *argv[])
{
    pthread_t tid; /* the thread identifier */
    pthread_attr_t attr; /* set of thread attributes */

    if (argc != 2) {
        fprintf(stderr,"usage:   a.out <integer value>\n");
        exit();
    }
    if (atoi(argv[1]) < 0) {
        fprintf(stderr,"%d must be >= 0\n",atoi(argv[1]));
        exit();
    }

    /* get the default attributes */
    pthread_attr_init(&attr);
    /* create the thread */
    pthread_create(&tid,&attr,runner,argv[1]);
    /* now wait for the thread to exit */
    pthread_join(tid,NULL);
    printf("sum = %d\n",sum);
}

/* The thread will begin control in this function */
void *runner(void *param)
{
    int i, upper = atoi(param);
    sum = 0;

    if (upper > 0) {
        for (i = 1; i <= upper; i++)
            sum += i;
    }

    pthread_exit(0);
}
```

Figure 5.7   Multithreaded C program using the Pthreads API.

A Windows XP application runs as a separate process. Each process may contain one or more threads. Windows XP uses the one-to-one mapping described in Section 5.2.2 where each user-level thread maps to an associated kernel thread. However, Windows XP also provides support for a **fiber library**, which provides the functionality of the many-to-many model (Section 5.2.3). Every thread belonging to a process can access the virtual address space of the process.

The general components of a thread include:

- A thread ID uniquely identifying the thread.

- A register set representing the status of the processor.

- A user stack used when the thread is running is user mode. Similarly, each thread has a kernel stack used when the thread is running in kernel mode.

- A private storage area used by various run-time libraries and dynamic link libraries (DLLs).

The register set, stacks, and private storage area are known as the **context** of the thread. The primary data structures of a thread include:

- ETHREAD (executive thread block).

- KTHREAD (kernel thread block).

- TEB (thread environment block).

The key components of the ETHREAD include a pointer to the process to which the thread belongs and the address of the routine in which the thread starts control. The ETHREAD also contains a pointer to the corresponding KTHREAD.

The KTHREAD includes scheduling and synchronization information for the thread. In addition, the KTHREAD includes the kernel stack (used when the thread is running in kernel mode) and a pointer to the TEB.

The ETHREAD and the KTHREAD exist entirely in kernel space; this means only the kernel can access them. The TEB is a user-space data structure that is accessed when the thread is running in user mode. Among other fields, the TEB contains a user mode stack and an array for thread-specific data (which Windows XP terms **thread-local storage**).

5.6 ■ Linux Threads

Linux provides a `fork()` system call with the traditional functionality of duplicating a process. Linux also provides the `clone()` system call, which is analogous to creating a thread. `clone()` behaves much like `fork()`, except that instead of creating a copy of the calling process, it creates a separate process that shares the address space of the calling process. This sharing of the address space of the parent process enables a cloned task to behave much like a separate thread.

The sharing of the address space is allowed because of the way a process is represented in the Linux kernel. A unique kernel data structure exists for each process in the system. However, the data structure, rather than storing the data for the process, contains pointers to other data structures where this data is stored—for example, data structures that represent the list of open files, signal-handling information, and virtual memory. When `fork()` is invoked, a new process is created along with a *copy* of all the associated data structures of the parent process. A new process is also created when the `clone()` system call is made. However, rather than copying all data structures, the new process *points* to the data structures of the parent process, thereby allowing the child process to share the memory and other process resources of the parent. A set of flags is passed as a parameter to the `clone()` system call. This set of flags is used to indicate how much of the parent process is to be shared with the child. If none of the flags is set, no sharing occurs; and `clone()` acts just like `fork()`. If all flags are set, the child process shares everything with the parent. Other combinations of flags allow various levels of sharing between these two extremes. The Linux kernel also creates several kernel threads that are designated for specific tasks; such as memory management.

Interestingly, Linux does not distinguish between processes and threads. In fact, Linux generally uses the term *task*—rather than *process* or *thread*—when referring to a flow of control within a program. Several Pthreads implementations are available for Linux, however; please consult the Bibliography for specifics.

5.7 ■ Java Threads

As we have already seen, support for threads may be provided at the user level with a library such as Pthreads. Furthermore, most operating systems provide support for threads at the kernel level as well. Java is one of a small number of languages that provide support at the language level for the creation and management of threads. However, because threads are managed by the Java virtual machine (JVM), not by a user-level library or kernel, it is difficult to classify Java threads as either user- or kernel-level. In this section, we present Java threads as an alternative to the strict user- or kernel-level models. We also discuss how a Java thread can be mapped to the underlying kernel thread.

All Java programs comprise at least a single thread of control. Even a simple Java program consisting of only a `main()` method runs as a single thread in the JVM. In addition, Java provides commands that allow the developer to create and manipulate additional threads of control within the program.

```
class Worker1 extends Thread
{
    public void run() {
        System.out.println("I am a worker thread");
    }
}

public class First
{
    public static void main(String args[]) {
        Thread runner = new Worker1();

        runner.start();

        System.out.println("I am the main thread");
    }
}
```

Figure 5.8 Thread creation by extending the Thread class.

5.7.1 Thread Creation

One way to create a thread explicitly is to create a new class that is derived from the Thread class and to override the run() method of the Thread class. This approach is shown in Figure 5.8.

An object of this derived class will run as a separate thread of control in the JVM. However, creating an object that is derived from the Thread class does not specifically create the new thread; rather, it is the start() method that actually creates the new thread. Calling the start() method for the new object (1) allocates memory and initializes a new thread in the JVM and (2) calls the run() method, making the thread eligible to be run by the JVM. (Note: Do not ever call the run() method directly. Call the start() method, and it will call the run() method on your behalf.)

When this program runs, two threads are created by the JVM. The first is the thread associated with the application—the thread that starts execution at the main() method. The second thread is the runner thread, created explicitly with the start() method. The runner thread begins execution in its run() method.

Another option to create a separate thread is to define a class that implements the Runnable interface. The Runnable interface is defined as follows:

```
public interface Runnable
{
    public abstract void run();
}
```

When a class implements Runnable, it must define a run() method. (The Thread class, in addition to defining static and instance methods, also implements the Runnable interface. That explains why a class derived from Thread must define a run() method.)

Implementing the Runnable interface is similar to extending the Thread class. The only change is that "extends Thread" is substituted for "implements Runnable":

```
class Worker2 implements Runnable
{
    public void run() {
        System.out.println("I am a worker thread.");
    }
}
```

Creating a new thread from a class that implements Runnable is slightly different from creating a thread from a class extending Thread, however. Since the new class does not extend Thread, it does not have access to the static or instance methods—such as the start() method—of the Thread class. However, an object of the Thread class is still needed because it is the start() method that creates a new thread of control. Figure 5.9 shows how threads can be created using the Runnable interface.

In the class Second, a new Thread object is created that is passed a Runnable object in its constructor. When the thread is created with the start() method, the new thread begins execution in the run() method of the Runnable object.

Why does Java support two approaches for creating threads? Which approach is more appropriate to use in what situations?

The first question is easy to answer. Since Java does not support multiple inheritance, if a class is already derived from another class, it will not also be able to extend the Thread class. A good example is that an applet already

```
public class Second
{
    public static void main(String args[]) {
        Thread thrd = new Thread(new Worker2());

        thrd.start();

        System.out.println("I am the main thread");
    }
}
```

Figure 5.9   Thread creation implementing the Runnable interface.

extends the Applet class. To multithread an applet, you extend the Applet class and implement the Runnable interface:

```
public class ThreadedApplet extends Applet implements Runnable
{
    .  .  .
}
```

The answer to the second question is less obvious. Object-oriented purists might say that, unless you are enhancing the Thread class, the class should not be extended. (This point may be moot, however, as many of the methods in the Thread class are defined as final.) We will not attempt to determine the correct answer in this debate. For this text, we adopt the practice of implementing the Runnable interface, as this approach seems more commonly used today.

5.7.2 Thread States

A Java thread can be in one of four states:

1. *New:* A thread is in this state when an object for the thread is created (that is, the new statement).

2. *Runnable:* Calling the start() method allocates memory for the new thread in the JVM and calls the run() method for the thread object. When a thread's run() method is invoked, the thread moves from the new to the runnable state. A thread in the runnable state is eligible to be run by the JVM. Note that Java does not distinguish between a thread that is eligible to run and a thread that is currently running. A running thread is still in the runnable state.

3. *Blocked:* A thread becomes blocked if it performs a blocking statement—for example, by doing I/O—or if it invokes certain Java Thread methods, such as sleep().

4. *Dead:* A thread moves to the dead state when its run() method terminates.

It is not possible to determine the exact state of a thread, although the isAlive() method returns a boolean value that a program can use to determine whether or not a thread is in the dead state. Figure 5.10 illustrates the different thread states and labels several possible transitions.

5.7.3 Joining Threads

The thread created in the program in Figure 5.9 runs independently of the thread that creates it (the thread associated with the main() method). In

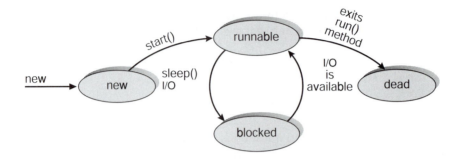

Figure 5.10   Java thread states.

situations where the creating thread wants to wait for any threads it has created, Java provides the `join()` method. By invoking `join()`, the creating thread is able to wait for the `run()` method of the joining thread to terminate before continuing its operation. The `join()` method is useful in situations where the creating thread can continue only after a worker thread has completed. For example, assume that thread *A* creates thread *B* and thread *B* will perform calculations that thread *A* requires. In this scenario, thread *A* will join on thread *B*.

We illustrate the `join()` method by modifying the code in Figure 5.9 as follows:

```
Thread thrd = new Thread(new Worker2());
thrd.start();

try {
    thrd.join();
} catch (InterruptedException ie) { }
```

Note that `join()` can throw an `InterruptedException`, which we will ignore for now. We will discuss handling this exception in Chapter 7.

5.7.4 Thread Cancellation

In Section 5.3.2, we discussed issues concerning thread cancellation. Java threads can be asynchronously terminated using the `stop()` method of the Thread class. However, this method was **deprecated**. Deprecated methods are still implemented in the current API; however, their use is discouraged. We discuss why `stop()` was deprecated in Chapter 8.

It is possible to cancel a thread using deferred cancellation as described in Section 5.3.2. Recall that deferred cancellation works by having the target thread periodically check whether it should terminate. In Java, checking involves use of the `interrupt()` method. The Java API defines the inter-

```
class InterruptibleThread implements Runnable
{
    /**
     * This thread will continue to run as long
     * as it is not interrupted.
     */
    public void run() {
        while (true) {
            /**
             * do some work for awhile
             * .   .   .
             */

            if (Thread.currentThread().isInterrupted()) {
                System.out.println("I'm interrupted!");
                break;
            }
        }
        // clean up and terminate
    }
}
```

Figure 5.11 Deferred cancellation using the isInterrupted() method.

rupt() method for the Thread class. When the interrupt() method is invoked, the **interruption status** of the target thread is set. A thread can periodically check its interruption status by invoking either the interrupted() method or the isInterrupted() method, both of which return true if the interruption status of the target thread is set. (It is important to note that the interrupted() method will clear the interruption status of the target thread, whereas the isInterrupted() method preserves the interruption status.) Figure 5.11 illustrates how deferred cancellation works when the isInterrupted() method is used.

An instance of an InterruptibleThread can be interrupted using the following code:

```
Thread thrd = new Thread(new InterruptibleThread());
thrd.start();
.   .   .
thrd.interrupt();
```

In this example, the target thread can periodically check its interruption status via the isInterrupted() method and—if it is set—clean up before terminating. Because the InterruptibleThread class does not extend Thread, it cannot directly invoke instance methods in the Thread class. To invoke instance methods in Thread, a program must first invoke the static method currentThread() which returns a Thread object representing the thread that is currently running. This return value can then be used to access instance methods in the Thread class.

It is important to recognize that interrupting a thread via the interrupt() method only sets the interruption status of a thread; it is up to the target thread to periodically check this interruption status. Traditionally, Java does not wake a thread that is blocked in an I/O operation using the java.io package. Any thread blocked doing I/O in this package will not be able to check its interruption status until the call to I/O is completed. However, the java.nio package introduced in Java 1.4 provides facilities for interrupting a thread that is blocked performing I/O.

5.7.5 Thread-Specific Data

In Section 5.3.5, we described thread-specific data, which allow a thread to have its own private copy of data. At first glance, it may appear that Java has no need

```
class Service
{
    private static ThreadLocal errorCode =
        new ThreadLocal();

    public static void transaction() {
        try {
            /**
             * some operation where an error may occur

             .   .   .

             */
        }
        catch (Exception e) {
            errorCode.set(e);
        }
    }

    /**
     * get the error code for this transaction
     */
    public static Object getErrorCode() {
        return errorCode.get();
    }
}
```

Figure 5.12   Using the ThreadLocal class.

for thread-specific data, and this viewpoint is partly correct. All that is required for each thread to have its own private data is to create threads by subclassing the Thread class and to declare instance data in this class. This approach works fine when threads are constructed in this way. However, when the developer has no control over the thread-creation process—for example, when a thread pool is being used—then an alternative approach is necessary.

The Java API provides the ThreadLocal class for declaring thread-specific data. ThreadLocal data can be initialized with either the initialValue() method or the set() method, and a thread can inquire as to the value of ThreadLocal data using the get() method. Typically, ThreadLocal data are declared as static. Consider the Service class shown in Figure 5.12, which declares errorCode as ThreadLocal data. The transaction() method in this class can be invoked by any number of threads. If an exception occurs, we assign the exception to errorCode using the set() method of the ThreadLocal class. Now consider a scenario in which two threads—say, thread 1 and thread 2— invoke transaction(). Assume that thread 1 generates exception A and thread 2 generates exception B. The value of errorCode for thread 1 and thread 2 will be A and B, respectively. Figure 5.13 illustrates how a thread can inquire as to the value of errorCode() after invoking transaction().

5.7.6 The JVM and the Host Operating System

The JVM is typically implemented on top of a host operating system. This setup allows the JVM to hide the implementation details of the underlying operating system and to provide a consistent, abstract environment that allows Java programs to operate on any platform that supports a JVM. The specification for the JVM does not indicate how Java threads are to be mapped to the underlying operating system, instead leaving that decision to the particular implementation of the JVM. For example, the Windows 2000 operating system use the one-to-one model; therefore, each Java thread for a JVM running on these systems maps to a kernel thread. On operating systems that use the many-to-many model (such as Tru64 UNIX), a Java thread is mapped according

```
class Worker implements Runnable
{
    private static Service provider;

    public void run() {
        provider.transaction();
        System.out.println(provider.getErrorCode());
    }
}
```

Figure 5.13   Inquiring the value of ThreadLocal data.

to the many-to-many model. Solaris initially implemented the JVM using the many-to-one model (called **green threads**). Later releases of the JVM were implemented using the many-to-many model. Beginning with Solaris 9, Java threads were mapped using the one-to-one model.

5.7.7 Multithreaded Solution Example

We conclude our discussion of Java threads with a complete multithreaded solution to the producer–consumer problem that uses message passing. The class Factory in Figure 5.14 first creates a mailbox for buffering messages, using the MessageQueue class developed in Chapter 4. It then creates separate producer and consumer threads (Figures 5.15 and 5.16, respectively) and passes each thread a reference to the shared mailbox. The producer thread alternates among sleeping for a while, producing an item, and entering that item into the mailbox. The consumer alternates between sleeping and then retrieving an item from the mailbox and consuming it. Because the receive() method of the MessageQueue class is nonblocking, the consumer must check to see whether the message that it retrieved is null.

```
public class Factory
{
    public Factory() {
        // First create the message buffer.
        Channel mailBox = new MessageQueue();

        // Create the producer and consumer threads and pass
        // each thread a reference to the mailBox object.
        Thread producerThread = new Thread(
          new Producer(mailBox));
        Thread consumerThread = new Thread(
          new Consumer(mailBox));

        // Start the threads.
        producerThread.start();
        consumerThread.start();
    }

    public static void main(String args[]) {
        Factory server = new Factory();
    }
}
```

Figure 5.14   The class Factory.

```
import java.util.Date;

class Producer implements Runnable
{
    private Channel mbox;

    public Producer(Channel mbox) {
        this.mbox = mbox;
    }

    public void run() {
        Date message;

        while (true) {
            // nap for awhile
            SleepUtilities.nap();

            // produce an item and enter it into the buffer
            message = new Date();

            System.out.println("Producer produced " + message);
            mbox.send(message);
        }
    }
}
```

Figure 5.15   Producer thread.

5.8 ■ Summary

A thread is a flow of control within a process. A multithreaded process contains several different flows of control within the same address space. The benefits of multithreading include increased responsiveness to the user, resource sharing within the process, economy, and the ability to take advantage of multiprocessor architectures.

User-level threads are threads that are visible to the programmer and are unknown to the kernel. A thread library in user space typically manages user-level threads. The operating-system kernel supports and manages kernel-level threads. In general, user-level threads are faster to create and manage than are kernel threads. Three different types of models relate user and kernel threads: The many-to-one model maps many user threads to a single kernel thread. The one-to-one model maps each user thread to a corresponding kernel thread. The many-to-many model multiplexes many user threads to a smaller or equal number of kernel threads.

```
import java.util.Date;

class Consumer implements Runnable
{
   private Channel mbox;

   public Consumer(Channel mbox) {
      this.mbox = mbox;
   }

   public void run() {
      Date message;

      while (true) {
         // nap for awhile
         SleepUtilities.nap();

         // consume an item from the buffer
         message = (Date)mbox.receive();

         if (message != null)
            System.out.println("Consumer consumed " + message);
      }
   }
}
```

Figure 5.16   Consumer thread.

Multithreaded programs introduce many challenges for the programmer, including the semantics of the fork() and exec() system calls. Other issues include thread cancellation, signal handling, and thread-specific data. Most modern operating systems provide kernel support for threads; among these are Windows NT and Windows, Solaris, and Linux. The Pthreads API provides a set of functions to create and manage threads at the user level. Java provides a similar API for supporting threads. However, because Java threads are managed by the JVM and not by a user-level thread library or kernel, they do not fall under the category of either user- or kernel-level threads.

■ Exercises

5.1 Provide two programming examples in which multithreading provides better performance than a single-threaded solution.

5.2 Provide two programming examples in which multithreading does *not* provide better performance than a single-threaded solution.

5.3 What are two differences between user-level threads and kernel-level threads? Under what circumstances is one type better than the other?

5.4 Describe the actions taken by a kernel to context-switch between kernel-level threads.

5.5 Describe the actions taken by a thread library to context-switch between user-level threads.

5.6 What resources are used when a thread is created? How do they differ from those used when a process is created?

5.7 Assume an operating system maps user-level threads to the kernel using the many-to-many model where the mapping is done through LWPs. Furthermore, the system allows the developers to create real-time threads. Is it necessary to bind a real-time thread to an LWP? Explain.

5.8 A Pthreads program that performs the summation function was provided in Section 5.4. Rewrite this program in Java.

5.9 Write a multithreaded Java or Pthreads program that generates the Fibonacci series. This program should work as follows: The user will run the program and will enter on the command line the number of Fibonacci numbers that the program is to generate. The program will then create a separate thread that will generate the Fibonacci numbers.

5.10 Write a multithreaded Java or Pthreads program that outputs prime numbers. This program should work as follows: The user will run the program and will enter a number on the command line. The program will then create a separate thread that outputs all the prime numbers less than or equal to the number that the user entered.

5.11 Write a multithreaded Java or Pthreads program that performs matrix multiplication. Specifically, use two matrices, A and B, where A is a matrix with M rows and K columns and matrix B contains K rows and N columns. The *matrix product* of A and B is C, where C contains M rows and N columns. The entry in matrix C for row i column j ($C_{i,j}$) is the sum of the products of elements for row i in matrix A and column j in matrix B. That is,

$$C_{i,j} = \sum_{n=1}^{K} A_{i,n} \times B_{n,j}$$

For example, if A were a 3-by-2 matrix and B were a 2-by-3 matrix, element $C_{3,1}$ would be the sum of $A_{3,1} \times B_{1,1}$ and $A_{3,2} \times B_{2,1}$. Calculate each element $C_{i,j}$ in a separate thread. This will involve creating $M \times N$ threads.

5.12 Modify the socket-based date server in Chapter 4 so that the server services each client request in a separate thread.

Bibliographical Notes

Thread performance issues were discussed by Anderson et al. [1989], who continued their work in Anderson et al. [1991] by evaluating the performance of user-level threads with kernel support. Bershad et al. [1990] described combining threads with RPC. Engelschall [2000] discusses a technique for supporting user-level threads. An analysis of an optimal thread pool size can be found in Ling et al. [2000]. Scheduler activations were first presented in Anderson et al. [1991] and Williams [2002] discusses scheduler activations in the NetBSD system. Zabatta and Young [1998] compare Windows NT and Solaris threads on a symmetric multiprocessor. Pinilla and Gill [2003] compare Java thread performance on Linux, Windows, and Solaris.

Vahalia [1996] covers threading in several versions of UNIX. Mauro and McDougall [2001] describe recent developments in threading the Solaris kernel. Solomon and Russinovich [2000] discusses threading in Windows 2000. Bovet and Cesati [2002] cover how Linux handles threading.

Information on Pthreads programming is given in Lewis and Berg [1998] and Butenhof [1997]. Oaks and Wong [1999], Lewis and Berg [2000], and Holub [2000] discuss multithreading in Java. Beveridge and Wiener [1997] discusses multithreading using Win32.

Chapter 6

CPU SCHEDULING

CPU scheduling is the basis of multiprogrammed operating systems. By switching the CPU among processes, the operating system can make the computer more productive. In this chapter, we introduce basic CPU scheduling concepts and present several CPU-scheduling algorithms. We also consider the problem of selecting an algorithm for a particular system.

In Chapter 5, we introduced threads to the process model. On operating systems that support them, it is kernel-level threads—not processes—that are being scheduled by the operating system. However, the terms **process scheduling** and **thread scheduling** are often used interchangeably. In this chapter, we use *process scheduling* when discussing general scheduling concepts and *thread scheduling* to refer to thread-specific ideas.

6.1 ■ Basic Concepts

In a uniprocessor system, only one process can run at a time; any others must wait until the CPU is free and can be rescheduled. The objective of multiprogramming is to have some process running at all times, to maximize CPU utilization. The idea is relatively simple. A process is executed until it must wait, typically for the completion of some I/O request. In a simple computer system, the CPU then just sits idle. All this waiting time is wasted; no useful work is accomplished. With multiprogramming, we try to use this time productively. Several processes are kept in memory at one time. When one process has to wait, the operating system takes the CPU away from that process and gives the CPU to another process. This pattern continues. Every time one process has to wait, another process can take over the use of the CPU.

Scheduling of this kind is a fundamental operating-system function. Almost all computer resources are scheduled before use. The CPU is, of course, one of the primary computer resources. Thus, its scheduling is central to operating-system design.

6.1.1 CPU–I/O Burst Cycle

The success of CPU scheduling depends on the following observed property of processes: Process execution consists of a **cycle** of CPU execution and I/O wait. Processes alternate between these two states. Process execution begins with a **CPU burst**. That is followed by an **I/O burst**, which is followed by another CPU burst, then another I/O burst, and so on. Eventually, the final CPU burst ends with a system request to terminate execution (Figure 6.1).

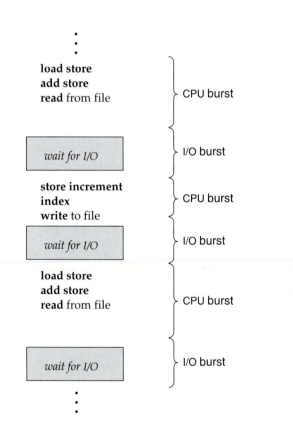

Figure 6.1   Alternating sequence of CPU and I/O bursts.

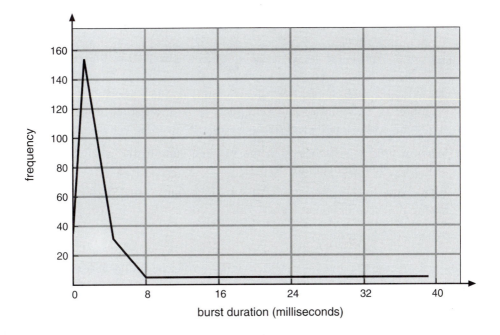

Figure 6.2   Histogram of CPU-burst times.

The durations of CPU bursts have been measured extensively. Although they vary greatly from process to process and from computer to computer, they tend to have a frequency curve similar to that shown in Figure 6.2. The curve is generally characterized as exponential or hyperexponential, with a large number of short CPU bursts and a small number of long CPU bursts. An I/O-bound program typically has many short CPU bursts. A CPU-bound program might have a few long CPU bursts. This distribution can be important in the selection of an appropriate CPU-scheduling algorithm.

6.1.2 CPU Scheduler

Whenever the CPU becomes idle, the operating system must select one of the processes in the ready queue to be executed. The selection process is carried out by the **short-term scheduler** (or CPU scheduler). The scheduler selects from among the processes in memory that are ready to execute and allocates the CPU to one of them.

Note that the ready queue is not necessarily a first-in, first-out (FIFO) queue. As we shall see when we consider the various scheduling algorithms, a ready queue may be implemented as a FIFO queue, a priority queue, a tree, or simply an unordered linked list. Conceptually, however, all the processes in the ready queue are lined up waiting for a chance to run on the CPU. The records in the queues are generally process-control blocks (PCBs) of the processes.

6.1.3 Preemptive Scheduling

CPU scheduling decisions may take place under the following four circumstances:

1. When a process switches from the running state to the waiting state (for example, as the result of an I/O request or an invocation of wait for the termination of one of the child processes)

2. When a process switches from the running state to the ready state (for example, when an interrupt occurs)

3. When a process switches from the waiting state to the ready state (for example, at completion of I/O)

4. When a process terminates

For situations 1 and 4, there is no choice in terms of scheduling. A new process (if one exists in the ready queue) must be selected for execution. There is a choice, however, for situations 2 and 3.

When scheduling takes place only under circumstances 1 and 4, we say that the scheduling scheme is **nonpreemptive** or **cooperative**; otherwise, it is **preemptive**. Under nonpreemptive scheduling, once the CPU has been allocated to a process, the process keeps the CPU until it releases the CPU either by terminating or by switching to the waiting state. This scheduling method was used by Microsoft Windows 3.x; Windows 95 introduced preemptive scheduling, and all subsequent versions of Windows operating systems have used preemptive scheduling. The OS X operating system for the Macintosh uses preemptive scheduling; previous versions of the Macintosh operating system relied on cooperative scheduling. Cooperative scheduling is the only method that can be used on certain hardware platforms, because it does not require the special hardware (for example, a timer) needed for preemptive scheduling.

Unfortunately, preemptive scheduling incurs a cost associated with access to shared data. Consider the case of two processes that share data. While one is updating the data, it is preempted so that the second process can run. The second process then tries to read the data, which are in an inconsistent state. In such situations, we need new mechanisms to coordinate access to shared data; we discuss this topic in Chapter 7.

Preemption also affects the design of the operating-system kernel. During the processing of a system call, the kernel may be busy with an activity on behalf of a process. Such activities may involve changing important kernel data (for instance, I/O queues). What happens if the process is preempted in the middle of these changes and the kernel (or the device driver) needs to read or modify the same structure? Chaos ensues. Certain operating systems, including most versions of UNIX, deal with this problem by waiting either for a system call to complete or for an I/O block to take place before doing a context switch.

This scheme ensures that the kernel structure is simple, since the kernel will not preempt a process while the kernel data structures are in an inconsistent state. Unfortunately, this kernel-execution model is a poor one for supporting real-time computing and multiprocessing. These problems, and their solutions, are described in Sections 6.4 and 6.5.

Because interrupts can, by definition, occur at any time, and because they cannot always be ignored by the kernel, the sections of code affected by interrupts must be guarded from simultaneous use. The operating system needs to accept interrupts at almost all times; otherwise, input might be lost or output overwritten. So that these sections of code are not accessed concurrently by several processes, they disable interrupts at entry and reenable interrupts at exit. It is important to note that sections of code that disable interrupts do not occur very often and typically contain few instructions.

6.1.4 Dispatcher

Another component involved in the CPU scheduling function is the **dispatcher**. The dispatcher is the module that gives control of the CPU to the process selected by the short-term scheduler. This function involves the following:

- Switching context

- Switching to user mode

- Jumping to the proper location in the user program to restart that program

The dispatcher should be as fast as possible, since it is invoked during every process switch. The time it takes for the dispatcher to stop one process and start another running is known as the **dispatch latency**.

6.2 ■ Scheduling Criteria

Different CPU scheduling algorithms have different properties and may favor one class of processes over another. In choosing which algorithm to use in a particular situation, we must consider the properties of the various algorithms.

Many criteria have been suggested for comparing CPU scheduling algorithms. Which characteristics are used for comparison can make a substantial difference in which algorithm is judged to be best. The criteria include the following:

- **CPU utilization:** We want to keep the CPU as busy as possible. Conceptually, CPU utilization can range from 0 to 100 percent. In a real system, it should range from 40 percent (for a lightly loaded system) to 90 percent (for a heavily used system).

- **Throughput:** If the CPU is busy executing processes, then work is being done. One measure of work is the number of processes that are completed per time unit, called *throughput*. For long processes, this rate may be one process per hour; for short transactions, it may be 10 processes per second.

- **Turnaround time:** From the point of view of a particular process, the important criterion is how long it takes to execute that process. The interval from the time of submission of a process to the time of completion is the *turnaround time*. Turnaround time is the sum of the periods spent waiting to get into memory, waiting in the ready queue, executing on the CPU, and doing I/O.

- **Waiting time:** The CPU scheduling algorithm does not affect the amount of time during which a process executes or does I/O; it affects only the amount of time that a process spends waiting in the ready queue. *Waiting time* is the sum of the periods spent waiting in the ready queue.

- **Response time:** In an interactive system, turnaround time may not be the best criterion. Often, a process can produce some output fairly early and can continue computing new results while previous results are being output to the user. Thus, another measure is the time from the submission of a request until the first response is produced. This measure, called *response time*, is the time it takes to start responding, not the time it takes to output the response. The turnaround time is generally limited by the speed of the output device.

It is desirable to maximize CPU utilization and throughput and to minimize turnaround time, waiting time, and response time. In most cases, we optimize the average measure. However, under some circumstances, it is desirable to optimize the minimum or maximum values rather than the average. For example, to guarantee that all users get good service, we may want to minimize the maximum response time.

Investigators have suggested that, for interactive systems (such as time-sharing systems), it is more important to minimize the *variance* in the response time than it is to minimize the average response time. A system with reasonable and *predictable* response time may be considered more desirable than a system that is faster on the average but is highly variable. However, little work has been done on CPU-scheduling algorithms that minimize variance.

As we discuss various CPU-scheduling algorithms in the following section, we will illustrate their operation. An accurate illustration should involve many processes, each being a sequence of several hundred CPU bursts and I/O bursts. For simplicity, though, we consider only one CPU burst (in milliseconds) per process in our examples. Our measure of comparison is the average waiting time. More elaborate evaluation mechanisms are discussed in Section 6.9.

6.3 ■ Scheduling Algorithms

CPU scheduling deals with the problem of deciding which of the processes in the ready queue is to be allocated the CPU. There are many different CPU scheduling algorithms. In this section, we describe several of them.

6.3.1 First-Come, First-Served Scheduling

By far the simplest CPU-scheduling algorithm is the **first-come, first-served (FCFS) scheduling algorithm**. With this scheme, the process that requests the CPU first is allocated the CPU first. The implementation of the FCFS policy is easily managed with a FIFO queue. When a process enters the ready queue, its PCB is linked onto the tail of the queue. When the CPU is free, it is allocated to the process at the head of the queue. The running process is then removed from the queue. The code for FCFS scheduling is simple to write and understand.

The average waiting time under the FCFS policy, however, is often quite long. Consider the following set of processes that arrive at time 0, with the length of the CPU-burst time given in milliseconds:

Process	Burst Time
P_1	24
P_2	3
P_3	3

If the processes arrive in the order P_1, P_2, P_3, and are served in FCFS order, we get the result shown in the following **Gantt chart**:

The waiting time is 0 milliseconds for process P_1, 24 milliseconds for process P_2, and 27 milliseconds for process P_3. Thus, the average waiting time is $(0 + 24 + 27)/3 = 17$ milliseconds. If the processes arrive in the order P_2, P_3, P_1, however, the results will be as shown in the following Gantt chart:

The average waiting time is now $(6 + 0 + 3)/3 = 3$ milliseconds. This reduction is substantial. Thus, the average waiting time under a FCFS policy is generally not minimal and may vary substantially if the process CPU-burst times vary greatly.

In addition, consider the performance of FCFS scheduling in a dynamic situation. Assume we have one CPU-bound process and many I/O-bound processes. As the processes flow around the system, the following scenario may result. The CPU-bound process will get and hold the CPU. During this time, all the other processes will finish their I/O and will move into the ready queue, waiting for the CPU. While the processes wait in the ready queue, the I/O devices are idle. Eventually, the CPU-bound process finishes its CPU burst and moves to an I/O device. All the I/O-bound processes, which have short CPU bursts, execute quickly and move back to the I/O queues. At this point, the CPU sits idle. The CPU-bound process will then move back to the ready queue and be allocated the CPU. Again, all the I/O processes end up waiting in the ready queue until the CPU-bound process is done. There is a **convoy effect**, as all the other processes wait for the one big process to get off the CPU. This effect results in lower CPU and device utilization than might be possible if the shorter processes were allowed to go first.

The FCFS scheduling algorithm is nonpreemptive. Once the CPU has been allocated to a process, that process keeps the CPU until it releases the CPU, either by terminating or by requesting I/O. The FCFS algorithm is particularly troublesome for time-sharing systems, where it is important that each user get a share of the CPU at regular intervals. It would be disastrous to allow one process to keep the CPU for an extended period.

6.3.2 Shortest-Job-First Scheduling

A different approach to CPU scheduling is the **shortest-job-first (SJF) scheduling algorithm**. This algorithm associates with each process the length of the process's next CPU burst. When the CPU is available, it is assigned to the process that has the smallest next CPU burst. If the next CPU bursts of two processes are the same, FCFS scheduling is used to break the tie. Note that a more appropriate term for this scheduling method would be the *shortest-next-CPU-burst algorithm,* because scheduling depends on the length of the next CPU burst of a process, rather than its total length. We use the term SJF because most people and textbooks refer to this type of scheduling as SJF.

As an example of SJF scheduling, consider the following set of processes, with the length of the CPU burst time given in milliseconds:

Process	Burst Time
P_1	6
P_2	8
P_3	7
P_4	3

Using SJF scheduling, we would schedule these processes according to the following Gantt chart:

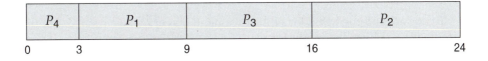

The waiting time is 3 milliseconds for process P_1, 16 milliseconds for process P_2, 9 milliseconds for process P_3, and 0 milliseconds for process P_4. Thus, the average waiting time is $(3 + 16 + 9 + 0)/4 = 7$ milliseconds. If we were using the FCFS scheduling scheme, then the average waiting time would be 10.25 milliseconds.

The SJF scheduling algorithm is provably *optimal*, in that it gives the minimum average waiting time for a given set of processes. Moving a short process before a long one decreases the waiting time of the short process more than it increases the waiting time of the long process. Consequently, the *average* waiting time decreases.

The real difficulty with the SJF algorithm is knowing the length of the next CPU request. For long-term (job) scheduling in a batch system, we can use as the length the process time limit that a user specifies when he submits the job. Thus, users are motivated to estimate the process time limit accurately, since a lower value may mean faster response. (Too low a value will cause a time-limit-exceeded error and require resubmission.) SJF scheduling is used frequently in long-term scheduling.

Although the SJF algorithm is optimal, it cannot be implemented at the level of short-term CPU scheduling. There is no way to know the length of the next CPU burst. One approach is to try to approximate SJF scheduling. We may not *know* the length of the next CPU burst, but we may be able to *predict* its value. We expect that the next CPU burst will be similar in length to the previous ones. Thus, by computing an approximation of the length of the next CPU burst, we can pick the process with the shortest predicted CPU burst.

The next CPU burst is generally predicted as an exponential average of the measured lengths of previous CPU bursts. Let t_n be the length of the nth CPU burst, and let τ_{n+1} be our predicted value for the next CPU burst. Then, for α, $0 \le \alpha \le 1$, define

$$\tau_{n+1} = \alpha\, t_n + (1 - \alpha)\tau_n.$$

This formula defines an **exponential average**. The value of t_n contains our most recent information; τ_n stores the past history. The parameter α controls the relative weight of recent and past history in our prediction. If $\alpha = 0$, then $\tau_{n+1} = \tau_n$, and recent history has no effect (current conditions are assumed to be transient); if $\alpha = 1$, then $\tau_{n+1} = t_n$, and only the most recent CPU burst matters (history is assumed to be old and irrelevant). More commonly, $\alpha = 1/2$, so recent history and past history are equally weighted. The initial τ_0 can be defined as a constant or as an overall system average. Figure 6.3 shows an exponential average with $\alpha = 1/2$ and $\tau_0 = 10$.

To understand the behavior of the exponential average, we can expand the formula for τ_{n+1} by substituting for τ_n, to find

$$\tau_{n+1} = \alpha t_n + (1 - \alpha)\alpha t_{n-1} + \cdots + (1 - \alpha)^j \alpha t_{n-j} + \cdots + (1 - \alpha)^{n+1} \tau_0.$$

Since both α and $(1 - \alpha)$ are less than or equal to 1, each successive term has less weight than its predecessor.

The SJF algorithm may be either preemptive or nonpreemptive. The choice arises when a new process arrives at the ready queue while a previous process is still executing. The next CPU burst of the new arriving process may be shorter than what is left of the currently executing process. A preemptive SJF algorithm will preempt the currently executing process, whereas a nonpreemptive SJF algorithm will allow the currently running process to finish its CPU burst. Preemptive SJF scheduling is sometimes called **shortest-remaining-time-first scheduling**.

As an example, consider the following four processes, with the length of the CPU-burst time given in milliseconds:

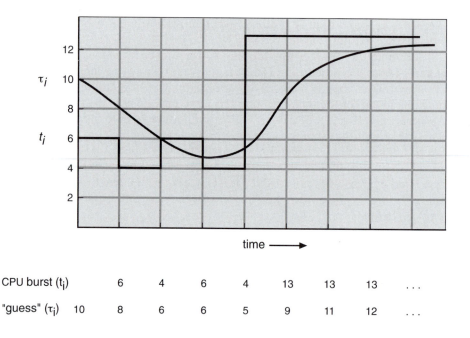

CPU burst (t_i)		6	4	6	4	13	13	13	...
"guess" (τ_i)	10	8	6	6	5	9	11	12	...

Figure 6.3   Prediction of the length of the next CPU burst.

Process	Arrival Time	Burst Time
P_1	0	8
P_2	1	4
P_3	2	9
P_4	3	5

If the processes arrive at the ready queue at the times shown and need the indicated burst times, then the resulting preemptive SJF schedule is as depicted in the following Gantt chart:

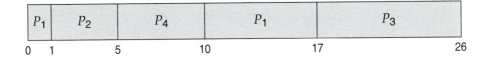

Process P_1 is started at time 0, since it is the only process in the queue. Process P_2 arrives at time 1. The remaining time for process P_1 (7 milliseconds) is larger than the time required by process P_2 (4 milliseconds), so process P_1 is preempted, and process P_2 is scheduled. The average waiting time for this example is $((10 - 1) + (1 - 1) + (17 - 2) + (5 - 3))/4 = 26/4 = 6.5$ milliseconds. Nonpreemptive SJF scheduling would result in an average waiting time of 7.75 milliseconds.

6.3.3 Priority Scheduling

The SJF algorithm is a special case of the general **priority scheduling algorithm**. A priority is associated with each process, and the CPU is allocated to the process with the highest priority. Equal-priority processes are scheduled in FCFS order. An SJF algorithm is simply a priority algorithm where the priority (p) is the inverse of the (predicted) next CPU burst. The larger the CPU burst, the lower the priority, and vice versa.

Note that we discuss scheduling in terms of *high* priority and *low* priority. Priorities are generally indicated by some fixed range of numbers, such as 0 to 7 or 0 to 4095. However, there is no general agreement on whether 0 is the highest or lowest priority. Some systems use low numbers to represent low priority; others use low numbers for high priority. This difference can lead to confusion. In this text, we assume that low numbers represent high priority.

As an example, consider the following set of processes, assumed to have arrived at time 0, in the order $P_1, P_2, \cdots, P_5$, with the length of the CPU-burst time given in milliseconds:

Process	Burst Time	Priority
P_1	10	3
P_2	1	1
P_3	2	4
P_4	1	5
P_5	5	2

Using priority scheduling, we would schedule these processes according to the following Gantt chart:

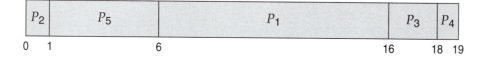

The average waiting time is 8.2 milliseconds.

Priorities can be defined either internally or externally. Internally defined priorities use some measurable quantity or quantities to compute the priority of a process. For example, time limits, memory requirements, the number of open files, and the ratio of average I/O burst to average CPU burst have been used in computing priorities. External priorities are set by criteria outside the operating system, such as the importance of the process, the type and amount of funds being paid for computer use, the department sponsoring the work, and other, often political, factors.

Priority scheduling can be either preemptive or nonpreemptive. When a process arrives at the ready queue, its priority is compared with the priority of the currently running process. A preemptive priority scheduling algorithm will preempt the CPU if the priority of the newly arrived process is higher than the priority of the currently running process. A nonpreemptive priority scheduling algorithm will simply put the new process at the head of the ready queue.

A major problem with priority scheduling algorithms is **indefinite blocking**, or **starvation**. A process that is ready to run but waiting for the CPU can be considered blocked. A priority scheduling algorithm can leave some low-priority processes waiting indefinitely. In a heavily loaded computer system, a steady stream of higher-priority processes can prevent a low-priority process from ever getting the CPU. Generally, one of two things will happen. Either the process will eventually be run (at 2 A.M. Sunday, when the system is finally lightly loaded), or the computer system will eventually crash and lose all unfinished low-priority processes. (Rumor has it that, when they shut down the IBM 7094 at MIT in 1973, they found a low-priority process that had been submitted in 1967 and had not yet been run.)

A solution to the problem of indefinite blockage of low-priority processes is **aging**. Aging is a technique of gradually increasing the priority of processes that wait in the system for a long time. For example, if priorities range from 127 (low) to 0 (high), we could increment the priority of a waiting process by 1 every 15 minutes. Eventually, even a process with an initial priority of 127 would have the highest priority in the system and would be executed. In fact, it would take no more than 32 hours for a priority-127 process to age to a priority-0 process.

6.3.4 Round-Robin Scheduling

The **round-robin (RR) scheduling algorithm** is designed especially for time-sharing systems. It is similar to FCFS scheduling, but preemption is added to switch between processes. A small unit of time, called a **time quantum** or time slice, is defined. A time quantum is generally from 10 to 100 milliseconds. The ready queue is treated as a circular queue. The CPU scheduler goes around the ready queue, allocating the CPU to each process for a time interval of up to 1 time quantum.

To implement RR scheduling, we keep the ready queue as a FIFO queue of processes. New processes are added to the tail of the ready queue. The CPU scheduler picks the first process from the ready queue, sets a timer to interrupt after 1 time quantum, and dispatches the process.

One of two things will then happen. The process may have a CPU burst of less than 1 time quantum. In this case, the process itself will release the CPU voluntarily. The scheduler will then proceed to the next process in the ready queue. Otherwise, if the CPU burst of the currently running process is longer than 1 time quantum, the timer will go off and will cause an interrupt to the operating system. A context switch will be executed, and the process will be put at the **tail** of the ready queue. The CPU scheduler will then select the next process in the ready queue.

The average waiting time under the RR policy is often long. Consider the following set of processes that arrive at time 0, with the length of the CPU-burst time given in milliseconds:

Process	Burst Time
P_1	24
P_2	3
P_3	3

If we use a time quantum of 4 milliseconds, then process P_1 gets the first 4 milliseconds. Since it requires another 20 milliseconds, it is preempted after the first time quantum, and the CPU is given to the next process in the queue, process P_2. Since process P_2 does not need 4 milliseconds, it quits before its time quantum expires. The CPU is then given to the next process, process P_3. Once each process has received 1 time quantum, the CPU is returned to process P_1 for an additional time quantum. The resulting RR schedule is

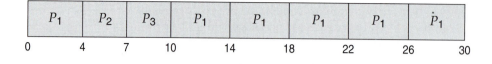

P_1	P_2	P_3	P_1	P_1	P_1	P_1	$\dot{P_1}$

0   4   7   10   14   18   22   26   30

The average waiting time is 17/3 = 5.66 milliseconds.

In the RR scheduling algorithm, no process is allocated the CPU for more than 1 time quantum in a row (unless it is the only runnable process). If a process's CPU burst exceeds 1 time quantum, that process is *preempted* and is put back in the ready queue. The RR scheduling algorithm is thus preemptive.

If there are n processes in the ready queue and the time quantum is q, then each process gets $1/n$ of the CPU time in chunks of at most q time units. Each process must wait no longer than $(n - 1) \times q$ time units until its next time quantum. For example, with five processes and a time quantum of 20 milliseconds, each process will get up to 20 milliseconds every 100 milliseconds.

The performance of the RR algorithm depends heavily on the size of the time quantum. At one extreme, if the time quantum is extremely large, the RR policy is the same as the FCFS policy. If the time quantum is extremely small (say 1 millisecond), the RR approach is called **processor sharing** and (in theory) creates the appearance that each of n processes has its own processor running at $1/n$ the speed of the real processor. This approach was used in Control Data Corporation (CDC) hardware to implement 10 peripheral processors with only one set of hardware and 10 sets of registers. The hardware executes one instruction for one set of registers, then goes on to the next. This cycle continues, resulting in 10 slow processors rather than one fast one. (Actually, since the processor was much faster than memory and each instruction referenced

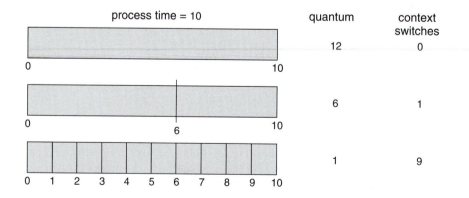

Figure 6.4   The way in which a smaller time quantum increases context switches.

memory, the processors were not much slower than 10 real processors would have been.)

In software, however, we need also to consider the effect of context switching on the performance of RR scheduling. Let us assume that we have only one process of 10 time units. If the quantum is 12 time units, the process finishes in less than 1 time quantum, with no overhead. If the quantum is 6 time units, however, the process requires 2 quanta, resulting in a context switch. If the time quantum is 1 time unit, then nine context switches will occur, slowing the execution of the process accordingly (Figure 6.4).

Thus, we want the time quantum to be large with respect to the context-switch time. If the context-switch time is approximately 10 percent of the time quantum, then about 10 percent of the CPU time will be spent in context switching. In practice, most modern systems have time quanta ranging from 10 to 100 milliseconds. The time required for a context switch is typically less than 10 microseconds; thus, the context-switch time is a small fraction of the time quantum.

Turnaround time also depends on the size of the time quantum. As we can see from Figure 6.5, the average turnaround time of a set of processes does not necessarily improve as the time-quantum size increases. In general, the average turnaround time can be improved if most processes finish their next

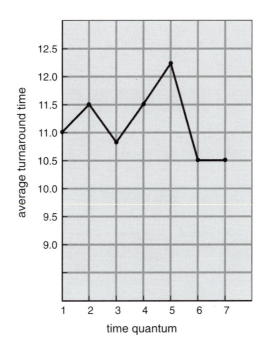

process	time
P_1	6
P_2	3
P_3	1
P_4	7

Figure 6.5   The way in which turnaround time varies with the time quantum.

CPU burst in a single time quantum. For example, given three processes of 10 time units each and a quantum of 1 time unit, the average turnaround time is 29. If the time quantum is 10, however, the average turnaround time drops to 20. If context-switch time is added in, the average turnaround time increases for a smaller time quantum, since more context switches are required.

Although the time quantum should be large compared with the context-switch time, it should not be too large. If the time quantum is too large, RR scheduling degenerates to FCFS policy. A rule of thumb is that 80 percent of the CPU bursts should be shorter than the time quantum.

6.3.5 Multilevel Queue Scheduling

Another class of scheduling algorithms has been created for situations in which processes are easily classified into different groups. For example, a common division is made between **foreground** (interactive) processes and **background** (batch) processes. These two types of processes have different response-time requirements and so might have different scheduling needs. In addition, foreground processes may have priority (externally defined) over background processes.

A **multilevel queue-scheduling algorithm** partitions the ready queue into several separate queues (Figure 6.6). The processes are permanently assigned to one queue, generally based on some property of the process, such as memory size, process priority, or process type. Each queue has its own scheduling

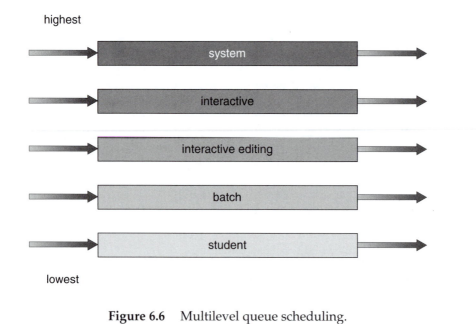

Figure 6.6   Multilevel queue scheduling.

algorithm. For example, separate queues might be used for foreground and background processes. The foreground queue might be scheduled by an RR algorithm, while the background queue is scheduled by an FCFS algorithm.

In addition, there must be scheduling among the queues, which is commonly implemented as fixed-priority preemptive scheduling. For example, the foreground queue may have absolute priority over the background queue.

Let us look at an example of a multilevel queue-scheduling algorithm with five queues, listed below in order of priority:

1. System processes

2. Interactive processes

3. Interactive editing processes

4. Batch processes

5. Student processes

Each queue has absolute priority over lower-priority queues. No process in the batch queue, for example, could run unless the queues for system processes, interactive processes, and interactive editing processes were all empty. If an interactive editing process entered the ready queue while a batch process was running, the batch process would be preempted.

Another possibility is to time-slice among the queues. Each queue gets a certain portion of the CPU time, which it can then schedule among the various processes in its queue. For instance, in the foreground–background queue example, the foreground queue can be given 80 percent of the CPU time for RR scheduling among its processes, whereas the background queue receives 20 percent of the CPU to give to its processes on an FCFS basis.

6.3.6 Multilevel Feedback-Queue Scheduling

Normally, in a multilevel queue-scheduling algorithm, processes are permanently assigned to a queue on entry to the system. Processes do not move between queues. If there are separate queues for foreground and background processes, for example, processes do not move from one queue to the other, since processes do not change their foreground or background nature. This setup has the advantage of low scheduling overhead, but it is inflexible.

Multilevel feedback-queue scheduling, in contrast, allows a process to move between queues. The idea is to separate processes with different CPU-burst characteristics. If a process uses too much CPU time, it will be moved to a lower-priority queue. This scheme leaves I/O-bound and interactive processes in the higher-priority queues. In addition, a process that waits too long in a lower-priority queue may be moved to a higher-priority queue. This form of aging prevents starvation.

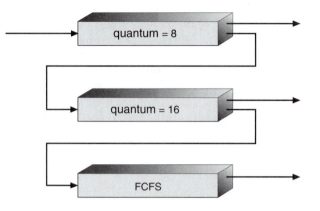

Figure 6.7   Multilevel feedback queues.

For example, consider a multilevel feedback-queue scheduler with three queues, numbered from 0 to 2 (Figure 6.7). The scheduler first executes all processes in queue 0. Only when queue 0 is empty will it execute processes in queue 1. Similarly, processes in queue 2 will only be executed if queues 0 and 1 are empty. A process that arrives for queue 1 will preempt a process in queue 2. A process in queue 1 will in turn be preempted by a process arriving for queue 0.

A process entering the ready queue is put in queue 0. A process in queue 0 is given a time quantum of 8 milliseconds. If it does not finish within this time, it is moved to the tail of queue 1. If queue 0 is empty, the process at the head of queue 1 is given a quantum of 16 milliseconds. If it does not complete, it is preempted and is put into queue 2. Processes in queue 2 are run on an FCFS basis but are run only when queues 0 and 1 are empty.

This scheduling algorithm gives highest priority to any process with a CPU burst of 8 milliseconds or less. Such a process will quickly get the CPU, finish its CPU burst, and go off to its next I/O burst. Processes that need more than 8, but less than 24, milliseconds are also served quickly, although with lower priority than shorter processes. Long processes automatically sink to queue 2 and are served in FCFS order with any CPU cycles left over from queues 0 and 1.

In general, a multilevel feedback-queue scheduler is defined by the following parameters:

- The number of queues

- The scheduling algorithm for each queue

- The method used to determine when to upgrade a process to a higher-priority queue

- The method used to determine when to demote a process to a lower-priority queue

- The method used to determine which queue a process will enter when that process needs service

The definition of a multilevel feedback-queue scheduler makes it the most general CPU-scheduling algorithm. It can be configured to match a specific system under design. Unfortunately, it is also the most complex algorithm, since defining the best scheduler requires some means by which to select values for all the parameters.

6.4 ■ Multiple-Processor Scheduling

Our discussion thus far has focused on the problems of scheduling the CPU in a system with a single processor. If multiple CPUs are available, the scheduling problem is correspondingly more complex. Many possibilities have been tried; and as we saw with single-processor CPU scheduling, there is no one best solution. Here, we briefly discuss concerns in multiprocessor scheduling. We concentrate on systems in which the processors are identical—**homogeneous** —in terms of their functionality; we can then use any available processor to run any processes in the queue.

Even within homogeneous multiprocessors, there are sometimes limitations on scheduling. Consider a system with an I/O device attached to a private bus of one processor. Processes that wish to use that device must be scheduled to run on that processor.

If several identical processors are available, then **load sharing** can occur. We could provide a separate queue for each processor. In this case, however, one processor could be idle, with an empty queue, while another processor was extremely busy. To prevent this situation, we can use a single common ready queue. All processes go into one queue and are scheduled onto any available processor.

In such a scheme, one of two scheduling approaches may be used. One approach has all scheduling decisions, I/O processing, and other system activities handled by a single processor—the master server. The other processors execute only user code. This **asymmetric multiprocessing** is simple because only one processor accesses the system data structures, alleviating the need for data sharing.

A second approach uses **symmetric multiprocessing (SMP)**, where each processor is self-scheduling. Each processor examines the common ready queue and selects a process to execute. As we shall see in Chapter 7, if we have multiple processors trying to access and update a common data structure, each processor must be programmed carefully: We must ensure that two processors do not choose the same process and that processes are not lost from the queue. Virtually all modern operating systems support SMP, including Windows NT, Windows 2000, Windows XP, Solaris, Linux, and Mac OS X.

6.5 ▪ Real-Time Scheduling

In Chapter 1, we discussed the growing importance of real-time operating systems. Here, we describe the scheduling facility needed to support real-time computing within a general-purpose computer system.

Real-time computing is of two types. **Hard real-time** systems are required to complete a critical task within a guaranteed amount of time. Generally, a process is submitted along with a statement of the amount of time within which it needs to complete or perform I/O. The scheduler then either admits the process, guaranteeing that the process will complete on time, or rejects the request as impossible. Such a guarantee, made under **resource reservation**, requires that the scheduler know exactly how long it takes to perform each type of operating-system function; therefore, each operation must be guaranteed to take a maximum amount of time. Such a guarantee is impossible in a system with secondary storage or virtual memory, as we show in Chapters 9 through 14, because these subsystems cause unavoidable and unforeseeable variation in the amount of time needed to execute a particular process. Therefore, hard real-time systems are composed of special-purpose software running on hardware dedicated to their critical process and lack the full functionality of modern computers and operating systems.

Soft real-time computing is less restrictive. It requires that critical processes receive priority over less fortunate ones. Although adding soft real-time functionality to a time-sharing system may cause an unfair allocation of resources and may result in longer delays, or even starvation, for some processes, it is at least possible to achieve. The result is a general-purpose system that can also support multimedia, high-speed interactive graphics, and a variety of tasks that will not function acceptably in an environment that does not support soft real-time computing.

Implementing soft real-time functionality requires careful design of the scheduler and related aspects of the operating system. First, the system must have priority scheduling, and real-time processes must have the highest priority. The priority of real-time processes must not degrade over time, even though the priority of non–real-time processes may. Second, the dispatch latency must be small. The smaller the latency, the faster a real-time process can start executing once it is runnable.

It is relatively simple to ensure that the former property holds. For example, we can disallow process aging on real-time processes, thereby guaranteeing that the priority of the various processes does not change. However, ensuring the latter property is much more involved. The problem is that many operating systems are forced to wait either for a system call to complete or for an I/O block to take place before they can do a context switch. The dispatch latency in such systems can be long, since some system calls are complex and some I/O devices are slow.

To keep dispatch latency low, we need to allow system calls to be pre-emptible. This goal can be achieved in several ways. One is to insert **pre-emption points** in long-duration system calls. A preemption point checks to see whether a high-priority process needs to be run. If so, a context switch takes place. Then, when the high-priority process terminates, the interrupted process continues with the system call. Preemption points can be placed at only *safe* locations in the kernel—only where kernel data structures are not being modified. Because it is impractical to add more than a few preemption points to a kernel, dispatch latency can be large even when preemption points are used.

Another method for dealing with preemption is to make the entire kernel preemptible. So that correct operation is ensured, all kernel data structures must be protected through the use of various synchronization mechanisms, which we discuss in Chapter 7. With this method, the kernel can always be preemptible, because any kernel data being updated are protected from modification by the high-priority process. This method is used in Solaris.

What happens if a process needs to read or modify kernel data that are currently being accessed by a lower-priority process—or a chain of lower-priority processes? The higher-priority process will have to wait for a lower-priority one to finish. This problem, known as **priority inversion**, can be solved by use of the **priority-inheritance protocol**, in which all processes that are accessing resources needed by a higher-priority process inherit the higher priority until they are finished with the resources in question. When they are finished, their priority reverts to its original value.

In Figure 6.8, we show the makeup of dispatch latency. The **conflict phase** of dispatch latency has two components:

1. Preemption of any process running in the kernel

2. Release by low-priority processes of resources needed by the high-priority process

As an example, in Solaris, the dispatch latency with preemption disabled is over 100 milliseconds. With preemption enabled, it is reduced to less than a millisecond.

6.6 ▪ Thread Scheduling

In Chapter 5, we introduced threads to the process model, distinguishing between *user-level* and *kernel-level* threads. On operating systems that support them, it is kernel-level threads—not processes—that are being scheduled by the operating system. User-level threads are managed by a thread library, and the kernel is unaware of them. To run on a CPU, user-level threads must ultimately be mapped to an associated kernel-level thread, although this mapping may be indirect and may use a lightweight process (LWP).

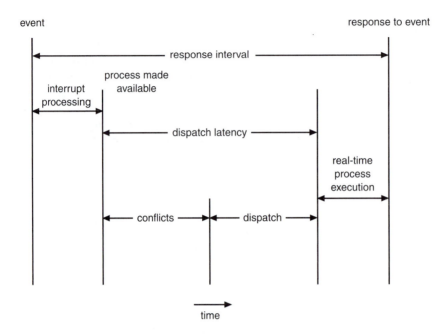

Figure 6.8   Dispatch latency.

In this section we explore scheduling issues between user-level and kernel-level threads and offer specific examples of scheduling for Pthreads.

6.6.1 Contention Scope

One distinction between user-level and kernel-level threads lies in how they are scheduled. On systems implementing the many-to-one (Section 5.2.1) and many-to-many (Section 5.2.3) models, the thread library schedules user-level threads to run on an available LWP, a scheme known as **process-contention scope (PCS)**, since competition for the CPU takes place among threads belonging to the same process. When we say the thread library *schedules* user threads onto available LWPs, we do not mean that the thread is actually running on a CPU; this would require the operating system to schedule the kernel thread onto a physical CPU. To decide which kernel thread to schedule onto a CPU, the kernel uses **system-contention scope (SCS)**. Competition for the CPU with SCS scheduling takes place among all threads in the system. Systems using the one-to-one model (such as Windows XP, Solaris 9, and Linux) schedule threads using only SCS.

Typically, PCS is done according to priority—the scheduler selects the runnable thread with the highest priority to run. User thread priorities are set by the programmer and are not adjusted by the thread library, although some thread libraries may allow the programmer to change the priority of a thread.

It is important to note that PCS will typically preempt the thread currently running in favor of a higher-priority thread; however, there is no guarantee of time slicing (Section 6.3.4) among threads of equal priority.

6.6.2 Pthread Scheduling

We gave an example POSIX Pthread program in Section 5.4. The POSIX standard also provides extensions for real-time computing—POSIX.1b. In this section, we cover some of the POSIX Pthread API related to thread scheduling.

Pthreads defines two scheduling classes for real-time threads:

- SCHED_FIFO

- SCHED_RR

SCHED_FIFO schedules threads according to an FCFS policy using a FIFO queue as outlined in Section 6.3.1. However, there is no time slicing among threads of equal priority. Therefore, the highest-priority real-time thread at the front of the FIFO queue will be granted the CPU until it terminates or blocks. SCHED_RR is similar to SCHED_FIFO except that it provides time slicing among threads of equal priority. Both SCHED_FIFO and SCHED_RR are designated as being for real-time threads. Pthreads provides an additional scheduling class —SCHED_OTHER, but its implementation is undefined and system specific; it may behave differently on different systems.

In addition, Pthreads allows two different thread-scheduling policies:

- PTHREAD_SCOPE_PROCESS schedules threads using PCS scheduling.

- PTHREAD_SCOPE_SYSTEM schedules threads using SCS scheduling.

On systems implementing the many-to-many model (Section 5.2.3), the PTHREAD_SCOPE_PROCESS policy schedules user-level threads onto available LWPs. The number of LWPs is maintained by the thread library, perhaps using scheduler activations (Section 5.3.6). The PTHREAD_SCOPE_SYSTEM scheduling policy will create and bind an LWP for each user-level thread on many-to-many systems, effectively mapping threads using the one-to-one policy (Section 5.2.2).

In Figure 6.9, we illustrate a Pthread program that creates five separate threads using the SCHED_OTHER scheduling algorithm and setting the scheduling policy to PTHREAD_SCOPE_SYSTEM. The SCHED_OTHER algorithm is set by setting the attributes for the thread attr with the function pthread_attr_setscope(&attr, PTHREAD_SCOPE_SYSTEM). The scheduling policy is set using the function call pthread_attr_setschedpolicy(&attr, SCHED_OTHER).

The Pthread API also allows the programmer to alter the priority of a thread.

```
#include <pthread.h>
#include <stdio.h>
#define NUM_THREADS 5

int main(int argc, char *argv[])
{
    int i;
    pthread_t tid[NUM_THREADS];
    pthread_attr_t attr;

    /* get the default attributes */
    pthread_attr_init(&attr);

    /* set the scheduling algorithm to PROCESS or SYSTEM */
    pthread_attr_setscope(&attr, PTHREAD_SCOPE_SYSTEM);

    /* set the scheduling policy - FIFO, RT, or OTHER */
    pthread_attr_setschedpolicy(&attr, SCHED_OTHER);

    /* create the threads */
    for (i = 0; i < NUM_THREADS; i++)
        pthread_create(&tid[i],&attr,runner,NULL);

    /* now join on each thread */
    for (i = 0; i < NUM_THREADS; i++)
        pthread_join(tid[i], NULL);
}

/* Each thread will begin control in this function */
void *runner(void *param)
{
    printf("I am a thread\n");
    pthread_exit(0);
}
```

Figure 6.9   Pthread Scheduling API.

6.7 ■ Operating System Examples

We turn next to a description of the scheduling policies of the Solaris, Windows XP, and Linux operating systems. It is important to remember that we are describing the scheduling of kernel threads.

6.7.1 Example: Solaris Scheduling

Solaris uses priority-based thread scheduling. It has defined four classes of scheduling, which are, in order of priority:

1. Real time

2. System

3. Time sharing

4. Interactive

Within each class there are different priorities and different scheduling algorithms. Solaris scheduling is illustrated in Figure 6.10.

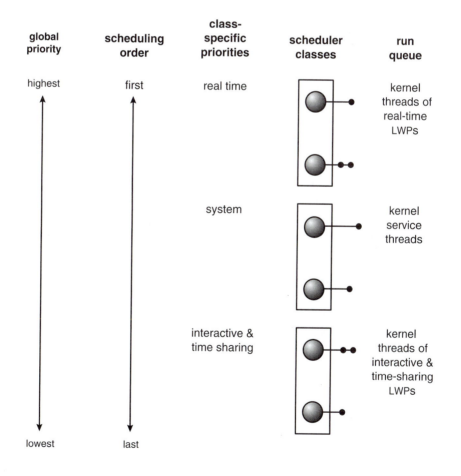

Figure 6.10   Solaris scheduling.

Priority	Time Quantum	Time Quantum Expired	Return From Sleep
0	200	0	50
5	200	0	50
10	160	0	51
15	160	5	51
20	120	10	52
25	120	15	52
30	80	20	53
35	80	25	54
40	40	30	55
45	40	35	56
50	40	40	58
55	40	45	58
59	20	49	59

Figure 6.11   Solaris dispatch table for interactive and timesharing threads.

The default scheduling class for a process is time sharing. The scheduling policy for time sharing dynamically alters priorities and assigns time slices of different lengths using a multilevel feedback queue. By default, there is an inverse relationship between priorities and time slices: The higher the priority, the smaller the time slice; and the lower the priority, the larger the time slice. Interactive processes typically have a higher priority; CPU-bound processes, a lower priority. This scheduling policy gives good response time for interactive processes and good throughput for CPU-bound processes. The interactive class uses the same scheduling policy as the time-sharing class, but it gives windowing applications a higher priority for better performance.

Figure 6.11 illustrates the dispatch table for scheduling interactive and time-sharing threads. These two scheduling classes include 60 priority levels, but for brevity, we will display only a handful of priorities to illustrate Solaris thread scheduling. The dispatch table shown in Figure 6.11 contains the following fields:

- **Priority:** The class-dependent priority for the time-sharing and interactive classes. A higher number indicates a higher priority.

- **Time quantum:** The time quantum for the associated priority. This illustrates the inverse relationship between priorities and time quanta: the lowest priority (priority 0) has the highest time quantum (200 milliseconds), the highest priority (priority 59) has the lowest time quantum (20 milliseconds).

- **Time quantum expired:** The new priority of a thread that has used its entire time quantum without blocking. Such threads are considered CPU-intensive. As shown in the table, such threads have their priorities lowered.

- **Return from sleep:** The priority of a thread that is returning from sleeping (such as waiting for I/O). As the table illustrates, when I/O is available for a waiting thread, its priority is boosted between 50 and 59, thus supporting the scheduling policy of providing good response time for interactive processes.

Solaris 9 introduced two new scheduling classes: **fixed priority** and **fair share**.   Threads in the fixed-priority class have the same priority range as those in the time-sharing class; however, their priorities are not dynamically adjusted. The fair-share scheduling class uses CPU **shares** instead of priorities to make scheduling decisions. CPU shares indicate entitlement to available CPU resources and are allocated to a set of processes (known as a **project**).

Solaris uses the system class to run kernel processes, such as the scheduler and paging daemon. Once established, the priority of a system process does not change. The system class is reserved for kernel use (user processes running in kernel mode are not in the systems class).

Threads in the real-time class are given the highest priority. This assignment allows a real-time process to have a guaranteed response from the system within a bounded period of time. A real-time process will run before a process in any other class. In general, however, few processes belong to the real-time class.

Each scheduling class includes a set of priorities. However, the scheduler converts the class-specific priorities into global priorities and selects to run the thread with the highest global priority. The selected thread runs on the CPU until it (1) blocks, (2) uses its time slice, or (3) is preempted by a higher-priority thread. If there are multiple threads with the same priority, the scheduler uses a round-robin queue. Solaris has traditionally used the many-to-many model (5.2.3) but with Solaris 9 switched to the one-to-one model (5.2.2).

6.7.2 Example: Windows xp Scheduling

Windows XP schedules threads using a priority-based, preemptive scheduling algorithm. The Windows XP scheduler ensures that the highest-priority thread will always run. The portion of the Windows XP kernel that handles scheduling is called the *dispatcher*. A thread selected to run by the dispatcher will run until it is preempted by a higher-priority thread, until it terminates, until its time quantum ends, or until it calls a blocking system call, such as for I/O. If a higher-priority real-time thread becomes ready while a lower-priority thread is running, the lower-priority thread will be preempted. This preemption gives a real-time thread preferential access to the CPU when the thread needs such access. Windows XP is not a hard real-time operating system, however, because it does not guarantee that a real-time thread will start to execute within any particular time limit.

The dispatcher uses a 32-level priority scheme to determine the order of thread execution. Priorities are divided into two classes. The **variable class** contains threads having priorities from 1 to 15, and the **real-time class** contains threads with priorities ranging from 16 to 31. (There is also a thread running at priority 0 that is used for memory management.) The dispatcher uses a queue for each scheduling priority and traverses the set of queues from highest to lowest until it finds a thread that is ready to run. If no ready thread is found, the dispatcher will execute a special thread called the **idle thread**.

There is a relationship between the numeric priorities of the Windows XP kernel and the Win32 API. The Win32 API identifies several priority classes to which a process can belong. These include:

- REALTIME_PRIORITY_CLASS

- HIGH_PRIORITY_CLASS

- ABOVE_NORMAL_PRIORITY_CLASS

- NORMAL_PRIORITY_CLASS

- BELOW_NORMAL_PRIORITY_CLASS

- IDLE_PRIORITY_CLASS

Priorities in all classes except the REALTIME_PRIORITY_CLASS are variable, meaning that the priority of a thread belonging to one of these classes can change.

Within each of the priority classes is a relative priority. The values for relative priority include:

- TIME_CRITICAL

- HIGHEST

- ABOVE_NORMAL

- NORMAL

- BELOW_NORMAL

- LOWEST

- IDLE

The priority of each thread is based on the priority class it belongs to and its relative priority within that class. This relationship is shown in Figure 6.12. The values of the priority classes appear in the top row. The left column contains the

	real-time	high	above normal	normal	below normal	idle priority
time-critical	31	15	15	15	15	15
highest	26	15	12	10	8	6
above normal	25	14	11	9	7	5
normal	24	13	10	8	6	4
below normal	23	12	9	7	5	3
lowest	22	11	8	6	4	2
idle	16	1	1	1	1	1

Figure 6.12   Windows XP priorities.

values for the relative priorities. For example, if the relative priority of a thread in the ABOVE_NORMAL_PRIORITY_CLASS is NORMAL, the numeric priority of that thread is 10.

Furthermore, each thread has a base priority representing a value in the priority range for the class the thread belongs to. By default, the base priority is the value of the NORMAL relative priority for that specific class. The base priorities for each priority class are:

- REALTIME_PRIORITY_CLASS—24.

- HIGH_PRIORITY_CLASS—13.

- ABOVE_NORMAL_PRIORITY_CLASS—10.

- NORMAL_PRIORITY_CLASS—8.

- BELOW_NORMAL_PRIORITY_CLASS—6.

- IDLE_PRIORITY_CLASS—4.

Processes are typically members of the NORMAL_PRIORITY_CLASS unless the parent of the process was of the IDLE_PRIORITY_CLASS or unless another class was specified when the process was created. The initial priority of a thread is typically the base priority of the process the thread belongs to.

When a thread's time quantum runs out, that thread is interrupted; if the thread is in the variable-priority class, its priority is lowered. The priority is never lowered below the base priority, however. Lowering the thread's priority tends to limit the CPU consumption of compute-bound threads. When a variable-priority thread is released from a wait operation, the dispatcher boosts the priority. The amount of the boost depends on what the thread was waiting for; for example, a thread that was waiting for keyboard I/O would get a large increase, whereas a thread waiting for a disk operation would get a moderate one. This strategy tends to give good response times to interactive threads that are using the mouse and windows. It also enables I/O-bound threads to keep the I/O devices busy while permitting compute-bound threads to use spare CPU cycles in the background. This strategy is used by several time-sharing operating systems, including UNIX. In addition, the window with which the user is currently interacting also receives a priority boost to enhance its response time.

When a user is running an interactive program, the system needs to provide especially good performance for that process. For this reason, Windows XP has a special scheduling rule for processes in the NORMAL_PRIORITY_CLASS. Windows XP distinguishes between the *foreground process* that is currently selected on the screen, and the *background processes* that are not currently selected. When a process moves into the foreground, Windows XP increases the scheduling quantum by some factor—typically by 3. This increase gives the foreground process three times longer to run before a time-sharing preemption occurs.

6.7.3 Example: Linux Scheduling

Linux provides two separate process-scheduling algorithms. One is a time-sharing algorithm for fair preemptive scheduling among multiple processes; the other is designed for real-time tasks where absolute priorities are more important than fairness. In Section 6.5, we described a situation in which real-time systems must allow the kernel to be preempted to keep dispatch latency low. Linux allows only processes running in user mode to be preempted. A process may not be preempted while it is running in kernel mode, even if a real-time process with a higher priority is available to run.

Part of every process's identity is a scheduling class that defines which of these algorithms to apply to the process. The scheduling classes used by Linux are defined in the POSIX standard's extensions for real-time computing which were covered in Section 6.6.2.

The first scheduling class is for time-sharing processes. For conventional time-shared processes, Linux uses a prioritized **credit-based** algorithm. Each process possesses a certain number of scheduling credits; when a new task must be chosen to run, the process with the most credits is selected. Every time that a timer interrupt occurs, the currently running process loses one credit; when its credits reaches zero, it is suspended, and another process is chosen.

If no runnable processes have any credits, then Linux performs a recrediting operation, adding credits to *every* process in the system (rather than to only the runnable ones), according to the following rule:

$$\text{credits} = \frac{\text{credits}}{2} + \text{priority}.$$

This algorithm tends to mix two factors: the process's history and its priority. Half of the credits that a process still holds will be retained after the algorithm has been applied, retaining some history of the process's recent behavior. Processes that are running all the time tend to exhaust their credits rapidly, but processes that spend much of their time suspended can accumulate credits over multiple recreditings and consequently end up with a higher credit count after a recredit. This crediting system automatically gives high priority to interactive or I/O-bound processes, for which a rapid response time is important.

The use of a process priority in calculating new credits allows the priority of a process to be fine-tuned. Background batch jobs can be given a low priority; they will automatically receive fewer credits than interactive users' jobs and hence will receive a smaller percentage of the CPU time than will similar jobs with higher priorities. Linux uses this priority system to implement the standard UNIX *nice* process-priority mechanism. Linux's real-time scheduling is simpler still. Linux implements the two real-time scheduling classes required by POSIX.1b: first come, first served (FCFS) and round-robin (RR) (Sections 6.3.1 and 6.3.4). In both cases, each process has a priority in addition to its scheduling class. In time-sharing scheduling, however, processes of different priorities can still compete with one another to some extent; in real-time scheduling, the scheduler always runs the process with the highest priority. Among processes of equal priority, it runs the process that has been waiting longest. The only difference between FCFS and RR scheduling is that FCFS processes continue to run until they either exit or block, whereas a round-robin process will be preempted after a while and will be moved to the end of the scheduling queue, so round-robin processes of equal priority will automatically time-share among themselves.

Note that Linux's real-time scheduling is soft—rather than hard—real time. The scheduler offers strict guarantees about the relative priorities of real-time processes, but the kernel does not offer any guarantees about how quickly a real-time process will be scheduled once that process becomes runable. Remember that Linux kernel code can never be preempted by user-mode code. If an interrupt arrives that wakes up a real-time process while the kernel is already executing a system call on behalf of another process, the real-time process will just have to wait until the currently running system call completes or blocks.

6.8 ■ Java Thread Scheduling

The specification for the JVM has a loosely defined scheduling policy that simply states that each thread has a priority and that higher-priority threads will run in preference to threads with lower priorities. However, unlike the case with strict priority-based scheduling, it is possible that a lower-priority thread may get an opportunity to run at the expense of a higher-priority thread. The specification does not say that a scheduling policy must be preemptive; it is possible that a thread with a lower priority may continue to run even as a higher-priority thread becomes runnable.

Furthermore, the specification for the JVM does not indicate whether or not threads are time-sliced using a round- robin scheduler (6.3.4)—it is up to the particular implementation of the JVM. If threads are time-sliced, then a runnable thread executes until one of the following events occur:

1. Its time quantum expires.

2. It blocks for I/O.

3. It exits its run() method.

On systems that support preemption, a thread running on a CPU may also be preempted by a higher-priority thread.

So that all threads have an equal amount of CPU time on a system that does not perform time slicing, a thread may yield control of the CPU with the yield() method. By invoking the yield() method, a thread *suggests* that it is willing to relinquish control of the CPU, allowing another thread an opportunity to run. This yielding of control is called **cooperative multitasking**. The use of the yield() method appears as

```
public void run() {
    while (true) {
        // perform a CPU-intensive task
         .   .   .
        // now yield control of the CPU
        Thread.yield();
    }
}
```

6.8.1 Thread Priorities

All Java threads are assigned a priority that is a positive integer within a given range. Threads are given a default priority when they are created. Unless they are changed explicitly by the program, they maintain the same priority throughout their lifetime; the JVM does not dynamically alter priorities. The Java Thread class identifies the following thread priorities:

Priority	Comment
Thread.MIN_PRIORITY	The minimum thread priority.
Thread.MAX_PRIORITY	The maximum thread priority.
Thread.NORM_PRIORITY	The default thread priority.

MIN_PRIORITY has a value of 1; MAX_PRIORITY, a value of 10; and NORM_PRIORITY, a value of 5. Every Java thread has a priority that falls

```
public class HighThread implements Runnable
{
  public void run() {
    Thread.currentThread().setPriority(Thread.NORM_PRIORITY + 1);
    // remainder of run() method
      .  .  .
  }
}
```

Figure 6.13   Setting a priority using `setPriority()`.

somewhere within this range. When a thread is created, it is given the same priority as the thread that created it. Unless otherwise specified, the default priority for all threads is NORM_PRIORITY. The priority of a thread can also be set explicitly with the `setPriority()` method. The priority can be set either before a thread is started or while a thread is active. The class HighThread (Figure 6.13) increases the priority of the thread by 1 more than the default priority prior to performing the remainder of its `run()` method.

Because the JVM is typically implemented on top of a host operating system, the priority of a Java thread is related to the priority of the kernel thread to which it is mapped. On systems that support relatively few priority levels, it is possible that different Java thread priorities may map to the same priority of the kernel thread. For example, Thread.NORM_PRIORITY +1, and Thread.NORM_PRIORITY +2 map to the same kernel priority on Windows NT. On this system, altering the priority of Java threads may have no effect on how such threads are scheduled.

6.9 ■ Algorithm Evaluation

How do we select a CPU scheduling algorithm for a particular system? As we saw in Section 6.3, there are many scheduling algorithms, each with its own parameters. As a result, selecting an algorithm can be difficult.

The first problem is defining the criteria to be used in selecting an algorithm. As we saw in Section 6.2, criteria are often defined in terms of CPU utilization, response time, or throughput. To select an algorithm, we must first define the relative importance of these measures. Our criteria may include several measures, such as:

- Maximizing CPU utilization under the constraint that the maximum response time is 1 second

- Maximizing throughput such that turnaround time is (on average) linearly proportional to total execution time

Once the selection criteria have been defined, we want to evaluate the various algorithms under consideration. We describe the various evaluation methods we can use in Sections 6.9.1 through 6.9.4.

6.9.1 Deterministic Modeling

One major class of evaluation methods is **analytic evaluation**. Analytic evaluation uses the given algorithm and the system workload to produce a formula or number that evaluates the performance of the algorithm for that workload.

One type of analytic evaluation is **deterministic modeling**. This method takes a particular predetermined workload and defines the performance of each algorithm for that workload. For example, assume that we have the workload shown. All five processes arrive at time 0, in the order given, with the length of the CPU-burst time given in milliseconds:

Process	Burst Time
P_1	10
P_2	29
P_3	3
P_4	7
P_5	12

Consider the FCFS, SJF, and RR (quantum = 10 milliseconds) scheduling algorithms for this set of processes. Which algorithm would give the minimum average waiting time?

For the FCFS algorithm, we would execute the processes as

The waiting time is 0 milliseconds for process P_1, 10 milliseconds for process P_2, 39 milliseconds for process P_3, 42 milliseconds for process P_4, and 49 milliseconds for process P_5. Thus, the average waiting time is $(0 + 10 + 39 + 42 + 49)/5 = 28$ milliseconds.

With nonpreemptive SJF scheduling, we execute the processes as

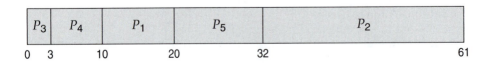

The waiting time is 10 milliseconds for process P_1, 32 milliseconds for process P_2, 0 milliseconds for process P_3, 3 milliseconds for process P_4, and 20 milliseconds for process P_5. Thus, the average waiting time is $(10 + 32 + 0 + 3 + 20)/5 = 13$ milliseconds.

With the RR algorithm, we execute the processes as

P_1	P_2	P_3	P_4	P_5	P_2	P_5	P_2

0   10   20 23   30   40   50 52   61

The waiting time is 0 milliseconds for process P_1, 32 milliseconds for process P_2, 20 milliseconds for process P_3, 23 milliseconds for process P_4, and 40 milliseconds for process P_5. Thus, the average waiting time is $(0 + 32 + 20 + 23 + 40)/5 = 23$ milliseconds.

We see that, *in this case*, the SJF policy results in less than one-half of the average waiting time obtained with FCFS scheduling; the RR algorithm gives us an intermediate value.

Deterministic modeling is simple and fast. It gives exact numbers, allowing the algorithms to be compared. However, it requires exact numbers for input, and its answers apply to only those cases. The main uses of deterministic modeling are in describing scheduling algorithms and providing examples. In cases where we may be running the same program over and over again and can measure the program's processing requirements exactly, we may be able to use deterministic modeling to select a scheduling algorithm. Furthermore, over a set of examples, deterministic modeling may indicate trends that can then be analyzed and proved separately. For example, it can be shown that, for the environment described (all processes and their times available at time 0), the SJF policy will always result in the minimum waiting time.

6.9.2 Queueing Models

The processes that are run on many systems vary from day to day, so there is no static set of processes (or times) to use for deterministic modeling. What can be determined, however, is the distribution of CPU and I/O bursts. These distributions can be measured and then approximated or simply estimated. The result is a mathematical formula describing the probability of a particular CPU burst. Commonly, this distribution is exponential and is described by its mean. Similarly, the distribution of times when processes arrive in the system (the arrival-time distribution) must be given. From these two distributions, it is possible to compute the average throughput, utilization, waiting time, and so on for most algorithms.

The computer system is described as a network of servers. Each server has a queue of waiting processes. The CPU is a server with its ready queue, as is the

I/O system with its device queues. Knowing arrival rates and service rates, we can compute utilization, average queue length, average wait time, and so on. This area of study is called **queueing-network analysis**.

As an example, let n be the average queue length (excluding the process being serviced), let W be the average waiting time in the queue, and let λ be the average arrival rate for new processes in the queue (such as three processes per second). Then, we expect that during the time W that a process waits, $\lambda \times W$ new processes will arrive in the queue. If the system is in a steady state, then the number of processes leaving the queue must be equal to the number of processes that arrive. Thus,

$$n = \lambda \times W.$$

This equation, known as **Little's formula**, is particularly useful because it is valid for any scheduling algorithm and arrival distribution.

We can use Little's formula to compute one of the three variables, if we know the other two. For example, if we know that 7 processes arrive every second (on average), and that there are normally 14 processes in the queue, then we can compute the average waiting time per process as 2 seconds.

Queueing analysis can be useful in comparing scheduling algorithms, but it also has limitations. At the moment, the classes of algorithms and distributions that can be handled are fairly limited. The mathematics of complicated algorithms and distributions can be difficult to work with. Thus, arrival and service distributions are often defined in mathematically tractable—but unrealistic—ways. It is also generally necessary to make a number of independent assumptions, which may not be accurate. As a result of these difficulties, queueing models are often only approximations of real systems, and the accuracy of the computed results may be questionable.

6.9.3 Simulations

To get a more accurate evaluation of scheduling algorithms, we can use **simulations**. Running simulations involves programming a model of the computer system. Software data structures represent the major components of the system. The simulator has a variable representing a clock; as this variable's value is increased, the simulator modifies the system state to reflect the activities of the devices, the processes, and the scheduler. As the simulation executes, statistics that indicate algorithm performance are gathered and printed.

The data to drive the simulation can be generated in several ways. The most common method uses a random-number generator, which is programmed to generate processes, CPU-burst times, arrivals, departures, and so on, according to probability distributions. The distributions can be defined mathematically (uniform, exponential, Poisson) or empirically. If the distribution is to be defined empirically, measurements of the actual system under study are taken.

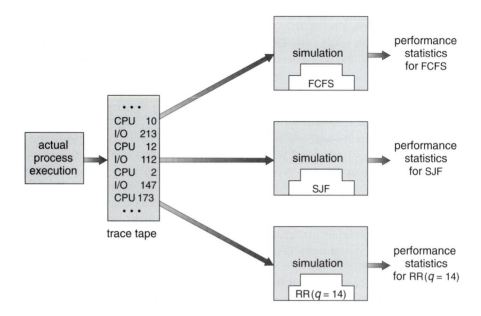

Figure 6.14 Evaluation of CPU schedulers by simulation.

The results define the distribution of events in the real system; this distribution can then be used to drive the simulation.

A distribution-driven simulation may be inaccurate, however, because of relationships between successive events in the real system. The frequency distribution indicates only how many of each event occur; it does not indicate anything about the order of their occurrence. To correct this problem, we can use **trace tapes**. We create a trace tape by monitoring the real system and recording the sequence of actual events (Figure 6.14). We then use this sequence to drive the simulation. Trace tapes provide an excellent way to compare two algorithms on exactly the same set of real inputs. This method can produce accurate results for its inputs.

Simulations can be expensive, often requiring hours of computer time. A more detailed simulation provides more accurate results, but it also requires more computer time. In addition, trace tapes can require large amounts of storage space. Finally, the design, coding, and debugging of the simulator can be a major task.

6.9.4 Implementation

Even a simulation is of limited accuracy. The only completely accurate way to evaluate a scheduling algorithm is to code it up, put it in the operating system, and see how it works. This approach puts the actual algorithm in the real system for evaluation under real operating conditions.

The major difficulty of this approach is the high cost. The expense is incurred not only in coding the algorithm and modifying the operating system to support it as well as its required data structures but also in the reaction of the users to a constantly changing operating system. Most users are not interested in building a better operating system; they merely want to get their processes executed and use their results. A constantly changing operating system does not help the users to get their work done.

The other difficulty with any algorithmic evaluation is that the environment in which the algorithm is used will change. The environment will change not only in the usual way, as new programs are written and the types of problems change, but also as a result of the performance of the scheduler. If short processes are given priority, then users may break larger processes into sets of smaller processes. If interactive processes are given priority over noninteractive processes, then users may switch to interactive use.

For example, researchers designed one system that classified interactive and noninteractive processes automatically by looking at the amount of terminal I/O. If a process did not input or output to the terminal in a 1-second interval, the process was classified as noninteractive and was moved to a lower-priority queue. This policy resulted in a situation where one programmer modified his programs to write an arbitrary character to the terminal at regular intervals of less than 1 second. The system gave his programs a high priority, even though the terminal output was completely meaningless.

The most flexible scheduling algorithms can be altered by the system managers or by the users so that they are tuned for a specific application or set of applications. For instance, a workstation that performs high-end graphical applications may have scheduling needs different from those of a web server or file server. Some operating systems—particularly several versions of UNIX—allow the system manager to fine-tune the scheduling parameters for a particular system configuration. Another approach is to use APIs such as yield() and setPriority(), thus enabling applications to act more predictably. The downfall of this approach is that performance tuning a system or application most often does not result in improved performance in more general situations.

6.10 ■ Summary

CPU scheduling is the task of selecting a waiting process from the ready queue and allocating the CPU to it. The CPU is allocated to the selected process by the dispatcher.

First-come, first-served (FCFS) scheduling is the simplest scheduling algorithm, but it can cause short processes to wait for very long processes. Shortest-job-first (SJF) scheduling is provably optimal, providing the shortest average waiting time. Implementing SJF scheduling is difficult because predicting the length of the next CPU burst is difficult. The SJF algorithm is a special case of the general priority-scheduling algorithm, which simply allocates the CPU to the highest-priority process. Both priority and SJF scheduling may suffer from starvation. Aging is a technique to prevent starvation.

Round-robin (RR) scheduling is more appropriate for a time-shared (interactive) system. RR scheduling allocates the CPU to the first process in the ready queue for q time units, where q is the time quantum. After q time units, if the process has not relinquished the CPU, it is preempted and the process is put at the tail of the ready queue. The major problem is the selection of the time quantum. If the quantum is too large, RR scheduling degenerates to FCFS scheduling; if the quantum is too small, scheduling overhead in the form of context-switch time becomes excessive.

The FCFS algorithm is nonpreemptive; the RR algorithm is preemptive. The SJF and priority algorithms may be either preemptive or nonpreemptive.

Multilevel queue algorithms allow different algorithms to be used for various classes of processes. The most common is a foreground interactive queue, which uses RR scheduling, and a background batch queue, which uses FCFS scheduling. Multilevel feedback queues allow processes to move from one queue to another.

Many contemporary computer systems support multiple processors where each processor schedules itself independently. Typically, there is a queue of processes (or threads), all of which are available to run. Each processor makes a scheduling decision and selects from this queue.

Operating systems supporting threads at the kernel level must schedule threads—not processes—for execution. This is the case with Solaris and Windows XP where both systems schedule threads using preemptive, priority-based scheduling algorithms including support for real-time threads. The Linux process scheduler also uses a priority-based algorithm with real-time support as well. The scheduling algorithms for these three operating systems typically favor interactive over batch and CPU-bound processes.

The JVM uses a priority-based thread-scheduling algorithm that favors higher-priority threads. The specification does not indicate whether the JVM should time-slice threads; that is up to the particular implementation of the JVM.

The wide variety of scheduling algorithms demands that we have methods to select among algorithms. Analytic methods use mathematical analysis to determine the performance of an algorithm. Simulation methods determine performance by imitating the scheduling algorithm on a "representative" sample of processes and computing the resulting performance.

▪ Exercises

6.1 A CPU-scheduling algorithm determines an order for the execution of its scheduled processes. Given n processes to be scheduled on one processor without preemption, how many possible schedules are there? Give a formula in terms of n.

6.2 Define the difference between preemptive and nonpreemptive scheduling.

6.3 Consider the following set of processes, with the length of the CPU-burst time given in milliseconds:

Process	Burst Time	Priority
P_1	10	3
P_2	1	1
P_3	2	3
P_4	1	4
P_5	5	2

The processes are assumed to have arrived in the order P_1, P_2, P_3, P_4, P_5, all at time 0.

a. Draw four Gantt charts that illustrate the execution of these processes using FCFS, SJF, a nonpreemptive priority (a smaller priority number implies a higher priority), and RR (quantum = 1) scheduling.

b. What is the turnaround time of each process for each of the scheduling algorithms in part a?

c. What is the waiting time of each process for each of the scheduling algorithms in part a?

d. Which of the schedules in part a results in the minimal average waiting time (over all processes)?

6.4 Suppose that the following processes arrive for execution at the times indicated. Each process will run the listed amount of time. In answering the questions, use nonpreemptive scheduling, and base all decisions on the information that you have at the time the decision must be made.

Process	Arrival Time	Burst Time
P_1	0.0	8
P_2	0.4	4
P_3	1.0	1

a. What is the average turnaround time for these processes with the FCFS scheduling algorithm?

b. What is the average turnaround time for these processes with the SJF scheduling algorithm?

c. The SJF algorithm is supposed to improve performance, but notice that we chose to run process P_1 at time 0 because we did not know that two shorter processes would arrive soon. Compute what the average turnaround time will be if the CPU is left idle for the first 1 unit and then SJF scheduling is used. Remember that processes P_1 and P_2 are waiting during this idle time, so their waiting time may increase. This algorithm could be known as *future-knowledge scheduling*.

6.5 Consider a variant of the RR scheduling algorithm where the entries in the ready queue are pointers to the PCBs.

a. What would be the effect of putting two pointers to the same process in the ready queue?

b. What would be two major advantages and two disadvantages of this scheme?

c. How would you modify the basic RR algorithm to achieve the same effect without the duplicate pointers?

6.6 What advantage is there in having different time-quantum sizes on different levels of a multilevel queueing system?

6.7 Consider the following preemptive priority-scheduling algorithm based on dynamically changing priorities. Larger priority numbers imply higher priority. When a process is waiting for the CPU (in the ready queue, but not running), its priority changes at a rate α; when it is running, its priority changes at a rate β. All processes are given a priority of 0 when they enter the ready queue. The parameters α and β can be set to give many different scheduling algorithms.

a. What is the algorithm that results from $\beta > \alpha > 0$?

b. What is the algorithm that results from $\alpha < \beta < 0$?

6.8 Many CPU-scheduling algorithms are parameterized. For example, the RR algorithm requires a parameter to indicate the time slice. Multilevel feedback queues require parameters to define the number of queues, the scheduling algorithms for each queue, the criteria used to move processes between queues, and so on.

These algorithms are thus really sets of algorithms (for example, the set of RR algorithms for all time slices, and so on). One set of algorithms may include another (for example, the FCFS algorithm is the RR algorithm with an infinite time quantum). What (if any) relation holds between the following pairs of sets of algorithms?

a. Priority and SJF

b. Multilevel feedback queues and FCFS

    c. Priority and FCFS

    d. RR and SJF

6.9 Suppose that a scheduling algorithm (at the level of short-term CPU scheduling) favors those processes that have used the least processor time in the recent past. Why will this algorithm favor I/O-bound programs and yet not permanently starve CPU-bound programs?

6.10 Explain the differences in the degree to which the following scheduling algorithms discriminate in favor of short processes:

    a. FCFS

    b. RR

    c. Multilevel feedback queues

6.11 Distinguish between PCS and SCS scheduling.

6.12 Assume an operating system maps user-level threads to the kernel using the many-to-many model where the mapping is done through the use of LWPs. Furthermore, the system allows program developers to create realtime threads. Is it necessary to bind a realtime thread to an LWP?

6.13 Using the Windows XP scheduling algorithm, what is the numeric priority of a thread for the following scenarios?

    a. A thread in the REALTIME_PRIORITY_CLASS with a relative priority of HIGHEST.

    b. A thread in the NORMAL_PRIORITY_CLASS with a relative priority of NORMAL.

    c. A thread in the HIGH_PRIORITY_CLASS with a relative priority of ABOVE_NORMAL.

6.14 Consider the scheduling algorithm in the Solaris operating system for time-sharing threads:

    a. What is the time quantum (in milliseconds) for a thread with priority 10? With priority 55?

    b. Assume a thread with priority 35 has used its entire time quantum without blocking. What new priority will the scheduler assign this thread?

    c. Assume a thread with priority 35 blocks for I/O before its time quantum has expired. What new priority will the scheduler assign this thread?

Bibliographical Notes

Feedback queues were originally implemented on the CTSS system described in Corbato et al. [1962]. This feedback queueing system was analyzed by Schrage [1967]. The preemptive priority-scheduling algorithm of Exercise 6.7 was suggested by Kleinrock [1975].

Anderson et al. [1989] and Lewis and Berg [1998] talked about thread scheduling. Discussions concerning multiprocessor scheduling were presented by Tucker and Gupta [1989], Zahorjan and McCann [1990], Feitelson and Rudolph [1990], and Leutenegger and Vernon [1990].

Discussions about scheduling in real-time systems were offered by Abbot [1984], Jensen et al. [1985], Hong et al. [1989], and Khanna et al. [1992]. A special issue on real-time operating systems was edited by Zhao [1989].

Fair-share schedulers were covered by Henry [1984], Woodside [1986], and Kay and Lauder [1988].

Discussion of scheduling policies used in the UNIX V operating system was presented by Bach [1987]; the one for UNIX BSD 4.4 was presented by McKusick et al. [1996]; and the one for the Mach operating system was presented by Black [1990]. Bovet and Cesati [2002] covers scheduling in Linux. Solaris scheduling was described by Mauro and McDougall [2001]. Solomon [1998] and Solomon and Russinovich [2000] discussed scheduling in Windows NT and Windows 2000, respectively. Butenhof [1997] and Lewis and Berg [1998] covers scheduling in Pthreads systems.

Java thread scheduling according to the specification of the JVM is described by Lindholm and Yellin [1999]. General-purpose books covering Java thread scheduling include Holub [2000], Lewis and Berg [2000], and Oaks and Wong [1999].

Chapter 7

PROCESS SYNCHRONIZATION

A cooperating process, as discussed in Chapter 4, is one that can affect or be affected by the other processes that are executing in the system. Cooperating processes may either directly share a logical address space (that is, both code and data) or be allowed to share data only through files or messages. The former case is achieved through the use of threads, which were discussed in Chapter 5. Concurrent access to shared data may result in data inconsistency. In this chapter, we discuss various mechanisms to ensure the orderly execution of cooperating processes or threads that share a logical address space, allowing data consistency to be maintained.

7.1 ■ Background

In Chapter 4, we developed a model of a system consisting of cooperating sequential processes or threads, all running asynchronously and possibly sharing data. We illustrated this model with the producer–consumer problem, which is representative of operating systems. The code fragment for the producer thread is as follows:

```
while (count == BUFFER_SIZE)
    ; // do nothing

// add an item to the buffer
++count;
buffer[in] = item;
in = (in + 1) % BUFFER_SIZE;
```

The code for the consumer is

```
while (count == 0)
   ; // do nothing

// remove an item from the buffer
--count;
item = buffer[out];
out = (out + 1) % BUFFER_SIZE;
```

Although both the producer and the consumer routines are correct separately, they may not function correctly when executed concurrently. The reason is that the threads share the variable count, which serves as the count for the number of items in the buffer. As an illustration, suppose that the value of the variable count is currently 5 and that the producer and consumer threads execute the statements ++count and --count concurrently. Following the execution of these two statements, the value of the variable count might be 4, 5, or 6! The only correct result for count is 5, which is generated correctly only if the producer and consumer execute sequentially.

We can show how the resulting value of count may be incorrect as follows. Note that the statement ++count may be implemented in machine language (on a typical machine) as

$$register_1 = count;$$
$$register_1 = register_1 + 1;$$
$$count = register_1;$$

where $register_1$ is a local CPU register. Similarly, the statement --count is implemented as follows:

$$register_2 = count;$$
$$register_2 = register_2 - 1;$$
$$count = register_2;$$

where again $register_2$ is a local CPU register. Remember that, even though $register_1$ and $register_2$ may be the same physical register (an accumulator, say), the contents of this register will be saved and restored by the interrupt handler (Section 2.1). Therefore, each thread sees only its own register values, not those of the other threads.

The concurrent execution of the statements ++count and --count is equivalent to a sequential execution where the lower-level statements presented previously are interleaved in some arbitrary order (but the order within each high-level statement is preserved). One such interleaving is

S_0:	producer	execute	$register_1 = count$	$\{register_1 = 5\}$
S_1:	producer	execute	$register_1 = register_1 + 1$	$\{register_1 = 6\}$
S_2:	consumer	execute	$register_2 = count$	$\{register_2 = 5\}$
S_3:	consumer	execute	$register_2 = register_2 - 1$	$\{register_2 = 4\}$
S_4:	producer	execute	$count = register_1$	$\{count = 6 \}$
S_5:	consumer	execute	$count = register_2$	$\{count = 4\}$

Notice that we have arrived at the incorrect state "$count = 4$," recording that there are four full buffers, when, in fact, there are five full buffers. If we reversed the order of the statements at S_4 and S_5, we would arrive at the incorrect state "$count = 6$."

We would arrive at this incorrect state because we allowed both threads to manipulate the variable count concurrently. This situation, where several threads access and manipulate the same data concurrently, and where the outcome of the execution depends on the particular order in which the access takes place, is called a **race condition**. Such situations occur frequently in operating systems as different parts of the system manipulate resources, and we do not want the changes to interfere with one another. Unexpected interference can cause data corruption and systems crashes. To guard against the race condition, we need to ensure that only one thread at a time can be manipulating the variable count. To make such a guarantee, we require some form of synchronization of the threads. A major portion of this chapter is concerned with thread synchronization and coordination.

7.2 ▪ The Critical-Section Problem

As a first method of controlling access to a shared resource, we declare a section of code to be *critical;* we then regulate access to that section. Consider a system consisting of n threads $\{T_0, T_1, ..., T_{n-1}\}$. Each thread has a segment of code, called a **critical section**, in which the thread may be changing common variables, updating a table, writing a file, and so on. The important feature of the system is that, when one thread is executing in its critical section, no other thread is to be allowed to execute in its critical section. Thus, the execution of critical sections by the threads is *mutually exclusive* in time. The critical-section challenge is creating a protocol that the threads can use to cooperate.

A solution to the critical-section problem must satisfy the following three requirements:

1. *Mutual exclusion:* If thread T_i is executing in its critical section, then no other threads can be executing in their critical sections.

2. *Progress:* If no thread is executing in its critical section and some threads wish to enter their critical sections, then only those threads that are not executing in their noncritical sections can participate in the decision on which

will enter its critical section next, and this selection cannot be postponed indefinitely.

3. *Bounded waiting:* There exists a bound on the number of times that other threads are allowed to enter their critical sections after a thread has made a request to enter its critical section and before that request is granted. This bound prevents *starvation* of any single thread.

We assume that each thread is executing at a nonzero speed. However, we can make no assumption concerning the *relative* speed of the n threads. In Section 7.3, we examine the critical-section problem and develop a solution that satisfies these three requirements. The solutions do not rely on any assumptions concerning the hardware instructions or the number of processors that the hardware supports. We do assume, however, that the basic machine-language instructions (the primitive instructions such as load, store, and test) are executed atomically. That is, if two such instructions are executed concurrently, the result is equivalent to their sequential execution in some unknown order. Thus, if a load and a store are executed concurrently, the load will get either the old value or the new value, but not some combination of the two.

7.3 ■ Two-Tasks Solutions

In this section, we consider three different Java implementations to coordinate the actions of two different threads. The threads are numbered T_0 and T_1. For convenience, when representing T_i, we use T_j to denote the other thread—that is, $j = 1 - i$. Before examining the different algorithms, we present the necessary Java class files.

The three algorithms will implement the MutualExclusion interface shown in Figure 7.1, with each algorithm implementing the methods enteringCriticalSection() and leavingCriticalSection().

We implement each thread using the Worker class shown in Figure 7.2. Before calling its critical section, each thread will call the method entering-CriticalSection(), passing its thread identifier (which will be either 0 or 1).

```
public interface MutualExclusion
{
    public static final int TURN_0 = 0;
    public static final int TURN_1 = 1;

    public abstract void enteringCriticalSection(int turn);
    public asbtract void leavingCriticalSection(int turn);
}
```

Figure 7.1   MutualExclusion interface.

```
public class Worker implements Runnable
{
    private String name;
    private int id;
    private MutualExclusion mutex;

    public Worker(String name, int id, MutualExclusion mutex) {
        this.name = name;
        this.id = id;
        this.mutex = mutex;
    }

    public void run() {
        while (true) {
            mutex.enteringCriticalSection(id);
            MutualExclusionUtilities.criticalSection(name);
            mutex.leavingCriticalSection(id);
            MutualExclusionUtilities.nonCriticalSection(name);
        }
    }
}
```

Figure 7.2   Worker thread.

A thread will not return from enteringCriticalSection() until it is able to enter its critical section. On finishing its critical section, a thread will call the method leavingCriticalSection().

Calls to the static methods criticalSection() and nonCriticalSection() represent where each thread performs its critical and noncritical sections. These methods are part of the MutualExclusionUtilities class and simulate critical and noncritical sections by sleeping for a random period of time. (The MutualExclusionUtilities class is available online.)

We use the AlgorithmFactory class (Figure 7.3) to create the two threads and to test each algorithm.

7.3.1 Algorithm 1

Our first approach is to let the threads share a common integer variable turn, initialized to either 0 or 1. If turn == i, then thread T_i is allowed to execute its critical section. A complete Java solution is shown in Figure 7.4.

This solution ensures that only one thread at a time can be in its critical section. However, it does not satisfy the progress requirement, since it requires strict alternation of threads in the execution of their critical sections. For example, if turn == 0 and thread T_1 is ready to enter its critical section, then T_1 cannot do so, even though T_0 may be in its noncritical section.

```
public class AlgorithmFactory
{
    public static void main(String args[]) {
        MutualExclusion alg = new Algorithm_1();

        Thread first = new Thread(
            new Worker("Worker 0", 0, alg));
        Thread second = new Thread(
            new Worker("Worker 1", 1, alg));

        first.start();
        second.start();
    }
}
```

Figure 7.3   The algorithm factory class.

Algorithm 1 uses the `yield()` method introduced in Section 6.8. Invoking the `yield()` method keeps the thread in the Runnable state but also allows the JVM to select another Runnable thread to run.

This solution also introduces a new Java keyword: `volatile`. The Java Language Specification allows a compiler to make certain optimizations, such as caching the value of a variable in a machine register rather than continually updating that value from main memory. Such optimizations occur when the

```
public class Algorithm_1 implements MutualExclusion
{
    private volatile int turn;

    public Algorithm_1() {
        turn = TURN_0;
    }

    public void enteringCriticalSection(int t) {
        while (turn != t)
            Thread.yield();
    }

    public void leavingCriticalSection(int t) {
        turn = 1 - t;
    }
}
```

Figure 7.4   Algorithm 1.

compiler recognizes that the value of the variable will remain unchanged, such as in the statement

```
while (turn != t)
    Thread.yield();
```

However, if another thread can change the value of turn—as happens in algorithm 1—then it is desirable that the value of turn be refreshed from main memory during every iteration. Declaring a variable as volatile prevents the compiler from making such optimizations.

7.3.2 Algorithm 2

The problem with algorithm 1 is that it does not retain sufficient information about the state of each thread; it remembers only which thread is allowed to enter its critical section. To remedy this problem, we can replace the variable turn with the following:

```
boolean flag0;
boolean flag1;
```

Each element is initialized to false. If an element is true, this value indicates that the associated thread is ready to enter its critical section. The complete Java solution is shown in Figure 7.5. (It should be noted that a two-element array of type boolean would be more appropriate than two separate boolean variables; however, the data must be declared as volatile, and the volatile keyword does not extend to arrays.)

In this algorithm, thread T_0 first sets flag0 to be true, signaling that it is ready to enter its critical section. Then, T_0 checks to verify that thread T_1 is not also ready to enter its critical section. If T_1 were ready, then T_0 would wait until T_1 had indicated that it no longer needed to be in the critical section (that is, until flag1 was false). At that point, T_0 would enter its critical section. On exiting the critical section, T_0 would set flag0 to false, allowing the other thread (if it is waiting) to enter its critical section.

In this solution, the mutual-exclusion requirement is satisfied. Unfortunately, the progress requirement is still not met. To illustrate this problem, consider the following execution sequence: Suppose that thread T_0 sets flag0 to true, indicating that it wishes to enter its critical section. Before it can begin executing the while loop, a context switch takes place, and thread T_1 sets flag1 to true. Each thread will loop forever in its while statement, because the value of flag for the other thread is true.

7.3.3 Algorithm 3

By combining the key ideas of algorithm 1 and algorithm 2, we obtain a correct solution to the critical-section problem—one that meets all three requirements.

```
public class Algorithm_2 implements MutualExclusion
{
    private volatile boolean flag0;
    private volatile boolean flag1;

    public Algorithm_2() {
        flag0 = false;
        flag1 = false;
    }

    public void enteringCriticalSection(int t) {
        if (t == 0) {
            flag0 = true;
            while(flag1 == true)
                Thread.yield();
        }
        else {
            flag1 = true;
            while (flag0 == true)
                Thread.yield();
        }
    }

    public void leavingCriticalSection(int t) {
        if (t == 0) {
            flag0 = false;
        else
            flag1 = false;
    }
}
```

Figure 7.5   Algorithm 2.

The threads share three variables:

```
boolean flag0;
boolean flag1;
int turn;
```

Initially, flag0 and flag1 are set to false, and the value of turn is immaterial (it is either 0 or 1). Figure 7.6 displays the complete Java solution.

To enter its critical section, thread T_0 first sets flag0 to be true and then asserts that it is the other thread's turn to enter if appropriate (turn == other). If both threads try to enter at the same time, turn is set to both 0 and 1 at roughly the same time. Only one of these assignments lasts; the other will occur but will be overwritten immediately. The eventual value of turn decides which of the two threads is allowed to enter its critical section first.

```java
public class Algorithm_3 implements MutualExclusion
{
    private volatile int turn;
    private volatile boolean flag0;
    private volatile boolean flag1;

    public Algorithm_3() {
        flag0 = false;
        flag1 = false;
        turn = TURN_0;
    }

    public void enteringCriticalSection(int t) {
        int other = 1 - t;
        turn = other;

        if (t == 0) {
            flag0 = true;
            while ( (flag1 == true) && (turn == other) )
                Thread.yield();
        }
        else {
            flag1 = true;
            while ( (flag0 == true) && (turn == other) )
                Thread.yield();
        }
    }

    public void leavingCriticalSection(int t) {
        if (t == 0)
            flag0 = false;
        else
            flag1 = false;
    }
}
```

Figure 7.6   Algorithm 3.

7.4 ■ Synchronization Hardware

As is true of other aspects of software, features of the hardware can make the programming task easier and improve system efficiency. In this section, we present simple hardware instructions that are available on many systems and show how they can be used effectively in solving the critical-section problem.

The critical-section problem could be solved simply in a uniprocessor environment if we could prevent interrupts from occurring while a shared variable was being modified. In this manner, we could be sure that the current sequence of instructions would be allowed to execute in order without preemption. No other instructions would be run, so no unexpected modifications could be made to the shared variable.

Unfortunately, this solution is not feasible in a multiprocessor environment. Disabling interrupts on a multiprocessor can be time consuming, as the disable and enable commands must be passed to all the processors. This message passing delays entry into each critical section and adds expense to exiting each

```java
public class HardwareData
{
    private boolean data;

    public HardwareData(boolean data) {
        this.data = data;
    }

    public boolean get() {
        return data;
    }

    public void set(boolean data) {
        this.data = data;
    }

    public boolean getAndSet(boolean data) {
        boolean oldValue = this.get();
        this.set(data);

        return oldValue;
    }

    public void swap(HardwareData other) {
        boolean temp = this.get();

        this.set(other.get());
        other.set(temp);
    }
}
```

Figure 7.7   Data structure for hardware solutions.

critical section. As a result, system efficiency decreases greatly. Systems that employ this method of synchronization lack scalability as CPUs are added, because the communication expense increases with the number of CPUs.

All modern machines therefore provide special hardware instructions that allow us either to test and modify the content of a word, or to swap the contents of two words, **atomically**—that is, as one uninterruptible unit. We can use these special instructions to solve the critical-section problem in a relatively simple manner. Rather than discussing one specific instruction for one specific machine, we will use Java to abstract the main concepts behind these types of instructions. The HardwareData class shown in Figure 7.7 will illustrate the instructions.

The getAndSet() method implementing the *Get-and-Set* instruction is shown in Figure 7.7. The important characteristic is that this instruction is executed atomically. Thus, if two *Get-and-Set* instructions are executed simultaneously (each on a different CPU), they will be executed sequentially in some arbitrary order.

If the machine supports the *Get-and-Set* instruction, then we can implement mutual exclusion by declaring lock to be an object of class HardwareData and initializing it to false. All threads will share access to lock. Figure 7.8 illustrates the structure of thread T_i.

The *Swap* instruction, defined in the swap() method in Figure 7.7, operates on the contents of two words; like the *Get-and-Set* instruction, it is executed atomically.

If the machine supports the *Swap* instruction, then mutual exclusion can be provided as follows. All threads share an object lock of class Hardware-Data that is initialized to false. In addition, each thread also has a local HardwareData object key. The structure of thread T_i is shown in Figure 7.9.

```
// lock is shared by all threads
HardwareData lock = new HardwareData(false);

while (true) {
    while (lock.getAndSet(true))
        Thread.yield();

    criticalSection();
    lock.set(false);
    nonCriticalSection();
}
```

Figure 7.8   Thread using *Get-and-Set* lock.

```
// lock is shared by all threads
HardwareData lock = new HardwareData(false);

// each thread has a local copy of key
HardwareData key = new HardwareData(true);

while (true) {
    key.set(true);

    do {
        lock.swap(key);
    }
    while (key.get() == true);

    criticalSection();
    lock.set(false);
    nonCriticalSection();
}
```

Figure 7.9   Thread using *Swap* instruction.

7.5 ■ Semaphores

The hardware-based solutions to the critical-section problem presented in Section 7.4 are complicated for application programmers to use. To overcome this difficulty, we can use a synchronization tool called a **semaphore**. A semaphore *S* is an integer variable that, apart from initialization, is accessed only through two standard operations: acquire() and release(). These operations were originally termed P (from the Dutch *proberen*, meaning "to test") and V (from *verhogen*, meaning "to increment"). The definitions of acquire() and release() are as follows:

```
acquire(S) {
    while S <= 0
        ; // no-op
    S--;
}

release(S) {
    S++;
}
```

Modifications to the integer value of the semaphore in the acquire() and release() operations must be executed indivisibly. That is, when one thread modifies the semaphore value, no other thread can simultaneously modify that same semaphore value. In addition, in the case of the acquire(S), the testing of the integer value of S (S <= 0) and of its possible modification (S--) must also be executed without interruption. We see in Section 7.5.2 how these operations can be implemented; first, let us see how semaphores can be used.

7.5.1   Usage

Operating systems often distinguish between counting and binary semaphores. The value of a **counting semaphore** can range over an unrestricted domain. The value of a **binary semaphore** can range only between 0 and 1. On some systems, binary semaphores are known as **mutex locks**, as they are locks that provide mutual exclusion.

The general strategy for using a binary semaphore to control access to a critical section is as follows (assuming that the semaphore is initialized to 1):

```
Semaphore S;

acquire(S);
criticalSection();
release(S);
```

Thus, we can use the semaphore to control access to the critical section for a process or thread. A generalized solution for multiple threads is shown in the Java program in Figure 7.10. Five separate threads are created, but only one can be in its critical section at a given time. The semaphore sem, which is shared by all the threads, controls access to the critical section.

Counting semaphores can be used to control access to a given resource consisting of a finite number of instances. The semaphore is initialized to the number of resources available. Each thread that wishes to use a resource performs an acquire() operation on the semaphore (thereby decrementing the count). When a thread releases a resource, it performs a release() operation (incrementing the count). When the count for the semaphore goes to 0, all resources are being used. After that, threads that wish to use a resource will block until the count becomes greater than 0.

7.5.2   Implementation

The main disadvantage of the mutual-exclusion solutions of Section 7.3, and of the type of semaphore just described, is that they all require busy waiting. While a process is in its critical section, any other process that tries to enter its critical section must loop continuously in the entry code. This continual looping is clearly a problem in a multiprogramming system, where a single CPU is shared among many processes. Busy waiting wastes CPU cycles that some other process might be able to use productively. A semaphore that produces this

```
public class Worker implements Runnable
{
    private Semaphore sem;
    private String name;

    public Worker(Semaphore sem, String name) {
        this.sem = sem;
        this.name = name;
    }

    public void run() {
        while (true) {
            sem.acquire();
            MutualExclusionUtilities.criticalSection(name);
            sem.release();
            MutualExclusionUtilities.nonCriticalSection(name);
        }
    }
}

public class SemaphoreFactory
{
    public static void main(String args[]) {
        Semaphore sem = new Semaphore(1);
        Thread[] bees = new Thread[5];

        for (int i = 0; i < 5; i++)
            bees[i] = new Thread(new Worker
                (sem, "Worker " + (new Integer(i)).toString() ));

        for (int i = 0; i < 5; i++)
            bees[i].start();
    }
}
```

Figure 7.10   Synchronization using semaphores.

result is also called a **spinlock**, because the process "spins" while waiting for the lock. (Spinlocks do have an advantage in that no context switch is required when a process must wait on a lock, and a context switch may take considerable time. Thus, when locks are expected to be held for short times, spinlocks are useful; they are often employed on multiprocessor systems where one thread can "spin" on one processor while another thread performs its critical section on another processor.)

To overcome the need for busy waiting, we can modify the definitions of the acquire() and release() semaphore operations. When a process executes the acquire() operation and finds that the semaphore value is not positive, it must wait. However, rather than using busy waiting, the process can *block* itself. The block operation places a process into a waiting queue associated with the semaphore, and the state of the process is switched to the waiting state. Then, control is transferred to the CPU scheduler, which selects another process to execute.

A process that is blocked, waiting on a semaphore S, should be restarted when some other process executes a release() operation. The process is restarted by a *wakeup* operation, which changes the process from the waiting state to the ready state. The process is then placed in the ready queue. (The CPU may or may not be switched from the running process to the newly ready process, depending on the CPU-scheduling algorithm.)

To implement semaphores under this definition, we define a semaphore as an integer value and a list of processes. When a process must wait on a semaphore, it is added to the list of processes for that semaphore. The release() operation removes one process from the list of waiting processes and awakens that process.

The semaphore operations can now be defined as

```
acquire(S){
    value--;
    if (value < 0) {
        add this process to list
        block;
    }
}

release(S){
    value++;
    if (value <= 0) {
        remove a process P from list
        wakeup(P);
    }
}
```

The block operation suspends the process that invokes it. The wakeup(P) operation resumes the execution of a blocked process P. These two operations are provided by the operating system as basic system calls.

Note that this implementation may have negative semaphore values, although under the classical definition of semaphores with busy waiting the semaphore value is never negative. If the semaphore value is negative, its magnitude is the number of processes waiting on that semaphore. This fact is a result of the switching of the order of the decrement and the test in the implementation of the `acquire()` operation.

The list of waiting processes can be easily implemented by a link field in each process control block (PCB). Each semaphore contains an integer value and a pointer to a list of PCBs. One way to add and remove processes from the list, which ensures bounded waiting, would be to use a FIFO queue, where the semaphore contains both head and tail pointers to the queue. In general, however, the list may use *any* queueing strategy. Correct use of semaphores does not depend on a particular queueing strategy for the semaphore lists.

The critical aspect of semaphores is that they are executed atomically. We must guarantee that no two processes can execute `acquire()` and `release()` operations on the same semaphore at the same time. This situation creates a critical-section problem, which can be solved in either of two ways.

In a uniprocessor environment, we can simply inhibit interrupts during the time the `acquire()` and `release()` operations are executing. Once interrupts are inhibited, instructions from different processes cannot be interleaved. Only the currently running process executes until interrupts are reenabled and the scheduler can regain control.

In a multiprocessor environment, however, inhibiting interrupts does not work. Instructions from different processes (running on different processors) may be interleaved in some arbitrary way. If the hardware does not provide any special instructions, we can employ any of the correct software solutions for the critical-section problem (Section 7.2), where the critical sections consist of the `acquire()` and `release()` operations.

We have not completely eliminated busy waiting with this definition of the `acquire()` and `release()` operations. Rather, we have moved busy waiting to the critical sections of application programs. Furthermore, we have limited busy waiting to only the critical sections of the `acquire()` and `release()` operations. These sections are short (if properly coded, they should be no more than about 10 instructions). Thus, the critical section is almost never occupied; busy waiting occurs rarely, and then for only a short time. An entirely different situation exists with application programs, whose critical sections may be long (minutes or even hours) or may almost always be occupied. In this case, busy waiting is extremely inefficient. Throughout this chapter, we address issues of performance and show techniques to avoid busy waiting.

In Section 7.8.5 we see how semaphores can be implemented in Java.

7.5.3 Deadlocks and Starvation

The implementation of a semaphore with a waiting queue may result in a situation where two or more processes are waiting indefinitely for an event that can be caused by only one of the waiting processes. The event in question is the execution of a `release()` operation. When such a state is reached, these processes are said to be **deadlocked**.

As an illustration, we consider a system consisting of two processes, P_0 and P_1, each accessing two semaphores, S and Q, set to the value 1:

P_0	P_1
`acquire(S);`	`acquire(Q);`
`acquire(Q);`	`acquire(S);`
.	.
.	.
.	.
`release(S);`	`release(Q);`
`release(Q);`	`release(S);`

Suppose that P_0 executes `acquire(S)`, and then P_1 executes `acquire(Q)`. When P_0 executes `acquire(Q)`, it must wait until P_1 executes `release(Q)`.

```
public class BoundedBuffer implements Buffer
{
    private static final int BUFFER_SIZE = 5;
    private Object[] buffer;
    private int in, out;
    private Semaphore mutex;
    private Semaphore empty;
    private Semaphore full;

    public BoundedBuffer() {
        // buffer is initially empty
        in = 0;
        out = 0;
        buffer = new Object[BUFFER_SIZE];

        mutex = new Semaphore(1);
        empty = new Semaphore(BUFFER_SIZE);
        full = new Semaphore(0);
    }

    public void insert(Object item) {
        // Figure 7.12
    }

    public Object remove() {
        // Figure 7.13
    }
}
```

Figure 7.11   Solution to the bounded-buffer problem that uses semaphores.

```
public void insert(Object item) {
    empty.acquire();
    mutex.acquire();

    // add an item to the buffer
    buffer[in] = item;
    in = (in + 1) % BUFFER_SIZE;

    mutex.release();
    full.release();
}
```

Figure 7.12   The insert() method.

Similarly, when P_1 executes acquire(S), it must wait until P_0 executes release(S). Since these signal operations cannot be executed, P_0 and P_1 are deadlocked.

We say that a set of processes is in a deadlock state when every process in the set is waiting for an event that can be caused by only another process in the set. The events with which we are mainly concerned here are resource acquisition and release; however, other types of events may result in deadlocks, as we show in Chapter 8. In that chapter, we describe various mechanisms for dealing with the deadlock problem.

Another problem related to deadlocks is **indefinite blocking** or **starvation** —a situation where processes wait indefinitely within the semaphore. Indefinite blocking may occur if we add and remove processes from the list associated with a semaphore in last-in first-out (LIFO) order.

```
public Object remove() {
    full.acquire();
    mutex.acquire();

    // remove an item from the buffer
    Object item = buffer[out];
    out = (out + 1) % BUFFER_SIZE;

    mutex.release();
    empty.release();

    return item;
}
```

Figure 7.13   The remove() method.

7.6 ■ Classical Synchronization Problems

In this section, we present a number of different synchronization problems that are important mainly because they are examples for a large class of concurrency-control problems. These problems are used for testing nearly every newly proposed synchronization scheme. Semaphores are used for synchronization in our solutions.

7.6.1 The Bounded-Buffer Problem

The bounded-buffer problem was introduced in Section 7.1; it is commonly used to illustrate the power of synchronization primitives. A solution was shown in Figure 7.11. A producer places an item in the buffer by calling the insert() method; consumers remove items by invoking remove().

The mutex semaphore provides mutual exclusion for accesses to the buffer pool and is initialized to 1. The empty and full semaphores count the number of empty and full buffers. The semaphore empty is initialized to the capacity of the buffer—BUFFER_SIZE; the semaphore full is initialized to 0.

```java
import java.util.Date;

public class Producer implements Runnable
{
   private Buffer buffer;

   public Producer(Buffer buffer) {
      this.buffer = buffer;
   }

   public void run() {
      Date message;

      while (true) {
         // nap for awhile
         SleepUtilities.nap();
         // produce an item & enter it into the buffer
         message = new Date();
         buffer.insert(message);
      }
   }
}
```

Figure 7.14   Producer thread.

```
import java.util.Date;

public class Consumer implements Runnable
{
   private Buffer buffer;

   public Consumer(Buffer buffer) {
      this.buffer = buffer;
   }

   public void run() {
      Date message;

      while (true) {
         // nap for awhile
         SleepUtilities.nap();
         // consume an item from the buffer
         message = (Date)buffer.remove();
      }
   }
}
```

Figure 7.15   Consumer thread.

The producer thread is shown in Figure 7.14. The producer alternates between sleeping for a while (the SleepUtilities class is available online) producing a message, and attempting to place that message into the buffer via the insert() method.

```
public class Factory
{
   public static void main(String args[]) {
      Buffer buffer = new BoundedBuffer();

      // now create the producer and consumer threads
      Thread producer = new Thread(new Producer(buffer));
      Thread consumer = new Thread(new Consumer(buffer));

      producer.start();
      consumer.start();
   }
}
```

Figure 7.16   The Factory class.

The consumer thread is shown in Figure 7.15. The consumer alternates between sleeping and consuming an item using the `remove()` method.

The `Factory` class (Figure 7.16) creates the producer and consumer threads, passing each a reference to the `BoundedBuffer` object.

7.6.2 The Readers–Writers Problem

A database is to be shared among several concurrent threads. Some of these threads may want only to read the database, whereas others may want to update (that is, to read and write) the database. We distinguish between these two types of threads by referring to the former as **readers** and to the latter as **writers**. Obviously, if two readers access the shared data simultaneously, no adverse affects will result. However, if a writer and some other thread (either a reader or a writer) access the database simultaneously, chaos may ensue.

To ensure that these difficulties do not arise, we require that the writers have exclusive access to the shared database. This requirement leads to the **reader–writers** problem. Since it was originally stated, this problem has been used to test nearly every new synchronization primitive. The problem has several variations, all involving priorities. The simplest one, referred to as

```
public class Reader implements Runnable
{
    private RWLock db;

    public Reader(RWLock db) {
        this.db = db;
    }

    public void run() {
        while (true) {
            // nap for awhile
            SleepUtilities.nap();

            db.acquireReadLock();

            // you have access to read from the database
            SleepUtilities.nap();

            db.releaseReadLock();
        }
    }
}
```

Figure 7.17   A reader.

the *first* readers–writers problem, requires that no reader will be kept waiting unless a writer has already obtained permission to use the shared database. In other words, no reader should wait for other readers to finish simply because a writer is waiting. The *second* readers–writers problem requires that, once a writer is ready, that writer performs its write as soon as possible. In other words, if a writer is waiting to access the object, no new readers can start reading.

We note that a solution to either problem may result in starvation. In the first case, writers may starve; in the second case, readers may starve. For this reason, other variants of the problem have been proposed. The following presents the Java class files for a solution to the first readers–writers problem. It does not address starvation. (In the exercises at the end of the chapter, you are asked to modify the solution to make it starvation-free.) Each reader thread alternates between sleeping and reading, as shown in Figure 7.17. When a reader wishes to read the database, it invokes the acquireReadLock() method; when it has finished reading, it calls releaseReadLock(). Each writer thread (Figure 7.18) performs similarly.

```java
public class Writer implements Runnable
{
    private RWLock db;

    public Writer(RWLock db) {
        this.db = db;
    }

    public void run() {
        while (true) {
            // nap for awhile
            SleepUtilities.nap();

            db.acquireWriteLock();

            // you have access to write to the database
            SleepUtilities.nap();

            db.releaseWriteLock();
        }
    }
}
```

Figure 7.18   A writer.

```
public interface RWLock
{
   public abstract void acquireReadLock();
   public abstract void acquireWriteLock();
   public abstract void releaseReadLock();
   public abstract void releaseWriteLock();
}
```

Figure 7.19   The interface for the readers–writers problem.

The methods called by each reader and writer thread are defined in the RWLock interface in Figure 7.19. The Database class in Figure 7.20 implements this interface. The readerCount keeps track of the number of readers. The

```
public class Database implements RWLock
{
    private int readerCount;
    private Semaphore mutex;
    private Semaphore db;

    public Database() {
       readerCount = 0;
       mutex = new Semaphore(1);
       db = new Semaphore(1);
    }

    public int acquireReadLock() {
       // Figure 7.21
    }

    public int releaseReadLock() {
       // Figure 7.21
    }

    public void acquireWriteLock() {
       // Figure 7.22
    }

    public void releaseWriteLock() {
       // Figure 7.22
    }
}
```

Figure 7.20   The database for the readers–writers problem.

```
public void acquireReadLock() {
    mutex.acquire();
    ++readerCount;

    // if I am the first reader tell all others
    // that the database is being read
    if (readerCount == 1)
        db.acquire();

    mutex.release();
}

public void releaseReadLock() {
    mutex.acquire();
    --readerCount;

    // if I am the last reader tell all others
    // that the database is no longer being read
    if (readerCount == 0)
        db.release();

    mutex.release();
}
```

Figure 7.21   Methods called by readers.

semaphore mutex is used to ensure mutual exclusion when readerCount is updated. The semaphore db functions as a mutual exclusion semaphore for the writers. It also is used by the readers to prevent writers from entering the database while the database is being read. The first reader performs an acquire() operation on db, thereby preventing any writers from entering the database. The final reader performs a release() operation on db. Note that, if a writer is active in the database and n readers are waiting, then one reader is queued on db and $n - 1$ readers are queued on mutex. Also observe that,

```
public void acquireWriteLock() {
    db.acquire();
}

public void releaseWriteLock() {
    db.release();
}
```

Figure 7.22   Methods called by writers.

when a writer executes db.release(), we may resume the execution of either the waiting readers or a single waiting writer. The selection is made by the scheduler.

Read–write locks are most useful in the following situations:

- In applications where it is easy to identify which threads only read shared data and which threads only write shared data.

- In applications that have more readers than writers. This is because read–write locks generally require more overhead to establish than semaphores or mutual exclusion locks, and the overhead for setting up a read–write lock is compensated by the increased concurrency of allowing multiple readers.

7.6.3 The Dining-Philosophers Problem

Consider five philosophers who spend their lives thinking and eating. The philosophers share a common circular table surrounded by five chairs, each belonging to one philosopher. In the center of the table there is a bowl of rice, and the table is laid with five single chopsticks (Figure 7.23). When a philosopher thinks, she does not interact with her colleagues. From time to time, a philosopher gets hungry and tries to pick up the two chopsticks that are closest to her (the chopsticks that are between her and her left and right neighbors). A philosopher may pick up only one chopstick at a time. Obviously, she cannot pick up a chopstick that is already in the hand of a neighbor. When a hungry philosopher has two chopsticks at the same time, she eats without releasing the chopsticks. When she is finished eating, she puts down both chopsticks and starts thinking again.

The **dining-philosophers problem** is considered a classic synchronization problem, not because of its practical importance nor because computer sci-

Figure 7.23   The situation of the dining philosophers.

entists dislike philosophers, but rather because it is an example of a large class of concurrency-control problems. It is a simple representation of the need to allocate several resources among several processes in a deadlock- and starvation-free manner.

One simple solution is to represent each chopstick by a semaphore. A philosopher tries to grab the chopstick by executing an acquire() operation on that semaphore; she releases a chopstick by executing the release() operation on the appropriate semaphores. Thus, the shared data are

```
Semaphore chopStick[] = new Semaphore[5];
```

where all the elements of chopstick are initialized to 1. The structure of philosopher i is shown in Figure 7.24.

Although this solution guarantees that no two neighboring philosophers are eating simultaneously, it nevertheless must be rejected because it has the possibility of creating a deadlock. Suppose that all five philosophers become hungry simultaneously and each grabs her left chopstick. All the elements of chopstick will now be equal to 0. When each philosopher tries to grab her right chopstick, she will be delayed forever.

Several possible remedies to the deadlock problem are listed next. These remedies prevent deadlock by placing restrictions on the philosophers:

- Allow at most four philosophers to be sitting simultaneously at the table.

- Allow a philosopher to pick up her chopsticks only if both chopsticks are available (note that she must pick them up in a critical section).

```
while (true) {
    // get left chopstick
    chopStick[i].acquire();
    // get right chopstick
    chopStick[(i + 1) % 5].acquire();

    eating();

    // return left chopstick
    chopStick[i].release();
    // return right chopstick
    chopStick[(i + 1) % 5].release();

    thinking();
}
```

Figure 7.24   The structure of philosopher i.

- Use an asymmetric solution; for example, an odd philosopher picks up first her left chopstick and then her right chopstick, whereas an even philosopher picks up her right chopstick and then her left chopstick.

In Section 7.7, we present a solution to the dining-philosophers problem that ensures freedom from deadlocks. Note, however, that any satisfactory solution to the dining-philosophers problem must guard against the possibility that one of the philosophers will starve to death. A deadlock-free solution does not necessarily eliminate the possibility of starvation.

7.7 ■ Monitors

Although semaphores provide a convenient and effective mechanism for process synchronization, their incorrect use can result in timing errors that are difficult to detect, since these errors happen only if some particular execution sequences take place, and these sequences do not always occur.

We have seen an example of such errors in the use of counters in our solution to the producer–consumer problem (Section 7.1). In that example, the timing problem happened only rarely, and even then the counter value appeared to be reasonable—off by only 1. Nevertheless, the solution is obviously not an acceptable one. It is for this reason that semaphores were introduced in the first place.

Unfortunately, such timing errors can still occur with the use of semaphores. To illustrate how, we review the semaphore solution to the critical-section problem. All processes share a semaphore variable `mutex`, which is initialized to 1. Each process must execute `mutex.acquire()` before entering the critical section and `mutex.release()` afterward. If this sequence is not observed, two processes may be in their critical sections simultaneously. Let us examine the various difficulties that may result. Note that these difficulties will arise even if a *single* process is not well behaved. This situation may be caused by an honest programming error or an uncooperative programmer.

- Suppose that a process interchanges the order in which the `acquire()` and `release()` operations on the semaphore `mutex` are executed, resulting in the following execution:

    ```
    mutex.release();
    criticalSection();
    mutex.acquire();
    ```

    In this situation, several processes may be executing in their critical sections simultaneously, violating the mutual-exclusion requirement. This error may be discovered only if several processes are simultaneously active in

their critical sections. Note that this situation may not always be repro-
ducible.

- Suppose   that   a   process   replaces   `mutex.release()`   with
  `mutex.acquire()`. That is, it executes

      ```
      mutex.acquire();
      criticalSection();
      mutex.acquire();
      ```

  In this case, a deadlock will occur.

- Suppose now that a process omits the `mutex.acquire()`, or the
  `mutex.release()`, or both.   In this case, either mutual exclusion is
  violated or a deadlock will occur.

These examples illustrate that various types of errors can be generated easily
when programmers use semaphores incorrectly to solve the critical-section
problem. Similar problems may arise in the other synchronization models that
we discussed in Section 7.6.

To deal with such errors, researchers have developed high-level language
constructs. In this section, we describe one fundamental high-level synchronization construct—the **monitor** type.

Remember that a type, or abstract data type, encapsulates private data
with public methods to operate on that data. A monitor type presents a set
of programmer-defined operations that are provided mutual exclusion within
the monitor. The monitor type also contains the declaration of variables whose
values define the state of an instance of that type, along with the bodies
of procedures or functions that operate on those variables.   The Java-like
pseudocode describing the syntax of a monitor is:

```
monitor monitor-name
{
    // variable declarations

    public entry p1 (. . .) {
        . . .
    }
    public entry p2 (. . .) {
        . . .
    }
}
```

The internal implementation of a monitor type cannot be accessed directly
by the various threads. A procedure defined within a monitor can access
only those variables that are declared locally within the monitor, along with

any formal parameters that are passed to the procedure. Similarly, the local variables can be accessed by only the local procedures.

The monitor construct prohibits concurrent access to procedures defined within the monitor. Therefore, only one thread (or process) can be active within the monitor at any one time. Consequently, the programmer does not need to code this synchronization explicitly; it is built into the monitor type.

Variables of type condition play a special role in monitors by virtue of the special operations wait and signal. A programmer who needs to write her own tailor-made synchronization scheme can define one or more variables of the condition type

        condition x,y;

The operation

        x.wait;

means that the thread invoking this operation is suspended until another thread invokes

        x.signal;

The signal operation resumes exactly one thread. If no thread is suspended, then the signal operation has no effect; that is, the state of x is as though the operation had never been executed (Figure 7.25). Contrast this scheme with the release() operation with semaphores, which always affects the state of the semaphore.

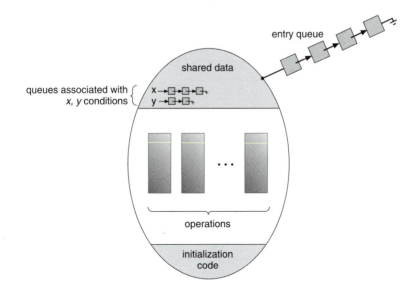

Figure 7.25   Monitor with condition variables.

Now suppose that, when the x.signal operation is invoked by a thread
P, there is a suspended thread Q associated with condition x. Clearly, if the
suspended thread Q is allowed to resume its execution, the signaling thread P
must wait. Otherwise, both P and Q would be active simultaneously within the
monitor. Note, however, that both threads can conceptually continue with their
execution. Two possibilities exist:

1. *Signal and wait:* P either waits until Q leaves the monitor or waits for
   another condition.

2. *Signal and continue:* Q either waits until P leaves the monitor or waits for
   another condition.

There are reasonable arguments in favor of adopting either option. On the
one hand, since P was already executing in the monitor, the *signal-and-continue*
method seems more reasonable. On the other hand, if we allow thread P to
continue, then by the time Q is resumed, the logical condition for which Q
was waiting may no longer hold. A compromise between these two choices
was adopted in the language Concurrent Pascal. When thread P executes the
signal operation, it immediately leaves the monitor. Hence, Q is immediately
resumed.

We illustrate these concepts by presenting a deadlock-free solution to the
dining-philosophers problem.   This solution imposes the restriction that a
philosopher may pick up her chopsticks only if both of them are available.
To code this solution, we need to distinguish among three states in which we
may find a philosopher. For this purpose, we introduce the following data
structures:

```
int[] state = new int[5];
static final int THINKING = 0;
static final int HUNGRY = 1;
static final int EATING = 2;
```

Philosopher i can set the variable state[i] = EATING only if her two neighbors are not eating; that is, the condition (state[(i + 4) % 5] != EATING)
and (state[(i + 1) % 5] != EATING) holds.

We also need to declare

```
condition[] self = new condition[5];
```

where philosopher i can delay herself when she is hungry but is unable to obtain
the chopsticks she needs.

We are now in a position to describe our solution to the dining-philosopher
problem. The distribution of the chopsticks is controlled by the monitor dp,
which is an instance of the monitor type DiningPhilosophers, whose definition using a Java-like pseudocode is shown in Figure 7.26. Each philosopher,

```
monitor DiningPhilosophers {
    int[] state = new int[5];
    static final int THINKING = 0;
    static final int HUNGRY = 1;
    static final int EATING = 2;
    condition[] self = new condition[5];

    public diningPhilosophers {
        for (int i = 0; i < 5; i++)
            state[i] = THINKING;
    }

    public entry pickUp(int i) {
        state[i] = HUNGRY;
        test(i);
        if (state[i] != EATING)
            self[i].wait;
    }

    public entry putDown(int i) {
        state[i] = THINKING;
        // test left and right neighbors
        test((i + 4) % 5);
        test((i + 1) % 5);
    }

    private test(int i) {
        if ( (state[(i + 4) % 5] != EATING) &&
            (state[i] == HUNGRY) &&
            (state[(i + 1) % 5] != EATING) ) {
                state[i] = EATING;
                self[i].signal;
        }
    }
}
```

Figure 7.26 A monitor solution to the dining-philosophers problem.

before starting to eat, must invoke the operation pickUp(). This act may result in the suspension of the philosopher thread. After the successful completion of the operation, the philosopher may eat. After she eats, the philosopher invokes the putDown() operation and starts to think. Thus, philosopher *i* must invoke the operations pickUp() and putDown() in the following sequence:

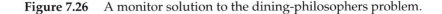

```
dp.pickUp(i);
eat();
dp.putDown(i);
```

It is easy to show that this solution ensures that no two neighboring philosophers are eating simultaneously and that no deadlocks will occur. We note,
however, that it is possible for a philosopher to starve to death. We do not
present a solution to that problem but rather ask you in the exercises to develop
one.

7.8 ■ Java Synchronization

Now that we have a grounding in synchronization theory, we can describe
how Java synchronizes the activity of threads, allowing the programmer to
develop generalized solutions enforcing mutual exclusion between threads.
When an application ensures that data remain consistent even when they are
being accessed concurrently by multiple threads, the application is said to be
thread-safe.

7.8.1 Bounded Buffer

The shared-memory solution to the bounded-buffer problem described in
Chapter 4 suffers from two problems. First, both the producer and the consumer use busy-wait loops if the buffer is either full or empty. Second, as shown
again in Section 7.1, the race condition on the variable count is shared by the
producer and the consumer. This section addresses these and other problems
while developing a solution using Java synchronization mechanisms.

7.8.1.1 Busy Wait

Busy waiting was introduced in Section 7.5.2, where we examined an implementation of the acquire() and release() semaphore operations. In that
section, we described how a process could block itself as an alternative to busy
waiting. One way to accomplish such blocking in Java is to have a thread call
the Thread.yield() method. Recall from Section 7.3.1 that, when a thread
invokes the yield() method, the thread stays in the runnable state but allows
the JVM to select another runnable thread to run. The yield() method makes
more effective use of the CPU than busy waiting does.

However, in this instance, using *either* busy waiting or yielding could lead
to another problem, known as **livelock**. Livelock is similar to deadlock; both
prevent two or more threads from proceeding, but the threads are unable to
proceed for different reasons. Deadlock occurs when every thread in a set is
blocked waiting for an event that can be caused by only another blocked thread

```
public synchronized void insert(Object item) {
    while (count == BUFFER_SIZE)
        Thread.yield();

    ++count;
    buffer[in] = item;
    in = (in + 1) % BUFFER_SIZE;
}


public synchronized Object remove() {
    Object item;

    while (count == 0)
        Thread.yield();

    --count;
    item = buffer[out];
    out = (out + 1) % BUFFER_SIZE;

    return item;
}
```

Figure 7.27   Synchronized `insert()` and `remove()` methods.

in the set. Livelock occurs when a thread continuously attempts an action that fails.

Here is one scenario that could cause livelock to occur. Recall that the JVM schedules threads using a priority-based algorithm, favoring high-priority threads over threads with lower priority. If the producer has a priority higher than that of the consumer and the buffer is full, the producer will enter the while loop and either busy-wait or yield() to another runnable thread while waiting for count to be decremented to less than BUFFER_SIZE. As long as the consumer has a priority lower than that of the producer, it may never be scheduled by the JVM to run and therefore may never be able to consume an item and free up buffer space for the producer. In this situation, the producer is livelocked waiting for the consumer to free buffer space. We see shortly that there is a better alternative than busy waiting or yielding while waiting for a desired condition to occur.

7.8.1.2 Race Condition

In Section 7.1, we saw an example of the consequences of a race condition on the shared variable count. Figure 7.27 illustrates how Java's handling of concurrent access to shared data prevents race conditions.

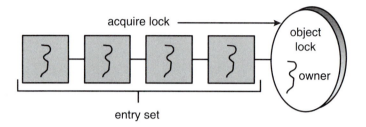

Figure 7.28   Entry set.

This situation introduces a new keyword: synchronized. Every object in Java has associated with it a single lock. (This protection is very much like that provided by a monitor. The differences are described in Section 7.8.7.) Ordinarily, when an object is being referenced (that is, when its methods are being invoked), the lock is ignored. When a method is declared to be synchronized, however, calling the method requires owning the lock for the object. If the lock is already owned by another thread, the thread calling the synchronized method blocks and is placed in the **entry set** for the object's lock. The entry set represents the set of threads waiting for the lock to become available. If the lock is available when a synchronized method is called, the calling thread becomes the owner of the object's lock and it can enter the method. The lock is released when the thread exits the method. If the entry set for the lock is not empty when the lock is released, the JVM arbitrarily selects a thread from this set to be the owner of the lock. (When we say "arbitrarily", we mean that the specification does not require that threads in this set be organized according to any specific ordering. However, in practice, most JVMs order threads in the wait set according to a FIFO policy.) Figure 7.28 illustrates how the entry set operates.

If the producer calls the insert() method, as shown in Figure 7.27, and the lock for the object is available, the producer becomes the owner of the lock; it can then enter the method, where it can alter the value of count and other shared data. If the consumer attempts to call the synchronized remove() method while the producer owns the lock, the consumer will block because the lock is unavailable. When the producer exits the insert() method, it releases the lock. The consumer can now acquire the lock and enter the remove() method.

7.8.1.3 Deadlock

At first glance, this approach appears at least to solve the problem of having a race condition on the variable count. Because both the insert() method and the remove() method are declared synchronized, we have ensured that only one thread can be active in either of these methods at a time. However, lock ownership has led to another problem.

Assume that the buffer is full and the consumer is sleeping. If the producer calls the `insert()` method, it will be allowed to continue, because the lock is available. When the producer invokes the `insert()` method, it sees that the buffer is full and performs the `yield()` method. All the while, the producer still owns the lock for the object. When the consumer awakens and tries to call the `remove()` method (which would ultimately free up buffer space for the producer), it will block because it does not own the lock for the object. Thus, both the producer and consumer are unable to proceed because (1) the

```java
public synchronized void insert(Object item) {
    while (count == BUFFER_SIZE) {
        try {
            wait();
        }
        catch (InterruptedException e) { }
    }

    ++count;
    buffer[in] = item;
    in = (in + 1) % BUFFER_SIZE;

    notify();
}

public synchronized Object remove() {
    Object item;

    while (count == 0) {
        try {
            wait();
        }
        catch (InterruptedException e) { }
    }

    --count;
    item = buffer[out];
    out = (out + 1) % BUFFER_SIZE;

    notify();

    return item;
}
```

Figure 7.29   insert() and remove() methods using wait() and notify().

producer is blocked waiting for the consumer to free space in the buffer, and (2) the consumer is blocked waiting for the producer to release the lock.

By declaring each method as synchronized, we have prevented the race condition on the shared variables. However, the presence of the yield() loop has led to a possible deadlock.

7.8.1.4 Wait and Notify

Figure 7.29 addresses the yield() loop by introducing two new Java methods: wait() and notify(). In addition to having a lock, every object also has associated with it a **wait set** consisting of a set of threads. This wait set is initially empty. When a thread enters a synchronized method, it owns the lock for the object. However, this thread may determine that it is unable to continue because a certain condition has not been met. That will happen, for example, if the producer calls the insert() method and the buffer is full. The thread then will release the lock and wait until the condition that will allow it to continue is met, thus avoiding the previous deadlock situation.

When a thread calls the wait() method, the following happens:

1. The thread releases the lock for the object.

2. The state of the thread is set to blocked.

3. The thread is placed in the wait set for the object.

Consider the example in Figure 7.29. If the producer calls the insert() method and sees that the buffer is full, it calls the wait() method. This call releases the lock, blocks the producer, and puts the producer in the wait set for the object. Because the producer has released the lock, the consumer ultimately enters the remove() method, where it frees space in the buffer for the producer. Figure 7.30 illustrates the entry and wait sets for a lock. (Note that wait() can result in an InterruptedException being thrown. We will cover this in Section 7.8.8.)

How does the consumer thread signal that the producer may now proceed? Ordinarily, when a thread exits a synchronized method, the default action is that the departing thread releases only the lock associated with the object,

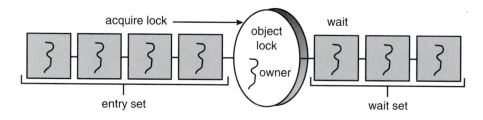

Figure 7.30   Entry and wait sets.

possibly removing a thread from the entry set and giving it ownership of the lock. However, at the end of the synchronized insert() and remove() methods, we have a call to the method notify(). The call to notify():

1. Picks an arbitrary thread T from the list of threads in the wait set

2. Moves T from the wait set to the entry set

3. Sets the state of T from blocked to runnable

T is now eligible to compete for the lock with the other threads. Once T has regained control of the lock, it returns from calling wait(), where it may check the value of count again.

Next, we describe the wait() and notify() methods in terms of the program shown in Figure 7.29. We assume that the buffer is full and the lock for the object is available.

- The producer calls the insert() method, sees that the lock is available, and enters the method. Once in the method, the producer determines that the buffer is full and calls wait(). The call to wait() releases the lock for the object, sets the state of the producer to blocked, and puts the producer in the wait set for the object.

- The consumer ultimately calls the remove() method because the lock for the object is now available. The consumer removes an item from the buffer and calls notify(). Note that the consumer still owns the lock for the object.

- The call to notify() removes the producer from the wait set for the object, moves the producer to the entry set, and sets the producer's state to runnable.

- The consumer exits the remove() method. Exiting this method releases the lock for the object.

- The producer tries to reacquire the lock and is successful. It resumes execution from the call to wait(). The producer tests the while loop, determines that room is available in the buffer, and proceeds with the remainder of the insert() method. If no thread is in the wait set for the object, the call to notify() is ignored. When the producer exits the method, it releases the lock for the object.

The BoundedBuffer class shown in Figure 7.31 represents the complete solution to the bounded-buffer problem using Java synchronization. This class may be substituted for the BoundedBuffer class that was used in the semaphore-based solution to this problem in Section 7.6.1.

```
public class BoundedBuffer implements Buffer
{
    private static final int BUFFER_SIZE = 5;

    private int count, in, out;
    private Object[] buffer;

    public BoundedBuffer() {
        // buffer is initially empty
        count = 0;
        in = 0;
        out = 0;
        buffer = new Object[BUFFER_SIZE];
    }

    public synchronized void insert(Object item) {
        // Figure 7.29
    }

    public synchronized Object remove() {
        // Figure 7.29
    }
}
```

Figure 7.31   Bounded buffer.

7.8.2 Multiple Notifications

As described in Section 7.8.1.4, the call to notify() arbitrarily selects a thread from the list of threads in the wait set for an object. This approach works fine when only one thread is in the wait set, but consider what can happen when there are multiple threads in the wait set and more than one condition for which to wait. It is possible that a thread whose condition has not yet been met will be the thread that receives the notification.

Suppose, for example, that there are five threads $\{T1, T2, T3, T4, T5\}$ and a shared variable turn indicating which thread's turn it is. When a thread wishes to do work, it calls the doWork() method in Figure 7.32. Only the thread whose number matches the value of turn can proceed; all other threads must wait their turn.

Assume the following:

- turn = 3.

- $T1, T2,$ and $T4$ are in the wait set for the object.

- $T3$ is currently in the doWork() method.

```
// myNumber is the number of the thread
// that wishes to do some work
public synchronized void doWork(int myNumber) {
    while (turn != myNumber) {
        try {
            wait();
        }
        catch (InterruptedException e) { }
    }

    // do some work for awhile .  .  .

    // Finished working.  Now indicate to the
    // next waiting thread that it is its
    // turn to do some work.

    if (turn < 5)
        ++turn;
    else
        turn = 1;

    notify();
}
```

Figure 7.32   doWork() method.

When thread *T3* is done, it sets turn to 4 (indicating that it is *T4*'s turn) and calls notify(). The call to notify() arbitrarily picks a thread from the wait set. If *T2* receives the notification, it resumes execution from the call to wait() and tests the condition in the while loop. *T2* sees that this is not its turn, so it calls wait() again. Ultimately, *T3* and *T5* will call doWork() and will also invoke the wait() method, since it is the turn for neither *T3* nor *T5*. Now, all five threads are blocked in the wait set for the object. Thus, we have another deadlock to handle.

Because the call to notify() picks a single thread at random from the wait set, the developer has no control over which thread is chosen. Fortunately, Java provides a mechanism that allows all threads in the wait set to be notified. The notifyAll() method is similar to notify(), except that *every* waiting thread is removed from the wait set and placed in the entry set. If the call to notify() in doWork() is replaced with a call to notifyAll(), when *T3* finishes and sets turn to 4, it calls notifyAll(). This call has the effect of removing *T1*, *T2*, and *T4* from the wait set. The three threads then compete for the object's lock once again. Ultimately, *T1* and *T2* call wait(), and only *T4* proceeds with the doWork() method.

In sum, the notifyAll() method is a mechanism that wakes up all waiting threads and lets the threads decide among themselves which of them should run next. In general, notifyAll() is a more expensive operation than notify() because it wakes up all threads, but it is regarded as a more conservative strategy appropriate for situations in which multiple threads may be in the wait set for an object.

In the following section, we look at a Java-based solution to the readers–writers problem that requires the use of both notify() and notifyAll().

7.8.3 The Readers–Writers Problem

We can now provide a solution to the first readers–writers problem by using Java synchronization. The methods called by each reader and writer thread are defined in the Database class in Figure 7.33 which implements the RWLock interface shown in Figure 7.19. The readerCount keeps track of the num-

```
public class Database implements RWLock {
    private int readerCount;
    private boolean dbWriting;

    public Database() {
        readerCount = 0;
        dbWriting = false;
    }

    public synchronized void acquireReadLock() {
        // Figure 7.34
    }

    public synchronized void releaseReadLock() {
        // Figure 7.34
    }

    public synchronized void acquireWriteLock() {
        // Figure 7.35
    }

    public synchronized void releaseWriteLock() {
        // Figure 7.35
    }
}
```

Figure 7.33   The database.

```
public synchronized void acquireReadLock() {
    while (dbWriting == true) {
        try {
            wait();
        }
        catch(InterruptedException e) { }
    }

    ++readerCount;
}

public synchronized int releaseReadLock() {
    --readerCount;

    // if I am the last reader tell writers
    // that the database is no longer being read
    if (readerCount == 0)
        notify();
}
```

Figure 7.34   Methods called by readers.

ber of readers; a value > 0 indicates that the database is currently being read. dbWriting is a boolean variable indicating whether the database is currently being accessed by a writer. acquireReadLock(), releaseRead-Lock(), acquireWriteLock(), and releaseWriteLock() are all declared as synchronized to ensure mutual exclusion to the shared variables.

When a writer wishes to begin writing, it first checks whether the database is currently being either read or written. If the database is being read or written, the writer enters the wait set for the object. Otherwise, it sets dbWriting to true. When a writer is finished, it sets dbWriting to false. When a reader invokes acquireReadLock(), it first checks whether the database is currently being written. If the database is unavailable, the reader enters the wait set for the object; otherwise, it increments readerCount. The final reader calling releaseReadLock() invokes notify(), thereby notifying a waiting writer. When a writer invokes releaseWriteLock(), however, it calls the notifyAll() method rather than notify(). Consider the effect on readers. If several readers wish to read the database while it is being written, and the writer invokes notify() once it has finished writing, only one reader will receive the notification. Other readers will remain in the wait set even though the database is available for reading. By invoking notifyAll(), a departing writer is ensured of notifying all waiting readers.

```
public synchronized void acquireWriteLock() {
    while (readerCount > 0 || dbWriting == true) {
        try {
            wait();
        }
        catch(InterruptedException e) { }
    }

    // once there are either no readers or writers
    // indicate that the database is being written
    dbWriting = true;
}

public synchronized void releaseWriteLock() {
    dbWriting = false;

    notifyAll();
}
```

Figure 7.35   Methods called by writers.

7.8.4 Block Synchronization

The amount of time between when a lock is acquired and when it is released is defined as the **scope** of the lock. Java also allows blocks of code to be declared as synchronized because a synchronized method that has only a small percentage of its code manipulating shared data may yield a scope that is too large. In such an instance, it may be better to synchronize only the block of code that manipulates shared data than to synchronize the entire method. Such a design results in a smaller lock scope. Thus, in addition to declaring synchronized methods, Java also allows block synchronization, as illustrated in Figure 7.36. Access to the criticalSection() method in Figure 7.36 requires ownership of the lock for the mutexLock object.

We can also use the wait() and notify() methods in a synchronized block. The only difference is that they must be invoked with the same object that is being used for synchronization. This approach is shown in Figure 7.37.

7.8.5 Java Semaphores

Java does not provide a semaphore, but we can easily construct one using standard synchronization mechanisms. Declaring the acquire() and release() methods as synchronized ensures that each operation is performed atomically. The Semaphore class shown in Figure 7.38 implements a basic counting semaphore. We leave it as an exercise to modify the Semaphore class so that it acts as a binary semaphore.

```
Object mutexLock = new Object();
    .   .   .
public void someMethod() {
    nonCriticalSection();

    synchronized(mutexLock) {
        criticalSection();
    }

    nonCriticalSection();
}
```

Figure 7.36   Block synchronization.

7.8.6 Synchronization Rules

The synchronized keyword is a straightforward construct, but it is important to know a few rules about its behavior.

1. A thread that owns the lock for an object can enter another synchronized method (or block) for the same object. This is known as a **recursive lock**.

2. A thread can nest synchronized method invocations for different objects. Thus, a thread can simultaneously own the lock for several different objects.

3. If a method is not declared synchronized, then it can be invoked regardless of lock ownership, even while another synchronized method for the same object is executing.

4. If the wait set for an object is empty, then a call to notify() or notifyAll() has no effect.

```
Object mutexLock = new Object();
    .   .   .
synchronized(mutexLock) {
    try {
        mutexLock.wait();
    }
    catch (InterruptedException ie) { }
}

synchronized(mutexLock) {
    mutexLock.notify();
}
```

Figure 7.37   Block synchronization using wait() and notify().

```
public class Semaphore
{
    private int value;

    public Semaphore() {
        value = 0;
    }

    public Semaphore(int value) {
        this.value = value;
    }

    public synchronized void acquire() {
        while (value == 0) {
            try {
                wait();
            }
            catch (InterruptedException e) { }
        }

        value--;
    }

    public synchronized void release() {
        ++value;

        notify();
    }
}
```

Figure 7.38   Java semaphore implementation.

5. wait(), notify(), and notifyAll() may only be invoked from synchronized methods or blocks; otherwise, an IllegalMonitorStateException is thrown.

7.8.7 Java Monitors

Many programming languages have incorporated the idea of the monitor (discussed in Section 7.7), including Concurrent Pascal, Mesa, NeWs, and Java. Many other modern programming languages have provided some type of concurrency support using a mechanism similar to monitors. We now discuss the relationship of monitors in the strict sense to Java monitors.

We have already described how Java synchronization uses an object's lock. In many ways, this lock acts as a monitor. Every Java object thus has an associated monitor. A thread can acquire an object's monitor by entering a synchronized method or block.

With monitors, the wait and signal operations can be applied to named condition variables, allowing a thread to wait for a specific condition or to be notified when a specific condition has been met. However, Java does not provide support for named condition variables. Furthermore, each Java monitor is associated with just one unnamed condition variable. The wait(), notify(), and notifyAll() operations may apply to only this single condition variable. When a Java thread is awakened via notify() or notifyAll(), it receives no information about why it was awakened. It is up to the reactivated thread to check for itself whether the condition for which it was waiting has been met.

Java monitors use the signal-and-continue approach: When a thread is signaled with the notify() method, it can acquire the lock for the monitor only when the notifying thread exits the synchronized method or block.

7.8.8 Handling InterruptedException

Note that invoking the wait() method requires placing it in a try-catch block, as wait() may result in an InterruptedException being thrown. Recall from Chapter 5 that the interrupt() method is the preferred technique for interrupting a thread in Java. When interrupt() is invoked on a thread, the **interruption status** of that thread is set. A thread can check its interruption status using the isInterrupted() method, which returns true if its interruption status is set.

The wait() method also checks the interruption status of a thread. If it is set, wait() will throw an InterruptedException. This allows interruption of a thread that is blocked in the wait set. (It should also be noted that once an InterruptedException is thrown, the interrupted status of the thread is cleared.) For code clarity and simplicity, we choose to ignore this exception in our code examples. That is, all calls to wait() appear as:

```
try {
    wait();
}
catch (InterruptedException ie) { /* ignore */ }
```

However, if we chose to handle InterruptedException, we would permit the interruption of a thread blocked in a wait set. Such a strategy allows for more robust multithreaded applications, as it provides a mechanism for interrupting a thread that is blocked trying to acquire a mutual exclusion lock. One strategy for handling this is to allow the InterruptedException to propagate. That is, in methods where wait() is invoked, we first remove the try-catch blocks when calling wait() and declare such methods as throwing InterruptedException. By doing this, we are allowing the InterruptedException to propagate from the method where wait() is being invoked.

```
public class Semaphore
{
    private int value;

    public Semaphore() {
        value = 0;
    }

    public Semaphore(int value) {
        this.value = value;
    }

    public synchronized void acquire()
            throws InterruptedException {
        while (value == 0)
            wait();

        value--;
    }

    public synchronized void release() {
        ++value;

        notify();
    }
}
```

Figure 7.39   Handling InterruptedException with Java semaphores.

As an example, the acquire() method in the Semaphore class shown in Figure 7.38 invokes wait(). The call to wait() is placed in a try-catch block; but if an InterruptedException is caught, we ignore it. Handling the InterruptedException according to the strategy outlined above results in the Semaphore class shown in Figure 7.39. Note that because acquire() is now declared as throwing an InterruptedException, this approach of handling InterruptedException now requires placing acquire() in a try-catch block. However, it does allow interrupting a thread that is blocked in the acquire() method of a semaphore.

7.9 ■ Synchronization Examples

We next describe the synchronization mechanisms provided by the Solaris, Windows XP, and Linux operating systems, as well as the Pthreads API. As will become clear in this section, there are subtle and significant variations in the synchronization methods available in differing systems.

7.9.1 Synchronization in Solaris

To control access to critical sections, Solaris provides adaptive mutexes, condition variables, semaphores, reader–writer locks, and turnstiles. Solaris implements semaphores and condition variables essentially as they arepresented in Sections 7.5 and 7.7. In this section, we describe the adaptive mutexes, reader–writer locks, and turnstiles.

An **adaptive mutex** protects access to every critical data item. On a multiprocessor system, an adaptive mutex starts as a standard semaphore implemented as a spinlock. If the data are locked and therefore already in use, the adaptive mutex does one of two things. If the lock is held by a thread that is currently running on another CPU, the thread spins while waiting for the lock to become available, because the thread holding the lock is likely to be done soon. If the thread holding the lock is not currently in run state, the thread blocks, going to sleep until it is awakened by the release of the lock. It is put to sleep so that it will avoid spinning when the lock will not be freed reasonably quickly. A lock held by a sleeping thread is likely to be in this category. On a uniprocessor system, the thread holding the lock is never running if the lock is being tested by another thread, because only one thread can run at a time. Therefore, on a uniprocessor system, threads always sleep rather than spin if they encounter a lock.

Solaris uses the adaptive-mutex method to protect only those data that are accessed by short code segments. That is, a mutex is used if a lock will be held for less than a few hundred instructions. If the code segment is longer than that, spin waiting will be exceedingly inefficient. For these longer code segments, condition variables and semaphores are used. If the desired lock is already held, the thread issues a wait and sleeps. When a thread frees the lock, it issues a signal to the next sleeping thread in the queue. The extra cost of putting a thread to sleep and waking it, and of the associated context switches, is less than the cost of wasting several hundred instructions waiting in a spinlock.

Readers–writers locks are used to protect data that are accessed frequently but are usually accessed in a read-only manner. In these circumstances, readers–writers locks are more efficient than semaphores, because multiple threads can read data concurrently, whereas semaphores always serialize access to the data. Readers–writers locks are relatively expensive to implement, so again they are used on only long sections of code.

Solaris uses turnstiles to order the list of threads waiting to acquire either an adaptive mutex or a reader–writer lock. A **turnstile** is a queue structure containing threads blocked on a lock. For example, if one thread currently owns the lock for a synchronized object, all other threads trying to acquire the lock will block and enter the turnstile for that lock. When the lock is released, the kernel selects a thread from the turnstile as the next owner of the lock. Each synchronized object with at least one thread blocked on the object's lock requires a separate turnstile. However, rather than associating a turnstile with each synchronized object, Solaris gives each kernel thread its own turnstile. Because a thread can be blocked only on one object at a time, this is more efficient than having a turnstile per object.

The turnstile for the first thread to block on a synchronized object becomes the turnstile for the object itself. Subsequent threads blocking on the lock will be added to this turnstile. When the initial thread ultimately releases the lock, it gains a new turnstile from a list of free turnstiles maintained by the kernel. To prevent a **priority inversion**, turnstiles are organized according to a **priority-inheritance protocol** (Section 6.5). This means that if a lower-priority thread currently holds a lock that a higher-priority thread is blocked on, the thread with the lower priority will temporarily inherit the priority of the higher-priority thread. Upon releasing the lock, the thread will revert to its original priority.

Note that the locking mechanisms used by the kernel are implemented for user-level threads as well, so the same types of locks are available inside and outside the kernel. A crucial implementation difference is the priority-inheritance protocol. Kernel-locking routines adhere to the kernel priority-inheritance methods used by the scheduler, as described in Section 6.5; user-level thread-locking mechanisms do not provide this functionality.

To optimize Solaris performance, developers have refined and fine-tuned the locking methods. Because locks are used frequently and typically are used for crucial kernel functions, tuning their implementation and use can produce great performance gains.

7.9.2 Synchronization in Windows XP

The Windows XP operating system is a multithreaded kernel that also provides support for real-time applications and multiple processors. When the Windows XP kernel accesses a global resource on a uniprocessor system, it temporarily masks interrupts for all interrupt handlers that may also access the global resource. On a multiprocessor system, Windows XP protects access to global resources using spinlocks. Just as in Solaris, the kernel uses spinlocks only to protect short code segments. Furthermore, for reasons of efficiency, the kernel ensures that a thread will never be preempted while holding a spinlock. For thread synchronization outside the kernel, Windows XP provides **dispatcher objects**. Using a dispatcher object, threads synchronize according to several different mechanisms, including mutexes, semaphores, and events. The system protects shared data by requiring a thread to gain ownership of a mutex to access the data and to release ownership when it is finished. **Events** are similar to condition variables; that is, they may notify a waiting thread when a desired condition occurs.

Dispatcher objects may be in either a **signaled** or a **nonsignaled** state. A signaled state indicates that an object is available and a thread will not block when acquiring the object. A nonsignaled state indicates that an object is not available and a thread will block when attempting to acquire the object. There is a relationship between the state of a dispatcher object and the state of a thread. When a thread blocks on a nonsignaled dispatcher object, its state changes from ready to waiting, and the thread is placed in a waiting queue for that object. When the state for the dispatcher object moves to signaled, the kernel checks whether any threads are waiting on the object. If so, the kernel moves one thread—or possibly more threads—from the waiting state to the ready state, where they can resume executing. The number of threads the kernel selects from the waiting queue depends on the type of dispatcher object they are waiting on. The kernel will select only one thread from the waiting queue for a mutex, since a mutex object may be "owned" by only a single thread. For an event object, the kernel will select all threads that are waiting for the event.

We can use a mutex lock as an illustrating example of dispatcher objects and thread states. If a thread tries to acquire a mutex dispatcher object that is in a nonsignaled state, that thread will be suspended and placed in a waiting queue for the mutex object. When the mutex moves to the signaled state (because another thread has released the lock on the mutex), the thread waiting at the front of the queue on the mutex will:

1. be moved from the wait to the ready state and

2. acquire the mutex lock.

7.9.3 Synchronization in Linux

The Linux kernel is nonpreemptive while running in kernel mode. This means that a process running in kernel mode cannot be preempted by a process with a higher priority. Such a policy simplifies the design of the kernel; race conditions on kernel data structures are avoided, since a process cannot be preempted while running in the kernel. It is possible, however, that an interrupt may occur while a process is running in kernel mode. Therefore, for critical sections consisting of short sections of code, Linux disables interrupts. This is only effective for short critical sections, as it is undesirable to disable interrupts for long periods of time. For longer critical sections, Linux uses semaphores to lock kernel data. Examples of kernel data structures that are locked by semaphores include structures for memory management and file systems. On multiprocessor machines, Linux uses spinlocks as well as semaphores to protect shared kernel data structures.

7.9.4 Synchronization in Pthreads

The Pthreads API provides mutex locks and condition variables for thread synchronization. This API is available for programmers and is not part of any particular kernel. Mutex locks are the fundamental synchronization technique used with Pthreads. A mutex lock is used to protect critical sections of code— that is, a thread acquires the lock before entering a critical section and releases it upon exiting the critical section. Condition variables in Pthreads behave much as described in Section 7.7. Many systems that implement Pthreads also provide semaphores, although they are not part of the Pthreads standard and instead belong to the POSIX standard POSIX.1b.

There are extensions to the Pthreads API, although they are not considered portable. Such extensions include read–write locks and spin locks.

7.10 ■ Atomic Transactions

The mutual exclusion of critical sections ensures that the critical sections are executed atomically. That is, if two critical sections are executed concurrently, the result is equivalent to their sequential execution in some unknown order. Although this property is useful in many application domains, in other cases we would like to make sure that a critical section forms a single logical unit of work that either is performed in its entirety or is not performed at all. An example is funds transfer, in which one account is debited and another is credited. Clearly, it is essential for data consistency to ensure either that both the credit and debit occur or that neither occur.

The remainder of this section is related to the field of database systems. **Databases** are concerned with the storage and retrieval of data and with the consistency of the data. Recently, there has been an upsurge of interest in using database-systems techniques in operating systems. Operating systems can be viewed as manipulators of data; as such, they can benefit from the advanced techniques and models available from database research. For instance, many of the ad hoc techniques used in operating systems to manage files could be more flexible and powerful if more formal database methods were used in their place. In Sections 7.10.2 to 7.10.4, we describe what these database techniques are and how they can be used by operating systems.

7.10.1 System Model

A collection of instructions (or operations) that performs a single logical function is called a **transaction**. A major issue in processing transactions is the preservation of atomicity despite the possibility of failures within the computer system. In this section, we describe various mechanisms for ensuring transaction atomicity. We first consider an environment where only one transaction can execute at a time. Then, we consider the case where multiple transactions are active simultaneously.

A transaction is a program unit that accesses and possibly updates various data items that may reside on the disk within some files. From our point of view, a transaction is simply a sequence of read and write operations, terminated by either a commit operation or an abort operation. A commit operation signifies that the transaction has terminated its execution successfully, whereas an abort operation signifies that the transaction had to cease its normal execution because of some logical error or because of a system failure. A terminated transaction that has completed its execution successfully is **committed**; otherwise, it is **aborted**. The effect of a committed transaction cannot be undone by abortion of the transaction.

Since an aborted transaction may already have modified the various data that it has accessed, the state of these data may not be the same as it would be had the transaction executed atomically. So that the atomicity property is ensured, an aborted transaction must have no effect on the state of the data that it has already modified. Thus, the state of the data accessed by an aborted transaction must be restored to what it was just before the transaction started executing. We say that such a transaction has been **rolled back**. It is part of the responsibility of the system to ensure this property.

To determine how the system should ensure atomicity, we need first to identify the properties of devices used for storing the various data accessed by the transactions. Various types of storage media are distinguished by their relative speed, capacity, and resilience to failure.

- **Volatile storage:** Information residing in volatile storage does not usually survive system crashes. Examples of such storage are main and cache memory. Access to volatile storage is extremely fast, both because of the speed of the memory access itself and because it is possible to access directly any data item in volatile storage.

- **Nonvolatile storage:** Information residing in nonvolatile storage usually survives system crashes. Examples of media for such storage are disks and magnetic tapes. Disks are more reliable than main memory but less reliable than magnetic tapes. Both disks and tapes, however, are subject to failure, which may result in loss of information. Currently, nonvolatile storage is slower than volatile storage by several orders of magnitude, because disk and tape devices are electromechanical and require physical motion to access data.

- **Stable storage:** Information residing in stable storage is *never* lost (*never* should be taken with a grain of salt, since theoretically such absolutes cannot be guaranteed). To implement an approximation of such storage, we need to replicate information in several nonvolatile storage caches (usually disk) with independent failure modes and to update the information in a controlled manner (Section 14.7).

Here, we are concerned only with ensuring transaction atomicity in an environment where failures result in the loss of information on volatile storage.

7.10.2 Log-Based Recovery

One way to ensure atomicity is to record, on stable storage, information describing all the modifications made by the transaction to the various data it accessed. The most widely used method for achieving this form of recording is **write-ahead logging**. The system maintains, on stable storage, a data structure called the **log**. Each log record describes a single operation of a transaction write and has the following fields:

- **Transaction name:** The unique name of the transaction that performed the `write` operation

- **Data item name:** The unique name of the data item written

- **Old value:** The value of the data item prior to the `write` operation

- **New value:** The value that the data item will have after the write

Other special log records exist to record significant events during transaction processing, such as the start of a transaction and the commit or abort of a transaction.

Before a transaction T_i starts its execution, the record $< T_i$ `starts`$>$ is written to the log. During its execution, any `write` operation by T_i is *preceded* by the writing of the appropriate new record to the log. When T_i commits, the record $< T_i$ `commits`$>$ is written to the log.

Because the information in the log is used in reconstructing the state of the data items accessed by the various transactions, we cannot allow the actual update to a data item to take place before the corresponding log record is written out to stable storage. We therefore require that, prior to the execution of a `write`(X) operation, the log records corresponding to X be written onto stable storage.

Note the performance penalty inherent in this system. Two physical writes are required for every logical write requested. Also, more storage is needed: for the data themselves and for the log of the changes. In cases where the data are extremely important and fast failure recovery is necessary, however, the price is worth the functionality.

Using the log, the system can handle any failure that does not result in the loss of information on nonvolatile storage. The recovery algorithm uses two procedures:

- undo(T_i), which restores the value of all data updated by transaction T_i to the old values

- redo(T_i), which sets the value of all data updated by transaction T_i to the new values

The set of data updated by T_i and their respective old and new values can be found in the log.

The undo and redo operations must be *idempotent* (that is, multiple executions of an operation must have the same result as does one execution) to
guarantee correct behavior, even if a failure occurs during the recovery process.

If a transaction T_i aborts, then we can restore the state of the data that
it has updated by simply executing undo(T_i). If a system failure occurs, we
restore the state of all updated data by consulting the log to determine which
transactions need to be redone and which need to be undone. This classification
of transactions is accomplished as follows:

- Transaction T_i needs to be undone if the log contains the $< T_i$ starts$>$
  record but does not contain the $< T_i$ commits$>$ record.

- Transaction T_i needs to be redone if the log contains both the $< T_i$ starts$>$
  and the $< T_i$ commits$>$ records.

7.10.3 Checkpoints

When a system failure occurs, we must consult the log to determine those
transactions that need to be redone and those that need to be undone. In
principle, we need to search the entire log to make these determinations. There
are two major drawbacks to this approach:

1. The searching process is time-consuming.

2. Most of the transactions that, according to our algorithm, need to be redone
   have already actually updated the data that the log says they need to
   modify. Although redoing the data modifications will cause no harm (due
   to idempotency), it will nevertheless cause recovery to take longer.

To reduce these types of overhead, we introduce the concept of **checkpoints**. During execution, the system maintains the write-ahead log. In addition, the system periodically performs checkpoints that require the following
sequence of actions to take place:

1. Output all log records currently residing in volatile storage (usually main
   memory) onto stable storage.

2. Output all modified data residing in volatile storage to the stable storage.

3. Output a log record <checkpoint> onto stable storage.

The presence of a <checkpoint> record in the log allows the system to
streamline its recovery procedure. Consider a transaction T_i that committed
prior to the checkpoint. The $< T_i$ commits$>$ record appears in the log before the
<checkpoint> record. Any modifications made by T_i must have been written

to stable storage either prior to the checkpoint or as part of the checkpoint itself. Thus, at recovery time, there is no need to perform a redo operation on T_i.

This observation allows us to refine our previous recovery algorithm. After a failure has occurred, the recovery routine examines the log to determine the most recent transaction T_i that started executing before the most recent checkpoint took place. It finds such a transaction by searching the log backward to find the first <checkpoint> record and then finding the subsequent $< T_i$ start> record.

Once transaction T_i has been identified, the redo and undo operations need be applied only to transaction T_i and all transactions T_j that started executing after transaction T_i. Let us denote these transactions by the set T. The remainder of the log can be ignored. The required recovery operations are as follows:

- For all transactions T_k in T such that the record $< T_k$ commits> appears in the log, execute redo(T_k).

- For all transactions T_k in T that have no $< T_k$ commits> record in the log, execute undo(T_k).

7.10.4 Concurrent Atomic Transactions

Because each transaction is atomic, the concurrent execution of transactions must be equivalent to the case where these transactions are executed serially in some arbitrary order. This property, called **serializability**, can be maintained by simply executing each transaction within a critical section. That is, all transactions share a common semaphore *mutex*, which is initialized to 1. When a transaction starts executing, its first action is to execute wait(*mutex*). After the transaction either commits or aborts, it executes signal(*mutex*).

Although this scheme ensures the atomicity of all concurrently executing transactions, it is nevertheless too restrictive. As we shall see, in many cases we can allow transactions to overlap their execution while maintaining serializability. A number of different **concurrency-control** algorithms ensure serializability. These are described below.

7.10.4.1 Serializability

Consider a system with two data items A and B that are both read and written by two transactions T_0 and T_1. Suppose that these transactions are executed atomically in the order T_0 followed by T_1. This execution sequence, which is called a **schedule,** is represented in Figure 7.40. In schedule 1 of Figure 7.40, the sequence of instruction steps is in chronological order from top to bottom, with instructions of T_0 appearing in the left column and instructions of T_1 appearing in the right column.

A schedule where each transaction is executed atomically is called a **serial schedule**. Each serial schedule consists of a sequence of instructions from

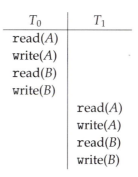

Figure 7.40 Schedule 1: A serial schedule in which T_0 is followed by T_1.

various transactions where the instructions belonging to one single transaction appear together. Thus, for a set of n transactions, there exist $n!$ valid serial schedules. Each serial schedule is correct, because it is equivalent to the atomic execution of the various participating transactions, in some arbitrary order.

If we allow the two transactions to overlap their execution, then the resulting schedule is no longer serial. A **nonserial schedule** does not necessarily imply an incorrect execution (that is, an execution that is not equivalent to one represented by a serial schedule). To see that this is the case, we need to define the notion of **conflicting operations**.

Consider a schedule S in which there are two consecutive operations O_i and O_j of transactions T_i and T_j, respectively. We say that O_i and O_j *conflict* if they access the same data item and at least one of these operations is a `write` operation. To illustrate the concept of conflicting operations, we consider the nonserial schedule 2 of Figure 7.41. The `write(A)` operation of T_0 conflicts with the `read(A)` operation of T_1. However, the `write(A)` operation of T_1 does not conflict with the `read(B)` operation of T_0, because the two operations access different data items.

Let O_i and O_j be consecutive operations of a schedule S. If O_i and O_j are operations of different transactions and O_i and O_j do not conflict, then we can

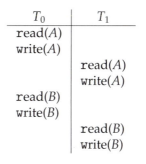

Figure 7.41 Schedule 2: A concurrent serializable schedule.

swap the order of O_i and O_j to produce a new schedule S'. We expect S to be equivalent to S', as all operations appear in the same order in both schedules, except for O_i and O_j, whose order does not matter.

We can illustrate the swapping idea by considering again schedule 2 of Figure 7.41. As the write(A) operation of T_1 does not conflict with the read(B) operation of T_0, we can swap these operations to generate an equivalent schedule. Regardless of the initial system state, both schedules produce the same final system state. Continuing with this procedure of swapping nonconflicting operations, we get:

- Swap the read(B) operation of T_0 with the read(A) operation of T_1.

- Swap the write(B) operation of T_0 with the write(A) operation of T_1.

- Swap the write(B) operation of T_0 with the read(A) operation of T_1.

The final result of these swaps is schedule 1 in Figure 7.40, which is a serial schedule. Thus, we have shown that schedule 2 is equivalent to a serial schedule. This result implies that, regardless of the initial system state, schedule 2 will produce the same final state as will some serial schedule.

If a schedule S can be transformed into a serial schedule S' by a series of swaps of nonconflicting operations, we say that a schedule S is **conflict serializable**. Thus, schedule 2 is conflict serializable, because it can be transformed into the serial schedule 1.

7.10.4.2 Locking Protocol

One way to ensure serializability is to associate with each data item a lock and to require that each transaction follow a **locking protocol** that governs how locks are acquired and released. There are various modes in which a data item can be locked. In this section, we restrict our attention to two modes:

- **Shared:** If a transaction T_i has obtained a shared-mode lock (denoted by S) on data item Q, then T_i can read this item but cannot write Q.

- **Exclusive:** If a transaction T_i has obtained an exclusive-mode lock (denoted by X) on data item Q, then T_i can both read and write Q.

We require that every transaction request a lock in an appropriate mode on data item Q, depending on the type of operations it will perform on Q.

To access a data item Q, transaction T_i must first lock Q in the appropriate mode. If Q is not currently locked, then the lock is granted, and T_i can now access it. However, if the data item Q is currently locked by some other transaction, then T_i may have to wait. More specifically, suppose that T_i requests an exclusive lock on Q. In this case, T_i must wait until the lock on Q is released. If T_i requests a shared lock on Q, then T_i must wait if Q is locked in exclusive mode. Otherwise, it can obtain the lock and access Q. Notice that this scheme is quite similar to the readers–writers algorithm discussed in Section 7.6.2.

A transaction may unlock a data item that it locked at an earlier point. It must, however, hold a lock on a data item as long as it accesses that item. Moreover, it is not always desirable for a transaction to unlock a data item immediately after its last access of that data item, because serializability may not be ensured.

One protocol that ensures serializability is the **two-phase locking protocol**. This protocol requires that each transaction issue lock and unlock requests in two phases:

- **Growing phase:** A transaction may obtain locks but may not release any lock.

- **Shrinking phase:** A transaction may release locks but may not obtain any new locks.

Initially, a transaction is in the growing phase. The transaction acquires locks as needed. Once the transaction releases a lock, it enters the shrinking phase, and no more lock requests can be issued.

The two-phase locking protocol generally ensures conflict serializability (Exercise 7.21). It does not, however, ensure freedom from deadlock. To improve performance over two-phase locking, we need either to have additional information about the transactions or to impose some structure or ordering on the set of data.

7.10.4.3 Timestamp-Based Protocols

In the locking protocols described above, the serializability order of every pair of conflicting transactions is determined at execution time by the first lock that they both request and that involves incompatible modes. Another method for determining the serializability order is to select an ordering among transactions in advance. The most common method for doing so is to use a **timestamp-ordering** scheme.

With each transaction T_i in the system, we associate a unique fixed timestamp, denoted by $TS(T_i)$. This timestamp is assigned by the system before the transaction T_i starts execution. If a transaction T_i has been assigned timestamp $TS(T_i)$, and later on a new transaction T_j enters the system, then $TS(T_i) < TS(T_j)$. There are two simple methods for implementing this scheme:

- Use the value of the system clock as the timestamp; that is, a transaction's timestamp is equal to the value of the clock when the transaction enters the system. This method will not work for transactions that occur on separate systems or for processors that do not share a clock.

- Use a logical counter as the timestamp; that is, a transaction's timestamp is equal to the value of the counter when the transaction enters the system. The counter is incremented after a new timestamp is assigned.

The timestamps of the transactions determine the serializability order. Thus, if $TS(T_i) < TS(T_j)$, then the system must ensure that the produced schedule is equivalent to a serial schedule in which transaction T_i appears before transaction T_j.

To implement this scheme, we associate with each data item Q two timestamp values:

- **W-timestamp**(Q), which denotes the largest timestamp of any transaction that executed `write`(Q) successfully

- **R-timestamp**(Q), which denotes the largest timestamp of any transaction that executed `read`(Q) successfully

These timestamps are updated whenever a new `read`(Q) or `write`(Q) instruction is executed.

The timestamp-ordering protocol ensures that any conflicting `read` and `write` operations are executed in timestamp order. This protocol operates as follows:

- Suppose that transaction T_i issues `read`(Q):

  - If $TS(T_i) <$ W-timestamp(), then T_i needs to read a value of Q that was already overwritten. Hence, the `read` operation is rejected, and T_i is rolled back.

  - If $TS(T_i) \geq$ W-timestamp(Q), then the `read` operation is executed, and R-timestamp(Q) is set to the maximum of R-timestamp(Q) and $TS(T_i)$.

- Suppose that transaction T_i issues `write`(Q):

  - If $TS(T_i) <$ R-timestamp(Q), then the value of Q that T_i is producing was needed previously and T_i assumed that this value would never be produced. Hence, the `write` operation is rejected, and T_i is rolled back.

  - If $TS(T_i) <$ W-timestamp(Q), then T_i is attempting to write an obsolete value of Q. Hence, this `write` operation is rejected, and T_i is rolled back.

  - Otherwise, the `write` operation is executed.

A transaction T_i that is rolled back by the concurrency-control scheme as a result of the issuing of either a `read` or `write` operation is assigned a new timestamp and is restarted.

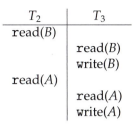

T_2	T_3
read(B)	
	read(B)
	write(B)
read(A)	
	read(A)
	write(A)

Figure 7.42 Schedule 3: A schedule possible under the timestamp protocol.

To illustrate the timestamp-ordering protocol, we consider schedule 3 of Figure 7.42 with transactions T_2 and T_3. We assume that a transaction is assigned a timestamp immediately before its first instruction. Thus, in schedule 3, $TS(T_2) < TS(T_3)$, and the schedule is possible under the timestamp protocol.

This execution can also be produced by the two-phase locking protocol. However, some schedules are possible under the two-phase locking protocol but not under the timestamp protocol, and vice versa (Exercise 7.22).

The timestamp-ordering protocol ensures conflict serializability. This capability follows from the fact that conflicting operations are processed in timestamp order. The protocol also ensures freedom from deadlock, because no transaction ever waits.

7.11 ▪ Summary

Given a collection of cooperating sequential processes or threads that share data, mutual exclusion must be provided to prevent the occurrence of a race condition on the shared data. One solution is to ensure that a critical section of code is in use by only one process or thread at a time. Different software solutions exist for solving the critical-section problem, with the assumption that only storage interlock is available.

The main disadvantage of software solutions is that they are not easy to generalize for multiple threads or for problems more complex than the critical-section problem. Semaphores overcome this difficulty. We can use semaphores to solve various synchronization problems and can implement them efficiently, especially if hardware support for atomic operations is available.

Various synchronization problems (such as the bounded-buffer, readers–writers, and dining-philosophers problems) are important mainly because they are examples of a large class of concurrency-control problems. These problems are used to test nearly every newly proposed synchronization scheme.

Java provides a mechanism to coordinate the activities of multiple threads when accessing shared data through the `synchronized`, `wait()`, `notify()`, and `notifyAll()` mechanisms. Java synchronization is provided at the language level. Java synchronization is an example of a higher-level synchronization mechanism called a monitor. In addition to Java, many languages have provided support for monitors, including Concurrent Pascal and Mesa.

Operating systems also provide support for thread synchronization. For example, Solaris, Windows XP, and Linux provide mechanisms such as semaphores, mutexes, spinlocks, and condition variables to control access to shared data. The Pthreads API provides support for mutexes and condition variables.

A transaction is a program unit that must be executed atomically; that is, either all the operations associated with it are executed to completion, or none are performed. To ensure atomicity despite system failure, we can use a write-ahead log. All updates are recorded on the log, which is kept in stable storage. If a system crash occurs, the information in the log is used in restoring the state of the updated data items, which is accomplished with the use of the undo and redo operations. To reduce the overhead in searching the log after a system failure has occurred, we can use a checkpoint scheme.

When several transactions overlap their execution, the resulting execution may no longer be equivalent to an execution in which these transactions execute atomically. To ensure correct execution, we must use a concurrency-control scheme to guarantee serializability. Various concurrency-control schemes ensure serializability by either delaying an operation or aborting the transaction that issued the operation. The most common ones are locking protocols and timestamp-ordering schemes.

■ Exercises

7.1 The first known correct software solution to the critical-section problem for two threads was developed by Dekker; it is shown in Figure 7.43. The two threads, T_0 and T_1, coordinate activity sharing an object of class Dekker. Show that the algorithm satisfies all three requirements for the critical-section problem.

7.2 In Chapter 5, we gave a multithreaded solution to the bounded-buffer problem that used message passing. The MessageQueue class is not considered thread-safe, meaning that a race condition is possible when multiple threads attempt concurrently to access the queue. Modify the MessageQueue class using Java synchronization to make it thread safe.

7.3 Implement the Channel interface from Chapter 4 so that the send() and receive() methods are blocking. To do this will require storing the messages in a fixed-length array. Ensure that your implementation is thread safe (using Java synchronization) and that the messages are stored in FIFO order.

7.4 The HardWareData class in Figure 7.7 abstracts the idea of the *Get-and-Set* and *Swap* instructions. However, this class is not considered thread safe,

```
public class Dekker implements MutualExclusion
{
    private volatile int turn = TURN_0;;
    private volatile boolean flag0 = false;
    private volatile boolean flag1 = false;

    public void enteringCriticalSection(int t) {
        int other = 1 - t;
        if (t == 0) {
            flag0 = true;
        else
            flag1 = true;

        if (t == 0) {
        while (flag1 == true) {
            if (turn == other) {
                flag0 = false;
                while (turn == other)
                        Thread.yield();
                flag0 = true;
            }
        }
        }
        else {
        while (flag0 == true) {
            if (turn == other) {
                flag1 = false;
                while (turn == other)
                        Thread.yield();
                flag1 = true;
            }
        }
        }
    }

    public void leavingCriticalSection(int t) {
        turn = 1 - t;
        if (t == 0)
            flag0 = false;
        else
            flag1 = false;
    }
}
```

Figure 7.43   Dekker's algorithm for mutual exclusion.

because multiple threads may concurrently access its methods and thread safety requires that each method be performed atomically. Rewrite the `HardwareData` class using Java synchronization so that it is thread safe.

7.5 Servers may be designed so that they limit the number of open connections. For example, a server may only wish to have N socket connections at any point in time. As soon as N connections are made, the server will not accept another incoming connection until an existing connection is released. Explain how semaphores can be used by a server to limit the number of concurrent connections.

7.6 Create a `BinarySemaphore` class that implements a binary semaphore.

7.7 The `wait()` statement in all Java program examples was part of a `while` loop. Explain why you would always need to use a `while` statement when using `wait()` and why you would never use an `if` statement.

7.8 The solution to the readers–writers problem does not prevent waiting writers from starving: If the database is currently being read and there is a waiting writer, subsequent readers will be allowed to read the database before the writer can write. Modify the solution so that it does not starve waiting writers.

7.9 A monitor-based solution to the dining-philosophers problem, written in Java-like pseudocode and using condition variables, was given in Section 7.7. Develop a solution to the dining-philosophers problem using Java synchronization.

7.10 The solution that we gave to the dining-philosophers problem does not prevent a philosopher from starving. For example, two philosophers—say, philosopher$_1$ and philosopher$_3$—could alternate eating and thinking such that philosopher$_2$ could never eat. Using Java synchronization, develop a solution to the dining-philosophers problem that prevents a philosopher from starving.

7.11 In Section 7.4, we mentioned that disabling interrupts frequently could affect the system's clock. Explain why it could and how such effects could be minimized.

7.12 Give the reasons why Solaris, Windows XP, and Linux implement multiple locking mechanisms. Describe the circumstances under which they use spinlocks, mutexes, semaphores, adaptive mutexes, and condition variables. In each case, explain why the mechanism is needed.

7.13 As described in Section 7.9.3, Linux uses nonpreemption and interrupt disabling to protect kernel data on uniprocessor systems, thus ensuring that at most one process at a time is active in the kernel. However, on symmetric multiprocessor systems (SMP), two processes may be active in the kernel concurrently while running on different processors.   The first version of Linux that supported SMP (the Linux 2.0 kernel) allowed multiple processes to run concurrently on different processors; however, only one process at a time could be running in kernel mode. Comment on the effectiveness of this SMP strategy.

7.14 A **barrier** is a thread synchronization mechanism that allows several threads to run for a period but then forces all threads to wait until all have reached a certain point. Once all threads have reached this certain point (the barrier), they may all continue.

The following code segment establishes a barrier and creates 10 Worker threads that will synchronize according to the barrier:

```
Barrier jersey = new Barrier(10);
for (int i = 0; i < 10; i++)
    (new Worker(jersey)).start();
```

Note that the barrier must be initialized to the number of threads that are being synchronized and that each thread has a reference to the same barrier object — jersey. Each Worker would run as follows:

```
// All threads have access to this barrier
Barrier jersey;
// do some work for a while .  .  .
// now wait for the others
jersey.waitForOthers();
// now do more work .  .  .
```

When a thread invokes the method waitForOthers(), it will block until all threads have reached this method (the barrier). Once all threads have reached this method, they may all proceed with the remainder of their code. Implement a barrier class using Java synchronization. This class will provide a constructor and the waitForOthers() method.

7.15 Create a thread pool (see Chapter 5) using Java synchronization. Your thread pool will implement the following API:

ThreadPool() – Create a default-sized thread pool.

ThreadPool(int size) – Create a thread pool of size size.

void add(Runnable task) – Add a task to be performed by
                          a thread in the pool.

void stopPool() – Stop all threads in the pool.

Your pool will first create a a number of idle threads that await work. Work will be submitted to the pool via the add() method that adds a task implementing the Runnable interface. The add() method will place the Runnable task into a queue. Once a thread in the pool becomes available for work, it will check the queue for any Runnable tasks. If there are such tasks, the idle thread will remove the task from the queue and invoke its run() method. If the queue is empty, the idle thread will wait to be notified once work becomes available. (The add() method will perform a notify() when it places a Runnable task into the queue to possibly awaken an idle thread awaiting work.) The stopPool() method will stop all threads in the pool by invoking their interrupt() method (Section 5.7.4). This of course requires that Runnable tasks being executed by the thread pool check their interruption status.

7.16 *The Sleeping-Barber Problem.* A barbershop consists of a waiting room with *n* chairs and a barber room with one barber chair. If there are no customers to be served, the barber goes to sleep. If a customer enters the barbershop and all chairs are occupied, then the customer leaves the shop. If the barber is busy, but chairs are available, then the customer sits in one of the free chairs. If the barber is asleep, the customer wakes up the barber. Write a program to coordinate the barber and the customers using Java synchronization.

7.17 *The Cigarette-Smokers Problem.* Consider a system with three *smoker* processes and one *agent* process. Each smoker continuously rolls a cigarette and then smokes it. But to roll and smoke a cigarette, the smoker needs three ingredients: tobacco, paper, and matches. One of the smoker processes has paper, another has tobacco, and the third has matches. The agent has an infinite supply of all three materials. The agent places two of the ingredients on the table. The smoker who has the remaining ingredient then makes and smokes a cigarette, signaling the agent on completion. The agent then puts out another two of the three ingredients, and the cycle repeats. Write a program to synchronize the agent and the smokers using Java synchronization.

7.18 Explain the differences, in terms of cost, among the three storage types: volatile, nonvolatile, and stable.

7.19 Explain the purpose of the checkpoint mechanism. How often should checkpoints be performed? Describe how the frequency of checkpoints affects:

- System performance when no failure occurs
- The time it takes to recover from a system crash
- The time it takes to recover from a disk crash

7.20 Explain the concept of transaction atomicity.

7.21 Show that the two-phase locking protocol ensures conflict serializability.

7.22 Show that some schedules are possible under the two-phase locking protocol but not possible under the timestamp protocol, and vice versa.

Bibliographical Notes

The mutual exclusion algorithms 1 and 2 for two tasks were first discussed in the classic paper by Dijkstra [1965a]. Dekker's algorithm (Exercise 7.1)—the first correct software solution to the two-process mutual-exclusion problem— was developed by the Dutch mathematician T. Dekker. This algorithm also was discussed by Dijkstra [1965a]. A simpler solution to the two-process mutual-exclusion problem has since been presented by Peterson [1981] (algorithm 3).

Dijkstra [1965b] presented the first solution to the mutual-exclusion problem for n processes. This solution, however, does not have an upper bound on the amount of time a process must wait before that process is allowed to enter the critical section. Knuth [1966] presented the first algorithm with a bound; his bound was 2^n turns. A refinement of Knuth's algorithm by deBruijn [1967] reduced the waiting time to n^2 turns, after which Eisenberg and McGuire [1972] succeeded in reducing the time to the lower bound of $n - 1$ turns. Lamport [1974] presented a different scheme for solving the mutual-exclusion problem— the bakery algorithm. It also requires $n - 1$ turns, but it is easier to program and to understand. Burns [1978] developed the hardware-solution algorithm that satisfies the bounded waiting requirement. General discussions concerning the mutual-exclusion problem were offered by Lamport [1986] and Lamport [1991]. A collection of algorithms for mutual exclusion was given by Raynal [1986].

Information on hardware solutions for process synchronization can be found Patterson and Hennessy [1998].

The semaphore concept was suggested by Dijkstra [1965a]. Patil [1971] examined the question of whether semaphores can solve all possible synchronization problems. Parnas [1975] discussed some of the flaws in Patil's arguments. Kosaraju [1973] followed up on Patil's work to produce a problem that cannot be solved by *wait* and *signal* operations. Lipton [1974] discussed the limitation of various synchronization primitives.

The classic process-coordination problems that we have described are paradigms for a large class of concurrency-control problems. The bounded-buffer problem, the dining-philosophers problem, and the sleeping-barber problem (Exercise 7.16) were suggested by Dijkstra [1965a] and Dijkstra [1971]. The cigarette-smokers problem (Exercise 7.17) was developed by Patil [1971]. The readers–writers problem was suggested by Courtois et al. [1971]. The matter of concurrent reading and writing was discussed by Lamport [1977].

The problem of synchronization of independent processes was discussed by Lamport [1976].

The monitor concept was developed by Brinch-Hansen [1973]. A complete description of the monitor was given by Hoare [1974]. Kessels [1977] proposed an extension to the monitor to allow automatic signaling. A paper describing the classifications for monitors was published by Buhr et al. [1995]. General discussions concerning concurrent programming were offered by Ben-Ari [1990] and Burns and Davies [1993].

Details of how Java synchronizes threads can be found in Oaks and Wong [1999], Holub [2000], and Lewis and Berg [2000]. Lea [2000] presents many design patterns for concurrent programming in Java. Java Report [1998] is devoted to advanced multithreading and synchronization topics in Java.

Synchronization primitives for Windows 2000 are discussed by Solomon and Russinovich [2000]. Details of the synchronization mechanisms used in Solaris and Linux are presented by Mauro and McDougall [2001] and Bovet and Cesati [2002], respectively. Butenhof [1997] discusses synchronization issues in the Pthreads API.

The write-ahead log scheme was first introduced in System R by Gray et al. [1981]. The concept of serializability was formulated by Eswaran et al. [1976] in connection with their work on concurrency control for System R. The two-phase locking protocol was introduced by Eswaran et al. [1976]. The timestamp-based concurrency-control scheme was provided by Reed [1983]. An exposition of various timestamp-based concurrency-control algorithms was presented by Bernstein and Goodman [1980].

Chapter 8

DEADLOCKS

In a multiprogramming environment, several processes may compete for a finite number of resources. A process requests resources; if the resources are not available at that time, the process enters a wait state. Waiting processes may never again change state, because the resources they have requested are held by other waiting processes. This situation is called a **deadlock**. We have already discussed this issue briefly in Chapter 7, in connection with semaphores.

Perhaps the best illustration of a deadlock can be drawn from a law passed by the Kansas legislature early in the 20th century. It said, in part: "When two trains approach each other at a crossing, both shall come to a full stop and neither shall start up again until the other has gone."

In this chapter, we describe methods that an operating system can use to prevent or deal with deadlocks. Most current operating systems do not provide deadlock-prevention facilities, but such features will probably be added soon. Deadlock problems can only become more common, given current trends, including larger numbers of processes, multithreaded programs, many more resources within a system, and an emphasis on long-lived file and database servers rather than batch systems.

8.1 ■ System Model

A system consists of a finite number of resources to be distributed among a number of competing processes. The resources are partitioned into several types, each of which consists of some number of identical instances. Memory space, CPU cycles, files, and I/O devices (such as printers and tape drives) are examples of resource types. If a system has two CPUs, then the resource type *CPU* has two instances. Similarly, the resource type *printer* may have five instances.

If a process requests an instance of a resource type, the allocation of *any* instance of the type will satisfy the request. If it will not, then the instances are not identical, and the resource type classes have not been defined properly. For example, a system may have two printers. These two printers may be defined to be in the same resource class if no one cares which printer prints which output. However, if one printer is on the ninth floor and the other is in the basement, then people on the ninth floor may not see both printers as equivalent, and separate resource classes may need to be defined for each printer.

A process must request a resource before using it and must release the resource after using it. A process may request as many resources as it requires to carry out its designated task. Obviously, the number of resources requested may not exceed the total number of resources available in the system. In other words, a process cannot request three printers if the system has only two.

Under the normal mode of operation, a process may utilize a resource in only the following sequence:

1. **Request:** If the request cannot be granted immediately (for example, if the resource is being used by another process), then the requesting process must wait until it can acquire the resource.

2. **Use:** The process can operate on the resource (for example, if the resource is a printer, the process can print on the printer).

3. **Release:** The process releases the resource.

The request and release of resources are system calls, as explained in Chapter 3. Examples are the `request` and `release device`, `open` and `close file`, and `allocate` and `free memory` system calls. Request and release of resources that are not managed by the operating system can be accomplished through the `acquire()` and `release()` operations on semaphores or through acquisition and release of a lock for a Java object via the `synchronized` keyword. For each use of a kernel-managed resource by a process or thread, the operating system checks to make sure that the process has requested and has been allocated the resource. A system table records whether each resource is free or allocated; for each resource that is allocated, it also records the process to which it is allocated. If a process requests a resource that is currently allocated to another process, it can be added to a queue of processes waiting for this resource.

A set of processes is in a deadlock state when every process in the set is waiting for an event that can be caused only by another process in the set. The events with which we are mainly concerned here are resource acquisition and release. The resources may be either physical resources (for example, printers, tape drives, memory space, and CPU cycles) or logical resources (for example, files, semaphores, and monitors). However, other types of events may result in deadlocks (for example, the IPC facilities discussed in Chapter 4).

To illustrate a deadlock state, consider a system with three tape drives. Suppose each of three processes holds one of these tape drives. If each process now requests another tape drive, the three processes will be in a deadlock state. Each is waiting for the event "tape drive is released," which can be caused only by one of the other waiting processes. This example illustrates a deadlock involving the same resource type.

Deadlocks may also involve different resource types. For example, consider a system with one printer and one tape drive. Suppose that process P_i is holding the tape drive and process P_j is holding the printer. If P_i requests the printer and P_j requests the tape drive, a deadlock occurs.

A programmer who is developing multithreaded applications must pay particular attention to this problem: Multithreaded programs are good candidates for deadlock because multiple threads can compete for shared resources (such as object locks).

8.2 ■ Deadlock Characterization

In a deadlock, processes never finish executing, and system resources are tied up, preventing other jobs from starting. Before we discuss the various methods for dealing with the deadlock problem, we look more closely at features that characterize deadlocks.

8.2.1 Necessary Conditions

A deadlock situation can arise if the following four conditions hold simultaneously in a system:

1. **Mutual exclusion:** At least one resource must be held in a nonsharable mode; that is, only one process at a time can use the resource. If another process requests that resource, the requesting process must be delayed until the resource has been released.

2. **Hold and wait:** A process must be holding at least one resource and waiting to acquire additional resources that are currently being held by other processes.

3. **No preemption:** Resources cannot be preempted; that is, a resource can be released only voluntarily by the process holding it, after that process has completed its task.

4. **Circular wait:** A set $\{P_0, P_1, ..., P_n\}$ of waiting processes must exist such that P_0 is waiting for a resource that is held by P_1, P_1 is waiting for a resource that is held by P_2, ..., P_{n-1} is waiting for a resource that is held by P_n, and P_n is waiting for a resource that is held by P_0.

We emphasize that all four conditions must hold for a deadlock to occur. The circular-wait condition implies the hold-and-wait condition, so the four conditions are not completely independent. We shall see in Section 8.4, however, that it is useful to consider each condition separately.

8.2.2 Resource-Allocation Graph

Deadlocks can be described more precisely in terms of a directed graph called a **system resource-allocation graph**. This graph consists of a set of vertices V and a set of edges E. The set of vertices V is partitioned into two different types of nodes: $P = \{P_1, P_2, ..., P_n\}$, the set consisting of all the active processes in the system, and $R = \{R_1, R_2, ..., R_m\}$, the set consisting of all resource types in the system.

A directed edge from process P_i to resource type R_j is denoted by $P_i \rightarrow R_j$; it signifies that process P_i requested an instance of resource type R_j and is currently waiting for that resource. A directed edge from resource type R_j to process P_i is denoted by $R_j \rightarrow P_i$; it signifies that an instance of resource type R_j has been allocated to process P_i. A directed edge $P_i \rightarrow R_j$ is called a **request edge**; a directed edge $R_j \rightarrow P_i$ is called an **assignment edge**.

Pictorially, we represent each process P_i as a circle and each resource type R_j as a rectangle. Since resource type R_j may have more than one instance, we represent each such instance as a dot within the rectangle. Note that a request edge points to only the rectangle R_j, whereas an assignment edge must also designate one of the dots in the rectangle.

When process P_i requests an instance of resource type R_j, a request edge is inserted in the resource-allocation graph. When this request can be fulfilled, the request edge is *instantaneously* transformed to an assignment edge. When the process no longer needs access to the resource, it releases the resource; as a result, the assignment edge is deleted.

The resource-allocation graph shown in Figure 8.1 depicts the following situation.

- The sets P, R, and E:
  - $P = \{P_1, P_2, P_3\}$
  - $R = \{R_1, R_2, R_3, R_4\}$
  - $E = \{P_1 \rightarrow R_1, P_2 \rightarrow R_3, R_1 \rightarrow P_2, R_2 \rightarrow P_2, R_2 \rightarrow P_1, R_3 \rightarrow P_3\}$
- Resource instances:

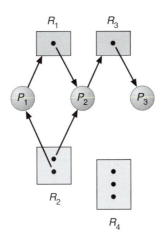

Figure 8.1   Resource-allocation graph.

- One instance of resource type R_1
- Two instances of resource type R_2
- One instance of resource type R_3
- Three instances of resource type R_4

• Process states:

- Process P_1 is holding an instance of resource type R_2 and is waiting for an instance of resource type R_1.

- Process P_2 is holding an instance of R_1 and R_2 and is waiting for an instance of resource type R_3.

- Process P_3 is holding an instance of R_3.

Given the definition of a resource-allocation graph, it can be shown that, if the graph contains no cycles, then no process in the system is deadlocked. If the graph does contain a cycle, then a deadlock may exist.

If each resource type has exactly one instance, then a cycle implies that a deadlock has occurred. If the cycle involves only a set of resource types, each of which has only a single instance, then a deadlock has occurred. Each process involved in the cycle is deadlocked. In this case, a cycle in the graph is both a necessary and a sufficient condition for the existence of deadlock.

If each resource type has several instances, then a cycle does not necessarily imply that a deadlock has occurred. In this case, a cycle in the graph is a necessary but not a sufficient condition for the existence of deadlock.

To illustrate this concept, let us return to the resource-allocation graph depicted in Figure 8.1. Suppose that process P_3 requests an instance of resource

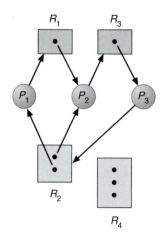

Figure 8.2   Resource-allocation graph with a deadlock.

type R_2. Since no resource instance is currently available, a request edge $P_3 \rightarrow R_2$ is added to the graph (Figure 8.2). At this point, two minimal cycles exist in the system:

$$P_1 \rightarrow R_1 \rightarrow P_2 \rightarrow R_3 \rightarrow P_3 \rightarrow R_2 \rightarrow P_1$$
$$P_2 \rightarrow R_3 \rightarrow P_3 \rightarrow R_2 \rightarrow P_2$$

Processes P_1, P_2, and P_3 are deadlocked. Process P_2 is waiting for the resource R_3, which is held by process P_3. Process P_3 is waiting for either process P_1 or process P_2 to release resource R_2. In addition, process P_1 is waiting for process P_2 to release resource R_1.

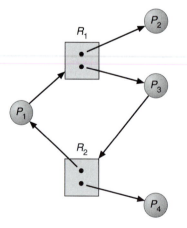

Figure 8.3   Resource-allocation graph with a cycle but no deadlock.

Now consider the resource-allocation graph in Figure 8.3. In this example, we also have a cycle

$$P_1 \rightarrow R_1 \rightarrow P_3 \rightarrow R_2 \rightarrow P_1$$

However, there is no deadlock. Observe that process P_4 may release its instance of resource type R_2. That resource can then be allocated to P_3, breaking the cycle.

In summary, if a resource-allocation graph does not have a cycle, then the system is *not* in a deadlocked state. If there is a cycle, then the system may or may not be in a deadlocked state. This observation is important when we deal with the deadlock problem.

Before we proceed to a discussion of handling deadlocks, let us see how deadlock can occur in a multithreaded Java program, as shown in Figure 8.4.

In that example, `threadA` attempts to acquire the objects' locks in the order of (1) `mutexX`, (2) `mutexY`; and `threadB` attempts using the order of (1) `mutexY`, (2) `mutexX`. Deadlock is possible in the following scenario:

$$\text{threadA} \rightarrow \text{mutexY} \rightarrow \text{threadB} \rightarrow \text{mutexX} \rightarrow \text{threadA}$$

Note that, even though deadlock is possible, it will not occur if `threadA` is able to acquire and release the locks for `mutexX` and `mutexY` before `threadB` attempts to acquire the locks. This example illustrates a problem with handling deadlocks: It is difficult to identify and test for deadlocks that may occur only under certain circumstances.

8.3 ▪ Methods for Handling Deadlocks

Principally, we can deal with the deadlock problem in one of three ways:

- We can use a protocol to prevent or avoid deadlocks, ensuring that the system will *never* enter a deadlock state.

- We can allow the system to enter a deadlock state, detect it, and recover.

- We can ignore the problem altogether and pretend that deadlocks never occur in the system.

The third solution is the one used by most operating systems, including UNIX and Windows. The JVM also does nothing to manage deadlocks. It is up to the application developer to write programs that handle deadlocks.

Next, we elaborate briefly on each of the three methods for handling deadlocks. Then, in Sections 8.4 through 8.7, we present detailed algorithms. However, before proceeding, it should be mentioned that some researchers have argued that none of the basic approaches alone is appropriate for the

```
class Mutex { }

class A implements Runnable
{
    private Mutex first, second;
    public A(Mutex first, Mutex second) {
        this.first = first;
        this.second = second;
    }

    public void run() {
        synchronized (first) {
            // do something
            synchronized (second) {
                // do something else
            }
        }
    }
}

class B implements Runnable
{
    private Mutex first, second;
    public B(Mutex first, Mutex second) {
        this.first = first;
        this.second = second;
    }

    public void run() {
        synchronized (second) {
            // do something
            synchronized (first) {
                // do something else
            }
        }
    }
}

public class DeadlockExample
{
    // Figure 8.5
}
```

Figure 8.4   Deadlock example.

```
public static void main(String arg[]) {
    Mutex mutexX = new Mutex();
    Mutex mutexY = new Mutex();

    Thread threadA = new Thread(new A(mutexX,mutexY));
    Thread threadB = new Thread(new B(mutexX,mutexY));

    threadA.start();
    threadB.start();
}
```

Figure 8.5   Creating the threads.

entire spectrum of resource-allocation problems in operating systems. The basic approaches can be combined, allowing the selection of an optimal approach for each class of resources in a system.

To ensure that deadlocks never occur, the system can use either a deadlock-prevention or a deadlock-avoidance scheme. **Deadlock prevention** is a set of methods for ensuring that at least one of the necessary conditions (Section 8.2.1) cannot hold. These methods prevent deadlocks by constraining how requests for resources can be made. We discuss these methods in Section 8.4.

Deadlock avoidance requires that the operating system be given in advance additional information concerning which resources a process will request and use during its lifetime. With this additional knowledge, we can decide for each request whether or not the process should wait. To decide whether the current request can be satisfied or must be delayed, the system must consider the resources currently available, the resources currently allocated to each process, and the future requests and releases of each process. We discuss these schemes in Section 8.5.

If a system does not employ either a deadlock-prevention or a deadlock-avoidance algorithm, then a deadlock situation may occur. In this environment, the system can provide an algorithm that examines the state of the system to determine whether a deadlock has occurred and an algorithm to recover from the deadlock (if a deadlock has indeed occurred). We discuss these issues in Section 8.6 and Section 8.7.

If a system neither ensures that a deadlock will never occur nor provides a mechanism for deadlock detection and recovery, then we may arrive at a situation where the system is in a deadlocked state yet has no way of recognizing what has happened. In this case, the undetected deadlock will result in deterioration of the system's performance, because resources are being held by processes that cannot run and because more and more processes, as they make requests for resources, enter a deadlocked state. Eventually, the system will stop functioning and will need to be restarted manually.

Although this method may not seem to be a viable approach to the deadlock problem, it is nevertheless used in most operating systems, as mentioned earlier. In many systems, deadlocks occur infrequently (say, once per year); thus, this method is cheaper than the prevention, avoidance, or detection and recovery methods, which must be used constantly. Also, in some circumstances, a system is in a frozen state but not in a deadlocked state. We see this situation, for example, with a real-time process running at the highest priority (or any process running on a nonpreemptive scheduler) and never returning control to the operating system. The system must have manual recovery methods for such nondeadlock conditions and may simply use those techniques for deadlock recovery.

As noted earlier, the JVM does nothing to manage deadlocks; it is up to the application developer to write programs that are deadlock-free. In the remainder of this section, we illustrate how deadlock is possible when selected methods of the core Java API are used and how the programmer can develop programs that appropriately handle deadlock.

In Chapter 5, we introduced Java threads and some of the API that allows users to create and manipulate threads. Two additional methods of theThread class are the suspend() and resume() methods, which were deprecated in Java 2 because they could lead to deadlock. The suspend() method suspends execution of the thread currently running. The resume() method resumes execution of a suspended thread. Once a thread has been suspended, it can continue only if another thread resumes it. Furthermore, a suspended thread continues to hold all locks while it is blocked. Deadlock is possible if a suspended thread holds a lock on an object and the thread that can resume it must own this lock before it can resume the suspended thread.

stop() has been deprecated as well, but not because it can lead to deadlock. Unlike the situation when a thread has been suspended, when a thread has been stopped, it releases all the locks that it owns. However, locks are generally used in the following progression: (1) acquire the lock, (2) access a shared data structure, and (3) release the lock. If a thread is in the middle of step 2 when it is stopped, it will release the lock; but it may leave the shared data structure in an inconsistent state. In Section 5.7.4, we discussed how to terminate a thread using a technique other than the stop() method. Here, we present a strategy for suspending and resuming a thread without using the deprecated suspend() and resume() methods.

The program shown in Figure 8.6 is a multithreaded applet that displays the time of day. When this applet starts, it creates a second thread (which we will call the *clock thread*) that outputs the time of day. The run() method of the clock thread alternates between sleeping for one second and then calling the repaint() method. The repaint() method ultimately calls the paint() method, which draws the current date and time in the browser's window.

This applet is designed so that the clock thread is running while the applet is visible; if the applet is not being displayed (as when the browser window has been minimized), the clock thread is suspended from execution. This is accomplished by overriding the start() and stop() methods of the Applet

```
import java.applet.*;
import java.awt.*;


public class ClockApplet extends Applet implements Runnable
{
    private Thread clockThread;
    private boolean ok = false;
    private Object mutex = new Object();

    public void run() {
        while (true) {
            try {
                // sleep for 1 second
                Thread.sleep(1000);

                // repaint the date and time
                repaint();

                // see if we need to suspend ourself
                synchronized (mutex) {
                    while (ok == false)
                        mutex.wait();
                }
            }
            catch (InterruptedException e) { }
        }
    }

    public void start() {
        // Figure 8.7
    }

    public void stop() {
        // Figure 8.7
    }

    public void paint(Graphics g) {
        g.drawString( new java.util.Date().toString(), 10, 30);
    }
}
```

Figure 8.6   Applet that displays the date and time of day.

```
// this method is called when the applet is
// started or we return to the applet
public void start() {
     ok = true;

     if (clockThread == null) {
         clockThread = new Thread(this);
         clockThread.start();
     }
     else {
         synchronized(mutex) {
             mutex.notify();
         }
     }
}

// this method is called when we
// leave the page the applet is on
public void stop() {
     synchronized(mutex) {
         ok = false;
     }
}
```

Figure 8.7   start() and stop() methods for the applet.

class. (Be careful not to confuse these with the start() and stop() methods of the Thread class.) The start() method of an applet is called when an applet is first created. If the user leaves the web page, if the applet scrolls off the screen, or if the browser window is minimized, the applet's stop() method is called. If the user returns to the applet's web page, the applet's start() method is called again.

The applet uses the boolean variable ok to indicate whether the clock thread can run or not. This variable will be set to true in the start() method of the applet, indicating that the clock thread can run. The stop() method of the applet will set it to false. The clock thread will check the value of this boolean variable in its run() method and will only proceed if it is true. Because the thread for the applet and the clock thread will be sharing this variable, access to it will be controlled through a synchronized block. This program is shown in Figure 8.6.

If the clock thread sees that the boolean value is false, it suspends itself by calling the wait() method for the object mutex. When the applet wishes to resume the clock thread, it sets the boolean variable to true and calls notify() for the mutex object. This call to notify() awakens the clock thread. It checks

the value of the boolean variable and, seeing that it is now true, proceeds in its
run() method, displaying the date and time.

8.4 ■ Deadlock Prevention

As we noted in Section 8.2.1, for a deadlock to occur, each of the four necessary
conditions must hold. By ensuring that at least one of these conditions cannot
hold, we can *prevent* the occurrence of a deadlock. We elaborate on this
approach by examining each of the four necessary conditions separately.

8.4.1 Mutual Exclusion

The mutual-exclusion condition must hold for nonsharable resources.   For
example, a printer cannot be simultaneously shared by several processes.
Sharable resources, in contrast, do not require mutually exclusive access and
thus cannot be involved in a deadlock. Read-only files are a good example of
a sharable resource. If several processes attempt to open a read-only file at the
same time, they can be granted simultaneous access to the file. A process never
needs to wait for a sharable resource. In general, however, we cannot prevent
deadlocks by denying the mutual-exclusion condition, because some resources
are intrinsically nonsharable.

8.4.2 Hold and Wait

To ensure that the hold-and-wait condition never occurs in the system, we must
guarantee that, whenever a process requests a resource, it does not hold any
other resources. One protocol that can be used requires each process to request
and be allocated all its resources before it begins execution. We can implement
this provision by requiring that system calls requesting resources for a process
precede all other system calls.

   An alternative protocol allows a process to request resources only when it
has none. A process may request some resources and use them. Before it can
request any additional resources, however, it must release all the resources that
it is currently allocated.

   To illustrate the difference between these two protocols, we consider a
process that copies data from a tape drive to a disk file, sorts the disk file, and
then prints the results to a printer. If all resources must be requested at the
beginning of the process, then the process must initially request the tape drive,
disk file, and printer. It will hold the printer for its entire execution, even though
it needs the printer only at the end.

   The second method allows the process to request initially only the tape
drive and disk file. It copies from the tape drive to the disk and then releases
both the tape drive and the disk file. The process must then again request the

disk file and the printer. After copying the disk file to the printer, it releases these two resources and terminates.

Both these protocols have two main disadvantages. First, resource utilization may be low, since resources may be allocated but unused for a long period. In the example given, for instance, we can release the tape drive and disk file, and then again request the disk file and printer, only if we can be sure that our data will remain on the disk file. If we cannot be assured that they will, then we must request all resources at the beginning for both protocols.

Second, starvation is possible. A process that needs several popular resources may have to wait indefinitely, because at least one of the resources that it needs is always allocated to some other process.

This solution also is impractical in Java, because a process requests resources (locks) by entering either synchronized methods or blocks. Because lock resources are requested in this manner, it is difficult to write an application that follows either of the protocols we have given.

8.4.3 No Preemption

The third necessary condition is that there be no preemption of resources that have already been allocated. To ensure that this condition does not hold, we can use the following protocol. If a process is holding some resources and requests another resource that cannot be immediately allocated to it (that is, the process must wait), then all resources currently being held are preempted. In other words, these resources are implicitly released. The preempted resources are added to the list of resources for which the process is waiting. The process will be restarted only when it can regain its old resources, as well as the new ones that it is requesting.

Alternatively, if a process requests some resources, we first check whether they are available. If they are, we allocate them. If they are not, we check whether they are allocated to some other process that is waiting for additional resources. If so, we preempt the desired resources from the waiting process and allocate them to the requesting process. If the resources are neither available nor held by a waiting process, the requesting process must wait. While it is waiting, some of its resources may be preempted, but only if another process requests them. A process can be restarted only when it is allocated the new resources it is requesting and recovers any resources that were preempted while it was waiting.

This protocol is often applied to resources whose state can be easily saved and restored later, such as CPU registers and memory space. It cannot generally be applied to such resources as printers and tape drives.

8.4.4 Circular Wait

The fourth and final condition for deadlocks is the circular-wait condition. One way to ensure that this condition never holds is to impose a total ordering of all resource types and to require that each process requests resources in an increasing order of enumeration.

To illustrate, we let $R = \{R_1, R_2, ..., R_m\}$ be the set of resource types. We assign to each resource type a unique integer number, which allows us to compare two resources and to determine whether one precedes another in our ordering. Formally, we define a one-to-one function $F: R \rightarrow N$, where N is the set of natural numbers. For example, if the set of resource types R includes tape drives, disk drives, and printers, then the function F might be defined as follows:

$$F(\text{tape drive}) = 1$$
$$F(\text{disk drive}) = 5$$
$$F(\text{printer}) = 12$$

We can now consider the following protocol to prevent deadlocks: Each process can request resources only in an increasing order of enumeration. That is, a process can initially request any number of instances of a resource type— say, R_i. After that, the process can request instances of resource type R_j if and only if $F(R_j) > F(R_i)$. If several instances of the same resource type are needed, a *single* request for all of them must be issued. For example, using the function defined previously, a process that wants to use the tape drive and printer at the same time must first request the tape drive and then request the printer. Alternatively, we can require that, whenever a process requests an instance of resource type R_j, it has released any resources R_i such that $F(R_i) \geq F(R_j)$.

If these two protocols are used, then the circular-wait condition cannot hold. We can demonstrate this fact by assuming that a circular wait exists (proof by contradiction). Let the set of processes involved in the circular wait be $\{P_0, P_1, ..., P_n\}$, where P_i is waiting for a resource R_i, which is held by process P_{i+1}. (Modulo arithmetic is used on the indexes, so that P_n is waiting for a resource R_n held by P_0.) Then, since process P_{i+1} is holding resource R_i while requesting resource R_{i+1}, we must have $F(R_i) < F(R_{i+1})$, for all i. But this condition means that $F(R_0) < F(R_1) < ... < F(R_n) < F(R_0)$. By transitivity, $F(R_0) < F(R_0)$, which is impossible. Therefore, there can be no circular wait.

We can accomplish this scheme in a Java application by developing an ordering among all objects in the system. All lock requests for objects must be made in increasing order. For example, if the lock ordering in the Java program shown in Figure 8.4 was

$$F(\mathtt{mutexX}) = 1$$
$$F(\mathtt{mutexY}) = 5$$

then `class` B could not request the locks out of order.

Keep in mind that developing an ordering, or hierarchy, in itself does not prevent deadlock. It is up to the application developers to write programs that follow the ordering. Also note that the function F should be defined according to the normal order of usage of the resources in a system. For example, because the tape drive is usually needed before the printer, it would be reasonable to define F(tape drive) $< F$(printer).

Although ensuring that resources are acquired in the proper order is the responsibility of application developers, certain software can be used to verify that locks are acquired in the proper order and to give appropriate warnings when locks are acquired out of order and deadlock is possible. One lock-order verifier, which works on BSD versions of UNIX such as FreeBSD, is known as **witness**. Witness works with mutual-exclusion locks that protect critical sections, as described in Chapter 7; it works by dynamically maintaining the relationship of lock orders in a system. Let's use the program shown in Figure 8.4 as an example. Assume that `threadA` is the first to acquire the locks and does so in the order (1) `mutexX`, (2) `mutexY`. Witness records the relationship that `mutexX` must be acquired before `mutexY`. If `threadB` later acquires the locks out of order, witness generates a warning message on the system console.

8.5 ■ Deadlock Avoidance

Deadlock-prevention algorithms, as discussed in Section 8.4, prevent deadlocks by restraining how requests can be made. The restraints ensure that at least one of the necessary conditions for deadlock cannot occur and, hence, that deadlocks cannot hold. Possible side effects of preventing deadlocks by this method, however, are low device utilization and reduced system throughput.

An alternative method for avoiding deadlocks is to require additional information about how resources are to be requested. For example, in a system with one tape drive and one printer, we might be told that process P will request first the tape drive, and later the printer, before releasing both resources. Process Q, however, will request first the printer and then the tape drive. With this knowledge of the complete sequence of requests and releases for each process, we can decide for each request whether or not the process should wait in order to avoid a possible future deadlock. Each request requires that in making this decision the system consider the resources currently available, the resources currently allocated to each process, and the future requests and releases of each process.

The various algorithms differ in the amount and type of information required. The simplest and most useful model requires that each process declare the *maximum number* of resources of each type that it may need. Given this a priori information, it is possible to construct an algorithm that ensures that the system will never enter a deadlocked state. Such an algorithm defines the **deadlock-avoidance** approach. A deadlock-avoidance algorithm dynamically examines the resource-allocation state to ensure that a circular-wait condition can never exist. The resource-allocation *state* is defined by the number of available and allocated resources and the maximum demands of the processes. In the following sections we explore two deadlock-avoidance algorithms.

8.5.1 Safe State

A state is *safe* if the system can allocate resources to each process (up to its maximum) in some order and still avoid a deadlock. More formally, a system is in a safe state only if there exists a **safe sequence**. A sequence of processes $<P_1, P_2, ..., P_n>$ is a safe sequence for the current allocation state if, for each P_i, the resource requests that P_i can still make can be satisfied by the currently available resources plus the resources held by all P_j, with $j < i$. In this situation, if the resources that process P_i needs are not immediately available, then P_i can wait until all P_j have finished. When they have finished, P_i can obtain all of its needed resources, complete its designated task, return its allocated resources, and terminate. When P_i terminates, P_{i+1} can obtain its needed resources, and so on. If no such sequence exists, then the system state is said to be *unsafe*.

A safe state is not a deadlocked state. Conversely, a deadlocked state is an unsafe state. Not all unsafe states are deadlocks, however (Figure 8.8). An unsafe state *may* lead to a deadlock. As long as the state is safe, the operating system can avoid unsafe (and deadlocked) states. In an unsafe state, the operating system cannot prevent processes from requesting resources such that a deadlock occurs: The behavior of the processes controls unsafe states.

To illustrate, we consider a system with 12 magnetic tape drives and 3 processes: P_0, P_1, and P_2. Process P_0 requires 10 tape drives, process P_1 may need as many as 4, and process P_2 may need up to 9 tape drives. Suppose that, at time t_0, process P_0 is holding 5 tape drives, process P_1 is holding 2, and process P_2 is holding 2 tape drives. (Thus, there are 3 free tape drives.)

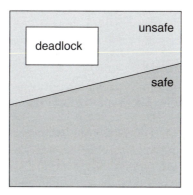

Figure 8.8   Safe, unsafe, and deadlock state spaces.

	Maximum Needs	Current Needs
P_0	10	5
P_1	4	2
P_2	9	2

At time t_0, the system is in a safe state. The sequence $<P_1, P_0, P_2>$ satisfies the safety condition. Process P_1 can immediately be allocated all its tape drives and then return them (the system will then have 5 available tape drives), then process P_0 can get all its tape drives and return them (the system will then have 10 available tape drives), and finally process P_2 can get all its tape drives and return them (the system will then have all 12 tape drives available).

A system may go from a safe state to an unsafe state. Suppose that, at time t_1, process P_2 requests and is allocated one more tape drive. The system is no longer in a safe state. At this point, only process P_1 can be allocated all its tape drives. When it returns them, the system will have only 4 available tape drives. Since process P_0 is allocated 5 tape drives but has a maximum of 10, it may request 5 more tape drives. Since they are unavailable, process P_0 must wait. Similarly, process P_2 may request an additional 6 tape drives and have to wait, resulting in a deadlock. Our mistake was in granting the request from process P_2 for one more tape drive. If we had made P_2 wait until either of the other processes had finished and released its resources, then we could have avoided the deadlock.

Given the concept of a safe state, we can define avoidance algorithms that ensure that the system will never deadlock. The idea is simply to ensure that the system will always remain in a safe state. Initially, the system is in a safe state. Whenever a process requests a resource that is currently available, the system must decide whether the resource can be allocated immediately or whether the process must wait. The request is granted only if the allocation leaves the system in a safe state.

In this scheme, if a process requests a resource that is currently available, it may still have to wait. Thus, resource utilization may be lower than it would be without a deadlock-avoidance algorithm.

8.5.2 Resource-Allocation-Graph Algorithm

If we have a resource-allocation system with only one instance of each resource type, a variant of the resource-allocation graph defined in Section 8.2.2 can be used for deadlock avoidance.

In addition to the request and assignment edges, we introduce a new type of edge, called a **claim edge**. A claim edge $P_i \rightarrow R_j$ indicates that process P_i may request resource R_j at some time in the future. This edge resembles a request edge in direction but is represented by a dashed line. When process P_i requests resource R_j, the claim edge $P_i \rightarrow R_j$ is converted to a request edge. Similarly, when a resource R_j is released by P_i, the assignment edge $R_j \rightarrow P_i$ is reconverted

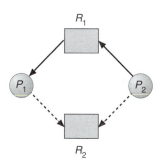

Figure 8.9 Resource-allocation graph for deadlock avoidance.

to a claim edge $P_i \rightarrow R_j$. We note that the resources must be claimed a priori in the system. That is, before process P_i starts executing, all its claim edges must already appear in the resource-allocation graph. We can relax this condition by allowing a claim edge $P_i \rightarrow R_j$ to be added to the graph only if all the edges associated with process P_i are claim edges.

Suppose that process P_i requests resource R_j. The request can be granted only if converting the request edge $P_i \rightarrow R_j$ to an assignment edge $R_j \rightarrow P_i$ does not result in the formation of a cycle in the resource-allocation graph. Note that we check for safety by using a cycle-detection algorithm. An algorithm for detecting a cycle in this graph requires an order of n^2 operations, where n is the number of processes in the system.

If no cycle exists, then the allocation of the resource will leave the system in a safe state. If a cycle is found, then the allocation will put the system in an unsafe state. Therefore, process P_i will have to wait for its requests to be satisfied.

To illustrate this algorithm, we consider the resource-allocation graph of Figure 8.9. Suppose that P_2 requests R_2. Although R_2 is currently free, we cannot allocate it to P_2, since this action will create a cycle in the graph (Figure 8.10). A cycle indicates that the system is in an unsafe state. If P_1 requests R_2, and P_2 requests R_1, then a deadlock will occur.

8.5.3 Banker's Algorithm

The resource-allocation graph algorithm is not applicable to a resource-allocation system with multiple instances of each resource type. The deadlock-avoidance algorithm that we describe next is applicable to such a system but is less efficient than the resource-allocation graph scheme. This algorithm is commonly known as the *banker's algorithm*. The name was chosen because the algorithm could be used in a banking system to ensure that the bank never allocates its available cash such that it can no longer satisfy the needs of all its customers.

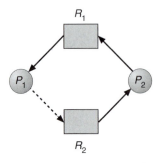

Figure 8.10   An unsafe state in a resource-allocation graph.

When a new process enters the system, it must declare the maximum number of instances of each resource type that it may need. This number may not exceed the total number of resources in the system. When a user requests a set of resources, the system must determine whether the allocation of these resources will leave the system in a safe state. If it will, the resources are allocated; otherwise, the process must wait until some other process releases enough resources.

Several data structures must be maintained to implement the banker's algorithm. These data structures encode the state of the resource-allocation system. Let n be the number of processes in the system and m be the number of resource types. We need the following data structures:

- **Available:** A vector of length m indicates the number of available resources of each type. If $Available[j]$ equals k, there are k instances of resource type R_j available.

- **Max:** An $n \times m$ matrix defines the maximum demand of each process. If $Max[i][j]$ equals k, then process P_i may request at most k instances of resource type R_j.

- **Allocation:** An $n \times m$ matrix defines the number of resources of each type currently allocated to each process. If $Allocation[i][j]$ equals k, then process P_i is currently allocated k instances of resource type R_j.

- **Need:** An $n \times m$ matrix indicates the remaining resource need of each process. If $Need[i][j]$ equals k, then process P_i may need k more instances of resource type R_j to complete its task. Note that $Need[i][j]$ equals $Max[i][j]$ − $Allocation[i][j]$.

These data structures vary over time in both size and value.

To simplify the presentation of the banker's algorithm, let us establish some notation. Let X and Y be vectors of length n. We say that $X \leq Y$ if and only if $X[i] \leq Y[i]$ for all $i = 1, 2, ..., n$. For example, if $X = (1,7,3,2)$ and $Y = (0,3,2,1)$, then $Y \leq X$. $Y < X$ if $Y \leq X$ and $Y \neq X$.

We can treat each row in the matrices *Allocation* and *Need* as vectors and refer to them as *Allocation$_i$* and *Need$_i$*, respectively. The vector *Allocation$_i$* specifies the resources currently allocated to process P_i; the vector *Need$_i$* specifies the additional resources that process P_i may still request to complete its task.

8.5.3.1 Safety Algorithm

The algorithm for finding out whether or not a system is in a safe state can be described as follows:

1. Let *Work* and *Finish* be vectors of length m and n, respectively. Initialize *Work* = *Available* and *Finish[i]* = *false* for i = 0, 1, ..., n-1.

2. Find an i such that both

    a. *Finish[i]* == *false*

    b. *Need$_i$* $\leq$ *Work*

   If no such i exists, go to step 4.

3. *Work* = *Work* + *Allocation$_i$*
   Finish[i] = *true*
   Go to step 2.

4. If *Finish[i]* == *true* for all i, then the system is in a safe state.

This algorithm may require an order of $m \times n^2$ operations to decide whether a state is safe.

8.5.3.2 Resource-Request Algorithm

Let *Request$_i$* be the request vector for process P_i. If *Request$_i$[j]* == k, then process P_i wants k instances of resource type R_j. When a request for resources is made by process P_i, the following actions are taken:

1. If *Request$_i$* $\leq$ *Need$_i$*, go to step 2. Otherwise, raise an error condition, since the process has exceeded its maximum claim.

2. If *Request$_i$* $\leq$ *Available*, go to step 3. Otherwise, P_i must wait, since the resources are not available.

3. Have the system pretend to have allocated the requested resources to process P_i by modifying the state as follows:

$$Available = Available - Request_i;$$
$$Allocation_i = Allocation_i + Request_i;$$
$$Need_i = Need_i - Request_i;$$

If the resulting resource-allocation state is safe, the transaction is completed, and process P_i is allocated its resources. However, if the new state is unsafe, then P_i must wait for $Request_i$, and the old resource-allocation state is restored.

8.5.3.3 An Illustrative Example

Consider a system with five processes P_0 through P_4 and three resource types A, B, C. Resource type A has 10 instances, resource type B has 5 instances, and resource type C has 7 instances. Suppose that, at time T_0, the following snapshot of the system has been taken:

	Allocation	Max	Available
	A B C	A B C	A B C
P_0	0 1 0	7 5 3	3 3 2
P_1	2 0 0	3 2 2	
P_2	3 0 2	9 0 2	
P_3	2 1 1	2 2 2	
P_4	0 0 2	4 3 3	

The content of the matrix $Need$ is defined to be $Max - Allocation$ and is

	Need
	A B C
P_0	7 4 3
P_1	1 2 2
P_2	6 0 0
P_3	0 1 1
P_4	4 3 1

We claim that the system is currently in a safe state. Indeed, the sequence $<P_1, P_3, P_4, P_2, P_0>$ satisfies the safety criteria. Suppose now that process P_1 requests one additional instance of resource type A and two instances of resource type C, so $Request_1 = (1,0,2)$. To decide whether this request can be immediately granted, we first check that $Request_1 \leq Available$—that is, $(1,0,2) \leq (3,3,2)$, which is true. We then pretend that this request has been fulfilled, and we arrive at the following new state:

	Allocation	Need	Available
	A B C	A B C	A B C
P_0	0 1 0	7 4 3	2 3 0
P_1	3 0 2	0 2 0	
P_2	3 0 2	6 0 0	
P_3	2 1 1	0 1 1	
P_4	0 0 2	4 3 1	

We must determine whether this new system state is safe. To do so, we execute our safety algorithm and find that the sequence <P_1, P_3, P_4, P_0, P_2> satisfies our safety requirement. Hence, we can immediately grant the request of process P_1.

You should be able to see, however, that when the system is in this state, a request for (3,3,0) by P_4 cannot be granted, since the resources are not available. Furthermore, a request for (0,2,0) by P_0 cannot be granted, even though the resources are available, since the resulting state is unsafe.

We leave it as an exercise to implement the banker's algorithm in Java.

8.6 ■ Deadlock Detection

If a system does not employ either a deadlock-prevention or a deadlock-avoidance algorithm, then a deadlock situation may occur. In this environment, the system must provide:

- An algorithm that examines the state of the system to determine whether a deadlock has occurred

- An algorithm to recover from the deadlock

In the following discussion, we elaborate on these two requirements as they pertain to systems with only a single instance of each resource type, as well as to systems with several instances of each resource type. At this point, however, let us note that a detection-and-recovery scheme requires overhead that includes not only the run-time costs of maintaining the necessary information and executing the detection algorithm but also the potential losses inherent in recovering from a deadlock.

8.6.1 Single Instance of Each Resource Type

If all resources have only a single instance, then we can define a deadlock-detection algorithm that uses a variant of the resource-allocation graph, called a *wait-for* graph. We obtain this graph from the resource-allocation graph by removing the resource nodes and collapsing the appropriate edges.

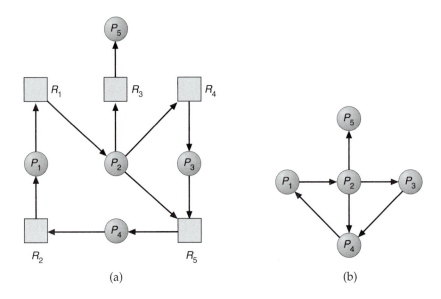

Figure 8.11   (a) Resource-allocation graph. (b) Corresponding wait-for graph.

More precisely, an edge from P_i to P_j in a wait-for graph implies that process P_i is waiting for process P_j to release a resource that P_i needs. An edge $P_i \rightarrow P_j$ exists in a wait-for graph if and only if the corresponding resource-allocation graph contains two edges $P_i \rightarrow R_q$ and $R_q \rightarrow P_j$ for some resource R_q. For example, in Figure 8.11, we present a resource-allocation graph and the corresponding wait-for graph.

As before, a deadlock exists in the system if and only if the wait-for graph contains a cycle. To detect deadlocks, the system needs to *maintain* the wait-for graph and periodically *invoke an algorithm* that searches for a cycle in the graph. An algorithm to detect a cycle in a graph requires an order of n^2 operations, where n is the number of vertices in the graph.

8.6.2 Several Instances of a Resource Type

The wait-for graph scheme is not applicable to a resource-allocation system with multiple instances of each resource type. We turn now to a deadlock-detection algorithm that is applicable to such a system. The algorithm employs several time-varying data structures that are similar to those used in the banker's algorithm (Section 8.5.3):

- **Available:** A vector of length m indicates the number of available resources of each type.

- **Allocation:** An $n \times m$ matrix defines the number of resources of each type currently allocated to each process.

- **Request:** An $n \times m$ matrix indicates the current request of each process. If $Request[i][j]$ equals k, then process P_i is requesting k more instances of resource type R_j.

The $\leq$ relation between two vectors is defined as in Section 8.5.3. To simplify notation, we again treat the rows in the matrices $Allocation$ and $Request$ as vectors; we refer to them as $Allocation_i$ and $Request_i$, respectively.   The detection algorithm described here simply investigates every possible allocation sequence for the processes that remain to be completed. Compare this algorithm with the banker's algorithm of Section 8.5.3.

1. Let $Work$ and $Finish$ be vectors of length m and n, respectively. Initialize $Work = Available$. For $i = 0, 1, ..., n\text{-}1$, if $Allocation_i \neq 0$, then $Finish[i] = false$; otherwise, $Finish[i] = true$.

2. Find an index i such that both

   a. $Finish[i] == false$

   b. $Request_i \leq Work$

   If no such i exists, go to step 4.

3. $Work = Work + Allocation_i$
   $Finish[i] = true$
   Go to step 2.

4. If $Finish[i] == false$, for some i, $0 \leq i < n$, then the system is in a deadlocked state. Moreover, if $Finish[i] == false$, then process P_i is deadlocked.

This algorithm requires an order of $m \times n^2$ operations to detect whether the system is in a deadlocked state.

You may wonder why we reclaim the resources of process P_i (in step 3) as soon as we determine that $Request_i \leq Work$ (in step 2b). We know that P_i is currently *not* involved in a deadlock (since $Request_i \leq Work$). Thus, we take an optimistic attitude and assume that P_i will require no more resources to complete its task; it will thus soon return all currently allocated resources to the system. If our assumption is incorrect, a deadlock may occur later. That deadlock will be detected the next time the deadlock-detection algorithm is invoked.

To illustrate this algorithm, we consider a system with five processes P_0 through P_4 and three resource types A, B, C. Resource type A has 7 instances, resource type B has 2 instances, and resource type C has 6 instances. Suppose that, at time T_0, we have the following resource-allocation state:

	Allocation	Request	Available
	A B C	A B C	A B C
P_0	0 1 0	0 0 0	0 0 0
P_1	2 0 0	2 0 2	
P_2	3 0 3	0 0 0	
P_3	2 1 1	1 0 0	
P_4	0 0 2	0 0 2	

We claim that the system is not in a deadlocked state. Indeed, if we execute our algorithm, we will find that the sequence $<P_0, P_2, P_3, P_1, P_4>$ results in $Finish[i] == true$ for all i.

Suppose now that process P_2 makes one additional request for an instance of type C. The $Request$ matrix is modified as follows:

	Request
	A B C
P_0	0 0 0
P_1	2 0 2
P_2	0 0 1
P_3	1 0 0
P_4	0 0 2

We claim that the system is now deadlocked. Although we can reclaim the resources held by process P_0, the number of available resources is not sufficient to fulfill the requests of the other processes. Thus, a deadlock exists, consisting of processes P_1, P_2, P_3, and P_4.

8.6.3 Detection-Algorithm Usage

When should we invoke the detection algorithm? The answer depends on two factors:

1. How *often* is a deadlock likely to occur?

2. How *many* processes will be affected by deadlock when it happens?

If deadlocks occur frequently, then the detection algorithm should be invoked frequently. Resources allocated to deadlocked processes will be idle until the deadlock can be broken. In addition, the number of processes involved in the deadlock cycle may grow.

Deadlocks occur only when some process makes a request that cannot be granted immediately. This request may be the final request that completes a chain of waiting processes. In the extreme, we could invoke the deadlock-detection algorithm every time a request for allocation cannot be granted immediately. In this case, we can identify not only the set of processes that is deadlocked but also the specific process that "caused" the deadlock. (In reality, each of the deadlocked processes is a link in the cycle in the resource graph, so all of them, jointly, caused the deadlock.) If there are many different resource types, one request may cause many cycles in the resource graph, each cycle completed by the most recent request and "caused" by the one identifiable process.

Of course, invoking the deadlock-detection algorithm for every request may incur a considerable overhead in computation time. A less expensive alternative is simply to invoke the algorithm at less frequent intervals—for example, once per hour or whenever CPU utilization drops below 40 percent. (A deadlock eventually cripples system throughput and will cause CPU utilization to drop.) If the detection algorithm is invoked at arbitrary points in time, there may be many cycles in the resource graph. We would generally not be able to tell which of the many deadlocked processes "caused" the deadlock.

8.7 ■ Recovery from Deadlock

When a detection algorithm determines that a deadlock exists, several alternatives are available. One possibility is to inform the operator that a deadlock has occurred and to let the operator deal with the deadlock manually. The other possibility is to let the system *recover* from the deadlock automatically. There are two options for breaking a deadlock. One is simply to abort one or more processes to break the circular wait. The other is to preempt some resources from one or more of the deadlocked processes.

8.7.1 Process Termination

To eliminate deadlocks by aborting a process, we use one of two methods. In both methods, the system reclaims all resources allocated to the terminated processes.

- **Abort all deadlocked processes:** This method clearly will break the deadlock cycle, but at great expense; the deadlocked processes may have computed for a long time, and the results of these partial computations must be discarded and probably will have to be recomputed later.

- **Abort one process at a time until the deadlock cycle is eliminated:** This method incurs considerable overhead, since, after each process is aborted, a deadlock-detection algorithm must be invoked to determine whether any processes are still deadlocked.

Aborting a process may not be easy. If the process was in the midst of updating a file, terminating it will leave that file in an incorrect state. Similarly, if the process was in the midst of printing data on a printer, the system must reset the printer to a correct state before printing the next job.

If the partial termination method is used, then we must determine which deadlocked process (or processes) should be terminated. This determination is a policy decision, similar to CPU-scheduling decisions. The question is basically an economic one; we should abort those processes whose termination will incur the minimum cost. Unfortunately, the term *minimum cost* is not a precise one. Many factors may affect which process is chosen, including:

1. What the priority of the process is

2. How long the process has computed and how much longer the process will compute before completing its designated task

3. How many and what type of resources the process has used (for example, whether the resources are simple to preempt)

4. How many more resources the process needs in order to complete

5. How many processes will need to be terminated

6. Whether the process is interactive or batch

8.7.2 Resource Preemption

To eliminate deadlocks using resource preemption, we successively preempt some resources from processes and give these resources to other processes until the deadlock cycle is broken.

If preemption is required to deal with deadlocks, then three issues need to be addressed:

1. **Selecting a victim:** Which resources and which processes are to be pre-empted? As in process termination, we must determine the order of pre-emption to minimize cost. Cost factors may include such parameters as the number of resources a deadlocked process is holding and the amount of time the process has thus far consumed during its execution.

2. **Rollback:** If we preempt a resource from a process, what should be done with that process? Clearly, it cannot continue with its normal execution; it is missing some needed resource. We must roll back the process to some safe state and restart it from that state.

    Since, in general, it is difficult to determine what a safe state is, the simplest solution is a total rollback: Abort the process and then restart it. Although it is more effective to roll back the process only as far as necessary to break the deadlock, this method requires the system to keep more information about the state of all running processes.

3. **Starvation:** How do we ensure that starvation will not occur? That is, how can we guarantee that resources will not always be preempted from the same process?

    In a system where victim selection is based primarily on cost factors, it may happen that the same process is always picked as a victim. As a result, this process never completes its designated task, a *starvation* situation that needs to be dealt with in any practical system. Clearly, we must ensure that a process can be picked as a victim only a (small) finite number of times. The most common solution is to include the number of rollbacks in the cost factor.

8.8 ■ Summary

A deadlock state occurs when two or more processes are waiting indefinitely for an event that can be caused only by one of the waiting processes. Principally, there are three methods for dealing with deadlocks:

- Use some protocol to prevent or avoid deadlocks, ensuring that the system will never enter a deadlock state.

- Allow the system to enter deadlock state, detect it, and then recover.

- Ignore the problem altogether and pretend that deadlocks never occur in the system.

The third solution is the one used by most operating systems, including UNIX and Windows, as well as the JVM.

A deadlock can occur only if four necessary conditions hold simultaneously in the system: mutual exclusion, hold and wait, no preemption, and circular wait. To prevent deadlocks, we can ensure that at least one of the necessary conditions never holds.

A method for avoiding deadlocks that is less stringent than the prevention algorithms requires that the operating system have a priori information on how each process will utilize the resources. The banker's algorithm, for example, requires a priori information about the maximum number of each resource class that may be requested by each process. Using this information, we can define a deadlock-avoidance algorithm.

If a system does not employ a protocol to ensure that deadlocks will never occur, then a detection-and-recovery scheme must be employed. A deadlock-detection algorithm must be invoked to determine whether a deadlock has occurred. If a deadlock is detected, the system must recover either by terminating some of the deadlocked processes or by preempting resources from some of the deadlocked processes.

Where preemption is used to deal with deadlocks, three issues must be addressed: selecting a victim, rollback, and starvation. In a system that selects victims for rollback primarily on the basis of cost factors, starvation may occur, and the selected process never completes its designated task.

Finally, researchers have argued that none of the basic approaches alone is appropriate for the entire spectrum of resource-allocation problems in operating systems. The basic approaches can be combined, allowing the selection of an optimal approach for each class of resources in a system.

■ Exercises

8.1 List three examples of deadlocks that are not related to a computer-system environment.

8.2 Is it possible to have a deadlock involving only one single-threaded process? Explain your answer.

8.3 Consider the traffic deadlock depicted in Figure 8.12.

   a. Show that the four necessary conditions for deadlock indeed hold in this example.

   b. State a simple rule for avoiding deadlocks in this system.

8.4 Suppose that a system is in an unsafe state. Show that it is possible for the processes to complete their execution without entering a deadlock state.

8.5 A possible solution for preventing deadlocks is to have a single, higher-order resource that must be requested before any other resource. For example, if multiple threads attempt to access the locks for five Java objects $A \cdots E$, deadlock is possible. We can prevent the deadlock by adding a sixth object F. Whenever a thread wants to acquire the lock for any object $A \cdots E$, it must first acquire the lock for object F. This solution is known as **containment**: The locks for objects $A \cdots E$ are contained within the lock for object F. Compare this scheme with the circular-wait scheme of Section 8.4.4.

8.6 In a real computer system, neither the resources available nor the demands of processes for resources are consistent over long periods (months). Resources break or are replaced, new processes come and go, new resources are bought and added to the system. If deadlock is controlled by the banker's algorithm, which of the following changes can be made

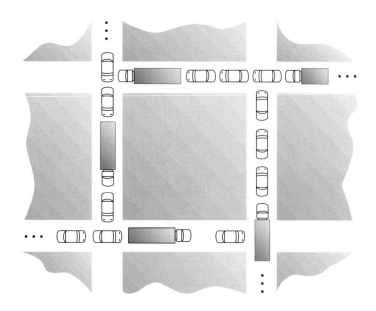

Figure 8.12   Traffic deadlock for Exercise 8.3.

safely (without introducing the possibility of deadlock), and under what circumstances?

- a. Increase *Available* (new resources added).

- b. Decrease *Available* (resource permanently removed from system).

- c. Increase *Max* for one process (the process needs more resources than allowed; it may want more).

- d. Decrease *Max* for one process (the process decides it does not need that many resources).

- e. Increase the number of processes.

- f. Decrease the number of processes.

8.7 Prove that the safety algorithm presented in Section 8.5.3 requires an order of $m \times n^2$ operations.

8.8 Consider a system consisting of four resources of the same type that are shared by three processes, each of which needs at most two resources. Show that the system is deadlock free.

8.9 Consider a system consisting of m resources of the same type being shared by n processes. Resources can be requested and released by processes only one at a time. Show that the system is deadlock free if the following two conditions hold:

a. The maximum need of each process is between 1 and m resources.

b. The sum of all maximum needs is less than $m + n$.

8.10 Consider a computer system that runs 5,000 jobs per month with no deadlock-prevention or deadlock-avoidance scheme. Deadlocks occur about twice per month, and the operator must terminate and rerun about 10 jobs per deadlock. Each job is worth about $2 (in CPU time), and the jobs terminated tend to be about half done when they are aborted.

A systems programmer has estimated that a deadlock-avoidance algorithm (like the banker's algorithm) could be installed in the system with an increase in the average execution time per job of about 10 percent. Since the machine currently has 30-percent idle time, all 5,000 jobs per month could still be run, although turnaround time would increase by about 20 percent on average.

a. What are the arguments for installing the deadlock-avoidance algorithm?

b. What are the arguments against installing the deadlock-avoidance algorithm?

8.11 We can obtain the banker's algorithm for a single resource type from the general banker's algorithm simply by reducing the dimensionality of the various arrays by 1. Show through an example that the multiple-resource-type banker's scheme cannot be implemented by individual application of the single-resource-type scheme to each resource type.

8.12 Can a system detect that some of its processes are starving? If you answer "yes," explain how it can. If you answer "no," explain how the system can deal with the starvation problem.

8.13 Consider the following snapshot of a system:

	Allocation	Max	Available
	A B C D	A B C D	A B C D
P_0	0 0 1 2	0 0 1 2	1 5 2 0
P_1	1 0 0 0	1 7 5 0	
P_2	1 3 5 4	2 3 5 6	
P_3	0 6 3 2	0 6 5 2	
P_4	0 0 1 4	0 6 5 6	

Answer the following questions using the banker's algorithm:

a. What is the content of the matrix *Need*?

b. Is the system in a safe state?

c. If a request from process P_1 arrives for (0,4,2,0), can the request be granted immediately?

8.14 Consider the following resource-allocation policy.   Requests for and releases of resources are allowed at any time. If a request for resources cannot be satisfied because the resources are not available, then we check any processes that are blocked, waiting for resources. If they have the desired resources, then these resources are taken away from them and are given to the requesting process. The vector of resources that a waiting process needs is increased to include the resources that were taken away.

For example, consider a system with three resource types and the vector *Available* initialized to (4,2,2). If process P_0 asks for (2,2,1), it gets them. If P_1 asks for (1,0,1), it gets them. Then, if P_0 asks for (0,0,1), it is blocked (resource not available). If P_2 now asks for (2,0,0), it gets the available one (1,0,0) along with one that was allocated to P_0 (since P_0 is blocked). P_0's *Allocation* vector goes down to (1,2,1), and its *Need* vector goes up to (1,0,1).

a. Can deadlock occur? If so, give an example. If not, which necessary condition cannot occur?

b. Can indefinite blocking occur?

8.15 Suppose that you have coded the deadlock-avoidance safety algorithm and now have been asked to implement the deadlock-detection algorithm. Can you do so by simply using the safety algorithm code and redefining $Max_i = Waiting_i + Allocation_i$, where $Waiting_i$ is a vector specifying the resources for which process i is waiting and $Allocation_i$ is as defined in Section 8.5? Explain your answer.

8.16 Write a Java program that illustrates deadlock by having `synchronized` methods calling other `synchronized` methods.

8.17 Write a Java program that illustrates deadlock by having separate threads attempt to perform operations on different semaphores.

8.18 Write a multithreaded Java program that implements the banker's algorithm discussed in Section 8.5.3. Create n threads that request and release resources from the bank. The banker will grant the request only if it leaves the system in a safe state. Ensure that access to shared data is thread-safe by employing Java thread synchronization as discussed in Section 7.8.

8.19 A railroad tunnel with a single set of tracks connects two Vermont villages. The railroad can become deadlocked if both a northbound and a southbound train enter the tunnel at the same time (the trains are unable to back up). Write a Java program that prevents deadlock using either semaphores or Java synchronization. Initially, do not be concerned about starvation (the situation in which northbound trains prevent southbound trains from using the tunnel, or vice versa), and do not be concerned about trains failing to stop and crashing into each other.

8.20 Modify your solution to Exercise 8.19 so that it is starvation-free.

Bibliographical Notes

Dijkstra [1965a] was one of the first and most influential contributors in the deadlock area. Holt [1972] was the first person to formalize the notion of deadlocks in terms of a graph-theoretical model similar to the one presented in this chapter. Starvation was covered by Holt [1972]. Hyman [1985] provided the deadlock example from the Kansas legislature. A recent study of deadlock handling is provided in Levine [2003].

The various prevention algorithms were suggested by Havender [1968], who devised the resource-ordering scheme for the IBM OS/360 system.

The banker's algorithm for avoiding deadlocks was developed for a single resource type by Dijkstra [1965a] and was extended to multiple resource types by Habermann [1969]. Exercises 8.8 and 8.9 are from Holt [1971].

The deadlock-detection algorithm for multiple instances of a resource type, which was described in Section 8.6.2, was presented by Coffman et al. [1971].

Bach [1987] describes how many of the algorithms in the traditional UNIX kernel handle deadlock.

The witness lock-order verifier is presented in Baldwin [2002].

Part Three

STORAGE MANAGEMENT

The main purpose of a computer system is to execute programs. These programs, together with the data they access, must be in main memory (at least partially) during execution.

To improve both the utilization of the CPU and the speed of its response to users, the computer must keep several processes in memory. Many memory-management schemes exist, reflecting various approaches, and the effectiveness of each algorithm depends on the situation. Selection of a memory-management scheme for a system depends on many factors, especially on the *hardware* design of the system. Each algorithm requires its own hardware support.

Since main memory is usually too small to accommodate all the data and programs permanently, the computer system must provide secondary storage to back up main memory. Modern computer systems use disks as the primary on-line storage medium for information (both programs and data). The file system provides the mechanism for on-line storage of and access to both data and programs residing on the disks. A file is a collection of related information defined by its creator. The files are mapped by the operating system onto physical devices. Files are normally organized into directories to ease their use.

Chapter 9

MEMORY MANAGEMENT

In Chapter 6, we showed how the CPU can be shared by a set of processes. As a result of CPU scheduling, we can improve both the utilization of the CPU and the speed of the computer's response to its users. To realize this increase in performance, however, we must keep several processes in memory; that is, we must *share* memory.

In this chapter, we discuss various ways to manage memory. The memory-management algorithms vary from a primitive bare-machine approach to paging and segmentation strategies. Each approach has its own advantages and disadvantages. Selection of a memory-management method for a specific system depends on many factors, especially on the *hardware* design of the system. As we shall see, many algorithms require hardware support, although recent designs have closely integrated the hardware and operating system.

9.1 ■ Background

As we saw in Chapter 1, memory is central to the operation of a modern computer system. Memory consists of a large array of words or bytes, each with its own address. The CPU fetches instructions from memory according to the value of the program counter. These instructions may cause additional loading from and storing to specific memory addresses.

A typical instruction-execution cycle, for example, first fetches an instruction from memory. The instruction is then decoded and may cause operands to be fetched from memory. After the instruction has been executed on the operands, results may be stored back in memory. The memory unit sees only a stream of memory addresses; it does not know how they are generated (by the instruction counter, indexing, indirection, literal addresses, and so on) or what they are for (instructions or data). Accordingly, we can ignore *how* a program generates a memory address. We are interested only in the sequence of memory addresses generated by the running program.

9.1.1 Address Binding

Usually, a program resides on a disk as a binary executable file. To be executed, the program must be brought into memory and placed within a process. Depending on the memory management in use, the process may be moved between disk and memory during its execution. The processes on the disk that are waiting to be brought into memory for execution form the **input queue**.

The normal procedure is to select one of the processes in the input queue and to load that process into memory. As the process is executed, it accesses instructions and data from memory. Eventually, the process terminates, and its memory space is declared available.

Most systems allow a user process to reside in any part of the physical memory. Thus, although the address space of the computer starts at 00000, the first address of the user process need not be 00000. This approach affects the addresses that the user program can use. In most cases, a user program will go through several steps—some of which may be optional—before being executed (Figure 9.1). Addresses may be represented in different ways during these steps. Addresses in the source program are generally symbolic (such as *count*). A compiler will typically **bind** these symbolic addresses to relocatable addresses (such as "14 bytes from the beginning of this module"). The linkage editor or loader will in turn bind the relocatable addresses to absolute addresses (such as 74014). Each binding is a mapping from one address space to another.

Classically, the binding of instructions and data to memory addresses can be done at any step along the way:

- **Compile time:** If you know at compile time where the process will reside in memory, then **absolute code** can be generated. For example, if you know that a user process will reside starting at location *R*, then the generated compiler code will start at that location and extend up from there. If, at some later time, the starting location changes, then it will be necessary to recompile this code. The MS-DOS .COM-format programs are bound at compile time.

- **Load time:** If it is not known at compile time where the process will reside in memory, then the compiler must generate **relocatable code**. In this case, final binding is delayed until load time. If the starting address changes, we need only reload the user code to incorporate this changed value.

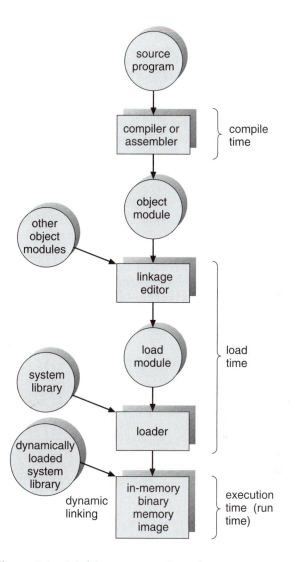

Figure 9.1 Multistep processing of a user program.

- **Execution time:** If the process can be moved during its execution from one memory segment to another, then binding must be delayed until run time. Special hardware must be available for this scheme to work, as will be discussed in Section 9.1.2. Most general-purpose operating systems use this method.

A major portion of this chapter is devoted to showing how these various bindings can be implemented effectively in a computer system and to discussing appropriate hardware support.

9.1.2 Logical- versus Physical-Address Space

An address generated by the CPU is commonly referred to as a **logical address**, whereas an address seen by the memory unit—that is, the one loaded into the **memory-address register** of the memory—is commonly referred to as a **physical address**.

The compile-time and load-time address-binding methods generate identical logical and physical addresses. However, the execution-time address-binding scheme results in differing logical and physical addresses. In this case, we usually refer to the logical address as a **virtual address**. We use *logical address* and *virtual address* interchangeably in this text. The set of all logical addresses generated by a program is a **logical-address space**; the set of all physical addresses corresponding to these logical addresses is a **physical-address space**. Thus, in the execution-time address-binding scheme, the logical- and physical-address spaces differ.

The run-time mapping from virtual to physical addresses is done by a hardware device called the **memory-management unit (MMU)**. We can choose from many different methods to accomplish such mapping, as we discuss in Sections 9.3 through 9.6. For the time being, we illustrate this mapping with a simple MMU scheme, which is a generalization of the base-register scheme described in Section 2.5.3.

As illustrated in Figure 9.2, this method requires hardware support slightly different from the hardware configuration discussed in Section 2.4. The base register is now called a **relocation register**. The value in the relocation register is *added* to every address generated by a user process at the time it is sent to memory. For example, if the base is at 14000, then an attempt by the user to address location 0 is dynamically relocated to location 14000; an access

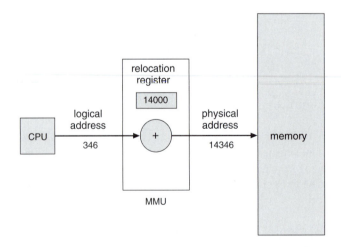

Figure 9.2   Dynamic relocation using a relocation register.

to location 346 is mapped to location 14346. The MS-DOS operating system running on the Intel 80x86 family of processors uses four relocation registers when loading and running processes.

The user program never sees the *real* physical addresses. The program can create a pointer to location 346, store it in memory, manipulate it, and compare it with other addresses—all as the number 346. Only when it is used as a memory address (in an indirect load or store, perhaps) is it relocated relative to the base register. The user program deals with *logical* addresses. The memory-mapping hardware converts logical addresses into physical addresses. This form of execution-time binding was discussed in Section 9.1.1. The final location of a referenced memory address is not determined until the reference is made.

We now have two different types of addresses: logical addresses (in the range 0 to *max*) and physical addresses (in the range $R + 0$ to $R + max$ for a base value R). The user generates only logical addresses and thinks that the process runs in locations 0 to *max*. The user program supplies logical addresses; these logical addresses must be mapped to physical addresses before they are used.

The concept of a *logical-address space* that is bound to a separate *physical-address space* is central to proper memory management.

9.1.3 Dynamic Loading

In our discussion so far, the entire program and all data of a process must be in physical memory for the process to execute. The size of a process is thus limited to the size of physical memory. To obtain better memory-space utilization, we can use **dynamic loading**. With dynamic loading, a routine is not loaded until it is called. All routines are kept on disk in a relocatable load format. The main program is loaded into memory and is executed. When a routine needs to call another routine, the calling routine first checks to see whether the other routine has been loaded. If not, the relocatable linking loader is called to load the desired routine into memory and to update the program's address tables to reflect this change. Then control is passed to the newly loaded routine.

The advantage of dynamic loading is that an unused routine is never loaded. This method is particularly useful when large amounts of code are needed to handle infrequently occurring cases, such as error routines. In this case, although the total program size may be large, the portion that is used (and hence loaded) may be much smaller.

Dynamic loading does not require special support from the operating system. It is the responsibility of the users to design their programs to take advantage of such a method. Operating systems may help the programmer, however, by providing library routines to implement dynamic loading.

9.1.4 Dynamic Linking and Shared Libraries

Figure 9.1 also shows **dynamically linked libraries**. Some operating systems support only **static linking**, in which system language libraries are treated like any other object module and are combined by the loader into the binary program image. The concept of dynamic linking is similar to that of dynamic loading. Here, though, linking, rather than loading, is postponed until execution time. This feature is usually used with system libraries, such as language subroutine libraries. Without this facility, each program on a system must have a copy of its language library (or at least the routines referenced by the program) included in the executable image. This requirement wastes both disk space and main memory.

With dynamic linking, a *stub* is included in the image for each library-routine reference. The stub is a small piece of code that indicates how to locate the appropriate memory-resident library routine or how to load the library if the routine is not already present. When the stub is executed, it checks to see whether the needed routine is already in memory. If not, the program loads the routine into memory. Either way, the stub replaces itself with the address of the routine and executes the routine. Thus, the next time that particular code segment is reached, the library routine is executed directly, incurring no cost for dynamic linking. Under this scheme, all processes that use a language library execute only one copy of the library code.

This feature can be extended to library updates (such as bug fixes). A library may be replaced by a new version, and all programs that reference the library will automatically use the new version. Without dynamic linking, all such programs would need to be relinked to gain access to the new library. So that programs will not accidentally execute new, incompatible versions of libraries, version information is included in both the program and the library. More than one version of a library may be loaded into memory, and each program uses its version information to decide which copy of the library to use. Minor changes retain the same version number, whereas major changes increment the version number. Thus, only programs that are compiled with the new library version are affected by the incompatible changes incorporated in it. Other programs linked before the new library was installed will continue using the older library. This system is also known as **shared libraries**.

Unlike dynamic loading, dynamic linking generally requires help from the operating system. If the processes in memory are protected from one another (Section 9.3), then the operating system is the only entity that can check to see whether the needed routine is in another process's memory space or that can allow multiple processes to access the same memory addresses. We elaborate on this concept when we discuss paging in Section 9.4.5.

9.1.5 Overlays

To enable a process to be larger than the amount of memory allocated to it, we can use **overlays**. The idea of overlays is to keep in memory only those instructions and data that are needed at any given time. When other instructions are needed, they are loaded into space occupied previously by instructions that are no longer needed.

As an example, consider a two-pass assembler. During pass 1, it constructs a symbol table; then, during pass 2, it generates machine-language code. We may be able to partition such an assembler into pass 1 code, pass 2 code, the symbol table, and common support routines used by both pass 1 and pass 2. Assume that the sizes of these components are as follows:

Pass 1	70 KB
Pass 2	80 KB
Symbol table	20 KB
Common routines	30 KB

To load everything at once, we would require 200 KB of memory. If only 150 KB is available, we cannot run our process. However, notice that pass 1 and pass 2 do not need to be in memory at the same time. We thus define two overlays: Overlay A is the symbol table, common routines, and pass 1; and overlay B is the symbol table, common routines, and pass 2.

We add an **overlay driver** (which manages the overlays and requires 10 KB itself) and start with overlay A in memory. When we finish pass 1, we jump to the overlay driver, which reads overlay B into memory, overwriting overlay A, and then transfers control to pass 2. Overlay A needs only 120 KB, whereas overlay B needs 130 KB (Figure 9.3). We can now run our assembler in the 150 KB of memory. It will load somewhat faster because fewer data need to be transferred before execution starts. However, it will run somewhat slower because of the extra I/O required to read the code for overlay B over the code for overlay A.

The code for overlay A and the code for overlay B are kept on disk as absolute memory images and are read by the overlay driver as needed. Special relocation and linking algorithms are needed to construct the overlays.

Overlays do not require any special support from the operating system. They can be implemented completely by the user with simple file structures. The operating system notices only that there is more I/O than usual.

The programmer, however, must design and program the overlay structure properly. This task can be a major undertaking, requiring complete knowledge of the structure of the program, its code, and its data structures. Because the program is, by definition, large—small programs do not need to be overlaid—obtaining a sufficient understanding of the program may be difficult. For these reasons, the use of overlays is currently limited to microcomputer and other systems that have limited amounts of physical memory and that lack hardware support for more advanced techniques. Some microcomputer compilers provide the programmer with support for overlays to make the task easier. Automatic techniques to run large programs in limited amounts of physical memory are certainly preferable.

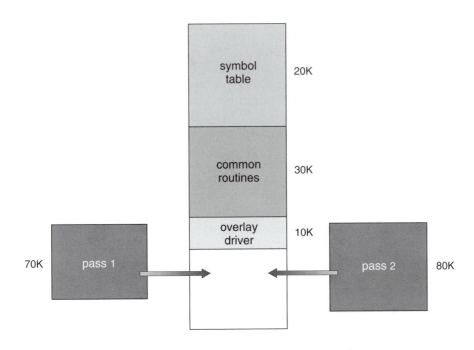

Figure 9.3   Overlays for a two-pass assembler.

9.2 ■ Swapping

A process must be in memory to be executed. A process, however, can be **swapped** temporarily out of memory to a **backing store** and then brought back into memory for continued execution. For example, assume a multiprogramming environment with a round-robin CPU-scheduling algorithm. When a quantum expires, the memory manager will start to swap out the process that just finished and to swap another process into the memory space that has been freed (Figure 9.4). In the meantime, the CPU scheduler will allocate a time slice to some other process in memory. When each process finishes its quantum, it will be swapped with another process. Ideally, the memory manager can swap processes fast enough that some processes will be in memory, ready to execute, when the CPU scheduler wants to reschedule the CPU. In addition, the quantum must be sufficiently large that reasonable amounts of computing are done between swaps.

A variant of this swapping policy is used for priority-based scheduling algorithms. If a higher-priority process arrives and wants service, the memory manager can swap out the lower-priority process and then load and execute the higher-priority process. When the higher-priority process finishes, the lower-priority process can be swapped back in and continued. This variant of swapping is sometimes called **roll out, roll in**.

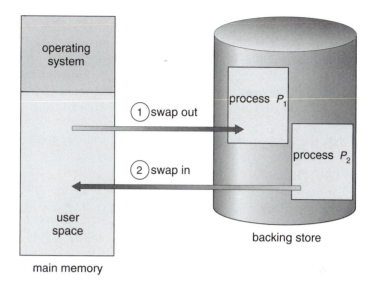

operating
system

(1) swap out

process P_1

(2) swap in

process P_2

user
space

backing store

main memory

Figure 9.4 Swapping of two processes using a disk as a backing store.

Normally, a process that is swapped out will be swapped back into the same memory space that it occupied previously. This restriction is dictated by the method of address binding. If binding is done at assembly or load time, then the process cannot be easily moved to a different location. If execution-time binding is being used, however, then a process can be swapped into a different memory space, because the physical addresses are computed during execution time.

Swapping requires a backing store. The backing store is commonly a fast disk. It must be large enough to accommodate copies of all memory images for all users, and it must provide direct access to these memory images. The system maintains a **ready queue** consisting of all processes whose memory images are on the backing store or in memory and are ready to run. Whenever the CPU scheduler decides to execute a process, it calls the dispatcher. The dispatcher checks to see whether the next process in the queue is in memory. If it is not, and if there is no free memory region, the dispatcher swaps out a process currently in memory and swaps in the desired process. It then reloads registers and transfers control to the selected process.

The context-switch time in such a swapping system is fairly high. To get an idea of the context-switch time, let us assume that the user process is of size 1 MB and the backing store is a standard hard disk with a transfer rate of 5 MB per second. The actual transfer of the 1-MB process to or from main memory takes

$$1000 \text{ KB}/5000 \text{ KB per second} = 1/5 \text{ second}$$
$$= 200 \text{ milliseconds}.$$

Assuming that no seeks are necessary and an average latency of 8 milliseconds, the swap time is 208 milliseconds. Since we must both swap out and
swap in, the total swap time is then about 416 milliseconds.

For efficient CPU utilization, we want the execution time for each process
to be long relative to the swap time. Thus, in a round-robin CPU-scheduling
algorithm, for example, the time quantum should be substantially larger than
0.416 seconds.

Notice that the major part of the swap time is transfer time. The total
transfer time is directly proportional to the *amount* of memory swapped. If
we have a computer system with 128 MB of main memory and a resident
operating system taking 5 MB, the maximum size of the user process is 123
MB. However, many user processes may be much smaller than this size—say,
1 MB. A 1-MB process could be swapped out in 208 milliseconds, compared
with the 24.6 seconds required for swapping 123 MB. Clearly, it would be useful
to know exactly how much memory a user process *is* using, not simply how
much it *might be* using. Then, we would need to swap only what is actually
used, reducing swap time. For this method to be effective, the user must keep
the system informed of any changes in memory requirements. Thus, a process
with dynamic memory requirements will need to issue system calls (`request
memory` and `release memory`) to inform the operating system of its changing
memory needs.

Swapping is constrained by other factors as well. If we want to swap
a process, we must be sure that it is completely idle. Of particular concern
is any pending I/O. A process may be waiting for an I/O operation when
we want to swap that process to free up memory. However, if the I/O is
asynchronously accessing the user memory for I/O buffers, then the process
cannot be swapped. Assume that the I/O operation is queued because the
device is busy. If we were to swap out process P_1 and swap in process P_2, the
I/O operation might then attempt to use memory that now belongs to process
P_2. There are two main solutions to this problem: Never swap a process with
pending I/O, or execute I/O operations only into operating-system buffers.
Transfers between operating-system buffers and process memory then occur
only when the process is swapped in.

The assumption, mentioned earlier, that swapping requires few, if any,
head seeks needs further explanation. We postpone discussing this issue until
Chapter 14, where secondary-storage structure is covered. Generally, swap
space is allocated as a chunk of disk, separate from the file system, so that its
use is as fast as possible.

Currently, standard swapping is used in few systems. It requires too
much swapping time and provides too little execution time to be a reasonable
memory-management solution. Modified versions of swapping, however, are
found on many systems.

A modification of swapping is used in many versions of UNIX. Swapping is
normally disabled but will start if many processes are running and are using a

threshold amount of memory. Swapping is again halted when the load on the system is reduced. Memory management in UNIX is described fully in Section A.6.

Early PCs—which lacked the sophistication to implement more advanced memory-management methods—ran multiple large processes by using a modified version of swapping. A prime example is the Microsoft Windows 3.1 operating system, which supports concurrent execution of processes in memory. If a new process is loaded and there is insufficient main memory, an old process is swapped to disk. This operating system, however, does not provide full swapping, because the user, rather than the scheduler, decides when it is time to preempt one process for another. Any swapped-out process remains swapped out (and not executing) until the user selects that process to run. Subsequent versions of Microsoft operating systems take advantage of advanced MMU features now found in PCs. We will explore such features in Section 9.4 and in Chapter 10, where we cover virtual memory.

9.3 ■ Contiguous-Memory Allocation

The main memory must accommodate both the operating system and the various user processes. We therefore need to allocate the parts of the main memory in the most efficient way possible. This section explains one common method, contiguous memory allocation.

The memory is usually divided into two partitions: one for the resident operating system and one for the user processes. We can place the operating system in either low memory or high memory. The major factor affecting this decision is the location of the interrupt vector. Since the interrupt vector is often in low memory, programmers usually place the operating system in low memory as well. Thus, in this text, we discuss only the situation where the operating system resides in low memory. The development of the other situation is similar.

We usually want several user processes to reside in memory at the same time. We therefore need to consider how to allocate available memory to the processes that are in the input queue waiting to be brought into memory. In this **contiguous-memory** allocation, each process is contained in a single contiguous section of memory.

9.3.1 Memory Protection

Before discussing memory allocation further, we must discuss the issue of memory protection—protecting the operating system from user processes and protecting user processes from one another. We can provide this protection by using a relocation register, as discussed in Section 9.1.2, with a limit register, as discussed in Section 2.5.3. The relocation register contains the value of

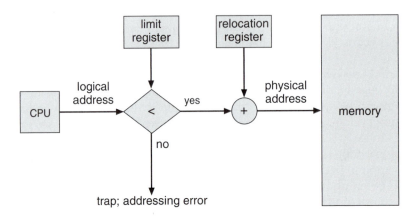

Figure 9.5   Hardware support for relocation and limit registers.

the smallest physical address; the limit register contains the range of logical addresses (for example, relocation = 100040 and limit = 74600). With relocation and limit registers, each logical address must be less than the limit register; the MMU maps the logical address *dynamically* by adding the value in the relocation register. This mapped address is sent to memory (Figure 9.5).

When the CPU scheduler selects a process for execution, the dispatcher loads the relocation and limit registers with the correct values as part of the context switch. Because every address generated by the CPU is checked against these registers, we can protect both the operating system and the other users' programs and data from being modified by this running process.

The relocation-register scheme provides an effective way to allow the operating-system size to change dynamically. This flexibility is desirable in many situations. For example, the operating system contains code and buffer space for device drivers. If a device driver (or other operating-system service) is not commonly used, we do not want to keep the code and data in memory, as we might be able to use that space for other purposes. Such code is sometimes called **transient** operating-system code; it comes and goes as needed. Thus, using this code changes the size of the operating system during program execution.

9.3.2 Memory Allocation

Now we are ready to turn to memory allocation. One of the simplest methods for memory allocation is to divide memory into several fixed-sized **partitions**. Each partition may contain exactly one process. Thus, the degree of multiprogramming is bound by the number of partitions. In this **multiple-partition method**, when a partition is free, a process is selected from the input queue and is loaded into the free partition. When the process terminates, the partition becomes available for another process. This method was originally used by the

IBM OS/360 operating system (called MFT); it is no longer in use. The method described next is a generalization of the fixed-partition scheme (called MVT); it is used primarily in a batch environment. Many of the ideas presented here are also applicable to a time-sharing environment in which pure segmentation is used for memory management (Section 9.5).

In the fixed-partition scheme, the operating system keeps a table indicating which parts of memory are available and which are occupied. Initially, all memory is available for user processes and is considered as one large block of available memory, a **hole**. When a process arrives and needs memory, we search for a hole large enough for this process. If we find one, we allocate only as much memory as is needed, keeping the rest available to satisfy future requests.

As processes enter the system, they are put into an input queue. The operating system takes into account the memory requirements of each process and the amount of available memory space in determining which processes are allocated memory. When a process is allocated space, it is loaded into memory, and it can then compete for the CPU. When a process terminates, it releases its memory, which the operating system may then fill with another process from the input queue.

At any given time, we have a list of available block sizes and the input queue. The operating system can order the input queue according to a scheduling algorithm. Memory is allocated to processes until, finally, the memory requirements of the next process cannot be satisfied — that is, no available block of memory (or hole) is large enough to hold that process. The operating system can then wait until a large enough block is available, or it can skip down the input queue to see whether the smaller memory requirements of some other process can be met.

In general, at any given time we have a *set* of holes of various sizes scattered throughout memory. When a process arrives and needs memory, the system searches the set for a hole that is large enough for this process. If the hole is too large, it is split into two parts. One part is allocated to the arriving process; the other is returned to the set of holes. When a process terminates, it releases its block of memory, which is then placed back in the set of holes. If the new hole is adjacent to other holes, these adjacent holes are merged to form one larger hole. At this point, the system may need to check whether there are processes waiting for memory and whether this newly freed and recombined memory could satisfy the demands of any of these waiting processes.

This procedure is a particular instance of the general **dynamic storage-allocation problem**, which concerns how to satisfy a request of size n from a list of free holes. There are many solutions to this problem. The **first-fit, best-fit**, and **worst-fit** strategies are the ones most commonly used to select a free hole from the set of available holes.

- *First fit:* Allocate the *first* hole that is big enough. Searching can start either at the beginning of the set of holes or where the previous first-fit search ended. We can stop searching as soon as we find a free hole that is large enough.

- *Best fit:* Allocate the *smallest* hole that is big enough. We must search the entire list, unless the list is ordered by size. This strategy produces the smallest leftover hole.

- *Worst fit:* Allocate the *largest* hole. Again, we must search the entire list, unless it is sorted by size. This strategy produces the largest leftover hole, which may be more useful than the smaller leftover hole from a best-fit approach.

Simulations have shown that both first fit and best fit are better than worst fit in terms of decreasing time and storage utilization. Neither first fit nor best fit is clearly better than the other in terms of storage utilization, but first fit is generally faster.

9.3.3 Fragmentation

Both the first-fit and the best-fit strategies for memory allocation suffer from **external fragmentation**. As processes are loaded and removed from memory, the free memory space is broken into little pieces. External fragmentation exists when there is enough total memory space to satisfy a request, but the available spaces are not contiguous; storage is fragmented into a large number of small holes. This fragmentation problem can be severe. In the worst case, we could have a block of free (or wasted) memory between every two processes. If all these small pieces of memory were in one big free block instead, we might be able to run several more processes.

Whether we are using the first-fit or best-fit strategy can affect the amount of fragmentation. (First fit is better for some systems, whereas best fit is better for others.) Another factor is which end of a free block is allocated. (Which is the leftover piece—the one on the top, or the one on the bottom?) No matter which algorithm is used, external fragmentation will be a problem.

Depending on the total amount of memory storage and the average process size, external fragmentation may be a minor or a major problem. Statistical analysis of first fit, for instance, reveals that, even with some optimization, given N allocated blocks, another $0.5N$ blocks will be lost to fragmentation. That is, one-third of memory may be unusable! This property is known as the **50-percent rule**.

Memory fragmentation can be internal as well as external. Consider a multiple-partition allocation scheme with a hole of 18,464 bytes. Suppose that the next process requests 18,462 bytes. If we allocate exactly the requested block, we are left with a hole of 2 bytes. The overhead to keep track of this hole will be substantially larger than the hole itself. The general approach to avoiding this problem is to break the physical memory into fixed-sized blocks and allocate memory in units based on block size. With this approach, the memory allocated to a process may be slightly larger than the requested memory. The difference between these two numbers is **internal fragmentation** —memory that is internal to a partition but is not being used.

One solution to the problem of external fragmentation is **compaction**. The goal is to shuffle the memory contents so as to place all free memory together in one large block. Compaction is not always possible, however. If relocation is static and is done at assembly or load time, compaction cannot be done; compaction is possible *only* if relocation is dynamic and is done at execution time. If addresses are relocated dynamically, relocation requires only moving the program and data and then changing the base register to reflect the new base address. When compaction is possible, we must determine its cost. The simplest compaction algorithm is to move all processes toward one end of memory; all holes move in the other direction, producing one large hole of available memory. This scheme can be expensive.

Another possible solution to the external-fragmentation problem is to permit the logical-address space of a process to be noncontiguous, thus allowing a process to be allocated physical memory wherever the latter is available. Two complementary techniques achieve this solution: paging (Section 9.4) and segmentation (Section 9.5). These techniques can also be combined (Section 9.6).

9.4 ■ Paging

Paging is a memory-management scheme that permits the physical-address space of a process to be noncontiguous. Paging avoids the considerable problem of fitting memory chunks of varying sizes onto the backing store; most memory-management schemes used before the introduction of paging suffered from this problem. The problem arises because, when some code fragments or data residing in main memory need to be swapped out, space must be found on the backing store. The backing store also has the fragmentation problems discussed in connection with main memory, except that access is much slower, so compaction is impossible. Because of its advantages over earlier methods, paging in its various forms is commonly used in most operating systems.

Traditionally, support for paging has been handled by hardware. However, recent designs have implemented paging by closely integrating the hardware and operating system, especially on 64-bit microprocessors.

9.4.1 Basic Method

The basic method for implementing paging involves breaking physical memory into fixed-sized blocks called **frames** and breaking logical memory into blocks of the same size called **pages**. When a process is to be executed, its pages are loaded into any available memory frames from the backing store. The backing

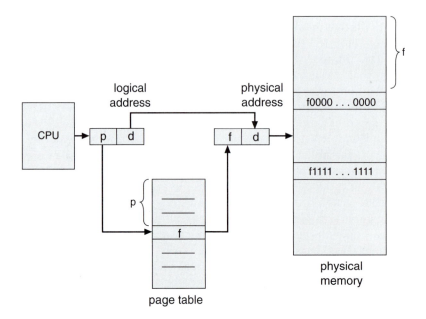

Figure 9.6   Paging hardware.

store is divided into fixed-sized blocks that are of the same size as the memory frames.

The hardware support for paging is illustrated in Figure 9.6. Every address generated by the CPU is divided into two parts: a **page number (p)** and a **page offset (d)**. The page number is used as an index into a **page table**. The page table contains the base address of each page in physical memory. This base address is combined with the page offset to define the physical memory address that is sent to the memory unit. The paging model of memory is shown in Figure 9.7.

The page size (like the frame size) is defined by the hardware. The size of a page is typically a power of 2, varying between 512 bytes and 16 MB per page, depending on the computer architecture. The selection of a power of 2 as a page size makes the translation of a logical address into a page number and page offset particularly easy. If the size of logical-address space is 2^m, and a page size is 2^n addressing units (bytes or words), then the high-order $m - n$ bits of a logical address designate the page number, and the n low-order bits designate the page offset. Thus, the logical address is as follows:

page number	page offset
p	d
$m - n$	n

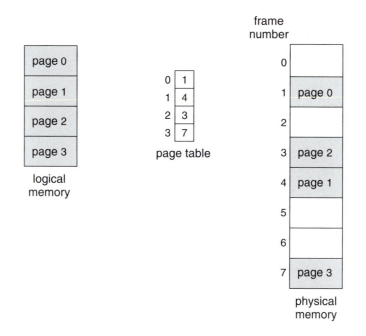

Figure 9.7 Paging model of logical and physical memory.

where p is an index into the page table and d is the displacement within the page.

As a concrete (although minuscule) example, consider the memory in Figure 9.8. Using a page size of 4 bytes and a physical memory of 32 bytes (8 pages), we show how the user's view of memory can be mapped into physical memory. Logical address 0 is page 0, offset 0. Indexing into the page table, we find that page 0 is in frame 5. Thus, logical address 0 maps to physical address 20 (= (5 × 4) + 0). Logical address 3 (page 0, offset 3) maps to physical address 23 (= (5 × 4) + 3). Logical address 4 is page 1, offset 0; according to the page table, page 1 is mapped to frame 6. Thus, logical address 4 maps to physical address 24 (= (6 × 4) + 0). Logical address 13 maps to physical address 9.

You may have noticed that paging itself is a form of dynamic relocation. Every logical address is bound by the paging hardware to some physical address. Using paging is similar to using a table of base (or relocation) registers, one for each frame of memory.

When we use a paging scheme, we have no external fragmentation: *Any* free frame can be allocated to a process that needs it. However, we may have some internal fragmentation. Notice that frames are allocated as units. If the memory requirements of a process do not happen to coincide with page boundaries, the *last* frame allocated may not be completely full. For example, if page size is 2,048 bytes, a process of 72,766 bytes would need 35 pages plus 1,086 bytes. It would be allocated 36 frames, resulting in an internal fragmentation

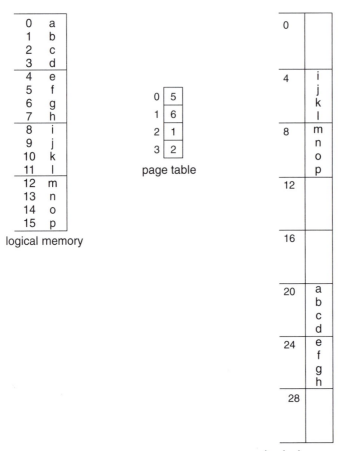

Figure 9.8   Paging example for a 32-byte memory with 4-byte pages.

of 2048 − 1086 = 962 bytes. In the worst case, a process would need n pages plus one byte. It would be allocated $n + 1$ frames, resulting in an internal fragmentation of almost an entire frame.

If process size is independent of page size, we expect internal fragmentation to average one-half page per process. This consideration suggests that small page sizes are desirable. However, overhead is involved in each page-table entry, and this overhead is reduced as the size of the pages increases. Also, disk I/O is more efficient when the number of data being transferred is larger (Chapter 14). Generally, page sizes have grown over time as processes, data sets, and main memory have become larger. Today, pages typically are between 4 KB and 8 KB in size, and some systems support even larger page sizes. Some CPUs and kernels even support multiple page sizes. For instance, Solaris uses page sizes of 8 KB and 4 MB, depending on the data stored by the pages. Researchers are now developing variable on-the-fly page-size support.

Usually, each page-table entry is 4 bytes long, but that size can vary as well. A 32-bit entry can point to one of 2^{32} physical page frames. If frame size is 4 KB, then a system with 4-byte entries can address 2^{44} bytes (or 16 TB) of physical memory.

When a process arrives in the system to be executed, its size, expressed in pages, is examined. Each page of the process needs one frame. Thus, if the process requires n pages, at least n frames must be available in memory. If n frames are available, they are allocated to this arriving process. The first page of the process is loaded into one of the allocated frames, and the frame number is put in the page table for this process. The next page is loaded into another frame, and its frame number is put into the page table, and so on (Figure 9.9).

An important aspect of paging is the clear separation between the user's view of memory and the actual physical memory. The user program views memory as one single space, containing only this one program. In fact, the user program is scattered throughout physical memory, which also holds other programs. The difference between the user's view of memory and the actual physical memory is reconciled by the address-translation hardware. The logical addresses are translated into physical addresses. This mapping is hidden from the user and is controlled by the operating system. Notice that the user process

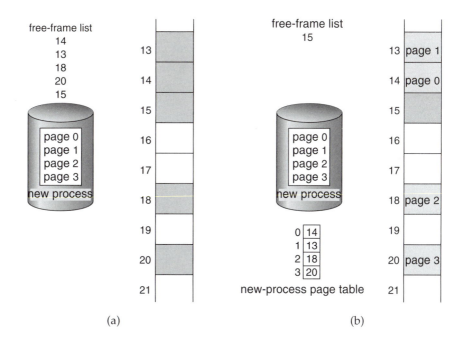

(a)   (b)

Figure 9.9   Free frames. (a) Before allocation. (b) After allocation.

by definition is unable to access memory it does not own. It has no way of addressing memory outside of its page table, and the table includes only those pages that the process owns.

Since the operating system is managing physical memory, it must be aware of the allocation details of physical memory—which frames are allocated, which frames are available, how many total frames there are, and so on. This information is generally kept in a data structure called a **frame table**. The frame table has one entry for each physical page frame, indicating whether the latter is free or allocated and, if it is allocated, to which page of which process or processes.

In addition, the operating system must be aware that user processes operate in user space, and all logical addresses must be mapped to produce physical addresses. If a user makes a system call (to do I/O, for example) and provides an address as a parameter (a buffer, for instance), that address must be mapped to produce the correct physical address. The operating system maintains a copy of the page table for each process, just as it maintains a copy of the instruction counter and register contents. This copy is used to translate logical addresses to physical addresses whenever the operating system must map a logical address to a physical address manually. It is also used by the CPU dispatcher to define the hardware page table when a process is to be allocated the CPU. Paging therefore increases the context-switch time.

9.4.2 Hardware Support

Each operating system has its own methods for storing page tables. Most allocate a page table for each process. A pointer to the page table is stored with the other register values (like the instruction counter) in the process control block. When the dispatcher is told to start a process, it must reload the user registers and define the correct hardware page-table values from the stored user page table.

The hardware implementation of the page table can be done in several ways. In the simplest case, the page table is implemented as a set of dedicated **registers**. These registers should be built with very high-speed logic to make the paging-address translation efficient. Every access to memory must go through the paging map, so efficiency is a major consideration. The CPU dispatcher reloads these registers, just as it reloads the other registers. Instructions to load or modify the page-table registers are, of course, privileged, so that only the operating system can change the memory map. The DEC PDP-11 is an example of such an architecture. The address consists of 16 bits, and the page size is 8 KB. The page table thus consists of eight entries that are kept in fast registers.

The use of registers for the page table is satisfactory if the page table is reasonably small (for example, 256 entries). Most contemporary computers, however, allow the page table to be very large (for example, 1 million entries). For these machines, the use of fast registers to implement the page table is not feasible. Rather, the page table is kept in main memory, and a **page-table base register (PTBR)** points to the page table. Changing page tables requires changing only this one register, substantially reducing context-switch time.

The problem with this approach is the time required to access a user memory location. If we want to access location *i*, we must first index into the page table, using the value in the PTBR offset by the page number for *i*. This task requires a memory access. It provides us with the frame number, which is combined with the page offset to produce the actual address. We can then access the desired place in memory. With this scheme, *two* memory accesses are needed to access a byte (one for the page-table entry, one for the byte). Thus, memory access is slowed by a factor of 2. This delay would be intolerable under most circumstances. We might as well resort to swapping!

The standard solution to this problem is to use a special, small, fast-lookup hardware cache, called **translation look-aside buffer (TLB)**. The TLB is associative, high-speed memory. Each entry in the TLB consists of two parts: a key (or tag) and a value. When the associative memory is presented with an item, the item is compared with all keys simultaneously. If the item is found, the corresponding value field is returned. The search is fast; the hardware, however, is expensive. Typically, the number of entries in a TLB is small, often numbering between 64 and 1,024.

The TLB is used with page tables in the following way. The TLB contains only a few of the page-table entries. When a logical address is generated by the CPU, its page number is presented to the TLB. If the page number is found, its frame number is immediately available and is used to access memory. The whole task may take less than 10 percent longer than it would if an unmapped memory reference were used.

If the page number is not in the TLB (known as a **TLB miss**), a memory reference to the page table must be made. When the frame number is obtained, we can use it to access memory (Figure 9.10). In addition, we add the page number and frame number to the TLB, so that they will be found quickly on the next reference. If the TLB is already full of entries, the operating system must select one for replacement. Replacement policies range from least recently used (LRU) to random. Furthermore, some TLBs allow entries to be **wired down**, meaning that they cannot be removed from the TLB. Typically, TLB entries for kernel code are wired down.

Some TLBs store **address-space identifiers (ASIDs)** in each TLB entry. An ASID uniquely identifies each process and is used to provide address-space protection for that process. When the TLB attempts to resolve virtual page numbers, it ensures that the ASID for the currently running process matches the ASID associated with the virtual page. If the ASIDs do not match, they are treated as a TLB miss. In addition to providing address-space protection, an ASID allows the TLB to contain entries for several different processes simultaneously. If the TLB does not support separate ASIDs, then every time a new page table is selected (for instance, each context switch), the TLB must be **flushed** (or erased) to ensure

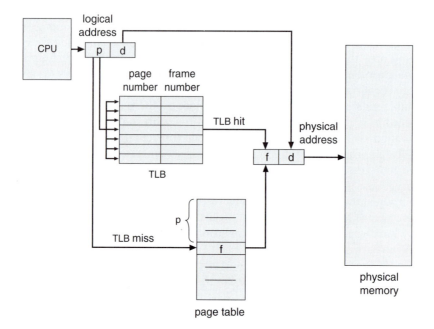

Figure 9.10   Paging hardware with TLB.

that the next executing process does not use the wrong translation information. Otherwise, the TLB could include old entries that contain valid virtual addresses but have incorrect or invalid physical addresses left over from the previous process.

The percentage of times that a particular page number is found in the TLB is called the **hit ratio**. An 80-percent hit ratio means that we find the desired page number in the TLB 80 percent of the time. If it takes 20 nanoseconds to search the TLB, and 100 nanoseconds to access memory, then a mapped-memory access takes 120 nanoseconds when the page number is in the TLB. If we fail to find the page number in the TLB (20 nanoseconds), then we must first access memory for the page table and frame number (100 nanoseconds) and then access the desired byte in memory (100 nanoseconds), for a total of 220 nanoseconds. To find the **effective memory-access time**, we must weigh each case by its probability:

$$\text{effective access time} = 0.80 \times 120 + 0.20 \times 220$$
$$= 140 \text{ nanoseconds.}$$

In this example, we suffer a 40-percent slowdown in memory-access time (from 100 to 140 nanoseconds).

For a 98-percent hit ratio, we have

$$\text{effective access time} = 0.98 \times 120 + 0.02 \times 220$$
$$= 122 \text{ nanoseconds.}$$

This increased hit rate produces only a 22 percent slowdown in access time. We will further explore the impact of the hit ratio on the TLB in Chapter 10.

9.4.3 Protection

Memory protection in a paged environment is accomplished by protection bits associated with each frame. Normally, these bits are kept in the page table.

One bit can define a page to be read–write or read-only. Every reference to memory goes through the page table to find the correct frame number. At the same time that the physical address is being computed, the protection bits can be checked to verify that no writes are being made to a read-only page. An attempt to write to a read-only page causes a hardware trap to the operating system (or memory-protection violation).

We can easily expand this approach to provide a finer level of protection. We can create hardware to provide read-only, read–write, or execute-only protection; or, by providing separate protection bits for each kind of access, we can allow any combination of these accesses. Illegal attempts will be trapped to the operating system.

One more bit is generally attached to each entry in the page table: a **valid –invalid** bit. When this bit is set to "valid," the associated page is in the process's logical-address space and is thus a legal (or valid) page. When the bit is set to"invalid," the page is not in the process's logical-address space. Illegal addresses are trapped by use of the valid–invalid bit. The operating system sets this bit for each page to allow or disallow accesses to the page.

Suppose, for example, that in a system with a 14-bit address space (0 to 16383), we have a program that should use only addresses 0 to 10468. Given a page size of 2 KB, we get the situation shown in Figure 9.11. Addresses in pages 0, 1, 2, 3, 4, and 5 are mapped normally through the page table. Any attempt to generate an address in pages 6 or 7, however, will find that the valid–invalid bit is set to invalid, and the computer will trap to the operating system (invalid page reference).

Notice that this scheme has created a problem. Because the program extends to only address 10468, any reference beyond that address is illegal. However, references to page 5 are classified as valid, so accesses to addresses up to 12287 are valid. Only the addresses from 12288 to 16383 are invalid. This problem is a result of the 2-KB page size and reflects the internal fragmentation of paging.

Rarely does a process use all its address range. In fact, many processes use only a small fraction of the address space available to them. It would be wasteful in these cases to create a page table with entries for every page in the address range. Most of this table would be unused but would take up valuable memory space. Some systems provide hardware, in the form of a **page-table length register (PTLR)**, to indicate the size of the page table. This value is checked against every logical address to verify that the address is in the valid

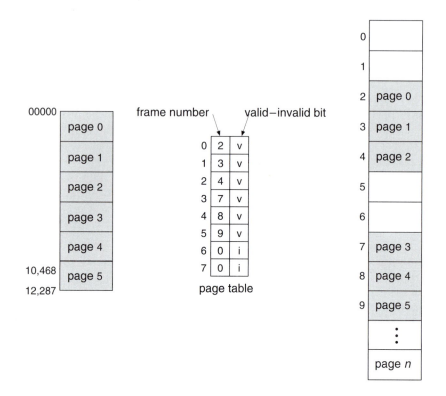

Figure 9.11   Valid (v) or invalid (i) bit in a page table.

range for the process. Failure of this test causes an error trap to the operating system.

9.4.4 Structure of the Page Table

In this section, we explore some of the most common techniques for structuring the page table.

9.4.4.1 Hierarchical Paging

Most modern computer systems support a large logical-address space (2^{32} to 2^{64}). In such an environment, the page table itself becomes excessively large. For example, consider a system with a 32-bit logical-address space. If the page size in such a system is 4 KB (2^{12}), then a page table may consist of up to 1 million entries ($2^{32}/2^{12}$). Assuming that each entry consists of 4 bytes, each process may need up to 4 MB of physical-address space for the page table alone. Clearly, we would not want to allocate the page table contiguously in main memory. One simple solution to this problem is to divide the page table into smaller pieces. We can accomplish this division in several ways.

One way is to use a two-level paging algorithm, in which the page table itself is also paged (Figure 9.12). Remember our example of a 32-bit machine with a page size of 4 KB. A logical address is divided into a page number consisting of 20 bits and a page offset consisting of 12 bits. Because we page the page table, the page number is further divided into a 10-bit page number and a 10-bit page offset. Thus, a logical address is as follows:

page number		page offset
p_1	p_2	d
10	10	1 2

where p_1 is an index into the outer page table and p_2 is the displacement within the page of the outer page table. The address-translation method for this architecture is shown in Figure 9.13. Because address translation works from the outer page table inward, this scheme is also known as a **forward-mapped page table**. The Pentium-II uses this architecture.

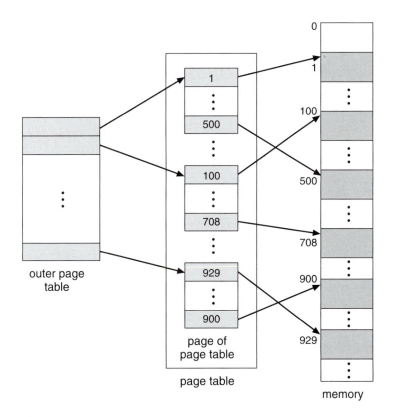

Figure 9.12 A two-level page-table scheme.

logical address

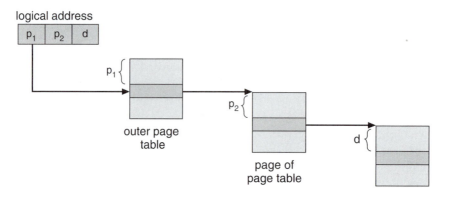

Figure 9.13   Address translation for a two-level 32-bit paging architecture.

The VAX architecture also supports a variation of two-level paging. The VAX is a 32-bit machine with a page size of 512 bytes. The logical-address space of a process is divided into four equal sections, each of which consists of 2^{30} bytes. Each section represents a different part of the logical-address space of a process. The first 2 high-order bits of the logical address designate the appropriate section. The next 21 bits represent the logical page number of that section, and the final 9 bits represent an offset in the desired page. By partitioning the page table in this manner, the operating system can leave partitions unused until a process needs them. An address on the VAX architecture is as follows:

section	page	offset
s	p	d
2	21	9

where s designates the section number, p is an index into the page table, and d is the displacement within the page.

Even when this scheme is used, the size of a one-level page table for a VAX process using one section still is 2^{21} bits $*$ 4 bytes per entry $= 8$ MB. So that main-memory use is reduced even further, the VAX pages the user-process page tables.

For a system with a 64-bit logical-address space, a two-level paging scheme is no longer appropriate. To illustrate this point, let us suppose that the page size in such a system is 4 KB (2^{12}). In this case, the page table will consist of up to 2^{52} entries. If we use a two-level paging scheme, then the inner page tables could conveniently be one page long, or contain 2^{10} 4-byte entries. The addresses would look like this:

outer page	inner page	offset
p1	p2	d
42	10	1 2

The outer page table will consist of 2^{42} entries, or 2^{44} bytes. The obvious method to avoid such a large table is to divide the outer page table into smaller pieces. This approach is also used on some 32-bit processors for added flexibility and efficiency.

We can divide the outer page table in various ways. We can page the outer page table, giving us a three-level paging scheme. Suppose that the outer page table is made up of standard-size pages (2^{10} entries, or 2^{12} bytes); a 64-bit address space is still daunting:

2nd outer page	outer page	inner page	offset
$p1$	$p2$	$p3$	d
32	10	1 0	12

The outer page table is still 2^{34} bytes in size.

The next step would be a four-level paging scheme, where the second-level outer page table itself is also paged. The SPARC architecture (with 32-bit addressing) supports a three-level paging scheme, whereas the 32-bit Motorola 68030 architecture supports a four-level paging scheme.

For 64-bit architectures, hierarchical page tables are generally considered inappropriate. For example, the 64-bit UltraSPARC would require seven levels of paging—a prohibitive number of memory accesses to translate each logical address.

9.4.4.2 Hashed Page Tables

A common approach for handling address spaces larger than 32 bits is to use a **hashed page table**, with the hash value being the virtual-page number. Each entry in the hash table contains a linked list of elements that hash to the same location (to handle collisions). Each element consists of three fields: (a) the virtual page number, (b) the value of the mapped page frame, and (c) a pointer to the next element in the linked list.

The algorithm works as follows: The virtual page number in the virtual address is hashed into the hash table. The virtual page number is compared with field a in the first element in the linked list. If there is a match, the corresponding page frame (field b) is used to form the desired physical address. If there is no match, subsequent entries in the linked list are searched for a matching virtual page number. This scheme is shown in Figure 9.14.

A variation of this scheme that is favorable for 64-bit address spaces has been proposed. This variation uses **clustered page tables**, which are similar to hashed page tables except that each entry in the hash table refers to several pages (such as 16) rather than a single page. Therefore, a single page-table entry can store the mappings for multiple physical-page frames. Clustered page tables are particularly useful for **sparse** address spaces, where memory references are noncontiguous and scattered throughout the address space.

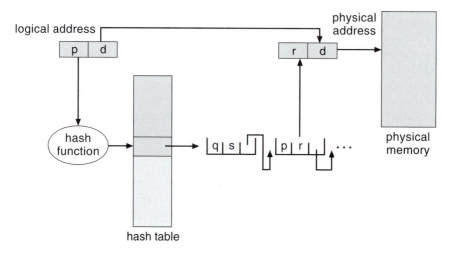

Figure 9.14   Hashed page table.

9.4.4.3 Inverted Page Tables

Usually, each process has an associated page table. The page table has one entry for each page that the process is using (or one slot for each virtual address, regardless of the latter's validity). This table representation is a natural one, since processes reference pages through the pages' virtual addresses. The operating system must then translate this reference into a physical memory address. Since the table is sorted by virtual address, the operating system is able to calculate where in the table the associated physical-address entry is and to use that value directly. One of the drawbacks of this method is that each page table may consist of millions of entries. These tables may consume large amounts of physical memory just to keep track of how the other physical memory is being used.

To solve this problem, we can use an **inverted page table**. An inverted page table has one entry for each real page (or frame) of memory. Each entry consists of the virtual address of the page stored in that real memory location, with information about the process that owns that page. Thus, only one page table is in the system, and it has only one entry for each page of physical memory. Figure 9.15 shows the operation of an inverted page table. Compare it with Figure 9.6, which depicts a standard page table in operation. Inverted page tables often require that an address-space identifier (Section 9.4.2) be stored in each entry of the page table, since the table usually contains several different address spaces mapping physical memory Storing the address-space identifier ensures that a logical page for a particular process is mapped to the corresponding physical page frame. Examples of systems using inverted page tables include the 64-bit UltraSPARC and PowerPC.

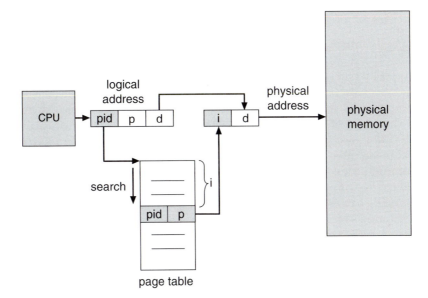

Figure 9.15 Inverted page table.

To illustrate this method, we describe a simplified version of the implementation of the inverted page table used in the IBM RT. Each virtual address in the system consists of a triple

<process-id, page-number, offset>.

Each inverted page-table entry is a pair <process-id, page-number> where the process-id assumes the role of the address-space identifier. When a memory reference occurs, part of the virtual address, consisting of <process-id, page-number>, is presented to the memory subsystem. The inverted page table is then searched for a match. If a match is found—say, at entry i—then the physical address <i, offset> is generated. If no match is found, then an illegal address access has been attempted.

Although this scheme decreases the amount of memory needed to store each page table, it increases the amount of time needed to search the table when a page reference occurs. Because the inverted page table is sorted by physical address, but lookups occur on virtual addresses, the whole table might need to be searched for a match. This search would take far too long. To alleviate this problem, we use a hash table, as described in Section 9.4.4.2, to limit the search to one—or at most a few—page-table entries. Of course, each access to the hash table adds a memory reference to the procedure, so one virtual-memory reference requires at least two real-memory reads: one for the hash-table entry and one for the page table. To improve performance, recall that the TLB is searched first, before the hash table is consulted.

9.4.5 Shared Pages

Another advantage of paging is the possibility of *sharing* common code. This consideration is particularly important in a time-sharing environment. Consider a system that supports 40 users, each of whom executes a text editor. If the text editor consists of 150 KB of code and 50 KB of data space, we need 8,000 KB to support the 40 users. If the code is **reentrant code** (or **pure code**), however, it can be shared, as shown in Figure 9.16. Here we see a three-page editor—each page 50 KB in size (the large page size is used to simplify the figure)—being shared among three processes. Each process has its own data page.

Reentrant code is non-self-modifying code; it never changes during execution. Thus, two or more processes can execute the same code at the same time. Each process has its own copy of registers and data storage to hold the data for the process's execution. The data for two different processes will, of course, vary for each process.

Only one copy of the editor need be kept in physical memory. Each user's page table maps onto the same physical copy of the editor, but data pages are mapped onto different frames. Thus, to support 40 users, we need only one

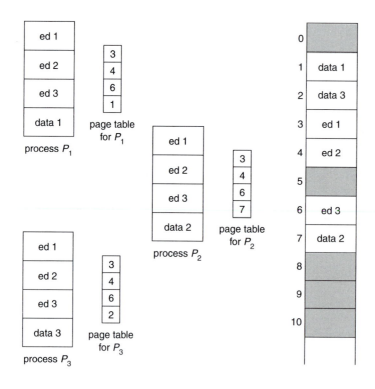

Figure 9.16   Sharing of code in a paging environment.

copy of the editor (150 KB), plus 40 copies of the 50 KB of data space per user. The total space required is now 2,150 KB instead of 8,000 KB—a significant savings.

Other heavily used programs can also be shared—compilers, window systems, run-time libraries, database systems, and so on. To be sharable, the code must be reentrant. The read-only nature of shared code should not be left to the correctness of the code; the operating system should enforce this property.

The sharing of memory among processes on a system is similar to the sharing of the address space of a task by threads, described in Chapter 5. Furthermore, recall that in Chapter 4 we described shared memory as a method of interprocess communication. Some operating systems implement shared memory using shared pages.

Systems that use inverted page tables have difficulty implementing shared memory. Shared memory is usually implemented as multiple virtual addresses (one for each process sharing the memory) that are mapped to one physical address. This standard method cannot be used with inverted page tables; because there is only one virtual page entry for every physical page, one physical page cannot have two (or more) shared virtual addresses.

Organizing memory according to pages provides numerous benefits in addition to allowing several processes to share the same physical pages. We will cover several other benefits in Chapter 10.

9.5 ▪ Segmentation

An important aspect of memory management that became unavoidable with paging is the separation of the user's view of memory and the actual physical memory. As we have already seen, the user's view of memory is not the same as the actual physical memory. The user's view is mapped onto physical memory. This mapping allows differentiation between logical memory and physical memory.

9.5.1 Basic Method

Do users think of memory as a linear array of bytes, some containing instructions and others containing data? Most people would say no. Rather, users prefer to view memory as a collection of variable-sized segments, with no necessary ordering among segments (Figure 9.17).

Consider how you think of a program when you are writing it. You think of it as a main program with a set of methods, procedures, or functions. It may also include various data structures: objects, arrays, stacks, variables, and so on. Each of these modules or data elements is referred to by name. You talk about "the symbol table," "method *Sqrt()*," "the main program," without caring

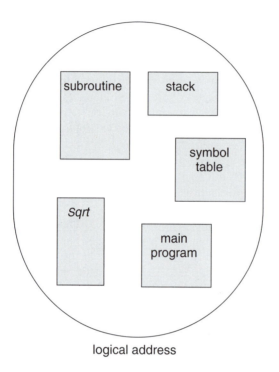

logical address

Figure 9.17   User's view of a program.

what addresses in memory these elements occupy. You are not concerned with whether the symbol table is stored before or after the *Sqrt()* method. Each of these segments is of variable length; the length is intrinsically defined by the purpose of the segment in the program. Elements within a segment are identified by their offset from the beginning of the segment: the first statement of the program, the seventeenth entry in the symbol table, the fifth instruction of the *Sqrt()* method, and so on.

Segmentation is a memory-management scheme that supports this user view of memory. A logical-address space is a collection of segments. Each segment has a name and a length. The addresses specify both the segment name and the offset within the segment. The user therefore specifies each address by two quantities: a segment name and an offset. (Contrast this scheme with the paging scheme, in which the user specifies only a single address, which is partitioned by the hardware into a page number and an offset, all invisible to the programmer.)

For simplicity of implementation, segments are numbered and are referred to by a segment number, rather than by a segment name. Thus, a logical address consists of a *two tuple*:

<segment-number, offset>.

Normally, the user program is compiled, and the compiler automatically constructs segments reflecting the input program. A Java compiler might create separate segments for the following:

1. The *method area*, which holds the code for all methods

2. The heap, from which memory for objects is allocated

3. The stacks used by each Java thread

4. The class loader

A C compiler might create a separate segment for global variables. Libraries that are linked in during compile time might be assigned separate segments. The loader would take all these segments and assign them segment numbers.

9.5.2 Hardware

Although the user can now refer to objects in the program by a two-dimensional address, the actual physical memory is still, of course, a one-dimensional sequence of bytes. Thus, we must define an implementation to map two-dimensional user-defined addresses into one-dimensional physical addresses. This mapping is effected by a **segment table**. Each entry in the segment table

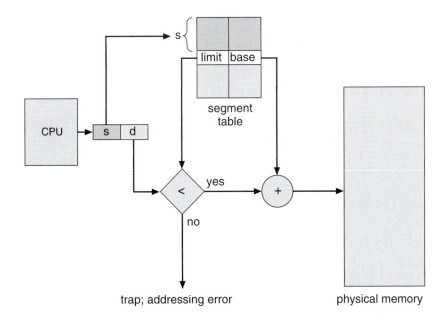

Figure 9.18 Segmentation hardware.

has a *segment base* and a *segment limit*. The segment base contains the starting physical address where the segment resides in memory, whereas the segment limit specifies the length of the segment.

The use of a segment table is illustrated in Figure 9.18. A logical address consists of two parts: a segment number, *s*, and an offset into that segment, *d*. The segment number is used as an index to the segment table. The offset *d* of the logical address must be between 0 and the segment limit. If it is not, we trap to the operating system (logical addressing attempt beyond end of segment). When an offset is legal, it is added to the segment base to produce the address in physical memory of the desired byte. The segment table is thus essentially an array of base–limit register pairs.

As an example, consider the situation shown in Figure 9.19. We have five segments numbered from 0 through 4. The segments are stored in physical memory as shown. The segment table has a separate entry for each segment, giving the beginning address of the segment in physical memory (or base) and

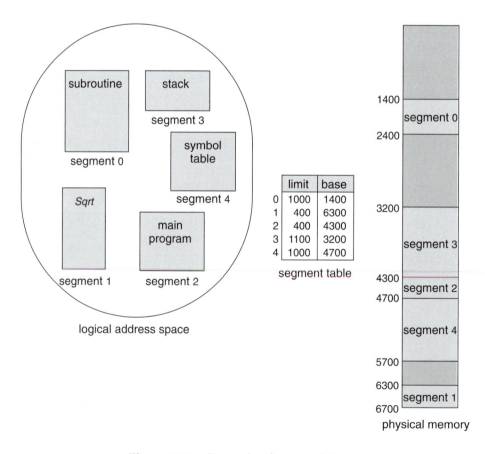

Figure 9.19   Example of segmentation.

the length of that segment (or limit). For example, segment 2 is 400 bytes long and begins at location 4300. Thus, a reference to byte 53 of segment 2 is mapped onto location 4300 + 53 = 4353. A reference to segment 3, byte 852, is mapped to 3200 (the base of segment 3) + 852 = 4052. A reference to byte 1222 of segment 0 would result in a trap to the operating system, as this segment is only 1,000 bytes long.

9.5.3 Protection and Sharing

A particular advantage of segmentation is the association of protection with the segments. Because the segments represent a semantically defined portion of the program, it is likely that all entries in the segment will be used the same way. Hence, some segments are instructions, whereas other segments are data. In a modern architecture, instructions are non-self-modifying, so instruction segments can be defined as read-only or execute-only. The memory-mapping hardware will check the protection bits associated with each segment-table entry to prevent illegal accesses to memory, such as attempts to write into a read-only segment or to use an execute-only segment as data. By placing an array in its own segment, the memory-management hardware will automatically check that array indexes are legal and do not stray outside the array boundaries. Thus, many common program errors will be detected by the hardware before they can cause serious damage.

Another advantage of segmentation involves the *sharing* of code or data. Each process has an associated segment table, which the dispatcher uses to define the hardware segment table when this process is given the CPU. Segments are shared when entries in the segment tables of two different processes point to the same physical location (Figure 9.20).

The sharing occurs at the segment level. Thus, any information can be shared if it is defined to be a segment. Several segments can be shared, so a program composed of several segments can be shared.

For example, consider the use of a text editor in a time-sharing system. A complete editor might be quite large, composed of many segments. These segments can be shared among all users, limiting the physical memory needed to support editing tasks. Rather than *n* copies of the editor, we need only one copy. For each user, we still need separate, unique segments to store local variables. These segments, of course, are not shared.

We can also share only parts of programs. For example, common subroutine packages can be shared among many users if they are defined as sharable, read-only segments. Two Java programs, for instance, may use the same math library containing methods such as sqrt(), log(), and sin(); but only one physical copy of the library is needed.

Although this sharing appears simple, there are subtle considerations. Code segments typically contain references to themselves. For example, a conditional jump normally has a transfer address, which consists of a segment

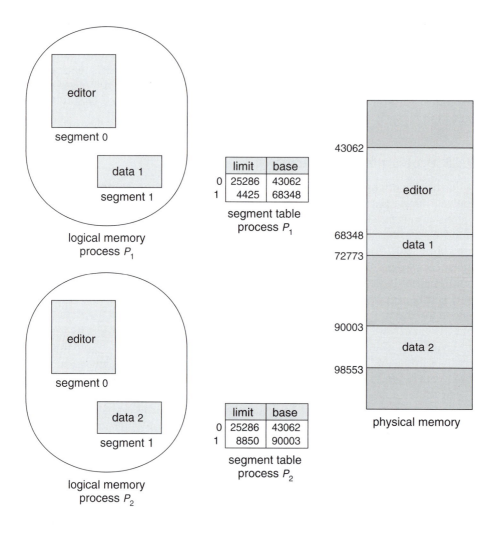

Figure 9.20   Sharing of segments in a segmented memory system.

number and an offset. The segment number of the transfer address will be the segment number of the code segment. If we try to share this segment, all sharing processes must define the shared code segment to have the same segment number.

For instance, suppose we want to share the math library, and one process wants to make it segment 4 and another wants to make it segment 17. How should the math library refer to itself? Because there is only one physical copy of the library, it must refer to itself in the same way for both users—it must have a unique segment number. As the number of users sharing the segment increases, so does the difficulty of finding an acceptable segment number.

Read-only data segments that contain no physical pointers may be shared as different segment numbers, as may code segments that refer to themselves only indirectly. For example, conditional branches that specify the branch address as an offset from the current program counter or relative to a register containing the current segment number would allow code to avoid direct reference to the current segment number.

9.5.4 Fragmentation

The long-term scheduler must find and allocate memory for all the segments of a user program. This situation is similar to paging except that the segments are of *variable* length, whereas pages are all the same size. Thus, as with the variable-sized partition scheme, memory allocation is a dynamic storage-allocation problem, usually solved with a best-fit or first-fit algorithm.

It follows that segmentation may cause external fragmentation. When all blocks of free memory are too small to accommodate a segment, the process may simply have to wait until more memory (or at least a larger hole) becomes available or until compaction creates a larger hole. Because segmentation is by its nature a dynamic-relocation algorithm, we can compact memory whenever we want. If the CPU scheduler must wait for one process because of a memory-allocation problem, it may (or may not) skip through the CPU queue looking for a smaller, lower-priority process to run.

How serious a problem is external fragmentation for a segmentation scheme? Would long-term scheduling with compaction help? The answers depend mainly on the average segment size. At one extreme, we could define each process to be one segment. This approach is analogous to the variable-sized partition scheme. At the other extreme, every byte could be put in its own segment and relocated separately. This arrangement eliminates external fragmentation altogether; however, every byte would need a base register for its relocation, doubling memory use! Of course, the next logical step—fixed-sized, small segments—is paging.

Generally, if the average segment size is small, external fragmentation will also be small. (By analogy, consider putting suitcases in the trunk of a car; they never quite seem to fit. However, if you open the suitcases and put the individual items in the trunk, everything is more likely to fit.) Because the individual segments are smaller than the overall process, they are more likely to fit in the available memory blocks.

9.6 ■ Segmentation with Paging

Both paging and segmentation have advantages and disadvantages. In fact, of the two most popular microprocessors now being used, one—the Motorola 68000 line—is based on a flat-address space, whereas the other—the Intel 80x86 and Pentium family—is based on segmentation. Both are merging memory models toward a mixture of paging and segmentation. We can combine these two methods to improve on each. This combination is best illustrated by the architecture of the Intel 80x86.

The 80x86 uses segmentation with paging for memory management. The maximum number of segments per process is 16 KB, and each segment can be as large as 4 gigabytes. The page size is 4 KB. We do not give a complete description of the memory-management structure of the 80x86 in this text. Rather, we present the major ideas.

The logical-address space of a process is divided into two partitions. The first partition consists of up to 8 KB segments that are private to that process. The second partition consists of up to 8 KB segments that are shared among all the processes. Information about the first partition is kept in the **local descriptor table (LDT)**; information about the second partition is kept in the **global descriptor table (GDT)**. Each entry in the LDT and GDT consists of an 8-byte segment descriptor with detailed information about a particular segment, including the base location and limit of that segment.

The logical address is a pair (selector, offset), where the selector is a 16-bit number:

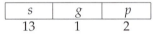

in which s designates the segment number, g indicates whether the segment is in the GDT or LDT, and p deals with protection. The offset is a 32-bit number specifying the location of the byte (or word) within the segment in question.

The machine has six segment registers, allowing six segments to be addressed at any one time by a process. It has six 8-byte microprogram registers to hold the corresponding descriptors from either the LDT or GDT. This cache lets the 80x86 avoid having to read the descriptor from memory for every memory reference.

The physical address on the 80x86 is 32 bits long and is formed as follows. The segment register points to the appropriate entry in the LDT or GDT. The base and limit information about the segment in question is used to generate a **linear address**. First, the limit is used to check for address validity. If the address is not valid, a memory fault is generated, resulting in a trap to the operating system. If it is valid, then the value of the offset is added to the value of the base, resulting in a 32-bit linear address. This address is then translated into a physical address.

As pointed out previously, each segment is paged, and each page is 4 KB. A page table may thus consist of up to 1 million entries. Because each entry consists of 4 bytes, each process may need up to 4 MB of physical-address space for the page table alone. Clearly, we would not want to allocate the page table contiguously in main memory. The solution adopted in the 80x86 is to use a two-level paging scheme. The linear address is divided into a page number consisting of 20 bits and a page offset consisting of 12 bits. Since we page the page table, the page number is further divided into a 10-bit page directory pointer and a 10-bit page table pointer. The logical address is as follows:

page number		page offset
p_1	p_2	d
10	10	12

The address-translation scheme for this architecture is similar to the scheme shown in Figure 9.13. The Intel address translation is shown in more detail in Figure 9.21. To improve the efficiency of physical-memory use, Intel 80x86

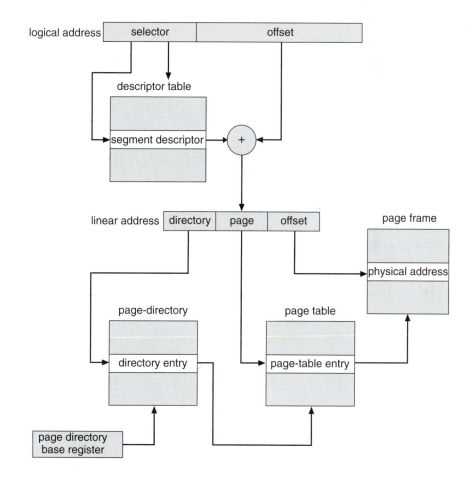

Figure 9.21   Intel 80x86 address translation.

page tables can be swapped to disk. In this case, an invalid bit is used in the page-directory entry to indicate whether the table to which the entry is pointing is in memory or on disk. If the table is on disk, the operating system can use the other 31 bits to specify the disk location of the table; the table then can be brought into memory on demand.

As an illustration, consider the Linux operating system running on the Intel 80x86 architecture. Because Linux is designed to run on a variety of processors —many of which may provide only limited support for segmentation—Linux does not rely on segmentation and uses it minimally. On the Intel 80x86, Linux uses only six segments:

1. A segment for kernel code

2. A segment for kernel data

3. A segment for user code

4. A segment for user data

5. A task-state segment (TSS)

6. A default LDT segment

The segments for user code and user data are shared by all processes running in user mode. This is possible because all processes use the same logical address space and all segment descriptors are stored in the global descriptor table (GDT). Furthermore, each process has its own task-state segment (TSS), and the descriptor for this segment is stored in the GDT. The TSS is used to store the hardware context of each process during context switches. The default LDT segment is normally shared by all processes and is usually not used. However, if a process requires its own LDT, it can create one and use that instead of the default LDT.

As noted, each segment selector includes a 2-bit field for protection. Thus, the 80x86 allows four levels of protection. Of these four levels, Linux only recognizes two: user mode and kernel mode.

9.7 ■ Summary

Memory-management algorithms for multiprogrammed operating systems range from the simple single-user system approach to paged segmentation. The most important determinant of the method used in a particular system is the hardware provided. Every memory address generated by the CPU must be checked for legality and possibly mapped to a physical address. The checking cannot be implemented (efficiently) in software. Hence, we are constrained by the hardware available.

The memory-management algorithms discussed (contiguous allocation, paging, segmentation, and combinations of paging and segmentation) differ in many aspects. In comparing different memory-management strategies, we use the following considerations:

- **Hardware support:** A simple base register or a pair of base and limit registers is sufficient for the single- and multiple-partition schemes, whereas paging and segmentation need mapping tables to define the address map.

- **Performance:** As the memory-management algorithm becomes more complex, the time required to map a logical address to a physical address increases. For the simple systems, we need only compare or add to the logical address—operations that are fast. Paging and segmentation can be as fast if the table is implemented in fast registers. If the table is in memory, however, user memory accesses can be degraded substantially. A TLB can reduce the performance degradation to an acceptable level.

- **Fragmentation:** A multiprogrammed system will generally perform more efficiently if it has a higher level of multiprogramming. For a given set of processes, we can increase the multiprogramming level only by packing more processes into memory. To accomplish this task, we must reduce memory waste, or fragmentation. Systems with fixed-sized allocation units, such as the single-partition scheme and paging, suffer from internal fragmentation. Systems with variable-sized allocation units, such as the multiple-partition scheme and segmentation, suffer from external fragmentation.

- **Relocation:** One solution to the external-fragmentation problem is compaction. Compaction involves shifting a program in memory in such a way that the program does not notice the change. This consideration requires that logical addresses be relocated dynamically, at execution time. If addresses are relocated only at load time, we cannot compact storage.

- **Swapping:** Swapping can be added to any algorithm. At intervals determined by the operating system, usually dictated by CPU-scheduling policies, processes are copied from main memory to a backing store and later are copied back to main memory. This scheme allows more processes to be run than can be fit into memory at one time.

- **Sharing:** Another means of increasing the multiprogramming level is to share code and data among different users. Sharing generally requires that either paging or segmentation be used, to provide small packets of information (pages or segments) that can be shared. Sharing is a means of running many processes with a limited amount of memory, but shared programs and data must be designed carefully.

- **Protection:** If paging or segmentation is provided, different sections of a user program can be declared execute-only, read-only, or read–write. This restriction is necessary with shared code or data and is generally useful in any case to provide simple run-time checks for common programming errors.

■ Exercises

9.1 Name two differences between logical and physical addresses.

9.2 Explain the difference between internal and external fragmentation.

9.3 Describe the following allocation algorithms:

    a. First fit

    b. Best fit

    c. Worst fit

9.4 When a process is rolled out of memory, it loses its ability to use the CPU (at least for a while). Describe another situation where a process loses its ability to use the CPU but where the process is not rolled out.

9.5 Given five memory partitions of 100 KB, 500 KB, 200 KB, 300 KB, and 600 KB (in order), how would each of the first-fit, best-fit, and worst-fit algorithms place processes of 212 KB, 417 KB, 112 KB, and 426 KB (in order)? Which algorithm makes the most efficient use of memory?

9.6 Consider a system in which a program can be separated into two parts: code and data. The CPU knows whether it wants an instruction (instruction fetch) or data (data fetch or store). Therefore, two base–limit register pairs are provided: one for instructions and one for data. The instruction base–limit register pair is automatically set to read-only, so programs can be shared among different users. Discuss the advantages and disadvantages of this scheme.

9.7 Why are page sizes always powers of 2?

9.8 Consider a logical-address space of eight pages of 1,024 words each, mapped onto a physical memory of 32 frames.

    a. How many bits are in the logical address?

    b. How many bits are in the physical address?

9.9 On a system with paging, a process cannot access memory that it does not own. Why? How could the operating system allow access to other memory? Why should it or should it not?

9.10 Consider a paging system with the page table stored in memory.

    a. If a memory reference takes 200 nanoseconds, how long does a paged memory reference take?

    b. If we add TLBs, and 75 percent of all page-table references are found in the TLBs, what is the effective memory reference time? (Assume that finding a page-table entry in the TLBs takes zero time, if the entry is there.)

9.11 What is the effect of allowing two entries in a page table to point to the same page frame in memory? Explain how you could use this effect to decrease the amount of time needed to copy a large amount of memory from one place to another. How would updating some byte on one page affect the other page?

9.12 Why are segmentation and paging sometimes combined into one scheme?

9.13 Describe a mechanism by which one segment could belong to the address space of two different processes.

9.14 Explain why sharing a reentrant module is easier when segmentation is used than when pure paging is used.

9.15 Sharing segments among processes without requiring the same segment number is possible in a dynamically linked segmentation system.

    a. Define a system that allows static linking and sharing of segments without requiring that the segment numbers be the same.

    b. Describe a paging scheme that allows pages to be shared without requiring that the page numbers be the same.

9.16 Consider the following segment table:

Segment	Base	Length
0	219	600
1	2300	14
2	90	100
3	1327	580
4	1952	96

What are the physical addresses for the following logical addresses?

    a. 0430

    b. 110

    c. 2500

d. 3400

e. 4112

9.17 Consider the Intel address-translation scheme shown in Figure 9.21.

a. Describe all the steps taken by the Intel 80x86 in translating a logical address into a physical address.

b. What are the advantages to the operating system of hardware that provides such complicated memory translation?

c. Are there any disadvantages to this address-translation system? If so, what are they? If not, why is it not used by every manufacturer?

9.18 In the IBM/370, memory protection is provided through the use of *keys*. A key is a 4-bit quantity. Each 2-KB block of memory has an associated key (the storage key). The CPU also has an associated key (the protection key). A store operation is allowed only if both keys are equal or if either is zero. Which of the following memory-management schemes could be used successfully with this hardware?

a. Bare machine

b. Single-user system

c. Multiprogramming with a fixed number of processes

d. Multiprogramming with a variable number of processes

e. Paging

f. Segmentation

Bibliographical Notes

Dynamic storage allocation was discussed by Knuth [1973] (Section 2.5), who found through simulation results that first fit is generally superior to best fit. Knuth [1973] discussed the 50-percent rule.

The concept of paging can be credited to the designers of the Atlas system, which has been described by Kilburn et al. [1961] and by Howarth et al. [1961]. The concept of segmentation was first discussed by Dennis [1965]. Paged segmentation was first supported in the GE 645, on which MULTICS was originally implemented (Organick [1972]).

Inverted page tables were discussed in an article about the IBM RT storage manager by Chang and Mergen [1988].

Address translation in software is covered in Jacob and Mudge [1997].

Hennessy and Patterson [2002] discussed the hardware aspects of TLBs, caches, and MMUs. Talluri et al. [1995] discusses page tables for 64-bit address spaces. Dougan et al. [1999] and Jacob and Mudge [2001] discuss techniques for managing the TLB. Fang et al. [2001] evaluate support for large pages.

Tanenbaum [2001] discusses Intel 80386 paging. Memory management for several architectures—such as the Pentium II, PowerPC, and UltraSPARC—was described by Jacob and Mudge [1998a]. Segmentation on Linux systems is presented in Bovet and Cesati [2002]

Chapter 10

VIRTUAL MEMORY

In Chapter 9, we discussed various memory-management strategies used in computer systems. All these strategies have the same goal: to keep many processes in memory simultaneously to allow multiprogramming. However, they tend to require that an entire process be in memory before it can execute.

Virtual memory is a technique that allows the execution of processes that are not completely in memory. One major advantage of this scheme is that programs can be larger than physical memory. Further, virtual memory abstracts main memory into an extremely large, uniform array of storage, separating logical memory as viewed by the user from physical memory. This technique frees programmers from the concerns of memory-storage limitations. Virtual memory also allows processes to share files easily and to implement shared memory. In addition, it provides an efficient mechanism for process creation. Virtual memory is not easy to implement, however, and may substantially decrease performance if it is used carelessly. In this chapter, we discuss virtual memory in the form of demand paging and examine its complexity and cost.

10.1 ■ Background

The memory-management algorithms outlined in Chapter 9 are necessary because of one basic requirement: The instructions being executed must be in physical memory. The first approach to meeting this requirement is to place the entire logical address space in physical memory. Overlays and dynamic loading can help to ease this restriction, but they generally require special precautions and extra work by the programmer.

This requirement that instructions must be in physical memory to be executed seems both necessary and reasonable; but it is also unfortunate, since it limits the size of a program to the size of physical memory. In fact, an examination of real programs shows us that, in many cases, the entire program is not needed. For instance, consider the following:

- Programs often have code to handle unusual error conditions. Since these errors seldom, if ever, occur in practice, this code is almost never executed.

- Arrays, lists, and tables are often allocated more memory than they actually need. An array may be declared 100 by 100 elements, even though it is seldom larger than 10 by 10 elements. An assembler symbol table may have room for 3,000 symbols, although the average program has less than 200 symbols.

- Certain options and features of a program may be used rarely. For instance, the routines on U.S. government computers that balance the budget are only rarely used.

Even in those cases where the entire program is needed, it may not all be needed at the same time (such is the case with overlays, for example).

The ability to execute a program that is only partially in memory would confer many benefits:

- A program would no longer be constrained by the amount of physical memory that is available. Users would be able to write programs for an extremely large *virtual* address space, simplifying the programming task.

- Because each user program could take less physical memory, more programs could be run at the same time, with a corresponding increase in CPU utilization and throughput but with no increase in response time or turnaround time.

- Less I/O would be needed to load or swap each user program into memory, so each user program would run faster.

Thus, running a program that is not entirely in memory would benefit both the system and the user.

Virtual memory involves the separation of logical memory as perceived by users from physical memory. This separation allows an extremely large virtual memory to be provided for programmers when only a smaller physical memory is available (Figure 10.1). Virtual memory makes the task of programming much easier, because the programmer no longer needs to worry about the amount of physical memory available or about what code can be placed in overlays; she can concentrate instead on the problem to be programmed. Indeed, on systems that support virtual memory, overlays have almost disappeared.

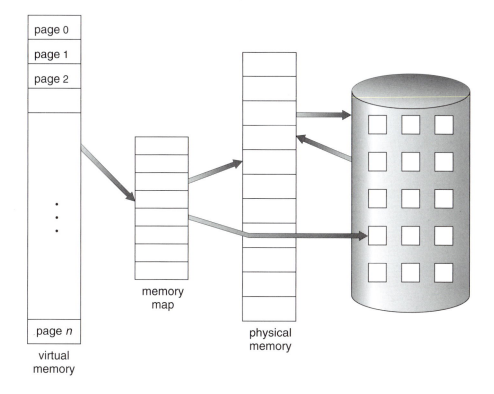

Figure 10.1 Diagram showing virtual memory that is larger than physical memory.

The **virtual-address space** of a process refers to the logical (or virtual) view of how a process is stored in memory. Typically, this view is that a process begins at a certain logical address—say, address 0—and exists in contiguous memory, as shown in Figure 10.2. Recall from Chapter 9, though, that in fact physical memory is organized in page frames and that the physical page frames assigned to a process may not be contiguous. It is up to the memory-management unit (MMU) to map logical pages to physical page frames in memory.

Note in Figure 10.2 that we have allowed for the heap to grow upward in memory (through dynamic memory allocation) and for the stack to grow downward in memory (through successive function calls). The large blank space (or hole) between the heap and the stack is part of the virtual address space but will require actual physical pages only if the heap or stack grows. Virtual address spaces that include holes are known as **sparse** address spaces. Using a sparse address space is beneficial because the holes can be filled as the stack or heap segments grow or if we wish to dynamically link libraries (or possibly other shared objects) during program execution.

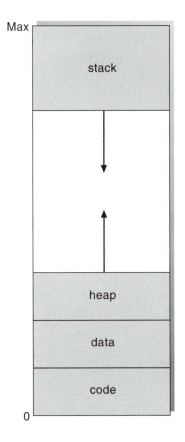

Figure 10.2   Virtual-address space.

In addition to separating logical memory from physical memory, virtual memory also allows files and memory to be shared by two or more different processes through page sharing (Section 9.4.5). This leads to the following benefits:

- System libraries can be shared by several different processes through mapping of the shared object into a virtual address space. Although each process considers the shared libraries to be part of its virtual address space, the actual pages where the libraries reside in physical memory are shared by all the processes (Figure 10.3). Typically, a library is mapped read only into the space of each process that is linked with it.

- Similarly, virtual memory enables processes to share memory. Recall from Chapter 4 that two or more processes can communicate through the use of shared memory. Virtual memory allows one process to create a region of memory that it can share with another process. Processes sharing this

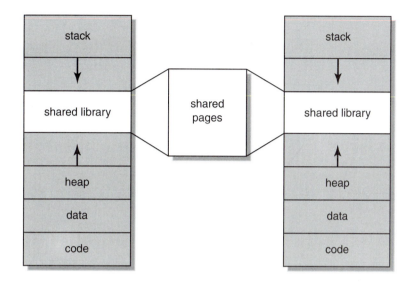

Figure 10.3   Shared library using virtual memory.

region consider it part of their virtual address space, yet the actual physical pages of memory are shared, much as is illustrated in Figure 10.3.

- Virtual memory can allow pages to be shared during process creation with the fork() system call, thus speeding up process creation. We will explain this in Section 10.3.

We will explore these—and other—benefits of virtual memory later in this chapter. First, we discuss the implementation of virtual memory.

10.2 ■ Demand Paging

Virtual memory is commonly implemented by **demand paging**. It can also be implemented in a segmentation system. Several systems provide a paged segmentation scheme, where segments are broken into pages. Thus, the user view is segmentation, but the operating system can implement this view with demand paging. **Demand segmentation** can also be used to provide virtual memory. Burroughs computer systems have used demand segmentation, and the IBM OS/2 operating system also uses demand segmentation. However, segment-replacement algorithms are more complex than are page-replacement algorithms because the segments have variable sizes. We do not cover demand segmentation in this text; refer to the Bibliographical Notes for relevant references.

A demand-paging system is similar to a paging system with swapping (Figure 10.4). Processes reside on secondary memory (which is usually a disk).

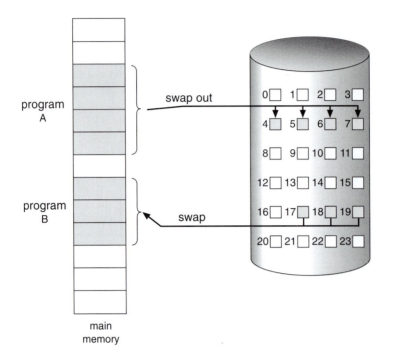

Figure 10.4   Transfer of a paged memory to contiguous disk space.

When we want to execute a process, we swap it into memory. Rather than swapping the entire process into memory, however, we use a **lazy swapper**. A lazy swapper never swaps a page into memory unless that page will be needed. Since we are now viewing a process as a sequence of pages, rather than as one large contiguous address space, use of the term *swapper* is technically incorrect. A swapper manipulates entire processes, whereas a **pager** is concerned with the individual pages of a process. We thus use *pager,* rather than *swapper,* in connection with demand paging.

10.2.1 Basic Concepts

When a process is to be swapped in, the pager guesses which pages will be used before the process is swapped out again. Instead of swapping in a whole process, the pager brings only those necessary pages into memory. Thus, it avoids reading into memory pages that will not be used anyway, decreasing the swap time and the amount of physical memory needed.

With this scheme, we need some form of hardware support to distinguish between the pages that are in memory and the pages that are on the disk. The valid–invalid bit scheme described in Section 9.4.4 can be used for this purpose. This time, however, when this bit is set to "valid," the associated page is both legal and in memory. If the bit is set to "invalid," the page either is not valid (that is, not in the logical address space of the process) or is valid but is currently on the disk. The page-table entry for a page that is brought into memory is set as usual, but the page-table entry for a page that is not currently in memory is either simply marked invalid or contains the address of the page on disk. This situation is depicted in Figure 10.5.

Notice that marking a page invalid will have no effect if the process never attempts to access that page. Hence, if we guess right and page in all and only those pages that are actually needed, the process will run exactly as though we had brought in all pages. While the process executes and accesses pages that are **memory resident,** execution proceeds normally.

But what happens if the process tries to access a page that was not brought into memory? Access to a page marked invalid causes a **page-fault trap**. The paging hardware, in translating the address through the page table, will notice

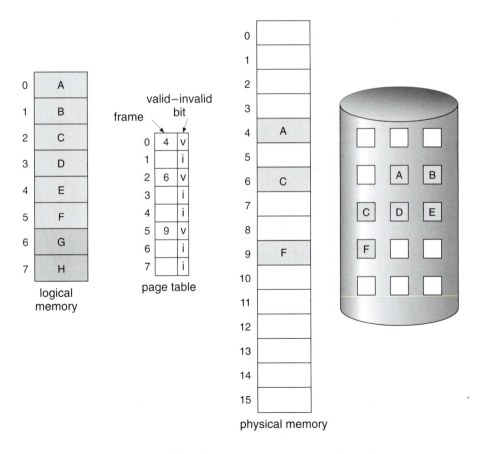

Figure 10.5   Page table when some pages are not in main memory.

that the invalid bit is set, causing a trap to the operating system. This trap is the result of the operating system's failure to bring the desired page into memory. The procedure for handling this page fault is straightforward (Figure 10.6):

1. We check an internal table (usually kept with the process control block) for this process to determine whether the reference was a valid or an invalid memory access.

2. If the reference was invalid, we terminate the process. If it was valid, but we have not yet brought in that page, we now page it in.

3. We find a free frame (by taking one from the free-frame list, for example).

4. We schedule a disk operation to read the desired page into the newly allocated frame.

5. When the disk read is complete, we modify the internal table kept with the process and the page table to indicate that the page is now in memory.

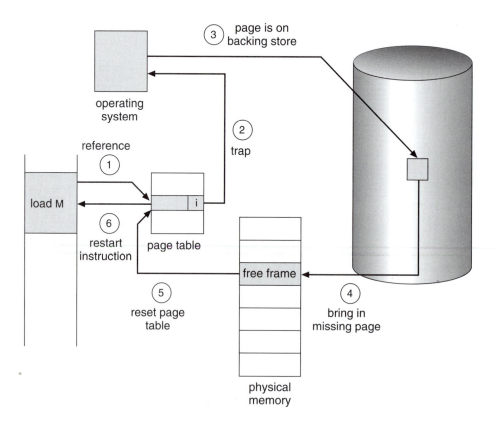

Figure 10.6   Steps in handling a page fault.

6. We restart the instruction that was interrupted by the trap. The process can now access the page as though it had always been in memory.

In the extreme case, we could start executing a process with *no* pages in memory. When the operating system sets the instruction pointer to the first instruction of the process, which is on a non-memory-resident page, the process immediately faults for the page. After this page is brought into memory, the process continues to execute, faulting as necessary until every page that it needs is in memory. At that point, it can execute with no more faults. This scheme is **pure demand paging:** Never bring a page into memory until it is required.

Theoretically, some programs may access several new pages of memory with each instruction execution (one page for the instruction and many for data), possibly causing multiple page faults per instruction. This situation would result in unacceptable system performance. Fortunately, analysis of running processes shows that this behavior is exceedingly unlikely. Programs tend to have **locality of reference**, described in Section 10.6.1, which results in reasonable performance from demand paging.

The hardware to support demand paging is the same as the hardware for paging and swapping:

- **Page table:** This table has the ability to mark an entry invalid through a valid–invalid bit or special value of protection bits.

- **Secondary memory:** This memory holds those pages that are not present in main memory. The secondary memory is usually a high-speed disk. It is known as the swap device, and the section of disk used for this purpose is known as **swap space**. Swap-space allocation is discussed in Chapter 14.

A crucial requirement for demand paging is the need to be able to restart any instruction after a page fault. Because we save the state (registers, condition code, instruction counter) of the interrupted process when the page fault occurs, we must be able to restart the process in *exactly* the same place and state, except that the desired page is now in memory and is accessible. In most cases, this restartability requirement is easy to meet. A page fault could occur at any memory reference. If the page fault occurs on the instruction fetch, we can restart by fetching the instruction again. If a page fault occurs while we are fetching an operand, we must fetch and decode the instruction again and then fetch the operand.

As a worst-case example, consider a three-address instruction such as ADD the content of A to B, placing the result in C. These are the steps to execute this instruction:

1. Fetch and decode the instruction (ADD).

2. Fetch A.

3. Fetch B.

4. Add A and B.

5. Store the sum in C.

If we faulted when we tried to store in C (because C is in a page not currently in memory), we would have to get the desired page, bring it in, correct the page table, and restart the instruction. The restart would require fetching the instruction again, decoding it again, fetching the two operands again, and then adding again. However, there is not much repeated work (less than one complete instruction), and the repetition is necessary only when a page fault occurs.

The major difficulty arises when one instruction may modify several different locations. For example, consider the IBM System 360/370 MVC (move character) instruction, which can move up to 256 bytes from one location to another (possibly overlapping) location. If either block (source or destination) straddles a page boundary, a page fault might occur after the move is partially done. In addition, if the source and destination blocks overlap, the source block may have been modified, in which case we cannot simply restart the instruction.

This problem can be solved in two different ways. In one solution, the microcode computes and attempts to access both ends of both blocks. If a page fault is going to occur, it will happen at this step, before anything is modified. The move can then take place; we know that no page fault can occur, since all the relevant pages are in memory. The other solution uses temporary registers to hold the values of overwritten locations. If there is a page fault, all the old values are written back into memory before the trap occurs. This action restores memory to its state before the instruction was started, so that the instruction can be repeated.

This is by no means the only architectural problem resulting from adding paging to an existing architecture to allow demand paging, but it illustrates some of the difficulties. Paging is added between the CPU and the memory in a computer system. It should be entirely transparent to the user process. Thus, people often assume that paging can be added to any system. Although this assumption is true for a non-demand-paging environment, where a page fault represents a fatal error, it is not true where a page fault means only that an additional page must be brought into memory and the process restarted.

10.2.2 Performance of Demand Paging

Demand paging can significantly affect the performance of a computer system. To see why, let us compute the **effective access time** for a demand-paged memory. For most computer systems, the memory-access time, denoted ma, ranges from 10 to 200 nanoseconds. As long as we have no page faults, the effective access time is equal to the memory access time. If, however, a page fault occurs, we must first read the relevant page from disk and then access the desired word.

Let p be the probability of a page fault ($0 \le p \le 1$). We would expect p to be close to zero—that is, we would expect to have only a few page faults. The **effective access time** is then

$$\text{effective access time} = (1 - p) \times ma + p \times \text{page fault time}.$$

To compute the effective access time, we must know how much time is needed to service a page fault. A page fault causes the following sequence to occur:

1. Trap to the operating system.

2. Save the user registers and process state.

3. Determine that the interrupt was a page fault.

4. Check that the page reference was legal and determine the location of the page on the disk.

5. Issue a read from the disk to a free frame:

    a. Wait in a queue for this device until the read request is serviced.

    b. Wait for the device seek and/or latency time.

    c. Begin the transfer of the page to a free frame.

6. While waiting, allocate the CPU to some other user (CPU scheduling; optional).

7. Receive an interrupt from the disk I/O subsystem (I/O completed).

8. Save the registers and process state for the other user (if step 6 is executed).

9. Determine that the interrupt was from the disk.

10. Correct the page table and other tables to show that the desired page is now in memory.

11. Wait for the CPU to be allocated to this process again.

12. Restore the user registers, process state, and new page table, and then resume the interrupted instruction.

Not all of these steps are necessary in every case. For example, we are assuming that, in step 6, the CPU is allocated to another process while the I/O occurs. This arrangement allows multiprogramming to maintain CPU utilization but requires additional time to resume the page-fault service routine when the I/O transfer is complete.

In any case, we are faced with three major components of the page-fault service time:

1. Service the page-fault interrupt.

2. Read in the page.

3. Restart the process.

The first and third tasks may be reduced, with careful coding, to several hundred instructions. These tasks may take from 1 to 100 microseconds each. The page-switch time, however, will probably be close to 8 milliseconds. A typical hard disk has an average latency of 3 milliseconds, a seek of 5 milliseconds, and a transfer time of .05 milliseconds. Thus, the total paging time is about 8 milliseconds, including hardware and software time. Remember also that we are looking at only the device-service time. If a queue of processes is waiting for the device (other processes that have caused page faults), we have to add device-queueing time as we wait for the paging device to be free to service our request, increasing even more the time to swap.

If we take an average page-fault service time of 8 milliseconds and a memory-access time of 200 nanoseconds, then the effective access time in nanoseconds is

$$\text{effective access time} = (1 - p) \times (200) + p \ (8 \text{ milliseconds})$$
$$= (1 - p) \times 200 + p \times 8,000,000$$
$$= 200 + 7,999,800 \times p.$$

We see, then, that the effective access time is directly proportional to the **page-fault rate**. If one access out of 1,000 causes a page fault, the effective access time is 8.2 microseconds. The computer would be slowed down by a factor of 40 because of demand paging! If we want less than 10-percent degradation, we need

$$220 > 200 + 7,999,800 \times p,$$
$$20 > 7,999,800 \times p,$$
$$p < 0.0000025.$$

That is, to keep the slowdown due to paging to a reasonable level, we can allow fewer than one memory access out of 399,990 to page fault. It is important to keep the page-fault rate low in a demand-paging system. Otherwise, the effective access time increases, slowing process execution dramatically.

An additional aspect of demand paging is the handling and overall use of swap space. Disk I/O to swap space is generally faster than that to the file system. It is faster because swap space is allocated in much larger blocks, and file lookups and indirect allocation methods are not used (Chapter 14). The system can therefore gain better paging throughput by copying an entire file image into the swap space at process startup and then performing demand paging from the swap space. Another option is to demand pages from the file system initially but to write the pages to swap space as they are replaced. This approach will ensure that only needed pages are read from the file system but that all subsequent paging is done from swap space.

Some systems attempt to limit the amount of swap space used through demand paging of binary files. Demand pages for such files are brought directly from the file system. However, when page replacement is called for, these frames can simply be overwritten (because they are never modified), and the pages can be read in from the file system again if needed. Using this approach, the file system itself serves as the backing store. However, swap space must still be used for pages not associated with a file; these pages include the **stack** and **heap** for a process. This method appears to be a good compromise and is used in several systems, including Solaris and BSD UNIX.

10.3 ■ Copy-on-Write

In Section 10.2, we illustrated how a process can start quickly by merely demand-paging in the page containing the first instruction. However, process creation using the fork() system call may initially bypass the need for demand paging by using a technique similar to page sharing (covered in Section 9.4.5). This technique provides for rapid process creation and minimizes the number of new pages that must be allocated to the newly created process.

Recall that the fork() system call creates a child process as a duplicate of its parent. Traditionally, fork() worked by creating a copy of the parent's address space for the child, duplicating the pages belonging to the parent. However, considering that many child processes invoke the exec() system call immediately after creation, the copying of the parent's address space may be unnecessary. Alternatively, we can use a technique known as **copy-on-write**. This works by allowing the parent and child processes initially to share the same pages. These shared pages are marked as copy-on-write pages, meaning that if either process writes to a shared page, a copy of the shared page is created. For example, assume that the child process attempts to modify a page containing portions of the stack, with the pages set to be copy-on-write. The operating system will then create a copy of this page, mapping it to the address space of the child process. The child process will then modify its copied page and not the page belonging to the parent process. Obviously, when the copy-on-write technique is used, only the pages that are modified by either process are copied; all unmodified pages may be shared by the parent and child processes. Note that only pages that may be modified need be marked as copy-on-write. Pages that cannot be modified (pages containing executable code) may be shared by the parent and child. Copy-on-write is a common technique used by several operating systems, including Windows XP, Linux, and Solaris.

When it is determined that a page is going to be duplicated using copy-on-write, it is important to note the location from which the free page will be allocated. Many operating systems provide a **pool** of free pages for such requests. These free pages are typically allocated when the stack or heap for a process must expand or for managing copy-on-write pages. Operating systems typically allocate these pages using a technique known as **zero-fill-on-demand**. Zero-fill-on-demand pages have been zeroed-out before being allocated, thus erasing the previous contents.

Several versions of UNIX (including Solaris and Linux) also provide a variation of the fork() system call—vfork() (for **virtual memory fork**). vfork() operates differently from fork() with copy-on-write. With vfork(), the parent process is suspended, and the child process uses the address space of the parent. Because vfork() does not use copy-on-write, if the child process changes any pages of the parent's address space, the altered pages will be visible to the parent once it resumes. Therefore, vfork() must be used with caution to ensure that the child process does not modify the address space of the parent. vfork() is intended to be used when the child process calls exec() immediately after creation. Because no copying of pages takes place, vfork() is an extremely efficient method of process creation and is sometimes used to implement UNIX command-line shell interfaces.

10.4 ■ Page Replacement

In our discussion of the page-fault rate, we have so far assumed that each page faults at most once, when it is first referenced. This representation is not strictly accurate. If a process of ten pages actually uses only half of them, then demand paging saves the I/O necessary to load the five pages that are never used. We could also increase our degree of multiprogramming by running twice as many processes. Thus, if we had forty frames, we could run eight processes, rather than the four that could run if each required ten frames (five of which were never used).

If we increase our degree of multiprogramming, we are **over-allocating** memory. If we run six processes, each of which is ten pages in size but actually uses only five pages, we have higher CPU utilization and throughput, with ten frames to spare. It is possible, however, that each of these processes, for a particular data set, may suddenly try to use all ten of its pages, resulting in a need for sixty frames, when only forty are available.

Further, consider that system memory is not used only for holding program pages. Buffers for I/O also consume a significant amount of memory. This use can increase the strain on memory-placement algorithms. Deciding how much memory to allocate to I/O and how much to program pages is a significant

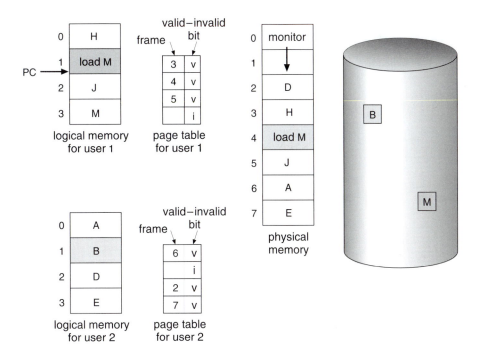

Figure 10.7   Need for page replacement.

challenge. Some systems allocate a fixed percentage of memory for I/O buffers, whereas others allow both user processes and the I/O subsystem to compete for all system memory.

Over-allocation manifests itself as follows. While a user process is executing, a page fault occurs. The operating system determines where the desired page is residing on the disk but then finds that there are *no* free frames on the free-frame list: All memory is in use (Figure 10.7).

The operating system has several options at this point. It could terminate the user process. However, demand paging is the operating system's attempt to improve the computer system's utilization and throughput. Users should not be aware that their processes are running on a paged system—paging should be logically transparent to the user. So this option is not the best choice.

The operating system could swap out a process, freeing all its frames and reducing the level of multiprogramming. This option is a good one in certain circumstances; we consider it further in Section 10.6. Here, we discuss the most common solution: **page replacement**.

10.4.1 Basic Page Replacement

Page replacement takes the following approach. If no frame is free, we find one that is not currently being used and free it. We can free a frame by writing its

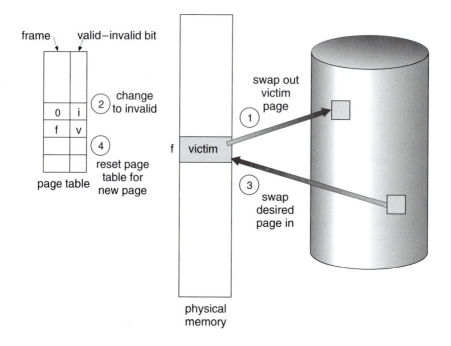

Figure 10.8   Page replacement.

contents to swap space and changing the page table (and all other tables) to indicate that the page is no longer in memory (Figure 10.8). We can now use the freed frame to hold the page for which the process faulted. We modify the page-fault service routine to include page replacement:

1. Find the location of the desired page on the disk.

2. Find a free frame:

    a. If there is a free frame, use it.

    b. If there is no free frame, use a page-replacement algorithm to select a **victim frame**.

    c. Write the victim frame to the disk; change the page and frame tables accordingly.

3. Read the desired page into the (newly) free frame; change the page and frame tables.

4. Restart the user process.

Notice that, if no frames are free, *two* page transfers (one out and one in) are required. This situation effectively doubles the page-fault service time and increases the effective access time accordingly.

We can reduce this overhead by using a **modify bit** (or **dirty bit**). Each page or frame may have a modify bit associated with it in the hardware. The modify bit for a page is set by the hardware whenever any word or byte in the page is written into, indicating that the page has been modified. When we select a page for replacement, we examine its modify bit. If the bit is set, we know that the page has been modified since it was read in from the disk. In this case, we must write that page to the disk. If the modify bit is not set, however, the page has *not* been modified since it was read into memory. Therefore, if the copy of the page on the disk has not been overwritten (by some other page, for example), then we can avoid writing the memory page to the disk: it is already there. This technique also applies to read-only pages (for example, pages of binary code). Such pages cannot be modified; thus, they may be discarded when desired. This scheme can reduce significantly the time required to service a page fault, since it reduces I/O time by one-half *if* the page has not been modified.

Page replacement is basic to demand paging. It completes the separation between logical memory and physical memory. With this mechanism, an enormous virtual memory can be provided for programmers on a smaller physical memory. With no demand paging, user addresses are mapped into physical addresses, so the two sets of addresses can be different. All the pages of a process still must be in physical memory, however. With demand paging, the size of the logical address space is no longer constrained by physical memory. If we have a user process of twenty pages, we can execute it in ten frames simply by using demand paging and using a replacement algorithm to find a free frame whenever necessary. If a page that has been modified is to be replaced, its contents are copied to the disk. A later reference to that page will cause a page fault. At that time, the page will be brought back into memory, perhaps replacing some other page in the process.

We must solve two major problems to implement demand paging: We must develop a **frame-allocation algorithm** and a **page-replacement algorithm**. If we have multiple processes in memory, we must decide how many frames to allocate to each process. Further, when page replacement is required, we must select the frames that are to be replaced. Designing appropriate algorithms to solve these problems is an important task, because disk I/O is so expensive. Even slight improvements in demand-paging methods yield large gains in system performance.

There are many different page-replacement algorithms. Every operating system probably has its own replacement scheme. How do we select a particular replacement algorithm? In general, we want the one with the lowest page-fault rate.

We evaluate an algorithm by running it on a particular string of memory references and computing the number of page faults. The string of memory references is called a **reference string**. We can generate reference strings artificially (by using a random-number generator, for example), or we can trace a given system and record the address of each memory reference. The latter

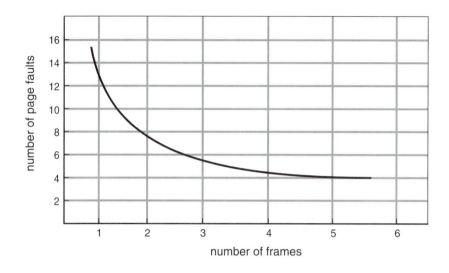

Figure 10.9   Graph of page faults versus the number of frames.

choice produces a large number of data (on the order of 1 million addresses per second). To reduce the number of data, we use two facts.

First, for a given page size (and the page size is generally fixed by the hardware or system), we need to consider only the page number, rather than the entire address. Second, if we have a reference to a page p, then any *immediately* following references to page p will never cause a page fault. Page p will be in memory after the first reference; the immediately following references will not fault.

For example, if we trace a particular process, we might record the following address sequence:

> 0100, 0432, 0101, 0612, 0102, 0103, 0104, 0101, 0611, 0102, 0103,
> 0104, 0101, 0610, 0102, 0103, 0104, 0101, 0609, 0102, 0105,

which, at 100 bytes per page, is reduced to the following reference string

$$1, 4, 1, 6, 1, 6, 1, 6, 1, 6, 1.$$

To determine the number of page faults for a particular reference string and page-replacement algorithm, we also need to know the number of page frames available. Obviously, as the number of frames available increases, the number of page faults decreases. For the reference string considered previously, for example, if we had three or more frames, we would have only three faults, one fault for the first reference to each page. In contrast, with only one frame available, we would have a replacement with every reference, resulting in 11 faults. In general, we expect a curve such as that in Figure 10.9. As the number of frames increases, the number of page faults drops to some minimal level. Of course, adding physical memory increases the number of frames.

We next illustrate several page-replacement algorithms. In doing so, we use the reference string

$$7, 0, 1, 2, 0, 3, 0, 4, 2, 3, 0, 3, 2, 1, 2, 0, 1, 7, 0, 1$$

for a memory with three frames.

10.4.2 FIFO Page Replacement

The simplest page-replacement algorithm is a FIFO algorithm. A FIFO replacement algorithm associates with each page the time when that page was brought into memory. When a page must be replaced, the oldest page is chosen. Notice that it is not strictly necessary to record the time when a page is brought in. We can create a FIFO queue to hold all pages in memory. We replace the page at the head of the queue. When a page is brought into memory, we insert it at the tail of the queue.

For our example reference string, our three frames are initially empty. The first three references (7, 0, 1) cause page faults and are brought into these empty frames. The next reference (2) replaces page 7, because page 7 was brought in first. Since 0 is the next reference and 0 is already in memory, we have no fault for this reference. The first reference to 3 results in replacement of page 0, since it is now first in line. Because of this replacement, the next reference, to 0, will fault. Page 1 is then replaced by page 0. This process continues as shown in Figure 10.10. Every time a fault occurs, we show which pages are in our three frames. There are 15 faults altogether.

The FIFO page-replacement algorithm is easy to understand and program. However, its performance is not always good. On the one hand, the page replaced may be an initialization module that was used a long time ago and is no longer needed. On the other hand, it could contain a heavily used variable that was initialized early and is in constant use.

reference string

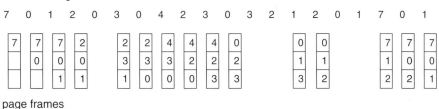

page frames

Figure 10.10 FIFO page-replacement algorithm.

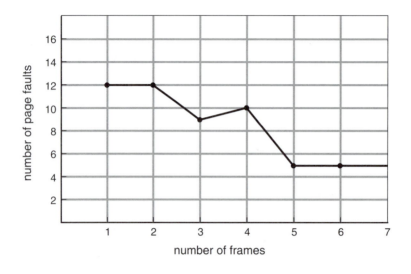

Figure 10.11   Page-fault curve for FIFO replacement on a reference string.

Notice that, even if we select for replacement a page that is in active use, everything still works correctly. After we replace an active page with a new one, a fault occurs almost immediately to retrieve the active page. Some other page will need to be replaced to bring the active page back into memory. Thus, a bad replacement choice increases the page-fault rate and slows process execution but does not cause incorrect execution.

To illustrate the problems that are possible with a FIFO page-replacement algorithm, we consider the reference string

$$1, 2, 3, 4, 1, 2, 5, 1, 2, 3, 4, 5.$$

Figure 10.11 shows the curve of page faults for this reference string versus the number of available frames. We notice that the number of faults for four frames (ten) is *greater* than the number of faults for three frames (nine)! This most unexpected result is known as **Belady's anomaly:** For some page-replacement algorithms, the page-fault rate may *increase* as the number of allocated frames increases. We would expect that giving more memory to a process would improve its performance. In some early research, investigators noticed that this assumption was not always true. Belady's anomaly was discovered as a result.

10.4.3 Optimal Page Replacement

One result of the discovery of Belady's anomaly was the search for an **optimal page-replacement algorithm**. An optimal page-replacement algorithm has the lowest page-fault rate of all algorithms and will never suffer from Belady's

reference string

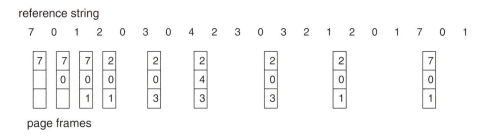

page frames

Figure 10.12   Optimal page-replacement algorithm.

anomaly. Such an algorithm does exist, and has been called OPT or MIN. It is simply this:

Replace the page that will not be used
for the longest period of time.

Use of this page-replacement algorithm guarantees the lowest possible page-fault rate for a fixed number of frames.

For example, on our sample reference string, the optimal page-replacement algorithm would yield nine page faults, as shown in Figure 10.12. The first three references cause faults that fill the three empty frames. The reference to page 2 replaces page 7, because 7 will not be used until reference 18, whereas page 0 will be used at 5, and page 1 at 14. The reference to page 3 replaces page 1, as page 1 will be the last of the three pages in memory to be referenced again. With only nine page faults, optimal replacement is much better than a FIFO algorithm, which had 15 faults. (If we ignore the first three, which all algorithms must suffer, then optimal replacement is twice as good as FIFO replacement.) In fact, no replacement algorithm can process this reference string in three frames with less than nine faults.

Unfortunately, the optimal page-replacement algorithm is difficult to implement, because it requires future knowledge of the reference string. (We encountered a similar situation with the SJF CPU-scheduling algorithm in Section 6.3.2.) As a result, the optimal algorithm is used mainly for comparison studies. For instance, it may be useful to know that, although a new algorithm is not optimal, it is within 12.3 percent of optimal at worst and within 4.7 percent on average.

10.4.4 LRU Page Replacement

If the optimal algorithm is not feasible, perhaps an approximation of the optimal algorithm is possible. The key distinction between the FIFO and OPT algorithms (other than looking backward or forward in time) is that the FIFO algorithm uses the time when a page was brought into memory, whereas the

reference string

7 0 1 2 0 3 0 4 2 3 0 3 2 1 2 0 1 7 0 1

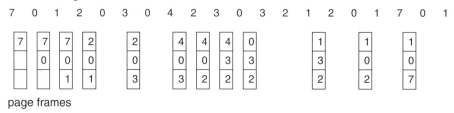

page frames

Figure 10.13   LRU page-replacement algorithm.

OPT algorithm uses the time when a page is to be *used*. If we use the recent past as an approximation of the near future, then we can replace the page that *has not been used* for the longest period of time (Figure 10.13). This approach is the **least-recently-used (LRU) algorithm**.

LRU replacement associates with each page the time of that page's last use. When a page must be replaced, LRU chooses the page that has not been used for the longest period of time. This strategy is the optimal page-replacement algorithm looking backward in time, rather than forward. (Strangely, if we let S^R be the reverse of a reference string S, then the page-fault rate for the OPT algorithm on S is the same as the page-fault rate for the OPT algorithm on S^R. Similarly, the page-fault rate for the LRU algorithm on S is the same as the page-fault rate for the LRU algorithm on S^R.)

The result of applying LRU replacement to our example reference string is shown in Figure 10.13. The LRU algorithm produces 12 faults. Notice that the first five faults are the same as those for optimal replacement. When the reference to page 4 occurs, however, LRU replacement sees that, of the three frames in memory, page 2 was used least recently. Thus, the LRU algorithm replaces page 2, not knowing that page 2 is about to be used. When it then faults for page 2, the LRU algorithm replaces page 3, since it is now the least recently used of the three pages in memory. Despite these problems, LRU replacement with 12 faults is still much better than FIFO replacement with 15.

The LRU policy is often used as a page-replacement algorithm and is considered to be good. The major problem is *how* to implement LRU replacement. An LRU page-replacement algorithm may require substantial hardware assistance. The problem is to determine an order for the frames defined by the time of last use. Two implementations are feasible:

- **Counters:** In the simplest case, we associate with each page-table entry a time-of-use field and add to the CPU a logical clock or counter. The clock is incremented for every memory reference. Whenever a reference to a page is made, the contents of the clock register are copied to the time-of-use field in the page-table entry for that page. In this way, we always have the "time" of the last reference to each page. We replace the page with the smallest time value. This scheme requires a search of the page table to find the LRU page and a write to memory (to the time-of-use field in the page table) for each memory access. The times must also be maintained when page tables are changed (due to CPU scheduling). Overflow of the clock must be considered.

- **Stack:** Another approach to implementing LRU replacement is to keep a stack of page numbers. Whenever a page is referenced, it is removed from the stack and put on the top. In this way, the top of the stack is always the most recently used page and the bottom is the LRU page (Figure 10.14). Because entries must be removed from the middle of the stack, it is best implemented by a doubly linked list, with a head and tail pointer. Removing a page and putting it on the top of the stack then requires changing six pointers at worst. Each update is a little more expensive, but there is no search for a replacement; the tail pointer points to the bottom of the stack, which is the LRU page. This approach is particularly appropriate for software or microcode implementations of LRU replacement.

Like optimal replacement, LRU replacement does not suffer from Belady's anomaly. They belong to a class of page-replacement algorithms, called **stack algorithms**, that can never exhibit Belady's anomaly. A stack algorithm is an algorithm for which it can be shown that the set of pages in memory for n frames is always a *subset* of the set of pages that would be in memory with $n + 1$ frames. For LRU replacement, the set of pages in memory would be the n most recently referenced pages. If the number of frames is increased, these n pages will still be the most recently referenced and so will still be in memory.

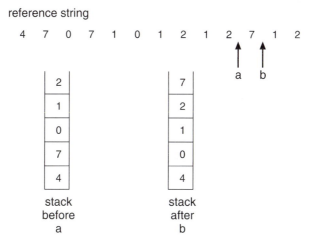

Figure 10.14   Use of a stack to record the most recent page references.

Note that neither implementation of LRU would be conceivable without hardware assistance beyond the standard TLB registers. The updating of the clock fields or stack must be done for *every* memory reference. If we were to use an interrupt for every reference, to allow software to update such data structures, it would slow every memory reference by a factor of at least ten, hence slowing every user process by a factor of ten. Few systems could tolerate that level of overhead for memory management.

10.4.5 LRU-Approximation Page Replacement

Few computer systems provide sufficient hardware support for true LRU page replacement. Some systems provide no hardware support, and other page-replacement algorithms (such as a FIFO algorithm) must be used. Many systems provide some help, however, in the form of a **reference bit**. The reference bit for a page is set, by the hardware, whenever that page is referenced (either a read or a write to any byte in the page). Reference bits are associated with each entry in the page table.

Initially, all bits are cleared (to 0) by the operating system. As a user process executes, the bit associated with each page referenced is set (to 1) by the hardware. After some time, we can determine which pages have been used and which have not been used by examining the reference bits. We do not know the *order* of use, but we know which pages were used and which were not used. This partial ordering information leads to many page-replacement algorithms that approximate LRU replacement.

10.4.5.1 Additional-Reference-Bits Algorithm

We can gain additional ordering information by recording the reference bits at regular intervals. We can keep an 8-bit byte for each page in a table in memory. At regular intervals (say, every 100 milliseconds), a timer interrupt transfers control to the operating system. The operating system shifts the reference bit for each page into the high-order bit of its 8-bit byte, shifting the other bits right 1 bit and discarding the low-order bit. These 8-bit shift registers contain the history of page use for the last eight time periods. If the shift register contains 00000000, for example, then the page has not been used for eight time periods; a page that is used at least once each period would have a shift register value of 11111111. A page with a history register value of 11000100 has been used more recently than has one with a value of 01110111. If we interpret these 8-bit bytes as unsigned integers, the page with the lowest number is the LRU page, and it can be replaced. Notice that the numbers are not guaranteed to be unique, however. We can either replace (swap out) all pages with the smallest value or use the FIFO method to choose among them.

The number of bits of history can be varied, of course, and would be selected (depending on the hardware available) to make the updating as fast as possible. In the extreme case, the number can be reduced to zero, leaving only the reference bit itself. This algorithm is called the **second-chance page-replacement algorithm**.

10.4.5.2 Second-Chance Algorithm

The basic algorithm of second-chance replacement is a FIFO replacement algorithm. When a page has been selected, however, we inspect its reference bit. If the value is 0, we proceed to replace this page; but if the reference bit is set to 1, we give the page a second chance and move on to select the next FIFO page. When a page gets a second chance, its reference bit is cleared, and its arrival time is reset to the current time. Thus, a page that is given a second chance will not be replaced until all other pages have been replaced (or given second chances). In addition, if a page is used often enough to keep its reference bit set, it will never be replaced.

One way to implement the second-chance algorithm (sometimes referred to as the *clock* algorithm) is as a circular queue. A pointer (that is, a hand on the clock) indicates which page is to be replaced next. When a frame is needed, the pointer advances until it finds a page with a 0 reference bit. As it advances, it clears the reference bits (Figure 10.15). Once a victim page is found, the page is replaced, and the new page is inserted in the circular queue in that position. Notice that, in the worst case, when all bits are set, the pointer cycles through the whole queue, giving each page a second chance. It clears all the reference bits before selecting the next page for replacement. Second-chance replacement degenerates to FIFO replacement if all bits are set.

10.4.5.3 Enhanced Second-Chance Algorithm

We can enhance the second-chance algorithm by considering both the reference bit and the modify bit (Section 10.4) as an ordered pair. With these two bits, we have the following four possible classes:

1. (0, 0) neither recently used nor modified—best page to replace

2. (0, 1) not recently used but modified—not quite as good, because the page will need to be written out before replacement

3. (1, 0) recently used but clean—it probably will be used again soon

4. (1, 1) recently used and modified—it probably will be used again soon, and the page will be need to be written out to disk before it can be replaced

Each page is in one of these four classes. When page replacement is called for, we use the same scheme as in the clock algorithm; but instead of examining whether the page to which we are pointing has the reference bit set to 1, we examine the class to which that page belongs. We replace the first page encountered in the lowest nonempty class. Notice that we may have to scan the circular queue several times before we find a page to be replaced.

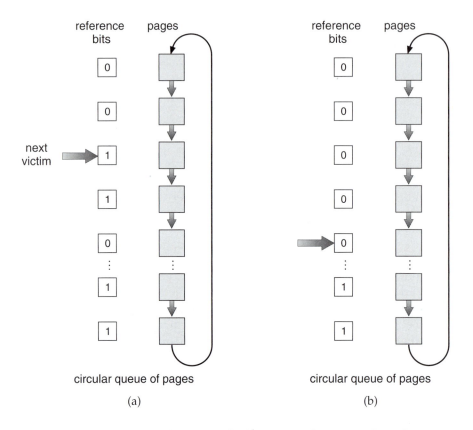

Figure 10.15   Second-chance (clock) page-replacement algorithm.

The major difference between this algorithm and the simpler clock algorithm is that here we give preference to those pages that have been modified to reduce the number of I/Os required.

10.4.6 Counting-Based Page Replacement

There are many other algorithms that can be used for page replacement. For example, we could keep a counter of the number of references that have been made to each page and develop the following two schemes.

- The **least frequently used (LFU) page-replacement algorithm** requires that the page with the smallest count be replaced. The reason for this selection is that an actively used page should have a large reference count. A problem arises, however, when a page is used heavily during the initial phase of a process but then is never used again. Since it was used heavily, it has a large count and remains in memory even though it is no longer needed. One solution is to shift the counts right by 1 bit at regular intervals, forming an exponentially decaying average usage count.

- The **most frequently used (MFU) page-replacement algorithm** is based on the argument that the page with the smallest count was probably just brought in and has yet to be used.

As you might expect, neither MFU nor LFU replacement is common. The implementation of these algorithms is expensive, and they do not approximate OPT replacement well.

10.4.7 Page-Buffering Algorithms

Other procedures are often used in addition to a specific page-replacement algorithm. For example, systems commonly keep a pool of free frames. When a page fault occurs, a victim frame is chosen as before. However, the desired page is read into a free frame from the pool before the victim is written out. This procedure allows the process to restart as soon as possible, without waiting for the victim page to be written out. When the victim is later written out, its frame is added to the free-frame pool.

An expansion of this idea is to maintain a list of modified pages. Whenever the paging device is idle, a modified page is selected and is written to the disk. Its modify bit is then reset. This scheme increases the probability that a page will be clean when it is selected for replacement and will not need to be written out.

Another modification is to keep a pool of free frames but to remember which page was in each frame. Since the frame contents are not modified when a frame is written to the disk, the old page can be reused directly from the free-frame pool if it is needed before that frame is reused. No I/O is needed in this case. When a page fault occurs, we first check whether the desired page is in the free-frame pool. If it is not, we must select a free frame and read into it.

This technique is used in the VAX/VMS system along with a FIFO replacement algorithm. When the FIFO replacement algorithm mistakenly replaces a page that is still in active use, that page is quickly retrieved from the free-frame pool, and no I/O is necessary. The free-frame buffer provides protection against the relatively poor, but simple, FIFO replacement algorithm. This method is necessary because the early versions of the VAX did not implement the reference bit correctly.

Some versions of UNIX use this method in conjunction with the second-chance algorithm. It can be a useful augmentation to any page replacement algorithm to reduce the penalty incurred if the wrong victim page is selected.

10.4.8 Applications and Page Replacement

In certain cases, applications accessing data through the operating system's virtual memory perform worse than if the operating system provided no buffering at all. A typical example is a database, which provides its own memory management and I/O buffering. Applications like this understand their memory use and disk use better than an operating system that is implementing algorithms for general-purpose use. If the operating system is buffering I/O, and the application is as well, then twice the memory is being used for a set of I/O.

In another example, data warehouses frequently perform massive sequential disk reads, followed by computations and writes. The LRU algorithm would be removing old pages and preserving new ones, while the application would more likely be reading older pages than newer ones (as it starts its sequential reads again). Here, MFU would actually be more efficient than LRU.

Because of this problem, some operating systems give special programs the ability to use a disk partition as a large sequential array of logical blocks, without any file-system data structures. This array is sometimes called the **raw disk**, and I/O to this array is termed raw I/O. Raw I/O bypasses all the file-system services, such as file I/O demand paging, file locking, prefetching, space allocation, file names, and directories. Although certain applications are more efficient when implementing their own special-purpose storage services on a raw partition, most applications perform better when they use the regular file-system services.

10.5 ■ Allocation of Frames

How do we allocate the fixed amount of free memory among the various processes? If we have 93 free frames and two processes, how many frames does each process get?

The simplest case of virtual memory is the single-user system. Consider a single-user system with 128 KB of memory composed of pages of size 1 KB. This system has 128 frames. The operating system may take 35 KB, leaving 93 frames for the user process. Under pure demand paging, all 93 frames would initially be put on the free-frame list. When a user process started execution, it would generate a sequence of page faults. The first 93 page faults would all get free frames from the free-frame list. When the free-frame list was exhausted, a page-replacement algorithm would be used to select one of the 93 in-memory pages to be replaced with the 94th, and so on. When the process terminated, the 93 frames would once again be placed on the free-frame list.

There are many variations on this simple strategy. We can require that the operating system allocate all its buffer and table space from the free-frame list. When this space is not in use by the operating system, it can be used to support user paging. We can try to keep three free frames reserved on the free-frame list at all times. Thus, when a page fault occurs, there is a free frame available to page into. While the page swap is taking place, a replacement can be selected, which is then written to the disk as the user process continues to execute. Other variants are also possible, but the basic strategy is clear: The user process is allocated any free frame.

10.5.1 Minimum Number of Frames

Our strategies for the allocation of frames are constrained in various ways. We cannot allocate more than the total number of available frames (unless there is page sharing). We must also allocate at least a minimum number of frames. Here, we look more closely at the latter requirement.

One reason for allocating at least a minimum number of frames involves performance. Obviously, as the number of frames allocated to each process decreases, the page-fault-rate increases, slowing process execution. In addition, remember that, when a page fault occurs before an executing instruction is complete, the instruction must be restarted. Consequently, we must have enough frames to hold all the different pages that any single instruction can reference.

For example, consider a machine in which all memory-reference instructions have only one memory address. In this case, we need at least one frame for the instruction and one frame for the memory reference. In addition, if one-level indirect addressing is allowed (for example, a `load` instruction on page 16 can refer to an address on page 0, which is an indirect reference to page 23), then paging requires at least three frames per process. Think about what might happen if a process had only two frames.

The minimum number of frames is defined by the computer architecture. For example, the move instruction for the PDP-11 includes more than one word for some addressing modes, and thus the instruction itself may straddle two pages. In addition, each of its two operands may be indirect references, for a total of six frames. Another example is the IBM 370 MVC instruction. Since the instruction is storage to storage, it takes 6 bytes and can straddle two pages. The block of characters to move and the area to which it is to be moved can each also straddle two pages. This situation would require six frames. The worst case occurs when the MVC instruction is the operand of an EXECUTE instruction that straddles a page boundary; in this case, we need eight frames.

The worst-case scenario occurs in computer architectures that allow multiple levels of indirection (for example, each 16-bit word could contain a 15-bit address plus a 1-bit indirect indicator). Theoretically, a simple load instruction could reference an indirect address that could reference an indirect address (on another page) that could also reference an indirect address (on yet another page), and so on, until every page in virtual memory had been touched. Thus, in the worst case, the entire virtual memory must be in physical memory. To overcome this difficulty, we must place a limit on the levels of indirection (for example, limit an instruction to at most 16 levels of indirection). When the first indirection occurs, a counter is set to 16; the counter is then decremented for each successive indirection for this instruction. If the counter is decremented to 0, a trap occurs (excessive indirection). This limitation reduces the maximum number of memory references per instruction to 17, requiring the same number of frames.

Whereas the minimum number of frames per process is defined by the architecture, the maximum number is defined by the amount of available physical memory. In between, we are still left with significant choice in frame allocation.

10.5.2 Allocation Algorithms

The easiest way to split m frames among n processes is to give everyone an equal share, m/n frames. For instance, if there are 93 frames and five processes, each process will get 18 frames. The leftover three frames can be used as a free-frame buffer pool. This scheme is called **equal allocation**.

An alternative is to recognize that various processes will need differing amounts of memory. Consider a system with a 1-KB frame size. If a small student process of 10 KB and an interactive database of 127 KB are the only two processes running in a system with 62 free frames, it does not make much sense to give each process 31 frames. The student process does not need more than 10 frames, so the other 21 are strictly wasted.

To solve this problem, we can use **proportional allocation**, in which we allocate available memory to each process according to its size. Let the size of the virtual memory for process p_i be s_i, and define

$$S = \sum s_i.$$

Then, if the total number of available frames is m, we allocate a_i frames to process p_i, where a_i is approximately

$$a_i = s_i/S \times m.$$

Of course, we must adjust each a_i to be an integer that is greater than the minimum number of frames required by the instruction set, with a sum not exceeding m.

For proportional allocation, we would split 62 frames between two processes, one of 10 pages and one of 127 pages, by allocating 4 frames and 57 frames, respectively, since

$$10/137 \times 62 \approx 4,$$
$$127/137 \times 62 \approx 57.$$

In this way, both processes share the available frames according to their "needs," rather than equally.

In both equal and proportional allocation, of course, the allocation to each process may vary according to the multiprogramming level. If the multiprogramming level is increased, each process will lose some frames to provide the memory needed for the new process. Conversely, if the multiprogramming level decreases, the frames that were allocated to the departed process can be spread over the remaining processes.

Notice that, with either equal or proportional allocation, a high-priority process is treated the same as a low-priority process. By its definition, however, we may want to give the high-priority process more memory to speed its execution, to the detriment of low-priority processes.

One approach is to use a proportional allocation scheme where the ratio of frames depends not on the relative sizes of processes but rather on the priorities of processes or on a combination of size and priority.

10.5.3   Global versus Local Allocation

Another important factor in the way frames are allocated to the various processes is page replacement. With multiple processes competing for frames, we can classify page-replacement algorithms into two broad categories: **global replacement** and **local replacement**. Global replacement allows a process to select a replacement frame from the set of all frames, even if that frame is currently allocated to some other process; that is, one process can take a frame from another. Local replacement requires that each process select from only its own set of allocated frames.

For example, consider an allocation scheme where we allow high-priority processes to select frames from low-priority processes for replacement. A process can select a replacement from among its own frames or the frames of any lower-priority process. This approach allows a high-priority process to increase its frame allocation at the expense of a low-priority process.

With a local replacement strategy, the number of frames allocated to a process does not change. With global replacement, a process may happen to select only frames allocated to other processes, thus increasing the number of frames allocated to it (assuming that other processes do not choose *its* frames for replacement).

One problem with a global replacement algorithm is that a process cannot control its own page-fault rate. The set of pages in memory for a process depends not only on the paging behavior of that process but also on the paging behavior of other processes. Therefore, the same process may perform quite differently (for example, taking 0.5 seconds for one execution and 10.3 seconds for the next execution) because of totally external circumstances. Such is not the case with a local replacement algorithm. Under local replacement, the set of pages in memory for a process is affected by the paging behavior of only that process. Local replacement might hinder a process, however, by not making available to it other, less used pages of memory. Thus, global replacement generally results in greater system throughput and is therefore the more common method.

10.6 ■ Thrashing

If the number of frames allocated to a low-priority process falls below the minimum number required by the computer architecture, we must suspend that process's execution. We should then page out its remaining pages, freeing all its allocated frames. This provision introduces a swap-in, swap-out level of intermediate CPU scheduling.

In fact, look at any process that does not have "enough" frames. If the process does not have the number of frames it needs to support pages in active use, it will quickly page fault. At this point, it must replace some page. However, since all its pages are in active use, it must replace a page that will be needed again right away. Consequently, it quickly faults again, and again, and again, replacing pages that it must bring back in right away.

This high paging activity is called **thrashing**. A process is thrashing if it is spending more time paging than executing.

10.6.1 Cause of Thrashing

Thrashing results in severe performance problems. Consider the following scenario, which is based on the actual behavior of early paging systems.

The operating system monitors CPU utilization. If CPU utilization is too low, we increase the degree of multiprogramming by introducing a new process to the system. A global page-replacement algorithm is used; it replaces pages with no regard to the process to which they belong. Now suppose that a process enters a new phase in its execution and needs more frames. It starts faulting and taking frames away from other processes. These processes need those pages, however, and so they also fault, taking frames from other processes. These faulting processes must use the paging device to swap pages in and out. As they queue up for the paging device, the ready queue empties. As processes wait for the paging device, CPU utilization decreases.

The CPU scheduler sees the decreasing CPU utilization and *increases* the degree of multiprogramming as a result. The new process tries to get started by taking frames from running processes, causing more page faults and a longer queue for the paging device. As a result, CPU utilization drops even further, and the CPU scheduler tries to increase the degree of multiprogramming even more. Thrashing has occurred, and system throughput plunges. The page-fault rate increases tremendously. As a result, the effective memory-access time increases. No work is getting done, because the processes are spending all their time paging.

This phenomenon is illustrated in Figure 10.16, in which CPU utilization is plotted against the degree of multiprogramming. As the degree of multi-programming increases, CPU utilization also increases, although more slowly, until a maximum is reached. If the degree of multiprogramming is increased even further, thrashing sets in, and CPU utilization drops sharply. At this point,

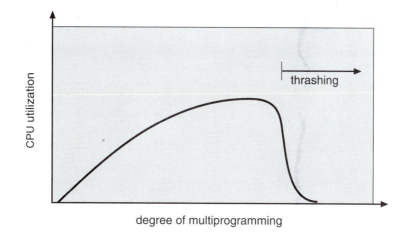

Figure 10.16   Thrashing.

to increase CPU utilization and stop thrashing, we must *decrease* the degree of multiprogramming.

We can limit the effects of thrashing by using a **local replacement algorithm** (or **priority replacement algorithm**). With local replacement, if one process starts thrashing, it cannot steal frames from another process and cause the latter to thrash also. Pages are replaced with regard to the process of which they are a part. However, the problem is not entirely solved. If processes are thrashing, they will be in the queue for the paging device most of the time. The average service time for a page fault will increase because of the longer average queue for the paging device. Thus, the effective access time will increase even for a process that is not thrashing.

To prevent thrashing, we must provide a process with as many frames as it needs. But how do we know how many frames it "needs"? There are several techniques. The working-set strategy (Section 10.6.2) starts by looking at how many frames a process is actually using. This approach defines the **locality model** of process execution.

The locality model states that, as a process executes, it moves from locality to locality. A locality is a set of pages that are actively used together (Figure 10.17). A program is generally composed of several different localities, which may overlap.

For example, when a subroutine is called, it defines a new locality. In this locality, memory references are made to the instructions of the subroutine, its local variables, and a subset of the global variables. When the subroutine is exited, the process leaves this locality, since the local variables and instructions of the subroutine are no longer in active use. We may return to this locality later.

Thus, we see that localities are defined by the program structure and its data structures. The locality model states that all programs will exhibit this

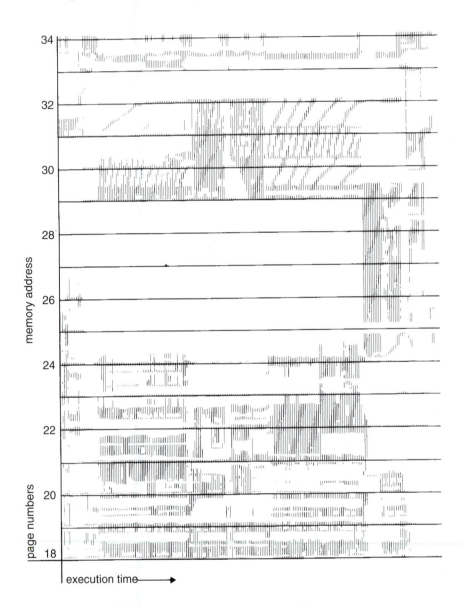

Figure 10.17   Locality in a memory-reference pattern.

basic memory reference structure. Note that the locality model is the unstated principle behind the caching discussions so far in this book. If accesses to any types of data were random rather than patterned, caching would be useless.

Suppose that we allocate enough frames to a process to accommodate its current locality. It will fault for the pages in its locality until all these pages are in memory; then, it will not fault again until it changes localities. If we allocate fewer frames than the size of the current locality, the process will thrash, since it cannot keep in memory all the pages that it is actively using.

10.6.2 Working-Set Model

The **working-set model** is based on the assumption of locality. This model uses a parameter, Δ, to define the **working-set window**. The idea is to examine the most recent Δ page references. The set of pages in the most recent Δ page references is the **working set** (Figure 10.18). If a page is in active use, it will be in the working set. If it is no longer being used, it will drop from the working set Δ time units after its last reference. Thus, the working set is an approximation of the program's locality.

For example, given the sequence of memory references shown in Figure 10.18, if $\Delta = 10$ memory references, then the working set at time t_1 is $\{1, 2, 5, 6, 7\}$. By time t_2, the working set has changed to $\{3, 4\}$.

The accuracy of the working set depends on the selection of Δ. If Δ is too small, it will not encompass the entire locality; if Δ is too large, it may overlap several localities. In the extreme, if Δ is infinite, the working set is the set of pages touched during the process execution.

The most important property of the working set, then, is its size. If we compute the working-set size, WSS_i, for each process in the system, we can then consider

$$D = \sum WSS_i,$$

where D is the total demand for frames. Each process is actively using the pages in its working set. Thus, process i needs WSS_i frames. If the total demand is greater than the total number of available frames ($D > m$), thrashing will occur, because some processes will not have enough frames.

Once Δ has been selected, use of the working-set model is simple. The operating system monitors the working set of each process and allocates to that working set enough frames to provide it with its working-set size. If there are enough extra frames, another process can be initiated. If the sum of the working-set sizes increases, exceeding the total number of available frames, the

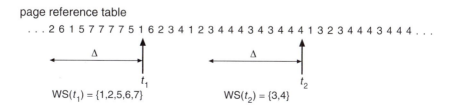

page reference table

... 2 6 1 5 7 7 7 7 5 1 6 2 3 4 1 2 3 4 4 4 3 4 3 4 4 4 1 3 2 3 4 4 4 3 4 4 4 ...

t_1

t_2

$WS(t_1) = \{1,2,5,6,7\}$ $WS(t_2) = \{3,4\}$

Figure 10.18   Working-set model.

operating system selects a process to suspend. The process's pages are written out (swapped), and its frames are reallocated to other processes. The suspended process can be restarted later.

This working-set strategy prevents thrashing while keeping the degree of multiprogramming as high as possible. Thus, it optimizes CPU utilization.

The difficulty with the working-set model is keeping track of the working set. The working-set window is a moving window. At each memory reference, a new reference appears at one end and the oldest reference drops off the other end. A page is in the working set if it is referenced anywhere in the working-set window. We can approximate the working-set model with a fixed interval timer interrupt and a reference bit.

For example, assume Δ is 10,000 references and we can cause a timer interrupt every 5,000 references. When we get a timer interrupt, we copy and clear the reference-bit values for each page. Thus, if a page fault occurs, we can examine the current reference bit and 2 in-memory bits to determine whether a page was used within the last 10,000 to 15,000 references. If it was used, at least 1 of these bits will be on. If it has not been used, these bits will be off. Those pages with at least 1 bit on will be considered to be in the working set. Note that this arrangement is not entirely accurate, because we cannot tell where, within an interval of 5,000, a reference occurred. We can reduce the uncertainty by increasing the number of our history bits and the frequency of interrupts (for example, 10 bits and interrupts every 1,000 references). However, the cost to service these more frequent interrupts will be correspondingly higher.

10.6.3 Page-Fault Frequency

The working-set model is successful, and knowledge of the working set can be useful for prepaging (Section 10.8.1), but it seems a clumsy way to control thrashing. A strategy that uses the **page-fault frequency (PFF)** takes a more direct approach.

The specific problem is how to prevent thrashing. Thrashing has a high page-fault rate. Thus, we want to control the page-fault rate. When it is too high, we know that the process needs more frames. Conversely, if the page-fault rate is too low, then the process may have too many frames. We can establish upper and lower bounds on the desired page-fault rate (Figure 10.19). If the actual page-fault rate exceeds the upper limit, we allocate that process another frame; if the page-fault rate falls below the lower limit, we remove a frame from that process. Thus, we can directly measure and control the page-fault rate to prevent thrashing.

As with the working-set strategy, we may have to suspend a process. If the page-fault rate increases and no free frames are available, we must select some process and suspend it. The freed frames are then distributed to processes with high page-fault rates.

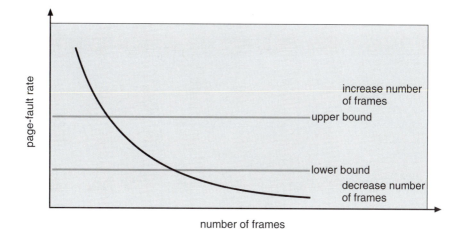

Figure 10.19   Page-fault frequency.

10.7 ■ Memory-Mapped Files

Consider a sequential read of a file on disk using the standard system calls open(), read(), and write(). Each file access requires a system call and disk access. Alternatively, we can use the virtual-memory techniques discussed so far to treat file I/O as routine memory accesses. This approach, known as **memory mapping** a file, allows a part of the virtual-address space to be logically associated with the file.

Memory mapping a file is accomplished by mapping a disk block to a page (or pages) in memory. Initial access to the file proceeds through ordinary demand paging, resulting in a page fault. However, a page-sized portion of the file is read from the file system into a physical page (some systems may opt to read in more than a page-sized chunk of memory at a time). Subsequent reads and writes to the file are handled as routine memory accesses, thereby simplifying file access and usage by allowing the system to manipulate files through memory rather than incurring the overhead of using the read() and write() system calls.

Note that writes to the file mapped in memory are not necessarily immediate (synchronous) writes to the file on disk. Some systems may choose to update the physical file when the operating system periodically checks whether the page in memory has been modified. When the file is closed, all the memory-mapped data is written back to disk and removed from the virtual memory of the process.

Some operating systems provide memory mapping only through a specific system call and use the standard system calls to perform all other file I/O. However, some systems choose to memory map a file regardless of whether the file was specified as memory mapped. Let's take Solaris as an example. If a file

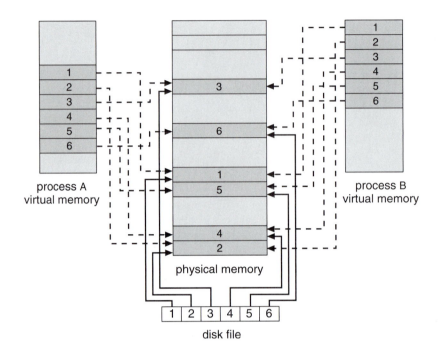

Figure 10.20   Memory-mapped files.

is specified as memory-mapped (using the mmap() system call), Solaris maps the file into the address space of the process. If a file is opened and accessed using ordinary system calls, such as open(), read(), and write(), Solaris still memory maps the file; however, the file is mapped to the kernel address space. Regardless how the file is opened, then, Solaris treats all file I/O as memory mapped, allowing file access to take place via the efficient memory subsystem.

Multiple processes may be allowed to map the same file concurrently, to allow sharing of data. Writes by any of the processes modify the data in virtual memory and can be seen by all others that map the same section of the file. Given our earlier discussions of virtual memory, it should be clear how the sharing of memory-mapped sections of memory is implemented: The virtual-memory map of each sharing process points to the same page of physical memory—the page that holds a copy of the disk block. This memory sharing is illustrated in Figure 10.20. The memory-mapping system calls can also support copy-on-write functionality, allowing processes to share a file in read-only mode but to have their own copies of any data they modify. So that access to the shared data is coordinated, the processes involved might use one of the mechanisms for achieving mutual exclusion described in Chapter 7.

On some systems, shared memory requires the use of memory mapping. On such systems, shared memory occurs when one process first creates a shared-memory object. Other processes can then access this shared memory by mapping the shared-memory object into their virtual address space.

10.7.1 Memory-Mapped Files in Java

Next, we present the facilities in the Java API for memory mapping files. To memory map a file requires first opening the file and then obtaining the FileChannel for the opened file. Once the FileChannel is obtained, we then invoke the map() method of this channel, which maps the file into memory. The map() method returns a MappedByteBuffer, which is a buffer of bytes that is mapped in memory. This is shown in Figure 10.21.

```java
import java.io.*;
import java.nio.*;
import java.nio.channels.*;

public class MemoryMapReadOnly
{
    // Assume the page size is 4 KB
    public static final int PAGE_SIZE = 4096;

    public static void main(String args[]) throws IOException {
        RandomAccessFile inFile = new RandomAccessFile(args[0],"r");

        FileChannel in = inFile.getChannel();
        MappedByteBuffer mappedBuffer =
          in.map(FileChannel.MapMode.READ_ONLY, 0, in.size());
        long numPages = in.size() / (long)PAGE_SIZE;
        if (in.size() % PAGE_SIZE > 0)
            ++numPages;

        // we will "touch" the first byte of every page
        int position = 0;
        for (long i = 0; i < numPages; i++) {
            byte item = mappedBuffer.get(position);
            position += PAGE_SIZE;
        }

        in.close();
        inFile.close();
    }
}
```

Figure 10.21 Memory mapping a file in Java.

The API for the map() method is as follows:

$$map(mode, position, size)$$

The mode refers to how the mapping occurs. Figure 10.21 maps the file as READ_ONLY. Files may also be mapped as READ_WRITE and PRIVATE. If the file is mapped as PRIVATE, memory mapping takes place using the copy-on-write technique described in Section 10.3 where any changes to the mapped file result in first copying the modified page so that the changes are made only to the object instance of the MappedByteBuffer performing the mapping.

The position refers to the byte position where the mapping is to begin, and the size indicates how many bytes are to be mapped from the starting position. Figure 10.21 maps the entire file—that is, from position 0 to the size of the FileChannel—in.size(). It is also possible to map only a portion of a file or to obtain several different mappings of the same file.

In Figure 10.21, we assume the page size mapping the file is 4,096 bytes. (Many operating systems provide a system call to determine the page size; however, this is not a feature of the Java API.) We then determine the number of pages necessary to map the file in memory and access the first byte of every page using the get() method of the MappedByteBuffer class. This has the effect of demand paging every page of the file into memory (on systems supporting that memory model). The API also provides the load() method of the MappedByteBuffer class, which loads the entire file into memory using demand paging.

Many operating systems provide a system call that releases (or unmaps) the mapping of a file. Such action releases the physical pages that mapped the file in memory. The Java API provides no such features. A mapping exists until the MappedByteBuffer object is garbage collected.

10.8 ■ Other Considerations

The major decisions that we make for a paging system are the selections of a replacement algorithm and an allocation policy, which we discussed earlier in this chapter. There are many other considerations as well, and we conclude the chapter by discussing several of them.

10.8.1 Prepaging

An obvious property of pure demand paging is the large number of page faults that occur when a process is started. This situation results from trying to get the initial locality into memory. The same situation may arise at other times. For instance, when a swapped-out process is restarted, all its pages are on the disk, and each must be brought in by its own page fault. **Prepaging** is an attempt to prevent this high level of initial paging. The strategy is to bring into memory at one time all the pages that will be needed. Some operating systems—notably Solaris—prepage the page frames for small files.

In a system using the working-set model, for example, we keep with each process a list of the pages in its working set. If we must suspend a process (due to an I/O wait or a lack of free frames), we remember the working set for that process. When the process is to be resumed (I/O completion or enough free frames), we automatically bring back into memory its entire working set before restarting the process.

Prepaging may offer an advantage in some cases. The question is simply whether the cost of using prepaging is less than the cost of servicing the corresponding page faults. It may well be the case that many of the pages brought back into memory by prepaging are not used.

Assume that s pages are prepaged and a fraction α of these s pages is actually used ($0 \leq \alpha \leq 1$). The question is whether the cost of the $s * \alpha$ saved page faults is greater or less than the cost of prepaging $s * (1 - \alpha)$ unnecessary pages. If α is close to zero, prepaging loses; if α is close to one, prepaging wins.

10.8.2 Page Size

The designers of an operating system for an existing machine seldom have a choice concerning the page size. However, when new machines are being designed, a decision regarding the best page size must be made. As you might expect, there is no single best page size. Rather, there is a set of factors that support various sizes. Page sizes are invariably powers of 2, generally ranging from 4,096 (2^{12}) to 4,194,304 (2^{22}) bytes.

How do we select a page size? One concern is the size of the page table. For a given virtual-memory space, decreasing the page size increases the number of pages and hence the size of the page table. For a virtual memory of 4 MB (2^{22}), for example, there would be 4,096 pages of 1,024 bytes but only 512 pages of 8,192 bytes. Because each active process must have its own copy of the page table, a large page size is desirable.

Memory is better utilized with smaller pages, however. If a process is allocated memory starting at location 00000 and continuing until it has as much as it needs, it probably will not end exactly on a page boundary. Thus, a part of the final page must be allocated (because pages are the units of allocation) but is unused (creating internal fragmentation). Assuming independence of process size and page size, we can expect that, on the average, one-half of the final page of each process will be wasted. This loss is only 256 bytes for a page of 512 bytes but is 4,096 bytes for a page of 8,192 bytes. To minimize internal fragmentation, then, we need a small page size.

Another problem is the time required to read or write a page. I/O time is composed of seek, latency, and transfer times. Transfer time is proportional to the amount transferred (that is, the page size)—a fact that would seem to argue for a small page size. Remember from Chapter 2, however, that latency and seek time normally dwarf transfer time. At a transfer rate of 2 MB per second, it takes only 0.2 milliseconds to transfer 512 bytes. Latency time, though, is perhaps 8 milliseconds and seek time 20 milliseconds. Of the total I/O time (28.2 milliseconds), therefore, only 1 percent is attributable to the actual transfer. Doubling the page size increases I/O time to only 28.4 milliseconds. It takes 28.4 milliseconds to read a single page of 1,024 bytes but 56.4 milliseconds to read the same amount as two pages of 512 bytes each. Thus, a desire to minimize I/O time argues for a larger page size.

With a smaller page size, however, total I/O should be reduced, since locality will be improved. A smaller page size allows each page to match program locality more accurately. For example, consider a process of size 200 KB, of which only one-half (100 KB) is actually used in an execution. If we have only one large page, we must bring in the entire page, a total of 200 KB transferred and allocated. If instead we had pages of only 1 byte, then we could bring in only the 100 KB that are actually used, resulting in only 100 KB being transferred and allocated. With a smaller page size, we have better **resolution**, allowing us to isolate only the memory that is actually needed. With a larger page size, we must allocate and transfer not only what is needed but also anything else that happens to be in the page, whether it is needed or not. Thus, a smaller page size should result in less I/O and less total allocated memory.

But did you notice that with a page size of 1 byte, we would have a page fault for *each* byte? A process of 200 KB, using only one-half of that memory, would generate only one page fault with a page size of 200 KB but 102,400 page faults with a page size of 1 byte. Each page fault generates the large amount of overhead needed for processing the interrupt, saving registers, replacing a page, queueing for the paging device, and updating tables. To minimize the number of page faults, we need to have a large page size.

Other factors must be considered as well (such as the relationship between page size and sector size on the paging device). The problem has no best answer. As we have seen, some factors (internal fragmentation, locality) argue for a small page size, whereas others (table size, I/O time) argue for a large page size. However, the historical trend is toward larger page sizes. Indeed, the first edition of *Operating Systems Concepts* (1983) used 4,096 bytes as the upper bound on page sizes, and this value was the most common page size in 1990. However, modern systems may now use much larger page sizes, as we will see in the following section.

10.8.3 TLB Reach

In Chapter 9, we introduced the **hit ratio** of the TLB. Recall that the hit ratio for the TLB refers to the percentage of virtual-address translations that are resolved in the TLB rather than the page table. Clearly, the hit ratio is related to the number of entries in the TLB, and the way to increase the hit ratio is by increasing the number of entries in the TLB. This, however, does not come cheaply, as the associative memory used to construct the TLB is both expensive and power hungry.

Related to the hit ratio is a similar metric: the **TLB reach**. The TLB reach refers to the amount of memory accessible from the TLB and is simply the number of entries multiplied by the page size. Ideally, the working set for a process is stored in the TLB. If not, the process will spend a considerable amount of time resolving memory references in the page table rather than the TLB. If we double the number of entries in the TLB, we double the TLB reach. However, for some memory-intensive applications, this may still prove insufficient for storing the working set.

Another approach for increasing the TLB reach is to either increase the size of the page or provide multiple page sizes. If we increase the page size—say, from 8 KB to 32 KB—we quadruple the TLB reach. However, this may lead to an increase in fragmentation for some applications that do not require such a large page size as 32 KB. Alternatively, an operating system may provide several different page sizes. For example, the UltraSPARC supports page sizes of 8 KB, 64 KB, 512 KB, and 4 MB. Of these available pages sizes, Solaris uses both 8 KB and 4 MB page sizes. And with a 64-entry TLB, the TLB reach for Solaris ranges from 512 KB with 8 KB pages to 256 MB with 4 MB pages. For the majority of applications, the 8 KB page size is sufficient, although Solaris maps the first 4 MB of kernel code and data with two 4 MB pages. Solaris also allows applications —such as databases—to take advantage of the large 4 MB page size.

Providing support for multiple pages requires the operating system— not hardware—to manage the TLB. For example, one of the fields in a TLB entry must indicate the size of the page frame corresponding to the TLB entry. Managing the TLB in software and not hardware comes at a cost in performance. However, the increased hit ratio and TLB reach offset the performance costs. Indeed, recent trends indicate a move toward software-managed TLBs and operating-system support for multiple page sizes. The UltraSPARC, MIPS, and Alpha architectures employ software-managed TLBs. The PowerPC and Pentium manage the TLB in hardware.

10.8.4 Inverted Page Table

Section 9.4.4.3 introduced the concept of an inverted page table. The purpose of this form of page management was to reduce the amount of physical memory needed to track virtual-to-physical address translations. We accomplish this savings by creating a table that has one entry per physical-memory page, indexed by the pair <process-id, page-number>.

Because they keep information about which virtual-memory page is stored in each physical frame, inverted page tables reduce the amount of physical memory needed to store this information. However, the inverted page table no longer contains complete information about the logical address space of a process, and that information is required if a referenced page is not currently in memory. Demand paging requires this information to process page faults. For the information to be available, an external page table (one per process) must be kept. Each such table looks like the traditional per-process page table and contains information on where each virtual page is located.

But do external page tables negate the utility of inverted page tables? Since these tables are referenced only when a page fault occurs, they do not need to be available quickly. Instead, they are themselves paged in and out of memory as necessary. Unfortunately, a page fault may now result in the virtual-memory manager causing another page fault as it pages in the external page table it needs to locate the virtual page on the backing store. This special case requires careful handling in the kernel and a delay in the page-lookup processing.

10.8.5 Program Structure

Demand paging is designed to be transparent to the user program. In many cases, the user is completely unaware of the paged nature of memory. In other cases, however, system performance can be improved if the user (or compiler) has an awareness of the underlying demand paging.

Let's look at a contrived but informative example. Assume that pages are 128 words in size. Consider a Java program whose function is to initialize to 0 each element of a 128-by-128 array. The following code is typical:

```
int data[][] = new int[128][128];

for (int j = 0; j < data.length; j++)
    for (int i = 0; i < data.length; i++)
        data[i][j] = 0;
```

Notice that the array is stored row major; that is, the array is stored data[0][0], data[0][1], ···, data[0][127], data[1][0], data[1][1], ···, data[127][127]. For pages of 128 words, each row takes one page. Thus, the preceding code zeros one word in each page, then another word in each page, and so on. If the operating system allocates less than 128 frames to the entire program, then its execution will result in $128 \times 128 = 16{,}384$ page faults. In contrast, changing the code to

```
int data[][] = new int[128][128];

for (int i = 0; i < data.length; i++)
    for (int j = 0; j < data.length; j++)
        data[i][j] = 0;
```

zeros all the words on one page before starting the next page, reducing the number of page faults to 128.

Careful selection of data structures and programming structures can increase locality and hence lower the page-fault rate and the number of pages in the working set. For example, a stack has good locality, since access is always made to the top. A hash table, in contrast, is designed to scatter references, producing bad locality. Of course, locality of reference is just one measure of the efficiency of the use of a data structure. Other heavily weighted factors include search speed, total number of memory references, and total number of pages touched.

At a later stage, the compiler and loader can have a significant effect on paging. Separating code and data and generating reentrant code means that code pages can be read-only and hence will never be modified. Clean pages do not have to be paged out to be replaced. The loader can avoid placing routines across page boundaries, keeping each routine completely in one page. Routines that call each other many times can be packed into the same page. This packaging is a variant of the bin-packing problem of operations research: Try to pack the variable-sized load segments into the fixed-sized pages so that interpage references are minimized. Such an approach is particularly useful for large page sizes.

The choice of programming language can affect paging as well. For example, C and C++ use pointers frequently, and pointers tend to randomize access to memory, thereby potentially diminishing a process's locality. Some studies have shown that object-oriented programs also tend to have a poor locality of reference.

10.8.6   I/O Interlock

When demand paging is used, we sometimes need to allow some of the pages to be **locked** in memory. One such situation occurs when I/O is done to or from user (virtual) memory. I/O is often implemented by a separate I/O processor. For example, a magnetic-tape controller is generally given the number of bytes to transfer and a memory address for the buffer (Figure 10.22). When the transfer is complete, the CPU is interrupted.

We must be sure the following sequence of events does not occur: A process issues an I/O request and is put in a queue for that I/O device. Meanwhile, the CPU is given to other processes. These processes cause page faults; and one of them, using a global replacement algorithm, replaces the page containing the memory buffer for the waiting process. The pages are paged out. Some time later, when the I/O request advances to the head of the device queue, the I/O occurs to the specified address. However, this frame is now being used for a different page belonging to another process.

There are two common solutions to this problem. One solution is never to execute I/O to user memory. Instead, data are always copied between system memory and user memory. I/O takes place only between system memory and the I/O device. To write a block on tape, we first copy the block to

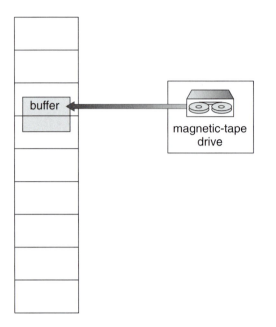

Figure 10.22   The reason why frames used for I/O must be in memory.

system memory and then write it to tape. This extra copying may result in unacceptably high overhead.

Another solution is to allow pages to be locked into memory. A lock bit is associated with every frame. If the frame is locked, it cannot be selected for replacement. Under this approach, to write a block on tape, we lock into memory the pages containing the block. The system can then continue as usual. Locked pages cannot be replaced. When the I/O is complete, the pages are unlocked.

Lock bits are used in various situations. Frequently, some or all of the operating-system kernel is locked into memory as many operating systems cannot tolerate a page fault caused by the kernel.

Another use for a lock bit involves normal page replacement. Consider the following sequence of events: A low-priority process faults. Selecting a replacement frame, the paging system reads the necessary page into memory. Ready to continue, the low-priority process enters the ready queue and waits for the CPU. Since it is a low-priority process, it may not be selected by the CPU scheduler for a time. While the low-priority process waits, a high-priority process faults. Looking for a replacement, the paging system sees a page that is in memory but has not been referenced or modified: It is the page that the low-priority process just brought in. This page looks like a perfect replacement: It is clean and will not need to be written out, and it apparently has not been used for a long time.

Whether the high-priority process should be able to replace the low-priority process is a policy decision. After all, we are simply delaying the low-priority process for the benefit of the high-priority process. However, we are wasting the effort spent to bring in the page for the low-priority process. If we decide to prevent replacement of a newly brought-in page until it can be used at least once, then we can use the lock bit to implement this mechanism. When a page is selected for replacement, its lock bit is turned on; it remains on until the faulting process is again dispatched.

Using a lock bit can be dangerous: The lock bit may get turned on but never turned off. Should this situation occur (because of a bug in the operating system, for example), the locked frame becomes unusable. On a single-user system, the overuse of locking would hurt only the user doing the locking. Multiuser systems must be less trusting of users. For instance, Solaris allows locking "hints," but it is free to disregard these hints if the free-frame pool becomes too small or if an individual process requests that too many pages be locked in memory.

10.8.7   Real-Time Processing

The discussions in this chapter have concentrated on providing the best overall utilization of a computer system by optimizing the use of memory. By using memory for active data and moving inactive data to disk, we increase overall system throughput. However, individual processes may suffer as a result, because they now may take additional page faults during their execution.

Consider a real-time process or thread, as described in Chapter 4. Such a process expects to gain control of the CPU and to run to completion with a minimum of delays. Virtual memory is the antithesis of real-time computing, because it can introduce unexpected long-term delays in the execution of a process while pages are brought into memory. Therefore, most real-time and embedded systems do not implement virtual memory.

In the case of Solaris, the developers at Sun Microsystems wanted both to provide time sharing and to allow real-time processes to have bounded and low dispatch latency. To solve the page-fault problem, Solaris allows a process to tell it which pages are important to that process. In addition to allowing "hints" on page use, the operating system allows privileged users to require pages to be locked into memory. If abused, this mechanism could lock all other processes out of the system.

10.9 ■ Operating-System Examples

In this section, we describe how Windows 2000 and Solaris implement virtual memory.

10.9.1 Windows XP

Windows XP implements virtual memory using demand paging with **clustering**. Clustering handles page faults by bringing in not only the faulting page but also several pages following the faulting page. When a process is first created, it is assigned a working-set minimum and maximum. The **working-set minimum** is the minimum number of pages the process is guaranteed to have in memory. If sufficient memory is available, a process may be assigned as many pages as its **working-set maximum**. For most applications, the value of working-set minimum and working-set maximum is 50 and 345 pages, respectively. (In some circumstances, a process may be allowed to exceed its working-set maximum.) The virtual-memory manager maintains a list of free page frames. Associated with this list is a threshold value that is used to indicate whether sufficient free memory is available. If a page fault occurs for a process that is below its working-set maximum, the virtual-memory manager allocates a page from this list of free pages. If a process is at its working-set maximum and it incurs a page fault, it must select a page for replacement using a local page-replacement policy.

When the amount of free memory falls below the threshold, the virtual-memory manager uses a tactic known as **automatic working-set trimming** to restore the value above the threshold. Automatic working-set trimming works by evaluating the number of pages allocated to processes. If a process has been allocated more pages than its working-set minimum, the virtual-memory manager removes pages until the process reaches its working-set minimum. A process that is at its working-set minimum may be allocated pages from the free-page frame list once sufficient free memory is available.

The algorithm used to determine which page to remove from a working set depends on the type of processor. On single-processor 80x86 systems, Windows XP uses a variation of the *clock* algorithm discussed in Section 10.4.5.2. On Alpha and multiprocessor x86 systems, clearing the reference bit may require invalidating the entry in the translation look-aside buffer on other processors. Rather than incurring this overhead, Windows XP uses a variation on the FIFO algorithm discussed in Section 10.4.2.

10.9.2 Solaris

In Solaris, when a thread incurs a page fault, the kernel assigns a page to the faulting thread from the list of free pages it maintains. Therefore, it is imperative that the kernel keep a sufficient amount of free memory available. Associated with this list of free pages is a parameter—*lotsfree*—which represents a threshold to begin paging. *lotsfree* is typically set to 1/64 of the size of the physical memory. Four times per second, the kernel checks whether the amount of free memory is less than *lotsfree*. If the number of free pages falls below *lotsfree*, a process known as the **pageout** starts up. The pageout process

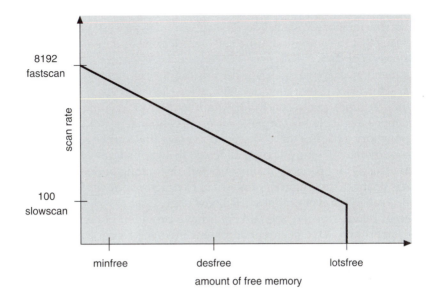

Figure 10.23   Solaris page scanner.

is similar to the second-chance algorithm described in Section 10.4.5.2, except that it uses two hands while scanning pages, rather than one as described in Section 10.4.5.2. The pageout process works as follows: The first hand of the clock scans all pages in memory, setting the reference bit to 0. At a later point in time, the second hand of the clock examines the reference bit for the pages in memory, appending those pages whose bit is still set to 0 to the free list and writing to disk their contents if modified. Solaris maintains a cache list of pages that have been "freed" but have not yet been overwritten. The free list contains frames that have invalid contents. Pages can be **reclaimed** from the cache list if they are accessed before being moved to the free list.

The pageout algorithm uses several parameters to control the rate at which pages are scanned (known as the *scanrate*). The scanrate is expressed in pages per second and ranges from *slowscan* to *fastscan*. When free memory falls below *lotsfree*, scanning occurs at *slowscan* pages per second and progresses to *fastscan*, depending on the amount of free memory available. The default value of *slowscan* is 100 pages per second. *fastscan* is typically set to (*TotalPhysicalPages*)/2 pages per second with a maximum of 8,192 pages per second. This is shown in Figure 10.23 (with *fastscan* set to the maximum).

The distance (in pages) between the hands of the clock is determined by a system parameter, *handspread*. The amount of time between the front hand's clearing a bit and the back hand's investigating its value depends on the *scanrate* and the *handspread*. If *scanrate* is 100 pages per second and *handspread* is 1,024 pages, 10 seconds can pass between the time a bit is set by the front hand and the time it is checked by the back hand. However, because of the demands placed on the memory system, a *scanrate* of several thousand is not uncommon. This means that the amount of time between clearing and investigating a bit is often a few seconds.

As mentioned above, the pageout process checks memory four times per second. However, if free memory falls below *desfree* (Figure 10.23), pageout will run 100 times per second with the intention of keeping at least *desfree* free memory available. If the pageout process is unable to keep the amount of free memory at *desfree* for a 30-second average, the kernel begins swapping processes, thereby freeing all pages allocated to swapped processes. In general, the kernel looks for processes that have been idle for long periods of time. If the system is unable to maintain the amount of free memory at *minfree*, the pageout process is called for every request for a new page.

Recent releases of the Solaris kernel have provided enhancements to the paging algorithm. One such enhancement involves recognizing pages from shared libraries. Pages belonging to libraries that are being shared by several processes—even if they are eligible to be claimed by the scanner—are skipped during the page-scanning process. Another enhancement concerns distinguishing pages that have been allocated to processes from pages allocated to regular files. This is known as **priority paging** and is covered in Section 12.6.2.

10.10 ■ Summary

It is desirable to be able to execute a process whose logical address space is larger than the available physical address space. The programmer can make such a process executable by restructuring it using overlays, but doing so is generally a difficult programming task. Virtual memory is a technique to allow a large logical address space to be mapped onto a smaller physical memory. Virtual memory allows extremely large processes to be run and also allows the degree of multiprogramming to be raised, increasing CPU utilization. Further, it frees application programmers from worrying about memory availability.

Virtual memory is commonly implemented by demand paging. Pure demand paging never brings in a page until that page is referenced. The first reference causes a page fault to the operating-system resident monitor. The operating system consults an internal table to determine where the page is located on the backing store. It then finds a free frame and reads the page in from the backing store. The page table is updated to reflect this change, and the instruction that caused the page fault is restarted. This approach allows a process to run even though its entire memory image is not in main memory at once. As long as the page-fault rate is reasonably low, performance is acceptable.

We can use demand paging to reduce the number of frames allocated to a process. This arrangement can increase the degree of multiprogramming (allowing more processes to be available for execution at one time) and—in theory, at least—the CPU utilization of the system. It also allows processes to be run even though their memory requirements exceed the total available physical memory. Such processes run in virtual memory.

If total memory requirements exceed the physical memory, then it may be necessary to replace pages from memory to free frames for new pages. Various page-replacement algorithms are used. FIFO page replacement is easy to program but suffers from Belady's anomaly. Optimal page replacement requires future knowledge. LRU replacement is an approximation of optimal page replacement, but even it may be difficult to implement. Most page-replacement algorithms, such as the second-chance algorithm, are approximations of LRU replacement.

In addition to a page-replacement algorithm, a frame-allocation policy is needed. Allocation can be fixed, suggesting local page replacement, or dynamic, suggesting global replacement. The working-set model assumes that processes execute in localities. The working set is the set of pages in the current locality. Accordingly, each process should be allocated enough frames for its current working set.

If a process does not have enough memory for its working set, it will thrash. Providing enough frames to each process to avoid thrashing may require process swapping and scheduling. In addition to requiring that we solve the major problems of page replacement and frame allocation, the proper design of a paging system requires that we consider page size, I/O, locking, prepaging, process creation, program structure, and other topics.

Many operating systems provide features for memory mapping files, thus allowing file I/O to be treated as routine memory access. Java provides an API for memory mapping as well. There are several other issues concerned with virtual memory including prepaging a file into memory, the size of a page, and the amount of memory that can be referenced in the translation lookaside buffer.

Virtual memory can be thought of as one level of a hierarchy of storage levels in a computer system. Each level has its own access time, size, and cost parameters. A full example of a hybrid, functional virtual-memory system is presented in the Mach chapter (Appendix B).

▪ Exercises

10.1 Under what circumstances do page faults occur? Describe the actions taken by the operating system when a page fault occurs.

10.2 Assume that you have a page-reference string for a process with m frames (initially all empty). The page-reference string has length p; n distinct page numbers occur in it. Answer these questions for any page-replacement algorithms:

    a. What is a lower bound on the number of page faults?

    b. What is an upper bound on the number of page faults?

10.3 A certain computer provides its users with a virtual-memory space of 2^{32} bytes. The computer has 2^{18} bytes of physical memory. The virtual memory is implemented by paging, and the page size is 4,096 bytes. A user process generates the virtual address 11123456. Explain how the system establishes the corresponding physical location. Distinguish between software and hardware operations.

10.4 Which of the following programming techniques and structures are "good" for a demand-paged environment? Which are "bad"? Explain your answers.

    a. Stack

    b. Hashed symbol table

    c. Sequential search

    d. Binary search

    e. Pure code

    f. Vector operations

    g. Indirection

10.5 Assume that we have a demand-paged memory. The page table is held in registers. It takes 8 milliseconds to service a page fault if an empty frame is available or if the replaced page is not modified and 20 milliseconds if the replaced page is modified. Memory-access time is 100 nanoseconds.

Assume that the page to be replaced is modified 70 percent of the time. What is the maximum acceptable page-fault rate for an effective access time of no more than 200 nanoseconds?

10.6 Consider the following page-replacement algorithms. Rank these algorithms on a five-point scale from "bad" to "perfect" according to their page-fault rate. Separate those algorithms that suffer from Belady's anomaly from those that do not.

    a. LRU replacement

    b. FIFO replacement

    c. Optimal replacement

    d. Second-chance replacement

10.7 When virtual memory is implemented in a computing system, it carries certain costs and certain benefits. List those costs and the benefits. It is possible for the costs to exceed the benefits. Explain what measures you can take to ensure that this imbalance does not occur.

10.8 An operating system supports a paged virtual memory using a central processor with a cycle time of 1 microsecond. It costs an additional 1 microsecond to access a page other than the current one. Pages have 1,000 words, and the paging device is a drum that rotates at 3,000 revolutions per minute and transfers one million words per second. The following statistical measurements were obtained from the system:

- One percent of all instructions executed accessed a page other than the current page.

- Of the instructions that accessed another page, 80 percent accessed a page already in memory.

- When a new page was required, the replaced page was modified 50 percent of the time.

Calculate the effective instruction time on this system, assuming that the system is running one process only and that the processor is idle during drum transfers.

10.9 Consider a demand-paging system with the following time-measured utilizations:

CPU utilization	20%
Paging disk	97.7%
Other I/O devices	5%

For each of the following, say whether it will (or is likely to) improve CPU utilization. Explain your answers.

a. Install a faster CPU.

b. Install a bigger paging disk.

c. Increase the degree of multiprogramming.

d. Decrease the degree of multiprogramming.

e. Install more main memory.

f. Install a faster hard disk or multiple controllers with multiple hard disks.

g. Add prepaging to the page-fetch algorithms.

h. Increase the page size.

10.10 Consider the two-dimensional array A:

```
int A[][] = new int[100][100];
```

where A[0][0] is stored at location 200 in a paged-memory system with pages of size 200. A small process resides in page 0 (locations 0 to 199) for manipulating the A matrix; thus, every instruction fetch will be from page 0.

For three page frames, indicate how many page faults are generated by the following array-initialization loops. Use LRU replacement and assume that page frame 1 has the process in it and the other two are initially empty:

```
a. for (int j = 0; j < 100; j++)
       for (int i = 0; i < 100; i++)
           A[i][j] = 0;

b. for (int i = 0; i < 100; i++)
       for (int j = 0; j < 100; j++)
           A[i][j] = 0;
```

10.11 Consider the following page-reference string:

$$1, 2, 3, 4, 2, 1, 5, 6, 2, 1, 2, 3, 7, 6, 3, 2, 1, 2, 3, 6.$$

How many page faults would occur for the following replacement algorithms, assuming one, two, three, four, five, six, or seven frames? Remember that all frames are initially empty, so all of your first unique pages will cost one fault each.

- LRU replacement

- FIFO replacement

- Optimal replacement

10.12 Suppose that you want to use a paging algorithm that requires a reference bit (such as second-chance replacement or working-set model), but the hardware does not provide one. Sketch how you could simulate a reference bit, and calculate the cost of doing so.

10.13 You have devised a new page-replacement algorithm that you think may be optimal. In some contorted test cases, Belady's anomaly occurs. Is the new algorithm optimal? Explain your answer.

10.14 Suppose that your replacement policy (in a paged system) is to examine each page regularly and to discard that page if it has not been used since the last examination. What would you gain and what would you lose by using this policy rather than LRU or second-chance replacement?

10.15 Segmentation is similar to paging but uses variable-sized "pages." Define two segment-replacement algorithms based on FIFO and LRU page-replacement schemes. Remember that, since segments are not the same size, the segment that is chosen to be replaced may not be big enough to leave enough consecutive locations for the needed segment. Consider strategies for systems where segments cannot be relocated and strategies for systems where they can.

10.16 A page-replacement algorithm should minimize the number of page faults. We can achieve this minimization by distributing heavily used pages evenly over all of memory, rather than having them compete for a small number of page frames. We can associate with each page frame a counter of the number of pages associated with that frame. Then, to replace a page, we can search for the page frame with the smallest counter.

    a. Define a page-replacement algorithm using this basic idea. Specifically address these problems:

       i. What the initial value of the counters is

       ii. When counters are increased

       iii. When counters are decreased

       iv. How the page to be replaced is selected

    b. How many page faults occur for your algorithm for the following reference string, with four page frames?

$$1, 2, 3, 4, 5, 3, 4, 1, 6, 7, 8, 7, 8, 9, 7, 8, 9, 5, 4, 5, 4, 2.$$

    c. What is the minimum number of page faults for an optimal page-replacement strategy for the reference string in part b with four page frames?

10.17 Consider a demand-paging system with a paging disk that has an average access and transfer time of 20 milliseconds. Addresses are translated through a page table in main memory, with an access time of 1 microsecond per memory access. Thus, each memory reference through the page table takes two accesses. To improve this time, we have added an associative memory that reduces access time to one memory reference if the page-table entry is in the associative memory.

Assume that 80 percent of the accesses are in the associative memory and that, of the remaining, 10 percent (or 2 percent of the total) cause page faults. What is the effective memory access time?

10.18 Consider a demand-paged computer system where the degree of multiprogramming is currently fixed at four. The system was recently measured to determine utilization of the CPU and the paging disk. The results are one of the following alternatives. For each case, what is happening? Can you increase the degree of multiprogramming to increase the CPU utilization? Is the paging helping to improve performance?

a. CPU utilization, 13 percent; disk utilization, 97 percent

b. CPU utilization, 87 percent; disk utilization, 3 percent

c. CPU utilization, 13 percent; disk utilization, 3 percent

10.19 We have an operating system for a machine that uses base and limit registers, but we have modified the machine to provide a page table. Can we set up the page tables to simulate base and limit registers? How can we do so, or why can we not do so?

10.20 What is the cause of thrashing? How does the system detect thrashing? Once it detects thrashing, what can the system do to eliminate this problem?

10.21 Write a program that implements the FIFO and LRU page-replacement algorithms presented in this chapter. First, generate a random page-reference string where page numbers range from 0 to 9. Apply the random page-reference string to each algorithm, and record the number of page faults incurred by each algorithm. Implement the replacement algorithms so that the number of page frames can vary from 1 to 7. Assume that demand paging is used.

Bibliographical Notes

Demand paging was first used in the Atlas system, implemented on the Manchester University MUSE computer around 1960 (Kilburn et al. [1961]). Another early demand-paging system was MULTICS, implemented on the GE 645 system (Organick [1972]).

Belady et al. [1969] were the first researchers to observe that the FIFO replacement strategy may produce the anomaly that bears Belady's name. Mattson et al. [1970] demonstrated that stack algorithms are not subject to Belady's anomaly.

The optimal replacement algorithm was presented by Belady [1966]. It was proved to be optimal by Mattson et al. [1970]. Belady's optimal algorithm is for a fixed allocation; Prieve and Fabry [1976] have an optimal algorithm for situations where the allocation can vary.

The enhanced clock algorithm was discussed by Carr and Hennessy [1981].

The working-set model was developed by Denning [1968]. Discussions concerning the working-set model were presented by Denning [1980].

The scheme for monitoring the page-fault rate was developed by Wulf [1969], who successfully applied this technique to the Burroughs B5500 computer system.

Solomon and Russinovich [2000] describe how Windows 2000 implements virtual memory. Mauro and McDougall [2001] discuss virtual memory in

Solaris. Virtual-memory techniques in Linux and BSD are described by Bovet and Cesati [2002] and McKusick et al. [1996], respectively. Ganapathy and Schimmel [1998] and Navarro et al. [2002] discuss operating system support for multiple page sizes. Ortix [2001] discusses virtual memory used in a real-time embedded operating system.

A comparison of an implementation of virtual memory in the MIPS, PowerPC, and Pentium architectures can be found in Jacob and Mudge [1998b]. A companion article (Jacob and Mudge [1998a]) describes the hardware support necessary for implementation of virtual memory in six different architectures, including the UltraSPARC.

Chapter 11

FILE-SYSTEM INTERFACE

For most users, the file system is the most visible aspect of an operating system. It provides the mechanism for on-line storage of and access to both data and programs of the operating system and all the users of the computer system. The file system consists of two distinct parts: a collection of *files*, each storing related data, and a *directory structure*, which organizes and provides information about all the files in the system. Some file systems have a third part, *partitions*, which are used to separate physically or logically large collections of directories. In this chapter, we consider the various aspects of files and the major directory structures. We also discuss the semantics of sharing files among multiple processes, users, and computers. Finally, we discuss ways to handle *file protection*, necessary when we have multiple users and we want to control who may access files and how files may be accessed.

11.1 ■ File Concept

Computers can store information on various storage media, such as magnetic disks, magnetic tapes, and optical disks. So that the computer system will be convenient to use, the operating system provides a uniform logical view of information storage. The operating system abstracts from the physical properties of its storage devices to define a logical storage unit, the *file*. Files are mapped by the operating system onto physical devices. These storage devices are usually nonvolatile, so the contents are persistent through power failures and system reboots.

A file is a named collection of related information that is recorded on secondary storage. From a user's perspective, a file is the smallest allotment of logical secondary storage; that is, data cannot be written to secondary storage unless they are within a file. Commonly, files represent programs (both source and object forms) and data. Data files may be numeric, alphabetic, alphanumeric, or binary. Files may be free form, such as text files, or may be formatted rigidly. In general, a file is a sequence of bits, bytes, lines, or records, the meaning of which is defined by the file's creator and user. The concept of a file is thus extremely general.

The information in a file is defined by its creator. Many different types of information may be stored in a file—source programs, object programs, executable programs, numeric data, text, payroll records, graphic images, sound recordings, and so on. A file has a certain defined **structure**, which depends on its type. A *text* file is a sequence of characters organized into lines (and possibly pages). A *source* file is a sequence of subroutines and functions, each of which is further organized as declarations followed by executable statements. An *object* file is a sequence of bytes organized into blocks understandable by the system's linker. An *executable* file is a series of code sections that the loader can bring into memory and execute.

11.1.1 File Attributes

A file is named, for the convenience of its human users, and is referred to by its name. A name is usually a string of characters, such as *example.c*. Some systems differentiate between uppercase and lowercase characters in names, whereas other systems do not. When a file is named, it becomes independent of the process, the user, and even the system that created it. For instance, one user might create the file *example.c,*, and another user might edit that file by specifying its name. The file's owner might write the file to a floppy disk, send it in an e-mail, or copy it across a network, and it could still be called *example.c* on the destination system.

A file has certain other attributes, which vary from one operating system to another but typically consist of these:

- **Name:** The symbolic file name is the only information kept in human-readable form.

- **Identifier:** This unique tag, usually a number, identifies the file within the file system; it is the non-human-readable name for the file.

- **Type:** This information is needed for those systems that support different types of files.

- **Location:** This information is a pointer to a device and to the location of the file on that device.

- **Size:** The current size of the file (in bytes, words, or blocks) and possibly the maximum allowed size are included in this attribute.

- **Protection:** Access-control information determines who can do reading, writing, executing, and so on.

- **Time, date, and user identification:** This information may be kept for creation, last modification, and last use. These data can be useful for protection, security, and usage monitoring.

The information about all files is kept in the directory structure, which also resides on secondary storage. Typically, a directory entry consists of the file's name and its unique identifier. The identifier in turn locates the other file attributes. It may take more than a kilobyte to record this information for each file. In a system with many files, the size of the directory itself may be megabytes. Because directories, like files, must be nonvolatile, they must be stored on the device and brought into memory piecemeal, as needed.

11.1.2 File Operations

A file is an **abstract data type**. To define a file properly, we need to consider the operations that can be performed on files. The operating system can provide system calls to create, write, read, reposition, delete, and truncate files. Let's examine what the operating system must do to perform each of these six basic file operations. It should then be easy to see how other, similar operations, such as renaming a file, would be implemented.

- **Creating a file:** Two steps are necessary to create a file. First, space in the file system must be found for the file. We discuss how to allocate space for the file in Chapter 12. Second, an entry for the new file must be made in the directory. The directory entry records the name of the file, its location in the file system, and possibly other information.

- **Writing a file:** To write a file, we make a system call specifying both the name of the file and the information to be written to the file. Given the name of the file, the system searches the directory to find the file's location. The system must keep a *write* pointer to the location in the file where the next write is to take place. The write pointer must be updated whenever a write occurs.

- **Reading a file:** To read from a file, we use a system call that specifies the name of the file and where (in memory) the next block of the file should be put. Again, the directory is searched for the associated entry, and the system needs to keep a *read* pointer to the location in the file where the next read is to take place. Once the read has taken place, the read pointer is updated. A given process is usually only reading or writing a given file, and the current operation location is kept as a per-process **current-file-position pointer**. Both the read and write operations use this same pointer, saving space and reducing the system complexity.

- **Repositioning within a file:** The directory is searched for the appropriate entry, and the current-file-position pointer is set to a given value. Repositioning within a file need not involve any actual I/O. This file operation is also known as a file *seek*.

- **Deleting a file:** To delete a file, we search the directory for the named file. Having found the associated directory entry, we release all file space, so that it can be reused by other files, and erase the directory entry.

- **Truncating a file:** The user may want to erase the contents of a file but keep its attributes. Rather than forcing the user to delete the file and then recreate it, this function allows all attributes to remain unchanged—except for file length—but lets the file be reset to length zero and its file space released.

These six basic operations comprise the minimal set of required file operations. Other common operations include *appending* new information to the end of an existing file and *renaming* an existing file. These primitive operations may then be combined to perform other file operations. For instance, creating a *copy* of a file, or copying the file to another I/O device, such as a printer or a display, can be accomplished by creating a new file and then reading from the old and writing to the new. We also want to have operations that allow a user to get and set the various attributes of a file. For example, we may want to have operations that allow a user to determine the status of a file, such as the file's length, and allow a user to set file attributes, such as the file's owner.

Most of the file operations mentioned involve searching the directory for the entry associated with the named file. To avoid this constant searching, many systems require that an open() system call be used before that file is first used actively. The operating system keeps a small table, called the **open-file table**, containing information about all open files. When a file operation is requested, the file is specified via an index into this table, so no searching is required. When the file is no longer being actively used, it is *closed* by the process, and the operating system removes its entry from the open-file table.

Some systems implicitly open a file when the first reference to it is made. The file is automatically closed when the job or program that opened the file terminates. Most systems, however, require that the programmer open a file explicitly with the open() system call before that file can be used. The open() operation takes a file name and searches the directory, copying the directory entry into the open-file table. The open() call can also accept access-mode information—create, read-only, read–write, append-only, and so on. This mode is checked against the file's permissions. If the request mode is allowed, the file is opened for the process. The open() system call will typically return a pointer to the entry in the open-file table. This pointer, not the actual file name, is used in all I/O operations, avoiding any further searching and simplifying the system-call interface.

The implementation of the open() and close() operations in a multiuser environment, such as UNIX, is more complicated. In such a system, several users may open the file at the same time. Typically, the operating system uses two levels of internal tables: a per-process table and a system-wide table. The per-process table tracks all files that a process has open. Stored in this table is information regarding the use of the file by the process. For instance, the current file pointer for each file is found here, indicating the location in the file that the next read() or write() call will affect. Access rights to the file and accounting information can also be included.

Each entry in the per-process table in turn points to a system-wide open-file table. The system-wide table contains process-independent information, such as the location of the file on disk, access dates, and file size. Once a file has been opened by one process, the system-wide table includes an entry for the file. When another process executes an open() call, a new entry is simply added to the process's open-file table pointing to the appropriate entry in the system-wide table. Typically, the open-file table also has an *open count* associated with each file to indicate how many processes have the file open. Each close() decreases this *count*, and when the *open count* reaches zero, the file is no longer in use, and the file's entry is removed from the open file table. In summary, several pieces of information are associated with an open file.

- **File pointer:** On systems that do not include a file offset as part of the read() and write() system calls, the system must track the last read–write location as a current-file-position pointer. This pointer is unique to each process operating on the file and therefore must be kept separate from the on-disk file attributes.

- **File-open count:** As files are closed, the operating system must reuse its open-file table entries, or it could run out of space in the table. Because multiple processes may have opened a file, the system must wait for the last file to close before removing the open-file table entry. The file-open counter tracks the number of opens and closes and reaches zero on the last close. The system can then remove the entry.

- **Disk location of the file:** Most file operations require the system to modify data within the file. The information needed to locate the file on disk is kept in memory so that the system does not have to read it from disk for each operation.

- **Access rights:** Each process opens a file in an access mode. This information is stored on the per-process table so the operating system can allow or deny subsequent I/O requests.

Some operating systems provide facilities for locking an open file (or sections of a file). File locks allow one process to lock a file and prevent other processes from gaining access to it. File locks are useful for files that are shared by several processes—for example, a system log file that can be accessed and modified by a number of processes in the system.

File locks provide functionality similar to readers–writers locks, covered in Section 7.6.2. A **shared lock** is akin to a reader lock in that several processes may acquire the lock concurrently. It is of course dependent upon the behavior of the processes to only read from—and not modify—a file that has been accessed via a shared lock; the operating system does not enforce this. An **exclusive lock** behaves like a writer lock; a file can have only a single concurrent exclusive lock (and no shared locks). It is important to note that not all operating systems provide both types of locks; some systems only provide exclusive file locking.

Furthermore, operating systems may provide either **mandatory** or **advisory** file-locking mechanisms. If a lock is mandatory, then once a process acquires a lock, the operating system will prevent any other process from accessing the locked file. For example, assume a process acquires an exclusive lock on the file *system.log*. If we attempt to open *system.log* from another process—for example, a text editor—the operating system will prevent access until the exclusive lock is released. This occurs even if the text editor is not written explicitly to acquire the lock. Alternatively, if the lock is advisory, then the operating system will not prevent the text editor from acquiring access to *system.log*. Rather, the text editor would have had to be written so that it manually acquired the lock before accessing the file. In other words, if the locking scheme is mandatory, the operating system ensures locking integrity. For advisory locking, it is up to the software developers to ensure that locks are appropriately acquired and released. As a general rule, Windows operating systems adopt mandatory locking, and UNIX systems employ advisory locks.

We now describe support for file locking in the Java API. Acquiring a lock first requires obtaining the `FileChannel` for the file intended to be locked. The `lock()` method of the `FileChannel` is used to acquire the lock. The API of the `lock()` method is

```
FileLock lock(long begin, long end, boolean shared)
```

where *begin* and *end* are the beginning and ending positions of the region being locked. Assigning *shared* to *true* is for shared locks; setting *shared* to *false* acquires the lock exclusively. The lock is released by invoking the `release()` of the `FileLock` returned by the `lock()` operation.

The program in Figure 11.1 illustrates file locking in Java. This program acquires two locks on the file *file.txt*. The first half of the file is acquired as an exclusive lock; the lock for the second half is a shared lock.

The use of file locks requires the same precautions as ordinary process synchronization. For example, programmers must be careful to hold exclusive file locks only while they are accessing the file; otherwise, they will prevent

```java
import java.io.*;
import java.nio.channels.*;

public class LockingExample {
  public static final boolean EXCLUSIVE = false;
  public static final boolean SHARED = true;

  public static void main(String arsg[]) throws IOException {
    FileLock sharedLock = null;
    FileLock exclusiveLock = null;

    try {
      RandomAccessFile raf = new RandomAccessFile("file.txt", "rw");

      // get the channel for the file
      FileChannel ch = raf.getChannel();

      // this locks the first half of the file - exclusive
      exclusiveLock = ch.lock(0, raf.length()/2, EXCLUSIVE);

      /** Now modify the data . . . */

      // release the lock
      exclusiveLock.release();

      // this locks the second half of the file - shared
      sharedLock = ch.lock(raf.length()/2+1, raf.length(), SHARED);

      /** Now read the data . . . */

      // release the lock
      exclusiveLock.release();
    } catch (java.io.IOException ioe) {
      System.err.println(ioe);
    }
    finally {
      if (exclusiveLock != null)
            exclusiveLock.release();
      if (sharedLock != null)
            sharedLock.release();
    }
  }
}
```

Figure 11.1   File-locking example in Java.

other processes from accessing the file as well. Furthermore, some measures must be taken to ensure that two or more processes do not become involved in a deadlock while trying to acquire locks.

11.1.3 File Types

When we design a file system—indeed, an entire operating system—we always consider whether the operating system should recognize and support file types. If an operating system recognizes the type of a file, it can then operate on the file in reasonable ways. For example, a common mistake occurs when a user tries to print the binary-object form of a program. This attempt normally produces garbage; however, the attempt can succeed *if* the operating system has been told that the file is a binary-object program.

A common technique for implementing file types is to include the type as part of the file name. The name is split into two parts—a name and an *extension*, usually separated by a period character (Figure 11.2). In this way, the user and the operating system can tell from the name alone what the type of a file is. For example, in MS-DOS, a name can consist of up to eight characters followed by a period and terminated by an extension of up to three characters. The system uses the extension to indicate the *type* of the file and the type of operations that can be done on that file. Only a file with a *.com*, *.exe*, or *.bat* extension can be *executed*, for instance. The *.com* and *.exe* files are two forms of binary executable files, whereas a *.bat* file is a **batch file** containing, in ASCII format, commands to the operating system. MS-DOS recognizes only a few extensions, but application programs also use extensions to indicate file types in which they are interested. For example, assemblers expect source files to have an *.asm* extension, and the WordPerfect word processor expects its file to end with a *.wp* extension. These extensions are not required, so a user may specify a file without the extension (to save typing), and the application will look for a file with the given name and the extension it expects. Because these extensions are not supported by the operating system, they can be considered as "hints" to applications that operate on them.

Another example of the utility of file types comes from the TOPS-20 operating system. If the user tries to execute an object program whose source file has been modified (or edited) since the object file was produced, the source file will be recompiled automatically. This function ensures that the user always runs an up-to-date object file. Otherwise, the user could waste a significant amount of time executing the old object file. For this function to be possible, the operating system must be able to discriminate the source file from the object file, to check the time that each file was created or last modified, and to determine the language of the source program (in order to use the correct compiler).

Consider the Apple Macintosh operating system. In this system, each file has a type, such as *text* or *pict*. Each file also has a creator attribute containing the name of the program that created it. This attribute is set by the operating

file type	usual extension	function
executable	exe, com, bin or none	ready-to-run machine-language program
object	obj, o	compiled, machine language, not linked
source code	c, cc, java, pas, asm, a	source code in various languages
batch	bat, sh	commands to the command interpreter
text	txt, doc	textual data, documents
word processor	wp, tex, rtf, doc	various word-processor formats
library	lib, a, so, dll	libraries of routines for programmers
print or view	ps, pdf, jpg	ASCII or binary file in a format for printing or viewing
archive	arc, zip, tar	related files grouped into one file, sometimes compressed, for archiving or storage
multimedia	mpeg, mov, rm	binary file containing audio or A/V information

Figure 11.2   Common file types.

system during the create() call, so its use is enforced and supported by the system. For instance, a file produced by a word processor has the word processor's name as its creator. When the user opens that file, by double-clicking the mouse on the icon representing the file, the word processor is invoked automatically, and the file is loaded, ready to be edited.

The UNIX system is unable to provide such a feature; it uses a crude **magic number** stored at the beginning of some files to indicate roughly the type of the file—executable program, batch file (or **shell script**), PostScript file, and so on. Not all files have magic numbers, so system features cannot be based solely on this type of information. UNIX does not record the name of the creating program, either. UNIX does allow file-name-extension hints, but these extensions are not enforced or depended on by the operating system; they are mostly to aid users in determining the type of contents of the file. Extensions

can be used or ignored by a given application, but that is up to the application's
programmer.

11.1.4 File Structure

File types also may be used to indicate the internal structure of the file. As
mentioned in Section 11.1.3, source and object files have structures that match
the expectations of the programs that read them. Further, certain files must
conform to a required structure that is understood by the operating system.
For example, the operating system may require that an executable file have a
specific structure so that it can determine where in memory to load the file and
what the location of the first instruction is. Some operating systems extend
this idea into a set of system-supported file structures, with sets of special
operations for manipulating files with those structures. For instance, DEC's VMS
operating system has a file system that supports three defined file structures.

This discussion brings us to one of the disadvantages of having the operating system support multiple file structures: The resulting size of the operating
system is cumbersome. If the operating system defines five different file structures, it needs to contain the code to support these file structures. In addition,
every file may need to be definable as one of the file types supported by the
operating system. When new applications require information structured in
ways not supported by the operating system, severe problems may result.

For example, assume that a system supports two types of files: text files
(composed of ASCII characters separated by a carriage return and line feed)
and executable binary files. Now, if we (as users) want to define an encrypted
file to protect our contents from being read by unauthorized people, we may
find neither file type to be appropriate. The encrypted file is not ASCII text lines
but rather is (apparently) random bits. Although it may appear to be a binary
file, it is not executable. As a result, we may have to circumvent or misuse the
operating system's file-types mechanism or abandon our encryption scheme.

Some operating systems impose (and support) a minimal number of file
structures. This approach has been adopted in UNIX, MS-DOS, and others. UNIX
considers each file to be a sequence of 8-bit bytes; no interpretation of these bits
is made by the operating system. This scheme provides maximum flexibility
but little support. Each application program must include its own code to
interpret an input file as to the appropriate structure. However, all operating
systems must support at least one structure—that of an executable file—so that
the system is able to load and run programs.

The Macintosh operating system also supports a minimal number of file
structures. It expects files to contain two parts: a **resource fork** and a **data
fork**. The resource fork contains information of interest to the user. For
instance, it holds the labels of any buttons displayed by the program. A
foreign user may want to relabel these buttons in his own language, and
the Macintosh operating system provides tools to allow modification of the

data in the resource fork. The data fork contains program code or data—the traditional file contents. To accomplish the same task on a UNIX or MS-DOS system, the programmer would need to change and recompile the source code, unless she created her own user-changeable data file. Clearly, it is useful for an operating system to support structures that will be used frequently and that will save the programmer substantial effort. Too few structures make programming inconvenient, whereas too many cause operating-system bloat and programmer confusion.

11.1.5 Internal File Structure

Internally, locating an offset within a file can be complicated for the operating system. Recall from Chapter 2 that disk systems typically have a well-defined block size determined by the size of a sector. All disk I/O is performed in units of one block (physical record), and all blocks are the same size. It is unlikely that the physical record size will exactly match the length of the desired logical record. Logical records may even vary in length. **Packing** a number of logical records into physical blocks is a common solution to this problem.

For example, the UNIX operating system defines all files to be simply streams of bytes. Each byte is individually addressable by its offset from the beginning (or end) of the file. In this case, the logical record is 1 byte. The file system automatically packs and unpacks bytes into physical disk blocks—say, 512 bytes per block—as necessary.

The logical record size, physical block size, and packing technique determine how many logical records are in each physical block. The packing can be done either by the user's application program or by the operating system.

In either case, the file may be considered to be a sequence of blocks. All the basic I/O functions operate in terms of blocks. The conversion from logical records to physical blocks is a relatively simple software problem.

Because disk space is always allocated in blocks, some portion of the last block of each file is generally wasted. If each block were 512 bytes, for example, then a file of 1,949 bytes would be allocated four blocks (2,048 bytes); the last 99 bytes would be wasted. The waste incurred to keep everything in units of blocks (instead of bytes) is *internal fragmentation*. All file systems suffer from internal fragmentation; the larger the block size, the greater the internal fragmentation.

11.2 ■ Access Methods

Files store information. When it is used, this information must be accessed and read into computer memory. The information in the file can be accessed in several ways. Some systems provide only one access method for files. Other systems, such as those of IBM, support many access methods, and choosing the right one for a particular application is a major design problem.

11.2.1 Sequential Access

The simplest access method is **sequential access**. Information in the file is processed in order, one record after the other. This mode of access is by far the most common; for example, editors and compilers usually access files in this fashion.

Reads and writes make up the bulk of the operations on a file. A read operation reads the next portion of the file and automatically advances a file pointer, which tracks the I/O location. Similarly, a write appends to the end of the file and advances to the end of the newly written material (the new end of file). Such a file can be reset to the beginning; and on some systems, a program may be able to skip forward or backward n records, for some integer n—perhaps only for $n = 1$. Sequential access, which is depicted in Figure 11.3, is based on a tape model of a file and works as well on sequential-access devices as it does on random-access ones.

11.2.2 Direct Access

Another method is **direct access** (or **relative access**). A file is made up of fixed-length **logical records** that allow programs to read and write records rapidly in no particular order. The direct-access method is based on a disk model of a file, since disks allow random access to any file block. For direct access, the file is viewed as a numbered sequence of blocks or records. A direct-access file allows blocks to be read or written in any order. Thus, we may read block 14, then read block 53, and then write block 7. There are no restrictions on the order of reading or writing for a direct-access file.

Direct-access files are of great use for immediate access to large amounts of information. Databases are often of this type. When a query concerning a particular subject arrives, we compute which block contains the answer and then read that block directly to provide the desired information.

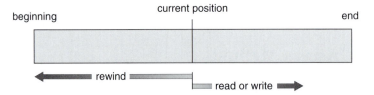

Figure 11.3   Sequential-access file.

As a simple example, on an airline-reservation system, we might store all the information about a particular flight (for example, flight 713) in the block identified by the flight number. Thus, the number of available seats for flight 713 is stored in block 713 of the reservation file. To store information about a larger set, such as people, we might compute a hash function on the people's names or search a small in-memory index to determine a block to read and search.

For the direct-access method, the file operations must be modified to include the block number as a parameter. Thus, we have *read n*, where *n* is the block number, rather than *read next*, and *write n* rather than *write next*. An alternative approach is to retain *read next* and *write next*, as with sequential access, and to add an operation *position file to n*, where *n* is the block number. Then, to effect a *read n*, we would *position to n* and then *read next*.

The block number provided by the user to the operating system is normally a **relative block number**. A relative block number is an index relative to the beginning of the file. Thus, the first relative block of the file is 0, the next is 1, and so on, even though the actual absolute disk address of the block may be 14703 for the first block and 3192 for the second. The use of relative block numbers allows the operating system to decide where the file should be placed (called the *allocation problem*, as discussed in Chapter 12) and helps to prevent the user from accessing portions of the file system that may not be part of her file. Some systems start their relative block numbers at 0; others start at 1.

Given a logical record length L, a request for record N is turned into an I/O request for L bytes starting at location $L * (N - 1)$ within the file (assuming the first record is $N = 1$). Since logical records are of a fixed size, it is also easy to read, write, or delete a record.

Not all operating systems support both sequential and direct access for files. Some systems allow only sequential file access; others allow only direct access. Some systems require that a file be defined as sequential or direct when it is created; such a file can be accessed only in a manner consistent with its declaration. We can easily simulate sequential access on a direct-access file by simply keeping a variable *cp* that defines our current position, as shown in Figure 11.4. Simulating a direct-access file on a sequential-access file, however, is extremely inefficient and clumsy.

11.2.3   Other Access Methods

Other access methods can be built on top of a direct-access method. These methods generally involve the construction of an index for the file. The **index**, like an index in the back of a book, contains pointers to the various blocks. To find a record in the file, we first search the index and then use the pointer to access the file directly and to find the desired record.

For example, a retail-price file might list the universal product codes (UPCs) for items, with the associated prices. Each record consists of a 10-digit UPC and

sequential access	implementation for direct access
reset	$cp = 0$;
read next	*read cp*; $cp = cp+1$;
write next	*write cp*; $cp = cp+1$;

Figure 11.4   Simulation of sequential access on a direct-access file.

a 6-digit price, for a 16-byte record. If our disk has 1,024 bytes per block, we can store 64 records per block. A file of 120,000 records would occupy about 2,000 blocks (2 million bytes). By keeping the file sorted by UPC, we can define an index consisting of the first UPC in each block. This index would have 2,000 entries of 10 digits each, or 20,000 bytes, and thus could be kept in memory. To find the price of a particular item, we can make a binary search of the index. From this search, we learn exactly which block contains the desired record and access that block. This structure allows us to search a large file doing little I/O.

With large files, the index file itself may become too large to be kept in memory. One solution is to create an index for the index file. The primary index file would contain pointers to secondary index files, which would point to the actual data items.

For example, IBM's indexed sequential-access method (ISAM) uses a small master index that points to disk blocks of a secondary index. The secondary index blocks point to the actual file blocks. The file is kept sorted on a defined key. To find a particular item, we first make a binary search of the master index, which provides the block number of the secondary index. This block is read in, and again a binary search is used to find the block containing the desired record. Finally, this block is searched sequentially. In this way, any record can be located from its key by at most two direct-access reads. Figure 11.5 shows a similar situation as implemented by VMS index and relative files.

11.3 ▪ Directory Structure

The file systems of computers can be extensive. Some systems store millions of files on terabytes of disk. To manage all these data, we need to organize them. This organization is usually done in two parts.

First, disks are split into one or more *partitions*, also known as *minidisks* in the IBM world or *volumes* in the PC and Macintosh arenas. Typically, each disk on a system contains at least one partition, which is a low-level structure in which files and directories reside. In some systems, partitions can be used to provide several separate areas within one disk, each treated as a separate

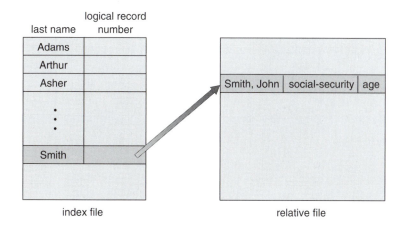

Figure 11.5   Example of index and relative files.

storage device, whereas other systems allow partitions to be larger than a disk so that disks can be grouped into one logical structure. These features allow the user to be concerned with only the logical directory and file structure and to ignore completely the problems of physically allocating space for files. For this reason, partitions can be thought of as virtual disks. Partitions can also store multiple operating systems, allowing a system to boot and run more than one.

Second, each partition contains information about files within it. This information is kept in entries in a **device directory** or **volume table of contents**. The device directory (more commonly known simply as a *directory*) records information—such as name, location, size, and type—for all files on that partition. Figure 11.6 shows the typical file-system organization.

The directory can be viewed as a symbol table that translates file names into their directory entries. If we take such a view, we see that the directory itself can be organized in many ways. We want to be able to insert entries, to delete entries, to search for a named entry, and to list all the entries in the directory. In Chapter 12, we discuss the data structures that can be used in the implementation of the directory structure. In this section, we examine several schemes for defining the logical structure of the directory system.

When considering a particular directory structure, we need to keep in mind the operations that are to be performed on a directory:

- **Search for a file:** We need to be able to search a directory structure to find the entry for a particular file. Since files have symbolic names and similar names may indicate a relationship between files, we may want to be able to find all files whose names match a particular pattern.

- **Create a file:** New files need to be created and added to the directory.

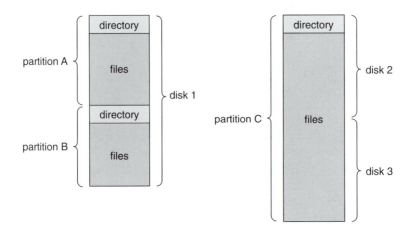

Figure 11.6   A typical file-system organization.

- **Delete a file:** When a file is no longer needed, we want to remove it from the directory.

- **List a directory:** We need to be able to list the files in a directory and the contents of the directory entry for each file in the list.

- **Rename a file:** Because the name of a file represents its contents to its users, we must be able to change the name when the contents or use of the file changes. Renaming a file may also allow its position within the directory structure to be changed.

- **Traverse the file system:** We may wish to access every directory and every file within a directory structure. For reliability, it is a good idea to save the contents and structure of the entire file system at regular intervals. Often, we do this by copying all files to magnetic tape. This technique provides a backup copy in case of system failure. In addition, if a file is no longer in use, the file can be copied to tape and the disk space of that file released for reuse by another file.

In Sections 11.3.1 through 11.3.5, we describe the most common schemes for defining the logical structure of a directory.

11.3.1 Single-Level Directory

The simplest directory structure is the single-level directory. All files are contained in the same directory, which is easy to support and understand (Figure 11.7).

A single-level directory has significant limitations, however, when the number of files increases or when the system has more than one user. Since all

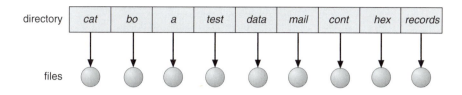

Figure 11.7   Single-level directory.

files are in the same directory, they must have unique names. If two users call their data file *test*, then the unique-name rule is violated. For example, in one programming class, 23 students called the program for their second assignment *prog2*; another 11 called it *assign2*. Although file names are generally selected to reflect the content of the file, they are often limited in length, complicating the task of making file names unique. The MS-DOS operating system allows only 11-character file names; UNIX, in contrast, allows 255 characters.

Even a single user on a single-level directory may find it difficult to remember the names of all the files as the number of files increases. It is not uncommon for a user to have hundreds of files on one computer system and an equal number of additional files on another system. Keeping track of so many files is a daunting task.

11.3.2 Two-Level Directory

As we have seen, a single-level directory often leads to confusion of file names between different users. The standard solution is to create a *separate* directory for each user.

In the two-level directory structure, each user has her own **user file directory (UFD)**. The UFDs have similar structures, but each lists only the files of a single user. When a user job starts or a user logs in, the system's **master file directory (MFD)** is searched. The MFD is indexed by user name or account number, and each entry points to the UFD for that user (Figure 11.8).

When a user refers to a particular file, only her own UFD is searched. Thus, different users may have files with the same name, as long as all the file names within each UFD are unique. To create a file for a user, the operating system searches only that user's UFD to ascertain whether another file of that name exists. To delete a file, the operating system confines its search to the local UFD; thus, it cannot accidentally delete another user's file that has the same name.

The user directories themselves must be created and deleted as necessary. A special system program is run with the appropriate user name and account information. The program creates a new UFD and adds an entry for it to the MFD. The execution of this program might be restricted to system administrators. The allocation of disk space for user directories can be handled with the techniques discussed in Chapter 12 for files themselves.

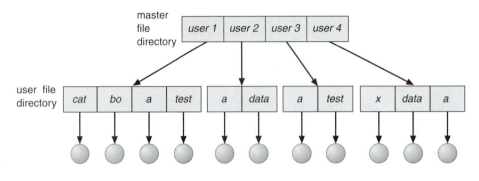

Figure 11.8   Two-level directory structure.

Although the two-level directory structure solves the name-collision problem, it still has disadvantages. This structure effectively isolates one user from
another. This isolation is an advantage when the users are completely independent but is a disadvantage when the users *want* to cooperate on some task and
to access one another's files. Some systems simply do not allow local user files
to be accessed by other users.

If access is to be permitted, one user must have the ability to name a file
in another user's directory. To name a particular file uniquely in a two-level
directory, we must give both the user name and the file name. A two-level
directory can be thought of as a tree, or an inverted tree, of height 2. The root of
the tree is the MFD. Its direct descendants are the UFDs. The descendants of the
UFDs are the files themselves. The files are the leaves of the tree. Specifying a
user name and a file name defines a path in the tree from the root (the MFD) to
a leaf (the specified file). Thus, a user name and a file name define a *path name*.
Every file in the system has a path name. To name a file uniquely, a user must
know the path name of the file desired.

For example, if user A wishes to access her own test file named *test*, she can
simply refer to *test*. To access the file named *test* of user B (with directory-entry
name *userb*), however, she might have to refer to */userb/test*. Every system has
its own syntax for naming files in directories other than the user's own.

Additional syntax is needed to specify the partition of a file. For instance,
in MS-DOS a partition is specified by a letter followed by a colon. Thus, a file
specification might be C:*userb**test*. Some systems go even further and separate
the partition, directory name, and file name parts of the specification. For
instance, in VMS, the file*login.com* might be specified as: *u:[sst.jdeck]login.com;1*,
where *u* is the name of the partition, *sst* is the name of the directory, *jdeck* is the
name of subdirectory, and *1* is the version number. Other systems simply treat
the partition name as part of the directory name. The first name given is that
of the partition, and the rest is the directory and file. For instance, */u/pbg/test*
might specify partition *u*, directory *pbg*, and file *test*.

A special case of this situation occurs in regard to the system files. Programs provided as a part of the system—loaders, assemblers, compilers, utility routines, libraries, and so on—are generally defined as files. When the appropriate commands are given to the operating system, these files are read by the loader and executed. Many command interpreters act by simply treating the command as the name of a file to load and execute. As the directory system is defined presently, this file name would be searched for in the current UFD. One solution would be to copy the system files into each UFD. However, copying all the system files would waste an enormous amount of space. (If the system files require 5 MB, then supporting 12 users would require $5 \times 12 = 60$ MB just for copies of the system files.)

The standard solution is to complicate the search procedure slightly. A special user directory is defined to contain the system files (for example, user 0). Whenever a file name is given to be loaded, the operating system first searches the local UFD. If the file is found, it is used. If it is not found, the system automatically searches the special user directory that contains the system files. The sequence of directories searched when a file is named is called the **search path**. The search path can be extended to contain an unlimited list of directories to search when a command name is given. This method is the one most used in UNIX and MS-DOS.

11.3.3 Tree-Structured Directories

Once we have seen how to view a two-level directory as a two-level tree, the natural generalization is to extend the directory structure to a tree of arbitrary height (Figure 11.9).   This generalization allows users to create their own subdirectories and to organize their files accordingly. The MS-DOS system, for instance, is structured as a tree. In fact, a tree is the most common directory structure.   The tree has a root directory, and every file in the system has a unique path name. A path name is the path from the root, through all the subdirectories, to a specified file.

A directory (or subdirectory) contains a set of files or subdirectories. A directory is simply another file, but it is treated in a special way. All directories have the same internal format. One bit in each directory entry defines the entry as a file (0) or as a subdirectory (1). Special system calls are used to create and delete directories.

In normal use, each user has a current directory. The **current directory** should contain most of the files that are of current interest to the user. When reference is made to a file, the current directory is searched. If a file is needed that is not in the current directory, then the user must either specify a path name or change the current directory to be the directory holding that file. To change directories, a system call is provided that takes a directory name as a parameter and uses it to redefine the current directory. Thus, the user can change his current directory whenever he desires. From one change directory system

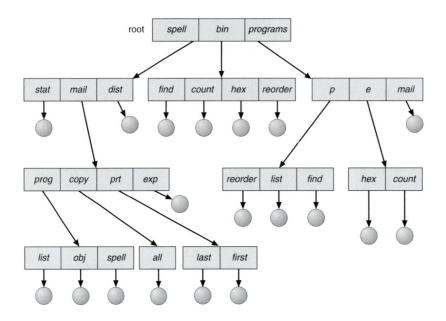

Figure 11.9   Tree-structured directory structure.

call to the next, all open system calls search the current directory for the specified file.

The initial current directory of a user is designated when the user job starts or the user logs in. The operating system searches the accounting file (or some other predefined location) to find an entry for this user (for accounting purposes). In the accounting file is a pointer to (or the name of) the user's initial directory. This pointer is copied to a local variable for this user that specifies the user's initial current directory.

Path names can be of two types: *absolute* path names or *relative* path names. An **absolute path name** begins at the root and follows a path down to the specified file, giving the directory names on the path. A **relative path name** defines a path from the current directory. For example, in the tree-structured file system of Figure 11.9, if the current directory is *root/spell/mail*, then the relative path name *prt/first* refers to the same file as does the absolute path name *root/spell/mail/prt/first*.

Allowing the user to define her own subdirectories permits her to impose a structure on his files. This structure might result in separate directories for files associated with different topics (for example, a subdirectory was created to hold the text of this book) or different forms of information (for example, the directory *programs* may contain source programs; the directory *bin* may store all the binaries).

An interesting policy decision in a tree-structured directory structure concerns how to handle the deletion of a directory. If a directory is empty, its entry in its containing directory can simply be deleted. However, suppose the directory to be deleted is not empty but contains several files or subdirectories: One of two approaches can be taken. Some systems, such as MS-DOS, will not delete a directory unless it is empty. Thus, to delete a directory, the user must first delete all the files in that directory. If any subdirectories exist, this procedure must be applied recursively to them, so that they can be deleted also. This approach may result in a substantial amount of work. An alternative approach, such as that taken by the UNIX rm command, is to provide the option that, when a request is made to delete a directory, all that directory's files and subdirectories are also to be deleted. Either approach is fairly easy to implement; the choice is one of policy. The latter policy is more convenient, but it is also more dangerous, because an entire directory structure can be removed with one command. If that command is issued in error, a large number of files and directories will need to be restored from backup tapes.

With a tree-structured directory system, users can access, in addition to their files, the files of other users. For example, user B can access files of user A by specifying their path names. User B can specify either an absolute or a relative path name. Alternatively, user B could change her current directory to be user A's directory and access the files by their file names. Some systems also allow users to define their own search paths. In this case, user B could define her search path to be (1) her local directory, (2) the system file directory, and (3) user A's directory, in that order. As long as the name of a file of user A does not conflict with the name of a local file or system file, it can be referred to simply by its name.

A path to a file in a tree-structured directory can be longer than that in a two-level directory. To allow users to access programs without having to remember these long paths, the Macintosh operating system automates the search for executable programs. It maintains a file, called the *Desktop File,* containing the names and locations of all executable programs it has seen. When a new hard disk or floppy disk is added to the system, or the network is accessed, the operating system traverses the directory structure, searching for executable programs on the device and recording the pertinent information. This mechanism supports the double-click execution functionality described previously. A double-click on a file causes its creator attribute to be read and the *Desktop File* to be searched for a match. Once the match is found, the appropriate executable program is started with the clicked-on file as its input. The Microsoft Windows family of operating systems (95, 98, NT, 2000, XP) maintains an extended two-level directory structure, with devices and partitions assigned a drive letter (Section 11.4).

11.3.4 Acyclic-Graph Directories

Consider two programmers who are working on a joint project. The files associated with that project can be stored in a subdirectory, separating them from

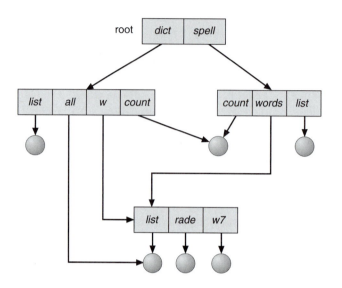

Figure 11.10   Acyclic-graph directory structure.

other projects and files of the two programmers. But since both programmers are equally responsible for the project, both want the subdirectory to be in their own directories. The common subdirectory should be *shared*. A shared directory or file will exist in the file system in two (or more) places at once.

A tree structure prohibits the sharing of files or directories. An **acyclic graph**—that is, a graph with no cycles—allows directories to share subdirectories and files (Figure 11.10). The *same* file or subdirectory may be in two different directories. The acyclic graphis a natural generalization of the tree-structured directory scheme.

It is important to note that a shared file (or directory) is not the same as two copies of the file. With two copies, each programmer can view the copy rather than the original, but if one programmer changes the file, the changes will not appear in the other's copy. With a shared file, only *one* actual file exists, so any changes made by one person are immediately visible to the other. Sharing is particularly important for subdirectories; a new file created by one person will automatically appear in all the shared subdirectories.

When people are working as a team, all the files they want to share can be put into one directory. The UFD of each team members will contain this directory of shared files as a subdirectory. Even in the case of a single user, the user's file organization may require some file to be placed into different subdirectories. For example, a program written for a particular project should be both in the directory of all programs and in the directory for that project.

Shared files and subdirectories can be implemented in several ways. A common way, exemplified by many of the UNIX systems, is to create a new directory entry called a link. A **link** is effectively a pointer to another file or subdirectory. For example, a link may be implemented as an absolute or a relative path name. When a reference to a file is made, we search the directory. If the directory entry is marked as a link, then the name of the real file (or directory) is given. We *resolve* the link by using the path name to locate the real file. Links are easily identified by their format in the directory entry (or by their having a special type on systems that support types) and are effectively named indirect pointers. The operating system ignores these links when traversing directory trees to preserve the acyclic structure of the system.

Another common approach to implementing shared files is simply to duplicate all information about them in both sharing directories. Thus, both entries are identical and equal. A link is clearly different from the original directory entry; thus, the two are not equal. Duplicate directory entries, however, make the original and the copy indistinguishable. A major problem with duplicate directory entries is maintaining consistency when a file is modified.

An acyclic-graph directory structure is more flexible than is a simple tree structure, but it is also more complex. Several problems must be considered carefully. A file may now have multiple absolute path names. Consequently, distinct file names may refer to the same file. This situation is similar to the aliasing problem for programming languages. If we are trying to traverse the entire file system—to find a file, to accumulate statistics on all files, or to copy all files to backup storage—this problem becomes significant, since we do not want to traverse shared structures more than once.

Another problem involves deletion. When can the space allocated to a shared file be deallocated and reused? One possibility is to remove the file whenever anyone deletes it, but this action may leave dangling pointers to the now-nonexistent file. Worse, if the remaining file pointers contain actual disk addresses, and the space is subsequently reused for other files, these dangling pointers may point into the middle of other files.

In a system where sharing is implemented by symbolic links, this situation is somewhat easier to handle. The deletion of a link does not need to affect the original file; only the link is removed. If the file entry itself is deleted, the space for the file is deallocated, leaving the links dangling. We can search for these links and remove them also, but unless a list of the associated links is kept with each file, this search can be expensive. Alternatively, we can leave the links until an attempt is made to use them. At that time, we can determine that the file of the name given by the link does not exist and can fail to resolve the link name; the access is treated just like any other illegal file name. (In this case, the system designer should consider carefully what to do when a file is deleted and another file of the same name is created, before a symbolic link to the original file is used.) In the case of UNIX, symbolic links are left when a file is deleted, and it is up to the user to realize that the original file is gone or has been replaced. Microsoft Windows (all flavors) uses the same approach.

Another approach to deletion is to preserve the file until all references to it are deleted. To implement this approach, we must have some mechanism for determining that the last reference to the file has been deleted. We could keep a list of all references to a file (directory entries or symbolic links). When a link or a copy of the directory entry is established, a new entry is added to the file-reference list. When a link or directory entry is deleted, we remove its entry on the list. The file is deleted when its file-reference list is empty.

The trouble with this approach is the variable and potentially large size of the file-reference list. However, we really do not need to keep the entire list—we need to keep only a count of the *number* of references. A new link or directory entry increments the reference count; deleting a link or entry decrements the count. When the count is 0, the file can be deleted; there are no remaining references to it. The UNIX operating system uses this approach for nonsymbolic links (or **hard links**), keeping a reference count in the file information block (or *inode*; see Appendix A.7.2). By effectively prohibiting multiple references to directories, we maintain an acyclic-graph structure.

To avoid problems such as the ones just discussed, some systems do not allow shared directories or links. For example, in MS-DOS, the directory structure is a tree structure rather than an acyclic graph.

11.3.5 General Graph Directory

A serious problem with using an acyclic-graph structure is ensuring that there are no cycles. If we start with a two-level directory and allow users to create subdirectories, a tree-structured directory results. It should be fairly easy to see that simply adding new files and subdirectories to an existing tree-structured directory preserves the tree-structured nature. However, when we add links to an existing tree-structured directory, the tree structure is destroyed, resulting in a simple graph structure (Figure 11.11).

The primary advantage of an acyclic graph is the relative simplicity of the algorithms to traverse the graph and to determine when there are no more references to a file. We want to avoid traversing shared sections of an acyclic graph twice, mainly for performance reasons. If we have just searched a major shared subdirectory for a particular file, without finding it, we want to avoid searching that subdirectory again; the second search would be a waste of time.

If cycles are allowed to exist in the directory, we likewise want to avoid searching any component twice, for reasons of correctness as well as performance. A poorly designed algorithm might result in an infinite loop continually searching through the cycle and never terminating. One solution is arbitrarily to limit the number of directories that will be accessed during a search.

A similar problem exists when we are trying to determine when a file can be deleted. With acyclic-graph directory structures, a value zero in the reference count means that there are no more references to the file or directory, and the file can be deleted. However, when cycles exist, the reference count may be nonzero, even when it is no longer possible to refer to a directory or file. This anomaly results from the possibility of self referencing (or a cycle) in the

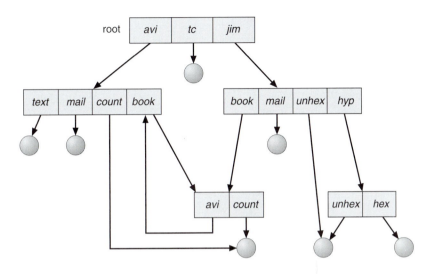

Figure 11.11   General graph directory.

directory structure. In this case, we generally need to use a garbage-collection scheme to determine when the last reference has been deleted and the disk space can be reallocated. Garbage collection involves traversing the entire file system, marking everything that can be accessed. Then, a second pass collects everything that is not marked onto a list of free space. (A similar marking procedure can be used to ensure that a traversal or search will cover everything in the file system once and only once.) Garbage collection for a disk-based file system, however, is extremely time-consuming and is thus seldom attempted.

Garbage collection is necessary only because of possible cycles in the graph. Thus, an acyclic-graph structure is much easier to work with. The difficulty is to avoid cycles as new links are added to the structure. How do we know when a new link will complete a cycle? There are algorithms to detect cycles in graphs; however, they are computationally expensive, especially when the graph is on disk storage. A simpler algorithm in the special case of directories and links is to bypass links during directory traversal. Cycles are avoided, and no extra overhead is incurred.

11.4 ■ File-System Mounting

Just as a file must be *open*ed before it is used, a file system must be *mount*ed before it can be available to processes on the system. More specifically, the directory structure can be built out of multiple partitions, which must be mounted to make them available within the file system name space.

The mount procedure is straightforward. The operating system is given the name of the device and the **mount point**—the location within the file structure

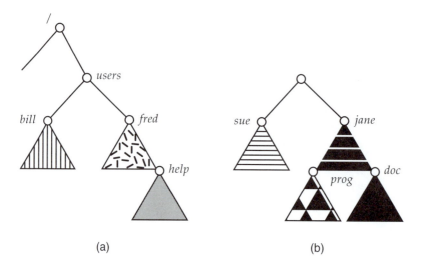

Figure 11.12   File system. (a) Existing. (b) Unmounted partition.

where the file system is to be attached. Typically, a mount point is an empty directory. For instance, on a UNIX system, a file system containing a user's home directories might be mounted as */home*; then, to access the directory structure within that file system, we could precede the directory names with */home*, as in */home/jane*. Mounting that file system under */users* would result in the path name */users/jane*, which we could use to reach the same directory.

Next, the operating system verifies that the device contains a valid file system. It does so by asking the device driver to read the device directory and verifying that the directory has the expected format. Finally, the operating system notes in its directory structure that a file system is mounted at the specified mount point. This scheme enables the operating system to traverse its directory structure, switching among file systems as appropriate.

To illustrate file mounting, consider the file system depicted in Figure 11.12, where the triangles represent subtrees of directories that are of interest. Figure 11.12(a) shows an existing file system, while Figure 11.12(b) shows an unmounted partition residing on */device/dsk*. At this point, only the files on the existing file system can be accessed. Figure 11.13 shows the effects of mounting the partition residing on */device/dsk* over */users*. If the partition is unmounted, the file system is restored to the situation depicted in Figure 11.12.

Systems impose semantics to clarify functionality. For example, a system may disallow a mount over a directory that contains files; or it may make the mounted file system available at that directory and obscure the directory's existing files until the file system is *unmounted*, terminating the use of the file system and allowing access to the original files in that directory. As another example, a system may allow the same file system to be mounted repeatedly, at different mount points; or it may only allow one mount per file system.

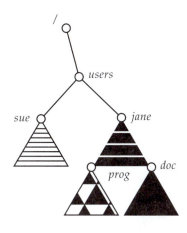

Figure 11.13   Mount point.

Consider the actions of the Macintosh operating system. Whenever the system encounters a disk for the first time (hard disks are found at boot time, and floppy disks are seen when they are inserted into the drive), the Macintosh operating system searches for a file system on the device. If it finds one, it automatically mounts the file system at the root level, adding a folder icon on the screen labeled with the name of the file system (as stored in the device directory). The user then is able to click on the icon and thus to display the newly mounted file system.

The Microsoft Windows family of operating systems (95, 98, NT, 2000, XP) maintains an extended two-level directory structure, with devices and partitions assigned a drive letter. Partitions have a general graph directory structure associated with the drive letter. The path to a specific file takes the form of *drive-letter:\path\to\file*. These operating systems automatically discover all devices and mount all located file systems at boot time. In some systems, like UNIX, the mount commands are explicit. A system configuration file contains a list of devices and mount points for automatic mounting at boot time, but other mounts may be executed manually.

File system mounting is further discussed in Section 12.2.2 and in Appendix A.7.5.

11.5 ■ File Sharing

In the previous sections, we explored the motivation for file sharing and some of the difficulties involved in allowing users to share files. Such file sharing is very desirable for users who want to collaborate and to reduce the effort required to achieve a computing goal. Therefore, user-oriented operating systems must accommodate the need to share files in spite of the inherent difficulties.

In this section, we examine more aspects of file sharing. We begin with the topic of multiple users and the sharing methods possible. Once multiple users are allowed to share files, the challenge is to extend sharing to multiple file systems, including remote file systems. Finally, we consider what to do about conflicting actions occurring on shared files. For instance, if multiple users are writing to a file, should all the writes be allowed to occur, or should the operating system protect the user actions from one another?

11.5.1 Multiple Users

When an operating system accommodates multiple users, the issues of file sharing, file naming, and file protection become preeminent. Given a directory structure that allows files to be shared by users, the system must mediate the file sharing. The system can either allow a user to access the files of other users by default or require that a user specifically grant access to the files. These are the issues of access control and protection, which are covered later in this chapter.

To implement sharing and protection, the system must maintain more file and directory attributes than are needed on a single-user system. Although many approaches have been taken to this requirement historically, most systems have evolved to use the concepts of file/directory *owner* (or *user*) and *group*. The owner is the user who may change attributes and grant access and who has the most control over the file or directory. The group attribute of a file is used to define a subset of users who may share access to the file. For example, the owner of a file on a UNIX system may issue all operations on a file, while members of the file's group may execute one subset of those operations, and all other users may execute another subset of operations. Exactly which operations can be executed by group members and other users is definable by the file's owner. More details on permission attributes are included in the next section.

Most systems implement owner attributes by managing a list of user names and associated **user identifiers (user IDs)**. In Windows NT parlance, this is a **security ID (SID)**. These numerical IDs are unique, one per user. When a user logs in to the system, the authentication stage determines the appropriate user ID for the user. That user ID is associated with all of the user's processes and threads. When an ID needs to be user readable, it is translated back to the user name via the user name list. Likewise, group functionality can be implemented as a system-wide list of group names and **group identifiers**. Every user can be in one or more groups, depending on operating system design decisions. The user's group IDs are also included in every associated process and thread.

The owner and group IDs of a given file or directory are stored with the other file attributes. When a user requests an operation on a file, the user ID can be compared to the owner attribute to determine if the requesting user is the owner of the file. Likewise, the group IDs can be compared. The result indicates which permissions are applicable. The system then applies those permissions to the requested operation and allows or denies it.

The user information within a process can be used for other purposes as well. One process may attempt to interact with another process, and user information can dictate the result, based on the design of the operating system. For example, a process may attempt to terminate, background, or lower the priority of another process. If the same user owns both processes, then the command may succeed; otherwise, it may be denied.

Many systems have multiple local file systems, including partitions of a single disk or multiple partitions on multiple attached disks. In these cases, the ID checking and permission matching are straightforward, once the file systems are mounted.

11.5.2 Remote File Systems

With the advent of networks (Chapter 15), communication between remote computers became possible. Networking allows the sharing of resources spread across a campus or even around the world. One obvious resource to share is data, in the form of files.

Through the evolution of network and file technology, file-sharing methods have changed. The first implemented method involves manually transferring files between machines via programs like ftp. The second major method uses a **distributed file system (DFS)** in which remote directories are visible from the local machine. In some ways, the third method, the **World Wide Web**, is a reversion to the first. A browser is needed to gain access to the remote files, and separate operations (essentially a wrapper for ftp) are used to transfer files.

ftp is used for both anonymous and authenticated access. **Anonymous access** allows a user to transfer files without having an account on the remote system. The World Wide Web uses anonymous file exchange almost exclusively. DFS involves a much tighter integration between the machine that is accessing the remote files and the machine providing the files. This integration adds complexity, which we describe in this section.

11.5.2.1 The Client–Server Model

Remote file systems allow a computer to mount one or more file systems from one or more remote machines. In this case, the machine containing the files is the *server*, and the machine seeking access to the files is the *client*. The client–server relationship is common with networked machines. Generally, the server declares that a resource is available to clients and specifies exactly which resource (in this case, which files) and exactly which clients. Files are usually specified on a partition or subdirectory level. A server can serve multiple clients, and a client can use multiple servers, depending on the implementation details of a given client–server facility.

Client identification is more difficult. A client can be specified by a network name or other identifier, such as *IP address*, but these can be **spoofed**, or imitated. As a result of spoofing, an unauthorized client could be allowed access to the server. More secure solutions include secure authentication of the client via encrypted keys. Unfortunately, with security come many challenges, including ensuring compatibility of the client and server (they must use the same encryption algorithms) and secure key exchanges (intercepted keys could again allow unauthorized access). These problems are difficult enough that, most commonly, unsecure authentication methods are used.

In the case of UNIX and its network file system (NFS), authentication takes place via the client networking information, by default. In this scheme, the user's IDs on the client and server must match. If they do not, the server will be unable to determine access rights to files. Consider the example of a user who has the ID of 1000 on the client and 2000 on the server. A request from the client to the server for a specific file will not be handled appropriately, as the server will determine if user 1000 has access to the file rather than basing the determination on the *real* user ID of 2000. Access is thus granted or denied based on incorrect authentication information. The server must trust the client to present the correct user ID. The NFS protocols allow many-to-many relationships. That is, many servers can provide files to many clients. In fact, a given machine can be both a server to other NFS clients and a client of other NFS servers.

Once the remote file system is mounted, file operation requests are sent on behalf of the user across the network to the server via the DFS protocol. Typically, a file open request is sent along with the ID of the requesting user. The server then applies the standard access checks to determine if the user has credentials to access the file in the mode requested. The request is either allowed or denied. If it is allowed, a file handle is returned to the client application, and the application then may perform read, write, and other operations on the file. The client closes the file when access is completed. The operating system may apply semantics similar to those for a local file-system mount or may have different semantics.

11.5.2.2 Distributed Information Systems

To make client–server systems easier to manage, **distributed information systems,** also known as **distributed naming services**, have been devised to provide unified access to the information needed for remote computing. The **domain name system (DNS)** provides host-name-to-network-address translations for the entire Internet (including the World Wide Web). Before DNS became widespread, files containing the same information were sent via e-mail or `ftp` between all networked hosts. This methodology was not scalable. DNS is further discussed in 15.3.1.

Other distributed information systems provide *user name/password/user ID/group ID* space for a distributed facility. UNIX systems have had a wide variety of distributed-information methods. Sun Microsystems introduced *yellow pages* (since renamed **network-information service (NIS)**), and most of the industry adopted its use. It centralizes storage of user names, host names, printer information, and the like. Unfortunately, it uses unsecure authentication methods, including sending user passwords unencrypted (in *clear text*) and identifying hosts by IP address. Sun's NIS+ is a much more secure replacement for NIS, but is also much more complicated and has not been widely adopted.

In the case of Microsoft networks (**CIFS**), network information is used in conjunction with user authentication (user name and password) to create a **network login** that the server uses to decide whether to allow or deny access to a requested file system. For this authentication to be valid, the user names must match between the machines (as with NFS). Microsoft uses two distributed-naming structures to provide a single namespace for users. The older naming technology is **domains**. The newer technology, available in Windows XP and Windows 2000, is **active directory**. Once established, the distributed naming facility is used by all clients and servers to authenticate users.

The industry is moving toward **lightweight directory-access protocol (LDAP)** as a secure distributed naming mechanism. In fact, active directory is based on LDAP. Sun Microsystems' Solaris 8 allows LDAP to be used for user authentication as well as system-wide retrieval of information, such as availability of printers. Conceivably, one distributed LDAP directory could be used by an organization to store all user and resource information for all computers within that organization. The result would be **secure single sign-on** for users, who would enter their authentication information once for access to all computers within the organization. It would also ease systems-administration efforts by combining, in one location, information that is currently scattered in various files on each system or in different distributed-information services.

11.5.2.3   Failure Modes

Local file systems can fail for a variety of reasons, including failure of the disk containing the file system, corruption of the directory structure or other disk management information (collectively called **metadata**), disk-controller failure, cable failure, or host-adapter failure. User or systems-administrator failure can also cause files to be lost or entire directories or partitions to be deleted. Many of these failures would cause a host to crash and an error condition to be displayed, and human intervention would be required to repair the damage.

Remote file systems have even more failure modes. Because of the complexity of network systems and the required interactions between remote machines, many more problems can interfere with the proper operation of remote file systems. In the case of networks, the network can be interrupted between the two hosts. Such interruptions can result from hardware failure, poor hardware configuration, or networking implementation issues. Although some networks have built-in resiliency, including multiple paths between hosts, many do not. Any single failure can thus interrupt the flow of DFS commands.

Consider a client in the midst of using a remote file system. It has mounted remote file systems and may have files open from the remote host; among other activities, it may be performing directory lookups to open files, reading or writing data to files, and closing files. Now consider a partitioning of the network, a crash of the server, or even a scheduled shutdown of the server. Suddenly, the remote file system is no longer reachable. This scenario is rather common, so it would not be appropriate for the client system to act as it would if a local file system were lost. Rather, the system can either terminate all operations to the lost server or delay operations until the server is again reachable. These failure semantics are defined and implemented as part of the remote-file-system protocol. Termination of all operations can result in users' losing data—and patience. Thus, most DFS protocols either enforce or allow delaying of file-system operations to remote hosts, with the hope that the remote host will become available again.

To implement this kind of recovery from failure, some kind of *state* information may be maintained on both the client and server. In the situation where the server crashes but must recognize that it has exported file systems, remotely mounted them, and opened certain files, NFS takes a simple approach, implementing a **stateless** DFS. In essence, it assumes that a client request for a file read or write would not have occurred unless the file system had been remotely mounted and the file had been previously open. The NFS protocol carries all the information needed to locate the appropriate file and perform the requested operation on a file. Similarly, it does not track which clients have its exported partitions mounted, again assuming that if a request comes it, it must be legitimate. While this stateless approach makes NFS resilient and rather easy to implement, it makes it unsecure. For example, forged read or write requests could be allowed by an NFS server even though the requisite mount request and permission check have not take place.

11.5.3 Consistency Semantics

Consistency semantics represent an important criterion for evaluating any file system that supports file sharing. These semantics specify how multiple users of a system are to access a shared file simultaneously. In particular, they should specify when modifications of data by one user will be observable by other users. These semantics are typically implemented as code with the file system.

Consistency semantics are directly related to the process-synchronization algorithms of Chapter 7. However, the complex algorithms of that chapter tend not to be implemented in the case of file I/O because of the great latencies and slow transfer rates of disks and networks. For example, performing an atomic transaction to a remote disk could involve several network communications, several disk reads and writes, or both. Systems that attempt such a full set of functionalities tend to perform poorly. A successful implementation of complex sharing semantics can be found in the Andrew file system.

For the following discussion, we assume that a series of file accesses (that is, reads and writes) attempted by a user to the same file is always enclosed between the open() and close() operations. The series of accesses between the open() and close() operations is a **file session**. To illustrate the concept, we sketch several prominent examples of consistency semantics.

11.5.4 UNIX Semantics

The UNIX file system (Chapter 16) uses the following consistency semantics:

- Writes to an open file by a user are visible immediately to other users that have this file open at the same time.

- One mode of sharing allows users to share the pointer of current location into the file. Thus, the advancing of the pointer by one user affects all sharing users. Here, a file has a single image that interleaves all accesses, regardless of their origin.

In the UNIX semantics, a file is associated with a single physical image that is accessed as an exclusive resource. Contention for this single image causes delays in user processes.

11.5.5 Session Semantics

The Andrew file system (AFS) (Chapter 16) uses the following consistency semantics:

- Writes to an open file by a user are not visible immediately to other users that have the same file open simultaneously.

- Once a file is closed, the changes made to it are visible only in sessions starting later. Already open instances of the file do not reflect these changes.

According to these semantics, a file may be associated temporarily with several (possibly different) images at the same time. Consequently, multiple users are allowed to perform both read and write accesses concurrently on their images of the file, without delay. Almost no constraints are enforced on scheduling accesses.

11.5.6 Immutable-Shared-Files Semantics

A unique approach is that of **immutable shared files**. Once a file is declared as *shared* by its creator, it cannot be modified. An immutable file has two key properties: Its name may not be reused, and its contents may not be altered. Thus, the name of an immutable file signifies that the contents of the file are fixed. The implementation of these semantics in a distributed system (Chapter 16) is simple, because the sharing is disciplined (read-only).

11.6 ■ Protection

When information is stored in a computer system, we want to keep it safe from physical damage (*reliability*) and improper access (*protection*).

Reliability is generally provided by duplicate copies of files. Many computers have systems programs that automatically (or through computer-operator intervention) copy disk files to tape at regular intervals (once per day or week or month) to maintain a copy should a file system be accidentally destroyed. File systems can be damaged by hardware problems (such as errors in reading or writing), power surges or failures, head crashes, dirt, temperature extremes, and vandalism. Files may be deleted accidentally. Bugs in the file-system software can also cause file contents to be lost. Reliability is covered in more detail in Chapter 14.

Protection can be provided in many ways. For a small single-user system, we might provide protection by physically removing the floppy disks and locking them in a desk drawer or file cabinet. In a multiuser system, however, other mechanisms are needed.

11.6.1 Types of Access

The need to protect files is a direct result of the ability to access files. Systems that do not permit access to the files of other users do not need protection. Thus, we could provide complete protection by prohibiting access. Alternatively, we could provide free access with no protection. Both approaches are too extreme for general use. What is needed is **controlled access**.

Protection mechanisms provide controlled access by limiting the types of file access that can be made. Access is permitted or denied depending on several factors, one of which is the type of access requested. Several different types of operations may be controlled:

- **Read:** Read from the file.

- **Write:** Write or rewrite the file.

- **Execute:** Load the file into memory and execute it.

- **Append:** Write new information at the end of the file.

- **Delete:** Delete the file and free its space for possible reuse.

- **List:** List the name and attributes of the file.

Other operations, such as renaming, copying, and editing the file, may also be controlled. For many systems, however, these higher-level functions may be implemented by a system program that makes lower-level system calls. Protection is provided at only the lower level. For instance, copying a file may be implemented simply by a sequence of read requests. In this case, a user with read access can also cause the file to be copied, printed, and so on.

Many protection mechanisms have been proposed, and we discuss some of them here. Each scheme has advantages and disadvantages and must be appropriate for its intended application. A small computer system that is used by only a few members of a research group, for example, may not need the same types of protection as a large corporate computer that is used for research, finance, and personnel operations. A complete treatment of the protection problem is deferred to Chapter 18.

11.6.2 Access Control

The most common approach to the protection problem is to make access dependent on the identity of the user. Different users may need different types of access to a file or directory. The most general scheme to implement identity-dependent access is to associate with each file and directory an **access-control list (ACL)** specifying user names and the types of access allowed for each user. When a user requests access to a particular file, the operating system checks the access list associated with that file. If that user is listed for the requested access, the access is allowed. Otherwise, a protection violation occurs, and the user job is denied access to the file.

This approach has the advantage of enabling complex access methodologies. The main problem with access lists is their length. If we want to allow everyone to read a file, we must list all users with read access. This technique has two undesirable consequences:

- Constructing such a list may be a tedious and unrewarding task, especially if we do not know in advance the list of users in the system.

- The directory entry, previously of fixed size, now needs to be of variable size, resulting in more complicated space management.

These problems can be resolved by use of a condensed version of the access list.

To condense the length of the access control list, many systems recognize three classifications of users in connection with each file:

- **Owner:** The user who created the file is the owner.

- **Group:** A set of users who are sharing the file and need similar access is a group, or work group.

- **Universe:** All other users in the system constitute the universe.

The most common recent approach is to combine access control lists with the more general (and easier to implement) owner, group, and universe access-control scheme just described. For example, Solaris 2.6 and beyond use the three categories of access by default but allow access control lists to be added to specific files and directories when more fine-grained access control is desired.

As an example, consider a person, Sara, who is writing a new book. She has hired three graduate students (Jim, Dawn, and Jill) to help with the project. The text of the book is kept in a file named *book*. The protection associated with this file is as follows:

- Sara should be able to invoke all operations on the file.

- Jim, Dawn, and Jill should be able only to read and write the file; they should not be allowed to delete the file.

- All other users should be able to read, but not write, the file. (Sara is interested in letting as many people as possible read the text so that she can obtain appropriate feedback.)

To achieve such protection, we must create a new group—say, *text*—with members Jim, Dawn, and Jill. The name of the group, *text*, must be then associated with the file *book,* and the access rights must be set in accordance with the policy we have outlined.

Now consider a visitor to whom Sara would like to grant temporary access to chapter 1. The visitor cannot be added to the *text* group because that would give the visitor access to all chapters. Because files can only be in one group, another group cannot be added to chapter 1. With the addition of access-control-list functionality, the visitor can be added to the access control list of chapter 1.

For this scheme to work properly, permissions and access lists must be controlled tightly. This control can be accomplished in several ways. For example, in the UNIX system, groups can be created and modified only by the manager of the facility (or by any superuser). Thus, this control is achieved through human interaction. In the VMS system, the owner of the file can create and modify this list. Access lists are discussed further in Section 18.4.2.

With the more limited protection classification, only three fields are needed to define protection. Each field is often a collection of bits, each of which either allows or prevents the access associated with it. For example, the UNIX system defines three fields of 3 bits each—rwx, where r controls read access, w controls write access, and x controls execution. A separate field is kept for the file owner, for the file's group, and for all other users. In this scheme, 9 bits per file are needed to record protection information. Thus, for our example, the protection fields for the file *book* are as follows: For the owner Sara, all 3 bits are set; for the group *text*, the r and w bits are set; and for the universe, only the r bit is set.

One difficulty in combining approaches comes in the user interface. Users must be able to tell when the optional ACL permissions are set on a file. In the Solaris example, a "+" appends the regular permissions, as in:

```
19 -rw-r--r--+ 1 jim staff 130 May 25 22:13 file1
```

A separate set of commands, setfacl and getfacl, are used to manage the ACLs.

Another difficulty is assigning precedence when permission and ACLs conflict. For example, if Joe is in a file's group, which has read permission, but the file has an ACL granting Joe read and write permissions, should a write by Joe be granted or denied? Solaris gives ACLs permission (as they are more fine-grained and are not assigned by default). This follows the general rule that specificity should have priority.

11.6.3 Other Protection Approaches

Another approach to the protection problem is to associate a password with each file. Just as access to the computer system is often controlled by a password, access to each file can be controlled by a password. If the passwords are chosen randomly and changed often, this scheme may be effective in limiting access to a file. This scheme, however, has several disadvantages. First, the number of passwords that a user needs to remember may become large, making the scheme impractical. Second, if only one password is used for all the files, then, once it is discovered, all files are accessible. Some systems (for example, TOPS-20) allow a user to associate a password with a subdirectory, rather than with an individual file, to deal with this problem. The IBM VM/CMS operating system allows three passwords for a minidisk—one each for read, write, and multiwrite access. Third, commonly, only one password is associated with all of a user's files. Thus, protection is on an all-or-nothing basis. To provide protection on a more detailed level, we must use multiple passwords.

Limited file protection is also currently available on single-user systems, such as the MS-DOS and Macintosh operating systems. These operating systems, when originally designed, essentially ignored the protection problem. However, since these systems are now being placed on networks where file sharing and communication are necessary, protection mechanisms must be **retrofitted** into them. Designing a feature for a new operating system is almost always easier than adding a feature to an existing one. Such updates are usually less effective and are not seamless.

In a multilevel directory structure, we need to protect not only individual files but also collections of files in subdirectories; that is, we need to provide a mechanism for directory protection. The directory operations that must be protected are somewhat different from the file operations. We want to control the creation and deletion of files in a directory. In addition, we probably want

-rw-rw-r–	1 pbg	staff	31200	Sep 3 08:30	intro.ps
drwx——	5 pbg	staff	512	Jul 8 09:33	private/
drwxrwxr-x	2 pbg	staff	512	Jul 8 09:35	doc/
drwxrwx—	2 pbg	student	512	Aug 3 14:13	student-proj/
-rw-r–r–	1 pbg	staff	9423	Feb 24 1999	program.c
-rwxr-xr-x	1 pbg	staff	20471	Feb 24 200	program
drwx–x–x	4 pbg	faculty	512	Jul 31 10:31	lib/
drwx——	3 pbg	staff	1024	Aug 29 06:52	mail/
drwxrwxrwx	3 pbg	staff	512	Jul 8 09:35	test/

Figure 11.14   A sample directory listing.

to control whether a user can determine the existence of a file in a directory. Sometimes, knowledge of the existence and name of a file may be significant in itself. Thus, listing the contents of a directory must be a protected operation. Therefore, if a path name refers to a file in a directory, the user must be allowed access to both the directory and the file. In systems where files may have numerous path names (such as acyclic or general graphs), a given user may have different access rights to a particular file, depending on the path name used.

11.6.4 An Example: UNIX

In the UNIX system, directory protection is handled similarly to file protection. That is, associated with each subdirectory are three fields—owner, group, and universe—each consisting of the 3 bits rwx. Thus, a user can list the content of a subdirectory only if the r bit is set in the appropriate field. Similarly, a user can change his current directory to another current directory (say *foo*) only if the x bit associated with the *foo* subdirectory is set in the appropriate field.

A sample directory listing from a UNIX environment is shown in Figure 11.14. The first field describes the file or directory's protection. A d as the first character indicates a subdirectory. Also shown are the number of links to the file, the owner's name, the group's name, the size of the file in bytes, the date of last modification, and finally the file's name (with optional extension).

11.7 ■ Summary

A file is an abstract data type defined and implemented by the operating system. It is a sequence of logical records. A logical record may be a byte, a line (of fixed or variable length), or a more complex data item. The operating system may specifically support various record types or may leave that support to the application program.

The major task for the operating system is to map the logical file concept onto physical storage devices such as magnetic tape or disk. Since the physical record size of the device may not be the same as the logical record size, it may be necessary to order logical records into physical records. Again, this task may be supported by the operating system or left for the application program.

Each device in a file system keeps a volume table of contents or device directory listing the location of the files on the device. In addition, it is useful to create directories to allow files to be organized. A single-level directory in a multiuser system causes naming problems, since each file must have a unique name. A two-level directory solves this problem by creating a separate directory for each user. Each user has her own directory, containing her own files. The directory lists the files by name and includes such information as the file's location on the disk, length, type, owner, time of creation, time of last use, and so on.

The natural generalization of a two-level directory is a tree-structured directory. A tree-structured directory allows a user to create subdirectories to organize her files. Acyclic-graph directory structures allow subdirectories and files to be shared but complicate searching and deletion. A general graph structure allows complete flexibility in the sharing of files and directories but sometimes requires garbage collection to recover unused disk space.

Disks are segmented into one or more partitions, each containing a file system or left "raw". File systems may be mounted into the system's naming structures to make them available. The naming scheme varies by operating system. Once mounted, the files within the partition are available for use. File systems may be unmounted to disable access or for maintenance.

File sharing depends on the semantics provided by the system. Files may have multiple readers, multiple writers, or limits on the sharing. Distributed file systems allow client hosts to mount partitions or directories from servers, as long as they can access each other across a network. Remote file systems present challenges in reliability, performance, and security. Distributed information systems maintain user, host, and access information so that clients and servers can share state information to manage use and access.

Since files are the main information-storage mechanism in most computer systems, file protection is needed. Access to files can be controlled separately for each type of access—read, write, execute, append, delete, list directory, and so on. File protection can be provided by passwords, by access lists, or by special ad hoc techniques.

■ Exercises

11.1 Consider a file system where a file can be deleted and its disk space reclaimed while links to that file still exist. What problems may occur if a new file is created in the same storage area or with the same absolute path name? How can these problems be avoided?

11.2 Some systems automatically delete all user files when a user logs off or a job terminates, unless the user explicitly requests that they be kept; other systems keep all files unless the user explicitly deletes them. Discuss the relative merits of each approach.

11.3 Why do some systems keep track of the type of a file, while others leave it to the user or simply do not implement multiple file types? Which system is "better"?

11.4 Similarly, some systems support many types of structures for a file's data, while others simply support a stream of bytes. What are the advantages and disadvantages?

11.5 What are the advantages and disadvantages of recording the name of the creating program with the file's attributes (as is done in the Macintosh operating system)?

11.6 Can you simulate a multilevel directory structure with a single-level directory structure in which arbitrarily long names can be used? If your answer is yes, explain how you can do so, and contrast this scheme with the multilevel directory scheme. If your answer is no, explain what prevents your simulation's success. How would your answer change if file names were limited to seven characters?

11.7 Explain the purpose of the open() and close() operations.

11.8 Some systems automatically open a file when it is referenced for the first time and close the file when the job terminates. Discuss the advantages and disadvantages of this scheme compared with the more traditional one, where the user has to open and close the file explicitly.

11.9 Give an example of an application in which data in a file should be accessed in the following order:

    a. Sequentially

    b. Randomly

11.10 Some systems provide file sharing by maintaining a single copy of a file; other systems maintain several copies, one for each of the users sharing the file. Discuss the relative merits of each approach.

11.11 In some systems, a subdirectory can be read and written by an authorized user, just as ordinary files can be.

    a. Describe the protection problems that could arise.

    b. Suggest a scheme for dealing with each of these protection problems.

11.12 Consider a system that supports 5,000 users. Suppose that you want to allow 4,990 of these users to be able to access one file.

    a. How would you specify this protection scheme in UNIX?

    b. Can you suggest a protection scheme that would be more effective for this purpose than the scheme provided by UNIX?

11.13 Researchers have suggested that, instead of having an access-control list associated with each file (specifying which users can access the file, and how), we should have a **user-control list** associated with each user (specifying which files a user can access, and how). Discuss the relative merits of these two schemes.

Bibliographical Notes

General discussions concerning file systems were offered by Grosshans [1986]. Golden and Pechura [1986] described the structure of microcomputer file systems. Database systems and their file structures were described in full in Silberschatz et al. [2001].

A multilevel directory structure was first implemented on the MULTICS system (Organick [1972]). Most operating systems now implement multilevel directory structures. These include Linux (Bovet and Cesati [2002]), Mac OS X (http://www.apple.com/macosx/), Solaris (Mauro and McDougall [2001]), and all versions of Windows including Windows 2000 (Solomon and Russinovich [2000]).

The Network File System (NFS), designed by Sun Microsystems, allows directory structures to be spread across networked computer systems. NFS is fully described in Chapter 16.

DNS was first proposed by Su [1982] and has gone through several revisions since, with Mockapetris [1987] adding several major features. Eastlake [1999] has proposed security extensions to let DNS hold security keys.

LDAP, also known as X.509, is a derivative subset of the X.500 distributed directory protocol. It was defined by Yeong et al. [1995] and has been implemented on many operating systems. Interesting research is ongoing in the area of file-system interfaces—in particular, on issues relating to file naming and attributes. For example, the Plan 9 operating system from Bell Laboratories (Lucent Technology) makes all objects look like file systems. Thus, to display a list of processes on a system, a user simply lists the contents of the /proc directory. Similarly, to display the time of day, a user need only type the file /dev/time.

Chapter 12

FILE-SYSTEM IMPLEMENTATION

As we saw in Chapter 11, the file system provides the mechanism for on-line storage and access to file contents, including data and programs. The file system resides permanently on *secondary storage*, which is designed to hold a large amount of data permanently. This chapter is primarily concerned with issues surrounding file storage and access on the most common secondary-storage medium, the disk. We explore ways to structure file use, to allocate disk space, to recover freed space, to track the locations of data, and to interface other parts of the operating system to secondary storage. Performance issues are considered throughout the chapter.

12.1 ■ File-System Structure

Disks provide the bulk of secondary storage on which a file system is maintained. They have two characteristics that make them a convenient medium for storing multiple files:

1. They can be rewritten in place; it is possible to read a block from the disk, to modify the block, and to write it back into the same place.

2. They can access directly any given block of information on the disk. Thus, it is simple to access any file either sequentially or randomly, and switching from one file to another requires only moving the read–write heads and waiting for the disk to rotate.

We discuss disk structure in great detail in Chapter 14.

463

Rather than transferring a byte at a time, to improve I/O efficiency, I/O transfers between memory and disk are performed in units of *blocks*. Each block is one or more sectors. Depending on the disk drive, sectors vary from 32 bytes to 4,096 bytes; usually, they are 512 bytes.

To provide an efficient and convenient access to the disk, the operating system imposes one or more **file systems** to allow the data to be stored, located, and retrieved easily. A file system poses two quite different design problems. The first problem is defining how the file system should look to the user. This task involves defining a file and its attributes, the operations allowed on a file, and the directory structure for organizing files. The second problem is creating algorithms and data structures to map the logical file system onto the physical secondary-storage devices.

The file system itself is generally composed of many different levels. The structure shown in Figure 12.1 is an example of a layered design. Each level in the design uses the features of lower levels to create new features for use by higher levels.

The lowest level, the *I/O control*, consists of **device drivers** and interrupt handlers to transfer information between the main memory and the disk system. A device driver can be thought of as a translator. Its input consists of high-level commands such as "retrieve block 123." Its output consists of low-level, hardware-specific instructions that are used by the hardware controller, which interfaces the I/O device to the rest of the system. The device driver usually writes specific bit patterns to special locations in the I/O controller's memory to tell the controller on which device location to act and what actions

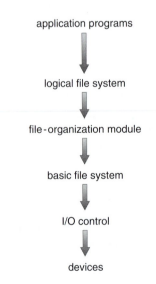

Figure 12.1   Layered file system.

to take. The details of device drivers and the I/O infrastructure are covered in Chapter 13.

The **basic file system** needs only to issue generic commands to the appropriate device driver to read and write physical blocks on the disk. Each physical block is identified by its numeric disk address (for example, drive 1, cylinder 73, track 2, sector 10).

The **file-organization module** knows about files and their logical blocks, as well as physical blocks. By knowing the type of file allocation used and the location of the file, the file-organization module can translate logical block addresses to physical block addresses for the basic file system to transfer. Each file's logical blocks are numbered from 0 (or 1) through N, whereas the physical blocks containing the data usually do not match the logical numbers, so a translation is needed to locate each block. The file-organization module also includes the free-space manager, which tracks unallocated blocks and provides these blocks to the file-organization module when requested.

Finally, the **logical file system** manages metadata information. Metadata includes all of the file-system structure, excluding the actual *data* (or contents of the files). The logical file system manages the directory structure to provide the file-organization module with the information the latter needs, given a symbolic file name. It maintains file structure via file control blocks. A **file control block (FCB)** contains information about the file, including ownership, permissions, and location of the file contents. The logical file system is also responsible for protection and security, as was discussed in Chapter 11 and will be further discussed in Chapter 18.

Many implemented file systems currently exist. Most operating systems support more than one file system. For example, most CD-ROMs are written in the *High Sierra* format, which is a standard format agreed upon by CD-ROM manufacturers. Without such a standard, there would be little or no interoperability between systems trying to use CD-ROMs. Aside from removable media file systems, each operating system has one (or more) disk-based file system. UNIX uses the **UNIX file system (UFS)** as a base. Windows NT supports disk file-system formats of FAT, FAT32 and NTFS (or Windows NT File System), as well as CD-ROM, DVD, and floppy-disk file-system formats. By using a layered structure for file-system implementation, duplication of code is minimized. The I/O control and sometimes the basic file-system code can be used by multiple file systems. Each file system may then have its own logical file system and file-organization modules.

12.2 ■ File-System Implementation

As was described in Section 11.1.2, operating systems implement open and close systems calls for processes to request access to file contents. In this section, we delve into the structures and operations used to implement file-system operations.

12.2.1 Overview

Several on-disk and in-memory structures are used to implement a file system. These vary depending on the operating system and the file system, but some general principles apply. On-disk, the file system may contain information about how to boot an operating system stored there, the total number of blocks, the number and location of free blocks, the directory structure, and individual files. Many of these structures are detailed throughout the remainder of this chapter.

The on-disk structures include:

- A **boot control block** can contain information needed by the system to boot an operating system from that partition. If the disk does not contain an operating system, this block can be empty. It is typically the first block of a partition. In UFS, this is called the **boot block**; in NTFS, it is the **partition boot sector**.

- A **partition control block** contains partition details, such as the number of blocks in the partition, size of the blocks, free-block count and free-block pointers, and free FCB count and FCB pointers. In UFS this is called a **superblock**; in NTFS, it is the **Master File Table**.

- A directory structure is used to organize the files.

- An FCB contains many of the file's details, including file permissions, ownership, size, and location of the data blocks. In UFS this is called the **inode**. In NTFS, this information is actually stored within the Master File Table, which uses a relational database structure, with a row per file.

The in-memory information is used for both file-system management and performance improvement via caching. The structures can include:

- An in-memory partition table containing information about each mounted partition.

- An in-memory directory structure that holds the directory information of recently accessed directories. (For directories at which partitions are mounted, it can contain a pointer to the partition table.)

- The **system-wide open-file table** contains a copy of the FCB of each open file, as well as other information.

- The **per-process open-file table** contains a pointer to the appropriate entry in the system-wide open-file table, as well as other information.

To create a new file, an application program calls the logical file system. The logical file system knows the format of the directory structures. To create a new file, it allocates a new FCB, reads the appropriate directory into memory, updates it with the new file name and FCB, and writes it back to the disk. A typical FCB is shown in Figure 12.2.

Some operating systems, including UNIX, treat a directory exactly as a file—one with a type field indicating that it is a directory. Other operating systems, including Windows NT, implement separate system calls for files and directories and treat directories as entities separate from files. No matter the larger structural issues, the logical file system can call the file-organization module to map the directory I/O into disk-block numbers, which are passed on to the basic file system and I/O control system. The file-organization module also allocates blocks for storage of the file's data.

Now that a file has been created, it can be used for I/O. First, though, it must be *opened*. The open call passes a file name to the file system. When a file is opened, the directory structure is searched for the given file name. Parts of the directory structure are usually cached in memory to speed directory operations. Once the file is found, the FCB is copied into a system-wide open-file table in memory. This table not only stores the FCB, but also has entries for a count of the number of processes that have the file open.

Next, an entry is made in the per-process open-file table, with a pointer to the entry in the system-wide open-file table and some other fields. These other fields can include a pointer to the current location in the file (for the next read or write operation) and the access mode in which the file is open. The open call returns a pointer to the appropriate entry in the per-process file-system table. All file operations are then performed via this pointer. The file name may not be part of the open-file table, as the system has no use for it once the appropriate FCB is located on disk. The name given to the entry varies.

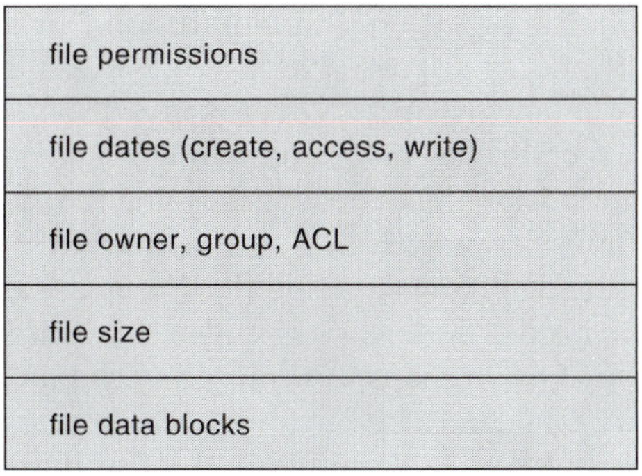

| file permissions |
| file dates (create, access, write) |
| file owner, group, ACL |
| file size |
| file data blocks |

Figure 12.2   A typical file control block.

UNIX systems refer to it as a **file descriptor**; Windows 2000 refers to it as a **file handle**. Consequently, as long as the file is not closed, all file operations are done on the open-file table.

When a process closes the file, the per-process table entry is removed, and the system-wide entry's open count is decremented. When all users that have opened the file close it, the updated file information is copied back to the disk-based directory structure and the system-wide open-file table entry is removed.

In reality, the open system call first searches the system-wide open-file table to see if the file is already in use by another process. If it is, a per-process open-file table entry is created pointing to the existing system-wide open-file table. This algorithm can save substantial overhead when opening files that are already open.

Some systems complicate this scheme even further by using the file system as an interface to other system aspects, such as networking. For example, in UFS, the system-wide open-file table holds the inodes and other information for files and directories. It also holds similar information for network connections and devices. In this way, one mechanism can be used for multiple system aspects.

The caching aspects of these structures should not be overlooked. Using this scheme, all information about an open file, except for its actual data blocks, is in memory. The BSD UNIX system is typical in its use of caches wherever disk I/O can be saved. Its average cache hit rate of 85 percent shows that these techniques are well worth implementing. The BSD UNIX system is described fully in Appendix A.

The operating structures of a file-system implementation are summarized in Figure 12.3.

12.2.2 Partitions and Mounting

The layout of a disk can have many variations, depending on the operating system. A disk can be sliced into multiple partitions, or a partition can span multiple disks. The former is discussed here, while the latter is more appropriately considered a form of RAID and is covered in Section 14.5.

Each partition can either be "raw," containing no file system, or "cooked," containing a file system. **Raw disk** is used where no file system is appropriate. UNIX swap space can use a raw partition, as it uses its own format on disk and does not use a file system. Likewise, some databases use raw disk and format the data to suit their needs. Raw disk can also hold information needed by disk RAID systems, such as bit maps indicating which blocks are mirrored and which have changed and need to be mirrored. Similarly, raw disk can contain a miniature database holding RAID configuration information, such as which disks are members of each RAID set. Raw disk use is further discussed in Section 14.3.1.

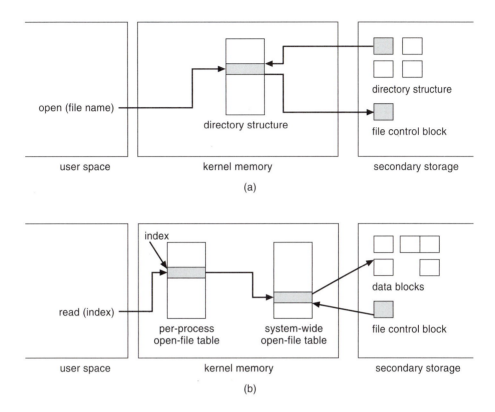

Figure 12.3   In-memory file-system structures. (a) File open. (b) File read.

Boot information can be stored in a separate partition. Again, it has its own format, because at boot time the system does not have file-system device drivers loaded and therefore cannot interpret the file-system format. Rather, it is usually a sequential series of blocks, loaded as an image into memory. Execution of the image starts at a predefined location, such as the first byte. This boot image can contain more than the instructions for how to boot a specific operating system. For instance, PCs and other systems can be **dual-booted**. Multiple operating systems can be installed on such a system. How does the system know which one to boot? A boot loader that understands multiple file systems and multiple operating systems can occupy the boot space. Once loaded, it can boot one of the operating systems available on the disk. The disk can have multiple partitions, each containing a different type of file system and a different operating system.

The **root partition**, which contains the operating-system kernel and potentially other system files, is mounted at boot time. Other partitions can be automatically mounted at boot or manually mounted later, depending on the operating system. As part of a successful mount operation, the operating system verifies that the device contains a valid file system. It does so by asking the device driver to read the device directory and verifying that the directory has the expected format. If the format is invalid, the partition must have its consistency checked and possibly corrected, either with or without user intervention. Finally, the operating system notes in its in-memory **mount table** structure that a file system is mounted, and the type of the file system. The details of this function depend on the operating system. Microsoft Windows-based systems mount each partition in a separate name space, denoted by a letter and a colon. To record that a file system is mounted at f:, for example, the operating system places a pointer to the file system in a field of the device structure corresponding to f:. When a process specifies the driver letter, the operating system finds the appropriate file-system pointer and traverses the directory structures on that device to find the specified file or directory.

On UNIX, file systems can be mounted at any directory. This is implemented by setting a flag in the in-memory copy of the inode for that directory. The flag indicates that the directory is a mount point. A field then points to an entry in the mount table, indicating which device is mounted there. The mount table entry contains a pointer to the superblock of the file system on that device. This scheme enables the operating system to traverse its directory structure, switching among file systems as appropriate.

12.2.3 Virtual File Systems

While the previous section makes it clear that modern operating systems must support concurrently multiple types of file systems, we now need to discuss some implementation details. How does an operating system allow multiple types of file systems to be integrated into a directory structure? How can users seamlessly move between file-system types as they navigate the file-system space?

An obvious but suboptimal method of implementing multiple types of file systems is to write directory and file routines for each type. Rather, most operating systems, including UNIX, use object-oriented techniques to simplify, organize, and modularize the implementation. The use of these methods allows very dissimilar file-system types to be implemented within the same structure, including network file systems, such as NFS. Users can access files that are contained within multiple file systems on the local disk, or even on file systems available across the network.

Data structures and procedures are used to isolate the basic system call functionality from the implementation details. Thus, the file-system implementation consists of three major layers; it is depicted schematically in Figure 12.4. The first layer is the file-system interface, based on the open, read, write, and close calls, and file descriptors.

The second layer is called the **Virtual File System (VFS)** layer; it serves two important functions:

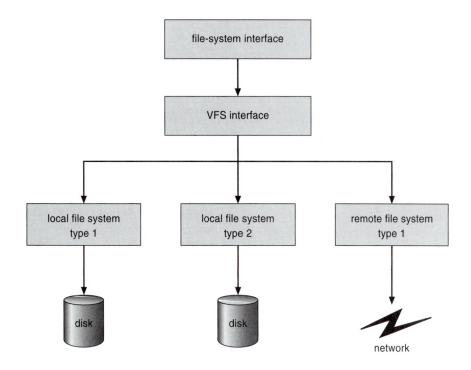

Figure 12.4   Schematic view of a virtual file system.

1. It separates file-system-generic operations from their implementation by defining a clean VFS interface. Several implementations for the VFS interface may coexist on the same machine, allowing transparent access to different types of file systems mounted locally.

2. The VFS is based on a file-representation structure, called a **vnode**, that contains a numerical designator for a network-wide unique file. (UNIX inodes are unique within only a single file system.) This network-wide uniqueness is required for support of network file systems. The kernel maintains one vnode structure for each active node (file or directory).

Thus, the VFS distinguishes local files from remote ones, and local files are further distinguished according to their file-system types.

The VFS activates file-system-specific operations to handle local requests according to their file-system types, and even calls the NFS protocol procedures for remote requests. File handles are constructed from the relevant vnodes and are passed as arguments to these procedures. The layer implementing the file-system type, or remote file system protocol, is the bottom layer of the architecture. An illustration of VFS operation is found in Section 12.9.

12.3 ▪ Directory Implementation

The selection of directory-allocation and directory-management algorithms has a large effect on the efficiency, performance, and reliability of the file system. Therefore, you need to understand the tradeoffs involved in these algorithms.

12.3.1 Linear List

The simplest method of implementing a directory is to use a linear list of file names with pointers to the data blocks. A linear list of directory entries requires a linear search to find a particular entry. This method is simple to program but time-consuming to execute. To create a new file, we must first search the directory to be sure that no existing file has the same name. Then, we add a new entry at the end of the directory. To delete a file, we search the directory for the named file, then release the space allocated to it. To reuse the directory entry, we can do one of several things. We can mark the entry as unused (by assigning it a special name, such as an all-blank name, or with a used–unused bit in each entry), or we can attach it to a list of free directory entries. A third alternative is to copy the last entry in the directory into the freed location, and to decrease the length of the directory. A linked list can also be used to decrease the time to delete a file.

The real disadvantage of a linear list of directory entries is the linear search to find a file. Directory information is used frequently, and users would notice a slow implementation of access to it. In fact, many operating systems implement a software cache to store the most recently used directory information. A cache hit avoids constantly rereading the information from disk. A sorted list allows a binary search and decreases the average search time. However, the requirement that the list must be kept sorted may complicate creating and deleting files, since we may have to move substantial amounts of directory information to maintain a sorted directory. A more sophisticated tree data structure, such as a B-tree, might help here. An advantage of the sorted list is that a sorted directory listing can be produced without a separate sort step.

12.3.2 Hash Table

Another data structure that has been used for a file directory is a **hash table**. In this method, a linear list stores the directory entries, but a hash data structure is also used. The hash table takes a value computed from the file name and returns a pointer to the file name in the linear list. Therefore, it can greatly decrease the directory search time. Insertion and deletion are also fairly straightforward, although some provision must be made for **collisions**—situations where two file names hash to the same location. The major difficulties with a hash table are its generally fixed size and the dependence of the hash function on that size.

For example, assume that we make a linear-probing hash table that holds 64 entries. The hash function converts file names into integers from 0 to 63, for instance, by using the remainder of a division by 64. If we later try to create a 65th file, we must enlarge the directory hash table—say, to 128 entries. As a result, we need a new hash function that must map file names to the range 0 to 127, and we must reorganize the existing directory entries to reflect their new hash-function values. Alternately, a chained-overflow hash table can be used. Each hash entry can be a linked list instead of an individual value, and we can resolve collisions by adding the new entry to the linked list. Lookups may be somewhat slowed, because searching for a name might require stepping through a linked list of colliding table entries, but this is likely to be much faster than a linear search through the entire directory.

12.4 ■ Allocation Methods

The direct-access nature of disks allows us flexibility in the implementation of files. In almost every case, many files will be stored on the same disk. The main problem is how to allocate space to these files so that disk space is utilized effectively and files can be accessed quickly. Three major methods of allocating disk space are in wide use: contiguous, linked, and indexed. Each method has advantages and disadvantages. Some systems (such as Data General's RDOS for its Nova line of computers) support all three. More commonly, a system will use one particular method for all files.

12.4.1 Contiguous Allocation

The **contiguous-allocation** method requires each file to occupy a set of contiguous blocks on the disk. Disk addresses define a linear ordering on the disk. With this ordering, assuming that only one job is accessing the disk, accessing block $b + 1$ after block b normally requires no head movement. When head movement is needed (from the last sector of one cylinder to the first sector of the next cylinder), it is only one track. Thus, the number of disk seeks required for accessing contiguously allocated files is minimal, as is seek time when a seek is finally needed. The IBM VM/CMS operating system uses contiguous allocation because it provides such good performance.

Contiguous allocation of a file is defined by the disk address and length (in block units) of the first block. If the file is n blocks long and starts at location b, then it occupies blocks $b, b + 1, b + 2, ..., b + n - 1$. The directory entry for each file indicates the address of the starting block and the length of the area allocated for this file (Figure 12.5).

Accessing a file that has been allocated contiguously is easy. For sequential access, the file system remembers the disk address of the last block referenced and, when necessary, reads the next block. For direct access to block i of a file that starts at block b, we can immediately access block $b + i$. Thus, both sequential and direct access can be supported by contiguous allocation.

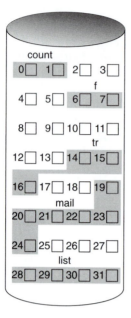

Figure 12.5   Contiguous allocation of disk space.

Contiguous allocation has some problems, however. One difficulty is finding space for a new file. The implementation of the free-space-management system, discussed in Section 12.5, determines how this task is accomplished. Any management system can be used, but some are slower than others.

The contiguous disk-space-allocation problem can be seen to be a particular application of the general **dynamic storage-allocation** problem discussed in Section 9.3, which is how to satisfy a request of size n from a list of free holes. First fit and best fit are the most common strategies used to select a free hole from the set of available holes. Simulations have shown that both first fit and best fit are more efficient than worst fit in terms of both time and storage utilization. Neither first fit nor best fit is clearly best in terms of storage utilization, but first fit is generally faster.

These algorithms suffer from the problem of **external fragmentation**. As files are allocated and deleted, the free disk space is broken into little pieces. External fragmentation exists whenever free space is broken into chunks. It becomes a problem when the largest contiguous chunk is insufficient for a request; storage is fragmented into a number of holes, no one of which is large enough to store the data. Depending on the total amount of disk storage and the average file size, external fragmentation may be a minor or a major problem.

Some older microcomputer systems used contiguous allocation on floppy disks. To prevent loss of significant amounts of disk space to external fragmentation, the user had to run a repacking routine that copied the entire file system onto another floppy disk or onto a tape. The original floppy disk was then freed completely, creating one large contiguous free space. The routine then copied the files back onto the floppy disk by allocating contiguous space from this one large hole. This scheme effectively **compacts** all free space into one contiguous space, solving the fragmentation problem. The cost of this compaction is time. The time cost is particularly severe for large hard disks that use contiguous allocation, where compacting all the space may take hours and may be necessary on a weekly basis. During this **down time**, normal system operation generally cannot be permitted, so such compaction is avoided at all costs on production machines.

Another problem with contiguous allocation is determining how much space is needed for a file. When the file is created, the total amount of space it will need must be found and allocated. How does the creator (program or person) know the size of the file to be created? In some cases, this determination may be fairly simple (copying an existing file, for example); in general, however, the size of an output file may be difficult to estimate.

If we allocate too little space to a file, we may find that the file cannot be extended. Especially with a best-fit allocation strategy, the space on both sides of the file may be in use. Hence, we cannot make the file larger in place. Two possibilities then exist. First, the user program can be terminated, with an appropriate error message. The user must then allocate more space and run the program again. These repeated runs may be costly. To prevent them, the user will normally overestimate the amount of space needed, resulting in considerable wasted space.

The other possibility is to find a larger hole, copy the contents of the file to the new space, and release the previous space. This series of actions may be repeated as long as space exists, although it can be time-consuming. However, in this case, the user never needs to be informed explicitly about what is happening; the system continues despite the problem, although more and more slowly.

Even if the total amount of space needed for a file is known in advance, preallocation may be inefficient. A file that grows slowly over a long period (months or years) must be allocated enough space for its final size, even though much of that space may be unused for a long time. The file, therefore, has a large amount of internal fragmentation.

To minimize these drawbacks, some operating systems use a modified contiguous-allocation scheme, in which a contiguous chunk of space is allocated initially, and then, when that amount is not large enough, another chunk of contiguous space, an **extent**, is added to the initial allocation. The location of a file's blocks is then recorded as a location and a block count, plus a link to the first block of the next extent. On some systems, the owner of the file can set the extent size, but this setting results in inefficiencies if the owner is incorrect. Internal fragmentation can still be a problem if the extents are too large, and external fragmentation can be a problem as extents of varying sizes are allocated and deallocated. The commercial Veritas File System uses extents to optimize performance. It is a high-performance replacement for the standard UFS.

12.4.2 Linked Allocation

Linked allocation solves all problems of contiguous allocation. With linked allocation, each file is a linked list of disk blocks; the disk blocks may be scattered anywhere on the disk. The directory contains a pointer to the first and last blocks of the file. For example, a file of five blocks might start at block 9, continue at block 16, then block 1, block 10, and finally block 25 (Figure 12.6). Each block contains a pointer to the next block. These pointers are not made available to the user. Thus, if each block is 512 bytes, and a disk address (the pointer) requires 4 bytes, then the user sees blocks of 508 bytes.

To create a new file, we simply create a new entry in the directory. With linked allocation, each directory entry has a pointer to the first disk block of the file. This pointer is initialized to *nil* (the end-of-list pointer value) to signify an empty file. The size field is also set to 0. A write to the file causes a free block to be found via the free-space-management system, and this new block is then written to, and is linked to the end of the file. To read a file, we simply read blocks by following the pointers from block to block. There is no external fragmentation with linked allocation, and any free block on the free-space list

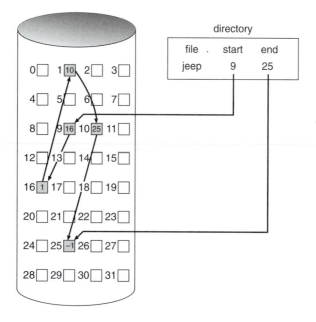

Figure 12.6   Linked allocation of disk space.

can be used to satisfy a request. The size of a file does not need to be declared when that file is created. A file can continue to grow as long as free blocks are available. Consequently, it is never necessary to compact disk space.

Linked allocation does have disadvantages, however. The major problem is that it can be used effectively only for sequential-access files. To find the ith block of a file, we must start at the beginning of that file, and follow the pointers until we get to the ith block. Each access to a pointer requires a disk read, and sometimes a disk seek. Consequently, it is inefficient to support a direct-access capability for linked allocation files.

Another disadvantage to linked allocation is the space required for the pointers. If a pointer requires 4 bytes out of a 512-byte block, then 0.78 percent of the disk is being used for pointers, rather than for information. Each file requires slightly more space than it would otherwise.

The usual solution to this problem is to collect blocks into multiples, called **clusters**, and to allocate the clusters rather than blocks. For instance, the file system may define a cluster as 4 blocks, and operate on the disk in only cluster units. Pointers then use a much smaller percentage of the file's disk space. This method allows the logical-to-physical block mapping to remain simple, but improves disk throughput (fewer disk head seeks) and decreases the space needed for block allocation and free-list management. The cost of this approach is an increase in internal fragmentation, because more space is wasted if a cluster is partially full than when a block is partially full. Clusters can be used to improve the disk-access time for many other algorithms, so they are used in most operating systems.

Yet another problem of linked allocation is reliability. Since the files are linked together by pointers scattered all over the disk, consider what would happen if a pointer were lost or damaged. A bug in the operating-system software or a disk hardware failure might result in picking up the wrong pointer. This error could result in linking into the free-space list or into another file. Partial solutions are to use doubly linked lists or to store the file name and relative block number in each block; however, these schemes require even more overhead for each file.

An important variation on the linked allocation method is the use of a **file-allocation table (FAT)**. This simple but efficient method of disk-space allocation is used by the MS-DOS and OS/2 operating systems. A section of disk at the beginning of each partition is set aside to contain the table. The table has one entry for each disk block, and is indexed by block number. The FAT is used much as is a linked list. The directory entry contains the block number of the first block of the file. The table entry indexed by that block number then contains the block number of the next block in the file. This chain continues until the last block, which has a special end-of-file value as the table entry. Unused blocks are indicated by a 0 table value. Allocating a new block to a file is a simple matter of finding the first 0-valued table entry, and replacing the previous end-of-file value with the address of the new block. The 0 is then

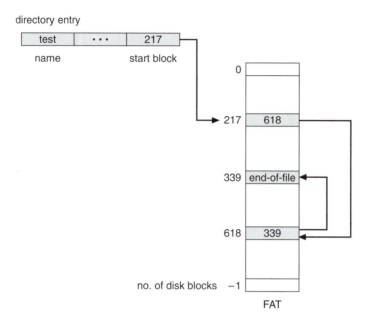

Figure 12.7   File-allocation table.

replaced with the end-of-file value. An illustrative example is the FAT structure of Figure 12.7 for a file consisting of disk blocks 217, 618, and 339.

The FAT allocation scheme can result in a significant number of disk head seeks, unless the FAT is cached. The disk head must move to the start of the partition to read the FAT and find the location of the block in question, then move to the location of the block itself. In the worst case, both moves occur for each of the blocks. A benefit is that random access time is improved, because the disk head can find the location of any block by reading the information in the FAT.

12.4.3 Indexed Allocation

Linked allocation solves the external-fragmentation and size-declaration problems of contiguous allocation. However, in the absence of a FAT, linked allocation cannot support efficient direct access, since the pointers to the blocks are scattered with the blocks themselves all over the disk and need to be retrieved in order. **Indexed allocation** solves this problem by bringing all the pointers together into one location: the **index block**.

Each file has its own index block, which is an array of disk-block addresses. The *i*th entry in the index block points to the *i*th block of the file. The directory contains the address of the index block (Figure 12.8). To read the *i*th block, we

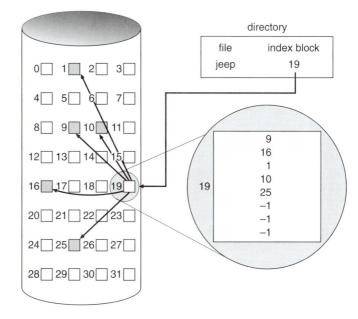

Figure 12.8   Indexed allocation of disk space.

use the pointer in the ith index-block entry to find and read the desired block. This scheme is similar to the paging scheme described in Chapter 9.

When the file is created, all pointers in the index block are set to *nil*. When the ith block is first written, a block is obtained from the free-space manager, and its address is put in the ith index-block entry.

Indexed allocation supports direct access, without suffering from external fragmentation, because any free block on the disk may satisfy a request for more space.

Indexed allocation does suffer from wasted space. The pointer overhead of the index block is generally greater than the pointer overhead of linked allocation. Consider a common case in which we have a file of only one or two blocks. With linked allocation, we lose the space of only one pointer per block (one or two pointers). With indexed allocation, an entire index block must be allocated, even if only one or two pointers will be non-*nil*.

This point raises the question of how large the index block should be. Every file must have an index block, so we want the index block to be as small as possible. If the index block is too small, however, it will not be able to hold enough pointers for a large file, and a mechanism will have to be available to deal with this issue:

- **Linked scheme:** An index block is normally one disk block. Thus, it can be read and written directly by itself. To allow for large files, we may link together several index blocks. For example, an index block might contain a small header giving the name of the file, and a set of the first 100 disk-block addresses. The next address (the last word in the index block) is *nil* (for a small file) or is a pointer to another index block (for a large file).

- **Multilevel index:** A variant of the linked representation is to use a first-level index block to point to a set of second-level index blocks, which in turn point to the file blocks. To access a block, the operating system uses the first-level index to find a second-level index block, and that block to find the desired data block. This approach could be continued to a third or fourth level, depending on the desired maximum file size. With 4,096-byte blocks, we could store 1,024 4-byte pointers in an index block. Two levels of indexes allow 1,048,576 data blocks, which allows a file of up to 4 GB.

- **Combined scheme:** Another alternative, used in the UFS, is to keep the first, say, 15 pointers of the index block in the file's inode. The first 12 of these pointers point to **direct blocks**; that is, they contain addresses of blocks that contain data of the file. Thus, the data for small (no more than 12 blocks) files do not need a separate index block. If the block size is 4 KB, then up to 48 KB of data may be accessed directly. The next 3 pointers point to **indirect blocks**. The first indirect block pointer is the address of a **single indirect block**. The single indirect block is an index block, containing not data, but rather the addresses of blocks that do contain data. Then there is a **double indirect block** pointer, which contains the address of a block that contains the addresses of blocks that contain pointers to the actual data blocks. The last pointer would contain the address of a **triple indirect block**. Under this method, the number of blocks that can be allocated to a file exceeds the amount of space addressable by the 4-byte file pointers used by many operating systems. A 32-bit file pointer reaches only 2^{32} bytes, or 4 GB. Many UNIX implementations, including Solaris and IBM's AIX, now support up to 64-bit file pointers. Pointers of this size allow files and file systems to be terabytes in size. An inode is shown in Figure 12.9.

Indexed-allocation schemes suffer from some of the same performance problems as does linked allocation. Specifically, the index blocks can be cached in memory, but the data blocks may be spread all over a partition.

12.4.4 Performance

The allocation methods that we have discussed vary in their storage efficiency and data-block access times. Both are important criteria in selecting the proper method or methods for an operating system to implement.

Before selecting an allocation method, we need to determine how the systems will be used. A system with mostly sequential access should use a method different from that for a system with mostly random access. For any type of access, contiguous allocation requires only one access to get a disk

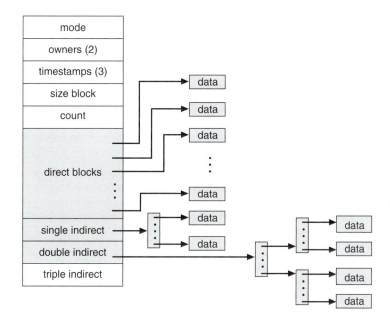

Figure 12.9   The UNIX inode.

block.   Since we can easily keep the initial address of the file in memory, we can calculate immediately the disk address of the ith block (or the next block) and read it directly.

For linked allocation, we can also keep the address of the next block in memory and read it directly. This method is fine for sequential access; for direct access, however, an access to the ith block might require i disk reads. This problem indicates why linked allocation should not be used for an application requiring direct access.

As a result, some systems support direct-access files by using contiguous allocation and sequential access by linked allocation. For these systems, the type of access to be made must be declared when the file is created. A file created for sequential access will be linked and cannot be used for direct access. A file created for direct access will be contiguous and can support both direct access and sequential access, but its maximum length must be declared when it is created. In this case, the operating system must have appropriate data structures and algorithms to support *both* allocation methods. Files can be converted from one type to another by the creation of a new file of the desired type, into which the contents of the old file are copied. The old file may then be deleted, and the new file renamed.

Indexed allocation is more complex. If the index block is already in memory, then the access can be made directly. However, keeping the index block in memory requires considerable space. If this memory space is not available, then we may have to read first the index block and then the desired data block. For a two-level index, two index-block reads might be necessary. For an extremely large file, accessing a block near the end of the file would require reading in all the index blocks to follow the pointer chain before the needed data block finally could be read. Thus, the performance of indexed allocation depends on the index structure, on the size of the file, and on the position of the block desired.

Some systems combine contiguous allocation with indexed allocation by using contiguous allocation for small files (up to three or four blocks), and automatically switching to an indexed allocation if the file grows large. Since most files are small, and contiguous allocation is efficient for small files, average performance can be quite good.

For instance, the version of the UNIX operating system from Sun Microsystems was changed in 1991 to improve performance in the file-system allocation algorithm. The performance measurements indicated that the maximum disk throughput on a typical workstation (12-MIPS SPARCstation1) took 50 percent of the CPU and produced a disk bandwidth of only 1.5 MB per second. To improve performance, Sun made changes to allocate space in clusters of size 56 KB whenever possible. (56 KB was the maximum size of a DMA transfer on Suns at that time.) This allocation reduced external fragmentation, and thus seek and latency times. In addition, the disk-reading routines were optimized to read in these large clusters. The inode structure was left unchanged. These changes, plus the use of read-ahead and free-behind (discussed in Section 12.6.2), resulted in 25 percent less CPU being used for substantially improved throughput.

Many other optimizations are possible and are in use. Given the disparity between CPU and disk speed, it is not unreasonable to add thousands of extra instructions to the operating system to save just a few disk-head movements. Furthermore, this disparity is increasing over time, to the point where hundreds of thousands of instructions reasonably could be used to optimize head movements.

12.5 ■ Free-Space Management

Since disk space is limited, we need to reuse the space from deleted files for new files, if possible. (Write-once optical disks only allow one write to any given sector, and thus such reuse is not physically possible.) To keep track of free disk space, the system maintains a **free-space list**. The free-space list records all *free* disk blocks—those not allocated to some file or directory. To create a file, we search the free-space list for the required amount of space, and allocate that space to the new file. This space is then removed from the free-space list. When a file is deleted, its disk space is added to the free-space list. The free-space list, despite its name, might not be implemented as a list, as we shall discuss.

12.5.1 Bit Vector

Frequently, the free-space list is implemented as a **bit map** or **bit vector**. Each block is represented by 1 bit. If the block is free, the bit is 1; if the block is allocated, the bit is 0.

For example, consider a disk where blocks 2, 3, 4, 5, 8, 9, 10, 11, 12, 13, 17, 18, 25, 26, and 27 are free, and the rest of the blocks are allocated. The free-space bit map would be

$$001111001111110001100000011100000 \ldots$$

The main advantage of this approach is its relative simplicity and efficiency in finding the first free block, or n consecutive free blocks on the disk. Indeed, many computers supply bit-manipulation instructions that can be used effectively for that purpose. For example, the Intel family starting with the 80386 and the Motorola family starting with the 68020 (processors that have powered PCs and Macintosh systems, respectively) have instructions that return the offset in a word of the first bit with the value 1. In fact, the Apple Macintosh operating system uses the bit-vector method to allocate disk space. To find the first free block, the Macintosh operating system checks sequentially each word in the bit map to see whether that value is not 0, since a 0-valued word has all 0 bits and represents a set of allocated blocks. The first non-0 word is scanned for the first 1 bit, which is the location of the first free block. The calculation of the block number is

(number of bits per word) × (number of 0-value words) + offset of first 1 bit.

Again, we see hardware features driving software functionality. Unfortunately, bit vectors are inefficient unless the entire vector is kept in main memory (and is written to disk occasionally for recovery needs). Keeping it in main memory is possible for smaller disks, such as on microcomputers, but not for larger ones. A 1.3-GB disk with 512-byte blocks would need a bit map of over 332 KB to track its free blocks. Clustering the blocks in groups of four reduces this number to over 83 KB per disk.

12.5.2 Linked List

Another approach to free-space management is to link together all the free disk blocks, keeping a pointer to the first free block in a special location on the disk and caching it in memory. This first block contains a pointer to the next free disk block, and so on. In our example (Section 12.5.1), we would keep a pointer to block 2 as the first free block. Block 2 would contain a pointer to block 3, which would point to block 4, which would point to block 5, which would point to block 8, and so on (Figure 12.10). However, this scheme is not efficient; to traverse the list, we must read each block, which requires substantial I/O

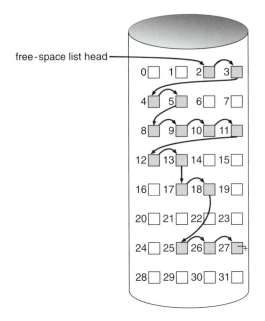

Figure 12.10   Linked free space list on disk.

time. Fortunately, traversing the free list is not a frequent action. Usually, the operating system simply needs a free block so that it can allocate that block to a file, so the first block in the free list is used. The FAT method incorporates free-block accounting into the allocation data structure. No separate method is needed.

12.5.3 Grouping

A modification of the free-list approach is to store the addresses of n free blocks in the first free block. The first $n-1$ of these blocks are actually free. The last block contains the addresses of another n free blocks, and so on. The importance of this implementation is that the addresses of a large number of free blocks can be found quickly, unlike in the standard linked-list approach.

12.5.4 Counting

Another approach is to take advantage of the fact that, generally, several contiguous blocks may be allocated or freed simultaneously, particularly when space is allocated with the contiguous-allocation algorithm or through clustering. Thus, rather than keeping a list of n free disk addresses, we can keep the address of the first free block and the number n of free contiguous blocks that follow the first block. Each entry in the free-space list then consists of a disk address and a count. Although each entry requires more space than would a simple disk address, the overall list will be shorter, as long as the count is generally greater than 1.

12.6 ■ Efficiency and Performance

Now that we have discussed the block-allocation and directory-management options, we can further consider their effect on performance and efficient disk use. Disks tend to be a major bottleneck in system performance, since they are the slowest main computer component. In this section, we discuss a variety of techniques used to improve the efficiency and performance of secondary storage.

12.6.1 Efficiency

The efficient use of disk space is heavily dependent on the disk allocation and directory algorithms in use. For instance, UNIX inodes are preallocated on a partition. Even an "empty" disk has a percentage of its space lost to inodes. However, by preallocating the inodes and spreading them across the partition, we improve the file system's performance. This improved performance is a result of the UNIX allocation and free-space algorithms, which try to keep a file's data blocks near that file's inode block to reduce seek time.

As another example, let us reconsider the clustering scheme discussed in Section 12.4, which aids in file-seek and file-transfer performance at the cost of internal fragmentation. To reduce this fragmentation, BSD UNIX varies the cluster size as a file grows. Large clusters are used where they can be filled, and small clusters are used for small files and the last cluster of a file. This system is described in Appendix A.

The types of data normally kept in a file's directory (or inode) entry also require consideration. Commonly, a "last write date" is recorded to supply information to the user and to determine whether the file needs to be backed up. Some systems also keep a "last access date," so that a user can determine when the file was last read. The result of keeping this information is that, whenever the file is read, a field in the directory structure must be written to. This change requires the block to be read into memory, a section changed, and the block written back out to disk, because operations on disks occur only in block (or cluster) chunks. So, any time a file is opened for reading, its directory entry must be read and written as well. This requirement can be inefficient for frequently accessed files, so we must weigh its benefit against its performance cost when designing a file system. Generally, *every* data item associated with a file needs to be considered for its effect on efficiency and performance.

As an example, consider how efficiency is affected by the size of the pointers used to access data. Most systems use either 16- or 32-bit pointers throughout the operating system. These pointer sizes limit the length of a file to either 2^{16} (64 KB) or 2^{32} bytes (4 GB). Some systems implement 64-bit pointers to increase this limit to 2^{64} bytes, which is a very large number indeed. However, 64-bit pointers take more space to store, and in turn make the allocation and free-space-management methods (linked lists, indexes, and so on) use more disk space.

One of the difficulties in choosing a pointer size, or indeed any fixed allocation size within an operating system, is planning for the effects of changing technology. Consider that the IBM PC XT had a 10-MB hard drive and an MS-DOS file system that could support only 32 MB. (Each FAT entry was 12 bits, pointing to an 8-KB cluster.) As disk capacities increased, larger disks had to be split into 32-MB partitions, because the file system could not track blocks beyond 32 MB. As hard disks of over 100-MB capacities became common, the disk data structures and algorithms in MS-DOS had to be modified to allow larger file systems. (Each FAT entry was expanded to 16 bits, and later to 32 bits.) The initial file-system decisions were made for efficiency reasons; however, with the advent of MS-DOS Version 4, millions of computer users were inconvenienced when they had to switch to the new, larger file system.

As another example, consider the evolution of Sun's Solaris operating system. Originally, many data structures were of fixed lengths, allocated at system startup. These structures included the process table and the open-file table. When the process table became full, no more processes could be created. When the file table became full, no more files could be opened. The system would fail to provide services to the users. These table sizes could be increased only by recompiling the kernel and rebooting the system. Since the release of Solaris 2, almost all kernel structures are allocated dynamically, eliminating these artificial limits on system performance. Of course, the algorithms that manipulate these tables are more complicated, and the operating system is a little slower because it must dynamically allocate and deallocate table entries, but that price is the usual one for more general functionality.

12.6.2 Performance

Once the basic file-system algorithms are selected, we can still improve performance in several ways. As noted in Chapter 2, most disk controllers include local memory to form an on-board **cache** that is sufficiently large to store entire tracks at a time. Once a seek is performed, the track is read into the disk cache starting at the sector under the disk head (alleviating latency time). The disk controller then transfers any sector requests to the operating system. Once blocks make it from the disk controller into main memory, the operating system may cache the blocks there.

Some systems maintain a separate section of main memory for a **disk cache**, where blocks are kept under the assumption that they will be used again shortly. Other systems cache file data using a **page cache**. The page cache uses virtual-memory techniques to cache file data as pages rather than as file-system-oriented blocks. Caching file data using virtual addresses is far more

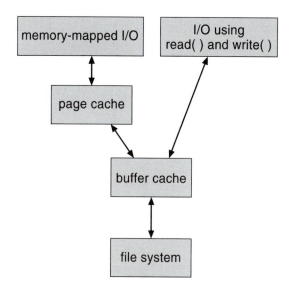

Figure 12.11   I/O without a unified buffer cache.

efficient than caching through physical disk blocks. Several systems, including Solaris, some new Linux releases, and Windows NT and 2000, use page caching to cache both process pages and file data. This is known as **unified virtual memory**. Solaris uses both a block cache and a page cache. The block cache is used for file-system metadata (such as inodes) and the page cache is used for all file-system data.

Some versions of UNIX provide a **unified buffer cache**. Consider the two alternatives of opening and accessing a file. One approach is to use memory mapping (Section 10.7), the second is to use the standard system calls read and write. Without a unified buffer cache, we have a situation similar to Figure 12.11. In this instance, the read and write system calls go through the buffer cache. The memory-mapping call requires using two caches—the page cache and buffer cache. A memory mapping proceeds by reading in disk blocks from the file system and storing them in the buffer cache. Because the virtual memory system cannot interface with the buffer cache, the contents of the file in the buffer cache must be copied into the page cache. This situation is known as **double caching** and requires caching file-system data twice. Not only is it wasteful of memory, but it wastes significant CPU and I/O cycles due to the extra data movement within system memory. Also, inconsistencies between the two caches can result in corrupt files. By providing a unified buffer cache, both memory mapping and the read and write system calls use the same page cache. This has the benefit of avoiding double caching and it allows the virtual memory system to manage file-system data. The unified buffer cache is shown in Figure 12.12.

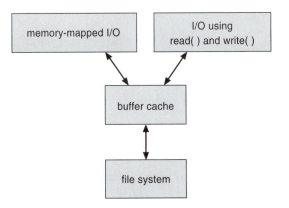

Figure 12.12   I/O using a unified buffer cache.

Regardless of whether we are caching disk blocks or pages, LRU seems a reasonable general-purpose algorithm for block or page replacement. However, the evolution of the Solaris page-caching algorithms reveals the difficulty in choosing an algorithm. Solaris allows processes and the page cache to share unused memory. Prior to Solaris 2.5.1, there was no distinction between allocating pages to a process or the page cache. As a result, a system performing many I/O operations uses most of the available memory for caching pages. Because of the high rates of I/O, the page scanner (Section 10.9.2) reclaims pages from processes—rather than the page cache—when free memory runs low. Solaris 2.6 and Solaris 7 optionally implemented *priority paging*, in which the page scanner gives priority to process pages over the page cache. Solaris 8 added a fixed limit between process pages and file-system page cache, preventing either from forcing the other out of memory.

The page cache, the file system, and the disk drivers have some interesting interactions. When data are written to a disk file, the pages are buffered in the cache, and the disk driver sorts its output queue according to disk address. These two actions allow the disk driver to minimize disk-head seeks and to write data at times optimized for disk rotation. Unless synchronous writes are required, a process writing to disk simply writes into the cache, and the system asynchronously writes the data to disk when convenient. The user process sees very fast writes. When data are read from a disk file, the block I/O system does some read-ahead; however, writes are much nearer to asynchronous than are reads. Thus, output to the disk through the file system is often faster than is input for large transfers, counter to intuition.

Synchronous writes occur in the order in which the disk subsystem receives them, and the writes are not buffered. Thus the calling routine must wait for the data to reach the disk drive before it can proceed. **Asynchronous writes** are done the majority of the time. In an asynchronous write the data is stored in the cache and returns control to the caller. Metadata writes, among others, can be synchronous. Operating systems frequently include a flag in the open system call to allow a process to request that writes be performed synchronously. For example, databases use this feature for atomic transactions, to assure that data reaches stable storage in the required order.

Some systems optimize their page cache by using different replacement algorithms, depending on the access type of the file. A file being read or written sequentially should not have its pages replaced in LRU order, because the most recently used page will be used last, or perhaps never again. Instead, sequential access may be optimized by techniques known as free-behind and read-ahead. **Free-behind** removes a page from the buffer as soon as the next page is requested. The previous pages are not likely to be used again and waste buffer space. With **read-ahead**, a requested page and several subsequent pages are read and cached. These pages are likely to be requested after the current page is processed. Retrieving this data from the disk in one transfer and caching it saves a considerable amount of time. A track cache on the controller does not eliminate the need for read-ahead on a multiprogrammed system, because of the high latency and overhead of many small transfers from the track cache to main memory.

Another method of using main memory to improve performance is common on PCs. A section of memory is set aside and treated as a **virtual disk** (or **RAM disk**). In this case, a RAM-disk device driver accepts all the standard disk operations but performs those operations on the memory section, instead of on a disk. All disk operations can then be executed on this RAM disk and, except for the lightning-fast speed, users will not notice a difference. Unfortunately, RAM disks are useful only for temporary storage, since a power failure or a reboot of the system will usually erase them. Commonly, temporary files such as intermediate compiler files are stored there.

The difference between a RAM disk and a disk cache is that the contents of the RAM disk are totally user controlled, whereas those of the disk cache are under the control of the operating system. For instance, a RAM disk will stay empty until the user (or programs, at a user's direction) creates files there. Figure 12.13 shows the possible caching locations in a system.

12.7 ■ Recovery

Since files and directories are kept both in main memory and on disk, care must taken to ensure that system failure does not result in loss of data or in data inconsistency.

12.7.1 Consistency Checking

As discussed in Section 12.3, part of the directory information is kept in main memory (or cache) to speed up access. The directory information in main

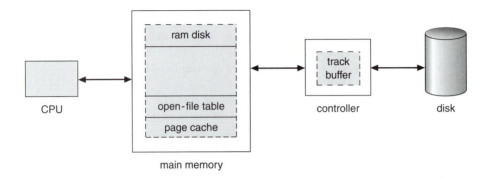

Figure 12.13   Various disk-caching locations.

memory is generally more up to date than is the corresponding information on the disk, because the write of cached directory information to disk does not necessarily occur as soon as the update takes place.

Consider the possible effect of a computer crash. In this case, the table of opened files is generally lost, and with it any changes in the directories of opened files. This event can leave the file system in an inconsistent state: The actual state of some files is not as described in the directory structure. Frequently, a special program is run at reboot time to check for and correct disk inconsistencies.

The **consistency checker** compares the data in the directory structure with the data blocks on disk, and tries to fix any inconsistencies it finds. The allocation and free-space-management algorithms dictate what types of problems the checker can find, and how successful it will be in fixing them. For instance, if linked allocation is used and there is a link from any block to its next block, then the entire file can be reconstructed from the data blocks, and the directory structure can be recreated. The loss of a directory entry on an indexed allocation system could be disastrous, because the data blocks have no knowledge of one another. For this reason, UNIX caches directory entries for reads, but any data write that results in space allocation, or other metadata changes, is done synchronously, before the corresponding data blocks are written.

12.7.2 Backup and Restore

Because magnetic disks sometimes fail, care must be taken to ensure that the data are not lost forever. To this end, system programs can be used to **back up** data from disk to another storage device, such as a floppy disk, magnetic tape, or optical disk. Recovery from the loss of an individual file, or of an entire disk, may then be a matter of **restoring** the data from backup.

To minimize the copying needed, we can use information from each file's directory entry. For instance, if the backup program knows when the last backup of a file was done, and the file's last write date in the directory indicates that the file has not changed since that date, then the file does not need to be copied again. A typical backup schedule may then be as follows:

- **Day 1:** Copy to a backup medium all files from the disk. This is called a **full backup**.

- **Day 2:** Copy to another medium all files changed since day 1. This is an **incremental backup**.

- **Day 3:** Copy to another medium all files changed since day 2.

  .
  .
  .

- **Day N:** Copy to another medium all files changed since day $N-1$. Then go back to Day 1.

The new cycle can have its backup written over the previous set, or onto a new set of backup media. In this manner, we can restore an entire disk by starting restores with the full backup, and continuing through each of the incremental backups. Of course, the larger N is, the more tapes or disks need to be read for a complete restore. An added advantage of this backup cycle is that we can restore any file accidentally deleted during the cycle by retrieving the deleted file from the backup of the previous day. The length of the cycle is a compromise between the amount of backup medium needed and the number of days back from which a restore can be done.

A user may notice that a particular file is missing or corrupted long after the damage was done. For this reason, we usually plan to take a full backup from time to time that will be saved "forever," rather than reusing that backup medium. It is a good idea to store these permanent backups far away from the regular backups to protect against hazard, such as a fire that destroys the computer and all the backups too. And if the backup cycle reuses media, one must take care not to reuse the media too many times—if the media wear out, it might not be possible to restore any data from the backups.

12.8 ■ Log-Structured File System

Frequently in computer science, algorithms and technologies transition from their original use to other applicable areas. Such is the case with the database log-based-recovery algorithms described in Section 7.10.2. These logging algorithms have been applied successfully to the problem of consistency checking. The resulting implementations are known as **log-based transaction-oriented** (or **journaling**) file systems.

Recall that on-disk file-system data structures—such as the directory structures, free-block pointers, free FCB pointers—can become inconsistent due to a system crash. Before the use of log-based techniques in operating systems, changes were usually applied to these structures in place. A typical operation, such as file create, can involve many structural changes within the file system on the disk. Directory structures are modified, FCBs are allocated, data blocks are allocated, and the free counts for all of these blocks are decreased. Those changes can be interrupted by a crash, with the result that the structures are inconsistent. For example, the free FCB count might indicate that an FCB had been allocated, but the directory structure might not point to the FCB. The FCB would be lost were it not for the consistency-check phase.

There are several problems with the approach of allowing the structures to break and repairing them on recovery. One is that the inconsistency may be irreparable. The consistency check may not be able to recover the structures, with the resulting loss of files and even entire directories. Consistency checking can require human intervention to resolve conflicts, and that is inconvenient if no human is available. The system can remain unavailable until the human tells the system how to proceed. Consistency checking also takes system and clock time. Terabytes of data can take hours of clock time to check.

The solution to this problem is to apply log-based-recovery techniques to file-system metadata updates. NTFS and the Veritas File System both use this method, and it is an option to UFS on Solaris 7 and beyond. In fact, it is becoming common on many operating systems.

Fundamentally, all metadata changes are written sequentially to a log. Each set of operations that perform a specific task is a **transaction**. Once the changes are written to this log, they are considered to be committed, and the system call can return to the user process, allowing it to continue execution. Meanwhile, these log entries are replayed across the actual file-system structures. As the changes are made, a pointer is updated to indicate which actions have completed and which are still incomplete. When an entire committed transaction is completed, it is removed from the log file, which is actually a circular buffer. The log may be in a separate section of the file system, or could even be on a separate disk spindle. It is more efficient, but more complex, to have it under separate read/write heads, thereby decreasing head contention and seek times.

If the system crashes, there will zero or more transactions in the log file. Those transactions were never completed to the file system even though they were committed by the operating system, so they must be completed. The transactions can be executed from the pointer until the work is complete, and the file-system structures remain consistent. The only problem occurs when a transaction has been aborted. That is, it was not committed before the system crashed. Any changes from those transactions that were applied to the file system must be undone, again preserving the consistency of the file system.

This recovery is all that is needed after a crash, eliminating all problems with consistency checking.

A side benefit of using logging on disk metadata updates is that those updates proceed much faster than when they are applied directly to the on-disk data structures. The reason for this improvement is found in the performance advantage of sequential I/O over random I/O. The costly synchronous random metadata writes are turned into much less costly synchronous sequential writes to the log-structured file systems logging area. Those changes in turn are replayed asynchronously via random writes to the appropriate structures. The overall result is a significant gain in performance of metadata-oriented operations, such as file creation and deletion.

12.9 ■ NFS

Network file systems are commonplace. They typically integrate with the overall directory structure and interface of the client system. NFS is a good example of a widely used, well-implemented client–server network file system. Here, we use it as an example to explore the implementation details of network file systems.

NFS is both an implementation and a specification of a software system for accessing remote files across LANs (or even WANs). NFS is part of ONC+, which most UNIX vendors and some PC operating systems are supporting. The implementation described here is part of the Solaris operating system, which is a modified version of UNIX SVR4, running on Sun workstations and other hardware. It uses either the TCP or UDP/IP protocol (depending on the interconnecting network). The specification and the implementation are intertwined in our description of NFS. Whenever detail is needed, we refer to the Sun implementation; whenever the description is general, it applies to the specification also.

12.9.1 Overview

NFS views a set of interconnected workstations as a set of independent machines with independent file systems. The goal is to allow some degree of sharing among these file systems (on explicit request) in a transparent manner. Sharing is based on a client–server relationship. A machine may be, and often is, both a client and a server. Sharing is allowed between any pair of machines, rather than with only dedicated server machines. To ensure machine independence, sharing of a remote file system affects only the client machine and no other machine.

So that a remote directory will be accessible in a transparent manner from a particular machine—say, from *M1*—a client of that machine has to carry out a mount operation first. The semantics of the operation are that a remote directory is mounted over a directory of a local file system. Once the mount

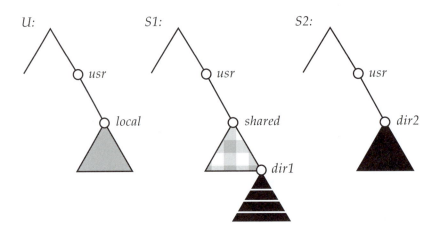

Figure 12.14   Three independent file systems.

operation is completed, the mounted directory looks like an integral subtree of the local file system, replacing the subtree descending from the local directory. The local directory becomes the name of the root of the newly mounted directory. Specification of the remote directory as an argument for the mount operation is done in a non-transparent manner; the location (or host name) of the remote directory has to be provided. However, from then on, users on machine *M1* can access files in the remote directory in a totally transparent manner.

To illustrate file mounting, consider the file system depicted in Figure 12.14, where the triangles represent subtrees of directories that are of interest. The figure shows three independent file systems of machines named *U*, *S1*, and *S2*. At this point, at each machine, only the local files can be accessed. In Figure 12.15(a), the effects of the mounting of *S1:/usr/shared* over *U:/usr/local* are shown. This figure depicts the view users on *U* have of their file system. Observe that they can access any file within the *dir1* directory, for instance, using the prefix */usr/local/dir1* on *U* after the mount is complete. The original directory */usr/local* on that machine is no longer visible.

Subject to access-rights accreditation, potentially any file system, or any directory within a file system, can be mounted remotely on top of any local directory. Diskless workstations can even mount their own roots from servers.

Cascading mounts are also permitted in some NFS implementations. That is, a file system can be mounted over another file system that is remotely mounted, not local. A machine is affected by only those mounts that it has itself invoked.

By mounting a remote file system, the client does not gain access to other file systems that were, by chance, mounted over the former file system. Thus, the mount mechanism does not exhibit a transitivity property. In Figure 12.15(b), we illustrate cascading mounts by continuing our previous exam-

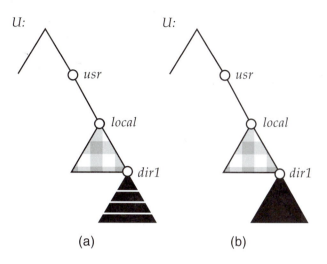

Figure 12.15 Mounting in NFS. (a) Mounts. (b) Cascading mounts.

ple. The figure shows the result of mounting *S2:/usr/dir2* over *U:/usr/local/dir1*, which is already remotely mounted from *S1*. Users can access files within *dir2* on *U* using the prefix */usr/local/dir1*. If a shared file system is mounted over a user's home directories on all machines in a network, a user can log into any workstation and get his home environment. This property permits **user mobility**.

One of the design goals of NFS was to operate in a heterogeneous environment of different machines, operating systems, and network architectures. The NFS specification is independent of these media and thus encourages other implementations. This independence is achieved through the use of RPC primitives built on top of an External Data Representation (XDR) protocol used between two implementation-independent interfaces. Hence, if the system consists of heterogeneous machines and file systems that are properly interfaced to NFS, file systems of different types can be mounted both locally and remotely.

The NFS specification distinguishes between the services provided by a mount mechanism and the actual remote-file-access services. Accordingly, two separate protocols are specified for these services: a mount protocol, and a protocol for remote file accesses, the **NFS protocol**. The protocols are specified as sets of RPCs. These RPCs are the building blocks used to implement transparent remote file access.

12.9.2 The Mount Protocol

The **mount protocol** establishes the initial logical connection between a server and a client. In Sun's implementation, each machine has a server process, outside the kernel, performing the protocol functions.

A mount operation includes the name of the remote directory to be mounted and the name of the server machine storing it. The mount request is mapped to the corresponding RPC and is forwarded to the mount server running on the specific server machine. The server maintains an **export list** —the */etc/dfs/dfstab* in Solaris, which can be edited only by a superuser—which specifies local file systems that it exports for mounting, along with names of machines that are permitted to mount them. The specification can also include access rights, such as read only. To simplify the maintenance of export lists and mount tables, a distributed naming scheme can be used to hold this information and make it available to appropriate clients.

Recall that any directory within an exported file system can be mounted remotely by an accredited machine. Hence, a component unit is such a directory. When the server receives a mount request that conforms to its export list, it returns to the client a **file handle** that serves as the key for further accesses to files within the mounted file system. The file handle contains all the information that the server needs to distinguish an individual file it stores. In UNIX terms, the file handle consists of a file-system identifier and an inode number to identify the exact mounted directory within the exported file system.

The server also maintains a list of the client machines and the corresponding currently mounted directories. This list is used mainly for administrative purposes—for instance, for notifying all clients that the server is going down. Addition and deletion of entries in this list are the only ways that the server state can be affected by the mount protocol.

Usually, a system has a static mounting preconfiguration that is established at boot time (*/etc/vfstab* in Solaris); however, this layout can be modified. In addition to the actual mount procedure, the mount protocol includes several other procedures, such as unmount and return export list.

12.9.3 The NFS Protocol

The NFS protocol provides a set of RPCs for remote file operations. The procedures support the following operations:

- Searching for a file within a directory

- Reading a set of directory entries

- Manipulating links and directories

- Accessing file attributes

- Reading and writing files

These procedures can be invoked only after a file handle for the remotely mounted directory has been established.

The omission of open and close operations is intentional. A prominent feature of NFS servers is that they are *stateless*. Servers do not maintain information about their clients from one access to another. No parallels to UNIX's open-files table or file structures exist on the server side. Consequently, each request has to provide a full set of arguments, including a unique file identifier and an absolute offset inside the file for the appropriate operations. The resulting design is robust; no special measures need to be taken to recover a server after a crash. File operations need to be idempotent for this purpose. Every NFS request has a sequence number, allowing the server to determine if a request is duplicated or if any are missing.

Maintaining the list of clients that we mentioned seems to violate the statelessness of the server. However, this list is not essential for the correct operation of the client or the server, and hence it does not need to be restored after a server crash. Consequently, it might include inconsistent data and is treated as only a hint.

A further implication of the stateless-server philosophy and a result of the synchrony of an RPC is that modified data (including indirection and status blocks) must be committed to the server's disk before results are returned to the client. That is, a client can cache write blocks, but when it flushes them to the server, it assumes that they have reached the server's disks. The server must write all NFS data synchronously. Thus, a server crash and recovery will be invisible to a client; all blocks that the server is managing for the client will be intact. The consequent performance penalty can be large, because the advantages of caching are lost. Performance can be increased by using storage with its own nonvolatile cache (usually battery-backed-up memory). The disk controller acknowledges the disk write when the write is stored in the nonvolatile cache. In essence the host sees a very fast synchronous write. These blocks remain intact even after system crash, and are written from this stable storage to disk periodically.

A single NFS write procedure call is guaranteed to be atomic, and also is not intermixed with other write calls to the same file. The NFS protocol, however, does not provide concurrency-control mechanisms. A write system call may be broken down into several RPC writes, because each NFS write or read call can contain up to 8 KB of data and UDP packets are limited to 1,500 bytes. As a result, two users writing to the same remote file may get their data intermixed. The claim is that, because lock management is inherently stateful, a service outside the NFS should provide locking (and Solaris does). Users are advised to coordinate access to shared files using mechanisms outside the scope of NFS.

NFS is integrated into the operating system via a VFS. As an illustration of the architecture, let us trace how an operation on an already open remote file is handled (follow the example in Figure 12.16). The client initiates the operation by a regular system call. The operating-system layer maps this call to a VFS operation on the appropriate vnode. The VFS layer identifies the file as a remote one and invokes the appropriate NFS procedure. An RPC call is made to the

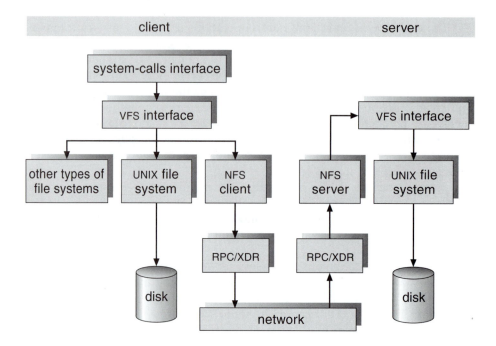

Figure 12.16   Schematic view of the NFS architecture.

NFS service layer at the remote server. This call is reinjected to the VFS layer on the remote system, which finds that it is local and invokes the appropriate file-system operation. This path is retraced to return the result. An advantage of this architecture is that the client and the server are identical; thus, a machine may be a client, or a server, or both.

The actual service on each server is performed by several kernel processes that provide a temporary substitute to a lightweight process (or threads) mechanism.

12.9.4 Path-Name Translation

Path-name translation is done by breaking the path into component names and performing a separate NFS lookup call for every pair of component name and directory vnode. Once a mount point is crossed, every component lookup causes a separate RPC to the server. This expensive path-name-traversal scheme is needed, since each client has a unique layout of its logical name space, dictated by the mounts it performed. It would have been much more efficient to hand a server a path name and to receive a target vnode once a mount point was encountered. At any point, however, there can be another mount point for the particular client of which the stateless server is unaware.

So that lookup is fast, a directory-name-lookup cache on the client side holds the vnodes for remote directory names. This cache speeds up references to files with the same initial path name. The directory cache is discarded when attributes returned from the server do not match the attributes of the cached vnode.

Recall that mounting a remote file system on top of another already mounted remote file system (cascading mount) is allowed in some implementations of NFS. However, a server cannot act as an intermediary between a client and another server. Instead, a client must establish a direct client–server connection with the second server by directly mounting the desired directory. When a client has a cascading mount, more than one server can be involved in a path-name traversal. However, each component lookup is performed between the original client and some server. Therefore, when a client does a lookup on a directory on which the server has mounted a file system, the client sees the underlying directory, instead of the mounted directory.

12.9.5 Remote Operations

With the exception of opening and closing files, there is almost a one-to-one correspondence between the regular UNIX system calls for file operations and the NFS protocol RPCs. Thus, a remote file operation can be translated directly to the corresponding RPC. Conceptually, NFS adheres to the remote-service paradigm, but in practice buffering and caching techniques are employed for the sake of performance. No direct correspondence exists between a remote operation and an RPC. Instead, file blocks and file attributes are fetched by the RPCs and are cached locally. Future remote operations use the cached data, subject to consistency constraints.

There are two caches: the file-attribute (inode-information) cache and the file-blocks cache. On a file open, the kernel checks with the remote server whether to fetch or revalidate the cached attributes. The cached file blocks are used only if the corresponding cached attributes are up to date. The attribute cache is updated whenever new attributes arrive from the server. Cached attributes are, by default, discarded after 60 seconds. Both read-ahead and delayed-write techniques are used between the server and the client. Clients do not free delayed-write blocks until the server confirms that the data have been written to disk. In contrast to the system used in Sprite, delayed-write is retained even when a file is opened concurrently, in conflicting modes. Hence, UNIX semantics are not preserved.

Tuning the system for performance makes it difficult to characterize the consistency semantics of NFS. New files created on a machine may not be visible elsewhere for 30 seconds. It is indeterminate whether writes to a file at one site are visible to other sites that have this file open for reading. New opens of that file observe only the changes that have already been flushed to the server. Thus, NFS provides neither strict emulation of UNIX semantics, nor the session semantics of Andrew. In spite of these drawbacks, the utility and high performance of the mechanism make it the most widely used multivendor distributed system in operation.

12.10 ■ Summary

The file system resides permanently on secondary storage, which is designed to hold a large amount of data permanently. The most common secondary-storage medium is the disk.

Physical disks may be segmented into partitions to control media use and to allow multiple, possibly varying, file systems per spindle. These file systems are mounted onto a logical file system architecture to make them available for use. File systems are often implemented in a layered or modular structure. The lower levels deal with the physical properties of storage devices. Upper levels deal with symbolic file names and logical properties of files. Intermediate levels map the logical file concepts into physical device properties.

Every file-system type can have different structures and algorithms. A VFS layer allows the upper layers to deal with each file-system type uniformly. Even remote file systems can be integrated into the system's directory structure and acted on by standard system calls via the VFS interface.

The various files can be allocated space on the disk in three ways: through contiguous, linked, or indexed allocation. Contiguous allocation can suffer from external fragmentation. Direct access is very inefficient with linked allocation. Indexed allocation may require substantial overhead for its index block. These algorithms can be optimized in many ways. Contiguous space may be enlarged through extents to increase flexibility and to decrease external fragmentation. Indexed allocation can be done in clusters of multiple blocks to increase throughput and to reduce the number of index entries needed. Indexing in large clusters is similar to contiguous allocation with extents.

Free-space allocation methods also influence the efficiency of use of disk space, the performance of the file system, and the reliability of secondary storage. The methods used include bit vectors and linked lists. Optimizations include grouping, counting, and the FAT, which places the linked list in one contiguous area.

The directory-management routines must consider efficiency, performance, and reliability. A hash table is the most frequently used method; it is fast and efficient. Unfortunately, damage to the table or a system crash could result in the directory information not corresponding to the disk's contents. A consistency checker—a systems program such as fsck in UNIX, or chkdsk in MS-DOS—can be used to repair the damage. Operating-system backup tools allow disk data to be copied to tape, to recover from data or even disk loss due to hardware failure, operating system bug, or user error.

Network file systems, such as NFS, use client–server methodology to allow users to access files and directories from remote machines as if they were on local file systems. System calls on the client are translated into network protocols, and retranslated into file-system operations on the server. Networking and multiple-client access create challenges in the areas of data consistency and performance.

Due to the fundamental role that file systems play in system operation, their performance and reliability is crucial. Techniques such as log structures and caching help improve the performance, while log structures and RAID improve reliability.

■ Exercises

12.1 Consider a file currently consisting of 100 blocks. Assume that the FCB (and the index block, in the case of indexed allocation) is already in memory. Calculate how many disk I/O operations are required for contiguous, linked, and indexed (single-level) allocation strategies if, for one block, the following conditions hold. In the contiguous-allocation case, assume that there is no room to grow in the beginning, but room to grow in the end. Assume that the block information to be added is stored in memory.

    a. The block is added at the beginning.

    b. The block is added in the middle.

    c. The block is added at the end.

    d. The block is removed from the beginning.

    e. The block is removed from the middle.

    f. The block is removed from the end.

12.2 Consider a system where free space is kept in a free-space list.

    a. Suppose that the pointer to the free-space list is lost. Can the system reconstruct the free-space list? Explain your answer.

    b. Suggest a scheme to ensure that the pointer is never lost as a result of memory failure.

12.3 What problems could occur if a system allowed a file system to be mounted simultaneously at more than one location?

12.4 Why must the bit map for file allocation be kept on mass storage, rather than in main memory?

12.5 Consider a system that supports the strategies of contiguous, linked, and indexed allocation. What criteria should be used in deciding which strategy is best utilized for a particular file?

12.6 Consider a file system on a disk that has both logical and physical block sizes of 512 bytes. Assume that the information about each file is already in memory. For each of the three allocation strategies (contiguous, linked, and indexed), answer these questions:

   a. How is the logical-to-physical address mapping accomplished in this system? (For the indexed allocation, assume that a file is always less than 512 blocks long.)

   b. If we are currently at logical block 10 (the last block accessed was block 10) and want to access logical block 4, how many physical blocks must be read from the disk?

12.7 One problem with contiguous allocation is that the user must preallocate enough space for each file. If the file grows to be larger than the space allocated for it, special actions must be taken. One solution is to define a file structure consisting of an initial contiguous area (of a specified size). If this area is filled, the operating system automatically defines an overflow area that is linked to the initial contiguous area. If the overflow area is filled, another overflow area is allocated. Compare this implementation of a file with the standard contiguous and linked implementations.

12.8 Fragmentation on a storage device could be eliminated by recompaction of the information. Typical disk devices do not have relocation or base registers (such as are used when memory is to be compacted), so how can we relocate files? Give three reasons why recompacting and relocation of files are often avoided.

12.9 How do caches help improve performance? Why do systems not use more or larger caches if they are so useful?

12.10 In what situations would using memory as a RAM disk be more useful than using it as a disk cache?

12.11 Why is it advantageous to the user for an operating system to dynamically allocate its internal tables? What are the penalties to the operating system for doing so?

12.12 Explain why logging metadata updates ensures recovery of a file system after a file system crash.

12.13 Explain how the VFS layer allows an operating system easily to support multiple types of file systems.

12.14 Consider the following backup scheme:

- **Day 1:** Copy to a backup medium all files from the disk.

- **Day 2:** Copy to another medium all files changed since day 1.

- **Day 3:** Copy to another medium all files changed since day 1.

This contrasts to the schedule given in Section 12.7.2 by having all subsequent backups copy all files modified since the first full backup. What
are the benefits of this system over the one in Section 12.7.2? What are
the drawbacks? Are restore operations made easier or more difficult?
Explain your answer.

Bibliographical Notes

The Apple Macintosh disk-space management scheme was discussed in Apple
[1987] and Apple [1991]. The MS-DOS FAT system was explained in Norton
and Wilton [1988], and the OS/2 description is found in Iacobucci [1988].
These operating systems use the Motorola MC68000 family (Motorola [1989])
and the Intel 8086 (Intel [1985b], Intel [1985a], Intel [1986], Intel [1990]) CPUs,
respectively. IBM allocation methods were described in Deitel [1990]. The
internals of the BSD UNIX system were covered in full in McKusick et al. [1996].
McVoy and Kleiman [1991] presented optimizations to these methods made in
SunOS.

Disk file allocation based on the buddy system was discussed by Koch
[1987]. A file-organization scheme that guarantees retrieval in one access was
discussed by Larson and Kajla [1984].

Disk caching was discussed by McKeon [1985] and Smith [1985]. Caching in
the experimental Sprite operating system was described in Nelson et al. [1988].
General discussions concerning mass-storage technology were offered by Chi
[1982] and Hoagland [1985]. Folk and Zoellick [1987] covered the gamut of file
structures. Silvers [2000] discusses implementing the page cache in the NetBSD
operating system.

The Network File System (NFS) is discussed in Sandberg et al. [1985],
Sandberg [1987], Sun [1990], and Callaghan [2000]. NFS and the UNIX File
System (UFS) are described in Vahalia [1996] and Mauro and McDougall [2001].
The Windows NT file system, NTFS, is described in Solomon [1998]. The Ext2
file system used in Linux is described in Bovet and Cesati [2002].

Part Four

I/O SYSTEMS

The devices that attach to a computer vary in many aspects. Some devices transfer a character or a block of characters at a time. Some can be accessed only sequentially, others randomly. Some transfer data synchronously, others asynchronously. Some are dedicated, some shared. They can be read-only or read–write. They vary greatly in speed. In many ways they are also the slowest major component of the computer.

Because of all this device variation, the operating system needs to provide a wide range of functionality to applications, to allow them to control all aspects of the devices. One key goal of an operating system's I/O subsystem is to provide the simplest interface possible to the rest of the system. Because devices are a performance bottleneck, another key is to optimize I/O for maximum concurrency. We initially describe the myriad variations of I/O devices and the ways in which operating systems control them. Afterwards we discuss the more complicated I/O devices used for secondary and tertiary storage, and we explain the special attention that operating systems must give them.

Chapter 13

I/O SYSTEMS

The two main jobs of a computer are I/O and processing. In many cases, the main job is I/O and the processing is merely incidental. For instance, when we browse a web page or edit a file, our immediate interest is to read or enter some information, not to compute an answer.

The role of the operating system in computer I/O is to manage and control I/O operations and I/O devices. Although related topics appear in other chapters, here we bring together the pieces to paint a complete picture of I/O. First, we describe the basics of I/O hardware, because the nature of the hardware interface places requirements on the internal facilities of the operating system. Next, we discuss the I/O services provided by the operating system, and the embodiment of these services in the application I/O interface. Then, we explain how the operating system bridges the gap between the hardware interface and the application interface. We also discuss the UNIX System V STREAMS mechanism, which enables an application to assemble pipelines of driver code dynamically. Finally, we discuss the performance aspects of I/O, and the principles of operating-system design that improve the I/O performance.

13.1 ■ Overview

The control of devices connected to the computer is a major concern of operating-system designers. Because I/O devices vary so widely in their function and speed (consider a mouse, a hard disk, and a CD-ROM jukebox), a variety of methods is needed to control them. These methods form the *I/O sub-system* of the kernel, which separates the rest of the kernel from the complexity of managing I/O devices.

I/O-device technology exhibits two conflicting trends. On one hand, we see increasing standardization of software and hardware interfaces. This trend helps us to incorporate improved device generations into existing computers and operating systems. On the other hand, we see an increasingly broad variety of I/O devices. Some new devices are so unlike previous devices that it is a challenge to incorporate them into our computers and operating systems. This challenge is met by a combination of hardware and software techniques. The basic I/O hardware elements, such as ports, buses, and device controllers, accommodate a wide variety of I/O devices. To encapsulate the details and oddities of different devices, the kernel of an operating system is structured to use device-driver modules. The **device drivers** present a uniform device-access interface to the I/O subsystem, much as system calls provide a standard interface between the application and the operating system.

13.2 ■ I/O Hardware

Computers operate a great many kinds of devices. Most fit into the general categories of storage devices (disks, tapes), transmission devices (network cards, modems), and human-interface devices (screen, keyboard, mouse). Other devices are more specialized, such as the steering of a military fighter jet or a space shuttle. In these aircraft, a human gives input to the flight computer via a joystick, and the computer sends output commands that cause motors to move rudders, flaps, and thrusters.

Despite the incredible variety of I/O devices, we need only a few concepts to understand how the devices are attached, and how the software can control the hardware.

A device communicates with a computer system by sending signals over a cable or even through the air. The device communicates with the machine via a connection point (or **port**), for example, a serial port. If one or more devices use a common set of wires, the connection is called a *bus*. A **bus** is a set of wires and a rigidly defined protocol that specifies a set of messages that can be sent on the wires. In terms of the electronics, the messages are conveyed by patterns of electrical voltages applied to the wires with defined timings. When device *A* has a cable that plugs into device *B*, and device *B* has a cable that plugs into device *C*, and device *C* plugs into a port on the computer, this arrangement is called a **daisy chain**. A daisy chain usually operates as a bus.

Buses are used widely in computer architecture. Figure 13.1 shows a typical PC bus structure. This figure shows a **PCI bus** (the common PC system bus) that connects the processor–memory subsystem to the fast devices, and an **expansion bus** that connects relatively slow devices such as the keyboard and

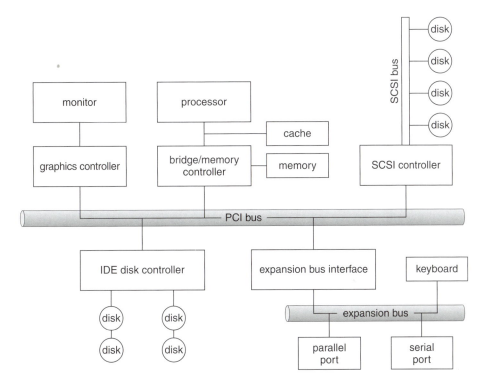

Figure 13.1   A typical PC bus structure.

serial and parallel ports. In the upper-right portion of the figure, four disks are connected together on a SCSI bus plugged into a SCSI controller.

A **controller** is a collection of electronics that can operate a port, a bus, or a device. A serial-port controller is a simple device controller. It is a single chip (or portion of a chip) in the computer that controls the signals on the wires of a serial port. By contrast, a SCSI bus controller is not simple. Because the SCSI protocol is complex, the SCSI bus controller is often implemented as a separate circuit board (or a **host adapter**) that plugs into the computer. It typically contains a processor, microcode, and some private memory to enable it to process the SCSI protocol messages. Some devices have their own built-in controllers. If you look at a disk drive, you will see a circuit board attached to one side. This board is the disk controller. It implements the disk side of the protocol for some kind of connection, SCSI or IDE, for instance. It has microcode and a processor to do many tasks, such as bad-sector mapping, prefetching, buffering, and caching.

How can the processor give commands and data to a controller to accomplish an I/O transfer? The short answer is that the controller has one or more registers for data and control signals. The processor communicates with the controller by reading and writing bit patterns in these registers. One way that this communication can occur is through the use of special I/O instructions that specify the transfer of a byte or word to an I/O port address. The I/O instruction triggers bus lines to select the proper device and to move bits into or out of a device register. Alternatively, the device controller can support **memory-mapped** I/O. In this case, the device-control registers are mapped into the address space of the processor. The CPU executes I/O requests using the standard data-transfer instructions to read and write the device-control registers.

Some systems use both techniques. For instance, PCs use I/O instructions to control some devices and memory-mapped I/O to control others. Figure 13.2 shows the usual PC I/O port addresses. The graphics controller has I/O ports for basic control operations, but the controller has a large memory-mapped region to hold screen contents. The process sends output to the screen by writing data into the memory-mapped region. The controller generates the screen image based on the contents of this memory. This technique is simple to use. Moreover, writing millions of bytes to the graphics memory is faster than issuing millions of I/O instructions. But the ease of writing to a memory-mapped I/O controller is offset by a disadvantage. Because a common type of software fault is a write through an incorrect pointer to an unintended region of memory, a memory-mapped device register is vulnerable to accidental modification. Of course, protected memory helps to reduce this risk.

An I/O port typically consists of four registers, called the *status, control, data-in,* and *data-out* registers.

I/O address range (hexadecimal)	device
000-00F	DMA controller
020-021	interrupt controller
040-043	timer
200-20F	game controller
2F8-2FF	serial port (secondary)
320-32F	hard-disk controller
378-37F	parallel port
3D0-3DF	graphics controller
3F0-3F7	diskette-drive controller
3F8-3FF	serial port (primary)

Figure 13.2   Device I/O port locations on PCs (partial).

- The *status* register contains bits that can be read by the host. These bits indicate states such as whether the current command has completed, whether a byte is available to be read from the data-in register, and whether there has been a device error.

- The *control* register can be written by the host to start a command or to change the mode of a device. For instance, a certain bit in the `control` register of a serial port chooses between full-duplex and half-duplex communication, another enables parity checking, a third bit sets the word length to 7 or 8 bits, and other bits select one of the speeds supported by the serial port.

- The *data-in* register is read by the host to get input.

- The *data-out* register is written by the host to send output.

The data registers are typically 1 to 4 bytes. Some controllers have FIFO chips that can hold several bytes of input or output data to expand the capacity of the controller beyond the size of the data register. A FIFO chip can hold a small burst of data until the device or host is able to receive those data.

13.2.1 Polling

The complete protocol for interaction between the host and a controller can be intricate, but the basic *handshaking* notion is simple. We explain handshaking by an example. We assume that 2 bits are used to coordinate the producer–consumer relationship between the controller and the host. The controller indicates its state through the *busy* bit in the *status* register. (Recall that to *set* a bit means to write a 1 into the bit, and to *clear* a bit means to write a 0 into it.) The controller sets the *busy* bit when it is busy working, and clears the *busy* bit when it is ready to accept the next command. The host signals its wishes via the *command-ready* bit in the *command* register. The host sets the *command-ready* bit when a command is available for the controller to execute. For this example, the host writes output through a port, coordinating with the controller by handshaking as follows.

1. The host repeatedly reads the *busy* bit until that bit becomes clear.

2. The host sets the *write* bit in the *command* register and writes a byte into the *data-out* register.

3. The host sets the *command-ready* bit.

4. When the controller notices that the *command-ready* bit is set, it sets the *busy* bit.

5. The controller reads the command register and sees the `write` command. It reads the *data-out* register to get the byte, and does the I/O to the device.

6. The controller clears the *command-ready* bit, clears the *error* bit in the status register to indicate that the device I/O succeeded, and clears the *busy* bit to indicate that it is finished.

This loop is repeated for each byte.

In step 1, the host is **busy-waiting** or **polling**: It is in a loop, reading the *status* register over and over until the *busy* bit becomes clear. If the controller and device are fast, this method is a reasonable one. But if the wait may be long, the host should probably switch to another task. How then does the host know when the controller has become idle? For some devices, the host must service the device quickly, or data will be lost. For instance, when data are streaming in on a serial port or from a keyboard, the small buffer on the controller will overflow and data will be lost if the host waits too long before returning to read the bytes.

In many computer architectures, three CPU-instruction cycles are sufficient to poll a device: *read* a device register, *logical–and* to extract a status bit, and *branch* if not zero. Clearly, the basic polling operation is efficient. But polling becomes inefficient when it is attempted repeatedly, yet rarely finds a device to be ready for service, while other useful CPU processing remains undone. In such instances, it may be more efficient to arrange for the hardware controller to notify the CPU when the device becomes ready for service, rather than to require the CPU to poll repeatedly for an I/O completion. The hardware mechanism that enables a device to notify the CPU is called an **interrupt**.

13.2.2 Interrupts

The basic interrupt mechanism works as follows. The CPU hardware has a wire called the **interrupt-request line** that the CPU senses after executing every instruction. When the CPU detects that a controller has asserted a signal on the interrupt request line, the CPU saves a small amount of state, such as the current value of the instruction pointer, and jumps to the **interrupt-handler** routine at a fixed address in memory. The interrupt handler determines the cause of the interrupt, performs the necessary processing, and executes a `return from interrupt` instruction to return the CPU to the execution state prior to the interrupt. We say that the device controller *raises* an interrupt by asserting a signal on the interrupt request line, the CPU *catches* the interrupt and *dispatches* to the interrupt handler, and the handler *clears* the interrupt by servicing the device. Figure 13.3 summarizes the interrupt-driven I/O cycle.

This basic interrupt mechanism enables the CPU to respond to an asynchronous event, such as a device controller becoming ready for service. In a modern operating system, we need more sophisticated interrupt-handling features. First, we need the ability to defer interrupt handling during critical processing. Second, we need an efficient way to dispatch to the proper interrupt handler for a device, without first polling all the devices to see which one raised the interrupt. Third, we need multilevel interrupts, so that the operating system

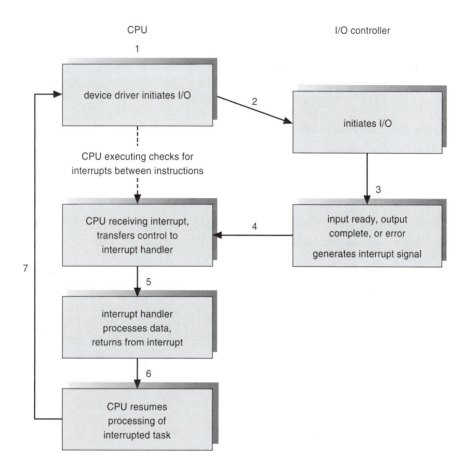

Figure 13.3   Interrupt-driven I/O cycle.

can distinguish between high- and low-priority interrupts, and can respond with the appropriate degree of urgency. In modern computer hardware, these three features are provided by the CPU and by the **interrupt-controller** hardware.

Most CPUs have two interrupt request lines. One is the **nonmaskable interrupt**, which is reserved for events such as unrecoverable memory errors. The second interrupt line is **maskable**: It can be turned off by the CPU before the execution of critical instruction sequences that must not be interrupted. The maskable interrupt is used by device controllers to request service.

The interrupt mechanism accepts an **address**—a number that selects a specific interrupt-handling routine from a small set. In most architectures, this address is an offset in a table called the **interrupt vector**. This vector contains the memory addresses of specialized interrupt handlers. The purpose of a vectored interrupt mechanism is to reduce the need for a single interrupt handler to search all possible sources of interrupts to determine which one needs service. In practice, however, computers have more devices (and hence, interrupt handlers) than they have address elements in the interrupt vector. A common way to solve this problem is to use the technique of **interrupt chaining**, in which each element in the interrupt vector points to the head of a list of interrupt handlers. When an interrupt is raised, the handlers on the corresponding list are called one by one, until one is found that can service the request. This structure is a compromise between the overhead of a huge interrupt table and the inefficiency of a dispatching to a single interrupt handler.

Figure 13.4 illustrates the design of the interrupt vector for the Intel Pentium processor. The events from 0 to 31, which are nonmaskable, are used to signal various error conditions. The events from 32 to 255, which are maskable, are used for purposes such as device-generated interrupts.

The interrupt mechanism also implements a system of **interrupt priority levels**. This mechanism enables the CPU to defer the handling of low-priority interrupts without masking off all interrupts, and makes it possible for a high-priority interrupt to preempt the execution of a low-priority interrupt.

A modern operating system interacts with the interrupt mechanism in several ways. At boot time, the operating system probes the hardware buses to determine what devices are present, and installs the corresponding interrupt handlers into the interrupt vector. During I/O, the various device controllers

vector number	description
0	divide error
1	debug exception
2	null interrupt
3	breakpoint
4	INTO-detected overflow
5	bound range exception
6	invalid opcode
7	device not available
8	double fault
9	coprocessor segment overrun (reserved)
10	invalid task state segment
11	segment not present
12	stack fault
13	general protection
14	page fault
15	(Intel reserved, do not use)
16	floating-point error
17	alignment check
18	machine check
19–31	(Intel reserved, do not use)
32–255	maskable interrupts

Figure 13.4   Intel Pentium processor event-vector table.

raise interrupts when they are ready for service. These interrupts signify that output has completed, or that input data are available, or that a failure has been detected. The interrupt mechanism is also used to handle a wide variety of **exceptions**, such as dividing by zero, accessing a protected or nonexistent memory address, or attempting to execute a privileged instruction from user mode. The events that trigger interrupts have a common property: They are occurrences that induce the CPU to execute an urgent, self-contained routine.

An operating system has other good uses for an efficient hardware mechanism that saves a small amount of processor state, and then calls a privileged routine in the kernel. For example, many operating systems use the interrupt mechanism for virtual-memory paging. A page fault is an exception that raises an interrupt. The interrupt suspends the current process and jumps to the page-fault handler in the kernel. This handler saves the state of the process, moves the process to the wait queue, performs page-cache management, schedules an I/O operation to fetch the page, schedules another process to resume execution, and then returns from the interrupt.

Another example is found in the implementation of system calls. A *system call* is a function called by an application to invoke a kernel service. The system call checks the arguments given by the application, builds a data structure to convey the arguments to the kernel, and then executes a special instruction called a **software interrupt** (or a **trap**). This instruction has an operand that identifies the desired kernel service. When the system call executes the trap instruction, the interrupt hardware saves the state of the user code, switches to supervisor mode, and dispatches to the kernel routine that implements the requested service. The trap is given a relatively low interrupt priority compared to those assigned to device interrupts—executing a system call on behalf of an application is less urgent than servicing a device controller before its FIFO queue overflows and loses data.

Interrupts can also be used to manage the flow of control within the kernel. For example, consider the processing required to complete a disk read. One step is to copy data from kernel space to the user buffer. This copying is time consuming but not urgent—it should not block other high-priority interrupt handling. Another step is to start the next pending I/O for that disk drive. This step has higher priority: If the disks are to be used efficiently, we need to start the next I/O as soon as the previous one completes. Consequently, a *pair* of interrupt handlers implements the kernel code that completes a disk read. The high-priority handler records the I/O status, clears the device interrupt, starts the next pending I/O, and raises a low-priority interrupt to complete the work. Later, when the CPU is not occupied with high-priority work, the low-priority interrupt will be dispatched. The corresponding handler completes the user-level I/O by copying data from kernel buffers to the application space, and then by calling the scheduler to place the application on the ready queue.

A threaded kernel architecture is well suited to implement multiple interrupt priorities and to enforce the precedence of interrupt handling over background processing in kernel and application routines. We illustrate this point with the Solaris kernel. In Solaris, interrupt handlers are executed as kernel threads. A range of high priorities is reserved for these threads. These priorities give interrupt handlers precedence over application code and kernel housekeeping, and implement the priority relationships among interrupt handlers. The priorities cause the Solaris thread scheduler to preempt low-priority interrupt handlers in favor of higher-priority ones, and the threaded implementation enables multiprocessor hardware to run several interrupt handlers concurrently. We describe the interrupt architecture of UNIX and WindowsXP in Appendices A and 21, respectively.

In summary, interrupts are used throughout modern operating systems to handle asynchronous events and to trap to supervisor-mode routines in the kernel. To enable the most urgent work to be done first, modern computers use a system of interrupt priorities. Device controllers, hardware faults, and system calls all raise interrupts to trigger kernel routines. Because interrupts are used so heavily for time-sensitive processing, efficient interrupt handling is required for good system performance.

13.2.3 Direct Memory Access

For a device that does large transfers, such as a disk drive, it seems wasteful to use an expensive general-purpose processor to watch status bits and to feed data into a controller register 1 byte at a time—a process termed **programmed I/O (PIO)**. Many computers avoid burdening the main CPU with PIO by offloading some of this work to a special-purpose processor called a **direct-memory-access (DMA)** controller. To initiate a DMA transfer, the host writes a DMA command block into memory. This block contains a pointer to the source of a transfer, a pointer to the destination of the transfer, and a count of the number of bytes to be transferred. The CPU writes the address of this command block to the DMA controller, then goes on with other work. The DMA controller proceeds to operate the memory bus directly, placing addresses on the bus to perform transfers without the help of the main CPU. A simple DMA controller is a standard component in PCs, and **bus-mastering** I/O boards for the PC usually contain their own high-speed DMA hardware.

Handshaking between the DMA controller and the device controller is performed via a pair of wires called DMA-request and DMA-acknowledge. The device controller places a signal on the DMA-request wire when a word of data is available for transfer. This signal causes the DMA controller to seize the memory bus, to place the desired address on the memory-address wires, and to place a signal on the DMA-acknowledge wire. When the device controller receives the DMA-acknowledge signal, it transfers the word of data to memory, and removes the DMA-request signal.

When the entire transfer is finished, the DMA controller interrupts the CPU. This process is depicted in Figure 13.5. When the DMA controller seizes the

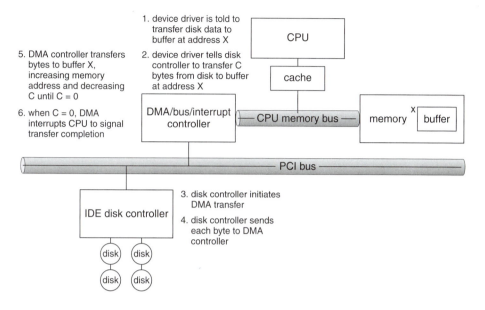

Figure 13.5   Steps in a DMA transfer.

memory bus, the CPU is momentarily prevented from accessing main memory, although it can still access data items in its primary and secondary cache. Although this **cycle stealing** can slow down the CPU computation, offloading the data-transfer work to a DMA controller generally improves the total system performance. Some computer architectures use physical memory addresses for DMA, but others perform **direct virtual-memory access (DVMA)**, using virtual addresses that undergo virtual- to physical-memory address translation. DVMA can perform a transfer between two memory-mapped devices without the intervention of the CPU or the use of main memory.

On protected-mode kernels, the operating system generally prevents processes from issuing device commands directly. This discipline protects data from access-control violations, and also protects the system from erroneous use of device controllers that could cause a system crash. Instead, the operating system exports functions that a sufficiently privileged process can use to access low-level operations on the underlying hardware. On kernels without memory protection, processes can access device controllers directly. This direct access can be used to obtain high performance, since it can avoid kernel communication, context switches, and layers of kernel software. Unfortunately, it interferes with system security and stability. The trend in general-purpose operating systems is to protect memory and devices, so that the system can try to guard against erroneous or malicious applications.

Although the hardware aspects of I/O are complex when considered at the level of detail of electronics-hardware designers, the concepts that we have just described are sufficient to understand many I/O aspects of operating systems. Let's review the main concepts:

- A bus

- A controller

- An I/O port and its registers

- The handshaking relationship between the host and a device controller

- The execution of this handshaking in a polling loop or via interrupts

- The offloading of this work to a DMA controller for large transfers

We gave a basic example of the handshaking that takes place between a device controller and the host in Section 13.2. In reality, the wide variety of available devices poses a problem for operating-system implementers. Each kind of device has its own set of capabilities, control-bit definitions, and protocol for interacting with the host—and they are all different. How can the operating system be designed so that new devices can be attached to the computer without the operating system being rewritten? Also, when the devices vary so widely, how can the operating system give a convenient, uniform I/O interface to applications?

13.3 ■ Application I/O Interface

In this section, we discuss structuring techniques and interfaces for the operating system that enable I/O devices to be treated in a standard, uniform way. We explain, for instance, how an application can open a file on a disk without knowing what kind of disk it is, and how new disks and other devices can be added to a computer without the operating system being disrupted.

Like other complex software-engineering problems, the approach here involves abstraction, encapsulation, and software layering. Specifically, we can abstract away the detailed differences in I/O devices by identifying a few general kinds. Each general kind is accessed through a standardized set of functions—an **interface**. The differences are encapsulated in kernel modules called device drivers that internally are custom tailored to each device, but that export one of the standard interfaces. Figure 13.6 illustrates how the I/O-related portions of the kernel are structured in software layers.

The purpose of the device-driver layer is to hide the differences among device controllers from the I/O subsystem of the kernel, much as the I/O system calls encapsulate the behavior of devices in a few generic classes that hide hardware differences from applications. Making the I/O subsystem independent of the hardware simplifies the job of the operating-system developer. It also benefits the hardware manufacturers. They either design new devices to be

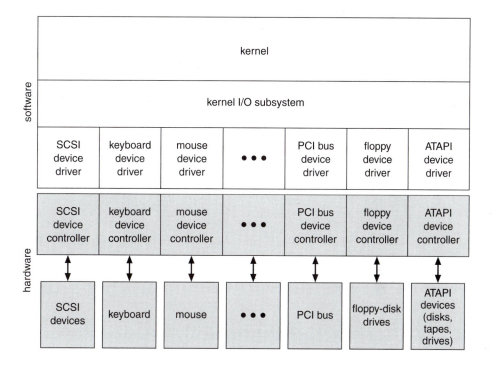

Figure 13.6   A kernel I/O structure.

compatible with an existing host controller interface (such as SCSI-2), or they write device drivers to interface the new hardware to popular operating systems. Thus, new peripherals can be attached to a computer without waiting for the operating-system vendor to develop support code.

Unfortunately for device-hardware manufacturers, each type of operating system has its own standards for the device-driver interface. A given device may ship with multiple device drivers—for instance, drivers for MS-DOS, Windows 95/98, Windows NT/2000, and Solaris. Devices vary in many dimensions, as illustrated in Figure 13.7.

- **Character-stream or block:** A character-stream device transfers bytes one by one, whereas a block device transfers a block of bytes as a unit.

- **Sequential or random-access:** A sequential device transfers data in a fixed order determined by the device, whereas the user of a random-access device can instruct the device to seek to any of the available data storage locations.

- **Synchronous or asynchronous:** A synchronous device is one that performs data transfers with predictable response times. An asynchronous device exhibits irregular or unpredictable response times.

aspect	variation	example
data-transfer mode	character block	terminal disk
access method	sequential random	modem CD-ROM
transfer schedule	synchronous asynchronous	tape keyboard
sharing	dedicated sharable	tape keyboard
device speed	latency seek time transfer rate delay between operations	
I/O direction	read only write only read–write	CD-ROM graphics controller disk

Figure 13.7   Characteristics of I/O devices.

- **Sharable or dedicated:** A sharable device can be used concurrently by several processes or threads; a dedicated device cannot.

- **Speed of operation:** Device speeds range from a few bytes per second to a few gigabytes per second.

- **Read–write, read only, or write only:** Some devices perform both input and output, but others support only one data direction.

For the purpose of application access, many of these differences are hidden by the operating system, and the devices are grouped into a few conventional types. The resulting styles of device access have been found to be useful and broadly applicable. Although the exact system calls may differ across operating systems, the device categories are fairly standard. The major access conventions include block I/O, character-stream I/O, memory-mapped file access, and network sockets. Operating systems also provide special system calls to access a few additional devices, such as a time-of-day clock and a timer. Some operating systems provide a set of system calls for graphical display, video, and audio devices.

Most operating systems also have an **escape** (or **back door**) that transparently passes arbitrary commands from an application to a device driver. In UNIX, this system call is ioctl() (for I/O control). The ioctl() system call enables an application to access any functionality that can be implemented by any device driver, without the need to invent a new system call. The ioctl()

system call has three arguments. The first is a file descriptor that connects the application to the driver by referring to a hardware device managed by that driver. The second is an integer that selects one of the commands implemented in the driver. The third is a pointer to an arbitrary data structure in memory, thus enabling the application and driver to communicate any necessary control information or data.

13.3.1   Block and Character Devices

The **block-device** interface captures all the aspects necessary for accessing disk drives and other block-oriented devices. The expectation is that the device understands commands such as read() and write(), and, if it is a random-access device, it has a seek() command to specify which block to transfer next. Applications normally access such a device through a file-system interface. The operating system itself, and special applications such as database-management systems, may prefer to access a block device as a simple linear array of blocks. This mode of access is sometimes called **raw I/O**. We can see that read(), write(), and seek() capture the essential behaviors of block-storage devices, so that applications are insulated from the low-level differences among those devices.

Memory-mapped file access can be layered on top of block-device drivers. Rather than offering read and write operations, a memory-mapped interface provides access to disk storage via an array of bytes in main memory. The system call that maps a file into memory returns the virtual-memory address of an array of characters that contains a copy of the file. The actual data transfers are performed only when needed to satisfy access to the memory image. Because the transfers are handled by the same mechanism as that used for demand-paged virtual-memory access, memory-mapped I/O is efficient. Memory mapping is also convenient for programmers—access to a memory-mapped file is as simple as reading and writing to memory. Operating systems that offer virtual memory commonly use the mapping interface for kernel services. For instance, to execute a program, the operating system maps the executable into memory, and then transfers control to the entry address of the executable. The mapping interface is also commonly used for kernel access to swap space on disk.

A keyboard is an example of a device that is accessed through a **character-stream** interface. The basic system calls in this interface enable an application to get() or put() one character. On top of this interface, libraries can be built that offer line-at-a-time access, with buffering and editing services (for example, when a user types a backspace, the preceding character is removed from the input stream). This style of access is convenient for input devices such as keyboards, mice, and modems, which produce data for input "spontaneously" —that is, at times that cannot necessarily be predicted by the application. This access style is also good for output devices such as printers or audio boards, which naturally fit the concept of a linear stream of bytes.

13.3.2 Network Devices

Because the performance and addressing characteristics of network I/O differ significantly from those of disk I/O, most operating systems provide a network I/O interface that is different from the read()–write()–seek() interface used for disks. One interface available in many operating systems, including UNIX and Windows NT, is the network **socket** interface.

Think of a wall socket for electricity: Any electrical appliance can be plugged in. By analogy, the system calls in the socket interface enable an application to create a socket, to connect a local socket to a remote address (which plugs this application into a socket created by another application), to listen for any remote application to plug into the local socket, and to send and receive packets over the connection. To support the implementation of servers, the socket interface also provides a function called select() that manages a set of sockets. A call to select() returns information about which sockets have a packet waiting to be received, and which sockets have room to accept a packet to be sent. The use of select() eliminates the polling and busy waiting that would otherwise be necessary for network I/O. These functions encapsulate the essential behaviors of networks, greatly facilitating the creation of distributed applications that can use any underlying network hardware and protocol stack.

Many other approaches to interprocess communication and network communication have been implemented. For instance, Windows NT provides one interface to the network interface card, and a second interface to the network protocols (Section C.6). In UNIX, which has a long history as a proving ground for network technology, we find half–duplex pipes, full–duplex FIFOs, full–duplex STREAMS, message queues, and sockets. Information on UNIX networking is given in Section A.9.

13.3.3 Clocks and Timers

Most computers have hardware clocks and timers that provide three basic functions:

- Give the current time
- Give the elapsed time
- Set a timer to trigger operation X at time T

These functions are used heavily by the operating system, and also by time-sensitive applications. Unfortunately, the system calls that implement these functions are not standardized across operating systems.

The hardware to measure elapsed time and to trigger operations is called a **programmable interval timer**. It can be set to wait a certain amount of time and then to generate an interrupt. It can be set to do this operation once, or to repeat the process, to generate periodic interrupts. The scheduler uses this mechanism to generate an interrupt that will preempt a process at the end of its time slice. The disk I/O subsystem uses it to invoke the flushing of dirty cache buffers to disk periodically, and the network subsystem uses it to cancel operations that are proceeding too slowly because of network congestion or failures. The operating system may also provide an interface for user processes to use timers. The operating system can support more timer requests than the number of timer hardware channels by simulating virtual clocks. To do so, the kernel (or the timer device driver) maintains a list of interrupts wanted by its own routines and by user requests, sorted in earliest-time-first order. It sets the timer for the earliest time. When the timer interrupts, the kernel signals the requester, and reloads the timer with the next earliest time.

On many computers, the interrupt rate generated by the ticking of the hardware clock is between 18 and 60 ticks per second. This resolution is coarse, since a modern computer can execute hundreds of millions of instructions per second. The precision of triggers is limited by the coarse resolution of the timer, together with the overhead of maintaining virtual clocks. And, if the timer ticks are used to maintain the system time-of-day clock, the system clock can drift. In most computers, the hardware clock is constructed from a high-frequency counter. In some computers, the value of this counter can be read from a device register, in which case the counter can be considered to be a high-resolution clock. Although this clock does not generate interrupts, it offers accurate measurements of time intervals.

13.3.4   Blocking and Nonblocking I/O

Another aspect of the system-call interface relates to the choice between blocking I/O and nonblocking (or asynchronous) I/O. When an application issues a **blocking** system call, the execution of the application is suspended. The application is moved from the operating system's run queue to a wait queue. After the system call completes, the application is moved back to the run queue, where it is eligible to resume execution, at which time it will receive the values returned by the system call. The physical actions performed by I/O devices are generally asynchronous—they take a varying or unpredictable amount of time. Nevertheless, most operating systems use blocking system calls for the application interface, because blocking application code is easier to understand than nonblocking application code.

Some user-level processes need **nonblocking** I/O. One example is a user interface that receives keyboard and mouse input while processing and displaying data on the screen. Another example is a video application that reads frames from a file on disk while simultaneously decompressing and displaying the output on the display.

One way that an application writer can overlap execution with I/O is to write a multithreaded application. Some threads can perform blocking system calls, while others continue executing. The Solaris developers used this technique to implement a user-level library for asynchronous I/O, freeing the application writer from that task. Some operating systems provide nonblocking I/O system calls. A nonblocking call does not halt the execution of the application for an extended time. Instead, it returns quickly, with a return value that indicates how many bytes were transferred.

An alternative to a nonblocking system call is an asynchronous system call. An asynchronous call returns immediately, without waiting for the I/O to complete. The application continues to execute its code. The completion of the I/O at some future time is communicated to the application, either through the setting of some variable in the address space of the application, or through the triggering of a signal or software interrupt or a call-back routine that is executed outside the linear control flow of the application. The difference between nonblocking and asynchronous system calls is that a nonblocking `read()` returns immediately with whatever data are available—the full number of bytes requested, fewer, or none at all. An asynchronous `read()` call requests a transfer that will be performed in its entirety, but that will complete at some future time.

A good example of nonblocking behavior is the `select()` system call for network sockets. This system call takes an argument that specifies a maximum waiting time. By setting it to 0, an application can poll for network activity without blocking. But using `select()` introduces extra overhead, because the `select()` call only checks whether I/O is possible. For a data transfer, `select()` must be followed by some kind of `read()` or `write()` command. A variation of this approach, found in Mach, is a blocking multiple-read call. It specifies desired reads for several devices in one system call, and returns as soon as any one of them completes.

13.4 ▪ Kernel I/O Subsystem

Kernels provide many services related to I/O. Several services—scheduling, buffering, caching, spooling, device reservation, and error handling—are provided by the kernel's I/O subsystem and build on the hardware and device-driver infrastructure.

13.4.1 I/O Scheduling

To schedule a set of I/O requests means to determine a good order in which to execute them. The order in which applications issue system calls rarely is the best choice. Scheduling can improve overall system performance, can share device access fairly among processes, and can reduce the average waiting time for I/O to complete. Here is a simple example to illustrate the opportunity. Suppose that a disk arm is near the beginning of a disk, and that three applications issue blocking read calls to that disk. Application 1 requests a block near the end of the disk, application 2 requests one near the beginning, and application 3 requests one in the middle of the disk. The operating system can reduce the distance that the disk arm travels by serving the applications in order 2, 3, 1. Rearranging the order of service in this way is the essence of I/O scheduling.

Operating-system developers implement scheduling by maintaining a queue of requests for each device. When an application issues a blocking I/O system call, the request is placed on the queue for that device. The I/O scheduler rearranges the order of the queue to improve the overall system efficiency and the average response time experienced by applications. The operating system may also try to be fair, so that no one application receives especially poor service, or it may give priority service for delay-sensitive requests. For instance, requests from the virtual-memory subsystem may take priority over application requests. Several scheduling algorithms for disk I/O are detailed in Section 14.2.

One way that the I/O subsystem improves the efficiency of the computer is by scheduling I/O operations. Another way is by using storage space in main memory or on disk, via techniques called buffering, caching, and spooling.

13.4.2 Buffering

A **buffer** is a memory area that stores data while they are transferred between two devices or between a device and an application. Buffering is done for three reasons. One reason is to cope with a speed mismatch between the producer and consumer of a data stream. Suppose, for example, that a file is being received via modem for storage on the hard disk. The modem is about a thousand times slower than the hard disk. So a buffer is created in main memory to accumulate the bytes received from the modem. When an entire buffer of data has arrived, the buffer can be written to disk in a single operation. Since the disk write is not instantaneous and the modem still needs a place to store additional incoming data, two buffers are used. After the modem fills the first buffer, the disk write is requested. The modem then starts to fill the second buffer while the first buffer is written to disk. By the time the modem has filled the second buffer, the disk write from the first one should have completed, so the modem can switch back to the first buffer while the disk writes the second one. This **double buffering** decouples the producer of data from the consumer, thus relaxing timing requirements between them. The need for this decoupling is illustrated in Figure 13.8, which lists the enormous differences in device speeds for typical computer hardware.

A second use of buffering is to adapt between devices that have different data-transfer sizes. Such disparities are especially common in computer

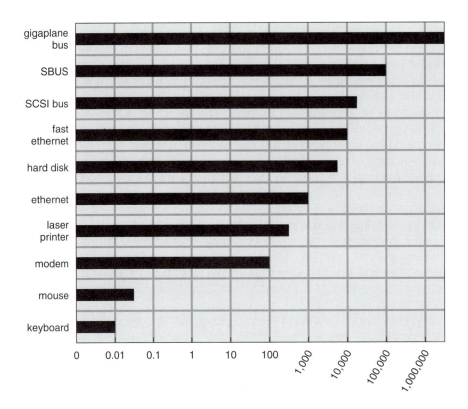

Figure 13.8   Sun Enterprise 6000 device-transfer rates (logarithmic).

networking, where buffers are used widely for fragmentation and reassembly of messages. At the sending side, a large message is fragmented into small network packets. The packets are sent over the network, and the receiving side places them in a reassembly buffer to form an image of the source data.

A third use of buffering is to support copy semantics for application I/O. An example will clarify the meaning of "copy semantics." Suppose that an application has a buffer of data that it wishes to write to disk. It calls the `write()` system call, providing a pointer to the buffer and an integer specifying the number of bytes to write. After the system call returns, what happens if the application changes the contents of the buffer? With **copy semantics**, the version of the data written to disk is guaranteed to be the version at the time of the application system call, independent of any subsequent changes in the application's buffer. A simple way that the operating system can guarantee copy semantics is for the `write()` system call to copy the application data into a kernel buffer before returning control to the application. The disk write is performed from the kernel buffer, so that subsequent changes to the application buffer have no effect. Copying of data between kernel buffers and application data space is common in operating systems, despite the overhead that this operation introduces, because of the clean semantics. The same effect can be obtained more efficiently by clever use of virtual-memory mapping and copy-on-write page protection.

13.4.3 Caching

A **cache** is a region of fast memory that holds copies of data. Access to the cached copy is more efficient than access to the original. For instance, the instructions of the currently running process are stored on disk, cached in physical memory, and copied again in the CPU's secondary and primary caches. The difference between a buffer and a cache is that a buffer may hold the only existing copy of a data item, whereas a cache, by definition, just holds a copy on faster storage of an item that resides elsewhere.

Caching and buffering are distinct functions, but sometimes a region of memory can be used for both purposes. For instance, to preserve copy semantics and to enable efficient scheduling of disk I/O, the operating system uses buffers in main memory to hold disk data. These buffers are also used as a cache, to improve the I/O efficiency for files that are shared by applications or that are being written and reread rapidly. When the kernel receives a file I/O request, the kernel first accesses the buffer cache to see whether that region of the file is already available in main memory. If so, a physical disk I/O can be avoided or deferred. Also, disk writes are accumulated in the buffer cache for several seconds, so that large transfers are gathered to allow efficient write schedules. This strategy of delaying writes to improve I/O efficiency is discussed, in the context of remote file access, in Section 16.3.

13.4.4 Spooling and Device Reservation

A **spool** is a buffer that holds output for a device, such as a printer, that cannot accept interleaved data streams. Although a printer can serve only one job at a time, several applications may wish to print their output concurrently, without having their output mixed together. The operating system solves this problem by intercepting all output to the printer. Each application's output is spooled to a separate disk file. When an application finishes printing, the spooling system queues the corresponding spool file for output to the printer. The spooling system copies the queued spool files to the printer one at a time. In some operating systems, spooling is managed by a system daemon process. In other operating systems, it is handled by an in-kernel thread. In either case, the operating system provides a control interface that enables users and system administrators to display the queue, to remove unwanted jobs before those jobs print, to suspend printing while the printer is serviced, and so on.

Some devices, such as tape drives and printers, cannot usefully multiplex the I/O requests of multiple concurrent applications. Spooling is one way that operating systems can coordinate concurrent output. Another way to deal with concurrent device access is to provide explicit facilities for coordination. Some operating systems (including VMS) provide support for exclusive device access, by enabling a process to allocate an idle device, and to deallocate that device when it is no longer needed. Other operating systems enforce a limit of one open file handle to such a device. Many operating systems provide functions that enable processes to coordinate exclusive access among themselves. For instance, Windows NT provides system calls to wait until a device object becomes available. It also has a parameter to the open() system call that declares the types of access to be permitted to other concurrent threads. On these systems, it is up to the applications to avoid deadlock.

13.4.5 Error Handling

An operating system that uses protected memory can guard against many kinds of hardware and application errors, so that a complete system failure is not the usual result of each minor mechanical glitch. Devices and I/O transfers can fail in many ways, either for transient reasons, such as a network becoming overloaded, or for "permanent" reasons, such as a disk controller becoming defective. Operating systems can often compensate effectively for transient failures. For instance, a disk read() failure results in a read() retry, and a network send() error results in a resend(), if the protocol so specifies. Unfortunately, if an important component experiences a permanent failure, the operating system is unlikely to recover.

As a general rule, an I/O system call will return 1 bit of information about the status of the call, signifying either success or failure. In the UNIX operating system, an additional integer variable named errno is used to return an error code—one of about 100 values—indicating the general nature of the failure (for example, argument out of range, bad pointer, or file not open). By contrast, some hardware can provide highly detailed error information, although many current operating systems are not designed to convey this information to the application. For instance, a failure of a SCSI device is reported by the SCSI protocol in terms of a **sense key** that identifies the general nature of the failure, such as a hardware error or an illegal request; an **additional sense code** that states the category of failure, such as a bad command parameter or a self-test failure; and an **additional sense-code qualifier** that gives even more detail, such as which command parameter was in error, or which hardware subsystem failed its self-test. Further, many SCSI devices maintain internal pages of error-log information that can be requested by the host, but that seldom are.

13.4.6 Kernel Data Structures

The kernel needs to keep state information about the use of I/O components. It does so through a variety of in-kernel data structures, such as the open-file table structure from Section 12.1. The kernel uses many similar structures to track network connections, character-device communications, and other I/O activities.

UNIX provides file-system access to a variety of entities, such as user files, raw devices, and the address spaces of processes. Although each of these entities supports a `read()` operation, the semantics differ. For instance, to read a user file, the kernel needs to probe the buffer cache before deciding whether to perform a disk I/O. To read a raw disk, the kernel needs to ensure that the request size is a multiple of the disk sector size, and is aligned on a sector boundary. To read a process image, it is merely necessary to copy data from memory. UNIX encapsulates these differences within a uniform structure by using an object-oriented technique. The open-file record, shown in Figure 13.9, contains a dispatch table that holds pointers to the appropriate routines, depending on the type of file.

Some operating systems use object-oriented methods even more extensively. For instance, Windows NT uses a message-passing implementation for I/O. An I/O request is converted into a message that is sent through the kernel to the I/O manager and then to the device driver, each of which may change the message contents. For output, the message contains the data to be written. For input, the message contains a buffer to receive the data. The message-passing approach can add overhead, by comparison with procedural techniques that use shared data structures, but it simplifies the structure and design of the I/O system, and adds flexibility.

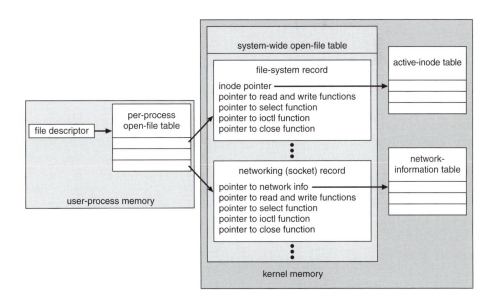

Figure 13.9   UNIX I/O kernel structure.

In summary, the I/O subsystem coordinates an extensive collection of services that are available to applications and to other parts of the kernel. The I/O subsystem supervises

- The management of the name space for files and devices
- Access control to files and devices
- Operation control (for example, a modem cannot `seek()`)
- File system space allocation
- Device allocation
- Buffering, caching, and spooling
- I/O scheduling
- Device-status monitoring, error handling, and failure recovery
- Device-driver configuration and initialization

The upper levels of the I/O subsystem access devices via the uniform interface provided by the device drivers.

13.5 ■ Transforming I/O to Hardware Operations

Earlier, we described the handshaking between a device driver and a device controller, but we did not explain how the operating system connects an application request to a set of network wires or to a specific disk sector. Let us consider the example of reading a file from disk. The application refers to the data by a file name. Within a disk, the file system maps from the file name through the file-system directories to obtain the space allocation of the file. For instance, in MS-DOS, the name maps to a number that indicates an entry in the file-access table, and that table entry tells which disk blocks are allocated to the file. In UNIX, the name maps to an inode number, and the corresponding inode contains the space-allocation information.

How is the connection made from the file name to the disk controller (the hardware port address or the memory-mapped controller registers)? First, we consider MS-DOS, a relatively simple operating system. The first part of an MS-DOS file name, preceding the colon, is a string that identifies a specific hardware device. For example, *c:* is the first part of every file name on the primary hard disk. The fact that *c:* represents the primary hard disk is built into the operating system; *c:* is mapped to a specific port address through a device table. Because of the colon separator, the device name space is separate from the file-system name space within each device. This separation makes it easy for the operating system to associate extra functionality with each device. For instance, it is easy to invoke spooling on any files written to the printer.

If, instead, the device name space is incorporated in the regular file-system name space, as it is in UNIX, the normal file-system name services are provided automatically. If the file system provides ownership and access control to all file names, then devices have owners and access control. Since files are stored on devices, such an interface provides access to the I/O system at two levels. Names can be used to access the devices themselves, or to access the files stored on the devices.

UNIX represents device names in the regular file-system name space. Unlike an MS-DOS file name, which has the colon separator, a UNIX path name has no clear separation of the device portion. In fact, no part of the path name is the name of a device. UNIX has a **mount table** that associates prefixes of path names with specific device names. To resolve a path name, UNIX looks up the name in the mount table to find the longest matching prefix; the corresponding entry in the mount table gives the device name. This device name also has the form of a name in the file-system name space. When UNIX looks up this name in the file-system directory structures, instead of finding an inode number, UNIX finds a <*major, minor*> device number. The major device number identifies a device driver that should be called to handle I/O to this device. The minor device number is passed to the device driver to index into a device table. The corresponding device-table entry gives the port address or the memory-mapped address of the device controller.

Modern operating systems obtain significant flexibility from the multiple stages of lookup tables in the path between a request and a physical device controller. The mechanisms that pass requests between applications and drivers are general. Thus, we can introduce new devices and drivers into a computer without recompiling the kernel. In fact, some operating systems have the ability to load device drivers on demand. At boot time, the system first probes the hardware buses to determine what devices are present, and then the system loads in the necessary drivers, either immediately, or when first required by an I/O request.

Now we describe the typical lifecycle of a blocking read request, as depicted in Figure 13.10. The figure suggests that an I/O operation requires a great many steps that together consume a tremendous number of CPU cycles.

1. A process issues a blocking `read()` system call to a file descriptor of a file that has been *open*ed previously.

2. The system-call code in the kernel checks the parameters for correctness. In the case of input, if the data are already available in the buffer cache, the data are returned to the process and the I/O request is completed.

3. Otherwise, a physical I/O needs to be performed, so the process is removed from the run queue and is placed on the wait queue for the device, and the

I/O request is scheduled. Eventually, the I/O subsystem sends the request
to the device driver. Depending on the operating system, the request is sent
via a subroutine call or via an in-kernel message.

4. The device driver allocates kernel buffer space to receive the data, and
   schedules the I/O. Eventually, the driver sends commands to the device
   controller by writing into the device control registers.

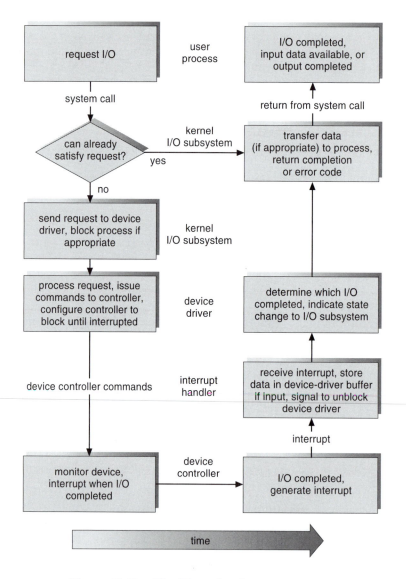

Figure 13.10   The life cycle of an I/O request.

5. The device controller operates the device hardware to perform the data transfer.

6. The driver may poll for status and data, or it may have set up a DMA transfer into kernel memory. We assume that the transfer is managed by a DMA controller, which generates an interrupt when the transfer completes.

7. The correct interrupt handler receives the interrupt via the interrupt-vector table, stores any necessary data, signals the device driver, and returns from the interrupt.

8. The device driver receives the signal, determines which I/O request completed, determines the request's status, and signals the kernel I/O subsystem that the request has been completed.

9. The kernel transfers data or return codes to the address space of the requesting process, and moves the process from the wait queue back to the ready queue.

10. Moving the process to the ready queue unblocks the process. When the scheduler assigns the process to the CPU, the process resumes execution at the completion of the system call.

13.6   ■   STREAMS

UNIX System V has an interesting mechanism, called **STREAMS**, that enables an application to assemble pipelines of driver code dynamically. A stream is a full-duplex connection between a device driver and a user-level process. It consists of a **stream head** that interfaces with the user process, a **driver end** that controls the device, and zero or more **stream modules** between them. The stream head, the driver end, and each module contain a pair of queues—a read queue and a write queue. Message passing is used to transfer data between queues. The STREAMS structure is shown in Figure 13.11.

Modules provide the functionality of STREAMS processing and they are *pushed* onto a stream using the ioctl() system call. For example, a process can open a serial-port device via a stream, and can push on a module to handle input editing. Because messages are exchanged between queues in adjacent modules, a queue in one module may overflow an adjacent queue. To prevent this from occurring, a queue may support **flow control**. Without flow control, a queue accepts all messages and immediately sends them on to the queue in the adjacent module without buffering them. A queue supporting flow control buffers messages and does not accept messages without sufficient buffer space. Flow control is supported by exchanging control messages between queues in adjacent modules.

A user process writes data to a device using either the write() or putmsg() system calls. The write() system call writes raw data to the stream

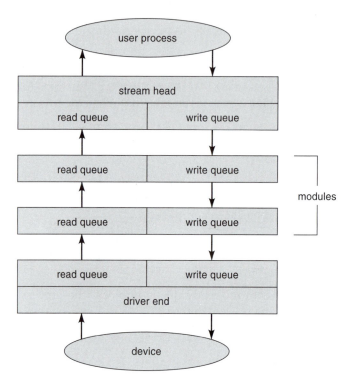

Figure 13.11   The STREAMS structure.

whereas putmsg() allows the user process to specify a message. Regardless of the system call used by the user process, the stream head copies the data into a message and delivers it to the queue for the next module in line. This copying of messages continues until the message is copied to the driver end and hence the device. Similarly, the user process reads data from the stream head using either the read() or getmsg() system calls. If read() is used, the stream head gets a message from its adjacent queue and returns ordinary data (an unstructured byte stream) to the process. If getmsg() is used, a message is returned to the process.

STREAMS I/O is asynchronous (or non-blocking) with the exception of when the user process communicates with the stream head. When writing to the stream, the user process will block, assuming the next queue uses flow control, until there is room to copy the message. Likewise, the user process will block when reading from the stream until data is available.

The driver end is similar to a stream head or a module in that it has a read and write queue. However, the driver end must respond to interrupts such as one triggered when a frame is ready to be read from a network. Unlike the stream head that may block if it is unable to copy a message to the next queue in line, the driver end must handle all incoming data. Drivers must support flow control as well. However, if a device's buffer is full, a device typically resorts to dropping incoming messages. Consider a network card whose input buffer is full. The network card must simply drop further messages until there is ample buffer space to store incoming messages.

The benefit of using STREAMS is that it provides a framework to a modular and incremental approach to writing device drivers and network protocols.

Modules may be used by different STREAMS and hence by different devices. For example, a networking module may be used by both an Ethernet network card and a token ring network card. Furthermore, rather than treating character device I/O as an unstructured byte stream, STREAMS allow support for message boundaries and control information between modules. Support for STREAMS is widespread among most UNIX variants and it is the preferred method for writing protocols and device drivers. For example, in System V UNIX and Solaris, the socket mechanism is implemented using STREAMS.

13.7 ■ Performance

I/O is a major factor in system performance. It places heavy demands on the CPU to execute device-driver code and to schedule processes fairly and efficiently as they block and unblock. The resulting context switches stress the CPU and its hardware caches. I/O also exposes any inefficiencies in the interrupt-handling mechanisms in the kernel, and I/O loads down the memory bus during data copy between controllers and physical memory, and again during copies between kernel buffers and application data space. Coping gracefully with all these demands is one of the major concerns of a computer architect.

Although modern computers can handle many thousands of interrupts per second, interrupt handling is a relatively expensive task: Each interrupt causes the system to perform a state change, to execute the interrupt handler, and then to restore state. Programmed I/O can be more efficient than interrupt-driven I/O, if the number of cycles spent busy-waiting is not excessive. An I/O completion typically unblocks a process, leading to the full overhead of a context switch.

Network traffic can also cause a high context-switch rate. Consider, for instance, a remote login from one machine to another. Each character typed on the local machine must be transported to the remote machine. On the local machine, the character is typed; a keyboard interrupt is generated; and the character is passed through the interrupt handler to the device driver, to the kernel, and then to the user process. The user process issues a network I/O system call to send the character to the remote machine. The character then flows into the local kernel, through the network layers that construct a network packet, and into the network device driver. The network device driver transfers the packet to the network controller, which sends the character and generates an interrupt. The interrupt is passed back up through the kernel to cause the network I/O system call to complete.

Now, the remote system's network hardware receives the packet, and an interrupt is generated. The character is unpacked from the network protocols and is given to the appropriate network daemon. The network daemon identifies which remote login session is involved, and passes the packet to the appropriate subdaemon for that session. Throughout this flow there are context switches and state switches (Figure 13.12). Usually, the receiver echoes the character back to the sender; that approach doubles the work.

The Solaris developers reimplemented the **telnet** daemon using in-kernel threads to eliminate the context switches involved in moving each character between daemons and the kernel. Sun estimates that this improvement

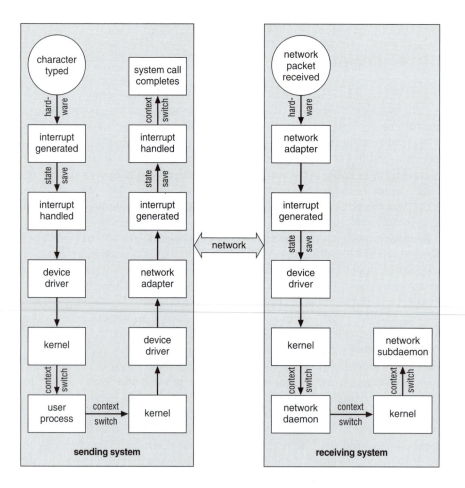

Figure 13.12   Intercomputer communications.

increased the maximum number of network logins from a few hundred to a few thousand on a large server.

Other systems use separate **front-end processors** for terminal I/O, to reduce the interrupt burden on the main CPU. For instance, a **terminal concentrator** can multiplex the traffic from hundreds of remote terminals into one port on a large computer. An **I/O channel** is a dedicated, special-purpose CPU found in mainframes and in other high-end systems. The job of a channel is to offload I/O work from the main CPU. The idea is that the channels keep the data flowing smoothly, while the main CPU remains free to process the data. Like the device controllers and DMA controllers found in smaller computers, a channel can process more general and sophisticated programs, so channels can be tuned for particular workloads.

We can employ several principles to improve the efficiency of I/O:

- Reduce the number of context switches.

- Reduce the number of times that data must be copied in memory while passing between device and application.

- Reduce the frequency of interrupts by using large transfers, smart controllers, and polling (if busy-waiting can be minimized).

- Increase concurrency by using DMA-knowledgeable controllers or channels to offload simple data copying from the CPU.

- Move processing primitives into hardware, to allow their operation in device controllers concurrent with the CPU and bus operation.

- Balance CPU, memory subsystem, bus, and I/O performance, because an overload in any one area will cause idleness in others.

Devices vary greatly in complexity. For instance, a mouse is simple. The mouse movements and button clicks are converted into numeric values that are passed from hardware, through the mouse device driver, to the application. By contrast, the functionality provided by the NT disk device driver is complex. It not only manages individual disks but also implements RAID arrays (Section 14.5). To do so, it converts an application's read or write request into a coordinated set of disk I/O operations. Moreover, it implements sophisticated error-handling and data-recovery algorithms, and takes many steps to optimize disk performance, because of the importance of secondary-storage performance to overall system performance.

Where should the I/O functionality be implemented—in the device hardware, in the device driver, or in application software? Sometimes we observe the progression depicted in Figure 13.13.

- Initially, we implement experimental I/O algorithms at the application level, because application code is flexible, and application bugs are unlikely to cause system crashes. Furthermore, by developing code at the application level, we avoid the need to reboot or reload device drivers after every change to the code. An application-level implementation can be inefficient, however, because of the overhead of context switches, and because the application cannot take advantage of internal kernel data structures and kernel functionality (such as efficient in-kernel messaging, threading, and locking).

- When an application-level algorithm has demonstrated its worth, we may reimplement it in the kernel. This can improve the performance, but the development effort is more challenging, because an operating-system kernel is a large, complex software system. Moreover, an in-kernel implementation must be thoroughly debugged to avoid data corruption and system crashes.

- The highest performance may be obtained by a specialized implementation in hardware, either in the device or in the controller. The disadvantages of a hardware implementation include the difficulty and expense of making further improvements or of fixing bugs, the increased development time (months rather than days), and the decreased flexibility. For instance, a hardware RAID controller may not provide any means for the kernel to influence the order or location of individual block reads and writes, even if the kernel has special information about the workload that would enable the kernel to improve the I/O performance.

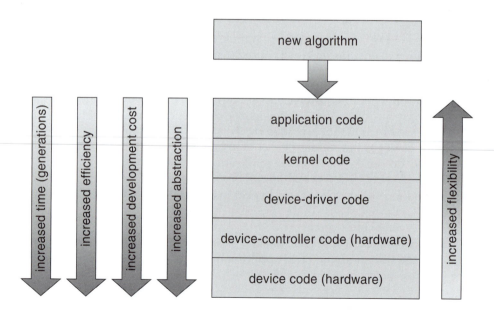

Figure 13.13 Device-functionality progression.

13.8 ■ Summary

The basic hardware elements involved in I/O are buses, device controllers, and the devices themselves. The work of moving data between devices and main memory is performed by the CPU as programmed I/O, or is offloaded to a DMA controller. The kernel module that controls a device is a device driver. The system-call interface provided to applications is designed to handle several basic categories of hardware, including block devices, character devices, memory-mapped files, network sockets, and programmed interval timers. The system calls usually block the process that issues them, but nonblocking and asynchronous calls are used by the kernel itself, and by applications that must not sleep while waiting for an I/O operation to complete.

The kernel's I/O subsystem provides numerous services. Among these are I/O scheduling, buffering, spooling, error handling, and device reservation. Another service is name translation, to make the connection between hardware devices and the symbolic file names used by applications. It involves several levels of mapping that translate from a character string name to a specific device driver and device address, and then to physical addresses of I/O ports or bus controllers. This mapping may occur within the file-system name space, as it does in UNIX, or in a separate device-name space, as it does in MS-DOS.

STREAMS is an implementation and methodology for making drivers reusable and easy to use. Through them, drivers can be stacked, with data passed through them sequentially and bidirectionally for processing.

I/O system calls are costly in terms of CPU consumption, because of the many layers of software between a physical device and the application. These layers imply the overheads of context switching to cross the kernel's protection boundary, of signal and interrupt handling to service the I/O devices, and of the load on the CPU and memory system to copy data between kernel buffers and application space.

■ Exercises

13.1 State three advantages of placing functionality in a device controller, rather than in the kernel. State three disadvantages.

13.2 Consider the following I/O scenarios on a single-user PC.

    a. A mouse used with a graphical user interface

    b. A tape drive on a multitasking operating system (assume no device preallocation is available)

    c. A disk drive containing user files

    d. A graphics card with direct bus connection, accessible through memory-mapped I/O

For each of these I/O scenarios, would you design the operating system to use buffering, spooling, caching, or a combination? Would you use polled I/O or interrupt-driven I/O? Give reasons for your choices.

13.3 The example of handshaking in Section 13.2 used 2 bits: a busy bit and a `command-ready` bit. Is it possible to implement this handshaking with only 1 bit? If it is, describe the protocol. If not, explain why 1 bit is insufficient.

13.4 Describe three circumstances under which blocking I/O should be used. Describe three circumstances under which nonblocking I/O should be used. Why not just implement nonblocking I/O and have processes busy-wait until their device is ready?

13.5 Why might a system use interrupt-driven I/O to manage a single serial port, but polling I/O to manage a front-end processor, such as a terminal concentrator?

13.6 Polling for an I/O completion can waste a large number of CPU cycles if the processor iterates a busy-waiting loop many times before the I/O completes. But if the I/O device is ready for service, polling can be much more efficient than is catching and dispatching an interrupt. Describe a hybrid strategy that combines polling, sleeping, and interrupts for I/O device service. For each of these three strategies (pure polling, pure interrupts, hybrid), describe a computing environment in which that strategy is more efficient than is either of the others.

13.7 UNIX coordinates the activities of the kernel I/O components by manipulating shared in-kernel data structures, whereas Windows NT uses object-oriented message passing between kernel I/O components. Discuss three pros and three cons of each approach.

13.8 How does DMA increase system concurrency? How does it complicate the hardware design?

13.9 Write (in pseudocode) an implementation of virtual clocks, including the queueing and management of timer requests for the kernel and applications. Assume that the hardware provides three timer channels.

13.10 Why is it important to scale up system bus and device speeds as the CPU speed increases?

13.11 Distinguish between a STREAMS driver and a STREAMS module.

Bibliographical Notes

Vahalia [1996] provides a good overview of I/O and networking in UNIX. Leffler et al. [1989] detail the I/O structures and methods employed in BSD UNIX.

Milenkovic [1987] discusses the complexity of I/O methods and implementation. The use and programming of the various interprocess-communication and network protocols in UNIX is explored in Stevens [1992]. Brain [1996] documents the Windows NT application interface. The I/O implementation in the sample MINIX OS is described in Tanenbaum and Woodhull [1997]. Custer [1994] includes detailed information on the NT message-passing implementation of I/O.

For details of hardware-level I/O handling and memory-mapping functionality, processor reference manuals (Motorola [1993] and Intel [1993]), are among the best sources. Hennessy and Patterson [2002] describe multiprocessor systems and cache-consistency issues. Tanenbaum [1990] describes hardware I/O design at a low level, and Sargent and Shoemaker [1995] provide a programmer's guide to low-level PC hardware and software. The IBM PC device I/O address map is given in IBM [1983]. An issue of the March 1994 *IEEE Computer* is devoted to advanced I/O hardware and software. Rago [1993] provides a good discussion on STREAMS.

Chapter 14

MASS-STORAGE STRUCTURE

The file system can be viewed logically as consisting of three parts. In Chapter 11, we saw the user and programmer interface to the file system. In Chapter 12, we described the internal data structures and algorithms used by the operating system to implement this interface. In this chapter, we discuss the lowest level of the file system: the secondary and tertiary storage structures. We first describe disk-scheduling algorithms that schedule the order of disk I/Os to improve performance. Next, we discuss disk formatting and management of boot blocks, damaged blocks, and swap space. We examine secondary storage structure, covering disk reliability and stable-storage implementation. We conclude with a brief description of tertiary storage devices, and the problems that arise when an operating system uses tertiary storage.

14.1 ■ Disk Structure

Disks provide the bulk of secondary storage for modern computer systems. Magnetic tape was used as an early secondary-storage medium, but the access time is much slower than for disks. Thus, tapes are currently used mainly for backup, for storage of infrequently used information, as a medium for transferring information from one system to another, and for storing quantities of data so large that they are impractical as disk systems. Tape storage is described in Section 14.8.

Modern disk drives are addressed as large one-dimensional arrays of **logical blocks**, where the logical block is the smallest unit of transfer. The size of a logical block is usually 512 bytes, although some disks can be **low-level formatted** to choose a different logical block size, such as 1,024 bytes. This option is described in Section 14.3.1.

The one-dimensional array of logical blocks is mapped onto the sectors of the disk sequentially. Sector 0 is the first sector of the first track on the outermost cylinder. The mapping proceeds in order through that track, then through the rest of the tracks in that cylinder, and then through the rest of the cylinders from outermost to innermost.

By using this mapping, we can—at least in theory—convert a logical block number into an old-style disk address that consists of a cylinder number, a track number within that cylinder, and a sector number within that track. In practice, it is difficult to perform this translation, for two reasons. First, most disks have some defective sectors, but the mapping hides this by substituting spare sectors from elsewhere on the disk. Second, the number of sectors per track is not a constant on some drives. On media that use **constant linear velocity (CLV)**, the density of bits per track is uniform. The farther a track is from the center of the disk, the greater its length, so the more sectors it can hold. As we move from outer zones to inner zones, the number of sectors per track decreases. Tracks in the outermost zone typically hold 40 percent more sectors than do tracks in the innermost zone. The drive increases its rotation speed as the head moves from the outer to the inner tracks to keep the same rate of data moving under the head. This method is used in CD-ROM and DVD-ROM drives. Alternatively, the disk rotation speed can stay constant, and the density of bits decreases from inner tracks to outer tracks to keep the data rate constant. This method is used in hard disks and is known as **constant angular velocity (CAV)**.

The number of sectors per track has been increasing as disk technology improves, and the outer zone of a disk usually has several hundred sectors per track. Similarly, the number of cylinders per disk has been increasing; large disks have tens of thousands of cylinders.

14.2 ■ Disk Scheduling

One of the responsibilities of the operating system is to use the hardware efficiently. For the disk drives, meeting this responsibility entails having a fast access time and disk bandwidth. The access time has two major components (also see Section 2.3.2). The **seek time** is the time for the disk arm to move the heads to the cylinder containing the desired sector. The **rotational latency** is the additional time waiting for the disk to rotate the desired sector to the disk head. The disk **bandwidth** is the total number of bytes transferred, divided by the total time between the first request for service and the completion of the last transfer. We can improve both the access time and the bandwidth by scheduling the servicing of disk I/O requests in a good order.

As we discussed in Chapter 2, whenever a process needs I/O to or from the disk, it issues a system call to the operating system. The request specifies several pieces of information:

- Whether this operation is input or output

- What the disk address for the transfer is

- What the memory address for the transfer is

- What the number of bytes to be transferred is

If the desired disk drive and controller are available, the request can be serviced immediately. If the drive or controller is busy, any new requests for service will be placed on the queue of pending requests for that drive. For a multiprogramming system with many processes, the disk queue may often have several pending requests. Thus, when one request is completed, the operating system chooses which pending request to service next.

14.2.1 FCFS Scheduling

The simplest form of disk scheduling is, of course, the first-come, first-served (FCFS) algorithm. This algorithm is intrinsically fair, but it generally does not provide the fastest service. Consider, for example, a disk queue with requests for I/O to blocks on cylinders

$$98, 183, 37, 122, 14, 124, 65, 67,$$

in that order. If the disk head is initially at cylinder 53, it will first move from 53 to 98, then to 183, 37, 122, 14, 124, 65, and finally to 67, for a total head movement of 640 cylinders. This schedule is diagrammed in Figure 14.1.

The wild swing from 122 to 14 and then back to 124 illustrates the problem with this schedule. If the requests for cylinders 37 and 14 could be serviced together, before or after the requests at 122 and 124, the total head movement could be decreased substantially, and performance could be thereby improved.

14.2.2 SSTF Scheduling

It seems reasonable to service all the requests close to the current head position, before moving the head far away to service other requests. This assumption is the basis for the **shortest-seek-time-first (SSTF) algorithm**. The SSTF algorithm selects the request with the minimum seek time from the current head position. Since seek time increases with the number of cylinders traversed by the head, SSTF chooses the pending request closest to the current head position.

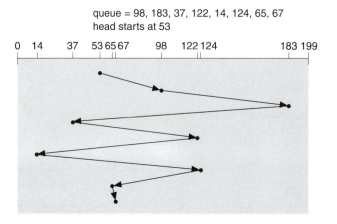

Figure 14.1   FCFS disk scheduling.

For our example request queue, the closest request to the initial head position (53) is at cylinder 65. Once we are at cylinder 65, the next closest request is at cylinder 67. From there, the request at cylinder 37 is closer than 98, so 37 is served next. Continuing, we service the request at cylinder 14, then 98, 122, 124, and finally 183 (Figure 14.2). This scheduling method results in a total head movement of only 236 cylinders—little more than one-third of the distance needed for FCFS scheduling of this request queue. This algorithm gives a substantial improvement in performance.

SSTF scheduling is essentially a form of shortest-job-first (SJF) scheduling, and, like SJF scheduling, it may cause starvation of some requests. Remember that requests may arrive at any time. Suppose that we have two requests in

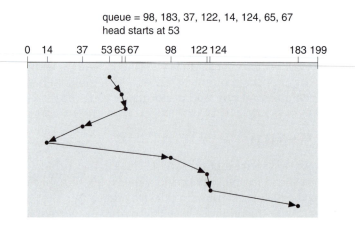

Figure 14.2   SSTF disk scheduling.

the queue, for cylinders 14 and 186, and while servicing the request from 14, a new request near 14 arrives. This new request will be serviced next, making the request at 186 wait. While this request is being serviced, another request close to 14 could arrive. In theory, a continual stream of requests near one another could arrive, causing the request for cylinder 186 to wait indefinitely. This scenario becomes increasingly likely if the pending-request queue grows long.

Although the SSTF algorithm is a substantial improvement over the FCFS algorithm, it is not optimal. In the example, we can do better by moving the head from 53 to 37, even though the latter is not closest, and then to 14, before turning around to service 65, 67, 98, 122, 124, and 183. This strategy reduces the total head movement to 208 cylinders.

14.2.3 SCAN Scheduling

In the **SCAN algorithm**, the disk arm starts at one end of the disk, and moves toward the other end, servicing requests as it reaches each cylinder, until it gets to the other end of the disk. At the other end, the direction of head movement is reversed, and servicing continues. The head continuously scans back and forth across the disk. We again use our example.

Before applying SCAN to schedule the requests on cylinders 98, 183, 37, 122, 14, 124, 65, and 67, we need to know the direction of head movement, in addition to the head's current position (53). If the disk arm is moving toward 0, the head will service 37 and then 14. At cylinder 0, the arm will reverse and will move toward the other end of the disk, servicing the requests at 65, 67, 98, 122, 124, and 183 (Figure 14.3). If a request arrives in the queue just in front of the head, it will be serviced almost immediately; a request arriving just behind

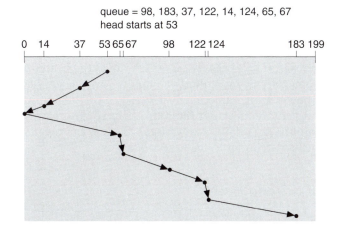

Figure 14.3   SCAN disk scheduling.

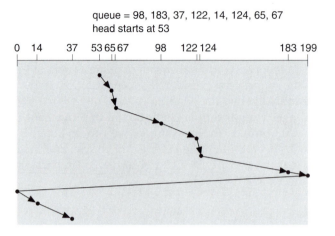

Figure 14.4   C-SCAN disk scheduling.

the head will have to wait until the arm moves to the end of the disk, reverses direction, and comes back.

The SCAN algorithm is sometimes called the **elevator algorithm**, since the disk arm behaves just like an elevator in a building, first servicing all the requests going up, and then reversing to service requests the other way.

Assuming a uniform distribution of requests for cylinders, consider the density of requests when the head reaches one end and reverses direction. At this point, relatively few requests are immediately in front of the head, since these cylinders have recently been serviced. The heaviest density of requests is at the other end of the disk. These requests have also waited the longest, so why not go there first? That is the idea of the next algorithm.

14.2.4 C-SCAN Scheduling

Circular SCAN (C-SCAN) scheduling is a variant of SCAN designed to provide a more uniform wait time. Like SCAN, C-SCAN moves the head from one end of the disk to the other, servicing requests along the way. When the head reaches the other end, however, it immediately returns to the beginning of the disk, without servicing any requests on the return trip (Figure 14.4). The C-SCAN scheduling algorithm essentially treats the cylinders as a circular list that wraps around from the final cylinder to the first one.

14.2.5 LOOK Scheduling

As we described them, both SCAN and C-SCAN move the disk arm across the full width of the disk. In practice, neither algorithm is implemented this way. More commonly, the arm goes only as far as the final request in each direction.

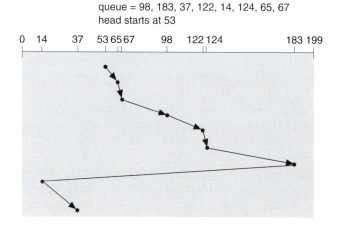

queue = 98, 183, 37, 122, 14, 124, 65, 67
head starts at 53

Figure 14.5   C-LOOK disk scheduling.

Then, it reverses direction immediately, without going all the way to the end of the disk. These versions of SCAN and C-SCAN are called **LOOK** and **C-LOOK scheduling**, because they *look* for a request before continuing to move in a given direction (Figure 14.5).

14.2.6 Selection of a Disk-Scheduling Algorithm

Given so many disk-scheduling algorithms, how do we choose the best one? SSTF is common and has a natural appeal because it increases performance over FCFS. SCAN and C-SCAN perform better for systems that place a heavy load on the disk, because they are less likely to have a starvation problem. For any particular list of requests, we can define an optimal order of retrieval, but the computation needed to find an optimal schedule may not justify the savings over SSTF or SCAN.

With any scheduling algorithm, however, performance depends heavily on the number and types of requests. For instance, suppose that the queue usually has just one outstanding request. Then, all scheduling algorithms are forced to behave the same, because they have only one choice for where to move the disk head: They all behave like FCFS scheduling.

The requests for disk service can be greatly influenced by the file-allocation method. A program reading a contiguously allocated file will generate several requests that are close together on the disk, resulting in limited head movement. A linked or indexed file, on the other hand, may include blocks that are widely scattered on the disk, resulting in greater head movement.

The location of directories and index blocks is also important. Since every file must be opened to be used, and opening a file requires searching the directory structure, the directories will be accessed frequently. Suppose that a directory entry is on the first cylinder and a file's data are on the final cylinder. In this case, the disk head has to move the entire width of the disk. If the directory entry were on the middle cylinder, the head would have to move, at most, one-half the width. Caching the directories and index blocks in main memory can also help to reduce the disk-arm movement, particularly for read requests.

Because of these complexities, the disk-scheduling algorithm should be written as a separate module of the operating system, so that it can be replaced with a different algorithm if necessary. Either SSTF or LOOK is a reasonable choice for the default algorithm.

The scheduling algorithms described here consider only the seek distances. For modern disks, the rotational latency can be nearly as large as the average seek time. But it is difficult for the operating system to schedule for improved rotational latency because modern disks do not disclose the physical location of logical blocks. Disk manufacturers have been alleviating this problem by implementing disk-scheduling algorithms in the controller hardware built into the disk drive. If the operating system sends a batch of requests to the controller, the controller can queue them and then schedule them to improve both the seek time and the rotational latency. If I/O performance were the only consideration, the operating system would gladly turn over the responsibility of disk scheduling to the disk hardware. In practice, however, the operating system may have other constraints on the service order for requests. For instance, demand paging may take priority over application I/O, and writes are more urgent than reads if the cache is running out of free pages. Also, it may be desirable to guarantee the order of a set of disk writes to make the file system robust in the face of system crashes. Consider what could happen if the operating system allocated a disk page to a file, and the application wrote data into that page before the operating system had a chance to flush the modified inode and free-space list back to disk. To accommodate such requirements, an operating system may choose to do its own disk scheduling and to spoon-feed the requests to the disk controller, one by one, for some types of I/O.

14.3 ■ Disk Management

The operating system is responsible for several other aspects of disk management, too. Here we discuss disk initialization, booting from disk, and bad-block recovery.

14.3.1 Disk Formatting

A new magnetic disk is a blank slate: It is just platters of a magnetic recording material. Before a disk can store data, it must be divided into sectors that the disk controller can read and write. This process is called low-level formatting (or **physical formatting**). **Low-level formatting** fills the disk with a special data structure for each sector. The data structure for a sector typically consists of a header, a data area (usually 512 bytes in size), and a trailer. The header and trailer contain information used by the disk controller, such as a sector number and an **error-correcting code (ECC)**. When the controller writes a sector of data during normal I/O, the ECC is updated with a value calculated from all the bytes in the data area. When the sector is read, the ECC is recalculated and is compared with the stored value. If the stored and calculated numbers are different, this mismatch indicates that the data area of the sector has become corrupted and that the disk sector may be bad (Section 14.3.3). The ECC is an error-*correcting* code because it contains enough information that, if only a few bits of data have been corrupted, the controller can identify which bits have changed and can calculate what their correct values should be. The controller automatically does the ECC processing whenever a sector is read or written.

Most hard disks are low-level formatted at the factory as a part of the manufacturing process. This formatting enables the manufacturer to test the disk and to initialize the mapping from logical block numbers to defect-free sectors on the disk. For many hard disks, when the disk controller is instructed to low-level format the disk, it can also be told how many bytes of data space to leave between the header and trailer of all sectors. It is usually possible to choose among a few sizes, such as 256, 512, and 1,024 bytes. Formatting a disk with a larger sector size means that fewer sectors can fit on each track, but that also means fewer headers and trailers are written on each track, and thus increases the space available for user data. Some operating systems can handle only a sector size of 512 bytes.

To use a disk to hold files, the operating system still needs to record its own data structures on the disk. It does so in two steps. The first step is to **partition** the disk into one or more groups of cylinders. The operating system can treat each partition as though it were a separate disk. For instance, one partition can hold a copy of the operating system's executable code, while another holds user files. After partitioning, the second step is **logical formatting** (or creation of a file system). In this step, the operating system stores the initial file-system data structures onto the disk. These data structures may include maps of free and allocated space (a FAT or inodes) and an initial empty directory.

Some operating systems give special programs the ability to use a disk partition as a large sequential array of logical blocks, without any file-system data structures. This array is sometimes called the raw disk, and I/O to this array is termed raw I/O. For example, some database systems prefer raw I/O because it enables them to control the exact disk location where each database record is stored. Raw I/O bypasses all the file-system services, such as the buffer cache, file locking, prefetching, space allocation, file names, and directories. We can make certain applications more efficient by implementing their own special-purpose storage services on a raw partition, but most applications perform better when they use the regular file-system services.

14.3.2 Boot Block

For a computer to start running—for instance, when it is powered up or rebooted—it needs to have an initial program to run. This initial bootstrap program tends to be simple. It initializes all aspects of the system, from CPU registers to device controllers and the contents of main memory, and then starts the operating system. To do its job, the bootstrap program finds the operating-system kernel on disk, loads that kernel into memory, and jumps to an initial address to begin the operating-system execution.

For most computers, the bootstrap is stored in **read-only memory (ROM)**. This location is convenient, because ROM needs no initialization and is at a fixed location that the processor can start executing when powered up or reset. And, since ROM is read only, it cannot be infected by a computer virus. The problem is that changing this bootstrap code requires changing the ROM hardware chips. For this reason, most systems store a tiny bootstrap loader program in the boot ROM, whose only job is to bring in a full bootstrap program from disk. The full bootstrap program can be changed easily: A new version is simply written onto the disk. The full bootstrap program is stored in a partition called the boot blocks, at a fixed location on the disk. A disk that has a boot partition is called a **boot disk** or **system disk**.

The code in the boot ROM instructs the disk controller to read the boot blocks into memory (no device drivers are loaded at this point), and then starts executing that code. The full bootstrap program is more sophisticated than the bootstrap loader in the boot ROM; it is able to load the entire operating system from a nonfixed location on disk, and to start the operating system running. Even so, the full bootstrap code may be small. For example, MS-DOS uses one 512-byte block for its boot program (Figure 14.6).

14.3.3 Bad Blocks

Because disks have moving parts and small tolerances (recall that the disk head flies just above the disk surface), they are prone to failure. Sometimes the failure is complete, and the disk needs to be replaced, and its contents restored from backup media to the new disk. More frequently, one or more sectors become defective. Most disks even come from the factory with **bad blocks**. Depending on the disk and controller in use, these blocks are handled in a variety of ways.

On simple disks, such as some disks with IDE controllers, bad blocks are handled manually. For instance, the MS-DOS format command does a logical format and, as a part of the process, scans the disk to find bad blocks. If format finds a bad block, it writes a special value into the corresponding FAT entry to tell the allocation routines not to use that block. If blocks go bad during normal operation, a special program (such as chkdsk) must be run manually to search for the bad blocks and to lock them away as before. Data that resided on the bad blocks usually are lost.

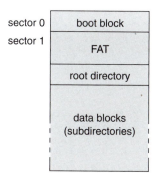

Figure 14.6   MS-DOS disk layout.

More sophisticated disks, such as the SCSI disks used in high-end PCs and most workstations and servers, are smarter about bad-block recovery. The controller maintains a list of bad blocks on the disk. The list is initialized during the low-level format at the factory, and is updated over the life of the disk. Low-level formatting also sets aside spare sectors not visible to the operating system. The controller can be told to replace each bad sector logically with one of the spare sectors. This scheme is known as **sector sparing** or **forwarding**.

A typical bad-sector transaction might be as follows:

- The operating system tries to read logical block 87.

- The controller calculates the ECC and finds that the sector is bad. It reports this finding to the operating system.

- The next time that the system is rebooted, a special command is run to tell the SCSI controller to replace the bad sector with a spare.

- After that, whenever the system requests logical block 87, the request is translated into the replacement sector's address by the controller.

Such a redirection by the controller could invalidate any optimization by the operating system's disk-scheduling algorithm! For this reason, most disks are formatted to provide a few spare sectors in each cylinder, and a spare cylinder as well. When a bad block is remapped, the controller uses a spare sector from the same cylinder, if possible.

As an alternative to sector sparing, some controllers can be instructed to replace a bad block by **sector slipping**. Here is an example: Suppose that logical block 17 becomes defective, and the first available spare follows sector 202. Then, sector slipping would remap all the sectors from 17 to 202, moving them all down one spot. That is, sector 202 would be copied into the spare, then sector 201 into 202, and then 200 into 201, and so on, until sector 18 is copied into sector 19. Slipping the sectors in this way frees up the space of sector 18, so sector 17 can be mapped to it.

The replacement of a bad block generally is not a totally automatic process because the data in the bad block are usually lost. Thus, whatever file was using that block must be repaired (for instance, by restoration from a backup tape), and that requires manual intervention.

14.4 ■ Swap-Space Management

Swap-space management is another low-level task of the operating system. Virtual memory uses disk space as an extension of main memory. Since disk access is much slower than memory access, using swap space significantly decreases system performance. The main goal for the design and implementation of swap space is to provide the best throughput for the virtual-memory system. In this section, we discuss how swap space is used, where swap space is located on disk, and how swap space is managed.

14.4.1 Swap-Space Use

Swap space is used in various ways by different operating systems, depending on the implemented memory-management algorithms. For instance, systems that implement swapping may use swap space to hold the entire process image, including the code and data segments. Paging systems may simply store pages that have been pushed out of main memory. The amount of swap space needed on a system can therefore vary depending on the amount of physical memory, the amount of virtual memory it is backing, and the way in which the virtual memory is used. It can range from a few megabytes of disk space to gigabytes.

Some operating systems, such as UNIX, allow the use of multiple swap spaces. These swap spaces are usually put on separate disks, so the load placed on the I/O system by paging and swapping can be spread over the system's I/O devices.

Note that it is safer to overestimate than to underestimate swap space, because if a system runs out of swap space it may be forced to abort processes or may crash entirely. Overestimation wastes disk space that could otherwise be used for files, but does no other harm.

14.4.2 Swap-Space Location

A swap space can reside in two places: Swap space can be carved out of the normal file system, or it can be in a separate disk partition. If the swap space is simply a large file within the file system, normal file-system routines can be used to create it, name it, and allocate its space. This approach, though easy to implement, is also inefficient. Navigating the directory structure and the disk-allocation data structures takes time and (potentially) extra disk accesses. External fragmentation can greatly increase swapping times by forcing multiple seeks during reading or writing of a process image. We can improve performance by caching the block location information in physical memory, and by using special tools to allocate physically contiguous blocks for the swap file, but the cost of traversing the file-system data structures still remains.

Alternatively, swap space can be created in a separate disk partition. No file system or directory structure is placed on this space. Rather, a separate swap-space storage manager is used to allocate and deallocate the blocks. This manager uses algorithms optimized for speed, rather than for storage efficiency. Internal fragmentation may increase, but this tradeoff is acceptable because data in the swap space generally live for much shorter amounts of time than do files in the file system, and the swap area may be accessed much more frequently. This approach creates a fixed amount of swap space during disk partitioning. Adding more swap space can be done only via repartitioning of the disk (which involves moving or destroying and restoring the other file-system partitions from backup), or via adding another swap space elsewhere.

Some operating systems are flexible and can swap both in raw partitions and in file-system space. Solaris 2 is an example. The policy and implementation are separate, allowing the machine's administrator to decide which type to use. The tradeoff is between the convenience of allocation and management in the file system, and the performance of swapping in raw partitions.

14.4.3 Swap-Space Management: An Example

To illustrate the methods used to manage swap space, we now follow the evolution of swapping and paging in UNIX. As discussed fully in Appendix A, UNIX started with an implementation of swapping that copied entire processes between contiguous disk regions and memory. UNIX evolved to a combination of swapping and paging, as paging hardware became available.

In 4.3 BSD, swap space is allocated to a process when the process is started. Enough space is set aside to hold the program, known as the **text pages** or the **text segment**, and the **data segment** of the process. Preallocating all the needed space in this way generally prevents a process from running out of swap space while it executes. When a process starts, its text is paged in from the file system. These pages are written out to swap when necessary, and are read back in from there, so the file system is consulted only once for each text page. Pages from the data segment are read in from the file system, or are created (if they are uninitialized), and are written to swap space and paged back in as needed. One optimization (for instance, when two users run the same editor) is that processes with identical text pages share these pages, both in physical memory and in swap space.

Two per-process **swap maps** are used by the kernel to track swap-space use. The text segment is a fixed size, so its swap space is allocated in 512 KB chunks, except for the final chunk, which holds the remainder of the pages, in 1 KB increments (Figure 14.7).

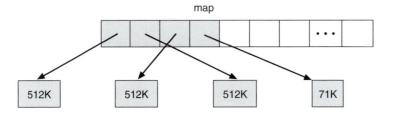

Figure 14.7   4.3 BSD text-segment swap map.

The data-segment swap map is more complicated, because the data segment can grow over time. The map is of fixed size, but contains swap addresses for blocks of varying size. Given index i, a block pointed to by swap-map entry i is of size $2^i \times 16$ KB, to a maximum of 2 MB. This data structure is shown in Figure 14.8. (The block size minimum and maximum are variable, and can be changed at system reboot.) When a process tries to grow its data segment beyond the final allocated block in its swap area, the operating system allocates another block, twice as large as the previous one. This scheme results in small processes using only small blocks. It also minimizes fragmentation. The blocks of large processes can be found quickly, and the swap map remains small.

In Solaris 1 (SunOS 4), the designers made changes to standard UNIX methods to improve efficiency and reflect technological changes. When a process executes, text-segment pages are brought in from the file system, accessed in main memory, and thrown away if selected for pageout. It is more efficient to reread a page from the file system than to write it to swap space and then to reread it from there.

More changes were made in Solaris 2. The biggest change is that Solaris 2 allocates swap space only when a page is forced out of physical memory, rather than when the virtual-memory page is first created. This change gives better performance on modern computers, which have more physical memory than older systems and tend to page less.

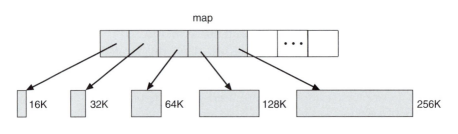

Figure 14.8   4.3 BSD data-segment swap map.

14.5 ■ RAID Structure

Disk drives have continued to get smaller and cheaper, so it is now economically feasible to attach a large number of disks to a computer system.

Having a large number of disks in a system presents opportunities for improving the rate at which data can be read or written, if the disks are operated in parallel. Furthermore, this setup offers the potential for improving the reliability of data storage, because redundant information can be stored on multiple disks. Thus, failure of one disk does not lead to loss of data. A variety of disk-organization techniques, collectively called redundant arrays of inexpensive disks (RAID), are commonly used to address the performance and reliability issues.

In the past, RAIDs composed of small cheap disks were viewed as a cost-effective alternative to large, expensive disks; today, RAIDs are used for their higher reliability and higher data-transfer rate, rather than for economic reasons. Hence, the *I* in *RAID* stands for "independent", instead of "inexpensive."

14.5.1 Improvement of Reliability via Redundancy

Let us first consider reliability. The chance that some disk out of a set of N disks will fail is much higher than the chance that a specific single disk will fail. Suppose that the **mean time to failure** of a single disk is 100,000 hours. Then, the mean time to failure of some disk in an array of 100 disks will be $100,000/100 = 1,000$ hours, or 41.66 days, which is not long at all! If we store only one copy of the data, then each disk failure will result in loss of a significant amount of data—such a high rate of data loss is unacceptable.

The solution to the problem of reliability is to introduce **redundancy**; we store extra information that is not needed normally, but that can be used in the event of failure of a disk to rebuild the lost information. Thus, even if a disk fails, data are not lost.

The simplest (but most expensive) approach to introducing redundancy is to duplicate every disk. This technique is called **mirroring** (or **shadowing**). A logical disk then consists of two physical disks, and every write is carried out on both disks. If one of the disks fails, the data can be read from the other. Data will be lost only if the second disk fails before the first failed disk is replaced.

The mean time to failure—where *failure* is the loss of data—of a mirrored disk depends on two factors: the mean time to failure of the individual disks, as well as on the **mean time to repair**, which is the time it takes (on average) to replace a failed disk and to restore the data on it. Suppose that the failures of the two disks are **independent**; that is, the failure of one disk is not connected to the failure of the other. Then, if the mean time to failure of a single disk is 100,000 hours and the mean time to repair is 10 hours, then the **mean time to data loss** of a mirrored disk system is $100,000^2/(2 * 10) = 500 * 10^6$ hours, or 57,000 years!

You should be aware that the assumption of independence of disk failures is not valid. Power failures and natural disasters, such as earthquakes, fires, and floods, may result in damage to both disks at the same time. Also, manufacturing defects in a batch of disks can cause correlated failures. As disks age, the probability of failure increases, increasing the chance that a second disk will fail while the first is being repaired. In spite of all these considerations, however, mirrored-disk systems offer much higher reliability than do single-disk systems.

Power failures are a particular source of concern, since they occur far more frequently than do natural disasters. However, even with mirroring of disks, if writes are in progress to the same block in both disks, and power fails before both blocks are fully written, the two blocks can be in an inconsistent state. The solution to this problem is to write one copy first, then the next, so that one of the two copies is always consistent. Some extra actions are required when we restart after a power failure, to recover from incomplete writes.

14.5.2 Improvement in Performance via Parallelism

Now let us consider the benefit of parallel access to multiple disks. With disk mirroring, the rate at which read requests can be handled is doubled, since read requests can be sent to either disk (as long as both disks in a pair are functional, as is almost always the case). The transfer rate of each read is the same as in a single-disk system, but the number of reads per unit time has doubled.

With multiple disks, we can improve the transfer rate as well (or instead) by striping data across multiple disks. In its simplest form, **data striping** consists of splitting the bits of each byte across multiple disks; such striping is called **bit-level striping**. For example, if we have an array of eight disks, we write bit i of each byte to disk i. The array of eight disks can be treated as a single disk with sectors that are eight times the normal size, and, more important, that have eight times the access rate. In such an organization, every disk participates in every access (read or write), so the number of accesses that can be processed per second is about the same as on a single disk, but each access can read eight times as many data in the same time as on a single disk.

Bit-level striping can be generalized to a number of disks that either is a multiple of 8 or divides 8. For example, if we use an array of four disks, bits i and $4+i$ of each byte go to disk i. Further, striping does not need to be at the level of bits of a byte: For example, in **block-level striping**, blocks of a file are striped across multiple disks; with n disks, block i of a file goes to disk $(i \bmod n) + 1$. Other levels of striping, such as bytes of a sector or sectors of a block, also are possible.

In summary, there are two main goals of parallelism in a disk system:

1. Increase the throughput of multiple small accesses (that is, page accesses) by load balancing.

2. Reduce the response time of large accesses.

14.5.3 RAID Levels

Mirroring provides high reliability, but it is expensive. Striping provides high data-transfer rates, but it does not improve reliability. Numerous schemes to provide redundancy at lower cost by using the idea of disk striping combined with "parity" bits (which we describe next) have been proposed. These schemes have different cost–performance tradeoffs and are classified into levels called **RAID levels**. We describe the various levels here; Figure 14.9 shows them pictorially (in the figure, P indicates error-correcting bits and C indicates a second copy of the data). In all cases depicted in the figure, four disks' worth of

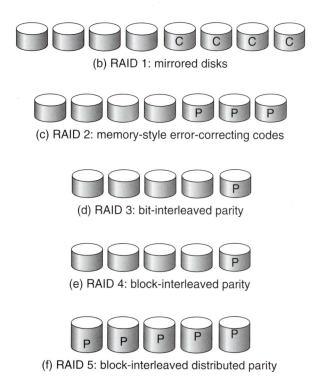

(a) RAID 0: non-redundant striping

(b) RAID 1: mirrored disks

(c) RAID 2: memory-style error-correcting codes

(d) RAID 3: bit-interleaved parity

(e) RAID 4: block-interleaved parity

(f) RAID 5: block-interleaved distributed parity

(g) RAID 6: P + Q redundancy

Figure 14.9   RAID levels.

data is stored, and the extra disks are used to store redundant information for failure recovery.

- **RAID Level 0:** RAID level 0 refers to disk arrays with striping at the level of blocks, but without any redundancy (such as mirroring or parity bits). Figure 14.9a shows an array of size 4.

- **RAID Level 1:** RAID level 1 refers to disk mirroring. Figure 14.9b shows a mirrored organization that holds four disks' worth of data.

- **RAID Level 2:** RAID level 2 is also known as **memory-style error-correcting-code (ECC) organization**. Memory systems have long implemented error detection using parity bits. Each byte in a memory system may have a parity bit associated with it that records whether the numbers of bits in the byte set to 1 is even (parity=0) or odd (parity=1). If one of the bits in the byte gets damaged (either a 1 becomes a 0, or a 0 becomes a 1), the parity of the byte changes and thus will not match the stored parity. Similarly, if the stored parity bit gets damaged, it will not match the computed parity. Thus, all single-bit errors are detected by the memory system. Error-correcting schemes store two or more extra bits, and can reconstruct the data if a single bit gets damaged. The idea of ECC can be used directly in disk arrays via striping of bytes across disks. For example, the first bit of each byte could be stored in disk 1, the second bit in disk 2, and so on until the eighth bit is stored in disk 8, and the error-correction bits are stored in further disks. This scheme is shown pictorially in Figure 14.9, where the disks labeled P store the error-correction bits. If one of the disks fails, the remaining bits of the byte and the associated error-correction bits can be read from other disks and be used to reconstruct the damaged data. Figure 14.9c shows an array of size 4; note RAID level 2 requires only three disks' overhead for four disks of data, unlike RAID level 1, which required four disks' overhead.

- **RAID level 3:** RAID level 3, or **bit-interleaved parity organization**, improves on level 2 by noting that, unlike memory systems, disk controllers can detect whether a sector has been read correctly, so a single parity bit can be used for error correction, as well as for detection. The idea is as follows. If one of the sectors gets damaged, we know exactly which sector it is, and, for each bit in the sector, we can figure out whether it is a 1 or a 0 by computing the parity of the corresponding bits from sectors in the other disks. If the parity of the remaining bits is equal to the stored parity, the missing bit is 0; otherwise, it is 1. RAID level 3 is as good as level 2 but is less expensive in the number of extra disks (it has only a one-disk overhead), so level 2 is not used in practice. This scheme is shown pictorially in Figure 14.9d.

  RAID level 3 has two benefits over level 1. Only one parity disk is needed for several regular disks, unlike one mirror disk for every disk in level 1, thus reducing the storage overhead. Since reads and writes of a byte are spread out over multiple disks, with N-way striping of data, the transfer rate for reading or writing a single block is N times as fast as with a RAID-level-1 organization using N-way striping. On the other hand, RAID level 3 supports a lower number of I/Os per second, since every disk has to participate in every I/O request. A further performance problem with RAID 3 (as with all parity-based RAID levels) is the expense of computing and writing the parity. This overhead results in significantly slower writes, as compared to non-parity RAID arrays. To moderate this performance penalty, many RAID storage arrays include a hardware controller with dedicated parity hardware. This offloads the parity computation from the CPU to the array. The array has a **nonvolatile RAM (NVRAM)** cache as well, to store the blocks while the parity is computed and to buffer the writes from the controller to the spindles. This combination can make parity RAID almost as fast as non-parity. In fact, a caching array doing parity RAID can outperform a non-caching non-parity RAID.

- **RAID Level 4:** RAID level 4, or **block-interleaved parity organization**, uses block-level striping, as in RAID 0, and in addition keeps a parity block on a separate disk for corresponding blocks from N other disks. This scheme is shown pictorially in Figure 14.9e. If one of the disks fails, the parity block can be used with the corresponding blocks from the other disks to restore the blocks of the failed disk.

  A block read accesses only one disk, allowing other requests to be processed by the other disks. Thus, the data-transfer rate for each access is slower, but multiple read accesses can proceed in parallel, leading to a higher overall I/O rate. The transfer rates for large reads is high, since all the disks can be read in parallel; large writes also have high transfer rates, since the data and parity can be written in parallel.

  Small independent writes, on the other hand, cannot be performed in parallel. A write of a block has to access the disk on which the block is stored, as well as the parity disk, since the parity block has to be updated. Moreover, both the old value of the parity block and the old value of the block being written have to be read for the new parity to be computed. This is known as the **read-modify-write**. Thus, a single write requires four disk accesses: two to read the two old blocks, and two to write the two new blocks.

- **RAID level 5:** RAID level 5, or **block-interleaved distributed parity**, differs from level 4 by spreading data and parity among all $N+1$ disks, rather than storing data in N disks and parity in one disk. For each block, one of the disks stores the parity, and the others store data. For example, with an array of five disks, the parity for the nth block is stored in disk $(n \bmod 5) + 1$; the nth blocks of the other four disks store actual data for that block. This setup is denoted pictorially in Figure 14.9f, where the Ps are distributed across all the disks. A parity block cannot store parity for blocks in the same disk, because a disk failure would result in loss of data as well as of parity, and hence would not be recoverable. By spreading the parity across all the disks in the set, RAID 5 avoids the potential overuse of a single parity disk that can occur with RAID 4.

- **RAID Level 6:** RAID level 6, also called the **P+Q redundancy scheme**, is much like RAID level 5, but stores extra redundant information to guard against multiple disk failures. Instead of using parity, error-correcting codes such as the **Reed–Solomon codes** are used. In the scheme shown in Figure 14.9g, 2 bits of redundant data are stored for every 4 bits of data— unlike 1 parity bit in level 5—and the system can tolerate two disk failures.

- **RAID level 0 + 1:** RAID level 0 + 1 refers to a combination of RAID levels 0 and 1. RAID 0 provides the performance, while RAID 1 provides the reliability. Generally, it provides better performance than RAID 5. It is common in environments where both performance and reliability are important. Unfortunately, it doubles the number of disks needed for storage, as does RAID 1, so it is also more expensive. In RAID 0 + 1, a set of disks are striped, and then the stripe is mirrored to another, equivalent stripe. Another RAID option that is becoming available commercially is RAID 1 + 0, in which disks are mirrored in pairs, and then the resulting mirror pairs are striped. This RAID has some theoretical advantages over RAID 0 + 1. For example, if a single disk fails in RAID 0 + 1, the entire stripe is inaccessible, leaving only the other stripe available. With a failure in RAID 1 + 0, the single disk is unavailable, but its mirrored pair is still available as are all the rest of the disks (Figure 14.10).

Finally, we note that numerous variations have been proposed to the basic RAID schemes described here. As a result, some confusion may exist about the exact definitions of the different RAID levels.

14.5.4 Selecting a RAID Level

If a disk fails, the time to rebuild its data can be significant and will vary with the RAID level used. Rebuilding is easiest for RAID level 1, since data can be copied from another disk; for the other levels, we need to access all the other disks in the array to rebuild data in a failed disk. The rebuild performance of a RAID system may be an important factor if continuous supply of data is required, as it is in high-performance or interactive database systems. Furthermore, rebuild performance influences the mean time to failure.

RAID level 0 is used in high-performance applications where data loss is not critical. RAID level 1 is popular for applications that require high reliability with fast recovery. RAID 0 + 1 and 1 + 0 are used where performance and reliability are important, for example for small databases. Due to RAID 1's high

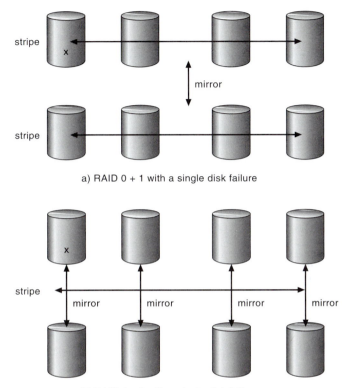

a) RAID 0 + 1 with a single disk failure

b) RAID 1 + 0 with a single disk failure

Figure 14.10   RAID 0 + 1 and 1 + 0.

space overhead, RAID level 5 is often preferred for storing large volumes of data. Level 6 is not supported currently by many RAID implementations, but it should offer better reliability than level 5.

RAID system designers have to make several other decisions as well. For example, how many disks should be in an array? How many bits should be protected by each parity bit? If more disks are in an array, data-transfer rates are higher, but the system is more expensive. If more bits are protected by a parity bit, the space overhead due to parity bits is lower, but the chance that a second disk will fail before the first failed disk is repaired is greater, and that will result in data loss.

One other aspect of most RAID implementations is a hot spare disk or disks. A **hot spare** is not used for data, but is configured to be used as a replacement should any other disk fail. For instance, a hot spare can be used to rebuild a mirror pair should one of the disks in the pair fail. In this way, the RAID level can be reestablished automatically, without waiting for the failed disk to be replaced. Allocating more than one hot spare allows more than one failure to be repaired without human intervention.

14.5.5 Extensions

The concepts of RAID have been generalized to other storage devices, including arrays of tapes, and even to the broadcast of data over wireless systems. When applied to arrays of tapes, the RAID structures are able to recover data even if one of the tapes in an array of tapes is damaged. When applied to broadcast of data, a block of data is split into short units and is broadcast along with a parity unit; if one of the units is not received for any reason, it can be reconstructed from the other units. Commonly, tape-drive robots containing multiple tape drives will stripe data across all the drives to increase throughput and decrease backup time.

14.6 ■ Disk Attachment

Computers access disk storage in two ways. One way is via I/O ports (or **host-attached storage**); this is common on small systems. The other way is via a remote host via a distributed file system; this is referred to as **network-attached storage**.

14.6.1 Host-Attached Storage

Host-attached storage is storage accessed via local I/O ports. These ports are available in several technologies. The typical desktop PC uses an I/O bus architecture called IDE or ATA. This architecture supports a maximum of two drives per I/O bus. High-end workstations and servers generally use more sophisticated I/O architectures such as SCSI and fibre channel (FC).

SCSI is a bus architecture. Its physical medium is usually a ribbon cable having a large number of conductors (typically 50 or 68). The SCSI protocol supports a maximum of 16 devices on the bus. Typically this consists of one controller card in the host (the **SCSI initiator**), and up to 15 storage devices (the **SCSI targets**). A SCSI disk is a typical SCSI target, but the protocol provides the ability to address up to 8 **logical units** in each SCSI target. A typical use of logical unit addressing is to direct commands to components of a RAID array, or components of a removable media library (such as a CD jukebox sending commands to the media changer mechanism or to one of the drives).

FC is a high-speed serial architecture. This architecture can operate over optical fiber or over a 4-conductor copper cable. It has two variants. One is a large switched fabric having a 24-bit address space. This method is expected to dominate in the future, and is the basis of **storage-area networks (SANs)**. Because of the large address space and the switched nature of the communication, multiple hosts and storage devices can attach to the fabric, allowing great flexibility in I/O communication. The other is an **arbitrated loop (FC-AL)** that can address 126 devices (drives and controllers).

A wide variety of storage devices are suitable for use as host-attached storage. Among these are hard disk drives, RAID arrays, and CD, DVD, and tape drives.

The I/O commands that initiate data transfers to a host-attached storage device are reads and writes of logical data blocks, directed to specifically identified storage units (such as bus ID, SCSI ID, and target logical unit, for example).

14.6.2 Network-Attached Storage

A network-attached storage device is a special-purpose storage system that is accessed remotely over a data network (Figure 14.11). Clients access network-attached storage (NAS) via a remote-procedure-call interface such as NFS for UNIX systems, or CIFS for Windows machines. The remote procedure calls (RPCs) are carried via TCP or UDP over an IP network—usually the same local-area network (LAN) that carries all data traffic to the clients. The network-attached storage unit is usually implemented as a RAID array with software that implements the remote procedure call interface. It is easiest to think of NAS as simply another storage-access protocol. For example, rather than using a SCSI device driver and SCSI protocols to access storage, a system using NAS would use RPC over TCP/IP.

Network-attached storage provides a convenient way for all the computers on a LAN to share a pool of storage, with the same ease of naming and access enjoyed with local host-attached storage. However, it tends to be less efficient and have lower performance than some direct-attached storage options.

14.6.3 Storage-Area Network

One drawback of network-attached storage systems is that the storage I/O operations consume bandwidth on the data network, thereby increasing the latency of network communication. This problem can be particularly acute

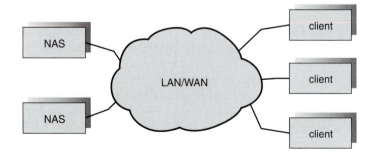

Figure 14.11   Network-attached storage.

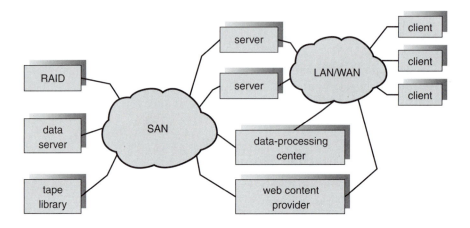

Figure 14.12   Storage-area network.

in large client–server installations—the communication between servers and clients competes for bandwidth with the communication among servers and storage devices.

A storage-area network (SAN) is a private network (using storage protocols rather than networking protocols) among the servers and storage units, separate from the LAN or WAN that connects the servers to the clients (Figure 14.12). The power of a SAN lies in its flexibility. Multiple hosts and multiple storage arrays can attach to the same SAN, and storage can be dynamically allocated to hosts. As one example, if a host is running low on disk space, the SAN can be configured to allocate more storage to that host. In 2003, many proprietary single-vendor SAN systems are available, but SAN components are not well standardized or interoperable. Most SAN systems in 2003 are based on fibre-channel loops or fibre-channel switched networks. One emerging alternative to a fibre-channel interconnect for the SAN is storage over IP network infrastructure such as Gigabit Ethernet. Another potential alternative is a special-purpose SAN architecture named Infiniband, which provides hardware and software support for high-speed interconnection networks for servers and storage units.

14.7 ■ Stable-Storage Implementation

In Chapter 7, we introduced the write-ahead log, which required the availability of stable storage. By definition, information residing in stable storage is *never* lost. To implement such storage, we need to replicate the needed information on multiple storage devices (usually disks) with independent failure modes. We need to coordinate the writing of updates in a way that guarantees that a failure during an update will not leave all the copies in a damaged state, and that, when we are recovering from a failure, we can force all copies to a consistent and correct value, even if another failure occurs during the recovery. In the remainder of this section, we discuss how to meet our needs.

A disk write results in one of three outcomes:

1. **Successful completion:** The data were written correctly on disk.

2. **Partial failure:** A failure occurred in the midst of transfer, so only some of the sectors were written with the new data, and the sector being written during the failure may have been corrupted.

3. **Total failure:** The failure occurred before the disk write started, so the previous data values on the disk remain intact.

We require that, whenever a failure occurs during writing of a block, the system detects it and invokes a recovery procedure to restore the block to a consistent state. To do that, the system must maintain two physical blocks for each logical block. An output operation is executed as follows:

1. Write the information onto the first physical block.

2. When the first write completes successfully, write the same information onto the second physical block.

3. Declare the operation complete only after the second write completes successfully.

During recovery from a failure, each pair of physical blocks is examined. If both are the same and no detectable error exists, then no further action is necessary. If one block contains a detectable error, then we replace its contents with the value of the other block. If both blocks contain no detectable error, but they differ in content, then we replace the content of the first block with the value of the second. This recovery procedure ensures that a write to stable storage either succeeds completely or results in no change.

We can extend this procedure easily to allow the use of an arbitrarily large number of copies of each block of stable storage. Although a large number of copies further reduces the probability of a failure, it is usually reasonable to simulate stable storage with only two copies. The data in stable storage are guaranteed to be safe unless a failure destroys all the copies.

Because waiting for disk writes to complete (synchronous I/O) is time consuming, many storage arrays add NVRAM as a cache. Because the memory is nonvolatile (usually it has battery power as a backup to the unit's power), it can be trusted to store the data on its way to the disks. It is thus considered part of the stable storage. Writes to it are much faster than to disk, so performance is greatly improved.

14.8 ■ Tertiary-Storage Structure

Would you buy a VCR that had inside it only one tape that you could not take out or replace? Or an audio cassette player or CD player that had one album sealed inside? Of course not. You expect to use a VCR or CD player with many relatively inexpensive tapes or disks. On a computer as well, using many inexpensive cartridges with one drive lowers the overall cost.

14.8.1 Tertiary-Storage Devices

Low cost is the defining characteristic of tertiary storage. So, in practice, tertiary storage is built with **removable media**. The most common examples of removable media are floppy disks, CD-ROMs, and tapes; many other kinds of tertiary-storage devices are available as well.

14.8.1.1 Removable Disks

Removable disks are one kind of tertiary storage. Floppy disks are an example of removable magnetic disks. They are made from a thin flexible disk coated with magnetic material, enclosed in a protective plastic case. Although common floppy disks can hold only about 1 MB, similar technology is used for removable magnetic disks that hold more than 1 GB. Removable magnetic disks can be nearly as fast as hard disks, although the recording surface is at greater risk of damage from scratches.

A **magneto-optic disk** is another kind of removable disk. It records data on a rigid platter coated with magnetic material, but the recording technology is quite different from that for a magnetic disk. The magneto-optic head flies much farther from the disk surface than a magnetic disk head does, and the magnetic material is covered with a thick protective layer of plastic or glass. This arrangement makes the disk much more resistant to head crashes.

The drive has a coil that produces a magnetic field; at room temperature, the field is too large and too weak to magnetize a bit on the disk. To write a bit, the disk head flashes a laser beam at the disk surface. The laser is aimed at a tiny spot where a bit is to be written. The laser heats this spot, which makes the spot susceptible to the magnetic field. So the large, weak magnetic field can record a tiny bit.

The magneto-optic head is too far from the disk surface to read the data by detecting the tiny magnetic fields in the way that the head of a hard disk does. Instead, the drive reads a bit using a property of laser light called the **Kerr effect**. When a laser beam is bounced off of a magnetic spot, the polarization of the laser beam is rotated clockwise or counter-clockwise, depending on the orientation of the magnetic field. This rotation is what the head detects to read a bit.

Another category of removable disk is the **optical disk**. These disks do not use magnetism at all. They use special materials that can be altered by laser light to have relatively dark or bright spots. One example of optical-disk technology is the phase-change disk.

The **phase-change disk** is coated with a material that can freeze into either a crystalline or an amorphous state. The crystalline state is more transparent, and hence a laser beam is brighter when it passes through the phase-change material and bounces off the reflective layer. The phase-change drive uses laser light at three different powers: low power to read data, medium power to erase the disk by melting and refreezing the recording medium into the crystalline state, and a high power to melt the medium into the amorphous state to write to the disk. The most common examples of this technology are the re-recordable CD-RW and DVD-RW.

The kinds of disks described here can be used over and over. They are called **read–write disks**. In contrast, **write-once, read-many-times (WORM) disks** form another category. An old way to make a WORM disk is to manufacture a thin aluminum film sandwiched between two glass or plastic platters. To write a bit, the drive uses a laser light to burn a small hole through the aluminum. Because this burning cannot be reversed, any sector on the disk can be written only once. Although it is possible to destroy the information on a WORM disk by burning holes everywhere, it is virtually impossible to alter data on the disk, because holes can only be added, and the ECC code associated with each sector is likely to detect such additions. WORM disks are considered to be durable and reliable because the metal layer is safely encapsulated between the protective glass or plastic platters, and magnetic fields cannot damage the recording. A newer write-once technology records on an organic polymer dye instead of an aluminum layer: the dye absorbs laser light to form marks. This technology is used in the recordable CD-R and DVD-R.

Read-only disks, such as CD-ROM and DVD, come from the factory with the data pre-recorded. They use technology similar to that of WORM disks (although the pits are pressed, not burnt), and they are very durable.

Most removable disks are slower than their non-removable counterparts. The writing process is slower, as are rotation and sometimes seek time.

14.8.1.2   Tapes

Magnetic tape is another type of removable medium. As a general rule, a tape holds more data than an optical or magnetic disk cartridge. Tape drives and disk drives have similar transfer rates. But random access to tape is much slower than a disk seek, because it requires a fast-forward or rewind operation that takes tens of seconds, or even minutes.

Although a typical tape drive is more expensive than a typical disk drive, the price of a tape cartridge is lower than the price of the equivalent capacity of magnetic disks. So tape is an economical medium for purposes that do not require fast random access. Tapes are commonly used to hold backup copies of disk data. They are also used in large supercomputer centers to hold the enormous volumes of data used in scientific research and by large commercial enterprises.

Some tapes can hold much more data than can a disk drive; the surface area of a tape is much larger than the surface area of a disk. The storage capacity of tapes could improve even further, because at present the **areal density** (or bits per square inch) of tape technology is much less than that for magnetic disks.

Large tape installations typically use robotic tape changers that move tapes between tape drives and storage slots in a tape library. These mechanisms give the computer automated access to a large number of tape cartridges.

A robotic tape library can lower the overall cost of data storage. A disk-resident file that will not be needed for a while can be **archived** to tape, where the cost per gigabyte can be lower; if the file is needed in the future, the computer can **stage** it back into disk storage for active use. A robotic tape library is sometimes called **near-line** storage, since it is between the high performance of **on-line** magnetic disks and the low cost of **off-line** tapes sitting on shelves in a storage room.

14.8.1.3 Future Technology

In the future, other storage technologies may become important. One promising storage technology, **holographic storage**, uses laser light to record holographic photographs on special media. We can think of a black-and-white photograph as a two-dimensional array of pixels. Each pixel represents one bit: 0 for black, or 1 for white. A sharp photograph can hold millions of bits of data. And all the pixels in a hologram are transferred in one flash of laser light, so the data rate is extremely high. With continued development, holographic storage may become commercially viable.

Another storage technology under active research is based on **micro-electronic mechanical systems (MEMS)**. The idea is to apply the fabrication technologies that produce electronic chips in order to manufacture small data-storage machines. One proposal calls for the fabrication of an array of 10,000 tiny disk heads, with a square centimeter of magnetic storage material suspended above the array. When the storage material is moved lengthwise over the heads, each head accesses its own linear track of data on the material. The storage material can be shifted sideways slightly to enable all the heads to access their next track. Although it remains to be seen whether this technology can be successful, it may provide a nonvolatile data storage technology that is faster than magnetic disk and cheaper than semiconductor DRAM.

Whether the storage medium is a removable magnetic disk, a DVD, or a magnetic tape, the operating system needs to provide several capabilities to use removable media for data storage. These capabilities are discussed in Section 14.8.2.

14.8.2 Operating-System Jobs

Two major jobs of an operating system are to manage physical devices and to present a virtual-machine abstraction to applications. In this chapter, we saw that, for hard disks, the operating system provides two abstractions. One is the raw device, which is just an array of data blocks. The other is a file system. For a file system on a magnetic disk, the operating system queues and schedules the interleaved requests from several applications. Now, we shall see how the operating system does its job when the storage media are removable.

14.8.2.1 Application Interface

Most operating systems can handle removable disks almost exactly as they do fixed disks. When a blank cartridge is inserted into the drive (or mounted), the cartridge must be formatted, and then an empty file system is generated on the disk. This file system is used just like a file system on a hard disk.

Tapes are often handled differently. The operating system usually presents a tape as a raw storage medium. An application does not open a file on the tape; it opens the whole tape drive as a raw device. Usually, the tape drive then is reserved for the exclusive use of that application until the application exits or closes the tape device. This exclusivity makes sense, because random access on a tape can take tens of seconds, or even a few minutes, so interleaving random accesses to tapes from more than one application would be likely to cause thrashing.

When the tape drive is presented as a raw device, the operating system does not provide file-system services. The application must decide how to use the array of blocks. For instance, a program that backs up a hard disk to tape might store a list of file names and sizes at the beginning of the tape, and then copy the data of the files to the tape in that order.

It is easy to see the problems that can arise from this way of using tape. Since every application makes up its own rules for how to organize a tape, a tape full of data can generally be used by only the program that created it. For instance, even if we know that a backup tape contains a list of file names and file sizes followed by the file data in that order, we still would find it difficult to use the tape. How exactly are the file names stored? Are the file sizes in binary or in ASCII? Are the files written one per block, or are they all concatenated together in one tremendously long string of bytes? We do not even know the block size on the tape, because this variable is generally one that can be chosen separately for each block written.

For a disk drive, the basic operations are read, write, and seek. Tape drives, on the other hand, have a different set of basic operations. Instead of seek, a tape drive uses the locate operation. The tape locate operation is more precise than the disk seek operation, because it positions the tape to a specific logical block, rather than an entire track. Locating to block 0 is the same as rewinding the tape.

For most kinds of tape drives, it is possible to locate to any block that has been written on a tape. In a partly filled tape, however, it is not possible to locate into the empty space beyond the written area, because most tape drives manage their physical space differently from disk drives. For a disk drive, the sectors have a fixed size, and the formatting process must be used to place empty sectors in their final positions before any data can be written. Most tape drives have a variable block size, and the size of each block is determined on the fly, when that block is written. If an area of defective tape is encountered during writing, the bad area is skipped and the block is written again. This operation explains why it is not possible to locate into the empty space beyond the written area—the positions and numbers of the logical blocks have not yet been determined.

Most tape drives have a `read position` operation that returns the logical block number where the tape head is. Many tape drives also support a `space` operation for relative motion. So, for example, the operation `space -2` would locate backward over two logical blocks.

For most kinds of tape drives, writing a block has the side effect of logically erasing everything beyond the position of the write. In practice, this side effect means that most tape drives are append-only devices, because updating a block in the middle of the tape also effectively erases everything beyond that block. The tape drive implements this appending by placing an end-of-tape (EOT) mark after a block that is written. The drive refuses to locate past the EOT mark, but it is possible to locate to the EOT and then to start writing. Doing so overwrites the old EOT mark, and places a new one at the end of the new blocks just written.

In principle, a file system can be implemented on a tape. But many of the file-system data structures and algorithms would be different from those used for disks, because of the append-only property of tape.

14.8.2.2 File Naming

Another question that the operating system needs to handle is how to name files on removable media. For a fixed disk, naming is not difficult. On a PC, the file name consists of a drive letter followed by a path name. In UNIX, the file name does not contain a drive letter, but the mount table enables the operating system to discover on what drive the file is located. But if the disk is removable, knowing a drive that contained the cartridge at some time in the past does not mean knowing how to find the file. If every removable cartridge in the world had a different serial number, the name of a file on a removable device could be prefixed with the serial number, but to ensure that no two serial numbers are the same would require each one to be about 12 digits in length. Who could remember the names of her files if she had to memorize a 12-digit serial number for each one?

The problem becomes even more difficult when we want to write data on a removable cartridge on one computer, and then use the cartridge in another computer. If both machines are of the same type and have the same kind of removable drive, the only difficulty is knowing the contents and data layout on the cartridge. But if the machines or drives are different, many additional problems can arise. Even if the drives are compatible, different computers may store bytes in different orders, and may use different encodings for binary numbers and even for letters (such as ASCII on PCs versus EBCDIC on mainframes).

Today's operating systems generally leave the name-space problem unsolved for removable media, and depend on applications and users to figure out how to access and interpret the data. Fortunately, a few kinds of removable media are so well standardized that all computers use them the same way. One example is the CD. Music CDs use a universal format that is understood by any CD drive. Data CDs are available in only a few different formats, so it is usual for a CD drive and the operating-system device driver to be programmed to handle all the common formats. DVD formats are also well standardized.

14.8.2.3 Hierarchical Storage Management

A **robotic jukebox** enables the computer to change the removable cartridge in a tape or disk drive without human assistance. Two major uses of this technology are for backups and hierarchical storage systems. The use of a jukebox for backups is simple: when one cartridge becomes full, the computer instructs the jukebox to switch to the next cartridge. Some jukeboxes hold tens of drives and thousands of cartridges, with robotic arms managing the movement of tapes to the drives.

A hierarchical storage system extends the storage hierarchy beyond primary memory and secondary storage (that is, magnetic disk) to incorporate tertiary storage. Tertiary storage is usually implemented as a jukebox of tapes or removable disks. This level of the storage hierarchy is larger, cheaper, and probably slower.

Although the virtual-memory system can be extended in a straightforward manner to tertiary storage, this extension is rarely carried out in practice. The reason is that a retrieval from a jukebox can take tens of seconds or even minutes, and such a long delay is intolerable for demand paging and for other forms of virtual-memory use.

The usual way to incorporate tertiary storage is to extend the file system. Small and frequently used files remain on magnetic disk, while large and old files that are not actively used are archived to the jukebox. In some file-archiving systems, the directory entry for the file continues to exist, but the contents of the file no longer occupy space in secondary storage. If an application tries to open the file, the open system call is suspended until the file contents can be staged in from tertiary storage. When the contents are again available from magnetic disk, the open operation returns control to the application, which proceeds to use the disk-resident copy of the data. **Hierarchical storage management (HSM)** has been implemented in ordinary time-sharing systems such as TOPS-20, which ran on minicomputers from Digital Equipment Corporation in the late 1970s. Today, HSM is usually found in supercomputing centers and other large installations that have enormous volumes of data.

14.8.3 Performance Issues

As with any component of the operating system, the three most important aspects of tertiary-storage performance are speed, reliability, and cost.

14.8.3.1 Speed

The speed of tertiary storage has two aspects: bandwidth and latency. We measure the bandwidth in bytes per second. The **sustained bandwidth** is the average data rate during a large transfer, that is, the number of bytes divided by the transfer time. The **effective bandwidth** calculates the average over the entire I/O time, including the time for seek or locate and any cartridge-switching time in a jukebox. In essence, the sustained bandwidth is the data rate when the data stream is actually flowing, and the effective bandwidth is the overall data rate provided by the drive. The *bandwidth of a drive* is generally understood to mean the sustained bandwidth.

For removable disks, the bandwidth ranges from less than 0.25 MB per second for the slowest, to several megabytes per second for the fastest. Tapes have an even wider range of bandwidths, from less than 0.25 MB per second to over 30 MB per second. The fastest tape drives have significantly higher bandwidth than do removable disk drives.

The second aspect of speed is the **access latency**. By this performance measure, disks are much faster than tapes: Disk storage is essentially two-dimensional—all the bits are out in the open. A disk access simply moves the arm to the selected cylinder and waits for the rotational latency, which may take less than 5 milliseconds. By contrast, tape storage is three-dimensional. At any time, a small portion of the tape is accessible to the head, whereas most of the bits are buried below hundreds or thousands of layers of tape wound on the reel. A random access on tape requires winding the tape reels until the selected block reaches the tape head, which can take tens or hundreds of seconds. So we can generally say that random access within a tape cartridge is more than a thousand times slower than random access on disk.

If a jukebox is involved, the access latency can be significantly higher. For a removable disk to be changed, the drive must stop spinning, then the robotic arm must switch the disk cartridges, and the drive must spin up the new cartridge. This operation takes several seconds—about a hundred times longer than the random-access time within one disk. So switching disks in a jukebox incurs a relatively high performance penalty.

For tapes, the robotic-arm time is about the same as for disk. But for tapes to be switched, the old tape generally must rewind before it can be ejected, and that operation can take as long as 4 minutes. And, after a new tape is loaded into the drive, many seconds can be required for the drive to calibrate itself to the tape and to prepare for I/O. Although a slow tape jukebox can have a tape switch time of 1 or 2 minutes, this time is not enormously larger than the random-access time within one tape.

So, to generalize, we say that random access in a disk jukebox has a latency of tens of seconds, whereas random access in a tape jukebox has a latency of hundreds of seconds; switching tapes is expensive, but switching disks is not. Be careful not to overgeneralize: Some expensive tape jukeboxes can rewind, eject, load a new tape, and fast forward to a random item of data all in less than 30 seconds.

If we pay attention to only the performance of the drives in a jukebox, the bandwidth and latency seem reasonable. But if we focus our attention on the cartridges instead, there is a terrible bottleneck. Consider first the bandwidth. By comparison with a fixed disk, the bandwidth-to-storage-capacity ratio of a robotic library is much less favorable. To read all the data stored on a large hard disk could take about an hour. To read all the data stored in a large tape library could take years. The situation with respect to access latency is nearly as bad. To illustrate this, if 100 requests are queued for a disk drive, the average waiting time will be about 1 second. If 100 requests are queued for a tape library, the average waiting time could be over 1 hour. The low cost of tertiary storage results from having many cheap cartridges share a few expensive drives. But a removable library is best devoted to the storage of infrequently used data, because the library can satisfy only a relatively small number of I/O requests per hour.

14.8.3.2 Reliability

Although we often think *good performance* means *high speed*, another important aspect of performance is *reliability*. If we try to read some data and are unable to do so because of a drive or media failure, for all practical purposes the access time is infinitely long and the bandwidth is infinitely small. So it is important to understand the reliability of removable media.

Removable magnetic disks are somewhat less reliable than are fixed hard disks because the cartridge is more likely to be exposed to harmful environmental conditions such as dust, large changes in temperature and humidity, and mechanical forces such as shock and bending. Optical disks are considered very reliable, because the layer that stores the bits is protected by a transparent plastic or glass layer. The reliability of magnetic tape varies widely, depending on the kind of drive. Some inexpensive drives wear out tapes after a few dozen uses; other kinds are gentle enough to allow millions of reuses. By comparison with a magnetic disk, the head in a magnetic-tape drive is a weak spot. A disk head flies above the media, but a tape head is in close contact with the tape. The scrubbing action of the tape can wear out the head after a few thousands or tens of thousands of hours.

In summary, we say that a fixed disk drive is likely to be more reliable than a removable disk or tape drive, and an optical disk is likely to be more reliable than a magnetic disk or tape. But a fixed magnetic disk has one weakness. A head crash in a hard disk generally destroys the data, whereas the failure of a tape drive or optical disk drive often leaves the data cartridge unharmed.

14.8.3.3 Cost

Storage cost is another important factor. Here is a concrete example of how removable media may lower the overall storage cost. Suppose that a hard disk that holds X GB has a price of $200; of this amount, $190 is for the housing, motor, and controller, and $10 is for the magnetic platters. Then, the storage cost for this disk is $200/X$ per gigabyte. Now, suppose that we can manufacture the platters in a removable cartridge. For one drive and 10 cartridges, the total price is $190 + $100 and the capacity is 10X GB, so the storage cost is $29/X$ per gigabyte. Even if it is a little more expensive to make a removable cartridge, the cost per gigabyte of removable storage may well be lower than the cost per gigabyte of a hard disk, because the expense of one drive is averaged with the low price of many removable cartridges.

Figures 14.13, 14.14, and 14.15 show the cost trends per megabyte for DRAM memory, magnetic hard disks, and tape drives. The prices in the graphs are the lowest price found in advertisements in *BYTE* magazine and *PC Magazine* at the end of each year. These prices reflect the small-computer marketplace of the

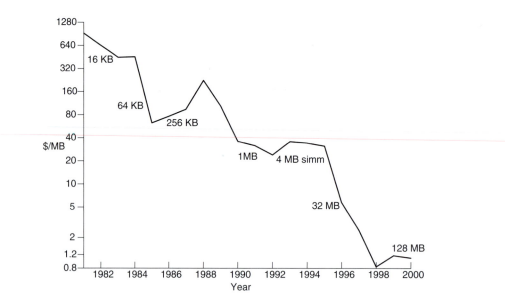

Figure 14.13   Price per megabyte of DRAM, from 1981 to 2000.

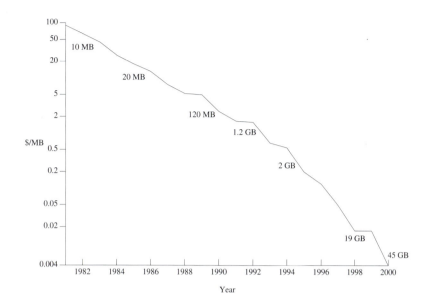

Figure 14.14   Price per megabyte of magnetic hard disk, from 1981 to 2000.

readership of these magazines, where prices are low by comparison with the mainframe and minicomputer markets. In the case of tape, the price is for a drive with one tape. The overall cost of tape storage becomes much lower as more tapes are purchased for use with the drive, because the price of a tape is a small fraction of the price of the drive. However, in a huge tape library containing thousands of cartridges, the storage cost is dominated by the cost of the tape cartridges. As of this writing in 2003, the cost per GB of tape cartridges can be approximated as $2.

The cost of DRAM fluctuates widely. In the period from 1981 to 2000, we can see three price crashes (around 1981, 1989, and 1996), as excess production caused a glut in the marketplace. We can also see two periods (around 1987 and 1993) where shortages in the marketplace caused significant price increases. In the case of hard disks, the price declines have been much steadier, although the price decline appears to have accelerated since 1992. Tape-drive prices also fell steadily up to 1997. Since 1997 the price per gigabyte of inexpensive tape drives has ceased its dramatic fall, although mid-range tape technology (such as DAT/DDS) has continued to fall, and is now approaching that of the inexpensive drives. Tape-drive prices are not shown prior to 1984, because *BYTE* magazine is targeted to the small-computer marketplace, and tape drives were not widely used with small computers prior to 1984.

By comparing these graphs we see that the price of disk storage has plummeted relative to the price of DRAM and tape.

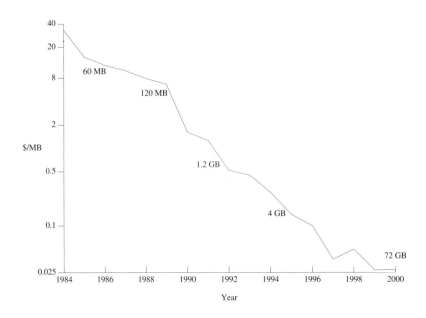

Figure 14.15   Price per megabyte of a tape drive, from 1984 to 2000.

The price per megabyte of magnetic disk has improved by more than four orders of magnitude during the past two decades, whereas the corresponding improvement for main memory has only been three orders of magnitude. Main memory today is more expensive than disk storage by a factor of 100.

The price per megabyte has dropped much more rapidly for disk drives than for tape drives. In fact, the price per megabyte of magnetic disk drives is approaching that of a tape cartridge without the tape drive. Consequently, small- and medium-size tape libraries have a higher storage cost than disk systems with equivalent capacity. The dramatic fall in disk prices has largely rendered tertiary storage obsolete: We no longer have any tertiary storage technology that is orders of magnitude less expensive than magnetic disk. It appears that the revival of tertiary storage must await a revolutionary technology breakthrough. Meanwhile, tape storage will find its use mostly limited to purposes such as backups of disk drives and archival storage in enormous tape libraries that greatly exceed the practical storage capacity of large disk farms.

14.9 ■ Summary

Disk drives are the major secondary-storage I/O device on most computers. Requests for disk I/O are generated by the file system and by the virtual-memory system. Each request specifies the address on the disk to be referenced, in the form of a logical block number.

Disk-scheduling algorithms can improve the effective bandwidth, the average response time, and the variance in response time. Algorithms such as SSTF, SCAN, C-SCAN, LOOK, and C-LOOK are designed to make such improvements by strategies for disk-queue ordering.

Performance can be harmed by external fragmentation. Some systems have utilities that scan the file system to identify fragmented files; they then move blocks around to decrease the fragmentation. Defragmenting a badly fragmented file system can significantly improve the performance, but the system may have reduced performance while the defragmentation is in progress. Sophisticated file systems, such as the UNIX Fast File System, incorporate many strategies to control fragmentation during space allocation, so that disk reorganization is not needed.

The operating system manages the disk blocks. First, a disk must be low-level formatted to create the sectors on the raw hardware—new disks usually come pre-formatted. Then, the disk is partitioned and file systems created, and boot blocks are allocated to store the system's bootstrap program. Finally, when a block is corrupted, the system must have a way to lock out that block, or to replace it logically with a spare.

Because an efficient swap space is a key to good performance, systems usually bypass the file system and use raw disk access for paging I/O. Some systems dedicate a raw disk partition to swap space, and others use a file within the file system instead. Other systems allow the user or system administrator to make the decision by providing both options.

The write-ahead log scheme requires the availability of stable storage. To implement such storage, we need to replicate the needed information on multiple nonvolatile storage devices (usually disks) with independent failure modes. We also need to update the information in a controlled manner to ensure that we can recover the stable data after any failure during data transfer or recovery.

Because of the amount of storage required on large systems, disks are frequently made redundant via RAID algorithms. These algorithms allow more than one disk to be used for a given operation, and allow continued operation and even automatic recovery in the face of a disk failure. RAID algorithms are organized into different levels where each level provides some combination of reliablity and high transfer rates.

Disks may be attached to a computer system one of two ways: (1) using the local I/O ports on the host computer or (2) using a network connection such as storage area networks.

Tertiary storage is built from disk and tape drives that use removable media. Many different technologies are available, including magnetic tape, removable magnetic and magneto-optic disks, and optical disks.

For removable disks, the operating system generally provides the full services of a file-system interface, including space management and request-queue scheduling. For many operating systems, the name of a file on a removable cartridge is a combination of a drive name and a file name within that drive. This convention is simpler but potentially more confusing than is using a name that identifies a specific cartridge.

For tapes, the operating system generally just provides a raw interface. Many operating systems have no built-in support for jukeboxes. Jukebox support can be provided by a device driver or by a privileged application designed for backups or for HSM.

Three important aspects of performance are bandwidth, latency, and reliability. A wide variety of bandwidths is available for both disks and tapes, but the random-access latency for a tape is generally much slower than that for a disk. Switching cartridges in a jukebox is also relatively slow. Because a jukebox has a low ratio of drives to cartridges, reading a large fraction of the data in a jukebox can take a long time. Optical media, which protect the sensitive layer by a transparent coating, are generally more robust than magnetic media, which expose the magnetic material to a greater possibility of physical damage.

■ Exercises

14.1 None of the disk-scheduling disciplines, except FCFS, are truly *fair* (starvation may occur).

    a. Explain why this assertion is true.

    b. Describe a way to modify algorithms such as SCAN to ensure fairness.

    c. Explain why fairness is an important goal in a time-sharing system.

    d. Give three or more examples of circumstances in which it is important that the operating system be *un*fair in serving I/O requests.

14.2 Suppose that a disk drive has 5,000 cylinders, numbered 0 to 4999. The drive is currently serving a request at cylinder 143, and the previous request was at cylinder 125. The queue of pending requests, in FIFO order, is

               86, 1470, 913, 1774, 948, 1509, 1022, 1750, 130.

Starting from the current head position, what is the total distance (in cylinders) that the disk arm moves to satisfy all the pending requests for each of the following disk-scheduling algorithms?

    a. FCFS

    b. SSTF

    c. SCAN

d. LOOK

e. C-SCAN

f. C-LOOK

14.3 Elementary physics states that when an object is subjected to a constant acceleration a, the relationship between distance d and time t is given by $d = \frac{1}{2}at^2$. Suppose that, during a seek, the disk in Exercise 14.2 accelerates the disk arm at a constant rate for the first half of the seek, then decelerates the disk arm at the same rate for the second half of the seek. Assume that the disk can perform a seek to an adjacent cylinder in 1 millisecond, and a full-stroke seek over all 5,000 cylinders in 18 milliseconds.

a. The distance of a seek is the number of cylinders that the head moves. Explain why the seek time is proportional to the square root of the seek distance.

b. Write an equation for the seek time as a function of the seek distance. This equation should be of the form $t = x + y\sqrt{L}$, where t is the time in milliseconds and L is the seek distance in cylinders.

c. Calculate the total seek time for each of the schedules in Exercise 14.2. Determine which schedule is the fastest (has the smallest total seek time).

d. The *percentage speedup* is the time saved divided by the original time. What is the percentage speedup of the fastest schedule over FCFS?

14.4 Suppose that the disk in Exercise 14.3 rotates at 7,200 RPM.

a. What is the average rotational latency of this disk drive?

b. What seek distance can be covered in the time that you found for part a?

14.5 The accelerating seek described in Exercise 14.3 is typical of hard-disk drives. By contrast, floppy disks (and many hard disks manufactured before the mid-1980s) typically seek at a fixed rate. Suppose that the disk in Exercise 14.3 has a constant-rate seek, rather than a constant-acceleration seek, so the seek time is of the form $t = x + yL$, where t is the time in milliseconds and L is the seek distance. Suppose that the time to seek to an adjacent cylinder is 1 millisecond, as before, and is 0.5 milliseconds for each additional cylinder.

a. Write an equation for this seek time as a function of the seek distance.

b. Using the seek-time function from part a, calculate the total seek time for each of the schedules in Exercise 14.2. Is your answer the same as it was for Exercise 14.3c? Explain why it is the same or why it is different.

c. What is the percentage speedup of the fastest schedule over FCFS in this case?

14.6 Write a Java program for disk scheduling using the SCAN and C-SCAN disk-scheduling algorithms.

14.7 Compare the performance of C-SCAN and SCAN scheduling, assuming a uniform distribution of requests. Consider the average response time (the time between the arrival of a request and the completion of that request's service), the variation in response time, and the effective bandwidth. How does performance depend on the relative sizes of seek time and rotational latency?

14.8 Is disk scheduling, other than FCFS scheduling, useful in a single-user environment? Explain your answer.

14.9 Explain why SSTF scheduling tends to favor middle cylinders over the innermost and outermost cylinders.

14.10 Requests are not usually uniformly distributed. For example, a cylinder containing the file system FAT or inodes can be expected to be accessed more frequently than a cylinder that contains only files. Suppose that you know that 50 percent of the requests are for a small, fixed number of cylinders.

a. Would any of the scheduling algorithms discussed in this chapter be particularly good for this case? Explain your answer.

b. Propose a disk-scheduling algorithm that gives even better performance by taking advantage of this "hot spot" on the disk.

c. File systems typically find data blocks via an indirection table, such as a FAT in DOS or inodes in UNIX. Describe one or more ways to take advantage of this indirection to improve the disk performance.

14.11 Why is rotational latency usually not considered in disk scheduling? How would you modify SSTF, SCAN, and C-SCAN to include latency optimization?

14.12 How would the use of a RAM disk affect your selection of a disk-scheduling algorithm? What factors would you need to consider? Do the same considerations apply to hard-disk scheduling, given that the file system stores recently used blocks in a buffer cache in main memory?

14.13 Why is it important to balance file system-I/O among the disks and controllers on a system in a multitasking environment?

14.14 What are the tradeoffs involved in rereading code pages from the file system, versus using swap space to store them?

14.15 Is there any way to implement truly stable storage? Explain your answer.

14.16 The reliability of a hard-disk drive is typically described in terms of a quantity called *mean time between failures* (MTBF). Although this quantity is called a "time," the MTBF actually is measured in drive-hours per failure.

a. If a system contains 1,000 disk drives, each of which has a 750,000 hour MTBF, which of the following best describes how often a drive failure will occur in that disk farm: once per thousand years, once per century, once per decade, once per year, once per month, once per week, once per day, once per hour, once per minute, or once per second?

b. Mortality statistics indicate that, on the average, a U.S. resident has about 1:1,000 chance of dying between ages 20 and 21 years. Deduce the MTBF hours for 20 year olds. Convert this figure from hours to years. What does this MTBF tell you about the expected lifetime of a 20 year old?

c. The manufacturer guarantees a 1-million hour MTBF for a certain model of disk drive. What can you conclude about the number of years for which one of these drives is under warranty?

14.17 The term *fast wide SCSI-II* denotes a SCSI bus that operates at a data rate of 20 MB per second when it moves a packet of bytes between the host and a device. Suppose that a fast wide SCSI-II disk drive spins at 7,200 RPM, has a sector size of 512 bytes, and holds 160 sectors per track.

a. Estimate the sustained transfer rate of this drive in megabytes per second.

b. Suppose that the drive has 7,000 cylinders, 20 tracks per cylinder, a head-switch time (from one platter to another) of 0.5 milliseconds, and an adjacent-cylinder seek time of 2 milliseconds. Use this additional information to give an accurate estimate of the sustained transfer rate for a huge transfer.

c. Suppose that the average seek time for the drive is 8 milliseconds. Estimate the I/Os per second and the effective transfer rate for a random-access workload that reads individual sectors scattered across the disk.

    d. Calculate the random-access I/Os per second and transfer rate for I/O sizes of 4 KB, 8 KB, and 64 KB.

    e. If multiple requests are in the queue, a scheduling algorithm such as SCAN should be able to reduce the average seek distance. Suppose that a random-access workload is reading 8 KB pages, the average queue length is 10, and the scheduling algorithm reduces the average seek time to 3 milliseconds. Calculate the I/Os per second and the effective transfer rate of the drive.

14.18 More than one disk drive can be attached to a SCSI bus. In particular, a fast wide SCSI-II bus (Exercise 14.17) can be connected to at most 15 disk drives. Recall that this bus has a bandwidth of 20 MB per second. At any time, only one packet can be transferred on the bus between some disk's internal cache and the host. However, a disk can be moving its disk arm while some other disk is transferring a packet on the bus. Also, a disk can be transferring data between its magnetic platters and its internal cache while some other disk is transferring a packet on the bus. Considering the transfer rates that you calculated for the various workloads in Exercise 14.17, discuss how many disks can be used effectively by one fast wide SCSI-II bus.

14.19 Remapping of bad blocks by sector sparing or sector slipping could influence performance. Suppose that the drive in Exercise 14.17 has a total of 100 bad sectors at random locations, and that each bad sector is mapped to a spare that is located on a different track, but within the same cylinder. Estimate the number of I/Os per second and the effective transfer rate for a random-access workload consisting of 8 KB reads, with a queue length of 1 (that is, the choice of scheduling algorithm is not a factor). What is the effect of a bad sector on performance?

14.20 Discuss the relative advantages and disadvantages of sector sparing and sector slipping.

14.21 The operating system generally treats removable disks as shared file systems, but assigns a tape drive to only one application at a time. Give three reasons that could explain this difference in treatment of disks and tapes. Describe the additional features that an operating system would need to support shared file-system access to a tape jukebox. Would the applications sharing the tape jukebox need any special properties, or could they use the files as though the files were disk-resident? Explain your answer.

14.22 In a disk jukebox, what would be the effect if the number of open files was greater than the number of drives in the jukebox?

14.23 What would be the effects on cost and performance if tape storage had the same areal density as disk storage?

14.24 If magnetic hard disks eventually have the same cost per gigabyte as do tapes, will tapes become obsolete, or will they still be needed? Explain your answer.

14.25 You can use simple estimates to compare the cost and performance of a terabyte storage system made entirely from disks with one that incorporates tertiary storage. Suppose that magnetic disks each hold 10 GB, cost $1,000, transfer 5 MB per second, and have an average access latency of 15 milliseconds. Suppose that a tape library costs $10 per gigabyte, transfers 10 MB per second, and has an average access latency of 20 seconds. Compute the total cost, the maximum total data rate, and the average waiting time for a pure disk system. If you make any assumptions about the workload, describe and justify them. Now, suppose that 5 percent of the data are frequently used, so they must reside on disk, but the other 95 percent are archived in the tape library. Further suppose that the disk system handles 95 percent of the requests, and the library handles the other 5 percent. What are the total cost, the maximum total data rate, and the average waiting time for this hierarchical storage system?

14.26 It is sometimes said that tape is a sequential-access medium, whereas magnetic disk is a random-access medium. In fact, the suitability of a storage device for random access depends on the transfer size. The term *streaming transfer rate* denotes the data rate for a transfer underway, excluding the effect of access latency. By contrast, the *effective transfer rate* is the ratio of total bytes per total seconds, including overhead time such as the access latency.

Suppose that, in a computer, the level-2 cache has an access latency of 8 nanoseconds and a streaming transfer rate of 800 MB per second, the main memory has an access latency of 60 nanoseconds and a streaming transfer rate of 80 MB per second, the magnetic disk has an access latency of 15 millisecond and a streaming transfer rate of 5 MB per second, and a tape drive has an access latency of 60 seconds and a streaming transfer rate of 2 MB per second.

   a. Random access causes the effective transfer rate of a device to decrease, because no data are transferred during the access time. For the disk described, what is the effective transfer rate if a streaming transfer of 512 bytes, 8 KB, 1 MB, and 16 MB follows an average access?

   b. The utilization of a device is the ratio of effective transfer rate to streaming transfer rate. Calculate the utilization of the disk drive for random access that performs transfers in each of the four sizes given in part a.

c. Suppose that a utilization of 25 percent (or higher) is considered acceptable. Using the performance figures given, compute the smallest transfer size for disk that gives acceptable utilization.

d. Complete the following sentence: A disk is a random-access device for transfers larger than _____ bytes, and is a sequential-access device for smaller transfers.

e. Compute the minimum transfer sizes that give acceptable utilization for cache, memory, and tape.

f. When is a tape a random-access device, and when is it a sequential-access device?

14.27 Imagine that a holographic storage drive has been invented. Suppose that the holographic drive costs $10,000 and has an average access time of 40 milliseconds. Suppose that it uses a $100 cartridge the size of a CD. This cartridge holds 40,000 images, and each image is a square black-and-white picture with resolution $6,000 \times 6,000$ pixels (each pixel stores 1 bit). Suppose that the drive can read or write one picture in 1 millisecond. Answer the following questions.

a. What would be some good uses for this device?

b. How would this device affect the I/O performance of a computing system?

c. Which other kinds of storage devices, if any, would become obsolete as a result of this device being invented?

14.28 Suppose that a one-sided 5.25-inch optical-disk cartridge has an areal density of 1 gigabit per square inch. Suppose that a magnetic tape has an areal density of 20 megabits per square inch, and is 1/2 inch wide and 1,800 feet long. Calculate an estimate of the storage capacities of these two kinds of storage cartridges. Suppose that an optical tape exists that has the same physical size as the tape, but the same storage density as the optical disk. What volume of data could the optical tape hold? What would be a marketable price for the optical tape if the magnetic tape cost $25?

14.29 Suppose that we agree that 1 KB is 1,024 bytes, 1 MB is $1,024^2$ bytes, and 1 GB is $1,024^3$ bytes. This progression continues through terabytes, petabytes, and exabytes ($1,024^6$). Several newly proposed scientific projects plan to be able to record and store a few exabytes of data during the next decade. To answer the following questions, you will need to make a few reasonable assumptions; state the assumptions that you make.

a. How many disk drives would be required to hold 4 exabytes of data?

b. How many magnetic tapes would be required to hold 4 exabytes of data?

c. How many optical tapes would be required to hold 4 exabytes of data (Exercise 14.28)?

d. How many holographic storage cartridges would be required to hold 4 exabytes of data (Exercise 14.27)?

e. How many cubic feet of storage space would each option require?

14.30 Discuss how an operating system could maintain a free-space list for a tape-resident file system. Assume that the tape technology is append-only, and that it uses the EOT mark and `locate`, `space`, and `read position` commands as described in Section 14.8.2.1.

Bibliographical Notes

Discussions of redundant arrays of independent disks (RAID) are presented by Patterson et al. [1988] and in the detailed survey of Chen et al. [1994]. Disk-system architectures for high-performance computing are discussed by Katz et al. [1989]. Teorey and Pinkerton [1972] present an early comparative analysis of disk-scheduling algorithms. They use simulations that model a disk for which seek time is linear in the number of cylinders crossed. For this disk, LOOK is a good choice for queue lengths below 140, and C-LOOK is good for queue lengths above 100. King [1990] describes ways to improve the seek time by moving the disk arm when the disk is otherwise idle. Seltzer et al. [1990] describe disk-scheduling algorithms that consider rotational latency in addition to seek time. Worthington et al. [1994] discuss disk performance, and show the negligible performance impact of defect management. The placement of hot data to improve seek times has been considered by Ruemmler and Wilkes [1991] and Akyurek and Salem [1993]. Ruemmler and Wilkes [1994] describe an accurate performance model for a modern disk drive. Worthington et al. [1995] tell how to determine low-level disk properties such as the zone structure, and this work is further advanced by Schindler and Gregory [1999].

The I/O size and randomness of the workload has a considerable influence on disk performance. Ousterhout et al. [1985] and Ruemmler and Wilkes [1993] report numerous interesting workload characteristics, including that most files are small, most newly created files are deleted soon thereafter, most files that are opened for reading are read sequentially in their entirety, and most seeks are short. McKusick et al. [1984] describe the Berkeley Fast File System, which uses many sophisticated techniques to obtain good performance for a wide variety of workloads. McVoy and Kleiman [1991] discuss further improvements to the basic FFS. Quinlan [1991] describes how to implement a file system on WORM storage with a magnetic disk cache; Richards [1990] discusses a file-system approach to tertiary storage. Maher et al. [1994] give an overview of the integration of distributed file systems and tertiary storage.

The concept of a storage hierarchy has been studied for more than a quarter of a century. For instance, a 1970 paper by Mattson et al. [1970] describes a mathematical approach to predict the performance of a storage hierarchy. Alt [1993] describes the accommodation of removable storage in a commercial operating system, and Miller and Katz [1993] describe the characteristics of tertiary-storage access in a supercomputing environment. Benjamin [1990] gives an overview of the massive storage requirements for the EOSDIS project at NASA.

Holographic-storage technology is the subject of an article by Psaltis and Mok [1995]; a collection of holographic-storage papers dating from 1963 has been assembled by Sincerbox [1994]. Asthana and Finkelstein [1995] describe several emerging storage technologies, including holographic storage, optical tape, and electron trapping. Toigo [2000] gives an in-depth description of modern disk technology and several potential future storage technologies.

Part Five

DISTRIBUTED SYSTEMS

A distributed system is a collection of processors that do not share memory or a clock. Instead, each processor has its own local memory, and the processors communicate with each other through communication lines such as local- or wide-area networks. The processors in a distributed system vary in size and function. Such systems may include small handheld or real-time devices, personal computers, workstations, and large mainframe computer systems.

The benefits of a distributed system include user access to the resources maintained by the system and therefore computation speedup and improved data availability and reliability. A distributed file system is a file-service system whose users, servers, and storage devices are dispersed among the sites of a distributed system. Accordingly, service activity has to be carried out across the network; instead of a single centralized data repository, there are multiple and independent storage devices.

Because a system is distributed, however, it must provide mechanisms for process synchronization and communication, for dealing with the deadlock problem, and for dealing with failures that are not encountered in a centralized system.

Chapter 15

DISTRIBUTED SYSTEM STRUCTURES

A distributed system is a collection of processors that do not share memory or a clock. Instead, each processor has its own local memory. The processors communicate with one another through various communication networks, such as high-speed buses or telephone lines. In this chapter, we discuss the general structure of distributed systems and the networks that interconnect them. We contrast the main differences in operating-system design between these systems and the centralized systems with which we were concerned previously. Detailed discussions are given in Chapters 16 and 17.

15.1 ■ Background

A **distributed system** is a collection of loosely coupled processors interconnected by a **communication network**. From the point of view of a specific processor in a distributed system, the rest of the processors and their respective resources are **remote**, whereas its own resources are local.

The processors in a distributed system may vary in size and function. They may include small microprocessors, workstations, minicomputers, and large general-purpose computer systems. These processors are referred to by a number of names, such as *sites, nodes, computers, machines,* or *hosts,* depending on the context in which they are mentioned. We mainly use *site* to indicate the location of a machine and *host* to refer to a specific system at a site. Generally, one host at one site, the *server,* has a resource that another host at another site, the *client* (or user), would like to use. The purpose of the distributed system is to

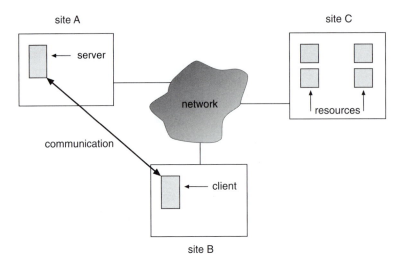

Figure 15.1   A distributed system.

provide an efficient and convenient environment for such sharing of resources. A distributed system is shown in Figure 15.1.

15.1.1 Advantages of Distributed Systems

The four major reasons for building distributed systems are: *resource sharing, computation speedup, reliability,* and *communication.* In this section, we briefly discuss each of them.

15.1.1.1 Resource Sharing

If a number of different sites (with different capabilities) are connected to one another, then a user at one site may be able to use the resources available at another. For example, a user at site A may be using a laser printer located at site B. Meanwhile, a user at B may access a file that resides at A. In general, **resource sharing** in a distributed system provides mechanisms for sharing files at remote sites, processing information in a distributed database, printing files at remote sites, using remote specialized hardware devices (such as a high-speed array processor), and performing other operations.

15.1.1.2 Computation Speedup

If a particular computation can be partitioned into subcomputations that can run concurrently, then a distributed system allows us to distribute the subcomputations among the various sites; the subcomputations can be run concurrently and thus provide **computation speedup**. In addition, if a particular site is currently overloaded with jobs, some of them may be moved to other, lightly loaded sites. This movement of jobs is called **load sharing**. Automated load sharing, in which the distributed operating system automatically moves jobs, is not yet common in commercial systems.

15.1.1.3 Reliability

If one site fails in a distributed system, the remaining sites can continue operating, giving the system better reliability. If the system is composed of multiple large autonomous installations (that is, general-purpose computers), the failure of one of them should not affect the rest. If, however, the system is composed of small machines, each of which is responsible for some crucial system function (such as terminal character I/O or the file system), then a single failure may halt the operation of the whole system. In general, with enough redundancy (in both hardware and data), the system can continue operation, even if some of its sites have failed.

The failure of a site must be detected by the system, and appropriate action may be needed to recover from the failure. The system must no longer use the services of that site. In addition, if the function of the failed site can be taken over by another site, the system must ensure that the transfer of function occurs correctly. Finally, when the failed site recovers or is repaired, mechanisms must be available to integrate it back into the system smoothly. As we shall see in Chapters 16 and 17, these actions present difficult problems that have many possible solutions.

15.1.1.4 Communication

When several sites are connected to one another by a communication network, the users at different sites have the opportunity to exchange information. At a low level, **messages** are passed between systems, much as messages are passed between processes in the single-computer message system discussed in Section 4.5. Given message passing, all the higher-level functionality found in standalone systems can be expanded to encompass the distributed system. Such functions include file transfer, login, mail, and remote procedure calls (RPCs).

The advantage of a distributed system is that these functions can be carried out over great distances. Two people at geographically disparate sites can collaborate on a project, for example. By transferring the files of the project, logging in to each other's remote systems to run programs, and exchanging mail to coordinate the work, users minimize the limitations inherent in long-distance work. We wrote this book by collaborating in such a manner.

The advantages of distributed systems have resulted in an industry-wide trend toward **downsizing**. Many companies are replacing their mainframes with networks of workstations or personal computers. Companies get a bigger bang for the buck (that is, better functionality for the cost), more flexibility in locating resources and expanding facilities, better user interfaces, and easier maintenance.

15.1.2 Types of Distributed Operating Systems

In this section, we describe the two general categories of network-oriented operating systems: network operating systems and distributed operating systems. Network operating systems are simpler to implement but generally more difficult for users to access and utilize than are distributed operating systems, which provide more features.

15.1.2.1 Network Operating Systems

A **network operating system** provides an environment in which users, who are aware of the multiplicity of machines, can access remote resources by either logging in to the appropriate remote machine or transferring data from the remote machine to their own machines.

Remote Login

An important function of a network operating system is to allow users to log in remotely. The Internet provides the **telnet** facility for this purpose. To illustrate this facility, let us suppose that a user at Westminster College wishes to compute on "cs.yale.edu," a computer that is located at Yale University. To do so, the user must have a valid account on that machine. To log in remotely, the user issues the command

```
telnet cs.yale.edu
```

This command results in the formation of a socket connection between the local machine at Westminster College and the "cs.yale.edu" computer. After this connection has been established, the networking software creates a transparent, bidirectional link such that all characters entered by the user are sent to a process on "cs.yale.edu," and all the output from that process is sent back to the user. The process on the remote machine asks the user for a login name and a password. Once the correct information has been received, the process acts as a proxy for the user, who can compute on the remote machine just as any local user can.

Remote File Transfer

Another major function of a network operating system is to provide a mechanism for **remote file transfer** from one machine to another. In such an environment, each computer maintains its own local file system. If a user at one site (say, "cs.uvm.edu") wants to access a file located on another computer (say, "cs.yale.edu"), then the file must be copied explicitly from the computer at Yale to the computer at the University of Vermont.

The Internet provides a mechanism for such a transfer with the File Transfer Protocol (FTP) program. Suppose that a user on cs.uvm.edu wants to copy a

Java program `Server.java` that resides on cs.yale.edu. The user must first invoke the FTP program, by executing

```
ftp cs.yale.edu
```

The program then asks the user for the login name and a password. Once the correct information has been received, the user must connect to the subdirectory where the file `Server.java` resides and then copy the file by executing

```
get Server.java
```

In this scheme, the file location is not transparent to the user; users must know exactly where each file is. Moreover, there is no real file sharing, because a user can only *copy* a file from one site to another. Thus, several copies of the same file may exist, resulting in a waste of space. In addition, if these copies are modified, the various copies will be inconsistent.

Notice that, in our example, the user at the University of Vermont must have login permission on "cs.yale.edu." FTP also provides a way to allow a user who does not have an account on the Yale computer to copy files remotely. This remote copying is accomplished through the "anonymous FTP" method, which works as follows. The file to be copied (that is, `Server.java`) must be placed in a special subdirectory (say, *ftp*) with the protection set to allow the public to read the file. A user who wishes to copy the file uses the `ftp` command as before. When the user is asked for the login name, the user supplies the name "anonymous" and an arbitrary password.

Once anonymous login is accomplished, care must be taken by the system to ensure that this partially authorized user does not access inappropriate files. Generally, the user is allowed to access only those files that are in the directory tree of user "anonymous." Any files placed here are accessible to any anonymous users, subject to the usual file-protection scheme used on that machine. Anonymous users, however, cannot access files outside of this directory tree.

The FTP mechanism is implemented in a manner similar to telnet implementation. There is a daemon on the remote site that watches for connection requests to the system's FTP port. Login authentication is accomplished, and the user is allowed to execute commands remotely. Unlike the telnet daemon, which executes any command for the user, the FTP daemon responds only to a predefined set of file-related commands. These include

- `get`: Transfer a file from the remote machine to the local machine.
- `put`: Transfer from the local machine to the remote machine.
- `ls` or `dir`: List files in the current directory on the remote machine.
- `cd`: Change the current directory on the remote machine.

There are also various commands to change transfer modes (for binary or ASCII files) and to determine connection status.

An important point about telnet and FTP is that they require the user to change paradigms. FTP requires the user to know a command set entirely different from the normal operating-system commands. Telnet requires a smaller shift: The user must know appropriate commands on the remote system. For instance, a user on a Windows machine who telnets to a UNIX machine must switch to UNIX commands for the duration of the telnet session. Facilities are more convenient for users if they do not require the use of a different set of commands. Distributed operating systems are designed to ameliorate this problem.

15.1.2.2 Distributed Operating Systems

In a distributed operating system, the users access remote resources in the same manner as they do local resources. Data and process migration from one site to another is under the control of the distributed operating system.

Data Migration

Suppose that a user on site A wants to access data (such as a file) that reside at site B. The system can transfer the data in one of two basic methods. One approach to **data migration** is to transfer the entire file to site A. From that point on, all access to the file is local. When the user no longer needs access to the file, a copy of the file (if it has been modified) is sent back to site B. Even if only a modest change has been made to a large file, all the data must be transferred. This mechanism can be thought of as an automated FTP system. This approach was used in the Andrew file system, as we discuss in Chapter 16, but it was found to be too inefficient.

The other approach is to transfer to site A only those portions of the file that are actually *necessary* for the immediate task. If another portion is required later, another transfer will take place. When the user no longer wants to access the file, any part of it that has been modified must be sent back to site B. (Note the similarity to demand paging.) The Sun Microsystems Network File System (NFS) protocol uses this method (Chapter 16), as do newer versions of Andrew. The Microsoft SMB protocol (running on top of either TCP/IP or the Microsoft NETBUI protocol) also allows file sharing over a network. SMB is described in Appendix C.6.1.

Clearly, if only a small part of a large file is being accessed, the latter approach is preferable. If significant portions of the file are being accessed, however, it is more efficient to copy the entire file.

In both methods, data migration includes more than the mere transfer of data from one site to another. The system must also perform various data translations if the two sites involved are not directly compatible (for instance, if they use different character-code representations or represent integers with a different number or order of bits).

Computation Migration

In some circumstances, we may want to transfer the computation, rather than the data, across the system; this approach is called **computation migration**. For example, consider a job that needs to access various large files that reside at different sites, to obtain a summary of those files. It would be more efficient to access the files at the sites where they reside and return the desired results to the site that initiated the computation. Generally, if the time to transfer the data is longer than the time to execute the remote command, the remote command should be used.

Such a computation can be carried out in different ways. Suppose that process P wants to access a file at site A. Access to the file is carried out at site A and could be initiated by an RPC. An RPC uses a **datagram protocol** (UDP on the Internet) to execute a routine on a remote system (Section 4.6.2). Process P invokes a predefined procedure at site A. The procedure executes appropriately and then returns the results to P.

Alternatively, process P can send a *message* to site A. The operating system at site A then creates a new process Q whose function is to carry out the designated task. When process Q completes its execution, it sends the needed result back to P via the message system. In this scheme, process P may execute concurrently with process Q and, in fact, may have several processes running concurrently on several sites.

Both methods could be used to access several files residing at various sites. One RPC might result in the invocation of another RPC or even in the transfer of messages to another site. Similarly, process Q could, during the course of its execution, send a message to another site, which in turn would create another process. This process might either send a message back to Q or repeat the cycle.

Process Migration

A logical extension of computation migration is **process migration**. When a process is submitted for execution, it is not always executed at the site at which it is initiated. The entire process, or parts of it, may be executed at different sites. This scheme may be used for several reasons:

- **Load balancing:** The processes (or subprocesses) may be distributed across the network to even the workload.

- **Computation speedup:** If a single process can be divided into a number of subprocesses that may run concurrently on different sites, then the total process turnaround time can be reduced.

- **Hardware preference:** The process may have characteristics that make it more suitable for execution on some specialized processor (such as matrix inversion on an array processor, rather than on a microprocessor).

- **Software preference:** The process may require software that is available at only a particular site, and either the software cannot be moved, or it is less expensive to move the process.

- **Data access:** Just as in computation migration, if the data being used in the computation are numerous, it may be more efficient to have a process run remotely than to transfer all the data locally.

We use two complementary techniques to move processes in a computer network. In the first, the system can attempt to hide the fact that the process has migrated from the client. This scheme has the advantage that the user does not need to code her program explicitly to accomplish the migration. This method is usually employed for achieving load balancing and computation speedup among homogeneous systems, as they do not need user input to help them execute programs remotely.

The other approach is to allow (or require) the user to specify explicitly how the process should migrate. This method is usually employed when the process must be moved to satisfy a hardware or software preference.

You have probably realized that the Web has many aspects of a distributed-computing environment. Certainly it provides data migration (between a web server and a web client). It also provides computation migration. For instance, a web client could trigger a database operation on a web server. Finally, with Java, it provides a form of process migration: Java applets are sent from the server to the client, where they are executed. A network operating system provides most of these features, but a distributed operating system makes them seamless and easily accessible. The result is a powerful and easy-to-use facility —one of the reasons for the huge growth of the World Wide Web.

15.1.3 Putting It All Together

Now that we understand the motivation for building distributed systems and the types of distributed operating systems, we can examine the pieces necessary to implement such systems. In the remainder of this chapter, we explore the lowest level: the underlying computer network. In Chapter 16, we discuss distributed file systems. This type of system is a distributed implementation of the classical time-sharing model of a file system (where multiple users share files and storage resources), where the files are physically dispersed among the various sites of a distributed system. Chapter 17 describes the methods necessary for distributed operating systems to coordinate their actions.

15.2 ■ Topology

The sites in a distributed system can be connected physically in a variety of ways. Each configuration has advantages and disadvantages. We can compare the configurations by using the following criteria:

- **Installation cost:** The cost of physically linking the sites in the system

- **Communication cost:** The cost in time and money to send a message from site A to site B

- **Availability:** The extent to which data can be accessed despite the failure of some links or sites

The various topologies are depicted in Figure 15.2 as graphs whose nodes correspond to sites. An edge from node A to node B corresponds to a direct communication link between the two sites. In a fully connected network, each site is directly connected to every other site. However, the number of links grows as the square of the number of sites, resulting in a huge installation cost. Therefore, fully connected networks are impractical in any large system.

In a **partially connected network**, direct links exist between some—but not all—pairs of sites. Hence, the installation cost of such a configuration is lower than that of the fully connected network. However, if two sites A and B are not directly connected, messages from one to the other must be **routed** through a sequence of communication links. This requirement results in a higher communication cost.

If a communication link fails, messages that would have been transmitted across the link must be rerouted. In some cases, another route through the network may be found, so that the messages are able to reach their destination. In other cases, a failure may mean that no connection exists between some pairs of sites. When a system is split into two (or more) subsystems that lack any connection between them, it is partitioned. Under this definition, a subsystem (or partition) may consist of a single node.

The various partially connected network types include tree-structured networks, ring networks, and star networks, as shown in Figure 15.2. They have different failure characteristics and installation and communication costs. Installation and communication costs are relatively low for a tree-structured network. However, the failure of a single link in a tree-structured network can result in the network's becoming partitioned. In a ring network, at least two links must fail for partition to occur. Thus, the ring network has a higher degree of availability than does a tree-structured network. However, the communication cost is high, since a message may have to cross a large number of links. In a star network, the failure of a single link results in a network partition, but one of the partitions has only a single site. Such a partition can be treated as a single-site failure. The star network also has a low communication cost, since

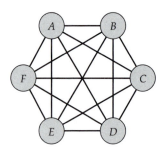

fully connected network

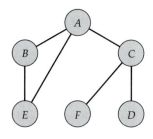

partially connected network

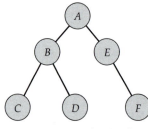

tree structured network

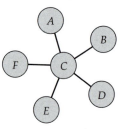

star network

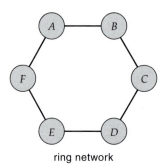

ring network

Figure 15.2   Network topology.

each site is at most two links away from every other site. However, if the central site fails, every site in the system becomes disconnected.

15.3 ■ Communication

Now that we have discussed the physical aspects of networking, we turn to the internal workings. The designer of a communication network must address five basic issues:

- **Naming and name resolution:** How do two processes locate each other to communicate?

- **Routing strategies:** How are messages sent through the network?

- **Packet strategies:** Are packets sent individually or as a sequence?

- **Connection strategies:** How do two processes send a sequence of messages?

- **Contention:** How do we resolve conflicting demands for the networks use, given that it is a shared resource?

In Sections 15.3.1 through 15.3.5, we elaborate on each of these issues.

15.3.1 Naming and Name Resolution

The first component of network communication is the naming of the systems in the network. For a process at site A to exchange information with a process at site B, each must be able to specify the other. Within a computer system, each process has a process identifier, and messages may be addressed with the process identifier. Because networked systems share no memory, a host within the system initially has no knowledge about the processes on other hosts.

To solve this problem, processes on remote systems are generally identified by the pair <host name, identifier>, where *host name* is a name unique within the network and *identifier* may be a process identifier or other unique number within that host. A *host name* is usually an alphanumeric identifier, rather than a number, to make it easier for users to specify. For instance, site A might have hosts named *homer, marge, bart,* and *lisa. Bart* is certainly easier to remember than is *12814831100.*

Names are convenient for humans to use, but computers prefer numbers for speed and simplicity. For this reason, there must be a mechanism to **resolve** the host name into a host-id that describes the destination system to the networking hardware. This resolve mechanism is similar to the name-to-address binding that occurs during program compilation, linking, loading, and execution (Chapter 9). In the case of host names, two possibilities exist. First, every host may have a data file containing the names and addresses of all the other hosts reachable on the network (similar to binding at compile time). The problem with this model is that adding or removing a host from the network requires updating the data files on all the hosts. The alternative is to distribute the information among systems on the network. The network must then use a protocol to distribute and retrieve the information. This scheme is like execution-time binding. The first method was the original method used on the Internet; as the Internet grew, however, it became untenable, so the second method, the **domain-name system** (**DNS**), is now in use.

DNS specifies the naming structure of the hosts, as well as name-to-address resolution. Hosts on the Internet are logically addressed with a multipart name. Names progress from the most specific to the most general part of the address, with periods separating the fields. For instance, *bob.cs.brown.edu* refers to host *bob* in the Department of Computer Science at Brown University within the domain *edu*. (Other top-level domains include *com* for commercial sites; *org* for organizations, and one for each country connected to the network, for systems specified by their country rather than organization type.) Generally, the system resolves addresses by examining the host name components in reverse order. Each component has a **name server**—simply a process on a system— that accepts a name and returns the address of the name server responsible for that name. As the final step, the name server for the host in question is contacted and a host-id is returned. For our example system, *bob.cs.brown.edu*, the following steps would be taken as result of a request made by a process on system A to communicate with *bob.cs.brown.edu*:

1. The kernel of system A issues a request to the name server for the *edu* domain, asking for the address of the name server for *brown.edu*. The name server for the *edu* domain must be at a known address, so that it can be queried.

2. The *edu* name server returns the address of the host on which the *brown.edu* name server resides.

3. The kernel on system A then queries the name server at this address and asks about *cs.brown.edu*.

4. An address is returned; and a request to that address for *bob.cs.brown.edu* now, finally, returns an **Internet address** host-id for that host (for example, 128.148.31.100).

This protocol may seem inefficient, but local caches are usually kept at each name server to speed the process. For example, the *edu* name server would have *brown.edu* in its cache and would inform system A that it could resolve two portions of the name, returning a pointer to the *cs.brown.edu* name server. Of course, the contents of these caches must be refreshed over time in case the name server is moved or its address changes. In fact, this service is so important that many optimizations have occurred in the protocol, as well as many safeguards. Consider what would happen if the primary *edu* name server crashed. It is possible that no *edu* hosts would be able to have their addresses resolved, making them all unreachable! The solution is to use secondary, back-up name servers that duplicate the contents of the primary servers.

Before the domain name service was introduced, all hosts on the Internet needed to have copies of a file that contained the names and addresses of each host on the network. All changes to this file had to be registered at one site

```
/**
 * Usage:   java DNSLookUp <IP name>
 * i.e.   java DNSLookUp www.wiley.com
 */
public class DNSLookUp {
   public static void main(String[] args) {
      InetAddress hostAddress;

      try {
         hostAddress = InetAddress.getByName(args[0]);
         System.out.println(hostAddress.getHostAddress());
      }
      catch (UnknownHostException uhe) {
         System.err.println("Unknown host:  " + args[0]);
      }
   }
}
```

Figure 15.3   Java program illustrating a DNS lookup.

(host SRI-NIC), and periodically all hosts had to copy the updated file from SRI-NIC to be able to contact new systems or find hosts whose addresses had changed. Under the domain-name service, each name server site is responsible for updating the host information for that domain. For instance, any host changes at Brown University are the responsibility of the name server for *brown.edu* and do not have to be reported anywhere else. DNS lookups will automatically retrieve the updated information because *brown.edu* is contacted directly. Within domains, there can be autonomous subdomains to distribute further the responsibility for host-name and host-id changes.

Java provides the necessary API to design a program that maps IP names to IP addresses. The program shown in Figure 15.3 is passed an IP name (such as "bob.cs.brown.edu") on the command line and either outputs the IP address of the host or returns a message indicating that the host name could not be resolved. An InetAddress is a Java class representing an IP name or address. The static method getByName() belonging to the InetAddress class is passed a string representation of an IP name and it returns the corresponding InetAddress. The program then invokes the getHostAddress() method, which internally uses DNS to lookup the IP address of the designated host.

Generally, the operating system is responsible for accepting from its processes a message destined for <host name, identifier> and for transferring that message to the appropriate host. The kernel on the destination host is then responsible for transferring the message to the process named by the identifier. This exchange is by no means trivial; it is described in Section 15.3.4.

15.3.2 Routing Strategies

When a process at site A wants to communicate with a process at site B, how is the message sent? If there is only one physical path from A to B (such as in a star or tree-structured network), the message must be sent through that path. However, if there are multiple physical paths from A to B, then several routing options exist. Each site has a **routing table** indicating the alternative paths that can be used to send a message to other sites. The table may include information about the speed and cost of the various communication paths, and it may be updated as necessary, either manually or via programs that exchange routing information. The three most common routing schemes are **fixed routing**, **virtual routing**, and **dynamic routing**.

- **Fixed routing:** A path from A to B is specified in advance and does not change unless a hardware failure disables it. Usually, the shortest path is chosen, so that communication costs are minimized.

- **Virtual routing:** A path from A to B is fixed for the duration of one **session**. Different sessions involving messages from A to B may use different paths. A session could be as short as a file transfer or as long as a remote-login period.

- **Dynamic routing:** The path used to send a message from site A to site B is chosen only when a message is sent. Because the decision is made dynamically, separate messages may be assigned different paths. Site A will make a decision to send the message to site C; C, in turn, will decide to send it to site D, and so on. Eventually, a site will deliver the message to B. Usually, a site sends a message to another site on that link that is the least used at that particular time.

There are tradeoffs among these three schemes. Fixed routing cannot adapt to link failures or load changes. In other words, if a path has been established between A and B, the messages must be sent along this path, even if the path is down or is used more heavily than another possible path. We can partially remedy this problem by using virtual routing and can avoid it completely by using dynamic routing. Fixed routing and virtual routing ensure that messages from A to B will be delivered in the order in which they were sent. In dynamic routing, messages may arrive out of order. We can remedy this problem by appending a sequence number to each message.

Dynamic routing is the most complicated to set up and run; however, it is the best way to manage routing in complicated environments. UNIX provides both fixed routing for use on hosts within simple networks and dynamic routing for complicated network environments. It is also possible to mix the two. Within a site, the hosts may just need to know how to reach the system that connects the local network to other networks (such as company-wide networks or the Internet). Such a node is known as a **gateway**. These individual hosts have a static route to the gateway. The gateway itself uses dynamic routing to reach any host on the rest of the network.

A router is the entity within the computer network responsible for routing messages. A router can be a host computer with routing software or a special-purpose device. Either way, a router must have at least two network connections, or else it would have nowhere to route messages. A router decides whether any given message needs to be passed from the network on which it is received to any other network connected to the router. It makes this determination by examining the destination Internet address of the message. The router checks its tables to determine the location of the destination host, or at least of the network to which it will send the message toward the destination host. In the case of static routing, this table is changed only by manual update (a new file is loaded onto the router). With dynamic routing, a **routing protocol** is used between routers to inform them of network changes and to allow them to update their routing tables automatically. Gateways and routers typically are dedicated hardware devices that run code out of firmware.

15.3.3 Packet Strategies

Messages are generally of variable length. To simplify the system design, we commonly implement communication with fixed-length messages called **packets**, **frames**, or **datagrams**. A communication implemented in one packet can be sent to its destination in a **connectionless message**. A connectionless message can be **unreliable**, in which case the sender has no guarantee that, and cannot tell whether, the packet reached its destination. Alternatively, the packet can be **reliable**; usually, in this case, a packet is returned from the destination indicating that the packet arrived. (Of course, the return packet could be lost along the way.) If a message is too long to fit within one packet, or if the packets need to flow back and forth between the two communicators, a connection is established to allow the reliable exchange of multiple packets.

15.3.4 Connection Strategies

Once messages are able to reach their destinations, processes may institute **communications sessions** to exchange information. Pairs of processes that want to communicate over the network can be connected in a number of ways. The three most common schemes are **circuit switching**, **message switching**, and **packet switching**.

- **Circuit switching:** If two processes want to communicate, a permanent physical link is established between them. This link is allocated for the duration of the communication session, and no other process can use that link during this period (even if the two processes are not actively communicating for a while). This scheme is similar to that used in the telephone system. Once a communication line has been opened between two parties (that is, party A calls party B), no one else can use this circuit until the communication is terminated explicitly (for example, when one of the parties hangs up).

- **Message switching:** If two processes want to communicate, a temporary link is established for the duration of one message transfer. Physical links are allocated dynamically among correspondents as needed and are allocated for only short periods. Each message is a block of data with system information—such as the source, the destination, and error-correction codes (ECC)—that allows the communication network to deliver the message to the destination correctly. This scheme is similar to the post-office mailing system. Each letter is considered a message that contains both the destination address and source (return) address. Many messages (from different users) can be shipped over the same link.

- **Packet switching:** One logical message may have to be divided into a number of packets. Each packet may be sent to its destination separately, and each therefore must include a source and destination address with its data. Furthermore, each packet may take a different path through the network. The packets must be reassembled into messages as they arrive. Note that it is not harmful for data to be broken into packets, possibly routed separately, and reassembled at the destination. Breaking up an audio signal (say, a telephone communication), in contrast, could cause great confusion if it was not done carefully.

There are obvious tradeoffs among these schemes. Circuit switching requires substantial set-up time and may waste network bandwidth, but it incurs less overhead for shipping each message. Conversely, message and packet switching require less set-up time but incur more overhead per message. Also, in packet switching, each message must be divided into packets and later reassembled. Packet switching is the method most commonly used on data networks because it makes the best use of network bandwidth.

15.3.5 Contention

Depending on the network topology, a link may connect more than two sites in the computer network, and several of these sites may want to transmit information over a link simultaneously. This situation occurs mainly in a ring or multiaccess bus network. In this case, the transmitted information may become scrambled. If it does, it must be discarded; and the sites must be notified about the problem so that they can retransmit the information. If no special provisions are made, this situation may be repeated, resulting in degraded performance. Several techniques have been developed to avoid repeated collisions, including **collision detection (CD)** and **token passing**.

- **CSMA/CD:** Before transmitting a message over a link, a site must listen to determine whether another message is currently being transmitted over that link; this technique is called **carrier sense with multiple access (CSMA)**. If the link is free, the site can start transmitting. Otherwise, it must wait (and continue to listen) until the link is free. If two or more sites begin transmitting at exactly the same time (each thinking that no other site is using the link), then they will register a **collision detection (CD)** and will stop transmitting. Each site will try again after some random time interval. The main problem with this approach is that, when the system is very busy, many collisions may occur, and thus performance may be degraded. Nevertheless, CSMA/CD has been used successfully in the Ethernet system, the most common network system. (The Ethernet protocol is defined by the IEEE 802.3 standard.) To limit the number of collisions, we limit the number of hosts per Ethernet network. Adding more hosts to a congested network could result in poor network throughput. As systems get faster, they are able to send more packets per time segment. As a result, the number of systems per Ethernet segment generally is decreasing so that networking performance is kept reasonable.

- **Token passing:** A unique message type, known as a **token**, continuously circulates in the system (usually a ring structure). A site that wants to transmit information must wait until the token arrives. It removes the token from the ring and begins to transmit its messages. When the site completes its round of message passing, it retransmits the token. This action, in turn, allows another site to receive and remove the token and to start its message transmission. If the token gets lost, then the systems must detect the loss and generate a new token. They usually do that by declaring an **election** to choose a unique site where a new token will be generated. Later, in Section 17.6, we present one election algorithm. A token-passing scheme has been adopted by the IBM and HP/Apollo systems. The benefit of a token-passing network is that performance is constant. Adding new systems to a network may lengthen the time a system waits for the token, but it will not cause a large performance decrease, as may happen on Ethernet. On lightly loaded networks, however, Ethernet is more efficient, because systems may send messages at any time.

15.4 ■ Communication Protocols

When we are designing a communication network, we must deal with the inherent complexity of coordinating asynchronous operations communicating in a potentially slow and error-prone environment. In addition, the systems on the network must agree on a protocol or a set of protocols for determining host names, locating hosts on the network, establishing connections, and so on. We can simplify the design problem (and related implementation) by partitioning

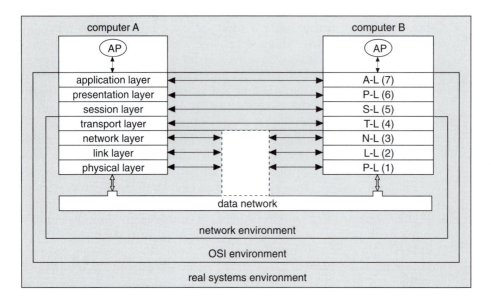

Figure 15.4   Two computers communicating via the ISO network model.

the problem into multiple layers. Each layer on one system communicates with the equivalent layer on other systems. Typically each layer has its own protocols and communication takes place between peer layers using a specific protocol. The protocols may be implemented in hardware or software. For instance, Figure 15.4 shows the logical communications between two computers, with the three lowest-level layers implemented in hardware. Following the International Standards Organization (ISO), we refer to the layers with the following descriptions:

1. **Physical layer:** The physical layer is responsible for handling both the mechanical and the electrical details of the physical transmission of a bit stream. At the physical layer, the communicating systems must agree on the electrical representation of a binary 0 and 1, so that when data are sent as a stream of electrical signals, the receiver is able to interpret the data properly as binary data. This layer is implemented in the hardware of the networking device.

2. **Data-link layer:** The data-link layer is responsible for handling the *frames,* or fixed-length parts of packets, including any error detection and recovery that occurred in the physical layer.

3. **Network layer:** The network layer is responsible for providing connections and for routing packets in the communication network, including handling the address of outgoing packets, decoding the address of incoming packets,

and maintaining routing information for proper response to changing load levels. Routers work at this layer.

4. **Transport layer:** The transport layer is responsible for low-level access to the network and for transfer of messages between the clients, including partitioning messages into packets, maintaining packet order, controlling flow, and generating physical addresses.

5. **Session layer:** The session layer is responsible for implementing sessions, or process-to-process communications protocols. Typically, these protocols

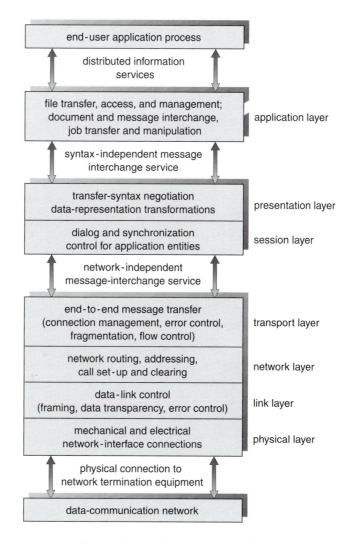

Figure 15.5 The ISO protocol layer.

are the actual communications for remote logins and for file and mail transfers.

6. **Presentation layer:** The presentation layer is responsible for resolving the differences in formats among the various sites in the network, including character conversions, and half duplex–full duplex modes (character echoing).

7. **Application layer:** The application layer is responsible for interacting directly with the users. This layer deals with file transfer, remote-login protocols, and electronic mail, as well as with schemas for distributed databases.

Figure 15.5 summarizes the **ISO protocol stack**—a set of cooperating protocols —showing the physical flow of data. As mentioned, logically each layer of a protocol stack communicates with the equivalent layer on other systems. But physically, a message starts at or above the application layer, and it is passed through each lower level in turn. Each layer may modify the message and include message-header data for the equivalent layer on the receiving side. Ultimately, the message makes it to the data-network layer and is transferred as one or more packets (Figure 15.6). The data-link layer of the target system

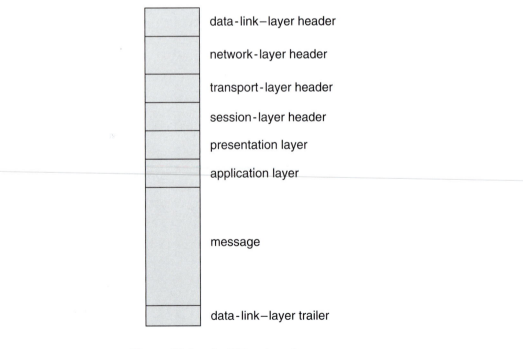

data-link–layer header

network-layer header

transport-layer header

session-layer header

presentation layer

application layer

message

data-link–layer trailer

Figure 15.6   An ISO network message.

receives these data, and the message is moved up through the protocol stack; it is analyzed, modified, and stripped of headers as it progresses. It finally reaches the application layer for use by the receiving process.

The ISO model formalizes some of the earlier work done in network protocols but was developed in late 1970s and is currently not in widespread use. Perhaps the most widely adopted protocol stack is the TCP/IP model, which has been adopted by virtually all Internet sites. The TCP/IP protocol stack has fewer layers than does the ISO model. Theoretically, because it combines several functions in each layer, it is more difficult to implement but more efficient than ISO networking. The relationship between the ISO and TCP/IP models is shown in Figure 15.7. The TCP/IP application layer identifies several protocols in widespread use in the Internet, including HTTP, FTP, Telnet, DNS, and SMTP. The transport layer identifies the unreliable, connectionless **User Datagram Protocol (UDP)** and the reliable, connection-oriented **Transmission Control Protocol (TCP)**. The Internet Protocol (**IP**) is responsible for routing IP datagrams through the Internet. The TCP/IP model does not formally identify a link or physical layer, allowing TCP/IP traffic to run across any physical network. In Section 15.7, we consider the TCP/IP model running over an Ethernet network.

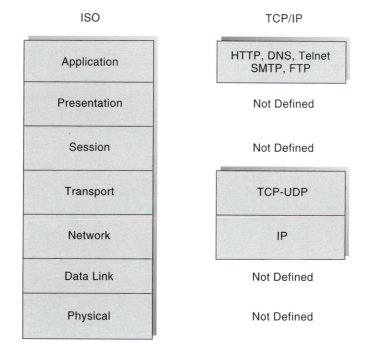

Figure 15.7   The ISO and TCP/IP protocol stacks.

15.5 ■ Robustness

A distributed system may suffer from various types of hardware failure. The failure of a link, the failure of a site, and the loss of a message are the most common failures. To ensure that the system is robust, we must **detect** any of these failures, **reconfigure** the system so that computation may continue, and **recover** when a site or a link is repaired.

15.5.1 Failure Detection

In an environment with no shared memory, we are generally unable to differentiate among link failure, site failure, and message loss. We can usually detect only that one of these failures has occurred. Once a failure has been detected, appropriate action must be taken. What action is appropriate depends on the particular application.

To detect link and site failure, we use a **handshaking** procedure. Suppose that sites A and B have a direct physical link between them. At fixed intervals, the sites send each other an *I-am-up* message. If site A does not receive this message within a predetermined time period, it can assume that site B has failed, that the link between A and B has failed, or that the message from B has been lost. At this point, site A has two choices. It can wait for another time period to receive an *I-am-up* message from B, or it can send an *Are-you-up?* message to B.

If time goes by and site A still has not received an *I-am-up* message, or if site A has sent an *Are-you-up?* message and has not received a reply, the procedure can be repeated. Again, the only conclusion that site A can draw safely is that some type of failure has occurred.

Site A can try to differentiate between link failure and site failure by sending an *Are-you-up?* message to B by another route (if one exists). If and when B receives this message, it immediately replies positively. This positive reply tells A that B is up and that the failure is in the direct link between them. Since we do not know in advance how long it will take the message to travel from A to B and back, we must use a **time-out scheme**. At the time A sends the *Are-you-up?* message, it specifies a time interval during which it is willing to wait for the reply from B. If A receives the reply message within that time interval, then it can safely conclude that B is up. If not, however (that is, if a time-out occurs), then A may conclude only that one or more of the following situations has occurred:

- Site B is down.

- The direct link (if one exists) from A to B is down.

- The alternative path from A to B is down.

- The message has been lost.

Site A cannot, however, determine which of these events has occurred.

15.5.2 Reconfiguration

Suppose that site A has discovered, through the mechanism described in the previous section, that a failure has occurred. It must then initiate a procedure that will allow the system to reconfigure and to continue its normal mode of operation.

- If a direct link from A to B has failed, this information must be broadcast to every site in the system, so that the various routing tables can be updated accordingly.

- If the system believes that a site has failed (because that site can be reached no longer), then every site in the system must be so notified, so that they will no longer attempt to use the services of the failed site. The failure of a site that serves as a central coordinator for some activity (such as deadlock detection) requires the election of a new coordinator. Similarly, if the failed site is part of a logical ring, then a new logical ring must be constructed. Note that, if the site has not failed (that is, if it is up but cannot be reached), then we may have the undesirable situation where two sites serve as the coordinator. When the network is partitioned, the two coordinators (each for its own partition) may initiate conflicting actions. For example, if the coordinators are responsible for implementing mutual exclusion, we may have a situation where two processes are executing simultaneously in their critical sections.

15.5.3 Recovery from Failure

When a failed link or site is repaired, it must be integrated into the system gracefully and smoothly.

- Suppose that a link between A and B has failed. When it is repaired, both A and B must be notified. We can accomplish this notification by continuously repeating the handshaking procedure described in Section 15.5.1.

- Suppose that site B has failed. When it recovers, it must notify all other sites that it is up again. Site B then may have to receive information from the other sites to update its local tables; for example, it may need routing-table information, a list of sites that are down, or undelivered messages and mail. If the site has not failed but simply could not be reached, then this information is still required.

15.6 ■ Design Issues

Making the multiplicity of processors and storage devices **transparent** to the users has been a key challenge to many designers. Ideally, a distributed system should look to its users like a conventional, centralized system. The user interface of a transparent distributed system should not distinguish between local and remote resources. That is, users should be able to access remote distributed systems as though the latter were local, and the distributed system should be responsible for locating the resources and for arranging for the appropriate interaction.

Another aspect of transparency is user mobility. It would be convenient to allow users to log into any machine in the system rather than forcing them to use a specific machine. A transparent distributed system facilitates user mobility by bringing over the user's environment (for example, home directory) to wherever she logs in. Both the Andrew file system from CMU and Project Athena from MIT provide this functionality on a large scale. NFS can provide this transparency on a smaller scale.

Another design issue involves fault tolerance. We use the term *fault tolerance* in a broad sense. Communication faults, machine failures (of type fail-stop), storage-device crashes, and decays of storage media should all be tolerated to some extent. A **fault-tolerant system** should continue to function, perhaps in a degraded form, when faced with these failures. The degradation can be in performance, in functionality, or in both. It should be proportional, however, to the failures that cause it. A system that grinds to a halt when only a few of its components fail is certainly not fault tolerant. Unfortunately, fault tolerance is difficult to implement. Most commercial systems provide only limited fault tolerance. For instance, the DEC VAXcluster allows multiple computers to share a set of disks. If a system crashes, users may still access their information from another system. Of course, if a disk fails, all systems will lose access. But in this case, RAID can ensure continued access to the data even in the event of a failure (Section 14.5).

Still another issue is **scalability**—the capability of a system to adapt to increased service load. Systems have bounded resources and can become completely saturated under increased load. For example, regarding a file system, saturation occurs either when a server's CPU runs at a high utilization rate or when disks are almost full. Scalability is a relative property, but it can be measured accurately. A scalable system reacts more gracefully to increased load than does a nonscalable one. First, its performance degrades more moderately; and second, its resources reach a saturated state later. Even perfect design cannot accommodate an ever-growing load. Adding new resources might solve the problem, but it might generate additional indirect load on other resources (for example, adding machines to a distributed system can clog the network and increase service loads). Even worse, expanding the system can incur expensive design modifications. A scalable system should have the potential to grow without these problems. In a distributed system, the ability to scale up gracefully is of special importance, since expanding the network by adding new machines or interconnecting two networks is commonplace. In short, a scalable design should withstand high service load, accommodate growth of the user community, and enable simple integration of added resources.

Fault tolerance and scalability are related to each other. A heavily loaded component can become paralyzed and behave like a faulty component. Also, shifting the load from a faulty component to that component's backup can saturate the latter. Generally, having spare resources is essential for ensuring reliability as well as for handling peak loads gracefully. An inherent advantage of a distributed system is a potential for fault tolerance and scalability because of the multiplicity of resources. However, inappropriate design can obscure this potential. Fault-tolerance and scalability considerations call for a design demonstrating distribution of control and data.

Very large-scale distributed systems, to a great extent, are still only theoretical. No magic guidelines ensure the scalability of a system. It is easier to point out why current designs are *not* scalable. We next discuss several designs that pose problems and propose possible solutions, all in the context of scalability.

One principle for designing very large-scale systems is that the service demand from any component of the system should be bounded by a constant that is independent of the number of nodes in the system. Any service mechanism whose load demand is proportional to the size of the system is destined to become clogged once the system grows beyond a certain size. Adding more resources will not alleviate such a problem. The capacity of this mechanism simply limits the growth of the system.

Central control schemes and central resources should not be used to build scalable (and fault-tolerant) systems. Examples of centralized entities are central authentication servers, central naming servers, and central file servers. Centralization is a form of functional asymmetry among machines constituting the system. The ideal alternative is a functionally symmetric configuration; that is, all the component machines have an equal role in the operation of the system, and hence each machine has some degree of autonomy. Practically, it is virtually impossible to comply with such a principle. For instance, incorporating diskless machines violates functional symmetry, since the workstations depend on a central disk. However, autonomy and symmetry are important goals to which we should aspire.

The practical approximation to symmetric and autonomous configuration is **clustering**, in which the system is partitioned into a collection of semi-autonomous clusters. A **cluster** consists of a set of machines and a dedicated cluster server. So that cross-cluster resource references are relatively infrequent, each cluster server should satisfy requests of its own machines most of the time. Of course, this scheme depends on the ability to localize resource references and to place the component units appropriately. If the cluster is well balanced—that is, if the server in charge suffices to satisfy all the cluster demands—it can be used as a modular building block to scale up the system.

Deciding on the process structure of the server is a major problem in the design of any service. Servers are supposed to operate efficiently in peak periods, when hundreds of active clients need to be served simultaneously. A single-process server is certainly not a good choice, since whenever a request necessitates disk I/O, the whole service will be blocked. Assigning a process for each client is a better choice; however, the expense of frequent context switches between the processes must be considered. A related problem occurs because all the server processes need to share information.

One of the best solutions for the server architecture is the use of lightweight processes, or threads, which we discussed in Chapter 5. We can think of a group of lightweight processes as multiple threads of control associated with some shared resources. Usually, a lightweight process is not bound to a particular client. Instead, it serves single requests of different clients. Scheduling of threads can be preemptive or nonpreemptive. If threads are allowed to run to completion (nonpreemptive), then their shared data do not need to be protected explicitly. Otherwise, some explicit locking mechanism must be used. Clearly, some form of lightweight-processes scheme is essential if servers are to be scalable.

15.7 ■ An Example: Networking

We now return to the name-resolution issue raised in Section 15.3.1 and examine its operation with respect to the TCP/IP protocol stack on the Internet. We consider the processing needed to transfer a packet between hosts on different Ethernet networks.

In a TCP/IP network, every host has a name and an associated 32-bit Internet number (or host-id). Both of these strings must be unique; and, so that the name space can be managed, they are segmented. The name is hierarchical (as explained in Section 15.3.1), describing the host name and then the organization with which the host is associated. The host-id is split into a network number and a host number. The proportion of the split varies, depending on the size of the network. Once the Internet administrators assign a network number, the site with that number is free to assign host-ids.

The sending system checks its routing tables to locate a router to send the packet on its way. The routers use the network part of the host-id to transfer the packet from its source network to the destination network. The destination system then receives the packet. The packet may be a complete message, or it may just be a component of a message, with more packets needed before the message is reassembled and passed to the TCP/UDP layer for transmission to the destination process.

Now we know how a packet moves from its source network to its destination. Within a network, how does a packet move from sender (host or router) to receiver? Every Ethernet device has a unique byte number, called the **Medium Access Control (MAC) address**, assigned to it for addressing. Two devices on a LAN communicate with each other only with this number. If a system needs to send data to another system, the kernel generates an **Address Resolution Protocol (ARP)** packet containing the IP address of the destination system. This packet is **broadcast** to all other systems on that Ethernet network. A broadcast uses a special network address (usually, the maximum address) to signal that all hosts should receive and process the packet. The broadcast is not re-sent by gateways, so only systems on the local network receive it. Only the system whose IP address matches the IP address of the ARP request responds and sends back its MAC address to the system that initiated the query. For efficiency, the host caches the IP-MAC address pair in an internal table. The cache entries are **aged**, so that they eventually are removed from the cache if an access to that system is not required in the given time. In this way, hosts that are removed from a network are eventually *forgotten*. For added performance, ARP entries for heavily used hosts may be hardwired in the ARP cache.

Once an Ethernet device has announced its host-id and address, communication can begin. A process may specify the name of a host with which to communicate. The kernel takes that name and determines the Internet number of the target, using a DNS lookup. The message is passed from the application layer, through the software layers, and to the hardware layer. At the hardware layer, the packet (or packets) has the Ethernet address at its start; a trailer indicates the end of the packet and contains a **checksum** for detection of packet damage (Figure 15.8). The packet is placed on the network by the Ethernet device. The data section of the packet may contain some or all of the data of the original message, but it may also contain some of the upper-level headers that compose the message. In other words, all parts of the original message must be sent from source to destination, and all headers above the 802.3 layer (data-link layer) are included as data in the Ethernet packets.

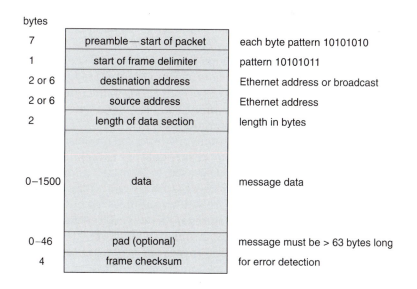

Figure 15.8   An Ethernet packet.

If the destination is on the same local network as the source, the system can look in its ARP cache, find the Ethernet address of the host, and place the packet on the wire. The destination Ethernet device then sees its address in the packet and reads in the packet, passing it up the protocol stack.

If the destination system is on a network different from that of the source, the source system finds an appropriate router on its network and sends the packet there. Routers then pass the packet along the WAN until it reaches its destination network. The router that connects the destination network checks its ARP cache, finds the Ethernet number of the destination, and sends the packet to that host. Through all of these transfers, the data-link-layer header may change as the Ethernet address of the next router in the chain is used, but the other headers of the packet remain the same until the packet is received and processed by the protocol stack and finally passed to the receiving process by the kernel.

15.8 ■ Summary

A distributed system is a collection of processors that do not share memory or a clock. Instead, each processor has its own local memory, and the processors communicate with one another through various communication lines, such as high-speed buses or telephone lines. The processors in a distributed system vary in size and function. They may include small microprocessors, workstations, minicomputers, and large general-purpose computer systems.

The processors in the system are connected through a communication network, which can be configured in a number of ways. The network may be fully or partially connected. It may be a tree, a star, a ring, or a multiaccess bus. The communication-network design must include routing and connection strategies, and it must solve the problems of contention and security.

A distributed system provides the user with access to the resources the system provides. Access to a shared resource can be provided by data migration, computation migration, or process migration.

Protocol stacks, as specified by network layering models, massage the message, adding information to it to ensure that it reaches its destination. A naming system such as DNS must be used to translate from a host name to network address, and another protocol (such as ARP) may be needed to translate the network number to a network device address (an Ethernet address, for instance). If systems are located on separate networks, routers are needed to pass packets from source network to destination network.

A distributed system may suffer from various types of hardware failure. For a distributed system to be fault tolerant, it must detect hardware failures and reconfigure the system. When the failure is repaired, the system must be reconfigured again.

■ Exercises

15.1 Contrast the various network topologies in terms of reliability.

15.2 Most WANs employ only a partially connected topology. Why is this so?

15.3 Even though the ISO model of networking specifies seven layers of functionality, most computer systems use fewer layers to implement a network. Why do they use fewer layers? What problems could the use of fewer layers cause?

15.4 Explain why a doubling of the speed of the systems on an Ethernet segment may result in decreased network performance. What changes could ameliorate the problem?

15.5 Under what circumstances is a token-passing network more effective than an Ethernet network?

15.6 Why would it be a bad idea for gateways to pass broadcast packets between networks? What would be the advantages of doing so?

15.7 What are the advantages of using dedicated hardware devices for routers and gateways? What are the disadvantages of using these devices compared with using general-purpose computers?

15.8 In what ways is using a name server better than using static host tables? What problems or complications are associated with name servers? What methods could you use to decrease the amount of traffic name servers generate to satisfy translation requests?

15.9 Run the program shown in Figure 15.3 and determine the IP addresses of the following host names:

- www.wiley.com
- www.cs.yale.edu
- www.javasoft.com
- www.westminstercollege.edu
- www.ietf.org

15.10 The original HTTP protocol uses TCP/IP as the underlying network protocol. For each page, graphic, or applet, a separate TCP session was constructed, used, and torn down. Because of the overhead of building and destroying TCP/IP connections, performance problems resulted from this implementation method. Would using UDP rather than TCP be a good alternative? What other changes could you make to improve HTTP performance?

15.11 Of what use is an address-resolution protocol? Why is it better to use such a protocol than to make each host read each packet to determine that packet's destination? Does a token-passing network need such a protocol? Explain your answer.

15.12 What are the advantages and the disadvantages of making the computer network transparent to the user?

15.13 What are two formidable problems that designers must solve to implement a network-transparent system?

15.14 Process migration within a heterogeneous network is usually impossible, given the differences in architectures and operating systems. Describe a method for process migration across different architectures running:

    a. The same operating system

    b. Different operating systems

15.15 To build a robust distributed system, you must know what kinds of failures can occur.

    a. List three possible types of failure in a distributed system.

    b. Specify which of the entries in your list also are applicable to a centralized system.

15.16 Is it always crucial to know that the message you have sent has arrived at its destination safely? If your answer is *yes*, explain why. If your answer is *no*, give appropriate examples.

15.17 Present an algorithm for reconstructing a logical ring after a process in the ring fails.

15.18 Consider a distributed system with two sites, A and B. Consider whether site A can distinguish among the following:

    a. B goes down.

    b. The link between A and B goes down.

    c. B is extremely overloaded and its response time is 100 times longer than normal.

What implications does your answer have for recovery in distributed systems?

Bibliographical Notes

Tanenbaum [2003], Stallings [2000a], and Kurose and Ross [2003] provide general overviews of computer networks. Williams [2001] provides coverage of computer networking from a computer-architecture viewpoint.

The Internet and its protocols were described in Comer [1999] and Comer [2000]. Coverage of small TCP/IP can be found in Stevens [1994] and Stevens [1995]. UNIX network programming was described thoroughly in Stevens [1997] and Stevens [1998].

Discussions concerning distributed operating-system structures have been offered by Coulouris et al. [2001] and Tanenbaum and van Steen [2002].

Discussions concerning load balancing and load sharing were presented by Harchol-Balter and Downey [1997] and Vee and Hsu [2000]. Harish and Owens [1999] discuss load-balancing DNS servers. Discussions concerning process migration were presented by Han and Ghosh [1998] and Milo et al. [2000].

Chapter 16

DISTRIBUTED FILE SYSTEMS

In the previous chapter, we discussed network construction and the low-level protocols needed for messages to be transferred between systems. Now we discuss one use of this infrastructure. A **distributed file system (DFS)** is a distributed implementation of the classical time-sharing model of a file system, where multiple users share files and storage resources (Chapter 12). The purpose of a DFS is to support the same kind of sharing when the files are physically dispersed among the sites of a distributed system.

In this chapter, we discuss the ways a DFS can be designed and implemented. First, we discuss common concepts on which DFSs are based. Then, we illustrate our concepts by examining one influential DFS—the Andrew File System (AFS).

16.1 ■ Background

A distributed system is a collection of loosely coupled machines interconnected by a communication network. We use the term *machine* to denote either a mainframe or a workstation. From the point of view of a specific machine in a distributed system, the rest of the machines and their respective resources are *remote*, whereas the machine's own resources are *local*.

In this chapter, we use the term *DFS* to mean distributed file systems in general, not the commercial Transarc DFS product. The latter is referenced as *Transarc DFS*.

To explain the structure of a DFS, we need to define the terms *service, server,* and *client*. A **service** is a software entity running on one or more machines and providing a particular type of function to a priori unknown clients. A **server** is the service software running on a single machine. A **client** is a process that can invoke a service using a set of operations that forms its **client interface**. Sometimes, a lower-level interface is defined for the actual cross-machine interaction; it is the **intermachine interface**.

Using this terminology, we say that a file system provides file services to clients. A client interface for a file service is formed by a set of primitive file operations, such as create a file, delete a file, read from a file, and write to a file. The primary hardware component that a file server controls is a set of local secondary-storage devices (usually, magnetic disks) on which files are stored, and from which they are retrieved according to the client requests.

A DFS is a file system whose clients, servers, and storage devices are dispersed among the machines of a distributed system. Accordingly, service activity has to be carried out across the network, and instead of a single centralized data repository, the system has multiple and independent storage devices. As you will see, the concrete configuration and implementation of a DFS may vary. In some configurations servers run on dedicated machines, in others a machine can be both a server and a client. A DFS can be implemented as part of a distributed operating system, or alternatively, by a software layer whose task is to manage the communication between conventional operating systems and file systems. The distinctive features of a DFS are the multiplicity and autonomy of clients and servers in the system.

Ideally, a DFS should appear to its clients to be a conventional, centralized file system. The multiplicity and dispersion of its servers and storage devices should be made invisible. That is, the client interface of a DFS should not distinguish between local and remote files. It is up to the DFS to locate the files and to arrange for the transport of the data. A **transparent** DFS facilitates user mobility by bringing the user's environment (that is, home directory) to wherever a user logs in.

The most important performance measurement of a DFS is the amount of time needed to satisfy service requests. In conventional systems, this time consists of disk-access time and a small amount of CPU-processing time. In a DFS, however, a remote access has the additional overhead attributed to the distributed structure. This overhead includes the time to deliver the request to a server, as well as the time to get the response across the network back to the client. For each direction, in addition to the transfer of the information, there is the CPU overhead of running the communication protocol software. The performance of a DFS can be viewed as another dimension of the DFS' transparency. That is, the performance of an ideal DFS would be comparable to that of a conventional file system.

The fact that a DFS manages a set of dispersed storage devices is the DFS' key distinguishing feature. The overall storage space managed by a DFS is composed of different and remotely located smaller storage spaces. Usually, these constituent storage spaces correspond to sets of files. A **component unit** is the smallest set of files that can be stored on a single machine, independently from other units. All files belonging to the same component unit must reside in the same location.

16.2 ■ Naming and Transparency

Naming is a mapping between logical and physical objects. For instance, users deal with logical data objects represented by file names, whereas the system manipulates physical blocks of data, stored on disk tracks. Usually, a user refers to a file by a textual name. The latter is mapped to a lower-level numerical identifier that in turn is mapped to disk blocks. This multilevel mapping provides users with an abstraction of a file that hides the details of how and where on the disk the file is stored.

In a transparent DFS, a new dimension is added to the abstraction: that of hiding where in the network the file is located. In a conventional file system, the range of the naming mapping is an address within a disk. In a DFS, this range is augmented to include the specific machine on whose disk the file is stored. Going one step farther with the concept of treating files as abstractions leads to the possibility of **file replication**. Given a file name, the mapping returns a set of the locations of this file's replicas. In this abstraction, both the existence of multiple copies and their location are hidden.

16.2.1 Naming Structures

We need to differentiate two related notions regarding name mappings in a DFS:

1. **Location transparency:** The name of a file does not reveal any hint of the file's physical storage location.

2. **Location independence:** The name of a file does not need to be changed when the file's physical storage location changes.

Both definitions are relative to the level of naming discussed previously, since files have different names at different levels (that is, user-level textual names and system-level numerical identifiers). A location-independent naming scheme is a dynamic mapping, since it can map the same file name to different locations at two different times. Therefore, location independence is a stronger property than is location transparency.

In practice, most of the current DFSs provide a static, location-transparent mapping for user-level names. These systems, however, do not support **file migration**; that is, changing the location of a file automatically is impossible.

Hence, the notion of location independence is irrelevant for these systems. Files are associated permanently with a specific set of disk blocks. Files and disks can be moved between machines manually, but file migration implies an automatic, operating-system-initiated action. Only AFS and a few experimental file systems support location independence and file mobility. AFS supports file mobility mainly for administrative purposes. A protocol provides migration of AFS component units to satisfy high-level user requests, without changing either the user-level names or the low-level names of the corresponding files.

A few aspects can further differentiate location independence and static location transparency:

- Divorce of data from location, as exhibited by location independence, provides better abstraction for files. A file name should denote the file's most significant attributes, which are its contents rather than its location. Location-independent files can be viewed as logical data containers that are not attached to a specific storage location. If only static location transparency is supported, the file name still denotes a specific, although hidden, set of physical disk blocks.

- Static location transparency provides users with a convenient way to share data. Users can share remote files by simply naming the files in a location-transparent manner, as though the files were local. Nevertheless, sharing the storage space is cumbersome, because logical names are still statically attached to physical storage devices. Location independence promotes sharing the storage space itself, as well as the data objects. When files can be mobilized, the overall, system-wide storage space looks like a single virtual resource. A possible benefit of such a view is the ability to balance the utilization of disks across the system.

- Location independence separates the naming hierarchy from the storage-devices hierarchy and from the intercomputer structure. By contrast, if static location transparency is used (although names are transparent), we can easily expose the correspondence between component units and machines. The machines are configured in a pattern similar to the naming structure. This configuration may restrict the architecture of the system unnecessarily and conflict with other considerations. A server in charge of a root directory is an example of a structure that is dictated by the naming hierarchy and contradicts decentralization guidelines.

Once the separation of name and location has been completed, clients may access files residing on remote server systems. In fact, these clients may be **diskless** and rely on servers to provide all files, including the operating-system kernel. Special protocols are needed for the boot sequence, however. Consider the problem of getting the kernel to a diskless workstation. The diskless workstation has no kernel, so it cannot use the DFS code to retrieve the kernel. Instead, a special boot protocol, stored in read-only memory (ROM) on the client, is invoked. It enables networking and retrieves only one special file (the kernel or boot code) from a fixed location. Once the kernel is copied over the network and loaded, its DFS makes all the other operating-system files available. The advantages of diskless clients are many, including lower cost (because no disk is needed on each machine) and greater convenience (when an operating-system upgrade occurs, only the server needs to be modified, rather than all the clients as well). The disadvantages are the added complexity of the boot protocols and the performance loss resulting from the use of a network rather than a local disk.

The current trend is to use clients with local disks. Disk drives are rapidly increasing in capacity and decreasing in cost, with new generations appearing every year or so. The same cannot be said for networks, which evolve every five to ten years. Overall, systems are growing more quickly than are networks, so extra work is needed to limit network access to improve system throughput.

16.2.2 Naming Schemes

There are three main approaches to naming schemes in a DFS. In the simplest approach, files are named by some combination of their host name and local name, which guarantees a unique system-wide name. In Ibis, for instance, a file is identified uniquely by the name *host:local-name*, where *local-name* is a UNIX-like path. This naming scheme is neither location transparent nor location independent. Nevertheless, the same file operations can be used for both local and remote files. The DFS is structured as a collection of isolated component units that are entire conventional file systems. In this first approach, component units remain isolated, although means are provided to refer to a remote file. We do not consider this scheme any further in this text.

The second approach was popularized by Sun's Network File System (NFS). NFS is the file-system component of ONC+, a networking package supported by many UNIX vendors. NFS provides means to attach remote directories to local directories, thus giving the appearance of a coherent directory tree. Early NFS versions allowed only previously mounted remote directories to be accessed transparently. With the advent of the **automount** feature, mounts are done on demand, based on a table of mount points and file-structure names. Components are integrated to support transparent sharing, although this integration is limited and is not uniform, because each machine may attach different remote directories to its tree. The resulting structure is versatile. Usually, it is a forest of UNIX trees with shared subtrees.

We can achieve total integration of the component file systems by using the third approach. A single global name structure spans all the files in the system. Ideally, the composed file-system structure is *isomorphic* to the structure of a conventional file system. In practice, however, the many special files (for example, UNIX device files and machine-specific binary directories) make this goal difficult to attain. To evaluate naming structures, we look at their **administrative complexity**. The most complex and most difficult-to-maintain structure is the NFS structure. Because any remote directory can be attached anywhere onto the local directory tree, the resulting hierarchy can be highly unstructured. If a server becomes unavailable, some arbitrary set of directories on different machines becomes unavailable. In addition, a separate accreditation mechanism controls which machine is allowed to attach which directory to its tree. Thus, a user might be able to access a remote directory tree on one client, but be denied access on another client.

16.2.3 Implementation Techniques

Implementation of transparent naming requires a provision for the mapping of a file name to the associated location. To keep this mapping manageable, we must aggregate sets of files into component units, and provide the mapping on a component-unit basis rather than on a single-file basis. This aggregation serves administrative purposes as well. UNIX-like systems use the hierarchical directory tree to provide name-to-location mapping and to aggregate files recursively into directories.

To enhance the availability of the crucial mapping information, we can use methods such as replication, local caching, or both. As we noted, location independence means that the mapping changes over time; hence, replicating the mapping renders a simple yet consistent update of this information impossible. A technique to overcome this obstacle is to introduce low-level, **location-independent file identifiers**. Textual file names are mapped to lower-level file identifiers that indicate to which component unit the file belongs. These identifiers are still location independent. They can be replicated and cached freely without being invalidated by migration of component units. A second level of mapping, which maps component units to locations and needs a simple yet consistent update mechanism, is the inevitable price. Implementing UNIX-like directory trees using these low-level, location-independent identifiers makes the whole hierarchy invariant under component-unit migration. The only aspect that does change is the component-unit location mapping.

A common way to implement these low-level identifiers is to use structured names. These names are bit strings that usually have two parts. The first part identifies the component unit to which the file belongs; the second part identifies the particular file within the unit. Variants with more parts are possible. The invariant of structured names, however, is that individual parts of the name are unique at all times only within the context of the rest of the parts. We can obtain uniqueness at all times by taking care not to reuse a name that is still used, by adding sufficiently more bits (this method is used in AFS), or by using a timestamp as one part of the name (as done in Apollo Domain). Another way to view this process is that we are taking a location-transparent system, such as Ibis, and adding another level of abstraction to produce a location-independent naming scheme.

The use of the techniques of aggregation of files into component units, and of lower-level location-independent file identifiers, is exemplified in AFS.

16.3 ■ Remote File Access

Consider a user who requests access to a remote file. Assuming that the server storing the file was located by the naming scheme, the actual data transfer to satisfy the user request for the remote access must take place.

One way to achieve this transfer is through a **remote-service mechanism**, whereby requests for accesses are delivered to the server, the server machine performs the accesses, and their results are forwarded back to the user. One of the most common ways of implementing remote service is the remote procedure call (RPC) paradigm, which we discussed in Chapter 4. A direct analogy exists between disk-access methods in conventional file systems and the remote-service method in a DFS: Using the remote-service method is analogous to performing a disk access for each access request.

To ensure reasonable performance of a remote-service mechanism, we can use a form of caching. In conventional file systems, the rationale for caching is to reduce disk I/O (thereby increasing performance), whereas in DFSs, the goal is to reduce both network traffic and disk I/O. In the following, we discuss the implementation of caching in a DFS and contrast it with the basic remote-service paradigm.

16.3.1 Basic Caching Scheme

The concept of caching is simple. If the data needed to satisfy the access request are not already cached, then a copy of those data is brought from the server to the client system. Accesses are performed on the cached copy. The idea is to retain recently accessed disk blocks in the cache, so that repeated accesses to the same information can be handled locally, without additional network traffic. A replacement policy (for example, least recently used) keeps the cache size bounded. No direct correspondence exists between accesses and traffic to the server. Files are still identified with one master copy residing at the server machine, but copies of (or parts of) the file are scattered in different caches. When a cached copy is modified, the changes need to be reflected on the master copy to preserve the relevant consistency semantics. The problem of keeping the cached copies consistent with the master file is the **cache-consistency problem**, which we discuss in Section 16.3.4. DFS caching could just as easily be called **network virtual memory**: It acts similarly to demand-paged virtual memory, except that the backing store usually is not a local disk, but rather a remote server.

The granularity of the cached data in a DFS can vary from blocks of a file to an entire file. Usually, more data are cached than are needed to satisfy a single access, so that many accesses can be served by the cached data. This procedure is much like disk read-ahead (Section 12.6.2). AFS caches files in large chunks (64 KB). The other systems discussed in this chapter support caching of individual blocks driven by client demand. Increasing the caching unit increases the hit ratio, but it also increases the miss penalty because each miss requires more data to be transferred. It also increases the potential for consistency problems. Selecting the unit of caching involves considering parameters such as the network transfer unit and the RPC protocol service unit (in case an RPC protocol is used). The network transfer unit (for Ethernet, a packet) is about 1.5 KB, so larger units of cached data need to be disassembled for delivery and reassembled on reception.

Block size and the total cache size are obviously of importance for block-caching schemes. In UNIX-like systems, common block sizes are 4 KB or 8 KB. For large caches (over 1 MB), large block sizes (over 8 KB) are beneficial. For smaller caches, large block sizes are less beneficial because they result in fewer blocks in the cache, and a lower hit ratio.

16.3.2 Cache Location

Where should the cached data be stored? Disk caches have one clear advantage over main-memory cache: They are reliable. Modifications to cached data are lost in a crash if the cache is kept in volatile memory. Moreover, if the cached data are kept on disk, they are still there during recovery and there is no need to fetch them again. On the other hand, main-memory caches have several advantages of their own:

- Main-memory caches permit workstations to be diskless.

- Data can be accessed more quickly from a cache in main memory than from one on a disk.

- The current technology trend is toward bigger and less expensive memories. The achieved performance speedup is predicted to outweigh the advantages of disk caches.

- The server caches (used to speed up disk I/O) will be in main memory regardless of where user caches are located; if we use main-memory caches on the user machine too, we can build a single caching mechanism for use by both servers and users.

Many remote-access implementations can be thought of as hybrids of caching and remote service. In NFS, for instance, the implementation is based on remote service but is augmented with client- and server-side memory caching for performance. On the other hand, Sprite's implementation is based on caching, but under certain circumstances a remote-service method is adopted. Thus, to evaluate the two methods, we evaluate to what degree either method is emphasized.

The NFS protocol and most implementations do not provide disk caching. Recent Solaris implementations of NFS (Solaris 2.6 and beyond) include a client-side disk caching option, the *cachefs* file system. Once the NFS client reads blocks of a file from the server, it caches them in memory as well as on disk. If the memory copy gets flushed, or even if the system reboots, the disk cache is referenced. If a needed block is not either in memory or in the cachefs disk cache, an RPC is sent to the server to retrieve the block, and the block is written into the disk cache as well as stored in the memory cache for client use.

16.3.3 Cache-Update Policy

The policy used to write modified data blocks back to the server's master copy has a critical effect on the system's performance and reliability. The simplest policy is to write data through to disk as soon as they are placed on any cache. The advantage of a **write-through policy** is reliability: Little information is lost when a client system crashes. However, this policy requires each write access to wait until the information is sent to the server, so it causes poor write performance. Caching with write-through is equivalent to using remote service for write accesses and exploiting caching only for read accesses.

An alternative is the **delayed-write policy**, where we delay updates to the master copy. Modifications are written to the cache, then are written through to the server at a later time. This policy has two advantages over write-through. First, because writes are to the cache, write accesses complete much more quickly. Second, data may be overwritten before they are written back, in which case only the last update needs to be written at all. Unfortunately, delayed-write schemes introduce reliability problems, since unwritten data are lost whenever a user machine crashes.

Variations of the delayed-write policy differ in when modified data blocks are flushed to the server. One alternative is to flush a block when it is about to be ejected from the client's cache. This option can result in good performance, but some blocks can reside in the client's cache a long time before they are written back to the server. A compromise between this alternative and the write- through policy is to scan the cache at regular intervals and to flush blocks that have been modified since the most recent scan, just as UNIX scans its local cache. Sprite uses this policy with a 30-second interval. NFS uses this policy as well for file data, but once a write is issued to the server during a cache flush, the write must reach the server's disk before it is considered to be complete. NFS treats metadata (directory data and file-attribute data) differently. Any metadata changes are issued synchronously to the server. Thus, file loss and directory-structure corruption are avoided on a client or server crash.

For NFS with cachefs, writes are also written to the local disk cache area when they are written to the server to keep all copies consistent. Thus NFS with cachefs improves performance over standard NFS on a read request with a cachefs cache hit, but decreases performance for read or write requests with a cache miss. As with all caches, it is vital to have a high cache hit rate to gain performance.

Yet another variation on delayed write is to write data back to the server when the file is closed. This **write-on-close policy** is used in AFS. In the case of files that are open for short periods or are modified rarely, this policy does not significantly reduce network traffic. In addition, the write-on-close policy requires the closing process to delay while the file is written through, which reduces the performance advantages of delayed writes. The performance advantages of this policy over delayed write with more frequent flushing are apparent for files that are open for long periods and are modified frequently.

16.3.4 Consistency

A client machine is faced with the problem of deciding whether or not a locally cached copy of the data is consistent with the master copy (and hence can be used). If the client machine determines that its cached data are out of date, accesses can no longer be served by those cached data. An up-to-date copy of the data needs to be cached. There are two approaches to verify the validity of cached data:

1. **Client-initiated approach:** The client initiates a validity check in which it contacts the server and checks whether the local data are consistent with the master copy. The frequency of the validity check is the crux of this approach and determines the resulting consistency semantics. It can range from a check before every access to a check only on first access to a file (on file open, basically). Every access coupled with a validity check is delayed, compared with an access served immediately by the cache. Alternatively, a check can be initiated every fixed interval of time. Depending on its frequency, the validity check can load both the network and the server.

2. **Server-initiated approach:** The server records, for each client, the files (or parts of files) that it caches. When the server detects a potential inconsistency, it must react. A potential for inconsistency occurs when two different clients in conflicting modes cache a file. If UNIX semantics (Section 11.5.3) is implemented, we can resolve the potential inconsistency by having the server play an active role. The server must be notified whenever a file is opened, and the intended mode (read or write mode) must be indicated for every open. Assuming such notification, the server can act when it detects a file that is opened simultaneously in conflicting modes by disabling caching for that particular file. Actually disabling caching results in switching to a remote-service mode of operation.

16.3.5 A Comparison of Caching and Remote Services

Essentially, the choice between caching and remote service trades off potentially increased performance with decreased simplicity. We evaluate this tradeoff by listing the advantages and disadvantages of the two methods:

- The local cache can handle a substantial number of the remote accesses efficiently when caching is used. Capitalizing on locality in file-access patterns makes caching even more attractive. Thus, most of the remote accesses will be served as fast as will local ones. Moreover, servers are contacted only occasionally, rather than for each access. Consequently, server load and network traffic are reduced, and the potential for scalability is enhanced. By contrast, every remote access is handled across the network when the remote-service method is used. The penalty in network traffic, server load, and performance is obvious.

- Total network overhead in transmitting big chunks of data (as is done in caching) is lower than when series of responses to specific requests are transmitted (as in the remote-service method). Furthermore, disk-access routines on the server may be better optimized if it is known that requests are always for large, contiguous segments of data, rather than for random disk blocks.

- The cache-consistency problem is the major drawback of caching. In access patterns that exhibit infrequent writes, caching is superior.   However, when writes are frequent, the mechanisms employed to overcome the consistency problem incur substantial overhead in terms of performance, network traffic, and server load.

- So that caching will confer a benefit, execution should be carried out on machines that have either local disks or large main memories. Remote access on diskless, small-memory-capacity machines should be done through the remote-service method.

- In caching, since data are transferred en masse between the server and client, rather than in response to the specific needs of a file operation, the lower intermachine interface is different from the upper-user interface. The remote-service paradigm, on the other hand, is just an extension of the local file-system interface across the network. Thus, the intermachine interface mirrors the local user-file-system interface.

16.4 ■ Stateful Versus Stateless Service

There are two approaches to server-side information: Either the server tracks each file being accessed by each client, or it simply provides blocks as they are requested by the client without knowledge of those blocks' usage.

The typical scenario of a **stateful file service** is as follows: A client must perform an open operation on a file before accessing that file. The server fetches information about the file from its disk, stores it in its memory, and gives the client a connection identifier that is unique to the client and the open file. (In UNIX terms, the server fetches the inode and gives the client a file descriptor, which serves as an index to an in-core table of inodes.) This identifier is used for subsequent accesses until the session ends. A stateful service is characterized as a connection between the client and the server during a session. Either on closing the file or by a garbage-collection mechanism, the server must reclaim the main-memory space used by clients that are no longer active. The key point regarding fault tolerance in a stateful service approach is that the server keeps main-memory information about its clients. AFS is a stateful file service.

A **stateless file server** avoids state information by making each request self-contained. That is, each request identifies the file and the position in the file (for read and write accesses) in full. The server does not need to keep a table of open files in main memory, although it usually does so for efficiency reasons. Moreover, there is no need to establish and terminate a connection by open and close operations. They are totally redundant, since each file operation stands on its own and is not considered as part of a session. A client process would open a file, and that open would not result in a remote message being sent. Reads and writes would take place as remote messages (or cache lookups). The final close by the client would again result in only a local operation. NFS is a stateless file service.

The advantage a stateful service has over a stateless service is increased performance. File information is cached in main memory and can be accessed easily via the connection identifier, thereby saving disk accesses. In addition, a stateful server would know whether a file was open for sequential access and could therefore read ahead the next blocks. Stateless servers cannot do so, since they have no knowledge of the purpose of the client's requests.

The distinction between stateful and stateless service becomes more evident when we consider the effects of a crash occurring during a service activity. A stateful server loses all its volatile state in a crash. Ensuring the graceful recovery of such a server involves restoring this state, usually by a recovery protocol based on a dialog with clients. Less graceful recovery requires that the operations that were underway when the crash occurred be aborted. A different problem is caused by client failures. The server needs to become aware of such failures, so that it can reclaim space allocated to record the state of crashed client processes. This phenomenon is sometimes referred to as **orphan detection and elimination**.

A stateless server avoids these problems, since a newly reincarnated server can respond to a self-contained request without any difficulty. Therefore, the effects of server failures and recovery are almost unnoticeable. There is no difference between a slow server and a recovering server from a client's point of view. The client keeps retransmitting its request if it receives no response.

The penalty for using the robust stateless service is longer request messages and slower processing of requests, since there is no in-core information to speed the processing. In addition, stateless service imposes additional constraints on the design of the DFS. First, since each request identifies the target file, a uniform, system-wide, low-level naming scheme should be used. Translating remote-to-local names for each request would cause even slower processing of the requests. Second, since clients retransmit requests for file operations, these operations must be idempotent; that is, each operation must have the same effect and return the same output if executed several times consecutively. Self-contained read and write accesses are idempotent, as long as they use an absolute byte count to indicate the position within the file they access and do not rely on an incremental offset (as done in UNIX `read` and `write` system calls). However, we must be careful when implementing destructive operations (such as deleting a file) to make them idempotent too.

In some environments, a stateful service is a necessity. If the server employs the server-initiated method for cache validation, it cannot provide stateless service, since it maintains a record of which files are cached by which clients.

The way UNIX uses file descriptors and implicit offsets is inherently stateful. Servers must maintain tables to map the file descriptors to inodes, and must store the current offset within a file. This requirement is why NFS, which employs a stateless service, does not use file descriptors and does include an explicit offset in every access.

16.5 ▪ File Replication

Replication of files on different machines is a useful redundancy for improving availability. Multimachine replication can benefit performance too: Selecting a nearby replica to serve an access request results in shorter service time.

The basic requirement of a replication scheme is that different replicas of the same file reside on failure-independent machines. That is, the availability of one replica is not affected by the availability of the rest of the replicas. This obvious requirement implies that replication management is inherently a location-opaque activity. Provisions for placing a replica on a particular machine must be available.

It is desirable to hide the details of replication from users. It is the task of the naming scheme to map a replicated file name to a particular replica. The existence of replicas should be invisible to higher levels. At lower levels, however, the replicas must be distinguished from one another by different lower-level names. Another transparency requirement is providing replication control at higher levels. Replication control includes determination of the degree of replication and of the placement of replicas. Under certain circumstances, we may want to expose these details to users. Locus, for instance, provides users and system administrators with mechanisms to control the replication scheme.

The main problem associated with replicas is their update. From a user's point of view, replicas of a file denote the same logical entity, and thus an update to any replica must be reflected on all other replicas. More precisely, the relevant consistency semantics must be preserved when accesses to replicas are viewed as virtual accesses to the replicas' logical files. If consistency is not of primary importance, it can be sacrificed for availability and performance. In this fundamental tradeoff in the area of fault tolerance, the choice is between preserving consistency at all costs, thereby creating a potential for indefinite blocking, and sacrificing consistency under some (we hope, rare) circumstances of catastrophic failures for the sake of guaranteed progress. Locus, for example, employs replication extensively and sacrifices consistency in the case of network partition, for the sake of availability of files for read and write accesses.

Ibis uses a variation of the primary-copy approach. The domain of the name mapping is a pair <*primary-replica-identifier, local-replica-identifier*>. If no local replica exists, a special value is used. Thus, the mapping is relative to a machine. If the local replica is the primary one, the pair contains two identical identifiers. Ibis supports demand replication, an automatic replication-control policy similar to whole-file caching. Under demand replication, reading of a nonlocal replica causes it to be cached locally, thereby generating a new nonprimary replica. Updates are performed only on the primary copy and cause all other replicas to be invalidated by sending appropriate messages. Atomic and serialized invalidation of all nonprimary replicas is not guaranteed. Hence, a stale replica may be considered valid. To satisfy remote write accesses, we migrate the primary copy to the requesting machine.

16.6 ■ An Example: AFS

Andrew is a distributed computing environment designed and implemented at Carnegie Mellon University starting in 1983. The Andrew file system (AFS) constitutes the underlying information-sharing mechanism among clients of the environment. The Transarc Corporation took over development of AFS, then was purchased by IBM. IBM has since produced several commercial implementations of AFS. AFS was subsequently chosen as the DFS for an industry coalition, with the result being *Transarc DFS,* part of the distributed computing environment (DCE) from the OSF organization.

In 2000, IBM's Transarc Lab announced that AFS would be an open-source product available under the IBM Public License. Transarc DFS continues as a commercial product. Many UNIX vendors, as well as Microsoft, have announced support for the DCE system. Work is continuing to make it a cross-platform, universally accepted DFS. AFS and Transarc DFS are very similar, so we describe AFS throughout this section, unless Transarc DFS is named specifically.

AFS seeks to solve many of the problems of the simpler DFSs, such as NFS, and is arguably the most feature-rich non-experimental DFS. It features a uniform name space, location-independent file sharing, client-side caching with cache consistency, and secure authentication via Kerberos. It also includes server-side caching in the form of replicas, with high availability through automatic switchover to a replica if the source server is unavailable. One of the most formidable attributes of AFS is scalability: The Andrew system is targeted to span over 5,000 workstations. Between AFS and Transarc DFS there are hundreds of implementations worldwide.

16.6.1 Overview

AFS distinguishes between *client machines* (sometimes referred to as *workstations*) and dedicated *server machines.* Servers and clients originally ran only 4.2BSD UNIX, but AFS has been ported to many operating systems. The clients and servers are interconnected by a network of LANs or WANs.

Clients are presented with a partitioned space of file names: a **local name space** and a **shared name space.** Dedicated servers, collectively called *Vice* after the name of the software they run, present the shared name space to the clients as a homogeneous, identical, and location-transparent file hierarchy. The local name space is the root file system of a workstation, from which the shared name space descends. Workstations run the *Virtue* protocol to communicate with Vice, and they are required to have local disks where they store their local name space. Servers collectively are responsible for the storage and management of the shared name space. The local name space is small, is distinct for each workstation, and contains system programs essential for autonomous operation and better performance. Also local are temporary files and files that the workstation owner, for privacy reasons, explicitly wants to store locally.

Viewed at a finer granularity, clients and servers are structured in clusters interconnected by a WAN. Each cluster consists of a collection of workstations on a LAN and a representative of Vice called a **cluster server**, and is connected to the WAN by a router. The decomposition into clusters is done primarily to address the problem of scale. For optimal performance, workstations should use the server on their own cluster most of the time, thereby making cross-cluster file references relatively infrequent.

The file-system architecture was also based on consideration of scale. The basic heuristic was to offload work from the servers to the clients, in light of experience indicating that server CPU speed is the system's bottleneck. Following this heuristic, the key mechanism selected for remote file operations is to cache files in large chunks (64 KB). This feature reduces file-open latency, and allows reads and writes to be directed to the cached copy without frequently involving the servers.

Briefly, here are a few additional issues in AFS' design:

- **Client mobility:** Clients are able to access any file in the shared name space from any workstation. They may notice some initial performance degradation due to the caching of files when accessing files from other than their usual workstations.

- **Security:** The Vice interface is considered the boundary of trustworthiness, because no client programs are executed on Vice machines. Authentication and secure-transmission functions are provided as part of a connection-based communication package, based on the RPC paradigm. After mutual authentication, a Vice server and a client communicate via encrypted messages. Encryption is performed by hardware devices or (more slowly) in software. Information about clients and groups is stored in a protection database replicated at each server.

- **Protection:** AFS provides **access lists** for protecting directories and the regular UNIX bits for file protection. The access list may contain information about those users allowed to access a directory, as well as information about those users *not* allowed to access it. Thus, with this scheme, it is simple to specify that everyone except, say, Jim can access a directory. AFS supports the access types read, write, lookup, insert, administer, lock, and delete.

- **Heterogeneity:** Defining a clear interface to Vice is a key for integration of diverse workstation hardware and operating system. So that heterogeneity is facilitated, some files in the local */bin* directory are symbolic links pointing to machine-specific executable files residing in Vice.

16.6.2 The Shared Name Space

AFS' shared name space is constituted of component units called **volumes**. AFS' volumes are unusually small component units. Typically, they are associated with the files of a single client. Few volumes reside within a single disk partition, and they may grow (up to a quota) and shrink in size. Conceptually, volumes are glued together by a mechanism similar to the UNIX mount mechanism. However, the granularity difference is significant, since in UNIX only an entire disk partition (containing a file system) can be mounted. Volumes are a key administrative unit and play a vital role in identifying and locating an individual file.

A Vice file or directory is identified by a low-level identifier called a *fid*. Each AFS directory entry maps a path-name component to a fid. A fid is 96 bits long and has three equal-length components: a *volume number*, a *vnode number*, and a *uniquifier*. The **vnode number** is used as an index into an array containing the inodes of files in a single volume. The **uniquifier** allows reuse of vnode numbers, thereby keeping certain data structures compact. Fids are location transparent; therefore, file movements from server to server do not invalidate cached directory contents.

Location information is kept on a volume basis in a **volume-location database** replicated on each server. A client can identify the location of every volume in the system by querying this database. The aggregation of files into volumes makes it possible to keep the location database at a manageable size.

To balance the available disk space and utilization of servers, volumes need to be migrated among disk partitions and servers. When a volume is shipped to its new location, its original server is left with temporary forwarding information, so that the location database does not need to be updated synchronously. While the volume is being transferred, the original server can still handle updates, which are shipped later to the new server. At some point, the volume is briefly disabled so that the recent modifications can be processed; then, the new volume becomes available again at the new site. The volume-movement operation is atomic; if either server crashes, the operation is aborted.

Read-only replication at the granularity of an entire volume is supported for system-executable files and for seldom updated files in the upper levels of the Vice name space. The volume-location database specifies the server containing the only read–write copy of a volume and a list of read-only replication sites.

16.6.3 File Operations and Consistency Semantics

The fundamental architectural principle in AFS is the caching of entire files from servers.   Accordingly, a client workstation interacts with Vice servers only during opening and closing of files, and even this interaction is not always necessary. Reading and writing files do not cause remote interaction (in contrast to the remote-service method). This key distinction has far-reaching ramifications for performance, as well as for semantics of file operations.

The operating system on each workstation intercepts file-system calls and forwards them to a client-level process on that workstation. This process, called *Venus,* caches files from Vice when they are opened, and stores modified copies of files back on the servers from which they came when they are closed. Venus may contact Vice only when a file is opened or closed; reading and writing of individual bytes of a file are performed directly on the cached copy and bypass Venus. As a result, writes at some sites are not visible immediately at other sites.

Caching is further exploited for future opens of the cached file. Venus assumes that cached entries (files or directories) are valid unless notified otherwise. Therefore, Venus does not need to contact Vice on a file open to validate the cached copy. The mechanism to support this policy, called **callback**, dramatically reduces the number of cache-validation requests received by servers. It works as follows. When a client caches a file or a directory, the server updates its state information recording this caching. We say that the client has a callback on that file. The server notifies the client before allowing a modification to the file by another client. In such a case, we say that the server removes the callback on the file for the former client. A client can use a cached file for open purposes only when the file has a callback. If a client closes a file after modifying it, all other clients caching this file lose their callbacks. Therefore, when these clients open the file later, they have to get the new version from the server.

Reading and writing bytes of a file are done directly by the kernel without Venus' intervention on the cached copy. Venus regains control when the file is closed and, if the file has been modified locally, it updates the file on the appropriate server. Thus, the only occasions on which Venus contacts Vice servers are on opens of files that either are not in the cache or have had their callback revoked, and on closes of locally modified files.

Basically, AFS implements session semantics. The only exceptions are file operations other than the primitive read and write (such as protection changes at the directory level), which are visible everywhere on the network immediately after the operation completes.

In spite of the callback mechanism, a small amount of cached validation traffic is still present, usually to replace callbacks lost because of machine or network failures. When a workstation is rebooted, Venus considers all cached files and directories suspect, and it generates a cache-validation request for the first use of each such entry.

The callback mechanism forces each server to maintain callback information and each client to maintain validity information. If the amount of callback information maintained by a server is excessive, the server can break callbacks and reclaim some storage by unilaterally notifying clients and revoking the validity of their cached files. If the callback state maintained by Venus gets out of sync with the corresponding state maintained by the servers, some inconsistency may result.

Venus also caches contents of directories and symbolic links, for path-name translation. Each component in the path name is fetched, and a callback is established for it if it is not already cached, or if the client does not have a callback on it. Lookups are done locally by Venus on the fetched directories using fids. No requests are forwarded from one server to another. At the end of a path-name traversal, all the intermediate directories and the target file are in the cache with callbacks on them. Future open calls to this file will involve no network communication at all, unless a callback is broken on a component of the path name.

The only exceptions to the caching policy are modifications to directories that are made directly on the server responsible for that directory for reasons of integrity. The Vice interface has well-defined operations for such purposes. Venus reflects the changes in its cached copy to avoid refetching the directory.

16.6.4 Implementation

Client processes are interfaced to a UNIX kernel with the usual set of system calls. The kernel is modified slightly to detect references to Vice files in the relevant operations and to forward the requests to the client-level Venus process at the workstation.

Venus carries out path-name translation component by component, as was described above. It has a mapping cache that associates volumes to server locations in order to avoid server interrogation for an already known volume location. If a volume is not present in this cache, Venus contacts any server to which it already has a connection, requests the location information, and enters that information into the mapping cache. Unless Venus already has a connection to the server, it establishes a new connection. It then uses this connection to fetch the file or directory. Connection establishment is needed for authentication and security purposes. When a target file is found and cached, a copy is created on the local disk. Venus then returns to the kernel, which opens the cached copy and returns its handle to the client process.

The UNIX file system is used as a low-level storage system for both AFS servers and clients. The client cache is a local directory on the workstation's disk. Within this directory are files whose names are placeholders for cache entries. Both Venus and server processes access UNIX files directly by the latter's inodes to avoid the expensive path-name-to-inode-translation routine (*namei*). Because the internal inode interface is not visible to client-level processes (both Venus and server processes are client-level processes), an appropriate set of additional system calls was added. DFS uses its own journaling file system to improve performance and reliability over UFS.

Venus manages two separate caches: one for status and the other for data. It uses a simple least-recently-used (LRU) algorithm to keep each of them bounded in size. When a file is flushed from the cache, Venus notifies the appropriate server to remove the callback for this file. The status cache is kept in virtual memory to allow rapid servicing of `stat` (file-status-returning) system calls. The data cache is resident on the local disk, but the UNIX I/O buffering mechanism does some caching of disk blocks in memory that is transparent to Venus.

A single client-level process on each file server services all file requests from clients. This process uses a lightweight-process package with non-preemptable scheduling to service many client requests concurrently. The RPC package is integrated with the lightweight-process package, thereby allowing the file server to be concurrently making or servicing one RPC per lightweight process. RPC is built on top of a low-level datagram abstraction. Whole file transfer is implemented as a side effect of these RPC calls. One RPC connection exists per client, but there is no a priori binding of lightweight processes to these connections. Instead, a pool of lightweight processes services client requests on all connections. The use of a single multithreaded server process allows the caching of data structures needed to service requests. On the other hand, a crash of a single server process has the disastrous effect of paralyzing this particular server.

16.7 ■ Summary

A DFS is a file-service system whose clients, servers, and storage devices are dispersed among the sites of a distributed system. Accordingly, service activity has to be carried out across the network; instead of a single centralized data repository, there are multiple and independent storage devices.

Ideally, a DFS should look to its clients like a conventional, centralized file system. The multiplicity and dispersion of its servers and storage devices should be made transparent. That is, the client interface of a DFS should not distinguish between local and remote files. It is up to the DFS to locate the files and to arrange for the transport of the data. A transparent DFS facilitates client mobility by bringing over the client's environment to the site where the client logs in.

There are several approaches to naming schemes in a DFS. In the simplest approach, files are named by some combination of their host name and local name, which guarantees a unique system-wide name. Another approach, popularized by NFS, provides a means to attach remote directories to local directories, thus giving the appearance of a coherent directory tree.

Requests to access a remote file are usually handled by two complementary methods. With remote service, requests for accesses are delivered to the server. The server machine performs the accesses, and their results are forwarded back to the client. With caching, if the data needed to satisfy the access request are not already cached, then a copy of those data is brought from the server to the client. Accesses are performed on the cached copy. The idea is to retain recently accessed disk blocks in the cache, so that repeated accesses to the same information can be handled locally, without additional network traffic. A replacement policy is used to keep the cache size bounded. The problem of keeping the cached copies consistent with the master file is the cache-consistency problem.

There are two approaches to server-side information. Either the server tracks each file the client accesses, or it simply provides blocks as the client requests them without knowledge of their use. These approaches are the stateful versus stateless service paradigms.

Replication of files on different machines is a useful redundancy for improving availability. Multimachine replication can benefit performance too, since selecting a nearby replica to serve an access request results in shorter service time.

AFS is a feature-rich DFS. It is an open-source predecessor to Transarc DFS. It features location independence and location transparency. It also imposes significant consistency semantics. Caching and replication are used to improve performance.

■ Exercises

16.1 What are the benefits of a DFS when compared to a file system in a centralized system?

16.2 Which of the example DFSs discussed in this chapter would handle a large, multiclient database application most efficiently? Explain your answer.

16.3 Under which circumstances would a client prefer a location-transparent DFS? Under which would she prefer a location-independent DFS? Discuss the reasons for these preferences.

16.4 What aspects of a distributed system would you select for a system running on a totally reliable network?

16.5 Compare and contrast the techniques of caching disk blocks locally, on a client system, and remotely, on a server.

16.6 What are the benefits of mapping objects into virtual memory, as Apollo Domain does? What are the detriments?

16.7 Describe some of the fundamental differences between AFS and NFS (see Chapter 12).

Bibliographical Notes

Discussions concerning consistency and recovery control for replicated files were offered by Davcev and Burkhard [1985]. Management of replicated files in a UNIX environment was covered by Brereton [1986] and Purdin et al. [1987]. Wah [1984] discussed the issue of file placement on distributed computer systems. A detailed survey of mainly centralized file servers was given in Svobodova [1984].

Sun's Network File System (NFS) was presented by Callaghan [2000]. The AFS system was discussed by Morris et al. [1986], Howard et al. [1988], and Satyanarayanan [1990]. Information about Transarc AFS and DFS is available from http://www.transarc.ibm.com/DFS.

Many different and interesting DFSs were not covered in detail in this text, including UNIX United, Sprite, and Locus. UNIX United was described by Brownbridge et al. [1982]. The Locus system was discussed by Popek and Walker [1985]. The Sprite system was described by Ousterhout et al. [1988] and Nelson et al. [1988].

Chapter 17

DISTRIBUTED COORDINATION

In Chapter 7, we described various mechanisms that allow processes to synchronize their actions. We also discussed a number of schemes to ensure the atomicity property of a transaction that executes either in isolation or concurrently with other transactions. In Chapter 8, we described various methods that an operating system can use to deal with the deadlock problem. In this chapter, we examine how the centralized synchronization mechanisms can be extended to a distributed environment. We also discuss methods for handling deadlocks in a distributed system.

17.1 ■ Event Ordering

In a centralized system, we can always determine the order in which two events occurred, since the system has a single common memory and clock. Many applications may require us to determine order. For example, in a resource-allocation scheme, we specify that a resource can be used only *after* the resource has been granted. A distributed system, however, has no common memory and no common clock. Therefore, it is sometimes impossible to say which of two events occurred first. The *happened-before* relation is only a partial ordering of the events in distributed systems. Since the ability to define a total ordering is crucial in many applications, we present a distributed algorithm for extending the *happened-before* relation to a consistent total ordering of all the events in the system.

17.1.1 The Happened-Before Relation

Since we are considering only sequential processes, all events executed in a single process are totally ordered. Also, by the law of causality, a message can be received only after it has been sent. Therefore, we can define the *happened-before* relation (denoted by $\rightarrow$) on a set of events as follows (assuming that sending and receiving a message constitutes an event):

1. If A and B are events in the same process, and A was executed before B, then A $\rightarrow$ B.

2. If A is the event of sending a message by one process and B is the event of receiving that message by another process, then A $\rightarrow$ B.

3. If A $\rightarrow$ B and B $\rightarrow$ C then A $\rightarrow$ C.

Since an event cannot happen before itself, the $\rightarrow$ relation is an irreflexive partial ordering.

If two events, A and B, are not related by the $\rightarrow$ relation (that is, A did not happen before B, and B did not happen before A), then we say that these two events were executed **concurrently**. In this case, neither event can causally affect the other. If, however, A $\rightarrow$ B, then it is possible for event A to affect event B causally.

A space–time diagram, such as that in Figure 17.1, can best illustrate the definitions of concurrency and *happened-before*. The horizontal direction represents space (that is, different processes), and the vertical direction represents time. The labeled vertical lines denote processes (or processors). The labeled dots denote events. A wavy line denotes a message sent from one process to another. From this diagram, events A and B are concurrent if and only if no path exists either from A to B or from B to A.

For example, consider Figure 17.1. Some of the events related by the *happened-before* relation are

$$p_1 \rightarrow q_2,$$
$$r_0 \rightarrow q_4,$$
$$q_3 \rightarrow r_4,$$
$$p_1 \rightarrow q_4 \text{ (since } p_1 \rightarrow q_2 \text{ and } q_2 \rightarrow q_4\text{).}$$

Some of the concurrent events in the system are

$$q_0 \text{ and } p_2,$$
$$r_0 \text{ and } q_3,$$
$$r_0 \text{ and } p_3,$$
$$q_3 \text{ and } p_3.$$

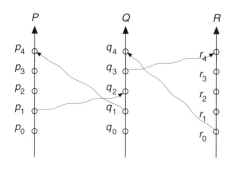

Figure 17.1   Relative time for three concurrent processes.

We cannot know which of two concurrent events, such as q_0 and p_2, happened first. However, since neither event can affect the other (there is no way for one of them to know whether the other has occurred yet), it is not important which happened first. It is important only that any processes that care about the order of two concurrent events agree on some order.

17.1.2 Implementation

To determine that an event A happened before an event B, we need either a common clock or a set of perfectly synchronized clocks. Since neither of these is available in a distributed system, we must define the *happened-before* relation without the use of physical clocks.

We associate with each system event a **timestamp**. We can then define the **global ordering** requirement: For every pair of events A and B, if A → B, then the timestamp of A is less than the timestamp of B. (Below we will see that the converse does not need to be true.)

How do we enforce the global ordering requirement in a distributed environment? We define within *each* process P_i a **logical clock**, LC_i. The logical clock can be implemented as a simple counter incremented between any two successive events executed within a process. Since the logical clock has a **monotonically** increasing value, it assigns a unique number to every event, and if an event A occurs before event B in process P_i, then $LC_i(A) < LC_i(B)$. The timestamp for an event is the value of the logical clock for that event. This scheme ensures that for any two events in the same process the global ordering requirement is met.

Unfortunately, this scheme does not ensure that the global ordering requirement is met across processes. To illustrate the problem, consider two proceses P_1 and P_2 that communicate with each other. Suppose that P_1 sends a message to P_2 (event A) with $LC_1(A) = 200$, and P_2 receives the message (event B) with $LC_2(B) = 195$ (because the processor for P_2 is slower than the processor for P_1, its logical clock ticks more slowly). This situation violates our requirement, since A → B, but the timestamp of A is greater than the timestamp of B.

To resolve this difficulty, we require a process to advance its logical clock when it receives a message whose timestamp is greater than the current value of its logical clock. In particular, if process P_i receives a message (event B) with timestamp t and $LC_i(B) \leq t$, then it should advance its clock such that $LC_i(B) = t + 1$. Thus, in our example, when P_2 receives the message from P_1, it will advance its logical clock such that $LC_2(B) = 201$.

Finally, to realize a total ordering, we need only to observe that, with our timestamp-ordering scheme, if the timestamps of two events, A and B, are the same, then the events are concurrent. In this case, we may use process identity numbers to break ties and to create a total ordering. The use of timestamps is discussed in Section 17.4.2.

17.2 ■ Mutual Exclusion

In this section, we present a number of different algorithms for implementing mutual exclusion in a distributed environment. We assume that the system consists of n processes, each of which resides at a different processor. To simplify our discussion, we assume that processes are numbered uniquely from 1 to n, and that a one-to-one mapping exists between processes and processors (that is, each process has its own processor).

17.2.1 Centralized Approach

In a centralized approach to providing mutual exclusion, one of the processes in the system is chosen to coordinate the entry to the critical section. Each process that wants to invoke mutual exclusion sends a *request* message to the coordinator. When the process receives a *reply* message from the coordinator, it can proceed to enter its critical section. After exiting its critical section, the process sends a *release* message to the coordinator and proceeds with its execution.

On receiving a *request* message, the coordinator checks to see whether some other process is in its critical section. If no process is in its critical section, the coordinator immediately sends back a *reply* message. Otherwise, the request is queued. When the coordinator receives a *release* message, it removes one of the *request* messages from the queue (in accordance with some scheduling algorithm) and sends a *reply* message to the requesting process.

It should be clear that this algorithm ensures mutual exclusion. In addition, if the scheduling policy within the coordinator is fair (such as first-come, first-served (FCFS) scheduling), no starvation can occur. This scheme requires three messages per critical-section entry: a *request*, a *reply*, and a *release*.

If the coordinator process fails, then a new process must take its place. In Section 17.6, we describe some algorithms for electing a unique new coordinator. Once a new coordinator has been elected, it must poll all the processes in the system, to reconstruct its *request* queue. Once the queue has been constructed, the computation may resume.

17.2.2 Fully Distributed Approach

If we want to distribute the decision making across the entire system, then the solution is far more complicated. We present an algorithm based on the event-ordering scheme described in Section 17.1.

When a process P_i wants to enter its critical section, it generates a new timestamp, TS, and sends the message *request*(P_i, TS) to all other processes in the system (including itself). On receiving a *request* message, a process may reply immediately (that is, send a *reply* message back to P_i), or it may defer sending a reply back (because it is already in its critical section, for example). A process that has received a *reply* message from all other processes in the system can enter its critical section, queueing incoming requests and deferring them. After exiting its critical section, the process sends *reply* messages to all its deferred requests.

The decision whether process P_i replies immediately to a *request*(P_j, TS) message or defers its reply is based on three factors:

1. If process P_i is in its critical section, then it defers its reply to P_j.

2. If process P_i does *not* want to enter its critical section, then it sends a reply immediately to P_j.

3. If process P_i wants to enter its critical section but has not yet entered it, then it compares its own *request* timestamp with the timestamp TS of the incoming request made by process P_j. If its own *request* timestamp is greater than TS, then it sends a reply immediately to P_j (P_j asked first). Otherwise, the reply is deferred.

This algorithm exhibits the following desirable behavior:

- Mutual exclusion is obtained.

- Freedom from deadlock is ensured.

- Freedom from starvation is ensured, since entry to the critical section is scheduled according to the timestamp ordering. The timestamp ordering ensures that processes are served in a FCFS order.

- The number of messages per critical-section entry is $2 \times (n - 1)$. This number is the minimum number of required messages per critical-section entry when processes act independently and concurrently.

To illustrate how the algorithm functions, we consider a system consisting of processes P_1, P_2, and P_3. Suppose that processes P_1 and P_3 want to enter their critical sections. Process P_1 then sends a message *request* (P_1, timestamp = 10) to processes P_2 and P_3, while process P_3 sends a message *request* (P_3, timestamp = 4) to processes P_1 and P_2. The timestamps 4 and 10 were obtained from the logical clocks described in Section 17.1. When process P_2 receives these *request* messages, it replies immediately. When process P_1 receives the *request* from process P_3 it replies immediately, since the timestamp (10) on its own *request* message is greater than the timestamp (4) for process P_3. When process P_3 receives the *request* message from process P_1, it defers its reply, since the timestamp (4) on its *request* message is less than the timestamp (10) for the message from process P_1. On receiving replies from both process P_1 and process P_2, process P_3 can enter its critical section. After exiting its critical section, process P_3 sends a reply to process P_1, which can then enter its critical section.

Because this scheme requires the participation of all the processes in the system, however, it has three undesirable consequences:

1. The processes need to know the identity of all other processes in the system. When a new process joins the group of processes participating in the mutual-exclusion algorithm, the following actions need to be taken:

   a. The process must receive the names of all the other processes in the group.

   b. The name of the new process must be distributed to all the other processes in the group.

   This task is not as trivial as it may seem, since some *request* and *reply* messages may be circulating in the system when the new process joins the group. The interested reader is referred to the Bibliographical Notes for more details.

2. If one process fails, then the entire scheme collapses. We can resolve this difficulty by continuously monitoring the state of all processes in the system. If one process fails, then all other processes are notified, so that they will no longer send *request* messages to the failed process. When a process recovers, it must initiate the procedure that allows it to rejoin the group.

3. Processes that have not entered their critical section must pause frequently to assure other processes that they intend to enter the critical section. This protocol is therefore suited for small, stable sets of cooperating processes.

17.2.3 Token-Passing Approach

Another method of providing mutual exclusion is to circulate a token among the processes in the system. A **token** is a special type of message that is passed around the system. Possession of the token entitles the holder to enter the critical section. Since there is only a single token, only one process can be in its critical section at a time.

We assume that the processes in the system are *logically* organized in a **ring structure**. The physical communication network does not need to be a ring. As long as the processes are connected to one another, it is possible to implement a logical ring. To implement mutual exclusion, we pass the token around the ring. When a process receives the token, it may enter its critical section, keeping the token. After the process exits its critical section, the token is passed around again. If the process receiving the token does not want to enter its critical section, it passes the token to its neighbor. This scheme is similar to algorithm 1 in Chapter 7, but a token is substituted for a shared variable.

If the ring is unidirectional, freedom from starvation is ensured. The number of messages required to implement mutual exclusion may vary from one message per entry, in the case of high contention (that is, every process wants to enter its critical section), to an infinite number of messages, in the case of low contention (that is, no process wants to enter its critical section).

Two types of failure must be considered. First, if the token is lost, an election must be called to generate a new token. Second, if a process fails, a new logical ring must be established. In Section 17.6, we present an election algorithm; others are possible. The development of an algorithm for reconstructing the ring is left to you in Exercise 17.6.

17.3 ■ Atomicity

In Chapter 7, we introduced the concept of an atomic transaction, which is a program unit that must be executed **atomically**. That is, either all the operations associated with it are executed to completion, or none are performed. When we are dealing with a distributed system, ensuring the atomicity property of a transaction becomes much more complicated than in a centralized system. This difficulty occurs because several sites may be participating in the execution of a single transaction. The failure of one of these sites, or the failure of a communication link connecting these sites, may result in erroneous computations.

The function of the **transaction coordinator** of a distributed system is to ensure that the execution of the transactions in the distributed system preserves atomicity. Each site has its own local transaction coordinator responsible for coordinating the execution of all the transactions initiated at that site. For each such transaction, the coordinator is responsible for the following:

- Starting the execution of the transaction

- Breaking the transaction into a number of subtransactions, and distributing these subtransactions to the appropriate sites for execution

- Coordinating the termination of the transaction, which may result in the transaction being committed at all sites or aborted at all sites

We assume that each local site maintains a log for recovery purposes.

17.3.1 The Two-Phase Commit Protocol

For atomicity to be ensured, all the sites in which a transaction T executed must agree on the final outcome of the execution. T must either commit at all sites or it must abort at all sites. To ensure this property, the transaction coordinator of T must execute a **commit protocol**. Among the simplest and most widely used commit protocols is the **two-phase commit (2PC) protocol**, which we discuss here.

Let T be a transaction initiated at site S_i, and let the transaction coordinator at S_i be C_i. When T completes its execution—that is, when all the sites at which T has executed inform C_i that T has completed—then C_i starts the 2PC protocol.

- **Phase 1:** C_i adds the record <prepare T> to the log and forces the record onto stable storage. It then sends a *prepare (T)* message to all the sites at which T executed. On receiving such a message, the transaction manager at that site determines whether it is willing to commit its portion of T. If the answer is *no*, it adds a record <no T> to the log, and then it responds by sending an *abort (T)* message to C_i. If the answer is *yes*, it adds a record <ready T> to the log, and forces all the log records corresponding to T onto stable storage. The transaction manager then replies with a *ready (T)* message to C_i.

- **Phase 2:** When C_i receives responses to the *prepare (T)* message it sent from all the sites, or when a prespecified interval of time has elapsed since the *prepare (T)* message was sent out, C_i can determine whether the transaction T can be committed or aborted. Transaction T can be committed if C_i received a *ready (T)* message from all the participating sites. Otherwise, transaction T must be aborted. Depending on the verdict, either a record <commit T> or a record <abort T> is added to the log and is forced onto stable storage. At this point, the fate of the transaction has been sealed. Following this, the coordinator sends either a *commit (T)* or an *abort (T)* message to all participating sites. When a site receives that message, it records the message in the log.

A site at which T executed can unconditionally abort T at any time prior to its sending the message *ready (T)* to the coordinator. The *ready (T)* message is, in effect, a promise by a site to follow the coordinator's order to commit T or to abort T. The only situation in which a site can make such a promise is if the needed information is stored in stable storage. Otherwise, if the site crashes after sending ready T, it may be unable to make good on its promise.

Since unanimity is required to commit a transaction, the fate of T is sealed as soon as at least one site responds with *abort (T)*. Since the coordinator site S_i is one of the sites at which T executed, the coordinator can decide unilaterally to abort T. The final verdict regarding T is determined at the time the coordinator writes that verdict (commit or abort) to the log and forces it to stable storage. In some implementations of the 2PC protocol, a site sends an acknowledge T message to the coordinator at the end of the second phase of the protocol. When the coordinator receives the acknowledge T message from all the sites, it adds the record <complete T> to the log.

17.3.2 Failure Handling in 2PC

We now examine in detail how 2PC responds to various types of failures. As we shall see, one major disadvantage of the 2PC protocol is that coordinator failure may result in blocking, where a decision either to commit or to abort T may have to be postponed until C_i recovers.

17.3.2.1 Failure of a Participating Site

When a participating site S_k recovers from a failure, it must examine its log to determine the fate of those transactions that were in the midst of execution when the failure occurred. Let T be one such transaction. We consider each of the possible cases:

- The log contains a <commit T> record. In this case, the site executes redo(T).

- The log contains an <abort T> record. In this case, the site executes undo(T).

- The log contains a <ready T> record. In this case, the site must consult C_i to determine the fate of T. If C_i is up, it notifies S_k regarding whether T committed or aborted. In the former case, it executes redo(T); in the latter case, it executes undo(T). If C_i is down, S_k must try to find the fate of T from other sites. It does so by sending a *query-status (T)* message to all the sites in the system. On receiving such a message, a site must consult its log to determine whether T has executed there, and if so, whether T committed or aborted. It then notifies S_k about this outcome. If no site has the appropriate information (that is, whether T committed or aborted), then S_k can neither abort nor commit T. The decision concerning T is postponed until S_k can obtain the needed information. Thus, S_k must periodically resend the *query-status (T)* message to the other sites. It does so until a site recovers that contains the needed information. The site at which C_i resides always has the needed information.

- The log contains no control records (abort, commit, ready) concerning T. The absence of control records implies that S_k failed before responding to the prepare T message from C_i. Since the failure of S_k precludes the sending of such a response, by our algorithm C_i must abort T. Hence, S_k must execute undo(T).

17.3.2.2 Failure of the Coordinator

If the coordinator fails in the midst of the execution of the commit protocol for transaction T, then the participating sites must decide on the fate of T. We shall see that, in certain cases, the participating sites cannot decide whether to commit or abort T, and therefore these sites must wait for the recovery of the failed coordinator.

- If an active site contains a <commit T> record in its log, then T must be committed.

- If an active site contains an <abort T> record in its log, then T must be aborted.

- If some active site does *not* contain a <ready T> record in its log, then the failed coordinator C_i cannot have decided to commit T. We can draw this conclusion because a site that does not have a <ready T> record in its log cannot have sent a *ready (T)* message to C_i. However, the coordinator may have decided to abort T, but not to commit T. Rather than wait for C_i to recover, it is preferable to abort T.

- If none of the preceding cases holds, then all the active sites must have a <ready T> record in their logs, but no additional control records (such as <abort T> or <commit T>). Since the coordinator has failed, it is impossible to determine whether a decision has been made, or what that decision is, until the coordinator recovers. Thus, the active sites must wait for C_i to recover. Since the fate of T remains in doubt, T may continue to hold system resources. For example, if locking is used, T may hold locks on data at active sites. Such a situation is undesirable because it may take hours or days before C_i is again active. During this time other transactions may be forced to wait for T. As a result, data are unavailable not only on the failed site (C_i) but on active sites as well. The number of unavailable data increases as the downtime of C_i grows. This situation is called the *blocking* problem, because T is blocked pending the recovery of site C_i.

17.3.2.3 Failure of the Network

When a link fails, all the messages in the process of being routed through the link do not arrive at their destination intact. From the viewpoint of the sites connected throughout that link, the other sites appears to have failed. Thus, our previous schemes apply here as well.

When a number of links fail, the network may partition. In this case, two possibilities exist. The coordinator and all its participants may remain in one partition; in this case, the failure has no effect on the commit protocol. Alternatively, the coordinator and its participants may belong to several partitions; in this case, messages between the participant and the coordinator are lost, reducing the case to a link failure, as discussed.

17.4 ■ Concurrency Control

In this section, we show how certain of the concurrency-control schemes discussed in Chapter 7 can be modified so that they can be used in a distributed environment.

The transaction manager of a distributed database system manages the execution of those transactions (or subtransactions) that access data stored in a local site. Each such transaction may be either a local transaction (that is, a transaction that executes only at that site) or part of a global transaction (that is, a transaction that executes at several sites). Each transaction manager is responsible for maintaining a log for recovery purposes, and for participating in an appropriate concurrency-control scheme to coordinate the concurrent execution of the transactions executing at that site. As we shall see, the concurrency schemes described in Chapter 7 need to be modified to accommodate the distribution of transactions.

17.4.1 Locking Protocols

The two-phase locking protocols described in Chapter 7 can be used in a distributed environment. The only change needed is in the way the lock manager is implemented. In this section, we present several possible schemes, the first of which deals with the case where no data replication is allowed. The other schemes apply to the more general case where data can be replicated in several sites. As in Chapter 7, we shall assume the existence of the **shared** and **exclusive lock modes**.

17.4.1.1 Nonreplicated Scheme

If no data are replicated in the system, then the locking schemes described in Section 7.10 can be applied as follows: Each site maintains a local lock manager whose function is to administer the lock and unlock requests for those data items stored in that site. When a transaction wishes to lock data item Q at site S_i, it simply sends a message to the lock manager at site S_i requesting a lock (in a particular lock mode). If data item Q is locked in an incompatible mode, then the request is delayed until that request can be granted. Once it has been determined that the lock request can be granted, the lock manager sends a message back to the initiator indicating that the lock request has been granted.

This scheme has the advantage of simple implementation. It requires two message transfers for handling lock requests and one message transfer for handling unlock requests. However, deadlock handling is more complex. Since the lock and unlock requests are no longer made at a single site, the various deadlock-handling algorithms discussed in Chapter 8 must be modified; these modifications will be discussed in Section 17.5.

17.4.1.2 Single-Coordinator Approach

Under the single-coordinator approach, the system maintains a *single* lock manager that resides in a *single* chosen site, say S_i. All lock and unlock requests are made at site S_i. When a transaction needs to lock a data item, it sends a lock request to S_i. The lock manager determines whether the lock can be granted immediately. If so, it sends a message to that effect to the site at which the lock request was initiated. Otherwise, the request is delayed until it can be granted, at which time a message is sent to the site at which the lock request was initiated. The transaction can read the data item from *any* one of the sites at which a replica of the data item resides. In the case of a `write`, all the sites where a replica of the data item resides must be involved in the writing.

The scheme has the following advantages:

- **Simple implementation:** This scheme requires two messages for handling lock requests and one message for handling unlock requests.

- **Simple deadlock handling:** Since all lock and unlock requests are made at one site, the deadlock-handling algorithms discussed in Chapter 8 can be applied directly to this environment.

The disadvantages of the scheme include the following:

- **Bottleneck:** The site S_i becomes a bottleneck, since all requests must be processed there.

- **Vulnerability:** If the site S_i fails, the concurrency controller is lost. Either processing must stop or a recovery scheme must be used.

A compromise between these advantages and disadvantages can be achieved through a **multiple-coordinator approach**, in which the lock-manager function is distributed over several sites.

Each lock manager administers the lock and unlock requests for a subset of the data items. Each lock manager resides in a different site. This distribution reduces the degree to which the coordinator is a bottleneck, but it complicates deadlock handling, since the lock and unlock requests are not made at a single site.

17.4.1.3 Majority Protocol

The majority protocol is a modification of the nonreplicated data scheme that we presented earlier. The system maintains a lock manager at each site. Each manager controls the locks for all the data or replicas of data stored at that site. When a transaction wishes to lock a data item Q that is replicated in n different sites, it must send a lock request to more than one-half of the n sites in which Q is stored. Each lock manager determines whether the lock can be granted immediately (as far as it is concerned). As before, the response is delayed until the request can be granted. The transaction does not operate on Q until it has successfully obtained a lock on a majority of the replicas of Q.

This scheme deals with replicated data in a decentralized manner, thus avoiding the drawbacks of central control. However, it suffers from its own disadvantages:

- **Implementation:** The majority protocol is more complicated to implement than the previous schemes. It requires $2(n/2 + 1)$ messages for handling lock requests, and $(n/2 + 1)$ messages for handling unlock requests.

- **Deadlock handling:** Since the lock and unlock requests are not made at one site, the deadlock-handling algorithms must be modified (Section 17.5). In addition, a deadlock can occur even if only one data item is being locked. To illustrate, consider a system with four sites and full replication. Suppose that transactions T_1 and T_2 wish to lock data item Q in exclusive mode. Transaction T_1 may succeed in locking Q at sites S_1 and S_3, while transaction T_2 may succeed in locking Q at sites S_2 and S_4. Each then must wait to acquire the third lock, and hence a deadlock has occurred.

17.4.1.4 Biased Protocol

The biased protocol is based on a model similar to that of the majority protocol. The difference is that requests for shared locks are given more favorable treatment than are requests for exclusive locks. The system maintains a lock manager at each site. Each manager manages the locks for all the data items stored at that site. **Shared** and **exclusive locks** are handled differently.

- **Shared locks:** When a transaction needs to lock data item Q, it simply requests a lock on Q from the lock manager at one site containing a replica of Q.

- **Exclusive locks:** When a transaction needs to lock data item Q, it requests a lock on Q from the lock manager at all sites containing a replica of Q.

As before, the response to the request is delayed until the request can be granted.

The scheme has the advantage of imposing less overhead on read operations than does the majority protocol. This advantage is especially significant in common cases in which the frequency of reads is much greater than is the frequency of writes. However, the additional overhead on writes is a disadvantage. Furthermore, the biased protocol shares the majority protocol's disadvantage of complexity in handling deadlock.

17.4.1.5 Primary Copy

In the case of data replication, we may choose one of the replicas as the primary copy. Thus, for each data item Q, the primary copy of Q must reside in precisely one site, which we call the *primary site of Q*.

When a transaction needs to lock a data item Q, it requests a lock at the primary site of Q. As before, the response to the request is delayed until the request can be granted.

Thus, the primary copy enables concurrency control for replicated data to be handled in a manner similar to that for unreplicated data. This method of handling allows for a simple implementation. However, if the primary site of Q fails, Q is inaccessible even though other sites containing a replica may be accessible.

17.4.2 Timestamping

The principal idea behind the timestamping scheme discussed in Section 7.10 is that each transaction is given a *unique* timestamp used to decide the serialization order. Our first task, then, in generalizing the centralized scheme to a distributed scheme is to develop a scheme for generating unique timestamps. Our previous protocols can then be applied directly to the nonreplicated environment.

17.4.2.1 Generation of Unique Timestamps

Two primary methods are used to generate unique timestamps; one is centralized and one is distributed. In the centralized scheme, a single site is chosen for distributing the timestamps. The site can use a logical counter or its own local clock for this purpose.

In the distributed scheme, each site generates a unique local timestamp using either a logical counter or the local clock. The global unique timestamp is obtained by concatenation of the unique local timestamp with the site identifier, which must be unique (Figure 17.2). The order of concatenation is important! We use the site identifier in the least significant position to ensure that the global timestamps generated in one site are not always greater than those generated in another site. Compare this technique for generating unique timestamps with the one we presented in Section 17.1.2 for generating unique names.

local unique timestamp

site identifier

global unique identifier

Figure 17.2 Generation of unique timestamps.

We may still have a problem if one site generates local timestamps at a faster rate than do other sites. In such a case, the fast site's logical counter will be larger than that of other sites. Therefore, all timestamps generated by the fast site will be larger than those generated by other sites. A mechanism is needed to ensure that local timestamps are generated fairly across the system. To accomplish the fair generation of timestamps, we define within each site S_i a logical clock (LC_i), which generates the unique local timestamp (see Section 17.1.2). To ensure that the various logical clocks are synchronized, we require that a site S_i advance its logical clock whenever a transaction T_i with timestamp $<x,y>$ visits that site and x is greater than the current value of LC_i. In this case, site S_i advances its logical clock to the value $x + 1$.

If the system clock is used to generate timestamps, then timestamps are assigned fairly, provided that no site has a system clock that runs fast or slow. Since clocks may not be perfectly accurate, a technique similar to that used for logical clocks must be used to ensure that no clock gets far ahead or far behind another clock.

17.4.2.2 Timestamp-Ordering Scheme

The basic timestamp scheme introduced in Section 7.10 can be extended in a straightforward manner to a distributed system. As in the centralized case, cascading rollbacks may result if no mechanism is used to prevent a transaction from reading a data item value that is not yet committed. To eliminate cascading rollbacks, we can combine the basic timestamp scheme of Section 7.10 with the 2PC protocol of Section 17.3 to obtain a protocol that ensures serializability with no cascading rollbacks. We leave the development of such an algorithm to you.

The basic timestamp scheme just described suffers from the undesirable property that conflicts between transactions are resolved through rollbacks, rather than through waits. To alleviate this problem, we can buffer the various **read** and **write** operations (that is, *delay* them) until a time when we are assured that these operations can take place without causing aborts. A **read**(x) operation by T_i must be delayed if there exists a transaction T_j that will perform a **write**(x) operation but has not yet done so and TS(T_j) < TS(T_i). Similarly, a write(x) operation by T_i must be delayed if there exists a transaction T_j that will perform either read(x) or write(x) operation and TS(T_j) < TS(T_i). Various methods are available for ensuring this property. One such method, called the **conservative timestamp-ordering scheme**, requires each site to maintain a read and write queue consisting of all the read and write requests, respectively, that are to be executed at the site and that must be delayed to preserve the above property. We shall not present the scheme here. Rather, we leave the development of the algorithm to you.

17.5 ■ Deadlock Handling

The deadlock-prevention, deadlock-avoidance, and deadlock-detection algorithms presented in Chapter 8 can be extended so that they can also be used in a distributed system. In the following, we describe several of these distributed algorithms.

17.5.1 Deadlock Prevention

The deadlock-prevention and deadlock-avoidance algorithms presented in Chapter 8 can also be used in a distributed system, provided that appropriate modifications are made. For example, we can use the resource-ordering deadlock-prevention technique by simply defining a global ordering among the system resources. That is, all resources in the entire system are assigned unique numbers, and a process may request a resource (at any processor) with unique number i only if it is not holding a resource with a unique number greater than i. Similarly, we can use the banker's algorithm in a distributed system by designating one of the processes in the system (the *banker*) as the process that maintains the information necessary to carry out the banker's algorithm. Every resource request must be channelled through the banker.

These two schemes can be used in dealing with the deadlock problem in a distributed environment. The global resource-ordering deadlock-prevention scheme is simple to implement and requires little overhead. The banker's algorithm can also be implemented easily, but it may require too much overhead. The banker may become a bottleneck, since the number of messages to and from the banker may be large. Thus, the banker's scheme does not seem to be of practical use in a distributed system.

In this section, we present a new deadlock-prevention scheme based on a timestamp-ordering approach with resource preemption. Although this approach can handle any deadlock situation that may arise in a distributed system, for simplicity we consider only the case of a single instance of each resource type.

To control the preemption, we assign a unique priority number to each process. These numbers are used to decide whether a process P_i should wait for a process P_j. For example, we can let P_i wait for P_j if P_i has a priority higher than that of P_j; otherwise P_i is rolled back. This scheme prevents deadlocks because, for every edge $P_i \rightarrow P_j$ in the wait-for graph, P_i has a higher priority than P_j. Thus, a cycle cannot exist.

One difficulty with this scheme is the possibility of starvation. Some processes with extremely low priority may always be rolled back. This difficulty can be avoided through the use of timestamps. Each process in the system is assigned a unique timestamp when it is created. Two complementary deadlock-prevention schemes using timestamps have been proposed:

1. **The wait–die scheme:** This approach is based on a nonpreemptive technique. When process P_i requests a resource currently held by P_j, P_i is allowed to wait only if it has a smaller timestamp than does P_j (that is, P_i is older than P_j). Otherwise, P_i is rolled back (dies). For example, suppose that processes P_1, P_2, and P_3 have timestamps 5, 10, and 15, respectively. If P_1 requests a resource held by P_2, P_1 will wait. If P_3 requests a resource held by P_2, P_3 will be rolled back.

2. **The wound–wait scheme:** This approach is based on a preemptive technique and is a counterpart to the wait–die system. When process P_i requests a resource currently held by P_j, P_i is allowed to wait only if it has a larger timestamp than does P_j (that is, P_i is younger than P_j). Otherwise, P_j is rolled back (P_j is *wounded* by P_i). Returning to our previous example, with processes P_1, P_2, and P_3, if P_1 requests a resource held by P_2, then the resource will be preempted from P_2 and P_2 will be rolled back. If P_3 requests a resource held by P_2, then P_3 will wait.

Both schemes can avoid starvation provided that, when a process is rolled back, it is *not* assigned a new timestamp. Since timestamps always increase, a process that is rolled back will eventually have the smallest timestamp. Thus, it will not be rolled back again. There are, however, significant differences in the way the two schemes operate.

- In the wait–die scheme, an older process must wait for a younger one to release its resource. Thus, the older the process gets, the more it tends to wait. By contrast, in the wound–wait scheme, an older process never waits for a younger process.

- In the wait–die scheme, if a process P_i dies and is rolled back because it requested a resource held by process P_j, then P_i may reissue the same sequence of requests when it is restarted. If the resource is still held by P_j, then P_i will die again. Thus, P_i may die several times before acquiring the needed resource. Contrast this series of events with what happens in the wound–wait scheme. Process P_i is wounded and rolled back because P_j requested a resource it holds. When P_i is restarted and requests the resource now being held by P_j, P_i waits. Thus, fewer rollbacks occur in the wound–wait scheme.

The major problem with both schemes is that unnecessary rollbacks may occur.

17.5.2 Deadlock Detection

The deadlock-prevention algorithm may preempt resources even if no deadlock has occurred. To prevent unnecessary preemptions, we can use a deadlock-detection algorithm. We construct a wait-for graph describing the resource-allocation state. Since we are assuming only a single resource of each type, a cycle in the wait-for graph represents a deadlock.

The main problem in a distributed system is deciding how to maintain the wait-for graph. We illustrate this problem by describing several common techniques to deal with this issue. These schemes require that each site keeps a *local* wait-for graph. The nodes of the graph correspond to all the processes (local as well as nonlocal) currently holding or requesting any of the resources local to that site. For example, in Figure 17.3 we have a system consisting of two sites, each maintaining its local wait-for graph. Note that processes P_2 and P_3 appear in both graphs, indicating that the processes have requested resources at both sites.

These local wait-for graphs are constructed in the usual manner for local processes and resources. When a process P_i in site S_1 needs a resource held by process P_j in site S_2, a request message is sent by P_i to site S_2. The edge $P_i \rightarrow P_j$ is then inserted in the local wait-for graph of site S_2.

Clearly, if any local wait-for graph has a cycle, deadlock has occurred. On the other hand, the fact that no cycles are in any of the local wait-for graphs does not mean that there are no deadlocks. To illustrate this problem, we consider the system depicted in Figure 17.3. Each wait-for graph is acyclic; nevertheless, a deadlock exists in the system. To prove that a deadlock has not occurred, we must show that the **union** of all local graphs is acyclic. The graph (Figure 17.4) that we obtain by taking the union of the two wait-for graphs of Figure 17.3 does indeed contain a cycle, implying that the system is in a deadlock state.

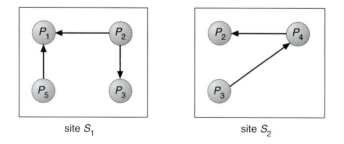

site S_1 site S_2

Figure 17.3   Two local wait-for graphs.

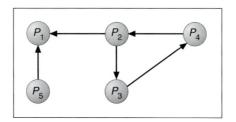

Figure 17.4   Global wait-for graph for Figure 17.3.

A number of methods are available to organize the wait-for graph in a distributed system. We shall describe several common schemes.

17.5.2.1 Centralized Approach

In the centralized approach, a global wait-for graph is constructed as the union of all the local wait-for graphs. It is maintained in a *single* process: the **deadlock-detection coordinator.** Since there is communication delay in the system, we must distinguish between two types of wait-for graphs. The *real* graph describes the real but unknown state of the system at any instance in time, as would be seen by an omniscient observer. The *constructed* graph is an approximation generated by the coordinator during the execution of its algorithm. The constructed graph must be generated such that, whenever the detection algorithm is invoked, the reported results are correct. By *correct* we mean the following:

- If a deadlock exists, then it is reported properly, and

- If a deadlock is reported, then the system is indeed in a deadlock state.

As we shall show, it is not easy to construct such correct algorithms.
     The wait-for graph may be constructed at three different points in time:

1. Whenever a new edge is inserted in or removed from one of the local wait-for graphs

2. Periodically, when a number of changes have occurred in a wait-for graph

3. Whenever the deadlock-detection coordinator needs to invoke the cycle-detection algorithm

Let us consider option 1. Whenever an edge is either inserted in or removed from a local graph, the local site must also send a message to the coordinator to notify it of this modification. On receiving such a message, the coordinator updates its global graph. Alternatively (option 2), a site can send a number of such changes in a single message periodically. Returning to our previous example, the coordinator process will maintain the global wait-for graph as depicted in Figure 17.4. When site S_2 inserts the edge $P_3 \rightarrow P_4$ in its local wait-for graph, it also sends a message to the coordinator. Similarly, when site S_1 deletes the edge $P_5 \rightarrow P_1$ because P_1 has released a resource that was requested by P_5, an appropriate message is sent to the coordinator.

When the deadlock-detection algorithm is invoked, the coordinator searches its global graph. If a cycle is found, a *victim* is selected to be rolled back. The coordinator must notify all the sites that a particular process has been selected as victim. The sites, in turn, roll back the victim process.

Note that, in this scheme (option 1), unnecessary rollbacks may occur, as a result of two situations:

1. **False cycles** may exist in the global wait-for graph. To illustrate this point, we consider a snapshot of the system as depicted in Figure 17.5. Suppose that P_2 releases the resource it is holding in site S_1, resulting in the deletion of the edge $P_1 \rightarrow P_2$ in site S_1. Process P_2 then requests a resource held by P_3 at site S_2, resulting in the addition of the edge $P_2 \rightarrow P_3$ in site S_2. If the *insert* $P_2 \rightarrow P_3$ message from site S_2 arrives before the *delete* $P_1 \rightarrow P_2$ message from site S_1, the coordinator may discover the false cycle $P_1 \rightarrow P_2 \rightarrow P_3 \rightarrow P_1$ after the *insert* (but before the *delete*). Deadlock recovery may be initiated, although no deadlock has occurred.

2. Unnecessary rollbacks may also result when a deadlock has indeed occurred and a victim has been picked, but *at the same time* one of the processes was aborted for reasons unrelated to the deadlock (such as the process exceeding its allocated time). For example, suppose that site S_1 in Figure 17.3 decides to abort P_2. At the same time, the coordinator has discovered a cycle and picked P_3 as a victim. Both P_2 and P_3 are now rolled back, although only P_2 needed to be rolled back.

The same problems are inherent in solutions employing options 2 and 3.

Let us now present a centralized deadlock-detection algorithm using option 3, which detects all deadlocks that actually occur, and does not detect false

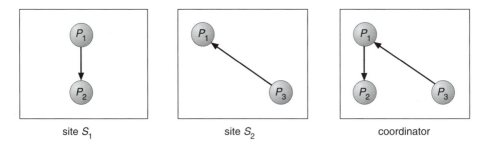

      site S_1 site S_2 coordinator

Figure 17.5   Local and global wait-for graphs.

deadlocks. To avoid the report of false deadlocks, we require that requests from different sites be appended with unique identifiers (or timestamps). When process P_i, at site S_1, requests a resource from P_j, at site S_2, a request message with timestamp TS is sent. The edge $P_i \rightarrow P_j$ with the label TS is inserted in the local wait-for graph of S_1. This edge is inserted in the local wait-for graph of site S_2 only if site S_2 has received the request message and cannot immediately grant the requested resource. A request from P_i to P_j in the same site is handled in the usual manner; no timestamps are associated with the edge $P_i \rightarrow P_j$. The detection algorithm is then as follows:

1. The controller sends an initiating message to each site in the system.

2. On receiving this message, a site sends its local wait-for graph to the coordinator. Each of these wait-for graphs contains all the local information the site has about the state of the real graph. The graph reflects an instantaneous state of the site, but it is not synchronized with respect to any other site.

3. When the controller has received a reply from each site, it constructs a graph as follows:

   a. The constructed graph contains a vertex for every process in the system.

   b. The graph has an edge $P_i \rightarrow P_j$ *if and only if* there is an edge $P_i \rightarrow P_j$ in one of the wait-for graphs, *or* an edge $P_i \rightarrow P_j$ with some label TS appears in more than one wait-for graph.

We assert that, if the constructed graph contains a cycle, then the system is in a deadlock state. If the constructed graph does not contain a cycle, then the system was not in a deadlock state when the detection algorithm was invoked as result of the initiating messages sent by the coordinator (in step 1).

17.5.2.2 Fully Distributed Approach

In the **fully distributed deadlock-detection algorithm**, all controllers share equally the responsibility for detecting deadlock. In this scheme, every site constructs a wait-for graph that represents a part of the total graph, depending on the dynamic behavior of the system. The idea is that, if a deadlock exists, a cycle will appear in (at least) one of the partial graphs. We present one such algorithm, which involves construction of partial graphs in every site.

Each site maintains its own local wait-for graph. A local wait-for graph in this scheme differs from the one described earlier in that we add one additional node P_{ex} to the graph. An arc $P_i \rightarrow P_{ex}$ exists in the graph if P_i is waiting for a data item in another site being held by *any* process. Similarly, an arc $P_{ex} \rightarrow P_j$ exists in the graph if a process at another site is waiting to acquire a resource currently being held by P_j in this local site.

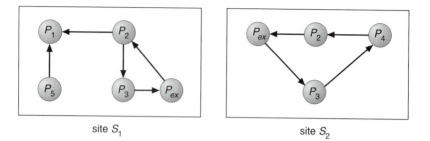

site S_1 site S_2

Figure 17.6   Augmented local wait-for graphs of Figure 17.3.

To illustrate this situation, we consider the two local wait-for graphs of Figure 17.3. The addition of the node P_{ex} in both graphs results in the local wait-for graphs shown in Figure 17.6.

If a local wait-for graph contains a cycle that does not involve node P_{ex}, then the system is in a deadlock state. If, however, a cycle involving P_{ex} exists, then this implies the *possibility* of a deadlock. To ascertain whether a deadlock does exist, we must invoke a distributed deadlock-detection algorithm.

Suppose that, at site S_i, the local wait-for graph contains a cycle involving node P_{ex}. This cycle must be of the form

$$P_{ex} \rightarrow P_{k_1} \rightarrow P_{k_2} \rightarrow \dots \rightarrow P_{k_n} \rightarrow P_{ex},$$

which indicates that process P_{k_n} in site S_i is waiting to acquire a data item located in some other site—say, S_j. On discovering this cycle, site S_i sends to site S_j a deadlock-detection message containing information about that cycle.

When site S_j receives this deadlock-detection message, it updates its local wait-for graph with the new information. Then, it searches the newly constructed wait-for graph for a cycle not involving P_{ex}. If one exists, a deadlock is found and an appropriate recovery scheme is invoked. If a cycle involving P_{ex} is discovered, then S_j transmits a deadlock-detection message to the appropriate site—say, S_k. Site S_k, in return, repeats the procedure. Thus, after a finite number of rounds, either a deadlock is discovered or the deadlock-detection computation halts.

To illustrate this procedure, we consider the local wait-for graphs of Figure 17.6. Suppose that site S_1 discovers the cycle

$$P_{ex} \rightarrow P_2 \rightarrow P_3 \rightarrow P_{ex}.$$

Since P_3 is waiting to acquire a data item in site S_2, a deadlock-detection message describing that cycle is transmitted from site S_1 to site S_2. When site S_2 receives this message, it updates its local wait-for graph, obtaining the wait-for graph of Figure 17.7. This graph contains the cycle

$$P_2 \rightarrow P_3 \rightarrow P_4 \rightarrow P_2,$$

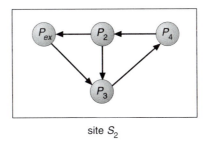

site S_2

Figure 17.7   Augmented local wait-for graph in site S_2 of Figure 17.6.

which does not include node P_{ex}. Therefore, the system is in a deadlock state and an appropriate recovery scheme must be invoked.

Note that the outcome would be the same if site S_2 discovered the cycle first in its local wait-for graph and sent the deadlock-detection message to site S_1. In the worst case, both sites will discover the cycle at about the same time, and two deadlock-detection messages will be sent: one by S_1 to S_2 and another by S_2 to S_1. This situation results in unnecessary message transfer and overhead in updating the two local wait-for graphs and searching for cycles in both graphs.

To reduce message traffic, we assign to each process P_i a unique identifier, which we denote by $ID(P_i)$. When site S_k discovers that its local wait-for graph contains a cycle involving node P_{ex} of the form

$$P_{ex} \rightarrow P_{K_1} \rightarrow P_{K_2} \rightarrow ... \rightarrow P_{K_n} \rightarrow P_{ex},$$

it sends a deadlock-detection message to another site only if

$$ID(P_{K_n}) < ID(P_{K_1}).$$

Otherwise, site S_k continues its normal execution, leaving the burden of initiating the deadlock-detection algorithm to some other site.

To illustrate this scheme, we consider again the wait-for graphs maintained at sites S_1 and S_2 of Figure 17.6. Suppose that

$$ID(P_1) < ID(P_2) < ID(P_3) < ID(P_4).$$

Let both sites discover these local cycles at about the same time. The cycle in site S_1 is of the form

$$P_{ex} \rightarrow P_2 \rightarrow P_3 \rightarrow P_{ex}.$$

Since $ID(P_3) > ID(P_2)$, site S_1 does not send a deadlock-detection message to site S_2.

The cycle in site S_2 is of the form

$$P_{ex} \rightarrow P_3 \rightarrow P_4 \rightarrow P_2 \rightarrow P_{ex}.$$

Since $ID(P_2) < ID(P_3)$, site S_2 does send a deadlock-detection message to site S_1, which, on receiving the message, updates its local wait-for graph. Site S_1 then searches for a cycle in the graph and discovers that the system is in a deadlock state.

17.6 ■ Election Algorithms

As we pointed out in Section 17.3, many distributed algorithms employ a coordinator process that performs functions needed by the other processes in the system. These functions include enforcing mutual exclusion, maintaining a global wait-for graph for deadlock detection, replacing a lost token, or controlling an input or output device in the system. If the coordinator process fails due to the failure of the site at which it resides, the system can continue execution only by restarting a new copy of the coordinator on some other site. The algorithms that determine where a new copy of the coordinator should be restarted are called **election algorithms**.

Election algorithms assume that a unique priority number is associated with each active process in the system. For ease of notation, we assume that the priority number of process P_i is i. To simplify our discussion, we assume a one-to-one correspondence between processes and sites, and thus refer to both as processes. The coordinator is always the process with the largest priority number. Hence, when a coordinator fails, the algorithm must elect that active process with the largest priority number. This number must be sent to each active process in the system. In addition, the algorithm must provide a mechanism for a recovered process to identify the current coordinator.

In this section, we present examples of election algorithms for two different configurations of distributed systems. The first algorithm applies to systems where every process can send a message to every other process in the system. The second algorithm applies to systems organized as a ring (logically or physically). Both algorithms require n^2 messages for an election, where n is the number of processes in the system. We assume that a process that has failed knows on recovery that it indeed has failed and thus takes appropriate actions to rejoin the set of active processes.

17.6.1 The Bully Algorithm

Suppose that process P_i sends a request that is not answered by the coordinator within a time interval T. In this situation, it is assumed that the coordinator has failed, and P_i tries to elect itself as the new coordinator. This task is completed through the following algorithm.

Process P_i sends an election message to every process with a higher priority number. Process P_i then waits for a time interval T for an answer from any one of these processes.

If no response is received within time T, P_i assumes that all processes with numbers greater than i have failed, and elects itself the new coordinator. Process P_i restarts a new copy of the coordinator and sends a message to inform all active processes with priority numbers less than i that P_i is the new coordinator.

However, if an answer is received, P_i begins a time interval T', waiting to receive a message informing it that a process with a higher priority number has been elected. (Some other process is electing itself coordinator, and should report the results within time T'.) If no message is sent within T', then the process with a higher number is assumed to have failed, and process P_i should restart the algorithm.

If P_i is not the coordinator, then, at any time during execution, P_i may receive one of the following two messages from process P_j:

1. P_j is the new coordinator ($j > i$). Process P_i, in turn, records this information.

2. P_j started an election ($j < i$). Process P_i sends a response to P_j and begins its own election algorithm, provided that P_i has not already initiated such an election.

The process that completes its algorithm has the highest number and is elected as the coordinator. It has sent its number to all active processes with smaller numbers. After a failed process recovers, it immediately begins execution of the same algorithm. If there are no active processes with higher numbers, the recovered process forces all processes with lower numbers to let it become the coordinator process, even if there is a currently active coordinator with a lower number. For this reason, the algorithm is termed the **bully algorithm**.

Let us demonstrate the operation of the algorithm with a simple example of a system consisting of processes P_1 through P_4. The operations are as follows:

1. All processes are active; P_4 is the coordinator process.

2. P_1 and P_4 fail. P_2 determines P_4 has failed by sending a request that is not answered within time T. P_2 then begins its election algorithm by sending a request to P_3.

3. P_3 receives the request, responds to P_2, and begins its own algorithm by sending an election request to P_4.

4. P_2 receives P_3's response and begins waiting for an interval T'.

5. P_4 does not respond within an interval T, so P_3 elects itself the new coordinator and sends the number 3 to P_2 and P_1 (which P_1 does not receive, since it has failed).

6. Later, when P_1 recovers, it sends an election request to P_2, P_3, and P_4.

7. P_2 and P_3 respond to P_1 and begin their own election algorithms. P_3 will again be elected, using the same events as before.

8. Finally, P_4 recovers and notifies P_1, P_2, and P_3 that it is the current coordinator. (P_4 sends no election requests, since it is the process with the highest number in the system.)

17.6.2 Ring Algorithm

The **ring algorithm** assumes that the links are unidirectional, and that processes send their messages to the neighbor on their right. The main data structure used by the algorithm is the **active list**, a list that contains the priority numbers of all active processes in the system when the algorithm ends; each process maintains its own active list. The algorithm works as follows:

1. If process P_i detects a coordinator failure, it creates a new active list that is initially empty. It then sends a message elect(i) to its right neighbor, and adds the number i to its active list.

2. If P_i receives a message elect(j) from the process on the left, it must respond in one of three ways:

   a. If this is the first elect message it has seen or sent, P_i creates a new active list with the numbers i and j. It then sends the message elect(i), followed by the message elect(j).

   b. If $i \neq j$, that is, the message received does not contain P_i's number, then P_i adds j to its active list and forwards the message to its right neighbor.

   c. If $i = j$, that is, P_i receives the message elect(i), then the active list for P_i now contains the numbers of all the active processes in the system. Process P_i can now determine the largest number in the active list to identify the new coordinator process.

This algorithm does not specify how a recovering process determines the number of the current coordinator process. One solution would require a recovering process to send an inquiry message. This message is forwarded around the ring to the current coordinator, which in turn sends a reply containing its number.

17.7 ■ Reaching Agreement

For a system to be reliable, we need a mechanism that allows a set of processes to agree on a common *value*. Such an agreement may not take place for several reasons. First, the communication medium may be faulty, resulting in lost or garbled messages. Second, the processes themselves may be faulty, resulting in unpredictable process behavior. The best we can hope for in this case is that processes fail in a clean way, stopping their execution without deviating from their normal execution pattern. In the worst case, processes may send garbled or incorrect messages to other processes, or even collaborate with other failed processes in an attempt to destroy the integrity of the system.

This problem has been expressed as the **Byzantine generals problem**. Several divisions of the Byzantine army, each commanded by its own general, surround an enemy camp. The Byzantine generals must reach agreement on whether or not to attack the enemy at dawn. It is crucial that all generals agree, since an attack by only some of the divisions would result in defeat. The various divisions are geographically dispersed and the generals can communicate with one another only via messengers who run from camp to camp. The generals may not be able to reach agreement for at least two major reasons:

1. Messengers may get caught by the enemy and thus may be unable to deliver their messages. This situation corresponds to unreliable communication in a computer system, and is discussed further in Section 17.7.1.

2. Generals may be *traitors*, trying to prevent the *loyal* generals from reaching an agreement. This situation corresponds to faulty processes in a computer system and is discussed further in Section 17.7.2.

17.7.1 Unreliable Communications

Let us assume that, if processes fail, they do so in a clean way, and that the communication medium is unreliable. Suppose that process P_i at site S_1, which has sent a message to process P_j at site S_2, needs to know whether P_j has received the message so that it can decide how to proceed with its computation. For example, P_i may decide to compute a function *foo* if P_j has received its message, or to compute a function *boo* if P_j has not received the message (because of some hardware failure).

To detect failures, we can use a **time-out scheme** similar to the one described in Section 15.5.1. When P_i sends out a message, it also specifies a time interval during which it is willing to wait for an acknowledgment message from P_j. When P_j receives the message, it immediately sends an acknowledgment to P_i. If P_i receives the acknowledgment message within the specified time interval, it can safely conclude that P_j has received its message. If, however, a time-out occurs, then P_i needs to retransmit its message and wait for an acknowledgment. This procedure continues until P_i either gets the acknowledgment message back, or is notified by the system that site S_2 is down. In the first case, it will compute S; in the latter case, it will compute F. Note that, if these are the only two viable alternatives, P_i must wait until it has been notified that one of the situations has occurred.

Suppose now that P_j also needs to know that P_i has received its acknowledgment message, to decide on how to proceed with its computation. For example, P_j may want to compute *foo* only if it is assured that P_i got its acknowledgment. In other words, P_i and P_j will compute *foo* if and only if both have agreed on it. It turns out that, in the presence of failure, it is not possible to accomplish this task. More precisely, it is not possible in a distributed environment for processes P_i and P_j to agree completely on their respective states.

Let us prove this claim. Suppose that a minimal sequence of message transfers exists such that, after the messages have been delivered, both processes agree to compute *foo*. Let m' be the last message sent by P_i to P_j. Since P_i does not know whether its message will arrive at P_j (since the message may be lost due to a failure), P_i will execute *foo* regardless of the outcome of the message delivery. Thus, m' could be removed from the sequence without affecting the decision procedure. Hence, the original sequence was not minimal, contradicting our assumption and showing that there is no sequence. The processes can never be sure that both will compute *foo*.

17.7.2 Faulty Processes

Let us assume that the communication medium is reliable, but that processes can fail in unpredictable ways. Consider a system of n processes, of which no more than m are faulty. Suppose that each process P_i has some private value of V_i. We wish to devise an algorithm that allows each nonfaulty process P_i to construct a vector $X_i = (A_{i,1}, A_{i,2}, ..., A_{i,n})$ such that the following conditions exist:

1. If P_j is a nonfaulty process, then $A_{i,j} = V_j$.

2. If P_i and P_j are both nonfaulty processes, then $X_i = X_j$.

There are many solutions to this problem, and they share the following properties:

1. A correct algorithm can be devised only if $n \geq 3 \times m + 1$.

2. The worst-case delay for reaching agreement is proportionate to $m + 1$ message-passing delays.

3. The number of messages required for reaching agreement is large. No single process is trustworthy, so all processes must collect all information and make their own decisions.

Rather than presenting a general solution, which would be complicated, we present an algorithm for the simple case where $m = 1$ and $n = 4$. The algorithm requires two rounds of information exchange:

1. Each process sends its private value to the other three processes.

2. Each process sends the information it has obtained in the first round to all other processes.

A faulty process obviously may refuse to send messages. In this case, a nonfaulty process can choose an arbitrary value and pretend that that value was sent by that process.

Once these two rounds are completed, a nonfaulty process P_i can construct its vector $X_i = (A_{i,1}, A_{i,2}, A_{i,3}, A_{i,4})$ as follows:

1. $A_{i,i} = V_i$.

2. For $j \neq i$, if at least two of the three values reported for process P_j (in the two rounds of exchange) agree, then the majority value is used to the value of $A_{i,j}$. Otherwise, a default value, say *nil*, is used to set the value of $A_{i,j}$.

17.8 ■ Summary

In a distributed system with no common memory and no common clock, it is sometimes impossible to determine the exact order in which two events occur. The *happened-before* relation is only a partial ordering of the events in distributed systems. Timestamps can be used to provide a consistent event ordering in a distributed system.

Mutual exclusion in a distributed environment can be implemented in a variety of ways. In a centralized approach, one of the processes in the system is chosen to coordinate the entry to the critical section. In the fully distributed approach, the decision making is distributed across the entire system. A distributed algorithm, which is applicable to ring-structured networks, is the token-passing approach.

For atomicity to be ensured, all the sites in which a transaction T executed must agree on the final outcome of the execution. T either commits at all sites or aborts at all sites. To ensure this property, the transaction coordinator of T must execute a commit protocol. The most widely used commit protocol is the 2PC protocol.

The various concurrency-control schemes that can be used in a centralized system can be modified for use in a distributed environment. In the case of locking protocols, the only change that needs to be incorporated is in the way that the lock manager is implemented. In the case of timestamping and validation schemes, the only needed change is the development of a mechanism for generating unique global timestamps. The mechanism can either concatenate a local timestamp with the site identification or advance local clocks whenever a message arrives that has a larger timestamp.

The primary method for dealing with deadlocks in a distributed environment is deadlock detection. The main problem is deciding how to maintain the wait-for graph. Different methods for organizing the wait-for graph include a centralized approach and a fully distributed approach.

Some of the distributed algorithms require the use of a coordinator. If the coordinator fails because of the failure of the site at which it resides, the system can continue execution only by restarting a new copy of the coordinator on some other site. It does so by maintaining a backup coordinator that is ready to assume responsibility if the coordinator fails. Another approach is to choose the new coordinator after the coordinator has failed. The algorithms that determine where a new copy of the coordinator should be restarted are called election algorithms. Two algorithms, the bully algorithm and a ring algorithm, can be used to elect a new coordinator in case of failures.

■ Exercises

17.1 Discuss the advantages and disadvantages of the two methods we presented for generating globally unique timestamps.

17.2 Your company is building a computer network, and you are asked to write an algorithm for achieving distributed mutual exclusion. Which scheme will you use? Explain your choice.

17.3 Why is deadlock detection much more expensive in a distributed environment than in a centralized environment?

17.4 Your company is building a computer network, and you are asked to develop a scheme for dealing with the deadlock problem.

   a. Would you use a deadlock-detection scheme or a deadlock-prevention scheme?

   b. If you were to use a deadlock-prevention scheme, which one would you use? Explain your choice.

   c. If you were to use a deadlock-detection scheme, which one would you use? Explain your choice.

17.5 Consider the following *hierarchical* deadlock-detection algorithm, in which the global wait-for graph is distributed over a number of different *controllers*, which are organized in a tree. Each nonleaf controller maintains a wait-for graph that contains relevant information from the graphs of the controllers in the subtree below it. In particular, let S_A, S_B, and S_C be controllers such that S_C is the lowest common ancestor of S_A and S_B (S_C must be unique, since we are dealing with a tree). Suppose that node T_i appears in the local wait-for graph of controllers S_A and S_B. Then, T_i must also appear in the local wait-for graph of

   • Controller S_C

   • Every controller in the path from S_C to S_A

   • Every controller in the path from S_C to S_B

In addition, if T_i and T_j appear in the wait-for graph of controller S_D and there exists a path from T_i to T_j in the wait-for graph of one of the children of S_D, then an edge $T_i \rightarrow T_j$ must be in the wait-for graph of S_D.

Show that, if a cycle exists in any of the wait-for graphs, then the system is deadlocked.

17.6 Derive an election algorithm for bidirectional rings that is more efficient than the one presented in this chapter. How many messages are needed for n processes?

17.7 Consider a failure that occurs during 2PC for a transaction. For each possible failure, explain how 2PC ensures transaction atomicity despite the failure.

Bibliographical Notes

The distributed algorithm for extending the *happened-before* relation to a consistent total ordering of all the events in the system was developed by Lamport [1978b].

The first general algorithm for implementing mutual exclusion in a distributed environment was developed by Lamport [1978b] also. Lamport's scheme requires $3 \times (n - 1)$ messages per critical-section entry. Subsequently, Ricart and Agrawala [1981] proposed a distributed algorithm that requires only $2 \times (n-1)$ messages. Their algorithm was presented in Section 17.2.2. A square-root algorithm for distributed mutual exclusion was presented by Maekawa [1985]. The token-passing algorithm for ring-structured systems presented in Section 17.2.3 was developed by Lann [1977]. Discussions concerning mutual exclusion in computer networks were presented by Carvalho and Roucairol [1983]. An efficient and fault-tolerant solution of distributed mutual-exclusion was presented by Agrawal and Abbadi [1991]. A simple taxonomy for distributed mutual-exclusion algorithms was presented by Raynal [1991].

The issue of distributed synchronization was discussed by Reed and Kanodia [1979] (shared-memory environment), Lamport [1978b], Lamport [1978a], and Schneider [1982] (totally disjoint processes). A distributed solution to the dining-philosophers problem was presented by Chang [1980].

The 2PC protocol was developed by Lampson and Sturgis [1976] and Gray [1978]. Mohan and Lindsay [1983] discussed two modified versions of 2PC, called presume commit and presume abort, that reduce the overhead of 2PC by defining default assumption regarding the fate of transactions.

Papers dealing with the problems of implementing the transaction concept in a distributed database were presented by Gray [1981], Traiger et al. [1982], and Spector and Schwarz [1983]. Comprehensive discussions covering distributed concurrency control were offered by Bernstein et al. [1987]. Rosenkrantz et al. [1978] reported the timestamp distributed deadlock-prevention algorithm.   The fully distributed deadlock-detection scheme presented in Section 17.5.2 was developed by Obermarck [1982]. The hierarchical deadlock-detection scheme of Exercise 17.3 appeared in Menasce and Muntz [1979]. A survey of deadlock detection in distributed systems is offered by Knapp [1987] and Singhal [1989].

The Byzantine generals problem was discussed by Lamport et al. [1982] and Pease et al. [1980]. The bully algorithm was presented by Garcia-Molina [1982]. The election algorithm for a ring-structured system was written by Lann [1977].

Part Six

PROTECTION
AND SECURITY

Protection mechanisms provide controlled access by limiting the types of file access permitted to users. In addition, protection must ensure that only those processes that have gained proper authorization from the operating system can operate on memory segments, the CPU, and other resources.

Protection is provided by a mechanism that controls the access of programs, processes, or users to the resources defined by a computer system. This mechanism must provide a means for specification of the controls to be imposed, together with a means of enforcement.

Security ensures the authentication of system users to protect the integrity of the information stored in the system (both data and code), as well as the physical resources of the computer system. The security system prevents unauthorized access to a system, malicious destruction or alteration of data, and accidental introduction of inconsistency.

Chapter 18

PROTECTION

The processes in an operating system must be protected from one another's activities. For that purpose, various mechanisms can be used to ensure that the files, memory segments, CPU, and other resources can be operated on by only those processes that have gained proper authorization from the operating system.

Protection refers to a mechanism for controlling the access of programs, processes, or users to the resources defined by a computer system. This mechanism must provide a means for specification of the controls to be imposed, together with some means of enforcement. We distinguish between protection and security, which is a measure of confidence that the integrity of a system and its data will be preserved. Security assurance is a much broader topic than is protection, and we address it in Chapter 19.

18.1 ■ Goals of Protection

As computer systems have become more sophisticated and pervasive in their applications, the need to protect their integrity has also grown. Protection was originally conceived as an adjunct to multiprogramming operating systems, so that untrustworthy users might safely share a common logical name space, such as a directory of files, or share a common physical name space, such as memory. Modern protection concepts have evolved to increase the reliability of any complex system that makes use of shared resources.

We need to provide protection for several reasons. The most obvious is the need to prevent mischievous, intentional violation of an access restriction by a user. Of more general importance, however, is the need to ensure that each program component active in a system uses system resources only in ways consistent with stated policies. This requirement is an absolute one for a reliable system.

Protection can improve reliability by detecting latent errors at the interfaces between component subsystems. Early detection of interface errors can often prevent contamination of a healthy subsystem by a malfunctioning subsystem. An unprotected resource cannot defend against use (or misuse) by an unauthorized or incompetent user. A protection-oriented system provides means to distinguish between authorized and unauthorized usage.

The role of protection in a computer system is to provide a mechanism for the enforcement of the policies governing resource use. These policies can be established in a variety of ways. Some are fixed in the design of the system, others are formulated by the management of a system. Still others are defined by the individual users to protect their own files and programs. A protection system must have the flexibility to enforce a variety of policies that can be declared to it.

Policies for resource use may vary by application, and they may change over time. For these reasons, protection is no longer the concern solely of the designer of an operating system. The application programmer needs to use protection mechanisms as well, to guard resources created and supported by an application subsystem against misuse. In this chapter, we describe the protection mechanisms the operating system should provide, so that an application designer can use them in designing her own protection software.

Policy is distinct from *mechanism*. Mechanisms determine *how* something will be done; policies decide *what* will be done. The separation of policy and mechanism is important for flexibility. Policies are likely to change from place to place or time to time. In the worst case, every change in policy would require a change in the underlying mechanism. General mechanisms are more desirable, because a policy change would require the modification of only some system parameters or tables.

18.2 ■ Domain of Protection

A computer system is a collection of processes and objects. By *objects,* we mean both **hardware objects** (such as the CPU, memory segments, printers, disks, and tape drives), and **software objects** (such as files, programs, and semaphores). Each object has a unique name that differentiates it from all other objects in the system, and each can be accessed only through well-defined and meaningful operations. Objects are essentially abstract data types.

The operations that are possible may depend on the object. For example, a CPU can only be executed on. Memory segments can be read and written, whereas a CD-ROM or DVD-ROM can only be read. Tape drives can be read, written, and rewound. Data files can be created, opened, read, written, closed, and deleted; program files can be read, written, executed, and deleted.

A process should be allowed to access only those resources for which it has authorization. Furthermore, at any time, a process should be able to access only those resources that it currently requires to complete its task. This second requirement, commonly referred to as the *need-to-know* principle, is useful in limiting the amount of damage a faulty process can cause in the system. For example, when process p invokes procedure A, the procedure should be allowed to access only its own variables and the formal parameters passed to it; it should not be able to access all the variables of process p. Similarly, consider the case where process p invokes a compiler to compile a particular file. The compiler should not be able to access any arbitrary files, but only a well-defined subset of files (such as the source file, listing file, and so on) related to the file to be compiled. Conversely, the compiler may have private files used for accounting or optimization purposes that process p should not be able to access.

18.2.1 Domain Structure

To facilitate this scheme, a process operates within a **protection domain**, which specifies the resources that the process may access. Each domain defines a set of objects and the types of operations that may be invoked on each object. The ability to execute an operation on an object is an **access right**. A **domain** is a collection of access rights, each of which is an ordered pair *<object-name, rights-set>*. For example, if domain D has the access right *<file F, {read,write}>*, then a process executing in domain D can both read and write file F; it cannot, however, perform any other operation on that object.

Domains do not need to be disjoint; they may share access rights. For example, in Figure 18.1, we have three domains: D_1, D_2, and D_3. The access right $<O_4, \{print\}>$ is shared by both D_2 and D_3, implying that a process executing in either of these two domains can print object O_4. Note that a process

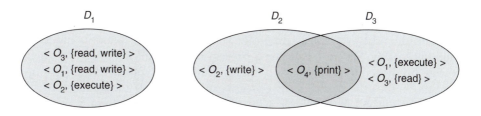

Figure 18.1   System with three protection domains.

must be executing in domain D_1 to read and write object O_1. On the other hand, only processes in domain D_3 may execute object O_1.

The association between a process and a domain may be either **static**, if the set of resources available to a process is fixed throughout the latter's lifetime, or **dynamic**. As might be expected, establishing dynamic protection domains is more complicated than establishing static protection domains.

If the association between processes and domains is fixed, and we want to adhere to the need-to-know principle, then a mechanism must be available to change the content of a domain. A process may execute in two different phases. For example, it may need read access in one phase and write access in another. If a domain is static, we must define the domain to include both read and write access. However, this arrangement provides more rights than are needed in each of the two phases, since we have read access in the phase where we need only write access, and vice versa. Thus, the need-to-know principle is violated. We must allow the contents of a domain to be modified, so that it always reflects the minimum necessary access rights.

If the association is dynamic, a mechanism is available to allow a process to switch from one domain to another. We may also want to allow the content of a domain to be changed. If we cannot change the content of a domain, we can provide the same effect by creating a new domain with the changed content, and switching to that new domain when we want to change the domain content.

A domain can be realized in a variety of ways:

- Each *user* may be a domain. In this case, the set of objects that can be accessed depends on the identity of the user. **Domain switching** occurs when the user is changed—generally when one user logs out and another user logs in.

- Each *process* may be a domain. In this case, the set of objects that can be accessed depends on the identity of the process. Domain switching corresponds to one process sending a message to another process, and then waiting for a response.

- Each *procedure* may be a domain. In this case, the set of objects that can be accessed corresponds to the local variables defined within the procedure. Domain switching occurs when a procedure call is made.

We discuss domain switching in greater detail in Section 18.3.

Consider the standard dual-mode (monitor–user mode) model of operating-system execution. When a process executes in monitor mode, it can execute privileged instructions and thus gain complete control of the computer system. On the other hand, if the process executes in user mode, it can invoke only nonprivileged instructions. Consequently, it can execute only within its predefined memory space. These two modes protect the operating system (executing in monitor domain) from the user processes (executing in user domain). In a multiprogrammed operating system, two protection domains are insufficient, since users also want to be protected from one another. Therefore, a more elaborate scheme is needed. We illustrate this scheme by examining two influential operating systems—UNIX and MULTICS—to see how these concepts have been implemented there.

18.2.2 An Example: UNIX

In the UNIX operating system, a domain is associated with the user. Switching the domain corresponds to changing the user identification temporarily. This change is accomplished through the file system as follows. An owner identification and a domain bit (known as the *setuid bit*) are associated with each file. When a user (with *user-id* = A) starts executing a file owned by B, whose associated domain bit is *off,* the *user-id* of the process is set to A. When the setuid bit is *on,* the user-id is set to that of the owner of the file: B. When the process exits, this temporary user-id change ends.

Other methods are used to change domains in operating systems in which user-ids are used for domain definition, because almost all systems need to provide such a mechanism. This mechanism is used when an otherwise privileged facility needs to be made available to the general user population. For instance, it might be desirable to allow users to access a network without letting them write their own networking programs. In such a case, on a UNIX system, the setuid bit on a networking program would be set, causing the user-id to change when the program is run. The user-id would change to that of a user with network access privilege (such as *root*, the most powerful user-id). One problem with this method is that if a user manages to create a file with user-id *root* and with its setuid bit *on,* that user can become *root* and do anything and everything on the system. The setuid mechanism is discussed further in Appendix A.

An alternative to this method used on other operating systems is to place privileged programs in a special directory. The operating system would be designed to change the user-id of any program run from this directory, either to the equivalent of *root* or to the user-id of the owner of the directory. This eliminates the setuid problem of secret setuid programs, because all these programs are in one location. This method is less flexible than that used in UNIX, however.

Even more restrictive, and thus more protective, are systems that simply do not allow a change of user-id. In these instances, special techniques must be used to allow users access to privileged facilities. For instance, a **daemon process** may be started at boot time and run as a special user-id. Users then run a separate program, which sends requests to this process whenever they need to use the facility. This method is used by the TOPS-20 operating system.

In any of these systems, great care must be taken in writing privileged programs. Any oversight can result in a total lack of protection on the system. Generally, these programs are the first to be attacked by people trying to break into a system; unfortunately, the attackers are frequently successful. For example, security has been breached on many UNIX systems because of the setuid feature. We discuss security in Chapter 19.

18.2.3 An Example: MULTICS

In the MULTICS system, the protection domains are organized hierarchically into a ring structure. Each ring corresponds to a single domain (Figure 18.2). The rings are numbered from 0 to 7. Let D_i and D_j be any two domain rings. If $j < i$, then D_i is a subset of D_j. That is, a process executing in domain D_j has more privileges than does a process executing in domain D_i. A process executing in domain D_0 has the most privileges. If only two rings exist, this scheme is equivalent to the monitor–user mode of execution, where monitor mode corresponds to D_0 and user mode corresponds to D_1.

MULTICS has a segmented address space; each segment is a file. Each segment is associated with one of the rings. A segment description includes an entry that identifies the ring number. In addition, it includes three access bits to control reading, writing, and execution. The association between segments and rings is a policy decision with which we are not concerned in this book. With each process, a *current-ring-number* counter is associated, identifying the ring in which the process is executing currently. When a process is executing in ring i, it cannot access a segment associated with ring $j, j < i$. It can, however, access a segment associated with ring $k, k \geq i$. The type of access, however, is restricted according to the access bits associated with that segment.

Domain switching in MULTICS occurs when a process crosses from one ring to another by calling a procedure in a different ring. Obviously, this switch must

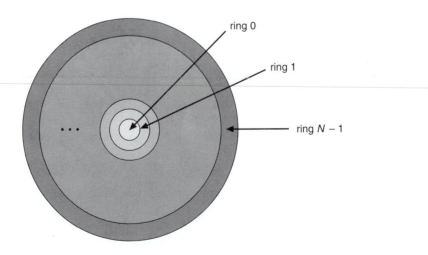

Figure 18.2   MULTICS ring structure.

be done in a controlled manner; otherwise, a process can start executing in ring 0, and no protection will be provided. To allow controlled domain switching, we modify the ring field of the segment descriptor to include the following:

- **Access bracket:** A pair of integers, $b1$ and $b2$, such that $b1 \leq b2$.

- **Limit:** An integer $b3$ such that $b3 > b2$.

- **List of gates:** Identifies the entry points (or **gates**) at which the segments may be called.

If a process executing in ring i calls a procedure (or segment) with access bracket $(b1,b2)$, then the call is allowed if $b1 \leq i \leq b2$, and the current ring number of the process remains i. Otherwise, a trap to the operating system occurs, and the situation is handled as follows:

- If $i < b1$, then the call is allowed to occur, because we have a transfer to a ring (or domain) with fewer privileges. However, if parameters are passed that refer to segments in a lower ring (that is, segments not accessible to the called procedure), then these segments must be copied into an area that can be accessed by the called procedure.

- If $i > b2$, then the call is allowed to occur only if $b3$ is greater than or equal to i, and the call has been directed to one of the designated entry points in the list of gates. This scheme allows processes with limited access rights to call procedures in lower rings that have more access rights, but only in a carefully controlled manner.

The main disadvantage of the ring (or hierarchical) structure is that it does not allow us to enforce the need-to-know principle. In particular, if an object must be accessible in domain D_j but not accessible in domain D_i, then we must have $j < i$. But this requirement means that every segment accessible in D_i is also accessible in D_j.

The MULTICS protection system is generally more complex and less efficient than are those used in current operating systems. If protection interferes with the ease of use of the system, or significantly decreases system performance, then its use must be weighed carefully against the purpose of the system. For instance, you would want to have a complex protection system on a computer used by a university to process students' grades, and also used by students for class work. A similar protection system would not be suited to a computer being used for number crunching in which performance is of utmost importance. We would prefer to separate the mechanism from the protection policy, allowing the same system to have complex or simple protection depending on the needs of its users. To separate mechanism from policy, we require more general models of protection.

18.3 ■ Access Matrix

Our model of protection can be viewed abstractly as a matrix, called an **access matrix**. The rows of the access matrix represent domains, and the columns represent objects. Each entry in the matrix consists of a set of access rights. Because the column defines objects explicitly, we can omit the object name from the access right. The entry access(i,j) defines the set of operations that a process, executing in domain D_i, can invoke on object O_j.

To illustrate these concepts, we consider the access matrix shown in Figure 18.3. There are four domains and four objects, three files (F_1, F_2, F_3) and one laser printer. When a process executes in domain D_1, it can read files F_1 and F_3. A process executing in domain D_4 has the same privileges as it does in domain D_1, but in addition, it can also write onto files F_1 and F_3. Note that the laser printer can be accessed only by a process executing in domain D_2.

The access-matrix scheme provides us with the mechanism for specifying a variety of policies. The mechanism consists of implementing the access matrix and ensuring that the semantic properties we have outlined indeed hold. More specifically, we must ensure that a process executing in domain D_i can access only those objects specified in row i, and then only as allowed by the access-matrix entries.

The access matrix can implement policy decisions concerning protection. The policy decisions involve which rights should be included in the (i,j)th entry. We must also decide the domain in which each process executes. This last policy is usually decided by the operating system.

The users normally decide the contents of the access-matrix entries. When a user creates a new object O_j, the column O_j is added to the access matrix with the appropriate initialization entries, as dictated by the creator. The user may decide to enter some rights in some entries in column j and other rights in other entries, as needed.

object domain	F_1	F_2	F_3	printer
D_1	read		read	
D_2				print
D_3		read	execute	
D_4	read write		read write	

Figure 18.3   Access matrix.

The access matrix provides an appropriate mechanism for defining and implementing strict control for both the static and dynamic association between processes and domains. When we switch a process from one domain to another, we are executing an operation (switch) on an object (the domain). We can control domain switching by including domains among the objects of the access matrix. Similarly, when we change the content of the access matrix, we are performing an operation on an object: the access matrix. Again, we can control these changes by including the access matrix itself as an object. Actually, since each entry in the access matrix may be modified individually, we must consider each entry in the access matrix as an object to be protected.

Now, we need to consider only the operations possible on these new objects (domains and the access matrix) and decide how we want processes to be able to execute these operations.

Processes should be able to switch from one domain to another. Domain switching from domain D_i to domain D_j is allowed to occur if and only if the access right switch $\in$ access(i, j). Thus, in Figure 18.4, a process executing in domain D_2 can switch to domain D_3 or to domain D_4. A process in domain D_4 can switch to D_1, and one in domain D_1 can switch to domain D_2.

Allowing controlled change to the contents of the access-matrix entries requires three additional operations: copy, owner, and control.

The ability to copy an access right from one domain (or row) of the access matrix to another is denoted by an asterisk (*) appended to the access right. The *copy* right allows the copying of the access right only within the column (that is, for the object) for which the right is defined. For example, in Figure 18.5(a), a process executing in domain D_2 can copy the read operation into any entry associated with file F_2. Hence, the access matrix of Figure 18.5(a) can be modified to the access matrix shown in Figure 18.5(b).

object domain	F_1	F_2	F_3	laser printer	D_1	D_2	D_3	D_4
D_1	read		read			switch		
D_2				print			switch	switch
D_3		read	execute					
D_4	read write		read write		switch			

Figure 18.4   Access matrix of Figure 18.3 with domains as objects.

object domain	F_1	F_2	F_3
D_1	execute		write*
D_2	execute	read*	execute
D_3	execute		

(a)

object domain	F_1	F_2	F_3
D_1	execute		write*
D_2	execute	read*	execute
D_3	execute	read	

(b)

Figure 18.5   Access matrix with *copy* rights.

This scheme has two variants:

1. A right is copied from access(i, j) to access(k, j); it is then removed from access(i, j); this action is a *transfer* of a right, rather than a copy.

2. Propagation of the *copy* right may be limited. That is, when the right R^* is copied from access(i, j) to access(k, j), only the right R (not R^*) is created. A process executing in domain D_k cannot further copy the right R.

A system may select only one of these three *copy* rights, or it may provide all three by identifying them as separate rights: *copy*, *transfer*, and *limited copy*.

We also need a mechanism to allow addition of new rights and removal of some rights. The *owner* right controls these operations. If access(i, j) includes the *owner* right, then a process executing in domain D_i can add and remove any right in any entry in column j. For example, in Figure 18.6(a), domain D_1 is the owner of F_1, and thus can add and delete any valid right in column F_1. Similarly, domain D_2 is the owner of F_2 and F_3, and thus can add and remove any valid right within these two columns. Thus, the access matrix of Figure 18.6(a) can be modified to the access matrix shown in Figure 18.6(b).

The *copy* and *owner* rights allow a process to change the entries in a column. A mechanism is also needed to change the entries in a row. The *control* right is applicable only to domain objects. If access(i, j) includes the *control* right,

domain \ object	F_1	F_2	F_3
D_1	owner execute		write
D_2		read* owner	read* owner write*
D_3	execute		

(a)

domain \ object	F_1	F_2	F_3
D_1	owner execute		
D_2		owner read* write*	read* owner write*
D_3		write	write

(b)

Figure 18.6   Access matrix with *owner* rights.

then a process executing in domain D_i can remove any access right from row j. For example, suppose that, in Figure 18.4, we include the *control* right in access(D_2, D_4). Then, a process executing in domain D_2 could modify domain D_4, as shown in Figure 18.7.

The *copy* and *owner* rights provide us with a mechanism to limit the propagation of access rights. However, they do not give us the appropriate tools for preventing the propagation (or disclosure) of information. The problem of guaranteeing that no information initially held in an object can migrate outside of its execution environment is called the **confinement problem**. This problem is in general unsolvable (see Bibliographical Notes for references).

These operations on the domains and the access matrix are not in themselves important. More importantly, they illustrate the ability of the access-matrix model to allow the implementation and control of dynamic protection requirements. New objects and new domains can be created dynamically and included in the access-matrix model. However, we have shown only that the basic mechanism is here; system designers and users must make the policy decisions concerning which domains are to have access to which objects in which ways.

object domain	F_1	F_2	F_3	laser printer	D_1	D_2	D_3	D_4
D_1	read		read			switch		
D_2				print			switch	switch control
D_3		read	execute					
D_4	write		write		switch			

Figure 18.7   Modified access matrix of Figure 18.4.

18.4 ▪ Implementation of Access Matrix

How can the access matrix be implemented effectively? In general, the matrix will be sparse; that is, most of the entries will be empty. Although data-structure techniques are available for representing sparse matrices, they are not particularly useful for this application, because of the way in which the protection facility is used.

18.4.1 Global Table

The simplest implementation of the access matrix is a global table consisting of a set of ordered triples <*domain, object, rights-set*>. Whenever an operation M is executed on an object O_j within domain D_i, the global table is searched for a triple <D_i, O_j, R_k>, with $M \in R_k$. If this triple is found, the operation is allowed to continue; otherwise, an exception (or error) condition is raised. This implementation suffers from several drawbacks. The table is usually large and thus cannot be kept in main memory, so additional I/O is needed. Virtual-memory techniques are often used for managing this table. In addition, it is difficult to take advantage of special groupings of objects or domains. For example, if everyone can read a particular object, it must have a separate entry in every domain.

18.4.2 Access Lists for Objects

Each column in the access matrix can be implemented as an access list for one object, as described in Section 11.6.2. Obviously, the empty entries can be discarded. The resulting list for each object consists of ordered pairs <*domain, rights-set*>, which define all domains with a nonempty set of access rights for that object.

This approach can be extended easily to define a list plus a *default* set of access rights. When an operation M on an object O_j is attempted in domain D_i, we search the access list for object O_j, looking for an entry $<D_i, R_k>$ with $M \in R_k$. If the entry is found, we allow the operation; if it is not, we check the default set. If M is in the default set, we allow the access. Otherwise, access is denied and an exception condition occurs. For efficiency, we may check the default set first and then search the access list.

18.4.3 Capability Lists for Domains

Rather than associating the columns of the access matrix with the objects as access lists, we can associate each row with its domain. A **capability list** for a domain is a list of objects together with the operations allowed on those objects. An object is often represented by its physical name or address, called a **capability**. To execute operation M on object O_j, the process executes the operation M, specifying the capability (or pointer) for object O_j as a parameter. Simple **possession** of the capability means that access is allowed.

The capability list is associated with a domain, but it is never directly accessible to a process executing in that domain. Rather, the capability list is itself a protected object, maintained by the operating system and accessed by the user only indirectly. Capability-based protection relies on the fact that the capabilities are never allowed to migrate into any address space directly accessible by a user process (where they could be modified). If all capabilities are secure, the object they protect is also secure against unauthorized access.

Capabilities were originally proposed as a kind of secure pointer, to meet the need for resource protection that was foreseen as multiprogrammed computer systems came of age. The idea of an inherently protected pointer (from the point of view of a system user) provides a foundation for protection that can be extended up to the applications level.

To provide inherent protection, we must distinguish capabilities from other kinds of objects, and must interpret them by an abstract machine on which higher-level programs run. Capabilities are usually distinguished from other data in one of two ways:

- Each object has a **tag** to denote its type as either a capability or as accessible data. The tags themselves must not be directly accessible by an application program. Hardware or firmware support may be used to enforce this restriction. Although only 1 bit is necessary to distinguish between capabilities and other objects, more bits are often used. This extension allows all objects to be tagged with their types by the hardware. Thus, the hardware can distinguish integers, floating-point numbers, pointers, Booleans, characters, instructions, capabilities, and uninitialized values by their tags.

- Alternatively, the address space associated with a program can be split into two parts. One part is accessible to the program and contains the program's normal data and instructions. The other part, containing the capability list, is accessible only by the operating system. A segmented memory space (Section 9.5) is useful to support this approach.

Several capability-based protection systems have been developed; we describe them briefly in Section 18.6. The Mach operating system also uses a version of capability-based protection; it is described in Appendix B.

18.4.4 A Lock–Key Mechanism

The **lock–key scheme** is a compromise between access lists and capability lists. Each object has a list of unique bit patterns, called **locks**. Similarly, each domain has a list of unique bit patterns, called **keys**. A process executing in a domain can access an object only if that domain has a key that matches one of the locks of the object.

As was the case with capability lists, the list of keys for a domain must be managed by the operating system on behalf of the domain. Users are not allowed to examine or modify the list of keys (or locks) directly.

18.4.5 Comparison

Access lists correspond directly to the needs of the users. When a user creates an object, she can specify which domains can access the object, as well as the operations allowed. However, because access-rights information for a particular domain is not localized, determining the set of access rights for each domain is difficult. In addition, every access to the object must be checked, requiring a search of the access list. In a large system with long access lists, this search can be time-consuming.

Capability lists do not correspond directly to the needs of the users; they are useful, however, for localizing information for a given process. The process attempting access must present a capability for that access. Then, the protection system needs only to verify that the capability is valid. Revocation of capabilities, however, may be inefficient (Section 18.5).

The lock–key mechanism is a compromise between these two schemes. The mechanism can be both effective and flexible, depending on the length of the keys. The keys can be passed freely from domain to domain. In addition, access privileges may be effectively revoked by the simple technique of changing some of the locks associated with the object (Section 18.5).

Most systems use a combination of access lists and capabilities. When a process first tries to access an object, the access list is searched. If access is denied, an exception condition occurs. Otherwise, a capability is created and is attached to the process. Additional references use the capability to demonstrate swiftly that access is allowed. After the last access, the capability is destroyed.

This strategy is used in the MULTICS system and in the CAL system; these systems use both access lists and capability lists.

As an example, consider a file system in which each file has an associated access list. When a process opens a file, the directory structure is searched to find the file, access permission is checked, and buffers are allocated. All this information is recorded in a new entry in a file table associated with the process. The operation returns an index into this table for the newly opened file. All operations on the file are made by specification of the index into the file table. The entry in the file table then points to the file and its buffers. When the file is closed, the file-table entry is deleted. Since the file table is maintained by the operating system, the user cannot accidentally corrupt it. Thus, the user can access only those files that have been opened. Since access is checked when the file is opened, protection is ensured. This strategy is used in the UNIX system.

The right to access *must* still be checked on each access, and the file-table entry has a capability only for the allowed operations. If a file is opened for reading, then a capability for read access is placed in the file-table entry. If an attempt is made to write onto the file, the system determines this protection violation by comparing the requested operation with the capability in the file-table entry.

18.5 ■ Revocation of Access Rights

In a dynamic protection system, we may sometimes need to revoke access rights to objects shared by different users. Various questions about revocation may arise:

- **Immediate versus delayed:** Does revocation occur immediately, or is it delayed? If revocation is delayed, can we find out when it will take place?

- **Selective versus general:** When an access right to an object is revoked, does it affect *all* the users who have an access right to that object, or can we specify a select group of users whose access rights should be revoked?

- **Partial versus total:** Can a subset of the rights associated with an object be revoked, or must we revoke all access rights for this object?

- **Temporary versus permanent:** Can access be revoked permanently (that is, the revoked access right will never again be available), or can access be revoked and later be obtained again?

With an access-list scheme, revocation is easy. The access list is searched for the access right(s) to be revoked, and they are deleted from the list. Revocation is immediate, and can be general or selective, total or partial, and permanent or temporary.

Capabilities, however, present a much more difficult revocation problem. Since the capabilities are distributed throughout the system, we must find them before we can revoke them. Schemes that implement revocation for capabilities include the following:

- **Reacquisition:** Periodically, capabilities are deleted from each domain. If a process wants to use a capability, it may find that that capability has been deleted. The process may then try to reacquire the capability. If access has been revoked, the process will not be able to reacquire the capability.

- **Back-pointers:** A list of pointers is maintained with each object, pointing to all capabilities associated with that object. When revocation is required, we can follow these pointers, changing the capabilities as necessary. This scheme was adopted in the MULTICS system. It is quite general, although its implementation is costly.

- **Indirection:** The capabilities point indirectly, not directly, to the objects. Each capability points to a unique entry in a global table, which in turn points to the object. We implement revocation by searching the global table for the desired entry and deleting it. When an access is attempted, the capability is found to point to an illegal table entry. Table entries can be reused for other capabilities without difficulty, since both the capability and the table entry contain the unique name of the object. The object for a capability and its table entry must match. This scheme was adopted in the CAL system. It does not allow selective revocation.

- **Keys:** A key is a unique bit pattern that can be associated with each capability. This key is defined when the capability is created, and it can be neither modified nor inspected by the process owning that capability. A **master key** associated with each object can be defined or replaced with the set-key operation. When a capability is created, the current value of the master key is associated with the capability. When the capability is exercised, its key is compared to the master key. If the keys match, the operation is allowed to continue; otherwise, an exception condition is raised. Revocation replaces the master key with a new value by the set-key operation, invalidating all previous capabilities for this object.

  This scheme does not allow selective revocation, since only one master key is associated with each object. If we associate a list of keys with each object, then selective revocation can be implemented. Finally, we can group all keys into one global table of keys. A capability is valid only if its key matches some key in the global table. We implement revocation by removing the matching key from the table. With this scheme, a key can be associated with several objects, and several keys can be associated with each object, providing maximum flexibility.

In key-based schemes, the operations of defining keys, inserting them into lists, and deleting them from lists should not be available to all users. In particular, it would be reasonable to allow only the owner of an object to set the keys for that object. This choice, however, is a policy decision that the protection system can implement but should not define.

18.6   ■   Capability-Based Systems

In this section, we survey two capability-based protection systems. These systems vary in their complexity and in the type of policies that can be implemented on them. Neither of them is widely used, but they are interesting proving grounds for protection theories.

18.6.1   An Example: Hydra

Hydra is a capability-based protection system that provides considerable flexibility. The system provides a fixed set of possible access rights that are known to and interpreted by the system. These rights include such basic forms of access as the right to read, write, or execute a memory segment. In addition, the system provides the means for a user (of the protection system) to declare additional rights. The interpretation of user-defined rights is performed solely by the user's program, but the system provides access protection for the use of these rights, as well as for the use of system-defined rights. These facilities constitute a significant development in protection technology.

Operations on objects are defined procedurally. The procedures that implement such operations are themselves a form of object, and they are accessed indirectly by capabilities. The names of user-defined procedures must be identified to the protection system if it is to deal with objects of the user-defined type. When the definition of an object is made known to Hydra, the names of operations on the type become **auxiliary rights**. Auxiliary rights can be described in a capability for an instance of the type. For a process to perform an operation on a typed object, the capability it holds for that object must contain the name of the operation being invoked among its auxiliary rights. This restriction enables discrimination of access rights to be made on an instance-by-instance and process-by-process basis.

Hydra also provides **rights amplification**. This scheme allows certification of a procedure as *trustworthy* to act on a formal parameter of a specified type, on behalf of any process that holds a right to execute the procedure. The rights held by a trustworthy procedure are independent of, and may exceed, the rights held by the calling process. However, such a procedure must not be regarded as universally trustworthy (the procedure is not allowed to act on other types, for instance), and the trustworthiness must not be extended to any other procedures or program segments that might be executed by a process.

Amplification allows implementation procedures access to the representation variables of an abstract data type. If a process holds a capability to a typed object A, for instance, this capability may include an auxiliary right to invoke some operation P, but would not include any of the so-called kernel rights, such as read, write, or execute, on the segment that represents A. Such a capability gives a process a means of indirect access (through the operation P) to the representation of A, but only for specific purposes.

On the other hand, when a process invokes the operation P on an object A, the capability for access to A may be amplified as control passes to the code body of P. This amplification may be necessary to allow P the right to access the storage segment representing A so as to implement the operation that P defines on the abstract data type. The code body of P may be allowed to read or to write to the segment of A directly, even though the calling process cannot. On return from P, the capability for A is restored to its original, unamplified state. This case is a typical one in which the rights held by a process for access to a protected segment must change dynamically, depending on the task to be performed. The dynamic adjustment of rights is performed to guarantee consistency of a programmer-defined abstraction. Amplification of rights can be stated explicitly in the declaration of an abstract type to the Hydra operating system.

When a user passes an object as an argument to a procedure, we may need to ensure that the procedure cannot modify the object. We can implement this restriction readily by passing an access right that does not have the modification (write) right. However, if amplification may occur, the right to modify may be reinstated. Thus, the user-protection requirement can be circumvented. In general, of course, a user may trust that a procedure indeed performs its task correctly. This assumption, however, is not always correct, because of hardware or software errors. Hydra solves this problem by restricting amplifications.

The procedure-call mechanism of Hydra was designed as a direct solution to the *problem of mutually suspicious subsystems*. This problem is defined as follows. Suppose that a program is provided that can be invoked as a service by a number of different users (for example, a sort routine, a compiler, a game). When users invoke this service program, they take the risk that the program will malfunction and will either damage the given data, or retain some access right to the data to be used (without authority) later. Similarly, the service program may have some private files (for accounting purposes, for example) that should not be accessed directly by the calling user program. Hydra provides mechanisms for directly dealing with this problem.

A Hydra subsystem is built on top of its protection kernel and may require protection of its own components. A subsystem interacts with the kernel through calls on a set of kernel-defined primitives that defines access rights to resources defined by the subsystem. Policies for use of these resources by user processes can be defined by the subsystem designer, but they are enforceable by use of the standard access protection afforded by the capability system.

A programmer can make direct use of the protection system, after acquainting himself with its features in the appropriate reference manual. Hydra provides a large library of system-defined procedures that can be called by user programs. A user of the Hydra system would explicitly incorporate calls on these system procedures into the code of his programs, or would use a program translator that had been interfaced to Hydra.

18.6.2 An Example: Cambridge CAP System

A different approach to capability-based protection has been taken in the design of the Cambridge CAP system. CAP's capability system is simpler and superficially less powerful than that of Hydra. However, closer examination shows that it too can be used to provide secure protection of user-defined objects. CAP has two kinds of capabilities. The ordinary kind is called a **data capability**. It can be used to provide access to objects, but the only rights provided are the standard read, write, or execute of the individual storage segments associated with the object. Data capabilities are interpreted by microcode in the CAP machine.

The second kind of capability is the so-called **software capability**, which is protected, but not interpreted, by the CAP microcode. It is interpreted by a *protected* (that is, a privileged) procedure, which may be written by an application programmer as part of a subsystem. A particular kind of rights amplification is associated with a protected procedure. When executing the code body of such a procedure, a process temporarily acquires the rights to read or write the contents of a software capability itself. This specific kind of rights amplification corresponds to an implementation of the seal and unseal primitives on capabilities. Of course, this privilege is still subject to type verification to ensure that only software capabilities for a specified abstract type are allowed to be passed to any such procedure. Universal trust is not placed in any code other than the CAP machine's microcode. See Bibliographical Notes for references.

The interpretation of a software capability is left completely to the subsystem, through the protected procedures it contains. This scheme allows a variety of protection policies to be implemented. Although a programmer can define her own protected procedures (any of which might be incorrect), the security of the overall system cannot be compromised. The basic protection system will not allow an unverified, user-defined, protected procedure access to any storage segments (or capabilities) that do not belong to the protection environment in which it resides. The most serious consequence of an insecure protected procedure is a protection breakdown of the subsystem for which that procedure has responsibility.

The designers of the CAP system have noted that the use of software capabilities allowed them to realize considerable economies in formulating and implementing protection policies commensurate with the requirements of abstract resources. However, a subsystem designer who wants to make use of this facility cannot simply study a reference manual, as is the case with Hydra. Instead, he must learn the principles and techniques of protection, since the system provides him with no library of procedures.

18.7 ■ Language-Based Protection

To the degree that protection is provided in existing computer systems, it is usually achieved through an operating-system kernel, which acts as a security agent to inspect and validate each attempt to access a protected resource. Since comprehensive access validation is potentially a source of considerable overhead, either we must give it hardware support to reduce the cost of each validation, or we must accept that the system designer may compromise the goals of protection. Satisfying all these goals is difficult if the flexibility to implement protection policies is restricted by the support mechanisms provided or if protection environments are made larger than necessary to secure greater operational efficiency.

As operating systems have become more complex, and particularly as they have attempted to provide higher-level user interfaces, the goals of protection have become much more refined. The designers of protection systems have drawn heavily on ideas that originated in programming languages and especially on the concepts of abstract data types and objects. Protection systems are now concerned not only with the identity of a resource to which access is attempted but also with the functional nature of that access. In the newest protection systems, concern for the function to be invoked extends beyond a set of system-defined functions, such as standard file-access methods, to include functions that may be user-defined as well.

Policies for resource use may also vary, depending on the application, and they may be subject to change over time. For these reasons, protection can no longer be considered as a matter of concern to only the designer of an operating system. It should also be available as a tool for use by the application designer, so that resources of an applications subsystem can be guarded against tampering or the influence of an error.

18.7.1 Compiler-Based Enforcement

At this point, programming languages enter the picture. Specifying the desired control of access to a shared resource in a system is making a declarative statement about the resource. This kind of statement can be integrated into a language by an extension of its typing facility. When protection is declared along with data typing, the designer of each subsystem can specify its requirements for protection, as well as its need for use of other resources in a system. Such a specification should be given directly as a program is composed, and in the language in which the program itself is stated. This approach has several significant advantages:

1. Protection needs are simply declared, rather than programmed as a sequence of calls on procedures of an operating system.

2. Protection requirements may be stated independently of the facilities provided by a particular operating system.

3. The means for enforcement do not need to be provided by the designer of a subsystem.

4. A declarative notation is natural because access privileges are closely related to the linguistic concept of data type.

A variety of techniques can be provided by a programming-language implementation to enforce protection, but any of these must depend on some degree of support from an underlying machine and its operating system. For example, suppose a language were used to generate code to run on the Cambridge CAP system. On this system, every storage reference made on the underlying hardware occurs indirectly through a capability. This restriction prevents any process from accessing a resource outside of its protection environment at any time. However, a program may impose arbitrary restrictions on how a resource may be used during execution of a particular code segment by any process. We can implement such restrictions most readily by using the software capabilities provided by CAP. A language implementation might provide standard protected procedures to interpret software capabilities that would realize the protection policies that could be specified in the language. This scheme puts policy specification at the disposal of the programmers, while freeing them from implementing its enforcement.

Even if a system does not provide a protection kernel as powerful as those of Hydra or CAP, mechanisms are still available for implementing protection specifications given in a programming language. The principal distinction is that the *security* of this protection will not be as great as that supported by a protection kernel, because the mechanism must rely on more assumptions about the operational state of the system. A compiler can separate references for which it can certify that no protection violation could occur from those for which a violation might be possible, and it can treat them differently. The security provided by this form of protection rests on the assumption that the code generated by the compiler will not be modified prior to or during its execution.

What, then, are the relative merits of enforcement based solely on a kernel, as opposed to enforcement provided largely by a compiler?

- **Security:** Enforcement by a kernel provides a greater degree of security of the protection system itself than does the generation of protection-checking code by a compiler. In a compiler-supported scheme, security rests on correctness of the translator, on some underlying mechanism of storage management that protects the segments from which compiled code is executed, and, ultimately, on the security of files from which a program is loaded. Some of these considerations also apply to a software-supported protection kernel, but to a lesser degree, since the kernel may reside in fixed physical storage segments and may be loaded from only a designated file. With a tagged-capability system, in which all address computation is performed either by hardware or by a fixed microprogram, even greater security is possible. Hardware-supported protection is also relatively immune to protection violations that might occur as a result of either hardware or system software malfunction.

- **Flexibility:** There are limits to the flexibility of a protection kernel in implementing a user-defined policy, although it may supply adequate facilities for the system to provide enforcement of its own policies. With a programming language, protection policy can be declared and enforcement provided as needed by an implementation. If a language does not provide sufficient flexibility, it can be extended or replaced, with less perturbation of a system in service than would be caused by the modification of an operating-system kernel.

- **Efficiency:** The greatest efficiency is obtained when enforcement of protection is supported directly by hardware (or microcode). Insofar as software support is required, language-based enforcement has the advantage that static access enforcement can be verified off-line at compile time. Also, since an intelligent compiler can tailor the enforcement mechanism to meet the specified need, the fixed overhead of kernel calls can often be avoided.

In summary, the specification of protection in a programming language allows the high-level description of policies for the allocation and use of resources. A language implementation can provide software for protection enforcement when automatic hardware-supported checking is unavailable. In addition, it can interpret protection specifications to generate calls on whatever protection system is provided by the hardware and the operating system.

One way of making protection available to the application program is through the use of a software capability that could be used as an object of computation. Inherent in this concept is the idea that certain program components might have the privilege of creating or examining these software capabilities. A capability-creating program would be able to execute a primitive operation that would seal a data structure, rendering the latter's contents inaccessible to any program components that did not hold either the seal or the unseal privileges. They might copy the data structure or pass its address to other program components, but they could not gain access to its contents. The reason for introducing such software capabilities is to bring a protection mechanism into the programming language. The only problem with the concept as proposed is that the use of the `seal` and `unseal` operations takes a procedural approach to specifying protection. A nonprocedural or declarative notation seems a preferable way to make protection available to the application programmer.

What is needed is a safe, dynamic access-control mechanism for distributing capabilities to system resources among user processes. To contribute to the overall reliability of a system, the access-control mechanism should be safe to use. To be useful in practice, it should also be reasonably efficient. This requirement has led to the development of a number of language constructs that allow the programmer to declare various restrictions on the use of a specific managed resource. (See the Bibliographical Notes for appropriate references.) These constructs provide mechanisms for three functions:

1. Distributing capabilities safely and efficiently among customer processes: In particular, mechanisms ensure that a user process will use the managed resource only if it was granted a capability to that resource.

2. Specifying the type of operations that a particular process may invoke on an allocated resource (for example, a reader of a file should be allowed only to read the file, whereas a writer should be able both to read and to write): It should not be necessary to grant the same set of rights to every user process, and it should be impossible for a process to enlarge its set of access rights, except with the authorization of the access control mechanism.

3. Specifying the order in which a particular process may invoke the various operations of a resource (for example, a file must be opened before it can be read): It should be possible to give two processes different restrictions on the order in which they can invoke the operations of the allocated resource.

The incorporation of protection concepts into programming languages, as a practical tool for system design, is in its infancy. Protection will likely become a matter of greater concern to the designers of new systems with distributed architectures and increasingly stringent requirements on data security. Then, the importance of suitable language notations in which to express protection requirements will be recognized more widely.

18.7.2 Protection in Java 2

Java is an object-oriented programming language from Sun Microsystems. Java programs are composed of **classes**, each of which is a collection of data fields and functions (called **methods**) that operate on those fields. The Java virtual machine (JVM) loads a class in response to a request to create instances (or objects) of that class. One of the most novel and useful features of Java is its support for dynamically loading untrusted classes over a network and for executing mutually distrusting classes within the same JVM.

Due to these capabilities of Java, protection is a paramount concern. Classes running in the same JVM may be from different sources and may not be equally trusted. As a result, enforcing protection at the granularity of the JVM process is insufficient. Intuitively, whether a request to open a file should be allowed will generally depend on which class requested the open. The operating system lacks this knowledge.

Thus, such protection decisions are handled within the JVM. When the JVM loads a class, it assigns the class to a protection domain that gives the permissions of that class. The protection domain to which the class is assigned depends on the URL from which the class was loaded and any digital signatures on the class file. (Digital signatures are covered in Section 19.7.1.) A configurable policy file determines the permissions granted to the domain (and its classes). For example, classes loaded from a trusted server might be placed in a protection domain that allows them to access files in the user's home directory, whereas classes loaded from an untrusted server might have no file access permissions at all.

It can be complicated for the JVM to determine what class is responsible for a request to access a protected resource. Accesses are often performed indirectly, through system libraries or other classes. For example, consider a class that is not allowed to open network connections. It could call a system library to request the load of the contents of a URL. The JVM must decide whether or not to open a network connection for this request. But which class should be used to determine if the connection should be allowed, the application or the system library?

The philosophy adopted in Java 2 is to require the library class explicitly to permit the network connection to load the requested URL. More generally, in order to access a protected resource, some method in the calling sequence that resulted in the request must explicitly assert the privilege to access the resource. By doing so, this method *takes responsibility* for the request; presumably, it will also perform whatever checks are necessary to ensure the safety of the request. Of course, not any method is allowed to assert a privilege; it can do so only if its class is in a protection domain that is itself allowed to exercise the privilege.

This implementation approach is called **stack inspection**. Every thread in the JVM has an associated stack of its ongoing method invocations. When its caller potentially is not trusted, a method executes an access request within a doPrivileged block to perform the access to a protected resource directly or indirectly. [1] When the doPrivileged block is entered, the stack frame for this method is annotated to indicate this fact. Then, the contents of the block are executed. When an access to a protected resource is subsequently requested, either by this method or a method it calls, a call to checkPermissions is used to invoke stack inspection to determine if the request should be allowed. The

---

[1] This is the approach taken in JDK 1.2, though more precisely, doPrivileged is a method of the AccessController class that is passed a class with a run method to invoke.

protection domain:	untrusted applet	URL loader	networking
socket permission:	none	*.lucent.com:80, connect	any

class:	gui:
	
	. . .
	get(url);
	open(addr);
	. . .
		get(URL u):
		
		. . .
		doPrivileged {
		  open('proxy.lucent.com:80');
		}
		<request u from proxy>
		. . .
			open(Addr a):
			
			. . .
			checkPermission(a, connect);
			connect (a);
			. . .

Figure 18.8   Stack inspection

inspection examines stack frames on the calling thread's stack, starting from the most recently added frame and working toward the oldest. If a stack frame is first found that has the doPrivileged annotation, then checkPermissions returns immediately and silently, allowing the access.   If a stack frame is first found for which access is disallowed based on the protection domain of the method's class, then checkPermissions throws an exception. If the stack inspection exhausts the stack without finding either type of frame, then whether access is allowed depends on the implementation (for example, Internet Explorer 4.0 and JDK 1.2 allow access, whereas Netscape 4.0 disallows it).

Stack inspection is illustrated in Figure 18.8. Here, the gui method of a class in the *untrusted applet* protection domain performs two operations, first a get and then an open. The former is an invocation of the get method of a class in the *URL loader* protection domain, which is permitted to open sessions to sites in the *lucent.com* domain, in particular a proxy server *proxy.lucent.com* for retrieving URLs. For this reason, the untrusted applet's get invocation will succeed: the checkPermissions call in the networking library encounters the stack frame of the get method, which performed its open in a doPrivileged block. However, the untrusted applet's open invocation will result in an exception, because the checkPermissions call finds no doPrivileged annotation before encountering the stack frame of the gui method.

Of course, for stack inspection to work, a program must be unable to modify the annotations on its own stack frame, or to do other manipulations of stack inspection. This is one of the most important differences between Java and many other languages (including C++). A Java program cannot directly access memory. Rather, it can manipulate only an object for which it has a reference. References are unforgeable, and the manipulations are made only through well-defined interfaces. Compliance is enforced through a sophisticated collection of load-time and run-time checks. As a result, an object cannot manipulate its run-time stack, because it cannot get a reference to the stack or other components of the protection system.

More generally, Java's load-time and run-time checks enforce **type safety** of Java classes. Type safety ensures that classes cannot treat integers as pointers, write past the end of an array, or otherwise access memory in arbitrary ways. Rather, a program can access an object only via the methods defined on that object by its class. This is the foundation of Java protection, since it enables a class to effectively **encapsulate** and protect its data and methods from other classes loaded in the same JVM. For example, a variable can be defined as *private* so that only the class that contains it can access it, or *protected* so that it can be accessed only by the class that contains it, subclasses of that class, or classes in the same package. Type safety ensures that these restrictions can be enforced.

18.8 ■ Summary

Computer systems contain many objects, and they need to be protected from misuse. Objects may be hardware (such as memory, CPU time, or I/O devices) or software (such as files, programs, and abstract data types). An access right is permission to perform an operation on an object. A domain is a set of access rights. Processes execute in domains and may use any of the access rights in the domain to access and manipulate objects. During its lifetime, a process may be either bound to a protection domain or it may be allowed to switch from one domain to another.

The access matrix is a general model of protection. The access matrix provides a mechanism for protection without imposing a particular protection policy on the system or its users. The separation of policy and mechanism is an important design property.

The access matrix is sparse. It is normally implemented either as access lists associated with each object, or as capability lists associated with each domain. We can include dynamic protection in the access-matrix model by considering domains and the access matrix itself as objects. Revocation of access rights in a dynamic protection model is typically easier to implement with an access list scheme than with a capability list.

Real systems are much more limited, and tend to provide protection only for files. UNIX is representative, providing read, write, and execution protection separately for the owner, group, and general public for each file. MULTICS uses a ring structure in addition to file access. Hydra, the Cambridge CAP system, and Mach are capability systems that extend protection to user-defined software objects.

Language-based protection provides finer-grained arbitration of requests and privileges than is possible from the operating system. For example, a single Java JVM can run several threads, each in a different protection class. It enforces the resource requests through sophisticated stack inspection and via the type safety of the language.

■ Exercises

18.1 What are the main differences between capability lists and access lists?

18.2 A Burroughs B7000/B6000 MCP file can be tagged as sensitive data. When such a file is deleted, its storage area is overwritten by some random bits. For what purpose would such a scheme be useful?

18.3 In a ring-protection system, level 0 has the greatest access to objects and level n (greater than 0) has fewer access rights. The access rights of a program at a particular level in the ring structure are considered as a set of capabilities. What is the relationship between the capabilities of a domain at level j and a domain at level i to an object (for $j > i$)?

18.4 Consider a computer system in which "computer games" can be played by students only between 10 P.M. and 6 A.M., by faculty members between 5 P.M. and 8 A.M., and by the computer center staff at all times. Suggest a scheme for implementing this policy efficiently.

18.5 The RC 4000 system (and other systems) have defined a tree of processes (called a process tree) such that all the descendants of a process are given resources (or objects) and access rights by their ancestors only. Thus, a descendant can never have the ability to do anything that its ancestors cannot do. The root of the tree is the operating system, which has the ability to do anything. Assume the set of access rights is represented by an access matrix, A. $A(x,y)$ defines the access rights of process x to object y. If x is a descendant of z, what is the relationship between $A(x,y)$ and $A(z,y)$ for an arbitrary object y?

18.6 What hardware features are needed in a computer system for efficient capability manipulation? Can these be used for memory protection?

18.7 Consider a computing environment where a unique number is associated with each process and each object in the system. Suppose that we allow a process with number n to access an object with number m only if $n > m$. What type of protection structure do we have?

18.8 What protection problems may arise if a shared stack is used for parameter passing?

18.9 Consider a computing environment where a process is given the privilege of accessing an object only n times. Suggest a scheme for implementing this policy.

18.10 If all the access rights to an object are deleted, the object can no longer be accessed. At this point, the object should also be deleted, and the space it occupies should be returned to the system. Suggest an efficient implementation of this scheme.

18.11 What is the need-to-know principle? Why is it important for a protection system to adhere to this principle?

18.12 Why is it difficult to protect a system in which users are allowed to do their own I/O?

18.13 Capability lists are usually kept within the address space of the user. How does the system ensure that the user cannot modify the contents of the list?

18.14 Describe how the Java protection model would be sacrificed if a Java program were allowed to directly alter the annotations of its stack frame.

Bibliographical Notes

The access-matrix model of protection between domains and objects was developed by Lampson [1969] and Lampson [1971]. Popek [1974], and Saltzer and Schroeder [1975] provided excellent surveys on the subject of protection. Harrison et al. [1976] used a formal version of this model to enable them to prove mathematically properties of a protection system.

The concept of a capability evolved from Iliffe's and Jodeit's *codewords*, which were implemented in the Rice University computer (Iliffe and Jodeit [1962]). The term *capability* was introduced by Dennis and Horn [1966].

The Hydra system was described by Wulf et al. [1981]. The CAP system was described by Needham and Walker [1977]. Organick [1972] discussed the MULTICS ring protection system.

Revocation was discussed by Redell and Fabry [1974], Cohen and Jefferson [1975], and Ekanadham and Bernstein [1979]. The principle of separation of policy and mechanism was advocated by the designer of Hydra (Levin et al. [1975]). The confinement problem was first discussed by Lampson [1973] and was further examined by Lipner [1975].

The use of higher-level languages for specifying access control was suggested first by Morris [1973], who proposed the use of the seal and unseal operations discussed in Section 18.7. Kieburtz and Silberschatz [1978], Kieburtz and Silberschatz [1983], and McGraw and Andrews [1979] proposed various language constructs for dealing with general dynamic resource-management schemes. Jones and Liskov [1978] considered how a static access-control scheme can be incorporated in a programming language that supports abstract data types.

A more detailed analysis of stack inspection, including comparisons to other approaches to Java security, can be found in Wallach et al. [1987] and Gong et al. [1997].

Chapter 19

SECURITY

Protection, as we discussed in Chapter 18, is strictly an *internal* problem: How do we provide controlled access to programs and data stored in a computer system? **Security**, on the other hand, requires not only an adequate protection system but also consideration of the *external* environment within which the system operates. Internal protection is not useful if the operator's console is exposed to unauthorized personnel or if files can simply be removed from the computer system on tapes and disks and taken to an unprotected system. These security problems are management, rather than operating-system, problems.

The information stored in the system (both data and code), as well as the physical resources of the computer system, need to be protected from unauthorized access, malicious destruction or alteration, and accidental introduction of inconsistency. In this chapter, we examine the ways in which information may be misused or intentionally made inconsistent. We then present mechanisms to guard against such occurrences.

19.1 ▪ The Security Problem

In Chapter 18, we discussed mechanisms that the operating system can provide (with appropriate aid from the hardware) that allow users to protect their resources (usually programs and data). These mechanisms work well only as long as the users conform to the intended use of and access to these resources. We say that a system is **secure** if its resources are used and accessed as intended under all circumstances. Unfortunately, total security cannot be achieved.

Nonetheless, we must have mechanisms to make security breaches a rare occurrence, rather than the norm.

Security violations (or misuse) of the system can be categorized as intentional (malicious) or accidental. It is easier to protect against accidental misuse than against malicious misuse. Among the forms of malicious access are the following:

- Unauthorized reading of data (or theft of information)

- Unauthorized modification of data

- Unauthorized destruction of data

- Preventing legitimate use of the system (or denial of service)

Absolute protection of the system from malicious abuse is not possible, but the cost to the perpetrator can be made sufficiently high to deter most, if not all, unauthorized attempts to access the information residing in the system.

To protect the system, we must take security measures at four levels:

1. **Physical:** The site or sites containing the computer systems must be physically secured against armed or surreptitious entry by intruders.

2. **Human:** Users must be screened carefully to reduce the chance of authorizing a user who then gives access to an intruder (in exchange for a bribe, for example).

3. **Network:** Much computer data in modern systems travels over private leased lines, shared lines like the Internet, or dial-up lines. Intercepting these data could be just as harmful as breaking into a computer; and interruption of communications could constitute a remote **denial-of-service attack**, diminishing users' use of and trust in the system.

4. **Operating system:** The system must protect itself from accidental or purposeful security breaches.

Security at the first two levels must be maintained if operating-system security is to be ensured. A weakness at a high level of security (physical or human) allows circumvention of strict low-level (operating-system) security measures.

Furthermore, the system hardware must provide protection (Chapter 18) to allow the implementation of security features. Most contemporary operating systems are now designed to provide security features.

In many applications, ensuring the security of the computer system is worth considerable effort. Large commercial systems containing payroll or other financial data are inviting targets to thieves. Systems that contain data pertaining to corporate operations may be of interest to unscrupulous competitors. Furthermore, loss of such data, whether by accident or fraud, can seriously impair the ability of the corporation to function.

In the remainder of this chapter, we address security at the network and operating-system levels. Security at the physical and human levels, although important, is far beyond the scope of this text. Security within the operating system and between operating systems is implemented in several ways, ranging from passwords for access to the system to the isolation of concurrent processes running within the system. The file system also provides some degree of protection.

19.2 ■ User Authentication

A major security problem for operating systems is **authentication**. The protection system depends on the ability to identify the programs and processes currently executing, which in turn depends on the ability to identify each user of the system. A user normally identifies himself. How do we determine whether a user's identity is authentic? Generally, authentication is based on one or more of three items: user possession (a key or card), user knowledge (a user identifier and password), and/or a user attribute (fingerprint, retina pattern, or signature).

19.2.1 Passwords

The most common approach to authenticating a user identity is the use of **passwords**. When the user identifies herself by user ID or account name, she is asked for a password. If the user-supplied password matches the password stored in the system, the system assumes that the user is legitimate.

Passwords are often used to protect objects in the computer system, in the absence of more complete protection schemes. They can be considered a special case of either keys or capabilities. For instance, a password could be associated with each resource (such as a file). Whenever a request is made to use the resource, the password must be given. If the password is correct, access is granted. Different passwords may be associated with different access rights. For example, different passwords may be used for reading files, appending files, and updating files.

19.2.2 Password Vulnerabilities

Passwords are extremely common because they are easy to understand and use. Unfortunately, passwords can often be guessed, accidentally exposed, sniffed, or illegally transferred from an authorized user to an unauthorized one, as we show next.

There are two common ways to guess a password. One way is for the intruder (either human or program) to know the user or to have information about the user. All too frequently, people use obvious information (such as the names of their cats or spouses) as their passwords. The other way is to use brute force, trying enumeration, or all possible combinations of letters, numbers, and punctuation, until the password is found. Short passwords are especially vulnerable to this method. For example, a four-decimal password provides only 10,000 variations. On average, guessing 5,000 times would produce a correct hit. A program that could try a password every 1 millisecond would take only about 5 seconds to guess a four-digit password. Enumeration is not as successful at finding passwords in systems that allow longer passwords, that differentiate between uppercase and lowercase letters, and that allow use of numbers and all punctuation characters in passwords. Of course, users must take advantage of the large password space and must not, for example, use only lowercase letters.

In addition to being guessed, passwords can be exposed as a result of visual or electronic monitoring. An intruder can look over the shoulder of a user (*shoulder surfing*) when the user is logging in and can learn the password easily by watching the keyboard. Alternatively, anyone with access to the network on which a computer resides could seamlessly add a network monitor, allowing her to watch all data being transferred on the network (*sniffing*), including user IDs and passwords. Encrypting the data stream containing the password solves this problem.

Exposure is a particularly severe problem if the password is written down where it can be read or lost. As we shall see, some systems force users to select hard-to-remember or long passwords, which may cause a user to record the password. As a result, such systems provide much less security than systems that allow easy passwords!

The final method of password compromise, illegal transfer, is the result of human nature. Most computer installations have a rule that forbids users to share accounts. This rule is sometimes implemented for accounting reasons but is often aimed at improving security. For instance, suppose one user ID is shared by several users, and a security breach occurs from that user ID. It is impossible to know who was using that user ID at the time the break occurred or even whether the user was an authorized one. With one user per user ID, any user can be questioned directly about use of her account. Sometimes, users break account-sharing rules to help friends or to circumvent accounting, and this behavior can result in a system's being accessed by unauthorized users—possibly harmful ones.

Passwords can be either generated by the system or selected by a user. System-generated passwords may be difficult to remember, and thus users may write them down. User-selected passwords, however, are often easy to guess (the user's name or favorite car, for example). At some sites, administrators occasionally check user passwords and notify a user if her password is too short or otherwise easy to guess. Some systems also *age* passwords, forcing users to change their passwords at regular intervals (every three months, for instance). This method is not foolproof either, because users can easily toggle between two passwords. The solution, as implemented on some systems, is to record a password history for each user. For instance, the system could record the last N passwords and not allow their reuse.

Several variants on these simple password schemes can be used.   For example, the password can be changed frequently. In the extreme, the password is changed from session to session. A new password is selected (either by the system or by the user) at the end of *each* session, and that password must be used for the next session. In such a case, even if a password is misused, it can be used only once. When the legitimate user tries to use a now-invalid password at the next session, he discovers the security violation. Steps can then be taken to repair the breached security.

19.2.3 Encrypted Passwords

One problem with all these approaches is the difficulty of keeping the password secret within the computer. How can the system store a password securely yet allow its use for authentication when the user presents her password? The UNIX system uses **encryption** to avoid the necessity of keeping its password list secret. Each user has a password. The system contains a function that is extremely difficult—the designers hope impossible—to invert but is simple to compute. That is, given a value x, it is easy to compute the function value $f(x)$. Given a function value $f(x)$, however, it is impossible to compute x. This function is used to encode all passwords. Only encoded passwords are stored. When a user presents a password, it is encoded and compared against the stored encoded password. Even if the stored encoded password is seen, it cannot be decoded, so the password cannot be determined. Thus, the password file does not need to be kept secret. The function $f(x)$ is typically an **encryption algorithm** that has been designed and tested rigorously, as discussed in Section 19.7.2.

The flaw in this method is that the system no longer has control over the passwords. Although the passwords are encrypted, anyone with a copy of the password file can run fast encryption routines against it—encrypting each word in a dictionary, for instance, and comparing the results against the passwords. If the user has selected a password that is also a word in the dictionary, the password is cracked. On sufficiently fast computers, or even on clusters of slow computers, such a comparison may take only a few hours. Furthermore, because UNIX systems use a well-known encryption algorithm, a hacker might keep a cache of passwords that have been cracked previously. For this reason, new versions of UNIX store the encrypted password entries in a file readable only by the **superuser**. The programs that compare a presented password to the stored password run `setuid` to root; so they can read this file, but other users cannot.

Another weakness in the UNIX password methods is that many UNIX systems treat only the first eight characters as significant. It is therefore extremely important for users to take advantage of the available password space. To avoid the dictionary encryption method, some systems disallow the use of dictionary words as passwords. A good technique is to generate your password by using the first letter of each word of an easily remembered phrase using both upper and lower characters with a number or punctuation thrown in for good measure. For example, the phrase "My mother's name is Katherine" might yield the password "MmnisK.!". The password is hard to crack but easy for the user to remember.

19.2.4 One-Time Passwords

To avoid the problems of password sniffing and shoulder surfing, a system could use a set of **paired passwords**. When a session begins, the system randomly selects and presents one part of a password pair; the user must supply the other part. In this system, the user is *challenged* and must *respond* with the correct answer to that challenge.

This approach can be generalized to the use of an algorithm as a password. The algorithm might be an integer function, for example. The system selects a random integer and presents it to the user. The user applies the function and replies with the correct result. The system also applies the function. If the two results match, access is allowed.

Such algorithmic passwords are not susceptible to exposure; that is, a user can type in a password, and no entity intercepting that password will be able to reuse it. In this variation, the system and the user share a secret. The secret is never transmitted over a medium that allows exposure. Rather, the secret is used as input to the function, along with a shared seed. A **seed** is a random number or alphanumeric sequence. The seed is the authentication challenge from the computer. The secret and the seed are used as input to the function $f(secret, seed)$. The result of this function is transmitted as the password to the computer. Because the computer also knows the secret and the seed, it can perform the same computation. If the results match, the user is authenticated. The next time that the user needs to be authenticated, another seed is generated, and the same steps ensue. This time, the password is different.

In this **one-time password** system, the password is different in each instance. Anyone capturing the password from one session and trying to reuse it in another session will fail. One-time passwords are among the only ways to prevent improper authentication due to password exposure. Commercial implementations of one-time password systems such as SecurID, for example, use hardware calculators. Most of these calculators are in the shape of a credit card but have a keypad and display. Some use the current time as the random seed. The user uses the keypad to enter the shared secret, also known as a **personal identification number (PIN)**. The display shows the one-time password. The use of both a one-time password generator and a PIN is one form of **two-factor authentication**. Two different types of components are needed in this case. Two-factor authentication offers far better authentication protection than single-factor authentication.

Another variation on one-time passwords is the use of a **code book**, or **one-time pad**, which is a list of single-use passwords. In this method, each password on the list is used, in order, once, and then is crossed out or erased. The commonly used S/Key system uses either a software calculator or a code book based on these calculations as a source of one-time passwords.

19.2.5 Biometrics

There are many other variations on the use of passwords for authentication. Palm- or hand-readers are commonly used to secure physical access—for example, access to a data center. These readers match stored parameters against what is being read from hand-reader pads. The parameters can include a temperature map, as well as finger length, finger width, and line patterns. These devices are currently too large and expensive to be used for normal computer authentication.

Fingerprint readers have become accurate and cost-effective and should become more common in the future. These devices read your finger's ridge patterns and convert them into a sequence of numbers. Over time, they can store a set of sequences to adjust for the location of the finger on the reading pad and other factors. Software can then scan a finger on the pad and compare its features with these stored sequences to determine if the finger on the pad is the same as the stored one. Of course, multiple users can have profiles stored, and the scanner can differentiate among them. A very accurate two-factor authentication scheme can result from requiring a password as well as a user name and fingerprint scan. If this information is encrypted in transit, the system can be very resistant to spoofing or replay attack.

19.3   ■   Program Threats

When a program written by one user may be used by another, misuse and unexpected behavior may result. In this section, we describe common methods by which users gain access to the programs of others: Trojan horses, trap doors, and stack and buffer overflow.

19.3.1 Trojan Horse

Many systems have mechanisms for allowing programs written by users to be executed by other users. If these programs are executed in a domain that provides the access rights of the executing user, the other users may misuse these rights. A text-editor program, for example, may include code to search the file to be edited for certain keywords. If any are found, the entire file may be copied to a special area accessible to the creator of the text editor. A code segment that misuses its environment is called a **Trojan horse**. Long search paths, such as are common on UNIX systems, exacerbate the Trojan-horse problem. The search path lists the set of directories to search when an ambiguous program name is given. The path is searched for a file of that name, and the file is executed. All the directories in the search path must be secure, or a Trojan horse could be slipped into the user's path and executed accidentally.

For instance, consider the use of the "." character in a search path. The "." tells the shell to include the current directory in the search. Thus, if a user has "." in her search path, has set her current directory to a friend's directory, and enters the name of a normal system command, the command may be executed from the friend's directory instead. The program would run within the user's domain, allowing the program to do anything that the user is allowed to do, including deleting the user's files, for instance.

A variation of the Trojan horse is a program that emulates a login program. An unsuspecting user starts to log in at a terminal and notices that he has apparently mistyped his password. He tries again and is successful. What has happened is that his authentication key and password have been stolen by the login emulator, which was left running on the terminal by the thief. The emulator stored away the password, printed out a login error message, and exited; the user was then provided with a genuine login prompt. This type of attack can be defeated by having the operating system print a usage message at the end of an interactive session or by a nontrappable key sequence, such as the control-alt-delete combination used by all Windows operating systems.

19.3.2 Trap Door

The designer of a program or system might leave a hole in the software that only she is capable of using. This type of security breach (or **trap door**) was shown in the movie *War Games*. For instance, the code might check for a specific user ID or password, and it might circumvent normal security procedures. Programmers have been arrested for embezzling from banks by including rounding errors in their code and having the occasional half-cent credited to their accounts. This account crediting can add up to a large amount of money, considering the number of transactions that a large bank executes.

A clever trap door could be included in a compiler. The compiler could generate standard object code as well as a trap door, regardless of the source code being compiled. This activity is particularly nefarious, since a search of the source code of the program will not reveal any problems. Only the source code of the compiler would contain the information.

Trap doors pose a difficult problem because, to detect them, we have to analyze all the source code for all components of a system. Given that software systems may consist of millions of lines of code, this analysis is not done frequently, and frequently it is not done at all!

19.3.3 Stack and Buffer Overflow

The stack- or buffer-overflow attack is the most common way for an attacker outside of the system, on a network or dial-up connection, to gain unauthorized access to the target system. An authorized user of the system may also use this exploit for **privilege escalation**, to gain privileges beyond those allowed for that user.

Essentially, the attack exploits a bug in a program. The bug can be a simple case of poor programming, in which the programmer neglected to code bounds checking on an input field. In this case, the attacker sends more data than the program was expecting. Using trial and error, or by examination of the source code of the attacked program if it is available, the attacker determines the vulnerability and writes a program to do the following:

1. Overflow an input field, command-line argument, or input buffer—for example, on a network daemon—until it writes into the stack

2. Overwrite the current return address on the stack with the address of the exploit code loaded in step 3

3. Write a simple set of code for the next space in the stack that includes the commands that the attacker wishes to execute—for instance, spawn a shell

The result of this attack program's execution will be a root shell or other privileged command execution.

For instance, if a web page form expects a user name to be entered into a field, the attacker could send the user name, plus extra characters to overflow the buffer and reach the stack, plus a new return address to load onto the stack, plus the code the attacker wants to run. When the buffer-reading subroutine returns from execution, the return address is the exploit code, and the code is run.

The buffer-overflow attack is especially pernicious, as it can be run within a system and can travel over allowed communications channels. Such attacks can occur within protocols that are expected to be used to communicate with the machine, and they can therefore be hard to detect and prevent. They can even bypass the security added by firewalls (Section 19.5).

One solution to this problem is for the CPU to have a feature that disallows execution of code in a stack section of memory. Recent versions of Sun's SPARC chip include this setting, and recent versions of Solaris enable it. The return address of the overflowed routine can still be modified; but when the return address is within the stack and the code there attempts to execute, an exception is generated, and the program is halted with an error.

19.4 ■ System Threats

Most operating systems provide a means by which processes can spawn other processes. In such an environment, it is possible to create a situation where operating-system resources and user files are misused. The two most common methods for achieving this misuse are worms and viruses. We discuss each below, along with a somewhat different form of system threat: denial of service.

19.4.1 Worms

A **worm** is a process that uses the **spawn** mechanism to ravage system performance. The worm spawns copies of itself, using up system resources and perhaps locking out all other processes. On computer networks, worms are particularly potent, since they may reproduce themselves among systems and thus shut down the entire network. Such an event occurred in 1988 to UNIX systems on the Internet, causing millions of dollars of lost system and system administrator time.

At the close of the workday on November 2, 1988, Robert Tappan Morris, Jr., a first-year Cornell graduate student, unleashed a worm program on one or more hosts connected to the Internet. Targeting Sun Microsystems' Sun 3 workstations and VAX computers running variants of Version 4 BSD UNIX, the worm quickly spread over great distances; within a few hours of its release, it had consumed system resources to the point of bringing down the infected machines.

Although Robert Morris designed the self-replicating program for rapid reproduction and distribution, some of the features of the UNIX networking environment provided the means to propagate the worm throughout the system. It is likely that Morris chose for initial infection an Internet host left open for and accessible to outside users. From there, the worm program exploited flaws in the UNIX operating system's security routines and took advantage of UNIX utilities that simplify resource sharing in local-area networks to gain unauthorized access to thousands of other connected sites. Morris's methods of attack are outlined next.

The worm was made up of two programs, a **grappling hook** (also called a **bootstrap** or **vector**) program and the main program. Named *l1.c*, the grappling hook consisted of 99 lines of C code compiled and run on each machine it accessed. Once established on the computer system under attack, the grappling hook connected to the machine where it originated and uploaded a copy of the main worm onto the *hooked* system (Figure 19.1). The main program proceeded to search for other machines to which the newly infected system could connect

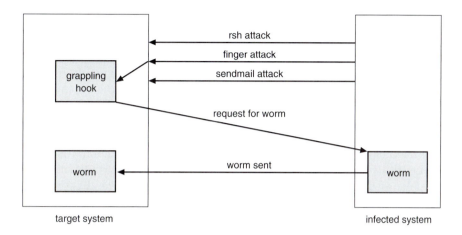

Figure 19.1   The Morris Internet worm.

easily. In these actions, Morris exploited the UNIX networking utility, `rsh`, for easy remote task execution. By setting up special files that list the host–login name pairs, users can omit entering a password each time they access a remote account on the paired list. The worm searched these special files for site names that would allow remote execution without a password. Where remote shells were established, the worm program was uploaded and began executing anew.

The attack via remote access was one of three infection methods built into the worm. The other two methods involved operating-system bugs in the UNIX *finger* and *sendmail* programs. The *finger* utility functions as an electronic telephone directory; the command

<code>finger user-name@hostname</code>

returns a person's real and login names along with other information that the user may have provided, such as office and home address and telephone number, research plan, or clever quotation. *Finger* runs as a background process (or daemon) at each BSD site and responds to queries throughout the Internet. The point vulnerable to malicious entry involved reading input without checking bounds for overflow. The code executed a buffer-overflow attack.

Morris's program queried *finger* with a 536-byte string crafted to exceed the buffer allocated for input and to overwrite the stack frame. Instead of returning to the *main* routine it was in before Morris's call, the *finger* daemon was routed to a procedure within the invading 536-byte string now residing on the stack. The new procedure executed */bin/sh*, which, if successful, gave the worm a remote shell on the machine under attack.

The bug exploited in *sendmail* also involved using a daemon process for malicious entry. *Sendmail* routes electronic mail in a network environment.

Debugging code in the utility permits testers to verify and display the state of the mail system. The debugging option is useful to system administrators and is often left on as a background process. Morris included in his attack arsenal a call to debug that, instead of specifying a user address, as would be normal in testing, issued a set of commands that mailed and executed a copy of the grappling-hook program.

Once in place, the main worm undertook systematic attempts to discover user passwords. It began by trying simple cases of no password or of passwords constructed of account–user-name combinations, then used comparisons with an internal dictionary of 432 favorite password choices, and then went to the final stage of trying each word in the standard UNIX on-line dictionary as a possible password. This elaborate and efficient three-stage password-cracking algorithm enabled the worm to gain access to other user accounts on the infected system. The worm then searched for *rsh* data files in these newly broken accounts and used them as described previously to gain access to user accounts on remote systems.

With each new access, the worm program searched for already active copies of itself. If it found one, the new copy exited, except in every seventh instance. Had the worm exited on all duplicate sightings, it might have remained undetected. Allowing every seventh duplicate to proceed (possibly to confound efforts to stop its spread by baiting with *fake* worms) created a wholesale infestation of Sun and VAX systems on the Internet.

The very features of the UNIX network environment that assisted the worm's propagation also helped to stop its advance. Ease of electronic communication, mechanisms to copy source and binary files to remote machines, and access to both source code and human expertise allowed cooperative efforts to develop solutions quickly. By the evening of the next day, November 3, methods of halting the invading program were circulated to system administrators via the Internet. Within days, specific software patches for the exploited security flaws were available.

Why did Morris unleash the worm? The action has been characterized as both a harmless prank gone awry and a serious criminal offense. Based on the complexity of starting the attack, it is unlikely that the worm's release or the scope of its spread was unintentional. The worm program took elaborate steps to cover its tracks and to repel efforts to stop its spread. Yet the program contained no code aimed at damaging or destroying the systems on which it ran. The author clearly had the expertise to include such commands; in fact, data structures were present in the bootstrap code that could have been used to transfer Trojan-horse or virus programs (Section 19.4.2). The behavior of the program may lead to interesting observations, but it does not provide a sound basis for inferring motive. What is not open to speculation, however, is the legal outcome: A federal court convicted Morris and handed down a sentence of three years' probation, 400 hours of community service, and a $10,000 fine. Morris' legal costs were probably in excess of $100,000.

A more recent event shows that worms are still a fact of life on the Internet. It also shows that as the Internet grows, the damage that even "harmless" worms can do also grows, and can be significant.

This example occurred during August, 2003.   The fifth version of the "Sobig" worm, more properly known as "W32.Sobig.F@mm", was released by persons at this time unknown. It is the fastest-spreading worm released to date, at its peak infecting hundreds of thousands of computers and one in seventeen e-mail messages on the Internet. It clogged e-mail inboxes, slowed networks, and took a huge number of man-hours to clean up.

Sobig.F was launched by being uploaded to a pornography newsgroup, via an account created using a stolen credit card. It was disguised as a photo. The virus targeted Microsoft Windows systems, and used its own SMTP engine to e-mail itself to all of the addresses found on an infected system. It used a variety of subject lines to help avoid detection, including "Thank You!, Your details," and "Re: Approved". It also used a random address on the host as the "From:" address, making it difficult to determine via the message which machine was the infected source. Sobig.F included an attachment for the target e-mail reader to click on, again with a variety of names. If the payload was executed, it stored a program called WINPPR32.EXE into the default Windows directory, along with a text file. It also modified the Windows registry.

It was also programmed to periodically attempt to connect to one of twenty servers, and download and execute a program from them.   Fortunately, the servers were disabled before the code could be downloaded. The contents of the program from these servers has not yet been determined. Should the code have been malevelent, untold damage to a vast number of machines could have resulted. Security experts are still evaluating methods to decrease or eliminate worms.

19.4.2 Viruses

Another form of computer attack is a **virus**. Like worms, viruses are designed to spread into other programs and can wreak havoc in a system by modifying or destroying files and causing system crashes and program malfunctions. Whereas a worm is structured as a complete, standalone program, a virus is a fragment of code embedded in a legitimate program. Viruses are a major problem for computer users, especially users of microcomputer systems. Multiuser computers generally are not susceptible to viruses because the executable programs are protected from writing by the operating system. Even if a virus does infect a program, its powers are limited because other aspects of the system are protected. Single-user systems have no such protections and, as a result, a virus has free run.

Viruses are usually spread when users download viral programs from public bulletin boards or exchange disks containing an infection. In February 1992, for example, two Cornell University students developed three Macintosh game programs with an embedded virus and distributed them to worldwide software archives via the Internet. The virus was discovered when a mathematics professor in Wales downloaded the games and antivirus programs on his system alerted him to an infection. Some 200 other users had already downloaded the games. Although the virus was not designed to destroy data, it could spread to application files and cause such problems as long delays and program malfunctions. The authors were easy to trace, since the games had been mailed electronically from a Cornell account. New York State authorities arrested the students on misdemeanor charges of computer tampering.

In recent years, a common form of virus transmission has been via the exchange of Microsoft Office files, such as Microsoft Word documents. These documents can contain so-called *macros* (or Visual Basic programs) that programs in the Office suite (Word, PowerPoint, or Excel) will execute automatically. Because these programs run under the user's own account, the macros can run largely unconstrained (for example, deleting user files at will).

On occasion, upcoming viral infections are announced in high-profile media events. Such was the case with the *Michelangelo* virus, which was scheduled to erase infected hard disk files on March 6, 1992, the Renaissance artist's 517th birthday. Because of the extensive publicity surrounding the virus, most sites had located and destroyed the virus before it was activated, so it caused little or no damage. Such cases both alert the general public to and alarm it about the virus problem. Antivirus programs are currently excellent sellers.

Most commercial antivirus packages are effective against only particular known viruses. They work by searching all the programs on a system for the specific pattern of instructions known to make up the virus. When they find a known pattern, they remove the instructions, *disinfecting* the program. These commercial packages have catalogs of thousands of viruses for which they search. Viruses and the antivirus software continue to become more sophisticated. Some viruses modify themselves as they infect other software to avoid the basic pattern-match approach of antivirus software. The antivirus software in turn now looks for families of patterns rather than a single pattern to identify a virus.

The best protection against computer viruses is prevention, or the practice of **safe computing**. Purchasing unopened software from vendors and avoiding free or pirated copies from public sources or disk exchange are the safest route to preventing infection. However, even new copies of legitimate software applications are not immune to virus infection: There have been cases where disgruntled employees of a software company have infected the master copies of software programs to do economic harm to the company selling the software. For macro viruses, one defense is to exchange Word documents in an alternative file format called **rich text format (RTF)**. Unlike the native Word format, RTF does not include the capability to attach macros.

Another defense is to avoid opening any e-mail attachments from unknown users. Unfortunately, history has shown that e-mail vulnerabilities appear as fast as they are fixed. For example, in 2000 the *love bug* virus became very widespread by appearing to be a love note sent by a friend of the receiver. Once the attached Visual Basic script was opened, the virus propagated by sending itself to the first users in the user's e-mail contact list. Fortunately, except for clogging e-mail systems and users' inboxes, it was relatively harmless. It did, however, effectively negate the defensive strategy of opening attachments only from people known to the receiver. A more effective defense method is to avoid opening any e-mail attachment that contains executable code. Some companies now enforce this as policy by removing all incoming attachments to e-mail messages.

Another safeguard, although it does not prevent infection, does permit early detection. A user must begin by completely reformatting the hard disk, especially the boot sector, which is often targeted for viral attack. Only secure software is uploaded, and a checksum for each file is calculated. The checksum list must then be kept free from unauthorized access. Periodically, a program can recompute the checksums and compare them to the original list; any differences serve as a warning of possible infection.

Because they usually work among systems and not programs, processes, or users, both worms and viruses generally pose security, rather than protection, problems.

19.4.3 Denial of Service

The last attack category, **denial of service**, is aimed not at gaining information or stealing resources but rather at disrupting legitimate use of a system or facility. An intruder could delete all the files on a system, for example. Most denial-of-service attacks involve systems that the attacker has not penetrated. Indeed, launching an attack that prevents legitimate use is frequently easier than breaking into a machine or facility.

Denial-of-service attacks are generally network based. They fall into two categories. The first case is an attack that uses so many facility resources that, in essence, no useful work can be done. For example, a web-site click could download a Java applet that proceeds to use all available CPU time. The second case involves disrupting the network of the facility. There have been several successful denial-of-service attacks against major web sites. They result from abuse of some of the fundamental functionality of TCP/IP. For instance, if the attacker sends the part of the protocol that says "I want to start a TCP connection," but never follows with the standard "The connection is now complete," the result can be several partially started TCP sessions. These sessions can eat up all the network resources of the system, disabling any further legitimate TCP connections. Such attacks, which can last hours or days, have caused partial or full failure of attempts to use the target facility. These attacks are usually stopped at the network level until the operating systems can be updated to reduce their vulnerability.

Generally, it is impossible to prevent denial-of-service attacks. The attacks use the same mechanisms as normal operation. Frequently, it is difficult to determine if a system slowdown is just a surge in use or an attack!

19.5 ■ Securing Systems and Facilities

Securing systems and facilities is intimately linked to intrusion detection (Section 19.6). Both techniques need to work together to assure that a system is secure and that, if a security breach happens, it is detected.

One method of improving system security is periodically to scan the system for security holes. These scans can be done at times when computer use is relatively low, so they will have less effect than logging. A scan can check a variety of aspects of the system:

- Short or easy-to-guess passwords

- Unauthorized privileged programs, such as *setuid* programs

- Unauthorized programs in system directories

- Unexpected long-running processes

- Improper directory protections on both user and system directories

- Improper protections on system data files, such as the password file, device drivers, or even the operating-system kernel itself

- Dangerous entries in the program search path (for example, the Trojan horse discussed in Section 19.3.1)

- Changes to system programs detected with checksum values

- Unexpected or hidden network daemons

Any problems found by a security scan can either be fixed automatically or reported to the managers of the system.

Networked computers are much more susceptible to security attacks than are standalone systems. Rather than attacks from a known set of access points, such as directly connected terminals, we face attacks from an unknown and large set of access points—a potentially severe security problem. To a lesser extent, systems connected to telephone lines via modems are also more exposed.

In fact, the U.S. government considers a system to be only as secure as its most far-reaching connection. For instance, a top-secret system may be accessed only from within a building also considered top-secret. The system loses its top-secret rating if any form of communication can occur outside that environment. Some government facilities take extreme security precautions. The connectors that plug a terminal into the secure computer are locked in a safe in the office when the terminal is not in use. A person must know a physical lock combination, as well as authentication information for the computer itself, to gain access to the computer.

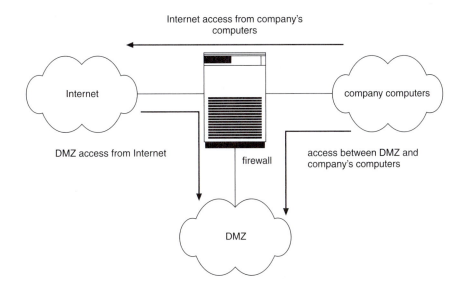

Figure 19.2   Network security through domain separation via firewall.

Unfortunately for systems administrators and computer-security professionals, it is frequently impossible to lock a machine in a room and disallow all remote access. For instance, the Internet network currently connects millions of computers. It is becoming a mission-critical, indispensable resource for many companies and individuals. If you consider the Internet a *club*, then, as in any club with millions of *members,* there are many good members and some bad members. The bad members have many tools they can use to attempt to gain access to the interconnected computers, just as Morris did with his worm.

How can trusted computers be connected safely to an untrustworthy network? One solution is the use of a firewall to separate trusted and untrusted systems. A **firewall** is a computer or router that sits between the trusted and the untrusted. It limits network access between the two **security domains** and monitors and logs all connections. It can also limit connections based on source or destination address, source or destination port, or direction of the connection. For instance, web servers use HTTP to communicate with web browsers. A firewall therefore may allow only HTTP to pass from all hosts outside the firewall only to the web server within the firewall. The Morris Internet worm used the finger protocol to break into computers, so *finger* would not be allowed to pass.

In fact, a firewall can separate a network into multiple domains. A common implementation has the Internet as the untrusted domain; a semitrusted and semisecure network, called the **demilitarized zone (DMZ)**, as another domain; and a company's computers as a third domain (Figure 19.2). Connections are allowed from the Internet to the DMZ computers and from the company computers to the Internet but are not allowed from the Internet or DMZ computers to the company computers. Optionally, controlled communications may be allowed between the DMZ and one or more company computers. For instance, a web server on the DMZ may need to query a database server on the corporate network. With a firewall, all access is contained, and any DMZ systems that are broken into based on the protocols allowed through the firewall still are unable to access the company computers.

Of course, a firewall itself must be secure and attack-proof; otherwise, its ability to secure connections can be compromised. Firewalls do not prevent attacks that **tunnel**, or travel within protocols or connections that the firewall allows. A buffer-overflow attack to a web server will not be stopped by the firewall, for example, because the HTTP connection is allowed; it is the contents of the HTTP connection that house the attack. Likewise, denial-of-service attacks can affect firewalls as much as any other machines. Another vulnerability of firewalls is **spoofing**, in which an unauthorized host pretends to be an authorized host by meeting some authorization criterion. For example, if a firewall rule allows a connection from a host and identifies that host by its IP address, then another host could send packets using that same address and be allowed through the firewall.

19.6 ■ Intrusion Detection

Intrusion detection, as its name suggests, strives to detect attempted or successful intrusions into computer systems and to initiate appropriate responses to the intrusions. Intrusion detection encompasses a wide array of techniques that vary on a number of *axes*. These axes include:

- The time that detection occurs. Detection can occur in real time (while the intrusion is occurring) or after the fact.

- The types of inputs examined to detect intrusive activity. These may include user shell commands, process system calls, and network packet headers or contents. Some forms of intrusions might be detected only by correlating information from several such sources.

- The range of response capabilities. Simple forms of response include alerting an administrator to the potential intrusion or somehow halting the potentially intrusive activity—for example, killing a process engaged in apparently intrusive activity. In a sophisticated form of response, a system might transparently divert an intruder's activity to a **honeypot**—a false resource exposed to the attacker. The resource appears real to the attacker and enables the system to monitor and gain information about the attack.

These degrees of freedom in the design space for detecting intrusions have yielded a wide range of solutions, known as **intrusion-detection systems (IDS)**.

19.6.1 What Constitutes an Intrusion?

Defining a suitable specification of intrusion turns out to be quite difficult, and thus automatic IDSs today typically settle for one of two less ambitious approaches. In the first, called **signature-based detection**, system input or network traffic is examined for specific behavior patterns (or **signatures**) known to indicate attacks. A simple example of signature-based detection is scanning network packets for the string */etc/passwd/* targeted for a UNIX system. Another example is virus-detection software, which scans binaries or network packets for known viruses.

The second approach, typically called **anomaly detection**, attempts through various techniques to detect anomalous behavior within computer systems. Of course, not all anomalous system activity indicates an intrusion, but the presumption is that intrusions often induce anomalous behavior. An example of anomaly detection is monitoring system calls of a daemon process to detect whether the system-call behavior deviates from normal patterns, possibly indicating that a buffer overflow has been exploited in the daemon to corrupt its behavior. Another example is monitoring shell commands to detect anomalous commands for a given user or detecting an anomalous login time for a user, either of which may indicate that an attacker has succeeded in gaining access to that user's account.

Signature-based detection and anomaly detection can be viewed as two sides of the same coin: Signature-based detection attempts to characterize dangerous behaviors and detects when one of these behaviors occurs, whereas anomaly detection attempts to characterize normal (or non-dangerous) behaviors and detects when something other than these behaviors occurs.

These different approaches yield IDSs with very different properties, however. In particular, anomaly detection can detect previously unknown methods of intrusion. Signature-based detection will identify only known attacks that can be codified in a recognizable pattern. Thus, new attacks that were not contemplated when the signatures were generated will evade signature-based detection. This problem is well known to vendors of virus-detection software, who must release new signatures with great frequency as new viruses are generated and detected manually.

Anomaly detection is not necessarily superior to signature-based detection, however. Indeed, a significant challenge for systems that attempt anomaly detection is to benchmark "normal" system behavior accurately. If the system is already penetrated when it is benchmarked, then the intrusive activity may be included in the "normal" benchmark. Even if the system is benchmarked cleanly, without influence from intrusive behavior, the benchmark must give a fairly complete picture of normal behavior. Otherwise, the number of false alarms will be excessive.

To illustrate the impact of even a marginally high rate of false alarms, consider an installation consisting of a few tens of UNIX workstations from which records of security-relevant events are recorded for purposes of intrusion detection. A small installation such as this could easily generate a million audit records per day. Only one or two might be worthy of an administrator's investigation. If we suppose, optimistically, that each such attack is reflected in ten audit records, we can then roughly compute the rate of occurrence of audit records reflecting truly intrusive activity as

$$\frac{2\dfrac{\text{intrusions}}{\text{day}} \cdot 10\dfrac{\text{records}}{\text{intrusion}}}{10^6\dfrac{\text{records}}{\text{day}}} = 0.00002$$

Interpreting this as a "probability of occurrence of intrusive records," we denote it as $P(I)$; that is, event I is the occurrence of a record reflecting truly intrusive behavior. Since $P(I) = 0.00002$, we also know that $P(\neg I) = 1 - P(I) = 0.99998$. Now let A denote the event of the IDS raising an alarm. An accurate IDS should maximize both $P(I|A)$ and $P(\neg I|\neg A)$—that is, the probabilities that an alarm indicates an intrusion and that no alarm indicates no intrusion. Focusing on $P(I|A)$ for the moment, we can compute it using **Bayes' theorem**:

$$P(I|A) = \frac{P(I) \cdot P(A|I)}{P(I) \cdot P(A|I) + P(\neg I) \cdot P(A|\neg I)} = \frac{0.00002 \cdot P(A|I)}{0.00002 \cdot P(A|I) + 0.99998 \cdot P(A|\neg I)}$$

Now consider the impact of the false-alarm rate $P(A|\neg I)$ on $P(I|A)$. Even with a very good, true alarm-rate $P(A|I) = 0.8$, a seemingly good false-alarm rate $P(A|\neg I) = 0.0001$ yields $P(I|A) \approx 0.14$. That is, fewer than one in every seven alarms indicates a real intrusion! In systems where a security administrator investigates each alarm, this rate of false alarms is exceedingly wasteful and would quickly teach the administrator to ignore alarms.

This example illustrates a general principle for IDSs: For usability, an IDS must offer an extremely low false-alarm rate. Achieving a sufficiently low false-alarm rate is a serious challenge for anomaly-detection systems, because of the difficulties of adequately benchmarking normal system behavior. However, research continues to improve anomaly-detection techniques.

19.6.2 Auditing and Logging

A common method of intrusion detection is **audit-trail processing**, in which security-relevant events are logged to an audit trail and then matched against attack signatures (in signature-based detection) or analyzed for anomalous behavior (in anomaly detection). On UNIX systems, a simple pair of programs that can be used to create and analyze audit trails and initiate responses are `syslog` and `swatch`. The program `syslog` creates audit trails and provides a dispatching facility for security-relevant messages. The program `swatch` applies simple signature-based detection to `syslog` audit trails as they are created and initiates responses as indications of intrusions are found.

When `syslog` is installed on a UNIX system, a daemon process called `syslogd` is created at system startup. Process `syslogd` waits for messages from various possible sources and dispatches them as instructed in the `syslog.conf` configuration file (usually in the */etc/* directory). The process `syslogd` can be set up to accept messages from a range of different sources, by default including the streams log driver */dev/log*; the process can also accept messages that come over a network from other machines. The file `syslog.conf` consists of pairs, each containing a selector field and an action field. The selector field identifies the messages to which the corresponding action should be applied. The types of actions that can be applied to messages include sending the message to a file, to a list of users, to the `syslogd` daemons on other machines, or to a program via a UNIX pipe. In this way, `syslogd` provides a centralized facility through which various security-relevant messages can be dispatched.

The `swatch` program is available from http://swatch.sourceforge.net/. It processes messages dispatched to it by the `syslogd` daemon (or other logging programs) and initiates activities when certain patterns are detected. These messages need not be dispatched to `swatch` directly but may be written to a file that `swatch` reads and analyzes. The `swatch` program matches each audit message against regular expressions listed in a configuration file. With each regular expression, actions to be taken if a match occurs are also listed. Allowable actions include echoing a line to `swatch`'s controlling terminal, ringing a bell at `swatch`'s controlling terminal, sending a message to a user list via e-mail or the `write` command, or executing a program with arguments drawn from the audit message.

Each regular expression listed in the `swatch` configuration file can be viewed as a primitive signature for use in signature-based intrusion detection. For example, a useful signature might match any string containing "permission denied" and instruct that a bell signal be directed to `swatch`'s controlling terminal. However, the signatures supported by `swatch` are fairly rudimentary, since they are applied to only a single audit message at a time. Attack signatures made up of multiple actions that would typically be reflected across multiple audit messages will not be detected by this approach. Commercial audit-trail-processing tools tend to offer richer processing capabilities.

19.6.3 Tripwire

An example of a simple anomaly-detection tool is the **Tripwire file system** integrity-checking tool for UNIX, developed at Purdue University. Tripwire operates on the premise that many intrusions result in anomalous modification of system directories and files. For example, an attacker might modify the */etc/passwd* file of a system to enable the intruder to gain access easily in the future. An intruder might modify system programs, perhaps inserting copies with Trojan horses, or insert new programs into directories commonly found in user shell search paths. Or an intruder might remove system log files to cover his tracks. Tripwire is a tool to monitor file systems for added, deleted, or changed files and to alert system administrators to these modifications.

The operation of Tripwire is controlled by a configuration file tw.config that enumerates the directories and files to be monitored for changes, deletions, or additions. Each entry in this configuration file includes a selection mask to specify the file attributes (inode attributes) to monitor for changes. For example, the selection mask might specify that a file's permissions be monitored but its access time be ignored. In addition, the selection mask can instruct that the file contents—or, more specifically, the results of applying a predefined hash function to the contents of the file—be monitored for changes. Tripwire offers several collision resistant hash functions for this purpose, where a hash function f is collision-resistant if, given the result $f(x)$ when f is applied to an input file x, it is computationally infeasible to compute a different file x' such that $f(x') = f(x)$. Thus, monitoring the hash of a file for changes is as good as monitoring the file itself, but storing hashes of files requires far less room than copying the files themselves.

When run initially, Tripwire takes as input the tw.config file and computes a signature for each file or directory consisting of its monitored attributes (inode attributes and hash values). These signatures are stored in a database. When run subsequently, Tripwire inputs both tw.config and the previously stored database, recomputes the signature for each file or directory named in tw.config, and compares this signature with the signature (if any) in the previously computed database. Events reported to an administrator include any monitored file or directory whose signature differs from that in the database (a changed file), any file or directory in a monitored directory for which a signature does not exist in the database (an added file), and any signature in the database for which the corresponding file or directory no longer exists (a deleted file).

Although effective for a wide class of attacks, Tripwire does have limitations. Perhaps the most obvious is the need to protect the Tripwire program and its associated files, especially the database file, from unauthorized modification. For this reason, Tripwire and its associated files should be stored on some tamper-proof medium, such as a write-protected disk or a secure server where logins can be tightly controlled. Unfortunately, this makes it less convenient to update the database after authorized updates to monitored directories and files. A second limitation is that some security-relevant files—for example, system log files—are *supposed* to change over time, and Tripwire does not provide a way to distinguish between an authorized and unauthorized change. So, for example, an attack that modifies (without deleting) a system log that would normally change anyway would escape Tripwire's detection capabilities. The best Tripwire can do in this case is to detect certain obvious inconsistencies (for example, if the log file shrinks). Free and commercial versions of Tripwire are available from http://tripwire.com and httpd://tripwire.org.

19.6.4 System-Call Monitoring

A more recent and speculative form of anomaly detection is system-call monitoring. This approach monitors process system calls to detect in real time when a process is deviating from its expected system-call behavior. It leverages the fact that a program implicitly defines the sequences of system calls that it can make, as determined by the set of possible execution paths through the program. For large and complex programs, the set of possible system-call sequences will be enormous and may not be easily determined, much less stored explicitly. Nevertheless, this approach attempts to characterize "usual" system-call behavior in an abbreviated form so that actual system-call traces can be compared against this characterization to detect anomalous behavior. A type of intrusion that might be detected this way is an attack that *takes over* the process—for example, by exploiting a buffer-overflow vulnerability in the process's program—and then causes the process to execute the attacker's code rather than the original program code. If the attacker's code induces an anomalous system-call sequence, then the intrusion detection system should detect this and take action (for example, kill the process).

One example of this approach, for UNIX processes, was initiated at the University of New Mexico. In this approach, the "usual" system-call sequence for a program is generated by running the program on various inputs, both actual user inputs and inputs designed to elicit a range of behaviors from the program. The system-call sequences thus generated (ignoring parameters) are recorded. For example, one such sequence might be:

$$\texttt{open, read, mmap, mmap, open, getrlimit, mmap, close}$$

This sequence is then used to populate a table indicating, for each system call, which system calls can follow it at a distance of one, two, and so forth, up to some distance k. For example, suppose we choose $k = 3$. Then, examining the first open, we see that read follows at distance one and mmap follows at distances two and three. Similarly, mmap follows the read at distances one and two, and open follows at distance three. Performing this exercise for each system call, we obtain the table depicted in Figure 19.3.

This table is then stored. During subsequent executions of the program, the system-call sequence is compared with this table to detect discrepancies. For example, if the sequence

$$\texttt{open, read, mmap, open, open, getrlimit, mmap, close}$$

is observed (that is, one mmap is replaced with an open), then the following discrepancies are noted: open follows open at a distance of three; open follows

system call	distance = 1	distance = 2	distance = 3
open	read getrlimit	mmap	mmap close
read	mmap	mmap	open
mmap	mmap open close	open getrlimit	getrlimit mmap
getrlimit	mmap	close	
close			

Figure 19.3   Data structure derived from system-call sequence.

read at a distance of two; open follows open at a distance of one; and getrlimit follows open at a distance of two. Whether the IDS determines that this behavior indicates an intrusion might depend on the number of discrepancies observed—perhaps as a fraction of the total possible number of discrepancies —or on the particular system calls involved.

This approach and others like it have been applied primarily to root processes, such as sendmail, in an attempt to detect intrusions. Root processes are attractive targets for this technique because they typically have a limited set of behaviors and do not change often. In addition, they are common targets for attackers because of their privileged status and because, in the case of network services that accept communication over the network, they can easily be probed by attackers from a distance.

Although system-call monitoring techniques can be useful, an attacker may craft an attack that does not perturb the sequence of system calls enough to alert the IDS. For example, the attacker may have a copy of the software that he plans to attack and may try various intrusions until one is found that leaves the system-call sequence largely intact. Additional security can be achieved by extending these detection techniques to take into account the parameters of the system calls.

19.7 ■ Cryptography

In an isolated computer, the operating system can reliably determine the sender and recipient of all interprocess communication, since it controls all communication channels in the computer. In a network of computers, the situation is quite different. A networked computer receives bits *from the wire* with no immediate and reliable way of determining what machine or application sent those bits. Similarly, the computer sends bits onto the network with no way of knowing who might eventually receive them.

Commonly, network addresses are used to infer the potential senders and receivers of network messages. Network packets arrive with a source address, such as an IP address. And when a computer sends a message, it names the intended receiver by specifying a destination address. However, for applications where security matters, we are asking for trouble if we assume that the source or destination address of a packet reliably determines who sent or received that packet. A rogue computer can send a message with a falsified source address, and numerous computers other than the one specified by the destination address can (and typically do) receive a packet. For example, all of the routers on the way to the destination will *receive* the packet, too. How, then, is an operating system to decide whether to grant a request to write a file when it cannot trust the named source of the request? And how is it supposed to provide read protection for a file when it cannot determine who will receive the file contents it sends over the network?

It is generally considered infeasible to build a network of any scale in which the source and destination addresses of packets can be *trusted* in this sense. Therefore, the only alternative is somehow to eliminate the need to trust the network. This is the job of cryptography. Abstractly, **cryptography** is used to constrain the potential senders and receivers of a message. Modern cryptography is based on secrets called **keys** that are selectively distributed to computers in a network and used to process messages. Cryptography enables a recipient of a message to verify that the message was created by some computer possessing a certain key—the key is the *source* of the message. Similarly, a sender can encode its message so that only a computer with a certain key can decode the message, so that the key becomes the *destination*. Unlike network addresses, however, keys are designed so that it is computationally infeasible to derive them from the messages they were used to generate or from any other public information. Thus, they provide a much more trustworthy means of constraining senders and receivers of messages.

19.7.1 Authentication

Constraining the set of potential senders of a message is called *authentication*. An authentication algorithm enables the recipient of a message to verify that a message was created by some computer possessing a certain key. More precisely, an authentication algorithm consists of the following components:

- A set K of keys.

- A set M of messages.

- A set A of authenticators.

- A function $S : K \rightarrow (M \rightarrow A)$. That is, for each $k \in K$, $S(k)$ is a function for generating authenticators from messages. Both S and $S(k)$ for any k should be efficiently computable functions.

- A function $V : K \rightarrow (M \times A \rightarrow \{\texttt{true}, \texttt{false}\})$. That is, for each $k \in K$, $V(k)$ is a function for verifying authenticators on messages. Both V and $V(k)$ for any k should be efficiently computable functions.

The critical property that an authentication algorithm must possess is this: For a message m, a computer can generate an authenticator $a \in A$ such that $V(k)(m, a) = \texttt{true}$ only if it possesses $S(k)$. Thus, a computer holding $S(k)$ can generate authenticators on messages so that any other computer possessing $V(k)$ can verify them. However, a computer not holding $S(k)$ is unable to generate authenticators on messages that can be verified using $V(k)$. Since authenticators are generally exposed (for example, they are sent on the network with the messages themselves), it must not be feasible to derive $S(k)$ from the authenticators.

Authentication algorithms come in two main varieties. In a **message-authentication code (MAC)**, knowledge of $V(k)$ and knowledge of $S(k)$ are equivalent: one can be derived from the other. For this reason, it is as important to protect $V(k)$ as it is to protect $S(k)$. A simple example of a MAC defines $S(k)(m) = f(k, m)$, where f is a function that is one-way on its first argument (that is, its first argument cannot be derived from its output) and collision-resistant on its second (that is, it is infeasible to find an $m' \neq m$ such that $f(k, m) = f(k, m')$). A suitable verification algorithm is then $V(k)(m, a) \equiv (f(k, m) = a)$. Note that k is needed to compute both $S(k)$ and $V(k)$; that is, anyone able to compute one can compute the other.

The second main type of authentication algorithm is a **digital-signature algorithm**, and the authenticators thus produced are called *digital signatures*. In a digital-signature algorithm, it is computationally infeasible to derive $S(k)$ from $V(k)$; in particular, V is a one-way function. Thus, $V(k)$ need not be kept secret and can be widely distributed. For this reason, $V(k)$ is called the **public key**, and conversely $S(k)$ (or just k) is the **private key**. Here we describe one digital signature algorithm, known as *RSA* after the names of its inventors. In the RSA scheme, the key k is a pair $\langle d, N \rangle$, where N is the product of two large, randomly chosen prime numbers p and q (for example, p and q are 512 bits each). The signature algorithm is $S(\langle d, N \rangle)(m) = f(m)^d \bmod N$, where f is a collision-resistant function. The verification algorithm is then $V(\langle d, N \rangle)(m, a) \equiv (a^e \bmod N = f(m))$, where e satisfies $ed \bmod (p - 1)(q - 1) = 1$. It is widely believed to be computationally infeasible for a computer possessing $V(\langle d, N \rangle)$ (that is, possessing $\langle e, N \rangle$ but not d) to generate $S(\langle d, N \rangle)$ (that is, d).

19.7.2 Encryption

Encryption is a means for constraining the possible receivers of a message. Encryption is thus complementary to authentication, and to emphasize this we provide a parallel treatment of it. An encryption algorithm enables the sender of a message to ensure that only a computer possessing a certain key can read the message. More precisely, an encryption algorithm consists of the following components:

- A set K of keys.

- A set M of messages.

- A set C of ciphertexts.

- A function $E : K \rightarrow (M \rightarrow C)$. That is, for each $k \in K$, $E(k)$ is a function for generating ciphertexts from messages. Both E and $E(k)$ for any k should be efficiently computable functions.

- A function $D : K \rightarrow (C \rightarrow M)$. That is, for each $k \in K$, $D(k)$ is a function for generating messages from ciphertexts. Both D and $D(k)$ for any k should be efficiently computable functions.

The essential property that an encryption algorithm must provide is that, given a ciphertext $c \in C$, a computer can compute m such that $E(k)(m) = c$ only if it possesses $D(k)$. Thus, a computer holding $D(k)$ can decrypt ciphertexts to the plaintexts used to produce them. However, a computer not holding $D(k)$ is unable to decrypt ciphertexts. Since ciphertexts are generally exposed (for example, they are sent on the network), it is important that it be infeasible to derive $D(k)$ from the ciphertexts.

Just as there are two types of authentication algorithms, there are two main types of encryption algorithms. In the first type, called a **symmetric encryption algorithm**, $E(k)$ can be derived from $D(k)$ and vice versa. Therefore, the secrecy of $E(k)$ must be protected to the same extent as that of $D(k)$. For the past 20 years or so, the most commonly used symmetric encryption algorithm in the United States for civilian applications has been the **data-encryption standard (DES)** adopted by the National Institute of Standards and Technology (NIST). However, DES is now considered insecure for many applications because its keys, of 56 bits in length, can be exhaustively searched with moderate computing resources. NIST has since adopted a new encryption algorithm, called the **advanced encryption standard (AES)**, to replace the DES.

In an **asymmetric encryption algorithm**, it is computationally infeasible to derive $D(k)$ from $E(k)$, and so $E(k)$ need not be kept secret and can be widely disseminated; $E(k)$ is the public key, and $D(k)$ (or just k) is the private key. Interestingly, the mechanism underlying the RSA signature algorithm can also be used to yield an asymmetric encryption algorithm. Again, the key k is a pair $\langle d, N \rangle$, where N is the product of two large, randomly chosen prime numbers p and q. The encryption algorithm is $E(\langle d, N \rangle)(m) = m^e \bmod N$, where e, d and N are as before. The decryption algorithm is then $D(\langle d, N \rangle)(c) = c^d \bmod N$.

19.7.3 An Example: SSL

SSL 3.0 is a cryptographic protocol that enables two computers to communicate securely—that is, so that each can limit the sender and receiver of messages to the other. It is perhaps the most commonly used cryptographic protocol on the Internet today, since it is the standard protocol by which web browsers communicate securely with web servers. SSL is a complex protocol with many options. Here, we present only a single variation of it, and even then in a very simplified and abstract form, so as to maintain focus on its use of cryptographic primitives.

The SSL protocol is initiated by a *client* to communicate securely with a *server*. Prior to the protocol's use, the server s is assumed have obtained a **certificate**, denoted $cert_s$, from another party called a **certification authority** CA. This certificate is a structure containing the following:

- Various attributes attrs of the server, such as its unique *distinguished* name and its *common* (DNS) name

- A public encryption algorithm $E(k_s)$ for the server

- A validity interval interval during which the certificate should be considered valid

- A digital signature a on the above information by the CA—that is, $a = S(k_{CA})(\langle attrs, E(k_s), interval \rangle)$

In addition, prior to the protocol's use, the client is presumed to have obtained the public verification algorithm $V(k_{CA})$ for CA. In the case of the Web, the user's browser is shipped from its vendor containing the verification algorithms of certain certification authorities. The user can add or delete the verification algorithms for certification authorities as she chooses.

When a client c connects to s, it sends a 28-byte random value n_c to the server. s responds with a random value n_s of its own, plus its certificate $cert_s$. The client verifies that $V(k_{CA})(\langle attrs, E(k_s), interval \rangle, a) =$ true and that the current time is in the validity interval interval. If both of these tests are satisfied, then the client generates a random 46-byte **premaster secret** pms and sends cpms $= E(k_s)$(pms) to the server. The server recovers pms $= D(k_s)$(cpms). Now both the client and the server are in possession of n_c, n_s and pms, and each can compute a shared 48-byte **master secret** ms $= f(n_c, n_s, \text{pms})$, where f is a one-way and collision-resistant function. Only the server and client can compute ms, since only they know pms. Moreover, the dependence of ms on n_c and n_s ensures that ms is a *fresh* value—that is, a value that has not been used in a previous protocol run. At this point, the client and the server both compute the following keys from the master secret ms:

- A symmetric encryption key k_{cs}^{crypt} for encrypting messages from the client to the server

- A symmetric encryption key k_{sc}^{crypt} for encrypting messages from the server to the client

- A MAC generation key k_{cs}^{mac} for generating authenticators on messages from the client to the server

- A MAC generation key k_{sc}^{mac} for generating authenticators on messages from the server to the client

To send a message m to the server, the client sends

$$c = E(k_{cs}^{crypt})(\langle m, S(k_{cs}^{mac})(m)\rangle).$$

Upon receiving c, the server recovers

$$\langle m, a\rangle = D(k_{cs}^{crypt})(c)$$

and accepts m if $V(k_{cs}^{mac})(m, a) = $ true. Similarly, to send a message m to the client, the server sends

$$c = E(k_{sc}^{crypt})(\langle m, S(k_{sc}^{mac})(m)\rangle)$$

and the client recovers

$$\langle m, a\rangle = D(k_{sc}^{crypt})(c)$$

and accepts m if $V(k_{sc}^{mac})(m, a) = $ true.

   This protocol enables the server to limit the recipients of its messages to the client that generated pms and to limit the senders of the messages it accepts to that same client. Similarly, the client can limit the recipients of the messages it sends and the sender of the messages it accepts to the party that knows $S(k_s)$ (that is, the party that can decrypt pms). In many applications, such as web transactions, the client needs to verify the identity of the party that knows $S(k_s)$. This is one purpose of the certificate cert$_s$; in particular, the attrs field contains information that the client can use to determine the identity—for example, the domain name—of the server with which it is communicating. For applications in which the server also needs information about the client, SSL supports an option by which a client can send a certificate to the server.

19.7.4 Use of Cryptography

Network protocols are typically organized in **layers**, each layer acting as a client to the one below it. That is, when one protocol generates a message to send to its protocol peer on another machine, it hands its message to the protocol below it in the network-protocol stack for delivery to its peer on that machine. For example, in an IP network, TCP (a *transport-layer* protocol) acts as a client of IP (a *network-layer* protocol): TCP packets are passed down to IP for delivery to the TCP peer at the other end of the TCP connection. IP encapsulates the TCP packet in an IP packet, which it similarly passes down to the *data-link layer* to be transmitted across the network to its IP peer on the destination computer. This IP peer then delivers the TCP packet up to the TCP peer on that machine. All in all, the OSI Reference Model, which has been almost universally adopted for data networking, defines seven such protocol layers. Any good networking book will cover this in detail.

Cryptography can be inserted at almost any layer in this model. SSL (Section 19.7.3) provides security at the transport layer. Network-layer security that has been standardized (or **IPSec**) defines IP packet formats that allow the insertion of authenticators and the encryption of packet contents. IPSec is becoming widely used as the basis for **virtual private networks**. Numerous protocols also have been developed for applications to use.

Where is cryptographic protection best placed in a protocol stack? In general, there is no definitive answer. On the one hand, more protocols benefit from protections placed lower in the stack. For example, since IP packets encapsulate TCP packets, encryption of IP packets (using IPSec, for example) also hides the contents of the encapsulated TCP packets. Similarly, authenticators on IP packets detect the modification of contained TCP header information.

On the other hand, protection at lower layers in the protocol stack may give insufficient protection to higher-layer protocols. For example, an application server that runs over IPSec might be able to authenticate the client computers from which requests are received. However, to authenticate a user at a client computer, the server may need to use an application-level protocol—for example, the user may be required to type a password.

19.8 ■ Computer-Security Classifications

The U.S. Department of Defense Trusted Computer System Evaluation Criteria specify four divisions of security in systems: A, B, C, and D. The lowest-level classification is division D, or minimal protection. Division D comprises only one class and is used for systems that have failed to meet the requirements of any of the other security classes. For instance, MS-DOS and Windows 3.1 are in division D.

Division C, the next level of security, provides discretionary protection and accountability of users and their actions through the use of audit capabilities. Division C has two levels: C1 and C2. A C1-class system incorporates some form of controls that allow users to protect private information and to keep other users from accidentally reading or destroying their data. A C1 environment is one in which cooperating users access data at the same levels of sensitivity. Most versions of UNIX are C1 class.

The sum total of all protection systems within a computer system (hardware, software, firmware) that correctly enforce a security policy is known as a

Trusted Computer Base (TCB). The TCB of a C1 system controls access between users and files by allowing the user to specify and control sharing of objects by named individuals or defined groups. In addition, the TCB requires that the users identify themselves before they start any activities that the TCB is expected to mediate. This identification is accomplished via a protected mechanism or password; the TCB protects the authentication data so that they are inaccessible to unauthorized users.

A C2-class system adds an individual-level access control to the requirements of a C1 system. For example, access rights of a file can be specified to the level of a single individual. In addition, the system administrator can selectively audit the actions of any one or more users based on individual identity. The TCB also protects itself from modification of its code or data structures. In addition, no information produced by a prior user is available to another user who accesses a storage object that has been released back to the system. Some special, secure versions of UNIX have been certified at the C2 level.

Division-B mandatory-protection systems have all the properties of a class-C2 system; in addition, they attach a sensitivity label to each object. The B1-class TCB maintains the security label of each object in the system; the label is used for decisions pertaining to mandatory access control. For example, a user at the confidential level could not access a file at the more sensitive secret level. The TCB also denotes the sensitivity level at the top and bottom of each page of any human-readable output. In addition to the normal user-name –password authentication information, the TCB also maintains the clearance and authorizations of individual users and will support at least two levels of security. These levels are hierarchical, so that a user may access any objects that carry sensitivity labels equal to or lower than his security clearance. For example, a secret-level user could access a file at the confidential level in the absence of other access controls. Processes are also isolated through the use of distinct address spaces.

A B2-class system extends the sensitivity labels to each system resource, such as storage objects. Physical devices are assigned minimum- and maximum-security levels that the system uses to enforce constraints imposed by the physical environments in which the devices are located. In addition, a B2 system supports covert channels and the auditing of events that may lead to the exploitation of a covert channel.

A B3-class system allows the creation of access-control lists that denote users or groups *not* granted access to a given named object. The TCB also contains a mechanism to monitor events that may indicate a violation of security policy. The mechanism notifies the security administrator and, if necessary, terminates the event in the least disruptive manner.

The highest-level classification is division A. A class-A1 system is functionally equivalent to a B3 system architecturally, but it uses formal design specifications and verification techniques, granting a high degree of assurance that the TCB has been implemented correctly. A system beyond class A1 might be designed and developed in a trusted facility by trusted personnel.

The use of a TCB merely ensures that the system can enforce aspects of a security policy; the TCB does not specify what the policy should be. Typically, a given computing environment develops a security policy for **certification** and has the plan **accredited** by a security agency, such as the National Computer Security Center. Certain computing environments may require other certification, such as by TEMPEST, which guards against electronic eavesdropping. For example, a TEMPEST-certified system has terminals that are shielded to prevent electromagnetic fields from escaping. This shielding ensures that equipment outside the room or building where the terminal is housed cannot detect what information is being displayed by the terminal.

19.9 ■ An Example: Windows NT

Microsoft Windows NT is a general-purpose operating system designed to support a variety of security features and methods. In this section, we examine features that Windows NT uses to perform security functions. For more information and background on Windows NT, see Chapter 21.

The NT security model is based on the notion of **user accounts**. NT allows the creation of any number of user accounts, which can be grouped in any manner. Access to system objects can then be permitted or denied as desired. Users are identified to the system by a *unique* Security ID. When a user logs on, NT creates a **security access token** that includes the Security ID for the user, Security IDs for any groups of which the user is a member, and a list of any special privileges that the user has. Examples of special privileges include backing up files and directories, shutting down the computer, logging on interactively, and changing the system clock. Every process that NT runs on behalf of a user will receive a copy of the access token. The system uses the Security IDs in the access token to permit or deny access to system objects whenever the user, or a process on behalf of the user, attempts to access the object. Authentication of a user account is typically accomplished via a user name and password, although the modular design of NT allows the development of custom authentication packages. For example, a retinal (or eye) scanner might be used to verify that the user is who she says she is.

NT uses the idea of a subject to ensure that programs run by a user do not get greater access to the system than the user is authorized to have. A **subject** is used to track and manage permissions for each program that a user runs; it is composed of the user's access token and the program acting on behalf of the user. Since NT operates with a client–server model, two classes of subjects are used to control access. An example of a **simple subject** is the typical application program that a user executes after she logs on. The simple subject is assigned a **security context** based on the security access token of the user. A **server subject** is a process implemented as a protected server that uses the security context of the client when acting on the client's behalf. The technique whereby one process takes on the security attributes of another is called **impersonation**.

As mentioned in Section 19.5, auditing is a useful security technique. NT has built-in auditing that allows many common security threats to be monitored. Examples include failure auditing for logon and logoff events to detect random password break-ins, success auditing for logon and logoff events to detect logon activity at strange hours, success and failure write-access auditing for executable files to track a virus outbreak, and success and failure auditing for file access to detect access to sensitive files.

Security attributes of an object in NT are described by a **security descriptor**. The security descriptor contains the Security ID of the owner of the object (who can change the access permissions), a group Security ID used only by the POSIX subsystem, a discretionary access-control list that identifies which users or groups are allowed (and which are not allowed) access, and a system access-control list that controls which auditing messages the system will generate. For example, the security descriptor of the file *foo.bar* might have owner avi and this discretionary access-control list:

- avi—all access

- group cs—read–write access

- user cliff—no access.

In addition, it might have a system access-control list of audit writes by every-one.

An access-control list is composed of access-control entries that contain the Security ID of the individual and an access mask that defines all possi-ble actions on the object, with a value of AccessAllowed or AccessDenied for each action. Files in NT may have the following access types: ReadData, WriteData, AppendData, Execute, ReadExtendedAttribute, WriteEx-tendedAttribute, ReadAttributes, and WriteAttributes. We can see how this allows a fine degree of control over access to objects.

NT classifies objects as either container objects or noncontainer objects. **Container objects**, such as directories, can logically contain other objects. By default, when an object is created within a container object, the new object inherits permissions from the parent object. It does so as well if the user copies a file from one directory to a new directory—the file will inherit the permissions of the destination directory. **Noncontainer objects** inherit no other permissions.

If a permission is changed on a directory, however, the new permissions do not automatically apply to existing files and subdirectories; the user may explicitly apply them if she so desires. Also, if the user moves a file into a new directory, the current permissions of the file move with it.

The system administrator can prohibit printing to a printer on the system for all or part of a day and can use the NT Performance Monitor to help her spot approaching problems. In general, NT does a good job of providing features to help ensure a secure computing environment. Many of these features are not enabled by default, however. For a real multiuser environment, the system administrator should formulate a security plan and implement it, using the features that NT provides.

19.10 ■ Summary

Protection is an internal problem. Security, in contrast, must consider both the computer system and the environment—people, buildings, businesses, valuable objects, and threats—within which the system is used.

The data stored in the computer system must be protected from unauthorized access, malicious destruction or alteration, and accidental introduction of inconsistency. It is easier to protect against accidental loss of data consistency than to protect against malicious access to the data. Absolute protection of the information stored in a computer system from malicious abuse is not possible; but the cost to the perpetrator can be made sufficiently high to deter most, if not all, attempts to access that information without proper authority.

Authentication methods are used to identify legitimate users of a system. In addition to standard user-name and password protection, several authentication methods are used. One-time passwords, for example, change from session to session to avoid replay attacks. Two-factor authentication requires two forms of authentication, such as a hardware calculator with an activation PIN. Along with biometric devices, these methods greatly decrease the chance of authentication forgery.

Several types of attacks can be launched against individual computers or the masses. Stack- and buffer-overflow techniques allow successful attackers to change their level of system access. Viruses and worms are self-perpetuating, sometimes infecting thousands of computers. Denial-of-service attacks prevent legitimate use of target systems.

Methods of preventing or detecting security incidents include intrusion-detection systems, auditing and logging of system events, monitoring of system software changes, and system-call monitoring. Cryptography can be used both within a system and between systems to prevent interception of information by hackers.

■ Exercises

19.1 A password may become known to other users in a variety of ways. Is there a simple method for detecting that such an event has occurred? Explain your answer.

19.2 The list of all passwords is kept within the operating system. Thus, if a user manages to read this list, password protection is no longer provided. Suggest a scheme that will avoid this problem. (Hint: Use different internal and external representations.)

19.3 An experimental addition to UNIX allows a user to connect a *watchdog* program to a file. The watchdog is invoked whenever a program requests access to the file. The watchdog then either grants or denies access to the file. Discuss two pros and two cons of using watchdogs for security.

19.4 The UNIX program COPS scans a given system for possible security holes and alerts the user to possible problems. What are two potential hazards of using such a system for security? How can these problems be limited or eliminated?

19.5 Discuss a means by which managers of systems connected to the Internet could have designed their systems to limit or eliminate the damage done by a worm. What are the drawbacks of making the change that you suggest?

19.6 Argue for or against the judicial sentence handed down against Robert Morris, Jr., for his creation and execution of the Internet worm.

19.7 Make a list of six security concerns for a bank's computer system. For each item on your list, state whether this concern relates to physical, human, or operating-system security.

19.8 What are two advantages of encrypting data stored in the computer system?

Bibliographical Notes

General discussions concerning security are given by Hsiao et al. [1979], Landwehr [1981], Denning [1982], Pfleeger [1989], and Russell and Gangemi [1991]. Also of general interest is the text by Lobel [1986].

Issues concerning the design and verification of secure systems are discussed by Rushby [1981] and by Silverman [1983]. A security kernel for a multiprocessor microcomputer is described by Schell [1983]. A distributed secure system is described by Rushby and Randell [1983].

Morris and Thompson [1979] discuss password security. Morshedian [1986] presents methods to fight password pirates. Password authentication with insecure communications is considered by Lamport [1981]. The issue of password cracking is discussed by Seely [1989]. Computer break-ins are discussed by Lehmann [1987] and by Reid [1987].

Discussions concerning UNIX security are offered by Grampp and Morris [1984], Wood and Kochan [1985], Farrow [1986b], Farrow [1986a], Filipski and Hanko [1986], Hecht et al. [1988], Kramer [1988], and Garfinkel and Spafford [1991]. Bershad and Pinkerton [1988] present the watchdog extension to BSDUNIX. The COPS security-scanning package for UNIX was written by Farmer at Purdue University. It is available to users on the Internet via the FTP program from host ftp.uu.net in directory /pub/security/cops.

Spafford [1989] presents a detailed technical discussion of the Internet worm. The Spafford article appears with three others in a special section on the Internet worm in *Communications of the ACM* (Volume 32, Number 6, June 1989).

Diffie and Hellman [1976] and Diffie and Hellman [1979] were the first researchers to propose the use of the public-key encryption scheme. The algorithm presented in Section 19.7.2 is based on the public-key encryption scheme; it was developed by Rivest et al. [1978]. Lempel [1979], Simmons [1979], Gifford [1982], Denning [1982], and Ahituv et al. [1987] explore the use of cryptography in computer systems. Discussions concerning protection of digital signatures are offered by Akl [1983], Davies [1983], Denning [1983], and Denning [1984].

The U.S. federal government is, of course, concerned about security. The *Department of Defense Trusted Computer System Evaluation Criteria* DoD [1985], known also as the *Orange Book,* describes a set of security levels and the features that an operating system must have to qualify for each security rating. Reading it is a good starting point for understanding security concerns. The *Microsoft Windows NT Workstation Resource Kit* (Microsoft [1996]) describes the security model of NT and how to use that model.

The RSA algorithm is presented in Rivest et al. [1978]. Information about NIST's AES activities can be found at http://www.nist.gov/aes/; information about other cryptographic standards for the United States can also be found at that site. More complete coverage of SSL 3.0 can be found at http://home.netscape.com/eng/ssl3/. In 1999, SSL 3.0 was modified slightly and presented in an IETF Request for Comments (RFC) under the name TLS.

The example in Section 19.6 illustrating the impact of false-alarm rate on the effectiveness of IDSs is based on Axelsson [1999]. A more complete description of the swatch program and its use with syslog can be found in Hansen and Atkins [1993]. The description of Tripwire in Section 19.6.3 is based on Kim and Spafford [1993]. The description and example in Section 19.6.4 are taken from Forrest et al. [1996].

Part Seven

CASE STUDIES

We can now integrate the concepts described in this book by describing real operating systems. Two such systems are covered in great detail—Linux and Windows XP. We chose Linux for several reasons: it is popular, it is freely available, and it has a representation of a full-featured UNIX system. This provides a student of operating systems an opportunity to read—and modify—*real* operating system source code.

We also cover Windows XP in great detail. This recent operating system from Microsoft is gaining popularity, not only for the stand-alone-machine market, but also in the workgroup–server market. We chose Windows XP because it provides an opportunity for us to study a modern operating system that has a design and implementation drastically different from those of UNIX.

In addition, we briefly discuss other highly influential operating systems. We have chosen the order of presentation to highlight the similarities and differences among the systems; it is not strictly chronological and does not reflect the relative importance of the system.

Finally, we provide on-line coverage of three other systems. The FreeBSD system is another UNIX system. However, whereas Linux adopted the approach of combining features from several UNIX systems, FreeBSD is based upon the BSD model of UNIX. Like Linux, FreeBSD source code is freely available. The Mach operating system is a modern operating system that provides compatibility with BSD UNIX. Windows 2000 is another modern operating system from Microsoft for Intel Pentium and later microprocessors, which is compatible with MS-DOS and Microsoft Windows applications.

Chapter 20

THE LINUX
SYSTEM

Appendix A discusses the internal workings of the 4.3BSD operating system. BSD is just one of the UNIX-like systems. Linux is another UNIX-like system that has gained popularity in recent years. In this chapter, we look at the history and development of Linux, and cover the user and programmer interfaces that Linux presents—interfaces that owe a great deal to the UNIX tradition. We also discuss the internal methods by which Linux implements these interfaces. However, since Linux has been designed to run as many standard UNIX applications as possible, it has much in common with existing UNIX implementations. We do not duplicate the basic description of UNIX given in Appendix A.

Linux is a rapidly evolving operating system. This chapter describes specifically the Linux 2.2 kernel, which was released in January, 1999.

20.1 ■ History

Linux looks and feels much like any other UNIX system; indeed, UNIX compatibility has been a major design goal of the Linux project. However, Linux is much younger than most UNIX systems. Its development began in 1991, when a Finnish student, Linus Torvalds, wrote and christened **Linux**, a small but self-contained kernel for the 80386 processor, the first true 32-bit processor in Intel's range of PC-compatible CPUs.

Early in its development, the Linux source code was made available free on the Internet. As a result, Linux's history has been one of collaboration by many users from all around the world, corresponding almost exclusively over the Internet. From an initial kernel that partially implemented a small subset of the UNIX system services, the Linux system has grown to include much UNIX functionality.

In its early days, Linux development revolved largely around the central operating-system kernel—the core, privileged executive that manages all system resources and that interacts directly with the computer hardware. We need much more than this kernel to produce a full operating system, of course. It is useful to make the distinction between the Linux kernel and a Linux system. The **Linux kernel** is an entirely original piece of software developed from scratch by the Linux community. The **Linux system**, as we know it today, includes a multitude of components, some written from scratch, others borrowed from other development projects, and others created in collaboration with other teams.

The basic Linux system is a standard environment for applications and user programming, but it does not enforce any standard means of managing the available functionality as a whole. As Linux has matured, there has been a need for another layer of functionality on top of the Linux system. A **Linux distribution** includes all the standard components of the Linux system, plus a set of administrative tools to simplify the initial installation and subsequent upgrading of Linux, and to manage installation and deinstallation of other packages on the system. A modern distribution also typically includes tools for management of file systems, creation and management of user accounts, administration of networks, and so on.

20.1.1 The Linux Kernel

The first Linux kernel released to the public was Version 0.01, dated May 14, 1991. It had no networking, ran on only 80386-compatible Intel processors and PC hardware, and had extremely limited device-driver support. The virtual-memory subsystem was also fairly basic and included no support for memory-mapped files; however, even this early incarnation supported shared pages with copy-on-write. The only file system supported was the Minix file system —the first Linux kernels were cross-developed on a Minix platform. However, the kernel did implement proper UNIX processes with protected address spaces.

The next milestone version, Linux 1.0, was released on March 14, 1994. This release culminated three years of rapid development of the Linux kernel. Perhaps the single biggest new feature was networking: 1.0 included support for UNIX's standard TCP/IP networking protocols, as well as a BSD-compatible socket interface for networking programming. Device-driver support was added for running IP over an Ethernet or (using PPP or SLIP protocols) over serial lines or modems.

The 1.0 kernel also included a new, much enhanced file system without the limitations of the original Minix file system, and supported a range of SCSI controllers for high-performance disk access. The developers extended the virtual-memory subsystem to support paging to swap files and memory mapping of arbitrary files (but only read-only memory mapping was implemented in 1.0).

A range of extra hardware support was also included in this release. Although still restricted to the Intel PC platform, hardware support had grown to include floppy-disk and CD-ROM devices, as well as sound cards, a range of mice, and international keyboards. Floating-point emulation was also provided in the kernel for 80386 users who had no 80387 math coprocessor, and System V UNIX-style **interprocess communication (IPC)**, including shared memory, semaphores, and message queues, was implemented. Simple support for dynamically loadable and unloadable kernel modules was also provided.

At this point, development started on the 1.1 kernel stream, but numerous bug-fix patches were released subsequently against 1.0. This pattern was adopted as the standard numbering convention for Linux kernels: Kernels with an odd minor-version number such as 1.1, 1.3, or 2.1 are **development kernels**; even-numbered minor-version numbers are stable, **production kernels**. Updates against the stable kernels are intended as only remedial versions, whereas the development kernels may include newer and relatively untested functionality.

In March, 1995, the 1.2 kernel was released. This release did not offer nearly the same improvement in functionality as the 1.0 release, but it did include support for a much wider variety of hardware, including the new PCI hardware bus architecture. Developers added another PC-specific feature—support for the 80386 CPU's virtual 8086 mode—to allow emulation of the DOS operating system for PC computers. They updated the networking stack to provide support for the IPX protocol, and made the IP implementation more complete by including accounting and firewalling functionality.

The 1.2 kernel also was the final PC-only Linux kernel. The source distribution for Linux 1.2 included partially implemented support for SPARC, Alpha, and MIPS CPUs, but full integration of these other architectures did not begin until after the 1.2 stable kernel was released.

The Linux 1.2 release concentrated on wider hardware support and more complete implementations of existing functionality. Much new functionality was under development at the time, but integration of the new code into the main kernel source code had been deferred until after the stable 1.2 kernel had been released. As a result, the 1.3 development stream saw a great deal of new functionality added to the kernel.

This work was finally released as Linux 2.0 in June, 1996. This release was given a major version-number increment on account of two major new capabilities: support for multiple architectures, including a fully 64-bit native Alpha port, and support for multiprocessor architectures. Linux distributions based on 2.0 are also available for the Motorola 68000-series processors and for Sun's SPARC systems. A derived version of Linux running on top of the Mach Microkernel also runs on PC and PowerMac systems.

The changes in 2.0 did not stop there. The memory-management code was substantially improved to provide a unified cache for file-system data independent of the caching of block devices. As a result of this change, the kernel offered greatly increased file-system and virtual-memory performance. For the first time, file-system caching was extended to networked file systems, and writable memory-mapped regions also were supported.

The 2.0 kernel also included much improved TCP/IP performance, and a number of new networking protocols were added, including AppleTalk, AX.25 amateur radio networking, and ISDN support. The ability to mount remote Netware and SMB (Microsoft LanManager) network volumes was added.

Other major improvements in 2.0 were support for internal kernel threads, for handling dependencies between loadable modules, and for automatic loading of modules on demand. Dynamic configuration of the kernel at run time was much improved through a new, standardized configuration interface. Additional, unrelated new features included file-system quotas and POSIX-compatible real-time process-scheduling classes.

In January, 1999, Linux 2.2 was released and continued the improvements added by Linux 2.0. A port for UltraSPARC systems was added. Networking was enhanced with more flexible firewalling, better routing and traffic management, as well as support for TCP large window and selective acks. Acorn, Apple, and NT disks can now be read and NFS was enhanced and a kernel-mode NFS daemon was added. Signal handling, interrupts, and some I/O are now locked at a finer level than before to improve SMP performance.

20.1.2 The Linux System

In many ways, the Linux kernel forms the core of the Linux project, but other components make up the complete Linux operating system. Whereas the Linux kernel is composed entirely of code written from scratch specifically for the Linux project, much of the supporting software that makes up the Linux system is not exclusive to Linux but is common to a number of UNIX-like operating systems. In particular, Linux uses many tools developed as part of Berkeley's BSD operating system, MIT's X Window System, and the Free Software Foundation's GNU project.

This sharing of tools has worked in both directions. The main system libraries of Linux were originated by the GNU project, but the Linux community greatly improved the libraries by addressing omissions, inefficiencies, and bugs. Other components such as the **GNU C compiler (gcc)** were already of sufficiently high quality to be used directly in Linux. The networking-administration tools under Linux were derived from code first developed for 4.3BSD, but more recent BSD derivatives such as FreeBSD have borrowed code from Linux in return, such as the Intel floating-point-emulation math library and the PC sound-hardware device drivers.

The Linux system as a whole is maintained by a loose network of developers collaborating over the Internet, with small groups or individuals having responsibility for maintaining the integrity of specific components. A small number of public Internet file-transfer-protocol (ftp) archive sites act as de facto standard repositories for these components. The **File System Hierarchy Standard** document is also maintained by the Linux community as a means of keeping compatibility across the various system components. This standard specifies the overall layout of a standard Linux file system; it determines under which directory names configuration files, libraries, system binaries, and run-time data files should be stored.

20.1.3 Linux Distributions

In theory, anybody can install a Linux system by fetching the latest revisions of the necessary system components from the ftp sites and compiling them. In Linux's early days, this operation was often precisely the one that a Linux user had to carry out. As Linux has matured, however, various individuals and groups have attempted to make this job less painful by providing a standard, precompiled set of packages for easy installation.

These collections, or distributions, include much more than just the basic Linux system. They typically include extra system-installation and management utilities, as well as precompiled and ready-to-install packages of many of the common UNIX tools, such as news servers, web browsers, text-processing and editing tools, and even games.

The first distributions managed these packages by simply providing a means of unpacking all the files into the appropriate places. One of the important contributions of modern distributions, however, is advanced package management. Today's Linux distributions include a package-tracking database that allows packages to be installed, upgraded, or removed painlessly.

In the early days of Linux, the SLS distribution was the first collection of Linux packages that was recognizable as a complete distribution. Although it could be installed as a single entity, SLS lacked the package-management tools now expected of Linux distributions. The **Slackware** distribution represented a great improvement in overall quality, despite also having poor package management; it is still one of the most widely installed distributions in the Linux community.

Since Slackware's release, a large number of commercial and noncommercial Linux distributions have become available. **Red Hat** and **Debian** are particularly popular distributions from a commercial Linux support company and from the free-software Linux community, respectively. Other commercially supported versions of Linux include distributions from **Caldera, Craftworks,** and **WorkGroup Solutions**. A large Linux following in Germany has resulted in several dedicated German-language distributions, including versions from **SuSE** and **Unifix**. There are too many Linux distributions in circulation for us to list here. The variety of distributions does not prohibit compatibility across Linux distributions. The RPM package file format is used, or at least understood, by the majority of distributions, and commercial applications distributed in this format can be installed and run on any distribution that can accept RPM files.

20.1.4 Linux Licensing

The Linux kernel is distributed under the GNU General Public License (GPL), the terms of which are set out by the Free Software Foundation. Linux is not public-domain software: **Public domain** implies that the authors have waived copyright over the software, but copyright over Linux code is still held by the code's various authors. Linux is *free* software, however, in the sense that people can copy it, modify it, use it in any manner they want, and give away their own copies, without any restrictions.

The main implications of Linux's licensing terms are that anybody using Linux, or creating her own derivative of Linux (a legitimate exercise), cannot make the derived product proprietary. Software released under the GPL cannot be redistributed as a binary-only product. If you release software that includes any components covered by the GPL, then, under the GPL, you must make source code available alongside any binary distributions. (This restriction does not prohibit making—or even selling—binary-only software distributions, as long as anybody who receives binaries is also given the opportunity to get source code too, for a reasonable distribution charge.)

20.2 ■ Design Principles

In its overall design, Linux resembles any other traditional, nonmicrokernel UNIX implementation. It is a multiuser, multitasking system with a full set of UNIX-compatible tools. Linux's file system adheres to traditional UNIX semantics, and the standard UNIX networking model is implemented fully. The internal details of Linux's design have been influenced heavily by the history of this operating system's development.

Although Linux runs on a wide variety of platforms, it was developed exclusively on PC architecture. A great deal of that early development was carried out by individual enthusiasts, rather than by well-funded development or research facilities, so from the start Linux attempted to squeeze as much functionality as possible from limited resources. Today, Linux can run happily on a multiprocessor machine with hundreds of megabytes of main memory and many gigabytes of disk space, but it is still capable of operating usefully in under 4 MB of RAM.

As PCs became more powerful and as memory and hard disks became cheaper, the original, minimalist Linux kernels grew to implement more UNIX functionality. Speed and efficiency are still important design goals, but much of the recent and current work on Linux has concentrated on a third major design goal: standardization. One of the prices paid for the diversity of UNIX implementations currently available is that source code written for one flavor may not necessarily compile or run correctly on another. Even when the same system calls are present on two different UNIX systems, they do not necessarily behave in exactly the same way. The POSIX standards comprise a set of specifications of different aspects of operating-system behavior. There are POSIX documents for common operating-system functionality and for extensions such as process threads and real-time operations. Linux is designed to be compliant with the relevant POSIX documents; at least two Linux distributions have achieved official POSIX certification.

Because it presents standard interfaces to both the programmer and the user, Linux presents few surprises to anybody familiar with UNIX. We do not detail these interfaces under Linux. The sections on the programmer interface (Section A.3) and user interface (Section A.4) of 4.3BSD apply equally well to Linux. By default, however, the Linux programming interface adheres to SVR4 UNIX semantics, rather than to BSD behavior. A separate set of libraries is available to implement BSD semantics in places where the two behaviors are significantly different.

Many other standards in the UNIX world exist, but full certification of Linux against them is sometimes slowed because they are often available only for a fee, and the expense involved in certifying an operating system's compliance with most standards is substantial. However, supporting a wide base of applications is important for any operating system, so implementation of standards is a major goal for Linux development even if the implementation is not formally certified. In addition to the basic POSIX standard, Linux currently supports the POSIX threading extensions and a subset of the POSIX extensions for real-time process control.

20.2.1 Components of a Linux System

The Linux system is composed of three main bodies of code, in line with most traditional UNIX implementations:

1. **Kernel:** The kernel is responsible for maintaining all the important abstractions of the operating system, including such things as virtual memory and processes.

2. **System libraries:** The system libraries define a standard set of functions through which applications can interact with the kernel, and that implement much of the operating-system functionality that does not need the full privileges of kernel code.

3. **System utilities:** The system utilities are programs that perform individual, specialized management tasks. Some system utilities may be invoked just once to initialize and configure some aspect of the system; others—known

as *daemons* in UNIX terminology—may run permanently, handling such tasks as responding to incoming network connections, accepting logon requests from terminals, or updating log files.

Figure 20.1 illustrates the various components that make up a full Linux system. The most important distinction here is between the kernel and everything else. All the kernel code executes in the processor's privileged mode with full access to all the physical resources of the computer. Linux refers to this privileged mode as **kernel mode**, equivalent to the monitor mode described in Section 2.5.1. Under Linux, no user-mode code is built into the kernel. Any operating-system-support code that does not need to run in kernel mode is placed into the system libraries instead.

Although various modern operating systems have adopted a message-passing architecture for their kernel internals, Linux retains UNIX's historical model: The kernel is created as a single, monolithic binary. The main reason is to improve performance: Because all kernel code and data structures are kept in a single address space, no context switches are necessary when a process calls an operating-system function or when a hardware interrupt is delivered. Not only the core scheduling and virtual-memory code occupies this address space; *all* kernel code, including all device drivers, file systems, and networking code, is present in the same single address space.

Just because all the kernel shares this same melting pot does not mean there is no scope for modularity. In the same way that user applications can load shared libraries at run time to pull in a needed piece of code, so the Linux kernel can load (and unload) modules dynamically at run time. The kernel does not necessarily need to know in advance which modules may be loaded—they are truly independent loadable components.

The Linux kernel forms the core of the Linux operating system. It provides all the functionality necessary to run processes, and it provides system services to give arbitrated and protected access to hardware resources. The kernel implements all the features required to qualify as an operating system. On

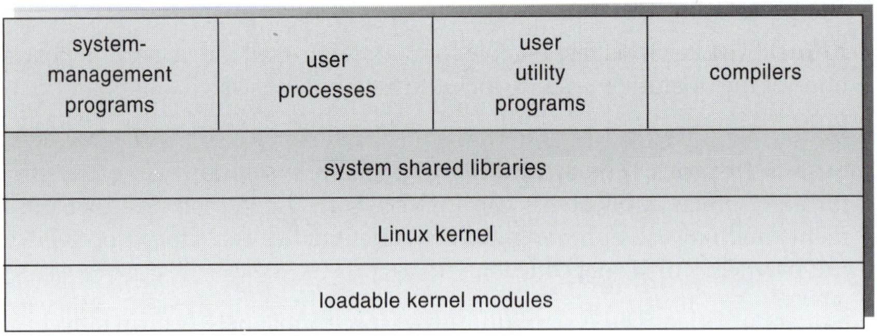

system- management programs	user processes	user utility programs	compilers
system shared libraries			
Linux kernel			
loadable kernel modules			

Figure 20.1   Components of the Linux system.

its own, however, the operating system provided by the Linux kernel looks nothing like a UNIX system. It is missing many of the extra features of UNIX, and the features that it does provide are not necessarily in the format in which a UNIX application expects them to appear. The operating-system interface visible to running applications is not maintained directly by the kernel. Rather, applications make calls to the system libraries, which in turn call the operating-system services as necessary.

The system libraries provide many types of functionality. At the simplest level, they allow applications to make kernel-system-service requests. Making a system call involves transferring control from unprivileged user mode to privileged kernel mode; the details of this transfer vary from architecture to architecture. The libraries take care of collecting the system-call arguments and, if necessary, arranging those arguments in the special form necessary to make the system call.

The libraries may also provide more complex versions of the basic system calls. For example, the C language's buffered file-handling functions are all implemented in the system libraries, providing more advanced control of file I/O than the basic kernel system calls. The libraries also provide routines that do not correspond to system calls at all, such as sorting algorithms, mathematical functions, and string-manipulation routines. All the functions necessary to support the running of UNIX or POSIX applications are implemented here in the system libraries.

The Linux system includes a wide variety of user-mode programs—both system utilities and user utilities. The system utilities include all the programs necessary to initialize the system, such as those to configure network devices or to load kernel modules. Continually running server programs also count as system utilities; such programs handle user login requests, incoming network connections, and the printer queues.

Not all the standard utilities serve key system-administration functions. The UNIX user environment contains a large number of standard utilities to do simple everyday tasks, such as listing directories, moving and deleting files, or displaying the contents of a file. More complex utilities can perform text-processing functions, such as sorting textual data or performing pattern searches on input text. Together, these utilities form a standard toolset that users can expect on any UNIX system; although they do not perform any operating-system function, they are an important part of the basic Linux system.

20.3 ■ Kernel Modules

The Linux kernel has the ability to load and unload arbitrary sections of kernel code on demand. These loadable kernel modules run in privileged kernel mode, and as a consequence have full access to all the hardware capabilities of the machine on which they run. In theory, there is no restriction on what a kernel module is allowed to do; typically, a module might implement a device driver, a file system, or a networking protocol.

Kernel modules are convenient for several reasons. Linux's source code is free, so anybody wanting to write kernel code is able to compile a modified kernel and to reboot to load that new functionality; however, recompiling, relinking, and reloading the entire kernel is a cumbersome cycle to undertake when you are developing a new driver. If you use kernel modules, you do not have to make a new kernel to test a new driver—the driver may be compiled on its own and loaded into the already-running kernel. Of course, once a new driver is written, it can be distributed as a module so that other users can benefit from it without having to rebuild their kernels.

This latter point has another implication. Because it is covered by the GPL license, the Linux kernel cannot be released with proprietary components added to it, unless those new components are also released under the GPL and the source code for them is made available on demand. The kernel's module interface allows third parties to write and distribute, on their own terms, device drivers or file systems that could not be distributed under the GPL.

Kernel modules allow a Linux system to be set up with a standard, minimal kernel, without any extra device drivers built in. Any device drivers that the user needs can be either loaded explicitly by the system at startup, or loaded automatically by the system on demand and unloaded when not in use. For example, a CD-ROM driver might be loaded when a CD is mounted, and unloaded from memory when the CD is dismounted from the file system.

The module support under Linux has three components:

1. The **module management** allows modules to be loaded into memory and to talk to the rest of the kernel.

2. The **driver registration** allows modules to tell the rest of the kernel that a new driver has become available.

3. A **conflict-resolution mechanism** allows different device drivers to reserve hardware resources and to protect those resources from accidental use by another driver.

20.3.1 Module Management

Loading a module requires more than just loading its binary contents into kernel memory. The system must also make sure that any references the module makes to kernel symbols or entry points get updated to point to the correct locations in the kernel's address space. Linux deals with this reference updating by splitting the job of module loading into two separate sections: the management of sections of module code in kernel memory, and the handling of symbols that modules are allowed to reference.

Linux maintains an internal symbol table in the kernel. This symbol table does not contain the full set of symbols defined in the kernel during the latter's compilation: rather, a symbol must be exported explicitly by the kernel. The set of exported symbols constitutes a well-defined interface by which a module may interact with the kernel.

Although exporting symbols from a kernel function requires an explicit request by the programmer, no special effort is needed to import those symbols into a module. A module writer just uses the standard external linking of the C language: Any external symbols referenced by the module but not declared by it are simply marked as unresolved in the final module binary produced by the compiler. When a module is to be loaded into the kernel, a system utility first scans the module for these unresolved references. All symbols that still need to be resolved are looked up in the kernel's symbol table, and the correct addresses of those symbols in the currently running kernel are substituted into the module's code. Only then is the module passed to the kernel for loading. If the system utility cannot resolve any references in the module by looking them up in the kernel's symbol table, then the module is rejected.

The loading of the module is performed in two stages. First, the module-loader utility asks the kernel to reserve a continuous area of virtual kernel memory for the module. The kernel returns the address of the memory allocated, and the loader utility can use this address to relocate the module's machine code to the correct loading address. A second system call then passes the module, plus any symbol table that the new module wants to export, to the kernel. The module itself is now copied verbatim into the previously allocated space, and the kernel's symbol table is updated with the new symbols for possible use by other modules not yet loaded.

The final module-management component is the module requestor. The kernel defines a communication interface to which a module-management program can connect. With this connection established, the kernel will inform the management process whenever a process requests a device driver, file system, or network service that is not currently loaded, and will give the manager the opportunity to load that service. The original service request will complete once the module is loaded. The manager process regularly queries the kernel to see whether a dynamically loaded module is still in use, and unloads that module when it is no longer actively needed.

20.3.2 Driver Registration

Once a module is loaded, it remains no more than an isolated region of memory unless it lets the rest of the kernel know what new functionality it provides. The kernel maintains dynamic tables of all known drivers, and provides a set of routines to allow drivers to be added to or removed from these tables at any time. The kernel makes sure that it calls a module's startup routine when that module is loaded, and calls the module's cleanup routine before that module is unloaded: These routines are responsible for registering the module's functionality.

A module may register many types of drivers. A single module may register drivers on any or all these types, and may register more than one driver if it wishes. For example, a device driver might want to register two separate mechanisms for accessing the device. Registration tables include the following items:

- **Device drivers:** These drivers include character devices (such as printers, terminals, or mice), block devices (including all disk drives), and network interface devices.

- **File systems:** The file system may be anything that implements Linux's virtual-file-system calling routines. It might implement a format for storing files on a disk, but it might equally well be a network file system, such as NFS, or a virtual file system whose contents are generated on demand, such as Linux's *proc* file system.

- **Network protocols:** A module may implement an entire networking protocol, such as IPX, or simply a new set of packet-filtering rules for a network firewall.

- **Binary format:** This format specifies a way of recognizing, and loading, a new type of executable file.

In addition, a module can register a new set of entries in the *sysctl* and */proc* tables, to allow that module to be configured dynamically (Section 20.7.3).

20.3.3 Conflict Resolution

Commercial UNIX implementations are usually sold to run on a vendor's own hardware. One advantage of a single-supplier solution is that the software vendor has a good idea about what hardware configurations are possible. IBM PC hardware, on the other hand, comes in a vast number of configurations, with large numbers of possible drivers for devices such as network cards, SCSI controllers, and video-display adapters. The problem of managing the hardware configuration becomes more severe when modular device drivers are supported, since the currently active set of devices becomes dynamically variable.

Linux provides a central conflict-resolution mechanism to help arbitrate access to certain hardware resources. Its aims are as follows:

- To prevent modules from clashing over access to hardware resources

- To prevent **autoprobes**—device-driver probes that auto-detect device configuration—from interfering with existing device drivers

- To resolve conflicts among multiple drivers trying to access the same hardware; for example, the parallel printer driver and parallel-line IP (PLIP) network driver might both try to talk to the parallel printer port

To these ends, the kernel maintains lists of allocated hardware resources. The PC has a limited number of possible I/O ports (addresses in its hardware I/O address space), interrupt lines, and DMA channels; when any device driver wants to access such a resource, it is expected to reserve the resource with the kernel database first. This requirement incidentally allows the system administrator to determine exactly which resources have been allocated by which driver at any given point.

A module is expected to use this mechanism to reserve in advance any hardware resources that it expects to use. If the reservation is rejected because the resource is not present or is already in use, then it is up to the module to decide how to proceed. It may fail its initialization and request that it be unloaded if it cannot continue, or it may carry on, using alternative hardware resources.

20.4 ■ Process Management

A process is the basic context within which all user-requested activity is serviced within the operating system. To be compatible with other UNIX systems, Linux must use a process model similar to those of other versions of UNIX. Linux operates differently from UNIX in a few key places, however. In this section, we review the traditional UNIX process model from Section A.3.2 and introduce Linux's own threading model.

20.4.1 The Fork/Exec Process Model

The basic principle of UNIX process management is to separate two distinct operations: the creation of processes and the running of a new program. A new process is created by the fork system call, and a new program is run after a call to execve. These are two distinctly separate functions. A new process may be created with fork without a new program being run—the new subprocess simply continues to execute exactly the same program that the first, parent process was running. Equally, running a new program does not require that a new process be created first: Any process may call execve at any time. The currently running program is immediately terminated, and the new program starts executing in the context of the existing process.

This model has the advantage of great simplicity. Rather than having to specify every detail of the environment of a new program in the system call that runs that program, new programs simply run in their existing environment. If a parent process wishes to modify the environment in which a new program is to be run, it can fork and then, still running the original program in a child process, make any system calls it requires to modify that child process before finally executing the new program.

Under UNIX, then, a process encompasses all the information that the operating system must maintain to track the context of a single execution of a single program. Under Linux, we can break down this context into a number of specific sections. Broadly, process properties fall into three groups: the process identity, environment, and context.

20.4.1.1 Process Identity

A process identity consists mainly of the following items:

- **Process ID (PID):** Each process has a unique identifier. PIDs are used to specify processes to the operating system when an application makes a system call to signal, modify, or wait for another process. Additional identifiers associate the process with a process group (typically, a tree of processes forked by a single user command) and login session.

- **Credentials:** Each process must have an associated user ID and one or more group IDs (user groups are discussed in Section 11.6.2; process groups are not) that determine the rights of a process to access system resources and files.

- **Personality:** Process personalities are not traditionally found on UNIX systems, but under Linux each process has an associated personality identifier that can modify slightly the semantics of certain system calls. Personalities are primarily used by emulation libraries to request that system calls be compatible with certain flavors of UNIX.

Most of these identifiers are under limited control of the process itself. The process group and session identifiers can be changed if the process wants to start a new group or session. Its credentials can be changed, subject to appropriate security checks. However, the primary PID of a process is unchangeable and uniquely identifies that process until termination.

20.4.1.2 Process Environment

A process's environment is inherited from its parent and is composed of two null-terminated vectors: the argument vector and the environment vector. The **argument vector** simply lists the command-line arguments used to invoke the running program, and conventionally starts with the name of the program itself. The **environment vector** is a list of "NAME=VALUE" pairs that associates named environment variables with arbitrary textual values. The environment is not held in kernel memory, but is stored in the process's own user-mode address space as the first datum at the top of the process's stack.

The argument and environment vectors are not altered when a new process is created: The new child process will inherit the environment that its parent possesses. However, a completely new environment is set up when a new program is invoked. On calling execve, a process must supply the environment for the new program. The kernel passes these environment variables to the next program, replacing the process's current environment. The kernel otherwise leaves the environment and command-line vectors alone—their interpretation is left entirely to the user-mode libraries and applications.

The passing of environment variables from one process to the next, and the inheriting of these variables by the children of a process, provide flexible ways to pass information to components of the user-mode system software. Various important environment variables have conventional meanings to related parts of the system software. For example, the TERM variable is set up to name the type of terminal connected to a user's login session; many programs use this variable to determine how to perform operations on the user's display, such as moving the cursor or scrolling a region of text. Programs with multilingual support use the LANG variable to determine in which language to display system messages for programs that include multilingual support.

The environment-variable mechanism custom tailors the operating system on a per-process basis, rather than for the system as a whole. Users can choose their own languages or select their own editors independently of one another.

20.4.1.3 Process Context

The process identity and environment properties are usually set up when a process is created, and not changed until that process exits. A process may choose to change some aspects of its identity if it needs to do so, or it may alter its environment. Process context, on the other hand, is the state of the running program at any one time; it changes constantly.

- **Scheduling context**: The most important part of the process context is its scheduling context: the information that the scheduler needs to suspend and restart the process. This information includes saved copies of all the process's registers. Floating-point registers are stored separately and are restored only when needed, so that processes that do not use floating-point arithmetic do not incur the overhead of saving that state. The scheduling context also includes information about scheduling priority and about any outstanding signals waiting to be delivered to the process. A key part of the scheduling context is the process's kernel stack: a separate area of kernel memory reserved for use exclusively by kernel-mode code. Both system calls and interrupts that occur while the process is executing will use this stack.

- **Accounting**: The kernel maintains information about the resources currently being consumed by each process, and the total resources consumed by the process in its entire lifetime so far.

- **File table**: The file table is an array of pointers to kernel file structures. When making file-I/O system calls, processes refer to files by their index into this table.

- **File-system context**: Whereas the file table lists the existing open files, the file-system context applies to requests to open new files. The current root and default directories to be used for new file searches are stored here.

- **Signal-handler table**: UNIX systems can deliver asynchronous signals to a process in response to various external events. The signal-handler table defines the routine in the process's address space to be called when specific signals arrive.

- **Virtual-memory context**: The virtual-memory context describes the full contents of a process's private address space; we discuss it in Section 20.6.

20.4.2 Processes and Threads

Most modern operating systems support both processes and threads. Although the precise difference between the two often varies by implementation, we distinguish them as follows: *Processes* represent the execution of single programs, whereas *threads* represent separate, concurrent execution contexts within a single process running a single program.

Any two separate processes have their own independent address spaces, even if they are using shared memory to share some (but not all) of the contents of their virtual memory. In contrast, two threads within the same process will share *the same*, rather than *similar*, address spaces. Any change to the virtual-memory layout made by one thread will be visible immediately to other threads in process, because they are all running in only one address space.

Threads can be implemented in several ways. A thread may be implemented in the operating system's kernel as an object owned by a process, or it may be a fully independent entity. It cannot be implemented in the kernel at all—threads may be implemented purely within application or library code with the help of kernel-supplied timer interruptions.

The Linux kernel deals simply with the difference between processes and threads: It uses exactly the same internal representation for each. A thread is just a new process that happens to share the same address space as its parent. The distinction between a process and a thread is made only when a new thread is created, by the `clone` system call. Whereas `fork` creates a new process that has its own entirely new process context, `clone` creates a new process that has its own identity but is allowed to share the data structures of its parent.

This distinction can be accomplished because Linux does not hold process's entire context within the main process data structure; rather, it holds context within independent subcontexts. A process's file-system context, file-descriptor table, signal-handler table, and virtual-memory context are held in separate data structures. The process data structure simply contains pointers to these other structures, so any number of processes can easily share one of these subcontexts by pointing to the same subcontexts as appropriate.

The `clone` system call accepts an argument that tells it which subcontexts to copy, and which to share, when it creates the new process. The new process always is given a new identity and a new scheduling context; according to the arguments passed, however, it may either create new subcontext data structures initialized to be a copy of the parent's, or set up the new process to use the same subcontext data structure being used by the parent. The `fork` system call is nothing more than a special case of `clone` that copies all subcontexts, sharing none. Using `clone` gives an application fine-grained control over exactly what is shared between two threads.

The POSIX working groups have defined a programming interface, specified in the POSIX.1c standard, to allow applications to run multiple threads. The Linux system libraries support two separate mechanisms that implement this single standard in different ways. An application may choose to use either Linux's user-mode–based thread package or its kernel-based one. The user-mode thread library avoids the overhead of kernel scheduling and kernel system calls when threads interact, but is limited by the fact that all threads run in a single process. The kernel-supported thread library uses the `clone` system call to implement the same programming interface, but, since multiple scheduling contexts are created, it has the advantage of allowing an application to run threads on multiple processors at once on a multiprocessor system. It also allows multiple threads to be executing kernel system calls simultaneously.

20.5 ■ Scheduling

Scheduling is the job of allocating CPU time to different tasks within an operating system. Normally, we think of scheduling as being the running and interrupting of processes, but another aspect of scheduling is also important to Linux: the running of the various kernel tasks. Kernel tasks encompass both tasks that are requested by a running process and tasks that execute internally on behalf of a device driver.

20.5.1 Kernel Synchronization

The way that the kernel schedules its own operations is fundamentally different from the way that it does process scheduling. A request for kernel-mode execution can occur in two ways. A running program may request an operating-system service, either explicitly via a system call, or implicitly—for example, when a page fault occurs. Alternatively, a device driver may deliver a hardware interrupt that causes the CPU to start executing a kernel-defined handler for that interrupt.

The problem posed to the kernel is that these tasks may all try to access the same internal data structures. If one kernel task is in the middle of accessing some data structure when an interrupt service routine executes, then that service routine cannot access or modify the same data without risking data corruption. This fact relates to the idea of critical sections: portions of code that access shared data and that must not be allowed to execute concurrently.

As a result, kernel synchronization involves much more than just process scheduling. A framework is required that will allow the kernel's critical sections to run without interruption by another critical section.

The first part of Linux's solution to this problem lies in making normal kernel code non-preemptible. Usually, when a timer interrupt is received by the kernel, it invokes the process scheduler, potentially so that it can suspend execution of the currently running process and resume running another one—the natural time sharing of any UNIX system. However, when a timer interrupt is received while a process is executing a kernel-system service routine, the rescheduling does not take place immediately. Rather, the kernel's need_resched flag is set to tell the kernel to run the scheduler after the system call has completed and control is about to be returned to user mode.

Once a piece of kernel code starts running, it can guarantee that it will be the only kernel code running until one of the following actions occurs:

- An interrupt

- A page fault

- A kernel-code call to the scheduler function itself

Interrupts are a problem only if they contain critical sections themselves. Timer interrupts never directly cause a process reschedule; they just request that a reschedule be performed later, so any incoming interrupts cannot affect the execution order of noninterrupt kernel code. Once the interrupt service is finished, execution will simply return to the same kernel code that was running when the interrupt was taken.

Page faults are a potential problem; if a kernel routine tries to read or write to user memory, it may incur a page fault that requires disk I/O to complete, and the running process will be suspended until the I/O completes. Similarly, if a system-call service routine calls the scheduler while it is in kernel mode, either explicitly by making a direct call to the scheduling code or implicitly by calling a function to wait for I/O to complete, then the process will be suspended and a reschedule will occur. When the process becomes runable again, it will continue to execute in kernel mode, continuing at the instruction after the call to the scheduler.

Kernel code can thus assume that it will never be preempted by another process and that no special care must be taken to protect critical sections. The only requirement is that critical sections do not contain references to user memory or waits for I/O completions.

The second protection technique that Linux uses applies to critical sections that occur in interrupt service routines. The basic tool is the processor's interrupt-control hardware. By disabling interrupts during a critical section, the kernel guarantees that it can proceed without the risk of concurrent access of shared data structures.

There is a penalty for disabling interrupts. On most hardware architectures, interrupt enable and disable instructions are expensive. Furthermore, as long as interrupts remain disabled, all I/O is suspended, and any device waiting for servicing will have to wait until interrupts are reenabled, so performance degrades. Linux's kernel uses a synchronization architecture that allows long critical sections to run for their entire duration without having interrupts disabled. This ability is especially useful in the networking code: An interrupt in a network device driver can signal the arrival of an entire network packet, which may result in a great deal of code being executed to disassemble, route, and forward that packet within the interrupt service routine.

Linux implements this architecture by separating interrupt service routines into two sections: the top half and bottom half. The **top half** is a normal interrupt service routine, and runs with recursive interrupts disabled; interrupts of a higher priority may interrupt the routine, but interrupts of the same or lower priority are disabled. The **bottom half** of a service routine is run, with all interrupts enabled, by a miniature scheduler that ensures that bottom halves never interrupt themselves. The bottom-half scheduler is invoked automatically whenever an interrupt service routine exits.

This separation means that any complex processing that has to be done in response to an interrupt can be completed by the kernel without the kernel worrying about being interrupted itself. If another interrupt occurs while a bottom half is executing, then that interrupt can request that the same bottom half execute, but the execution will be deferred until the currently running one completes. Each execution of the bottom half can be interrupted by a top half, but can never be interrupted by a similar bottom half.

The top-half bottom-half architecture is completed by a mechanism for disabling selected bottom halves while executing normal, foreground kernel code. The kernel can code critical sections easily using this system: Interrupt handlers can code their critical sections as bottom halves, and when the foreground kernel wants to enter a critical section, it can disable any relevant bottom halves to prevent any other critical sections from interrupting it. At the end of the critical section, the kernel can reenable the bottom halves and run any bottom-half tasks that have been queued by top-half interrupt service routines during the critical section.

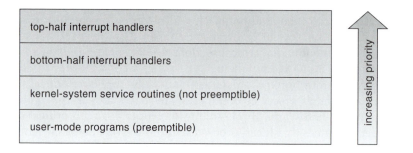

Figure 20.2   Interrupt protection levels.

Figure 20.2 summarizes the various levels of interrupt protection within the kernel. Each level may be interrupted by code running at a higher level, but will never be interrupted by code running at the same or a lower level; except for user-mode code, user processes can always be preempted by another process when a time-sharing scheduling interrupt occurs.

20.5.2 Process Scheduling

Once the kernel has reached a rescheduling point—either a rescheduling interrupt has occurred or a running kernel process has blocked waiting for some wakeup signal—it must decide what process to run next. Linux has two separate process-scheduling algorithms. One is a time-sharing algorithm for fair preemptive scheduling among multiple processes; the other is designed for real-time tasks where absolute priorities are more important than fairness.

Part of every process identity is a scheduling class that defines which of these algorithms to apply to the process. The scheduling classes used by Linux are defined in the POSIX standard's extensions for real-time computing (POSIX.4, now known as POSIX.1b).

For time-sharing processes, Linux uses a prioritized, credit-based algorithm. Each process possesses a certain number of scheduling credits; when a new task must be chosen to run, the process with the most credits is selected. Every time that a timer interrupt occurs, the currently running process loses one credit; when its credits reaches zero, it is suspended and another process is chosen.

If no runable processes have any credits, then Linux performs a recrediting operation, adding credits to *every* process in the system, rather than to just the runable ones, according to the following rule:

$$\text{credits} = \frac{\text{credits}}{2} + \text{priority}$$

This algorithm tends to mix two factors, the process's history and priority. One-half of the credits that a process still holds since the previous recrediting operation will be retained after the algorithm has been applied, retaining some history of the process's recent behavior. Processes that run all the time tend to exhaust their credits rapidly, but processes that spend much of their time suspended can accumulate credits over multiple recreditings and consequently end up with a higher credit count after a recredit. This crediting system automatically gives high priority to interactive or I/O-bound processes, for which a rapid response time is important.

The use of a process priority in calculating new credits allows the priority of a process to be fine-tuned. Background batch jobs can be given a low priority; they will automatically receive fewer credits than interactive users' jobs, and hence will receive a smaller percentage of the CPU time than will similar jobs that have higher priorities. Linux uses this priority system to implement the standard UNIX *nice* process-priority mechanism.

Linux's real-time scheduling is simpler still. Linux implements the two real-time scheduling classes required by POSIX.1b: first-come, first-served (FCFS) and round-robin (Sections 6.3.1 and 6.3.4, respectively). In both cases, each process has a priority in addition to its scheduling class. In time-sharing scheduling, however, processes of different priorities can still compete with one another to some extent; in real-time scheduling, the scheduler always runs the process with the highest priority. Among processes of equal priority, it runs the process that has been waiting longest. The only difference between FCFS and round-robin scheduling is that FCFS processes continue to run until they either exit or block, whereas a round-robin process will be preempted after a while and will be moved to the end of the scheduling queue, so round-robin processes of equal priority will automatically time share among themselves.

Linux's real-time scheduling is soft—rather than hard—real time. The scheduler offers strict guarantees about the relative priorities of real-time processes, but the kernel does not offer any guarantees about how quickly a real-time process will be scheduled once that process becomes runable. Remember that Linux kernel code cannot ever be preempted by user-mode code. If an interrupt arrives that wakes up a real-time process while the kernel is already executing a system call on behalf of another process, the real-time process will just have to wait until the currently running system call completes or blocks.

20.5.3 Symmetric Multiprocessing

The Linux 2.0 kernel was the first stable Linux kernel to support **symmetric multiprocessor (SMP)** hardware. Separate processes or threads can execute in parallel on separate processors. However, to preserve the non-preemptible synchronization requirements of the kernel, the implementation of SMP in this kernel imposes the restriction that only one processor at a time can be executing kernel-mode code. SMP uses a single kernel spinlock to enforce this rule. This spinlock does not pose a problem for computation-bound tasks, but tasks that involve a lot of kernel activity can become seriously bottlenecked.

The Linux 2.2 kernel makes the SMP implementation more scalable by splitting the single-kernel spinlock into multiple locks that each protect against reentrance only a small subset of the kernel's data structures. Currently, signal handling, interrupts, and some I/O routines use multiple locks to let multiple processors execute kernel-mode code simultaneously. The development kernel 2.3 (Linux 2.4) seems to have completely removed the single-kernel spinlock.

20.6 ▪ Memory Management

Memory management under Linux has two components. The first deals with allocating and freeing physical memory: pages, groups of pages, and small blocks of memory. The second handles virtual memory, which is memory mapped into the address space of running processes.

We describe these two components, and then examine the mechanisms by which the loadable components of a new program are brought into a process's virtual memory in response to an `exec` system call.

20.6.1 Management of Physical Memory

The primary physical-memory manager in the Linux kernel is the **page allocator**. This allocator is responsible for allocating and freeing all physical pages, and it is capable of allocating ranges of physically contiguous pages on request. The allocator uses a **buddy-heap algorithm** to keep track of available physical pages. A buddy-heap allocator pairs adjacent units of allocatable memory together (hence its name). Each allocatable memory region has an adjacent partner (or buddy) and whenever two allocated partner regions are both freed up, they are combined to form a larger region. That larger region also has a partner, with which it can combine to form a still larger free region. Alternatively, if a small memory request cannot be satisfied by allocation of an existing small free region, then a larger free region will be subdivided into two partners to satisfy the request. Separate linked lists are used to record the free memory regions of each allowable size; under Linux, the smallest size allocatable under this mechanism is a single physical page. Figure 20.3 shows an example of buddy-heap allocation: A 4 KB region is being allocated, but the smallest available region is 16 KB. The region is broken up recursively until a piece of the desired size is available.

Ultimately, all memory allocations in the Linux kernel occur either statically, by drivers that reserve a contiguous area of memory during system boot time, or dynamically, by the page allocator. However, kernel functions do not have to use the basic allocator to reserve memory. Several specialized memory-management subsystems use the underlying page allocator to manage their own pool of memory. The most important are the virtual-memory

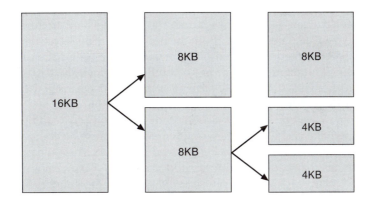

Figure 20.3   Splitting of memory in a buddy heap.

system, described in Section 20.6.2; the kmalloc variable-length allocator; and the kernel's two persistent data caches, the buffer cache and the page cache.

Many components of the Linux operating system need to allocate entire pages at will, but often smaller blocks of memory are required. The kernel provides an additional allocator for arbitrary-sized requests, where the size of a request is not known in advance and may be only a few bytes, rather than an entire page. Analogous to the C language's malloc function, this **kmalloc** service allocates entire pages on demand, but then splits them into smaller pieces. The kernel maintains a set of lists of pages in use by the kmalloc service, where all the pages on a given list have been split into pieces of a specific size. Allocating memory involves working out the appropriate list and either taking the first free piece available on the list or allocating a new page and splitting it up.

Both the page and kmalloc allocators are safe from interrupts. A function that wants to allocate memory passes a request priority to the allocation function. Interrupt routines use an atomic priority that guarantees that the request either is satisfied or, if there is no more memory, fails immediately. In contrast, normal user processes that require a memory allocation will start attempting to find existing memory to free, and will stall until memory becomes available. The allocation priority can also be used for specifying that the memory is required for DMA, for use on architectures such as the PC where certain DMA requests are not supported on all pages of physical memory.

Memory regions claimed by the **kmalloc** system are allocated permanently until they are freed explicitly. The **kmalloc** system cannot relocate or reclaim these regions in response to memory shortages.

The other three main subsystems that do their own management of physical pages are closely related. These are the buffer cache, the page cache, and the virtual-memory system. The **buffer cache** is the kernel's main cache for block-oriented devices such as disk drives, and is the main mechanism through which I/O to these devices is performed. Both the native Linux disk-based file systems and the NFS networked file system use the page cache. The page cache caches entire pages of file contents, and is not limited to block devices; it can also cache networked data. The *virtual-memory system* manages the contents of each process's virtual-address space.

These three systems interact closely with one another. Reading a page of data into the page cache requires going temporarily through the buffer cache; pages in the page cache can also be mapped into the virtual-memory system if a process has mapped a file into its address space. The kernel maintains a reference count on each page of physical memory, so that pages shared by two or more of these subsystems can be released when they are no longer in use anywhere.

20.6.2 Virtual Memory

The Linux virtual-memory system is responsible for maintaining the address space visible to each process. It creates pages of virtual memory on demand, and manages the loading of those pages from disk or their swapping back out to disk as required. Under Linux, the virtual-memory manager maintains two separate views of a process's address space: as a set of separate regions, and as a set of pages.

The first view of an address space is the logical view, describing instructions that the virtual-memory system has received concerning the layout of the address space. In this view, the address space consists of a set of nonoverlapping regions, each region representing a continuous, page-aligned subset of the address space. Each region is described internally by a single **vm_area_struct** structure that defines the properties of the region, including the process's read, write, and execute permissions in the region, and information about any files associated with the region. The regions for each address space are linked into a balanced binary tree to allow fast lookup of the region corresponding to any virtual address.

The kernel also maintains a second, physical view of each address space. This view is stored in the hardware page tables for the process. The page-table entries determine the exact current location of each page of virtual memory, whether it is on disk or in physical memory. The physical view is managed by a set of routines invoked from the kernel's software-interrupt handlers whenever a process tries to access a page that is not currently present in the page tables. Each **vm_area_struct** in the address-space description contains a field that points to a table of functions that implement the key page-management functions for any given virtual-memory region. All requests to read or write an unavailable page are eventually dispatched to the appropriate handler in **vm_area_struct**'s function table, so that the central memory-management routines do not have to know the details of managing each possible type of memory region.

20.6.2.1 Virtual-Memory Regions

Linux implements several types of virtual-memory regions. The first property that characterizes a type of virtual memory is the backing store for the region: This store describes from where the pages for a region come. Most memory regions are backed either by a file, or by nothing. A region backed by nothing is the simplest type of virtual memory. Such a region represents **demand-zero memory**: When a process tries to read a page in such a region, it is simply given back a page of memory filled with zeros.

A region backed by a file acts as a viewport onto a section of that file: Whenever the process tries to access a page within that region, the page table is filled with the address of a page within the kernel's page cache corresponding to the appropriate offset in the file. The same page of physical memory is used both by the page cache and by the process's page tables, so any changes made to the file by the file system are immediately visible to any processes that have mapped that file into their address space. Any number of processes can map the same region of the same file, and they will all end up using the same page of physical memory for the purpose.

A virtual-memory region is also defined by its reaction to writes. The mapping of a region into the process's address space can be either *private* or *shared*. If a process writes to a privately mapped region, then the pager detects that a copy-on-write is necessary to keep the changes local to the process. On the other hand, writes to a shared region result in the object mapped into that region being updated, so that the change will be visible immediately to any other process that is mapping that object.

20.6.2.2 Lifetime of a Virtual Address Space

The kernel will create a new virtual address space in exactly two situations: When a process runs a new program with the exec system call, and on creation of a new process by the fork system call. The first case is easy: When a new program is executed, the process is given a new, completely empty virtual address space. It is up to the routines for loading the program to populate the address space with virtual-memory regions.

In the second case, creating a new process with fork involves creating a complete copy of the existing process's virtual address space. The kernel copies the parent process's **vm_area_struct** descriptors, then creates a new set of page tables for the child. The parent's page tables are copied directly into the child's, with the reference count of each page covered being incremented; thus, after the fork, the parent and child share the same physical pages of memory in their address spaces.

A special case occurs when the copying operation reaches a virtual-memory region that is mapped privately. Any pages to which the parent process has written within such a region are private, and subsequent changes to these pages by either the parent or the child must not update the page in the other process's address space. When the page-table entries for such regions are copied, they are set to be read only and are marked for copy-on-write. As long as neither process modifies these pages, the two processes share the same page of physical memory. However, if either process tries to modify a copy-on-write page, the reference count on the page is checked. If the page is still shared, then the process copies the page's contents to a brand-new page of physical memory and uses its copy instead. This mechanism ensures that private data pages are shared between processes whenever possible; copies are made only when absolutely necessary.

20.6.2.3 Swapping and Paging

An important task for a virtual-memory system is to relocate pages of memory from physical memory out to disk when that memory is needed. Early UNIX systems performed this relocation by swapping out the contents of entire processes at once, but modern versions of UNIX rely more on paging—the movement of individual pages of virtual memory between physical memory and disk. Linux does not implement whole-process swapping; it uses the newer paging mechanism exclusively.

The paging system can be divided into two sections. First, the **policy algorithm** decides which pages to write out to disk, and when to write them. Second, the **paging mechanism** carries out the transfer and pages data back into physical memory when they are needed again.

Linux's **pageout policy** uses a modified version of the standard clock (or second-chance) algorithm described in Section 10.4.5.2. Under Linux, a multiple-pass clock is used, and every page has an *age* that is adjusted on each pass of the clock. The age is more precisely a measure of the page's youthfulness, or how much activity the page has seen recently. Frequently accessed pages will attain a higher age value, but the age of infrequently accessed pages will drop toward zero with each pass. This age valuing allows the pager to select pages to page out based on a least-frequently-used (LFU) policy.

The paging mechanism supports paging both to dedicated swap devices and partitions, and to normal files, although swapping to a file is significantly slower due to the extra overhead incurred by the file system. Blocks are allocated from the swap devices according to a bitmap of used blocks, which is maintained in physical memory at all times. The allocator uses a next-fit algorithm to try to write out pages to continuous runs of disk blocks for improved performance. The allocator records the fact that a page has been paged out to disk by using a feature of the page tables on modern processors: The page-table entry's page-not-present bit is set, allowing the rest of the page-table entry to be filled with an index identifying where the page has been written.

20.6.2.4 Kernel Virtual Memory

Linux reserves for its own internal use a constant, architecture-dependent region of the virtual address space of every process. The page-table entries that map to these kernel pages are marked as protected, so that the pages are not visible or modifiable when the processor is running in user mode. This kernel virtual-memory area contains two regions. The first section is a static area that contains page-table references to every available physical page of memory in the system, so that a simple translation from physical to virtual addresses occurs when kernel code is run. The core of the kernel, plus all pages allocated by the normal page allocator, resides in this region.

The remainder of the kernel's reserved section of address space is not reserved for any specific purpose. Page-table entries in this address range can be modified by the kernel to point to any other areas of memory as desired. The kernel provides a pair of facilities that allow processes to use this virtual memory. The vmalloc function allocates an arbitrary number of physical pages of memory, and maps them into a single region of kernel virtual memory, allowing allocation of large contiguous memory chunks even if there are not sufficient adjacent free physical pages to satisfy the request. The vremap function maps a sequence of virtual addresses to point to an area of memory used by a device driver for memory-mapped I/O.

20.6.3 Execution and Loading of User Programs

The Linux kernel's execution of user programs is triggered by a call to the exec system call. This call commands the kernel to run a new program within the current process, completely overwriting the current execution context with the initial context of the new program. The first job of this system service is to verify that the calling process has permission rights to the file being executed. Once that matter has been checked, the kernel invokes a loader routine to start running the program. The loader does not necessarily load the contents of the program file into physical memory, but it does at least set up the mapping of the program into virtual memory.

There is no single routine in Linux for loading a new program. Instead, Linux maintains a table of possible loader functions, and it gives each such function the opportunity to try loading the given file when an exec system call is made. The initial reason for this loader table was that, between the release of the 1.0 and 1.2 kernels, the standard format for Linux's binary files was changed. Older Linux kernels understood the a.out format for binary files —a relatively simple format common on older UNIX systems. Newer Linux systems use the more modern **ELF** format, now supported by most current UNIX implementations. ELF has a number of advantages over a.out, including flexibility and extensibility: New sections can be added to an ELF binary (for example, to add extra debugging information), without the loader routines becoming confused. By allowing registration of multiple loader routines, Linux can easily support the ELF and a.out binary formats in a single running system.

In Sections 20.6.3.1 and 20.6.3.2, we concentrate exclusively on the loading and running of ELF-format binaries. The procedure for loading a.out binaries is simpler, but is similar in operation.

20.6.3.1 Mapping of Programs into Memory

Under Linux, the binary loader does not load a binary file into physical memory. Rather, the pages of the binary file are mapped into regions of virtual memory. Only when the program tries to access a given page will a page fault result in the loading of that page into physical memory.

It is the responsibility of the kernel's binary loader to set up the initial memory mapping. An ELF-format binary file consists of a header followed by several page-aligned sections. The ELF loader works by reading the header and mapping the sections of the file into separate regions of virtual memory.

Figure 20.4 shows the typical layout of memory regions set up by the ELF loader. In a reserved region at one end of the address space sits the kernel, in its own privileged region of virtual memory inaccessible to normal user-mode programs. The rest of virtual memory is available to applications, which can use the kernel's memory-mapping functions to create regions that map a portion of a file or that are available for application data.

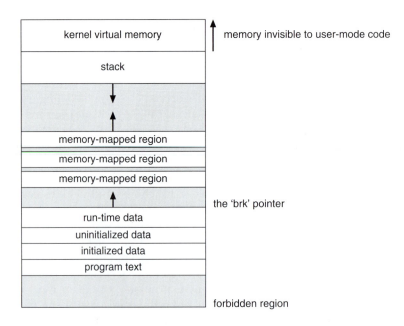

Figure 20.4   Memory layout for ELF programs.

The loader's job is to set up the initial memory mapping to allow the execution of the program to start. The regions that need to be initialized include the stack and the program's text and data regions.

The stack is created at the top of the user-mode virtual memory; it grows downward toward lower-numbered addresses. It includes copies of the arguments and environment variables given to the program in the exec system call. The other regions are created near the bottom end of virtual memory. The sections of the binary file that contain program text or read-only data are mapped into memory as a write-protected region. Writable initialized data are mapped next; then any uninitialized data are mapped in as a private demand-zero region.

Directly beyond these fixed-sized regions is a variable-sized region that programs can expand as needed to hold data allocated at run time. Each process has a pointer, *brk*, which points to the current extent of this data region, and processes can extend or contract their *brk* region with a single system call.

Once these mappings have been set up, the loader initializes the process's program-counter register with the starting point recorded in the ELF header, and the process can be scheduled.

20.6.3.2 Static and Dynamic Linking

Once the program has been loaded and has started running, all the necessary contents of the binary file have been loaded into the process's virtual address space. However, most programs also need to run functions from the system libraries, and these library functions also need to be loaded. In the simplest case, when a programmer builds an application, the necessary library functions are embedded directly in the program's executable binary file. Such a program is statically linked to its libraries, and statically linked executables can commence running as soon as they are loaded.

The main disadvantage of static linking is that every program generated must contain copies of exactly the same common system library functions. It is much more efficient, in terms of both physical memory and disk-space usage, to load the system libraries into memory only once. Dynamic linking allows this single loading to happen.

Linux implements dynamic linking in user mode through a special linker library. Every dynamically linked program contains a small statically linked function that is called when the program starts. This static function just maps the link library into memory and runs the code that the function contains. The link library reads a list of the dynamic libraries required by the program and the names of the variables and functions needed from those libraries by reading the information contained in sections of the ELF binary. It then maps the libraries into the middle of virtual memory, and resolves the references to the symbols contained in those libraries. It does not matter exactly where in memory these shared libraries get mapped: They are compiled into **position-independent code (PIC)**, which can run at any address in memory.

20.7 ■ File Systems

Linux retains UNIX's standard file-system model. In UNIX, a file does not have to be an object stored on disk or fetched over a network from a remote file server. Rather, UNIX files can be anything capable of handling the input or output of a stream of data. Device drivers can appear as files, and interprocess-communication channels or network connections also look like files to the user.

The Linux kernel handles all these types of file by hiding the implementation details of any single file type behind a layer of software, the virtual file system (VFS).

20.7.1 The Virtual File System

The Linux VFS is designed around object-oriented principles. It has two components: a set of definitions that define what a file object is allowed to look like, and a layer of software to manipulate those objects. The three main object types defined by the VFS are the **inode-object** and the **file-object** structures, which represent individual files, and the **file-system-object**, which represents an entire file system.

For each of these three types of object, the VFS defines a set of operations that must be implemented by that structure. Every object of one of these types contains a pointer to a function table. The function table lists the addresses of the actual functions that implement those operations for that particular object. Thus, the VFS software layer can perform an operation on one of these objects by calling the appropriate function from that object's function table, without having to know in advance exactly with what kind of an object it is dealing. The VFS does not know, or care, whether an inode represents a networked file, a disk file, a network socket, or a directory file. The appropriate function for that file's `read data` operation will always be at the same place in its function table, and the VFS software layer will call that function without caring how the data are actually read.

The file-system object represents a connected set of files that forms a self-contained directory hierarchy. The operating-system kernel maintains a single file-system object for each disk device mounted as a file system and for each networked file system currently connected. The file-system object's main responsibility is to give access to inodes. The VFS identifies every inode by a unique (file-system-inode number) pair, and it finds the inode corresponding to a particular inode number by asking the file-system object to return the inode with that number.

The inode- and file-objects are the mechanisms used to access files. An inode-object represents the file as a whole, and a file-object represents a point of access to the data in the file. A process cannot access an inode's data contents without first obtaining a file-object pointing to the inode. The file-object keeps track of where in the file the process is currently reading or writing, to keep track of sequential file I/O. It also remembers whether the process asked for write permissions when the file was opened, and keeps track of the process's activity if necessary to perform adaptive read-ahead, fetching file data into memory in advance of the process requesting it, to improve performance.

File-objects typically belong to a single process, but inode-objects do not. Even once a file is no longer being used by any processes, its inode-object may still be cached by the VFS to improve performance if the file is used again in the near future. All cached file data are linked onto a list in the file's inode-object. The inode also maintains standard information about each file, such as the owner, size, and time most recently modified.

Directory files are dealt with slightly differently from other files. The UNIX programming interface defines a number of operations on directories, such as creating, deleting, and renaming a file in a directory. Unlike reading and writing data, for which a file must first be opened, the system calls for these directory operations do not require that the user open the files concerned. The VFS therefore defines these directory operations in the inode-object, rather than in the file-object.

20.7.2 The Linux ext2fs File System

The standard on-disk file system used by Linux is called *ext2fs*, for historical reasons. Linux was originally programmed with a Minix-compatible file system, to ease exchanging data with the Minix development system, but that file system was severely restricted by 14-character file-name limits and the maximum file-system size of 64 MB. The Minix file system was superseded by a new file system, which was christened the **extended file system (extfs)**. A later redesign of this file system to improve performance and scalability and to add a few missing features led to the **second extended file system (ext2fs)**.

ext2fs has much in common with the BSD Fast File System (ffs) (Section A.7.7). It uses a similar mechanism for locating the data blocks belonging to a specific file, storing data-block pointers in indirect blocks throughout the file system with up to three levels of indirection. As they are in ffs, directory files are stored on disk just like normal files, although their contents are interpreted differently. Each block in a directory file consists of a linked list of entries, where each entry contains the length of the entry, the name of a file, and the inode number of the inode to which that entry refers.

The main differences between ext2fs and ffs lie in the disk-allocation policies. In ffs, the disk is allocated to files in blocks of 8 KB, with blocks being subdivided into fragments of 1 KB to store small files or partially filled blocks at the end of a file. In contrast, ext2fs does not use fragments at all, but performs all its allocations in smaller units. The default block size on ext2fs is 1 KB, although 2 KB and 4 KB blocks are also supported.

To maintain high performance, the operating system must try to perform I/Os in large chunks whenever possible by clustering physically adjacent I/O requests. Clustering reduces the per-request overhead incurred by device drivers, disks, and disk-controller hardware. A 1 KB I/O request size is too small to maintain good performance, so ext2fs uses allocation policies designed to place logically adjacent blocks of a file into physically adjacent blocks on disk, so that it can submit an I/O request for several disk blocks as a single operation.

The ext2fs allocation policy comes in two parts. As in ffs, an ext2fs file system is partitioned into multiple **block groups**. ffs uses the similar concept of **cylinder groups**, where each group corresponds to a single cylinder of a physical disk. However, modern disk-drive technology packs sectors onto the disk at different densities, and thus with different cylinder sizes, depending on how far the disk head is from the center of the disk. Therefore, fixed-sized cylinder groups do not necessarily correspond to the disk's geometry.

When allocating a file, ext2fs must first select the block group for that file. For data blocks, it attempts to choose the same block group as that in which the file's inode has been allocated. For inode allocations, it selects the same block group as the file's parent directory, for nondirectory files. Directory files are not kept together, but rather are dispersed throughout the available block groups. These policies are designed to keep related information within the same block group, but also to spread out the disk load among the disk's block groups to reduce the fragmentation of any one area of the disk.

Within a block group, ext2fs tries to keep allocations physically contiguous if possible, reducing fragmentation if it can. It maintains a bitmap of all free blocks in a block group. When allocating the first blocks for a new file, it starts searching for a free block from the beginning of the block group; when extending a file, it continues the search from the block most recently allocated to the file. The search is performed in two stages. First, it searches for an entire free byte in the bitmap; if it fails to find one, it looks for any free bit. The search for free bytes aims to allocate disk space in chunks of at least eight blocks where possible.

Once a free block has been identified, the search is extended backward until an allocated block is encountered. When a free byte is found in the bitmap, this backward extension prevents ext2fs from leaving a hole between the most recently allocated block in the previous nonzero byte and the zero byte found. Once the next block to be allocated has been thus found by either bit or byte search, ext2fs extends the allocation forward for up to eight blocks and **preallocates** these extra blocks to the file. This preallocation helps to reduce fragmentation during interleaved writes to separate files, and also reduces the CPU cost of disk allocation by allocating multiple blocks simultaneously. The preallocated blocks are returned to the free-space bitmap when the file is closed.

Figure 20.5 illustrates the allocation policies. Each row represents a sequence of set and unset bits in an allocation bitmap, indicating used and free blocks on disk. In the first case, if we can find any free blocks sufficiently near the start of the search, then we allocate them no matter how fragmented they may be. The fragmentation is partially compensated by the fact that the

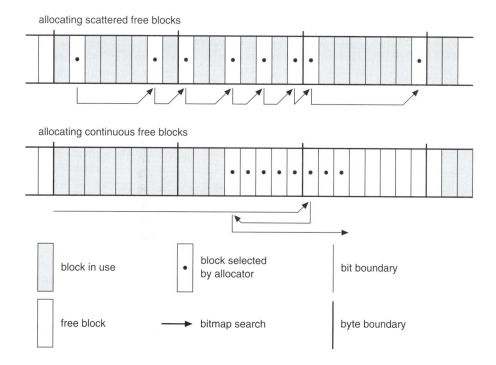

allocating scattered free blocks

allocating continuous free blocks

block in use

block selected by allocator

bit boundary

free block

bitmap search

byte boundary

Figure 20.5 ext2fs block-allocation policies.

blocks are close together and can probably all be read without any disk seeks being incurred, and allocating them all to one file is better in the long run than allocating isolated blocks to separate files once large free areas become scarce on disk. In the second case, we have not immediately found a free block close by, so we search forward for an entire free byte in the bitmap. If we allocated that byte as a whole, we would end up creating a fragmented area of free space before it, so before allocating we back up to make this allocation flush with the allocation preceding it, and then we allocate forward to satisfy the default allocation of eight blocks.

20.7.3 The Linux Proc File System

The Linux VFS is sufficiently flexible that it is possible to implement a file system that does not store data persistently at all, but rather simply provides an interface to some other functionality. The Linux **process file system**, known as the *proc* file system, is an example of a file system whose contents are not actually stored anywhere but are computed on demand according to user file I/O requests.

A *proc* file system is not unique to Linux. SVR4 UNIX introduced a *proc* file system as an efficient interface to the kernel's process debugging support:

Each subdirectory of the file system corresponded not to a directory on any disk, but rather to an active process on the current system. A listing of the file system reveals one directory per process, with the directory name being the ASCII decimal representation of the process's unique process identifier (PID).

Linux implements such a *proc* file system, but extends it greatly by adding a number of extra directories and text files under the file system's root directory. These new entries correspond to various statistics about the kernel and the associated loaded drivers. The *proc* file system provides a way for programs to access this information as plain text files, which the standard UNIX user environment provides powerful tools to process. For example, in the past, the traditional UNIX ps command for listing the states of all running processes has been implemented as a privileged process that reads the process state directly from the kernel's virtual memory. Under Linux, this command is implemented as an entirely unprivileged program that simply parses and formats the information from *proc*.

The *proc* file system must implement two things: a directory structure and the file contents within. Given that a UNIX file system is defined as a set of file and directory inodes identified by their inode numbers, the *proc* file system must define a unique and persistent inode number for each directory and the associated files. Once such a mapping exists, it can use this inode number to identify just what operation is required when a user tries to read from a particular file inode or to perform a lookup in a particular directory inode. When data are read from one of these files, the *proc* file system will collect the appropriate information, format it into textual form, and place it into the requesting process's read buffer.

The mapping from inode number to information type splits the inode number into two fields. In Linux, a PID is 16 bits wide, but an inode number is 32 bits. The top 16 bits of the inode number are interpreted as a PID, and the remaining bits define what type of information is being requested about that process.

A PID of zero is not valid, so a zero PID field in the inode number is taken to mean that this inode contains global—rather than process-specific—information. Separate global files exist in *proc* to report information such as the kernel version, free memory, performance statistics, and drivers currently running.

Not all the inode numbers in this range are reserved: The kernel can allocate new *proc* inode mappings dynamically, maintaining a bitmap of allocated inode numbers. It also maintains a tree data structure of registered global *proc* file-system entries: Each entry contains the file's inode number, file name, access permissions, and the special functions used to generate the file's contents. Drivers can register and deregister entries in this tree at any time, and a special section of the tree—appearing under the */proc/sys* directory—is reserved for kernel variables. Files under this tree are dealt with by a set of common handlers that allow both reading and writing of these variables, so a system administrator can tune the value of kernel parameters simply by writing the new desired values out in ASCII decimal to the appropriate file.

To allow efficient access to these variables from within applications, the */proc/sys* subtree is made available through a special system call, sysctl, that reads and writes the same variables in binary, rather than in text, without the overhead of the file system. sysctl is not an extra facility; it simply reads the *proc* dynamic entry tree to decide to which variables the application is referring.

20.8 ■ Input and Output

To the user, the I/O system in Linux looks much like it does in any UNIX. That is, to the extent possible, all device drivers appear as normal files. A user can open an access channel to a device in the same way as she can open any other file—devices can appear as objects within the file system. The system administrator can create special files within a file system that contain references to a specific device driver, and a user opening such a file will be able to read from and write to the device referenced. By using the normal file-protection system, which determines who can access which file, the administrator can set access permissions for each device.

Linux splits all devices into three classes: block devices, character devices, and network devices. Figure 20.6 illustrates the overall structure of the device-driver system. **Block devices** include all devices that allow random access to completely independent, fixed-sized blocks of data, including hard disks, floppy disks, and CD-ROMs. Block devices are typically used to store file systems, but direct access to a block device is also allowed so that programs can create and repair the file system that the device contains. Applications can also access these block devices directly if they wish; for example, a database

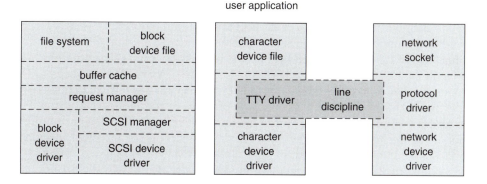

Figure 20.6   Device-driver block structure.

application may prefer to perform its own, fine-tuned laying out of data onto the disk, rather than using the general-purpose file system.

Character devices include most other devices, with the main exception of network devices. Character devices do not need to support all the functionality of regular files. For example, a loudspeaker device would allow data to be written to it, but it would not support reading of data back from it. Similarly, seeking to a certain position in the file might be supported for a magnetic-tape device but would make no sense to a pointing device such as a mouse.

Network devices are dealt with differently from block and character devices. Users cannot directly transfer data to network devices; instead, they must communicate indirectly by opening a connection to the kernel's networking subsystem. We discuss the interface to network devices separately in Section 20.10.

20.8.1 Block Devices

Block devices provide the main interface to all disk devices in a system. Performance is particularly important for disks, and the block-device system must provide functionality to ensure that disk access is as fast as possible. This functionality is achieved through the use of two system components, the **block buffer cache** and the **request manager**.

20.8.1.1 The Block Buffer Cache

The Linux **block buffer cache** serves two main purposes: It acts as both a pool of buffers for active I/O and a cache for completed I/O. The buffer cache consists of two parts. First, the buffers themselves are a dynamically sized set of pages allocated directly from the kernel's main memory pool. Each page is split up into a number of equally sized buffers. Second, a set of corresponding buffer descriptors, the *buffer_heads*, includes one for each buffer in the cache.

The *buffer_heads* contain all the information that the kernel maintains about the buffers. The primary information is the buffer's identity. Each buffer is identified by a 3-tuple: the block device to which the buffer belongs, the offset of the data within that block device, and the size of the buffer. Buffers are also held on a number of lists, with separate lists for clean, dirty, and locked buffers, plus a list of free buffers. Buffers enter the free list by being placed there either by a file system (for example, when a file is deleted), or by a `refill_freelist` function, which is called whenever the kernel needs more buffers. The kernel fills the free list by expanding the pool of buffers or by recycling existing buffers, according to whether sufficient free memory is available. Finally, each buffer not on the free list is indexed by a hash function on its device and block number, and is linked onto a corresponding hash lookup list.

The kernel's buffer management automatically deals with the writing of dirty buffers back to disk. Two background daemons assist. One simply wakes up at a regular interval and requests that all data be written back to disk if it has been dirty for longer than a certain interval. The other is a kernel thread that is woken up whenever the `refill_freelist` function finds that too high a proportion of the buffer cache is dirty.

20.8.1.2 The Request Manager

The request manager is the layer of software that manages the reading and writing of buffer contents to and from a block-device driver. The request system revolves around a function, `ll_rw_block`, that performs low-level read and write of block devices. This function takes a list of `buffer_head` buffer descriptors and a read–write flag as its argument, and sets the I/O in progress for all those buffers. It does not wait for that I/O to complete.

Outstanding I/O requests are recorded in `request` structures. A `request` represents an outstanding I/O request for the read or write of a contiguous range of sectors on a single block device. Since more than one buffer may be involved in the transfer, the `request` contains a pointer to the first in a linked list of *buffer_heads* to be used for the transfer.

A separate list of requests is kept for each block-device driver, and these requests are scheduled according to a unidirectional elevator (C-SCAN) algorithm that exploits the order in which requests are inserted and removed from the per-device lists. The request lists are maintained in sorted order of increasing starting-sector number. When a request is accepted for processing by a block-device driver, it is not removed from the list. It is removed only after the I/O is complete, at which point the driver continues with the next request in the list, even if new requests have been inserted into the list before the active request.

As new I/O requests are made, the request manager attempts to merge requests in the per-device lists. Passing a single, large request, instead of many smaller requests, is often much more efficient in terms of the overhead of the underlying devices. All the *buffer_heads* in such an aggregate request are locked as soon as the initial I/O request is made. As the request is processed by a device driver, the individual *buffer_heads* constituting the aggregate request are unlocked one at a time; a process waiting on one buffer does not need to wait for all the other buffers in the request to become unlocked, too. This factor is particularly important because it ensures that read-ahead can be performed efficiently.

One final feature of the request manager is that I/O requests can be made that bypass the buffer cache entirely. The low-level page I/O function, `brw_page`, creates a set of temporary *buffer_heads* to label the contents of a page of memory for the purpose of submitting I/O requests to the request manager. However, these temporary *buffer_heads* are not linked into the buffer cache, and once the final buffer on the page has completed its I/O, the entire page is unlocked and the *buffer_heads* are discarded.

This cache-bypassing mechanism is used in the kernel whenever the caller is doing independent caching of data, or whenever the data are known to be no longer cachable. The page cache fills its pages in this way, to avoid unnecessary caching of the same data in both the page cache and the buffer cache. The virtual-memory system also bypasses the cache when performing I/O to swap devices.

20.8.2 Character Devices

A character-device driver can be almost any device driver that does not offer random access to fixed blocks of data. Any character-device drivers registered to the Linux kernel must also register a set of functions that implements the file I/O operations that the driver can handle. The kernel performs almost no preprocessing of a file read or write request to a character device, but simply passes the request to the device in question, and lets the device deal with the request.

The main exception to this rule is the special subset of character-device drivers that implement terminal devices. The kernel maintains a standard interface to these drivers by means of a set of *tty_struct* structures. Each of these structures provides buffering and flow control on the data stream from the terminal device and feeds those data to a line discipline.

A **line discipline** is an interpreter for the information from the terminal device. The most common line discipline is the `tty` discipline, which glues the terminal's data stream onto the standard input and output streams of a user's running processes, allowing those processes to communicate directly with the user's terminal. This job is complicated by the fact that more than one such process may be running simultaneously, and the `tty` line discipline is responsible for attaching and detaching the terminal's input and output from the various processes connected to it as those processes are suspended or are woken up by the user.

Other line disciplines also are implemented that have nothing to do with I/O to a user process. The PPP and SLIP networking protocols are ways of encoding a networking connection over a terminal device such as a serial line. These protocols are implemented under Linux as drivers that at one end appear to the terminal system as line disciplines, and at the other end appear to the networking system as a network-device driver. After one of these line disciplines has been enabled on a terminal device, any data appearing on that terminal will be routed directly to the appropriate network device driver.

20.9 ■ Interprocess Communication

UNIX provides a rich environment for allowing processes to communicate with each other. Communication may be just a matter of letting another process know that some event has occurred, or it may involve transferring data from one process to another.

20.9.1 Synchronization and Signals

The standard UNIX mechanism for informing a process that an event has occurred is the **signal**. Signals can be sent from any process to any other process. with restrictions on signals sent to processes owned by another user. However, a limited number of signals are available and they cannot carry information: Only the fact that a signal occurred is available to a process. Signals do not need to be generated by another process. The kernel also generates signals internally; for example, it can send a signal to a server process when data arrive on a network channel, to a parent process when a child terminates, or when a timer expires.

Internally, the Linux kernel does not use signals to communicate with processes running in kernel mode: If a kernel-mode process is expecting an event to occur, it will not normally use signals to receive notification of that event. Rather, communication about incoming asynchronous events within the kernel is performed through the use of scheduling states and `wait_queue` structures. These mechanisms allow kernel-mode processes to inform one another about relevant events, and they also allow events to be generated by device drivers or by the networking system. Whenever a process wants to wait for some event to complete, it places itself on a `wait_queue` associated with that event and tells the scheduler that it is no longer eligible for execution. Once the event has completed, it will wake up every process on the `wait_queue`. This procedure allows multiple processes to wait for a single event. For example, if several processes are trying to read a file from a disk, then they will all be woken up once the data have been read into memory successfully.

Although signals have always been the main mechanism for communicating asynchronous events among processes, Linux also implements the semaphore mechanism of System V UNIX. A process can wait on a semaphore as easily as it can wait for a signal, but semaphores have two advantages: large numbers of semaphores can be shared among multiple independent processes, and operations on multiple semaphores can be performed atomically. Internally, the standard Linux `wait_queue` mechanism synchronizes processes that are communicating with semaphores.

20.9.2 Passing of Data Among Processes

Linux offers several mechanisms for passing data among processes. The standard UNIX **pipe** mechanism allows a child process to inherit a communication channel from its parent; data written to one end of the pipe can be read at the other. Under Linux, pipes appear as just another type of inode to virtual-file-system software, and each pipe has a pair of `wait_queues` to synchronize the reader and writer. UNIX also defines a set of networking facilities that can send streams of data to both local and remote processes. Networking is covered in Section 20.10.

Two other methods of sharing data among processes are available. First, shared memory offers an extremely fast way to communicate large or small numbers of data; any data written by one process to a shared-memory region can be read immediately by any other process that has mapped that region into its address space. The main disadvantage of shared memory is that, on its own, it offers no synchronization: A process can neither ask the operating system whether a piece of shared memory has been written to, nor suspend execution until such a write occurs. Shared memory becomes particularly powerful when used in conjunction with another interprocess-communication mechanism that provides the missing synchronization.

A shared-memory region in Linux is a persistent object that can be created or deleted by processes. Such an object is treated as though it were a small independent address space: The Linux paging algorithms can elect to page out to disk shared-memory pages, just as they can page out a process's data pages. The shared-memory object acts as a backing store for shared-memory regions, just as a file can act as a backing store for a memory-mapped memory region. When a file is mapped into a virtual-address-space region, then any page faults that occur cause the appropriate page of the file to be mapped into virtual memory. Similarly, shared-memory mappings direct page faults to map in pages from a persistent shared-memory object. Also just as for files, shared-memory objects remember their contents even if no processes are currently mapping them into virtual memory.

20.10 ■ Network Structure

Networking is a key area of functionality for Linux. Not only does Linux support the standard Internet protocols used for most UNIX-to-UNIX communications, but it also implements a number of protocols native to other, non-UNIX operating systems. In particular, since Linux was originally implemented primarily on PCs, rather than on large workstations or on server class systems, it supports many of the protocols typically used on PC networks, such as AppleTalk and IPX.

Internally, networking in the Linux kernel is implemented by three layers of software:

1. The socket interface

2. Protocol drivers

3. Network-device drivers

User applications perform all networking requests through the socket interface. This interface is designed to look like the BSD4.3 socket layer, so that any programs designed to make use of Berkeley sockets will run on Linux without any source-code changes. This interface is described in Section A.9.1. The BSD socket interface is sufficiently general purpose to represent network addresses for a wide range of networking protocols. This single interface is used in Linux to access not just those protocols implemented on standard BSD systems, but all the protocols supported by the system.

The next layer of software is the protocol stack, which is similar in organization to BSD's own framework. Whenever any networking data arrive at this layer, either from an application's socket or from a network-device driver, the data are expected to have been tagged with an identifier specifying which network protocol they contain. Protocols can communicate with one another if they desire; for example, within the Internet protocol set, separate protocols manage routing, error reporting, and reliable retransmission of lost data.

The protocol layer may rewrite packets, create new packets, split or reassemble packets into fragments, or simply discard incoming data. Ultimately, once it has finished processing a set of packets, it passes them on, up to the socket interface if the data are destined for a local connection or downward to a device driver if the packet needs to be transmitted remotely. The protocol layer decides to which socket or device to send the packet.

All communication between the layers of the networking stack is performed by passing single **skbuff** structures. An skbuff contains a set of pointers into a single continuous area of memory, representing a buffer inside which network packets can be constructed. The valid data in an skbuff do not need to start at the beginning of the skbuff's buffer, and they do not need to run to the end. The networking code can add data to or trim data from either end of the packet, as long as the result still fits into the skbuff. This capacity is especially important on modern microprocessors where improvements in CPU speed have far outstripped the performance of main memory: The skbuff architecture allows flexibility in manipulating packet headers and checksums while avoiding any unnecessary data copying.

The most important set of protocols in the Linux networking system is the Internet protocol (IP) suite. This suite comprises a number of separate protocols. The IP protocol implements routing between different hosts anywhere on the network. On top of the routing protocol are built the UDP, TCP, and ICMP protocols. The UDP protocol carries arbitrary individual datagrams between hosts. The TCP protocol implements reliable connections between hosts with guaranteed in-order delivery of packets and automatic retransmission of lost data. The ICMP protocol is used to carry various error and status messages between hosts.

Packets (skbuffs) arriving at the networking stack's protocol software are expected to be already tagged with an internal identifier indicating to which protocol the packet is relevant. Different networking-device drivers encode the protocol type in different ways over their communications media; thus, identifying the protocol for incoming data must be done in the device driver. The device driver uses a hash table of known networking-protocol identifiers to look up the appropriate protocol, and passes the packet to that protocol. New protocols can be added to the hash table as kernel-loadable modules.

Incoming IP packets are delivered to the IP driver. The job of this layer is to perform routing: It decides where the packet is destined and forwards it to the appropriate internal protocol driver to be delivered locally, or injects it back into a selected network-device-driver queue to be forwarded to another host. It performs the routing decision using two tables: the persistent forwarding information base (FIB), and a cache of recent routing decisions. The FIB holds routing-configuration information and can specify routes based either on a specific destination address or on a wildcard representing multiple destinations. The FIB is organized as a set of hash tables indexed by destination address; the tables representing the most specific routes are always searched first. Successful lookups from this table are added to the route-caching table, which caches routes only by specific destination; no wildcards are stored in the cache, so lookups can be made quickly. An entry in the route cache expires after a fixed period with no hits.

At various stages, the IP software passes packets to a separate section of code for **firewall management**: selective filtering of packets according to arbitrary criteria, usually for security purposes. The firewall manager maintains a number of separate **firewall chains**, and allows an skbuff to be matched against any chain. Chains are reserved for separate purposes: One is used for forwarded packets, one for packets being input to this host, and one for data generated at this host. Each chain is held as an ordered list of rules, where a rule specifies one of a number of possible firewall-decision functions plus some arbitrary data to match against.

Two other functions performed by the IP driver are disassembly and reassembly of large packets. If an outgoing packet is too large to be queued to a device, it is simply split up into smaller **fragments**, which are all queued to the driver. At the receiving host, these fragments must be reassembled. The IP driver maintains an ipfrag object for each fragment awaiting reassembly, and an ipq for each datagram being assembled. Incoming fragments are matched against each known ipq. If a match is found, the fragment is added to it; otherwise, a new ipq is created. Once the final fragment has arrived for a ipq, a completely new skbuff is constructed to hold the new packet, and this packet is passed back into the IP driver.

Packets matched by the IP as destined for this host are passed on to one of the other protocol drivers. The UDP and TCP protocols share a means of associating packets with source and destination sockets: Each connected pair of sockets is uniquely identified by its source and destination addresses and by the source and destination port numbers. The socket lists are linked onto hash tables keyed on these four address–port values for socket lookup on incoming packets. The TCP protocol has to deal with unreliable connections, so it maintains ordered lists of unacknowledged outgoing packets to retransmit after a timeout, and of incoming out-of-order packets to be presented to the socket when the missing data have arrived.

20.11 ■ Security

Linux's security model is closely related to typical UNIX security mechanisms. The security concerns can be classified in two groups:

1. **Authentication:** Making sure that nobody can access the system without first proving that she has entry rights

2. **Access control:** Providing a mechanism for checking whether a user has the right to access a certain object, and preventing access to objects as required

20.11.1 Authentication

Authentication in UNIX has typically been performed through the use of a publicly readable password file. A user's password is combined with a random "salt" value and the result is encoded with a one-way transformation function and stored in the password file. The use of the one-way function means that the original password cannot be deduced from the password file except by trial and error. When a user presents a password to the system, the password is recombined with the salt value stored in the password file and passed through the same one-way transformation. If the result matches the contents of the password file, then the password is accepted.

Historically, UNIX implementations of this mechanism have had several problems. Passwords were often limited to eight characters, and the number of possible salt values was so low that an attacker could easily combine a dictionary of commonly used passwords with every possible salt value and have a good chance of matching one or more passwords in the password file, gaining unauthorized access to any accounts compromised as a result. Extensions to the password mechanism have been introduced that keep the encrypted password secret in a file that is not publicly readable, that allow longer passwords, or that use more secure methods of encoding the password. Other authentication mechanisms have been introduced that limit the times during which a user is permitted to connect to the system or to distribute authentication information to all the related systems in a network.

A new security mechanism has been developed by UNIX vendors to address these issues. The **pluggable authentication modules (PAM)** system is based on a shared library that can be used by any system component that needs to authenticate users. An implementation of this system is available under Linux. PAM allows authentication modules to be loaded on demand as specified in a system-wide configuration file. If a new authentication mechanism is added at a later date, it can be added to the configuration file and all system components will immediately be able to take advantage of it. PAM modules can specify authentication methods, account restrictions, session-setup functions, or password-changing functions (so that, when users change their passwords, all the necessary authentication mechanisms can be updated at once).

20.11.2 Access Control

Access control under UNIX systems, including Linux, is performed through the use of unique numeric identifiers. A user identifier (uid) identifies a single user or a single set of access rights. A group identifier (gid) is an extra identifier that can be used to identify rights belonging to more than one user.

Access control is applied to various objects in the system. Every file available in the system is protected by the standard access-control mechanism. In addition, other shared objects, such as shared-memory sections and semaphores, employ the same access system.

Every object in a UNIX system under user and group access control has a single uid and a single gid associated with it. User processes also have a single uid, but they may have more than one gid. If a process's uid matches the uid of an object, then the process has **user rights** or **owner rights** to that object. If the uids do not match but any of the process's gids match the object's gid, then **group rights** are conferred; otherwise, the process has **world rights** to the object.

Linux performs access control by assigning objects a **protection mask** that specifies which access modes—read, write, or execute—are to be granted to processes with owner, group, or world access. Thus, the owner of an object might have full read, write, and execute access to a file; other users in a certain group might be given read access but denied write access; and everybody else might be given no access at all.

The only exception is the privileged **root** uid. A process with this special uid is granted automatic access to any object in the system, bypassing normal access checks. Such processes are also granted permission to perform privileged operations such as reading any physical memory or opening reserved network sockets. This mechanism allows the kernel to prevent normal users from accessing these resources: Most of the kernel's key internal resources are implicitly owned by this root uid.

Linux implements the standard UNIX setuid mechanism described in Section A.3.2. This mechanism allows a program to run with privileges different from those of the user running the program: For example, the lpr program (which submits a job onto a print queue) has access to the system's print queues even if the user running that program does not. The UNIX implementation of setuid distinguishes between a process's *real* and *effective* uid: The real uid is that of the user running the program; the effective uid is that of the file's owner.

Under Linux, this mechanism is augmented in two ways. First, Linux implements the POSIX specification's saved user-id mechanism, which allows a process to drop and reacquire its effective uid repeatedly. For security reasons, a program may want to perform most of its operations in a safe mode, waiving the privileges granted by its `setuid` status, but may wish to perform selected operations with all its privileges. Standard UNIX implementations achieve this capacity only by swapping the real and effective uids; the previous effective uid is remembered but the program's real uid does not always correspond to the uid of the user running the program. Saved uids allow a process to set its effective uid to its real uid and then back to the previous value of its effective uid, without having to modify the real uid at any time.

The second enhancement provided by Linux is the addition of a process characteristic that grants just a subset of the rights of the effective uid. The **fsuid** and **fsgid** process properties are used when access rights are granted to files, and are set every time the effective uid or gid is set. However, the fsuid and fsgid can be set independently of the effective ids, allowing a process to access files on behalf of another user without taking on the identity of that other user in any other way. Specifically, server processes can use this mechanism to serve files to a certain user without the process becoming vulnerable to being killed or suspended by that user.

Linux provides another mechanism that has become common in modern versions of UNIX for flexible passing of rights from one program to another. When a local network socket has been set up between any two processes on the system, either of those processes may send to the other process a file descriptor for one of its open files; the other process receives a duplicate file descriptor for the same file. This mechanism allows a client to pass access to a single file selectively to some server process, without granting that process any other privileges. For example, it is no longer necessary for a print server to be able to read all the files of a user who submits a new print job; the print client could simply pass the server file descriptors for any files to be printed, denying the server access to any of the user's other files.

20.12 ■ Summary

Linux is a modern, free operating system based on UNIX standards. It has been designed to run efficiently and reliably on common PC hardware; it also runs on a variety of other platforms. It provides a programming interface and user interface compatible with standard UNIX systems, and can run a large number of UNIX applications, including an increasing number of commercially supported applications.

Linux has not evolved in a vacuum. A complete Linux system includes many components that were developed independently of Linux. The core Linux operating-system kernel is entirely original, but it allows much existing free UNIX software to run, resulting in an entire UNIX-compatible operating system free from proprietary code.

The Linux kernel is implemented as a traditional monolithic kernel for performance reasons, but it is modular enough in design to allow most drivers to be dynamically loaded and unloaded at run time.

Linux is a multiuser system, providing protection between processes and running multiple processes according to a time-sharing scheduler. Newly created processes can share selective parts of their execution environment with their parent processes, allowing multithreaded programming. Interprocess communication is supported by both System V mechanisms—message queues, semaphores, and shared memory—and BSD's socket interface. Multiple networking protocols can be accessed simultaneously through the socket interface.

To the user, the file system appears as a hierarchical directory tree that obeys UNIX semantics. Internally, Linux uses an abstraction layer to manage multiple different file systems. Device-oriented, networked, and virtual file systems are supported. Device-oriented file systems access disk storage through two caches: Data are cached in the page cache that is unified with the virtual-memory system, and metadata are cached in the buffer cache—a separate cache indexed by physical disk block.

The memory-management system uses page sharing and copy-on-write to minimize the duplication of data shared by different processes. Pages are loaded on demand when they are first referenced, and are paged back out to backing store according to an LFU algorithm if physical memory needs to be reclaimed.

■ Exercises

20.1 Linux runs on a variety of hardware platforms. What steps must the Linux developers take to ensure that the system is portable to different processors and memory-management architectures, and to minimize the amount of architecture-specific kernel code?

20.2 Dynamically loadable kernel modules give flexibility when drivers are added to a system. Do they also have disadvantages? Under what circumstances would a kernel be compiled into a single binary file? When would it be better to keep it split into modules? Explain your answers.

20.3 Multithreading is a commonly used programming technique. Describe three ways that threads could be implemented. Explain how these ways compare to the Linux clone mechanism. When might each alternative mechanism be better or worse than using clones?

20.4 What extra costs are incurred by the creation and scheduling of a process, as compared to the cost of a cloned thread?

20.5 The Linux scheduler implements *soft* real-time scheduling. What features necessary for certain real-time programming tasks are missing? How might they be added to the kernel?

20.6 The Linux kernel does not allow paging out of kernel memory. What effect does this restriction have on the kernel's design? What are two advantages and two disadvantages of this design decision?

20.7 In Linux, shared libraries perform many operations central to the operating system. What is the advantage of keeping this functionality out of the kernel? Are there any drawbacks? Explain your answer.

20.8 What are three advantages of dynamic (or shared) linking of libraries compared to static linking? What are two cases where static linking is preferable?

20.9 Compare the use of networking sockets with the use of shared memory as a mechanism for communicating data between processes on a single computer. Name two of the advantages of each method. When might each be preferred?

20.10 UNIX systems used to use disk-layout optimizations based on the rotation position of disk data, but modern implementations, including Linux, simply optimize for sequential data access. Why do they do so? Of what hardware characteristics does sequential access take advantage? Why is rotational optimization no longer so useful?

20.11 The Linux source code is freely and widely available over the Internet or from CD-ROM vendors. What are three implications of this availability for the security of the Linux system?

Bibliographical Notes

The Linux system is a product of the Internet; as a result, most of the available documentation on Linux is available in some form on the Internet. The following key sites reference most of the useful information available:

- The Linux Cross-Reference Pages at http://lxr.linux.no/ maintain current listings of the Linux kernel, browsable via the Web and fully cross-referenced.

- Linux-HQ at http://www.linuxhq.com/ hosts a large amount of information relating to the Linux 2.x kernels. This site also includes links to the home pages of most Linux distributions, as well as archives of the major mailing lists.

- The Linux Documentation Project at http://sunsite.unc.edu/linux/ lists many books on Linux that are available in source format as part of the Linux Documentation Project. The project also hosts the Linux *How-To* guides, which contain a series of hints and tips relating to aspects of Linux.

- The *Kernel Hackers' Guide* is an Internet-based guide to kernel internals in general. This constantly expanding site is located at http://www.redhat.com:8080/HyperNews/get/khg.html.

In addition, many mailing lists devoted to Linux are available. The most important are maintained by a mailing-list manager that can be reached at the email address `majordomo@vger.rutgers.edu`. Send e-mail to this address with the single line "help" in the mail's body for information on how to access the list server and to subscribe to any lists.

The one book that currently describes the internal details of the Linux kernel is *Linux Kernel Internals* by Beck et al. [1998]. For further reading on UNIX in general, a good place to start is Vahalia's *Unix Internals: The New Frontiers* (Vahalia [1996]).

Finally, the Linux system itself can be obtained over the Internet. Complete Linux distributions can be obtained from the home sites of the companies concerned, and the Linux community also maintains archives of current system components at several places on the Internet. The most important are these:

- ftp://tsx-11.mit.edu/pub/linux/

- ftp://sunsite.unc.edu/pub/Linux/

- ftp://linux.kernel.org/pub/linux/

Chapter 21

WINDOWS XP

The Microsoft Windows XP operating system is a 32/64-bit preemptive multitasking operating system for AMD K6/K7, Intel IA32/IA64 and later microprocessors. The successor to Windows NT/2000, Windows XP is also intended to replace the Windows 95/98 operating system. Key goals for the system are security, reliability, ease of use, Windows and POSIX application compatibility, high performance, extensibility, portability and international support. In this chapter, we discuss the key goals for Windows XP, the layered architecture of the system that makes it so easy to use, the file system, networks, and the programming interface.

21.1 ■ History

In the mid-1980s, Microsoft and IBM cooperated to develop the OS/2 operating system, which was written in assembly language for single-processor Intel 80286 systems. In 1988, Microsoft decided to make a fresh start and to develop a "new technology" (or NT) portable operating system that supported both the OS/2 and POSIX application-programming interfaces (APIs). In October, 1988, Dave Cutler, the architect of the DEC VAX/VMS operating system, was hired and given the charter of building this new operating system.

Originally, the team planned for NT to use the OS/2 API as its native environment, but during development, NT was changed to use the 32-bit Windows API (or Win32 API), reflecting the popularity of Windows 3.0. The first versions of NT were Windows NT 3.1 and Windows NT 3.1 Advanced Server.

(At that time, 16-bit Windows was at Version 3.1.) Windows NT version 4.0 adopted the Windows 95 user interface and incorporated Internet web-server and web-browser software. In addition, user-interface routines and all graphics code were moved into the kernel to improve performance, with the side effect of decreased system reliability. Although previous versions of NT had been ported to other microprocessor architectures, the Windows 2000 version, released in February 2000, discontinued support for other than Intel (and compatible) processors due to marketplace factors. Windows 2000 incorporated significant changes over Windows NT. It added Active Directory (an X.500-based directory service), better networking and laptop support, support for plug-and-play devices, a distributed file system, and support for more processors and more memory.

In October 2001 Windows XP was released as both an update to the Windows 2000 desktop operating system and a replacement for Windows 95/98. In 2002 the server versions of Windows XP became available (called Windows .Net Server). Windows XP updates the graphical user interface with a visual design that takes advantage of more recent hardware advances and many new **ease-of-use** features. Numerous features have been added to automatically repair problems in applications and the operating system itself. Windows XP provides better networking and device experience (including zero-configuration wireless, instant messaging, streaming media, digital photography/video), dramatic performance improvements both for the desktop and large multiprocessors, and better reliability and security than even Windows 2000.

Windows XP uses a client–server architecture (like Mach) to implement multiple operating-system personalities, such as Win32 and POSIX, with user-level processes called subsystems. The subsystem architecture allows enhancements to be made to one operating system personality without affecting the other's application compatibility.

Windows XP is a multiuser operating system, supporting simultaneous access through distributed services, or through multiple instances of the graphical user interface (GUI) via the Windows terminal server. The server versions of Windows XP support simultaneous terminal server sessions from Windows desktop systems. The desktop versions of terminal server multiplex the keyboard, mouse, and monitor between virtual terminal sessions for each logged-on user. This feature, called fast-user switching, allows users to preempt each other at the console of a PC without having to log off and on the system.

Windows XP is the first version of Windows to ship a 64-bit version. The native NT File System (NTFS) and many of the Win32 APIs have always used 64-bit integers where appropriate—so the major extension to 64-bit in Windows XP is support for large addresses.

There are two desktop versions of Windows XP. Windows XP Professional is the premium desktop system for power users at work and at home. For home users migrating from Windows 95/98, Windows XP Personal provides the relia-

bility and ease of use of Windows XP, but without the more advanced features needed to work seamlessly with Active Directory or run POSIX applications.

The members of the Windows .Net Server family use the same core components as the desktop versions, but add a range of features needed for uses such as webserver farms, print/file servers, clustered systems, and large datacenter machines. The large datacenter machines can reach to 64 GB of memory and 32 processors on IA32 systems, and 128 GB and 64 processors on IA64 systems.

21.2 ■ Design Principles

Microsoft's design goals for Windows XP include security, reliability, Windows and POSIX application compatibility, high performance, extensibility, portability, and international support.

21.2.1 Security

Windows XP **security** goals required more than just adherence to the design standards that enabled Windows NT4.0 to receive C-2 security classification from the U.S. government (which signifies a moderate level of protection from defective software and malicious attacks). Extensive code review and testing were combined with sophisticated automatic analysis tools to identify and investigate potential defects that might represent security vulnerabilities.

21.2.2 Reliability

Windows 2000 was the most reliable, stable operating system Microsoft ever shipped to that point. Much of this reliability came from maturity in the source code, extensive stress testing of the system, and automatic detection of many serious errors in drivers. The **reliability** requirements for Windows XP were even more stringent. Microsoft used extensive manual and automatic code review to identify over 63,000 lines in the source files that might contain issues not detected by testing, and set about reviewing each area to verify that the code was indeed correct.

Windows XP extends driver verification to catch more subtle bugs, improves the facilities for catching programming errors in user-level code, and subjects third-party applications, drivers, and devices to a rigorous certification process. Furthermore, Windows XP adds new facilities for monitoring the health of the PC including downloading fixes for problems before they are encountered by users. The perceived reliability of Windows XP was also improved by making the graphical user interface easier to use through better visual design, simpler menus, and measured improvements in the discoverability of how to perform common tasks.

21.2.3 Windows and Posix Application Compatibility

Windows XP is not only an update of Windows 2000; it is a replacement for Windows 95/98. Windows 2000 focused primarily on compatibility for business applications. The requirements for Windows XP include a much higher compatibility with consumer applications that run on Windows 95/98. **Application compatibility** is difficult to achieve because each application checks for a particular version of Windows, may have dependence on the quirks of the implementation of APIs, and may have latent application bugs that were masked in the previous system, and other similar dependencies.

Windows XP introduces a compatibility layer that falls between applications and the Win32 APIs. This layer makes Windows XP look (almost) bug-for-bug compatible with previous versions of Windows. Windows XP, like earlier NT releases, maintains support for running many 16-bit applications using a thunking layer that translates 16-bit API calls into equivalent 32-bit calls. Similarly, the 64-bit version of Windows XP provides a thunking layer that translates 32-bit API calls into native 64-bit calls. Posix support in Windows XP is much improved. A new POSIX subsystem called Interix is now available. Most available UNIX-compatible software compiles and runs under Interix without modification.

21.2.4 High Performance

Windows XP is designed to provide **high performance** on desktop systems (which are largely constrained by I/O performance), server systems (where CPU is often the bottleneck), and large multithreaded and multiprocessor environments (where locking and cache-line management are key to scalability). High performance has been an increasingly important goal for Windows XP. Windows 2000 with SQL 2000 on Compaq hardware achieved top TPC-C numbers at the time it shipped.

To satisfy performance requirements NT uses a variety of techniques such as asynchronous I/O, optimized protocols for networks (e.g. optimistic locking of distributed data, batching of requests), kernel-based graphics, and sophisticated caching of file-system data. The memory-management and synchronization algorithms are designed with an awareness of the performance considerations related to cache-lines and multiprocessors.

Windows XP has further improved performance by reducing the code-path length in critical functions, using better algorithms and per-processor data structures, using memory coloring for NUMA (Non-Uniform Memory Access) machines, and implementing more scalable locking protocols, such as queued spinlocks. The new locking protocols help reduce system bus cycles, lock-free lists and queues, use of atomic read-modify-write operations (like interlocked increment), and other advanced locking techniques.

The subsystems that constitute Windows XP communicate with one another efficiently by a local procedure call (LPC) facility that provides

high-performance message passing. Except while executing in the kernel dispatcher, threads in the subsystems of Windows XP can be preempted by higher-priority threads. Thus, the system responds quickly to external events. In addition, Windows XP is designed for symmetrical multiprocessing; on a multiprocessor computer, several threads can run at the same time.

21.2.5 Extensibility

Extensibility refers to the capacity of an operating system to keep up with advances in computing technology. So that changes are facilitated over time, the developers implemented Windows XP using a layered architecture. The Windows XP executive runs in kernel or protected mode and provides the basic system services. On top of the executive, several server subsystems operate in user-mode. Among them are **environmental subsystems** that emulate different operating systems. Thus, programs written for MS-DOS, Microsoft Windows, and POSIX all run on Windows XP in the appropriate environment. (See Section 21.4 for more information on environmental subsystems.) Because of the modular structure, additional environmental subsystems can be added without affecting the executive. In addition, Windows XP uses loadable drivers in the I/O system, so new file systems, new kinds of I/O devices, and new kinds of networking can be added while the system is running. Windows XP uses a client–server model like the Mach operating system, and supports distributed processing by remote procedure calls (RPCs) as defined by the Open Software Foundation.

21.2.6 Portability

An operating system is **portable** if it can be moved from one hardware architecture to another with relatively few changes. Windows XP is designed to be portable. As is true of the UNIX operating system, the majority of the system is written in C and C++. Most processor-dependent code is isolated in a dynamic link library (DLL) called the **hardware-abstraction layer (HAL)**. A DLL is a file that gets mapped into a process's address space such that any functions in the DLL appear to be part of the process. The upper layers of Windows XP kernel depend on the HAL interfaces rather than on the underlying hardware, bolstering Windows XP portability. The HAL manipulates hardware directly, isolating the rest of Windows XP from hardware differences among the platforms on which it runs.

Although for market reasons Windows 2000 only shipped on Intel IA32-compatible platforms, it was also tested on IA32 and DEC Alpha platforms until just prior to release to ensure portability. Windows XP runs on IA32-compatible and IA64 processors. Microsoft recognizes the importance of multiplatform development and testing, since, as a practical matter, maintaining portability is a matter of *use it or lose it*.

21.2.7 International Support

Windows XP is also designed for **international** and **multinational** use. It provides support for different locales via the **national-language-support (NLS) API**. The NLS API provides specialized routines to format dates, time, and money in accordance with various national customs. String comparisons are specialized to account for varying character sets. UNICODE is Windows XP's native character code. Windows XP supports ANSI characters by converting them to UNICODE characters before manipulating them (8-bit to 16-bit conversion). System text strings are kept in resource files that can be replaced to localize the system for different languages. Multiple locales can be used concurrently, which is important to multilingual individuals and businesses.

21.3 ■ System Components

The architecture of Windows XP is a layered system of modules, as shown in Figure 21.1. The main layers are the HAL, the kernel, and the executive, all of which run in protected mode, and a collection of subsystems and services that run in user mode. The user-mode subsystems fall into two categories. The environmental subsystems emulate different operating systems; the **protection subsystems** provide security functions. One of the chief advantages of this type of architecture is that interactions between modules are kept simple. The remainder of this section describes these layers and subsystems.

21.3.1 Hardware-Abstraction Layer

The HAL is the layer of software that hides hardware differences from upper levels of the operating system, to help make Windows XP portable. The HAL exports a virtual-machine interface that is used by the kernel dispatcher, the executive, and the device drivers. One advantage of this approach is that only a single version of each device driver is required—it runs on all hardware platforms without porting the driver code. The HAL also provides support for symmetric multiprocessing. Device drivers map devices and access them directly, but the administrative details of mapping memory, configuring I/O busses, setting up DMA and coping with motherboard-specific facilities are all provided by the HAL interfaces.

21.3.2 Kernel

The kernel of Windows XP provides the foundation for the executive and the subsystems. The kernel remains in memory, and its execution is never preempted. It has four main responsibilities: thread scheduling, interrupt and exception handling, low-level processor synchronization, and recovery after a power failure.

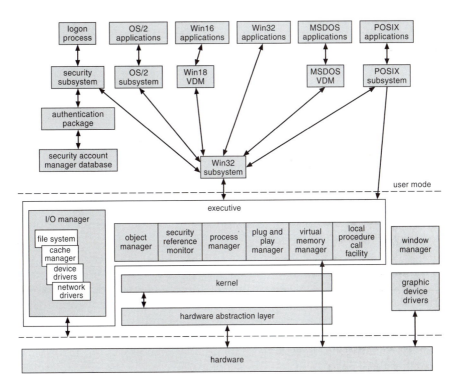

Figure 21.1   Windows XP block diagram.

The kernel is object oriented. An *object type* in Windows 2000 is a system-defined data type that has a set of attributes (data values) and a set of methods (for example, functions or operations). An *object* is an instance of an object type. The kernel performs its job by using a set of kernel objects whose attributes store the kernel data, and whose methods perform the kernel activities.

21.3.2.1 Kernel Dispatcher

The kernel dispatcher provides the foundation for the executive and the subsystems. Most of the dispatcher is never paged out of memory, and its execution is never preempted. Its main responsibilities are thread scheduling, implementation of synchronization primitives, timer management, software interrupts (asynchronous and deferred procedure calls), and exception dispatching.

21.3.2.2 Threads and Scheduling

As do many modern operating systems, Windows XP uses the concepts of processes and threads for executable code. The process has a virtual-memory address space, and information used to initialize each thread, such as a base priority and an affinity for either one or more processors. Each process has one or more threads, each of which is an executable unit dispatched by the kernel. Each thread has its own scheduling state, including actual priority, processor affinity, and CPU-usage information.

The six possible thread states are ready, standby, running, waiting, transition, and terminated. **Ready** indicates waiting to run. The highest-priority ready thread is moved to the **standby** state, which means it is the next thread to run. In a multiprocessor system, each process keeps one thread in a standby state. A thread is **running** when it is executing on a processor. It runs until it is preempted by a higher-priority thread, it terminates, its alloted execution time (**quantum**) ends, or it blocks on a dispatcher object, such as an event signaling I/O completion. A thread is in the **waiting** state when it is waiting for a dispatcher object to be signaled. A new thread is in the **transition** state while it waits for resources necessary for execution. A thread enters the **terminated** state when it finishes execution.

The dispatcher uses a 32-level priority scheme to determine the order of thread execution. Priorities are divided into two classes: variable class and real-time class. The variable class contains threads having priorities from 0 to 15, and the real-time class contains threads with priorities ranging from 16 to 31. The dispatcher uses a queue for each scheduling priority, and traverses the set of queues from highest to lowest until it finds a thread that is ready to run. If a thread has a particular processor affinity but that processor is not available, the dispatcher skips past it, and continues looking for a ready thread that is willing to run on the available processor. If no ready thread is found, the dispatcher executes a special thread called the idle thread.

When a thread's time quantum runs out, the clock interrupt queues a quantum-end DPC to the processor in order to reschedule the processor. If the preempted thread is in the variable-priority class, its priority is lowered. The priority is never lowered below the base priority. Lowering the thread's priority tends to limit the CPU consumption of compute-bound threads. When a variable-priority thread is released from a wait operation, the dispatcher boosts the priority. The amount of the boost depends on the device for which the thread was waiting; for example, a thread that was waiting for keyboard I/O would get a large priority increase, whereas a thread waiting for a disk operation would get a moderate one. This strategy tends to give good response times to interactive threads using a mouse and windows, and enables I/O-bound threads to keep the I/O devices busy, while permitting compute-bound threads to use spare CPU cycles in the background. This strategy is used by several time-sharing operating systems, including UNIX. In addition, the thread associated with the user's active GUI window receives a priority boost to enhance its response time.

Scheduling occurs when a thread enters the ready or wait state, when a thread terminates, or when an application changes a thread's priority or processor affinity. If a higher-priority real-time thread becomes ready while a lower-priority thread is running, the lower-priority thread is preempted. This preemption gives a real-time thread preferential access to the CPU when the thread needs such access. Windows XP is not a hard real-time operating system, however, because it does not guarantee that a real-time thread will start to execute within a particular time limit.

21.3.2.3 Implementation of Synchronization Primitives

Key operating-system data structures are managed as objects using common facilities for allocation, reference counting, and security. **Dispatcher objects** control dispatching and synchronization in the system. Examples of these objects are events, mutants, mutexes, semaphores, processes, threads, and timers. The **event object** is used to record an event occurrence and to synchronize the latter with some action. Notification events signal all waiting threads, and synchronization events signal a single waiting thread. The **mutant** provides kernel-mode or user-mode mutual exclusion with the notion of ownership. The **mutex**, available only in kernel mode, provides deadlock-free mutual exclusion. A **semaphore object** acts as a counter or gate to control the number of threads that access a resource. The **thread object** is the entity that is scheduled by the kernel dispatcher and is associated with a **process object** which encapsulates a virtual address space. **Timer objects** are used to keep track of time and to signal timeouts when operations take too long and need to be interrupted, or a periodic activity needs to be scheduled.

Many of the dispatcher objects are accessed from user mode via an open operation that returns a handle. The user-mode code polls and/or waits on handles to synchronize with other threads as well as the operating system (see Section 21.7.1).

21.3.2.4 Software Interrupt: Asynchronous Procedure Calls

The dispatcher implements two types of software interrupts: asynchronous procedure calls and deferred procedure calls. Asynchronous procedure calls (APCs) break into an executing thread and call a procedure. APCs are used to begin execution of a new thread, terminate processes, and deliver notification that an asynchronous I/O has completed. APCs are queued to specific threads, and allow the system to execute both system and user code within a process's context.

21.3.2.5 Software Interrupt: Deferred Procedure Calls

Deferred procedure calls (DPCs) are used to postpone interrupt processing. After handling all blocked device-interrupt processes, the interrupt service routine (ISR) schedules the remaining processing by queuing a DPC. The dispatcher schedules software interrupts at a lower priority than the device interrupts so that DPCs do not block other ISRs.

In addition to deferring device-interrupt processing, the dispatcher uses DPCs to process timer expirations and to preempt thread execution at the end of the scheduling quantum.

Execution of DPCs prevents threads from being scheduled on the current processor, and also keeps APCs from signaling the completion of I/O. This is done so DPC routines do not take an extended amount of time to complete. As an alternative, the dispatcher maintains a pool of worker threads. ISRs and DPCs queue work items to the worker threads. DPC routines are restricted such that they cannot take page faults, call system services, or take any other action that might possibly result in an attempt to block execution on a dispatcher object. Unlike APCs, DPC routines make no assumptions about what process context the processor is executing.

21.3.2.6 Exceptions and Interrupts

The kernel dispatcher also provides trap handling for exceptions and interrupts generated by hardware or software. Windows XP defines several architecture-independent exceptions, including: memory-access violation, integer overflow, floating-point overflow or underflow, integer divide by zero, floating-point divide by zero, illegal instruction, data misalignment, privileged instruction, page-read error, access violation, paging file quota exceeded, debugger break-point, and debugger single step.

The trap handlers deal with simple exceptions. Elaborate exception handling is performed by the kernel's exception dispatcher. The **exception dispatcher** creates an exception record containing the reason for the exception and finds an exception handler to deal with it.

When an exception occurs in kernel mode, the exception dispatcher simply calls a routine to locate the exception handler. If no handler is found, a fatal system error occurs and the user is left with the infamous "blue screen of death" that signifies system failure.

Exception handling is more complex for user-mode processes, because an environmental subsystem (such as the POSIX system) sets up a debugger port and an exception port for every process it creates. If a debugger port is registered, the exception handler sends the exception to the port. If the debugger port is not found or does not handle that exception, the dispatcher attempts to find an appropriate exception handler. If a handler is not found, the debugger is called again to catch the error for debugging. If a debugger is not running, a message is sent to the process's exception port to give the environmental subsystem a chance to translate the exception. For example, the POSIX environment translates Windows XP exception messages into POSIX signals before sending them to the thread that caused the exception. Finally, if nothing else works, the kernel simply terminates the process that contains the thread that caused the exception.

The interrupt dispatcher in the kernel handles interrupts by calling either an interrupt service routine (ISR) supplied by a device driver, or a kernel trap-handler routine. The interrupt is represented by an interrupt object that contains all the information needed to handle the interrupt. Using an interrupt object makes it easy to associate interrupt-service routines with an interrupt without having to access the interrupt hardware directly.

Various processor architectures, such as Intel or DEC Alpha, have different types and numbers of interrupts. For portability, the interrupt dispatcher maps the hardware interrupts into a standard set. The interrupts are prioritized and are serviced in priority order. There are 32 interrupt request levels (**IRQLs**) in Windows XP. Eight are reserved for use by the kernel; the remaining 24 represent hardware interrupts via the HAL (although most IA32 systems use only 16). The Windows XP interrupts are defined in Figure 21.2.

The kernel uses an **interrupt-dispatch table** to bind each interrupt level to a service routine. In a multiprocessor computer, Windows XP keeps a separate interrupt-dispatch table for each processor, and each processor's IRQL can be set independently to mask out interrupts. All interrupts that occur at a level equal to or less than the IRQL of a processor get blocked until the IRQL is lowered by a kernel-level thread or by an ISR returning from interrupt processing. Windows XP takes advantage of this property and uses software interrupts to deliver APCs and DPCs, to perform system functions such as synchronizing threads with I/O completion, to start thread dispatches, and to handle timers.

21.3.3 Executive

The Windows XP executive provides a set of services that all environmental subsystems use. The services are grouped as follows: object manager, virtual-memory manager, process manager, local procedure call facility, I/O manager, security reference monitor, plug-and-play and security managers, registry, and booting.

interrupt levels	types of interrupts
31	machine check or bus error
30	power fail
29	interprocessor notification (request another processor to act; e.g., dispatch a process or update the TLB)
28	clock (used to keep track of time)
27	profile
3-26	traditional PC IRQ hardware interrupts
2	dispatch and deferred procedure call (DPC) (kernel)
1	asynchronous procedure call (APC)
0	passive

Figure 21.2 Windows XP interrupt request levels.

21.3.3.1 Object Manager

Windows XP uses a generic set of interfaces for managing the kernel-mode entities that is manipulated by user-mode programs. Windows XP calls these entities *objects*, and the executive component that manipulates them is the **object manager**. Each process has an object table containing entries that track the objects used by the process. User-mode code accesses these objects using an opaque value called a *handle* that is returned by many APIs. Object handles can also be created by duplicating an existing handle, either from the same process or a different process.

Examples of objects are semaphores, mutexes, events, processes and threads. These are all *dispatcher objects*. Threads can block in the kernel dispatcher waiting for any of these objects to be signaled. The process, thread, and virtual-memory APIs use process and thread handles to identify the process or thread to be operated on. Other examples of objects include files, sections, ports, and various internal I/O objects. File objects are used to maintain the open state of files and devices. Sections are used to map files. Open files are described in terms of file objects. Local-communication endpoints are implemented as port objects.

The object manager maintains the Windows XP internal namespace. In contrast to UNIX, which roots the system namespace in the file system, Windows XP uses an abstract namespace and connects the file systems as devices.

The object manager provides interfaces for defining both object types and object instances, translating names to objects, maintaining the abstract namespace (through internal directories and symbolic links), and managing object creation and deletion. Objects are typically managed using reference counts in protected-mode code and handles in user-mode. However, some kernel-mode components use the same APIs as user-mode code and thus use handles to manipulate objects. If a handle needs to exist beyond the lifetime of the current process, it is marked as a kernel handle and stored in the object table for the system process. The abstract namespace does not persist across reboots, but is built up from configuration information stored in the system registry, plug-and-play device discovery, and creation of objects by system components.

The Windows XP executive allows any object to be given a **name**. One process may create a named object, while a second process opens a handle to the object and shares it with the first process. Processes can also share objects by duplicating handles between processes, in which case the objects need not be named.

A name can be either permanent or temporary. A permanent name represents an entity, such as a disk drive, that remains even if no process is accessing it. A temporary name exists only while a process holds a handle to the object.

Object names are structured like file path names in MS-DOS and UNIX. Namespace directories are represented by a **directory object** that contains the names of all the objects in the directory. The object namespace is extended by the addition of device objects representing volumes containing file systems.

Objects are manipulated by a set of virtual functions with implementations provided for each object type: `create`, `open`, `close`, `delete`, `query name`, `parse`, and `security`. The latter three objects need explanation:

- `query name` is called when a thread has a reference to an object, but wants to know the object's name.

- `parse` is used by the object manager to search for an object given the object's name.

- `security` is called to make security checks on all object operations, such as when a process opens or closes an object, makes changes to the security descriptor, or duplicates a handle for an object.

The parse procedure is used to extend the abstract namespace to include files. The translation of a pathname to a file object begins at the root of the abstract namespace. Pathname components are separated by whack characters ('\') rather than the slashes ('/') used in UNIX. Each component is looked up in the current parse directory of the namespace. Internal nodes within the namespace are either directories or symbolic links. If a leaf object is found and there are no pathname components remaining, the leaf object is returned. Otherwise the leaf object's parse procedure is invoked with the remaining pathname.

Parse procedures are only used with a small number of objects belonging to the Windows GUI, the configuration manager (registry), and— most notably —device objects representing file systems.

The parse procedure for the device object type allocates a file object and initiates an open or create I/O operation on the file system. If successful, the file object fields are filled in to describe the file.

In summary, the pathname to a file is used to traverse the object-manager namespace, translating the original absolute pathname into a (device object, relative pathname) pair. This pair is then passed to the file system via the I/O manager, which fills in the file object. The file object itself has no name, but is referred to by a handle.

UNIX file systems have **symbolic links**, permitting multiple nicknames or aliases for the same file. The **symbolic-link object** implemented by the Windows XP object manager is used within the abstract namespace, not to alias files on a file system. Even so, symbolic links are still very useful. They are used to organize the namespace, similar to the organization of the /devices directory in UNIX. They are also used to map standard MS-DOS drive letters to drive names. Drive letters are symbolic links that can be remapped to suit the convenience of the user or administrator.

Drive letters are one place where the abstract namespace in Windows XP is not global. Each logged-on user has their own set of drive letters so they avoid interfering with one another. On the other hand, terminal server sessions share all processes within a session. BaseNamedObjects contain the named objects created by most applications.

Although the namespace is not directly visible across a network, the object manager's parse method is used to help access a named object on another system. When a process attempts to open an object that resides on a remote computer, the object manager calls the parse method for the device object corresponding to a network redirector. This results in an I/O operation which accesses the file across the network.

Objects are instances of an **object type**. The object type specifies how instances are to be allocated, the definitions of the data fields, and the implementation of the standard set of virtual functions used for all objects. These functions implement operations such as mapping names to objects, closing and deleting, and applying security.

The object manager keeps track of two counts for each object. The pointer count is the number of distinct references made to an object. Protected-mode code that refers to objects must keep a reference on the object to ensure the object isn't deleted while in use. The handle count is the number of handle table entries referring to an object. Each handle is also reflected in the reference count.

When a handle for an object is closed, the object's close routine is called. In the case of file objects this call causes the I/O manager to do a cleanup operation at the close of the last handle. The cleanup operation tells the file system that the file is no longer accessed by user mode so that it removes sharing restrictions, range locks, and other states specific to the corresponding open routine.

Each handle close removes a reference from the pointer count, but internal system components may retain additional references. When the final reference is removed, the object's delete procedure is called. Again using file objects as an example, the delete procedure causes the I/O manager to send the file system a close operation on the file object. This causes the file system to deallocate any internal data structures that were allocated for the file object.

After the delete procedure for a temporary object completes, the object is deleted from memory. Objects can be made permanent (at least with respect to the current boot of the system) by asking the object manager to take an extra reference against the object. Thus permanent objects are not deleted even when the last reference outside the object manager is removed. When a permanent object is made temporary again, the object manager removes the extra reference. If this was the last reference, the object is deleted. Permanent objects are rare, used mostly for devices, drive-letter mappings and the directory and symbolic link objects.

The job of the **object manager** is to supervise the use of all managed objects. When a thread wants to use an object, it calls the object manager's open method to get a reference to the object. If the object is being opened from a user-mode API, the reference is inserted into the process's object table and a handle is returned.

A process gets a handle by creating an object, by opening an existing object, by receiving a duplicated handle from another process, or by inheriting a handle from a **parent process**, similar to the way a UNIX process gets a file descriptor. These handles are all stored in the process's **object table**. An entry in the object table contains the object's access rights and states whether the handle should be inherited by **child processes**. When a process terminates, Windows XP automatically closes all the process's open handles.

Handles are a standardized interface to all kinds of objects. Like a file descriptor in UNIX, an object handle is an identifier unique to a process that confers the ability to access and manipulate a system resource. Handles can be duplicated within a process, or between processes. The latter case is used when creating child processes or implementing out-of-process execution contexts.

Since the object manager is the only entity that generates object handles, it is the natural place to check security. The object manager checks whether a process has the right to access an object when the process tries to open the object. The object manager also enforces quotas, such as the maximum amount of memory a process may use, by charging a process for the memory occupied by all its referenced objects and refusing to allocate more memory when the accumulated charges exceed the process's quota.

When the login process authenticates a user, an access-token is attached to the user's process. The access token contains information such as the security id, group ids, privileges, primary group, and default access-control list. The services and objects a user can access are determined by these attributes.

The token that controls access is associated with the thread making the access. Normally the thread token is missing and defaults to the process token, but services often need to execute code on behalf of their client. Windows XP allows threads to impersonate temporarily by using a client's token. Thus, the thread token is not necessarily the same as the process token.

In Windows XP, each object is protected by an access-control list that contains the security ids and access rights granted. When a thread attempts to access an object, the system compares the security id in the thread's access token with the object's access-control list to determine whether access should be permitted. The check is performed only when an object is opened, so it is not possible to deny access after the open occurs. Operating-system components executing in kernel mode bypass the access check, since kernel-mode code is assumed to be trusted. Therefore, kernel-mode code must avoid security vulnerabilities, such as leaving checks disabled while creating a user-mode-accessible handle in an untrusted process.

Generally, the creator of the object determines the access-control list for the object. If none is explicitly supplied, one may be set to a default by the object-type's open routine, or a default list may be obtained from the user's access-token object.

The access token has a field that controls auditing of object accesses. Operations that are being audited get logged to the system's security log with an identification of the user. An administrator monitors this log to discover attempts to break into the system or to access protected objects.

21.3.3.2 Virtual-Memory Manager

The executive component that manages the virtual address space, physical memory allocation, and paging is the **virtual-memory (VM) manager**. The design of the VM manager assumes that the underlying hardware supports virtual-to-physical mapping, a paging mechanism, and transparent cache coherence on multiprocessor systems, and allows multiple page-table entries to map to the same physical page frame. The VM manager in Windows XP uses a page- based management scheme with a page size of 4 KB on IA32-compatible processors and 8 KB on the IA64. Pages of data allocated to a process that are not in physical memory are stored in either the **paging files** on disk or mapped directly to a regular file on a local or remote file-system. Pages can also be marked zero-on-demand.

On IA32 processors each process has a 4 GB virtual address space. The upper 2 GB are mostly identical for all processes, and are used by Windows XP in kernel mode to access the operating system code and data structures. Key areas of the kernel-mode region that are not identical in each process are the **page-table self-map**, **hyperspace** and **session space**. The hardware references a process's page tables using physical page-frame numbers. The VM manager maps the page tables into a single 4 MB region in the process's address space so they are accessed through virtual addresses. Hyperspace maps the current process's working-set information into the kernel-mode address space.

Session space is used to share the Win32 and other session-specific drivers between all the processes in the same terminal-server session rather than with all the processes in the system. The lower 2 GB are specific to every process, and are accessible by both user- and kernel-mode threads. Certain configurations of Windows XP reserve only 1 GB for operating system use, allowing a process to use 3 GB of address space. Running the system in 3GB mode drastically reduces the amount of data caching in the kernel. However, for large applications that manage their own I/O, such as SQL databases, the advantage of a larger user-mode address space may be worth the loss of caching.

The Windows XP VM manager uses a two-step process to allocate user memory. The first step *reserves* a portion of the process's virtual address space. The second step *commits* the allocation by assigning virtual memory space (physical memory or space in the paging files). Windows XP limits the amount of virtual memory space a process consumes by enforcing a quota on committed memory. A process decommits memory that it is no longer using to free up virtual memory for use by other processes. The APIs used to reserve virtual addresses and commit virtual memory take a handle on a process object as a parameter. This allows one process to control the virtual memory of another. This is how environmental subsystems manage the memory of their client processes.

For performance, the VM manager allows a privileged process to lock selected pages in physical memory, thus ensuring the pages are not paged out to the paging file. Processes also allocate raw physical memory and then map regions into its virtual address space. IA32 processors with the Physical Address Extension (PAE) feature can have up to 64 GB of physical memory on a system. This memory cannot all be mapped in a process's address space at once, but Windows XP makes it available using the Address Windowing Extension (AWE) APIs that allocate physical memory and then map regions of virtual addresses in the process's address space onto part of the physical memory. The AWE facility is primarily used by very large applications such as the SQL database.

Windows XP implements shared memory by defining a **section object**. After getting a handle to a section object, a process maps the memory portion it needs into its address space. This portion is called a **view**. A process redefines its view of an object to gain access to the entire object, one region at a time.

A process can control the use of a shared-memory section object in many ways. The maximum size of a section can be bounded. The section can be backed by disk space either in the system-paging file or by a regular file (a **memory-mapped file**). A section can be *based*, meaning the section appears at the same virtual address for all processes attempting to access it. Finally, the memory protection of pages in the section can be set to read–only, read–write, read–write–execute, execute–only, no access, or copy–on–write. The last two of these protection settings need some explanation:

- A no-access page raises an exception if accessed; the exception is used, for example, to check whether a faulty program iterates beyond the end of an array. Both the user-mode memory allocator and the special kernel allocator used by the device verifier can be configured to map each allocation onto the end of a page followed by a no-access page in order to detect buffer overruns.

- The copy–on–write mechanism increases the efficient use of physical memory by the VM manager. When two processes want independent copies of an object, the VM manager places a single shared copy into virtual memory and activates the copy–on–write property for that region of memory. If one of the processes tries to modify data in a copy–on–write page, the VM manager makes a private copy of the page for the process.

The virtual-address translation in Windows XP uses a multilevel page table. For IA32 processors, without the Physical Address Extensions enabled, each process has a **page directory** that contains 1024 **page-directory entries** (PDEs) of size 4 bytes. Each PDE points to a **page table** that contains 1024 **page-table entries (PTEs)** of size 4 bytes. Each PTE points to a 4 KB **page frame** in physical memory. The total size of all page tables for a process is 4 MB, so the VM manager pages out individual tables to disk when necessary. See Figure 21.3 for a diagram of this structure.

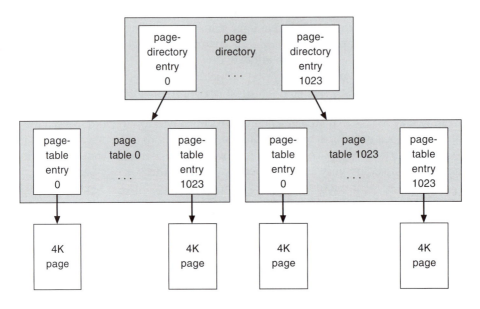

Figure 21.3   Page table layout.

The page directory and page tables are referenced by the hardware via physical addresses. To improve performance the VM manager self-maps the page directory and page tables into a 4 MB region of virtual addresses. The self-map allows the VM manager to translate a virtual address into the corresponding PDE or PTE without additional memory accesses. When a process context is changed, a single page-directory entry needs to be changed to map the new process's page tables. For a variety of reasons the hardware requires that each page directory or page table occupy a single page. Thus the number of PDEs or PTEs that fit in a page determine how virtual addresses are translated.

The following describes how virtual addresses are translated into physical addresses on IA32 compatible processors (without PAE enabled). A 10-bit value can represent all the values from 0 to 1023. Thus, a 10-bit value can select any entry in the page directory, or in a page table. This property is used when a virtual-address pointer is translated to a byte address in physical memory. A 32-bit virtual-memory address is split into three values, as shown in Figure 21.4. The first 10 bits of the virtual address are used as an index into the page directory. This address selects one page-directory entry (PDE), which contains the physical page frame of a page table. The memory management unit (MMU) uses the next 10 bits of the virtual address to select a PTE from the page table. The PTE specifies a page frame in physical memory. The remaining 12 bits of the virtual address are the offset of a specific byte in the page frame. The MMU creates a pointer to the specific byte in physical memory by concatenating the 20 bits from the PTE with the lower 12 bits from the virtual address. Thus, the 32-bit PTE has 12 bits to describe the state of the physical page. The IA32

31   0

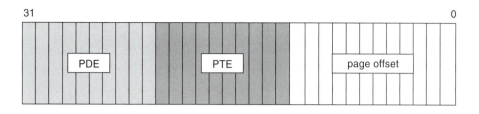

| PDE | PTE | page offset |

Figure 21.4   Virtual-to-physical address translation on IA32.

hardware reserves 3 bits for use by the operating system. The rest of the bits specify whether the page has been accessed or written, the caching attributes, the access mode, if the page is global, and whether the PTE is valid.

IA32 processors running with PAE enabled use 64-bit PDEs and PTEs in order to represent the larger 24-bit page-frame number field. Thus the second-level page directories and the page tables contain only 512 PDEs and PTEs, respectively. To provide 4 GB of virtual address space requires an extra level of page directory containing four PDEs. Translation of a 32-bit virtual address uses 2 bits for the top-level directory index, and 9 bits for each of the second-level page directories and the page tables.

To avoid the overhead of translating every virtual address by looking up the PDE and PTE, processors use a **translation-lookaside buffer** (TLB) which contains an associative memory cache for mapping virtual pages to PTEs. Unlike the IA32 architecture where the TLB is maintained by the hardware MMU, the IA64 invokes a software-trap routine to supply translations missing from the TLB. This gives the VM manager flexibility in choosing the data structures to use. In Windows XP a three-level tree structure is chosen for mapping user-mode virtual addresses on the IA64.

On IA64 processors the page size is 8 KB, but the PTEs occupy 64-bits, so a page still contains only 1024 (10 bits' worth) of PDEs or PTEs. Therefore, with 10 bits worth of top-level PDEs, 10 bits of second-level, 10 bits of page table, and 13 bits of page offset, the user portion of the process's virtual address space for Windows XP on the IA64 is 8 TB (43 bits' worth). The 8 TB limitation in the current version of Windows XP is less than the capabilities of the IA64 processor, but represents a tradeoff between the number of memory references required to handle TLB misses and the size of the user-mode address space supported.

A physical page can be in one of six states: valid, free, zeroed, standby, modified, bad, or in transition. A *valid* page is in use by an active process. A *free* page is a page that is not referenced in a PTE. A *zeroed* page is a free page that has been zeroed out and is ready for immediate use to satisfy zero-on-demand faults. A *modified* page is one that has been written by a process, and must be sent to the disk before it is allocated for another process. *Standby* pages are copies of information already stored on disk. They can be pages that were not modified, modified pages that have already been written to the disk, or pages that were prefetched to exploit locality. A *bad* page is unusable because a hardware error has been detected. Finally, a *transition* page is one that is on its way in from disk to a page frame allocated in physical memory.

When the valid bit in a PTE is zero, the VM manager defines the format of the other bits. Invalid pages can have a number of states represented by bits in the PTE. Page file pages that have never been faulted in are marked zero-on-demand. Files mapped through section objects encode a pointer to that section object. Pages that have been written to the page file contain enough information to find the page on disk, etc.

The actual structure of the page-file PTE is shown in Figure 21.5. The PTE contains 5 bits for page protection, 20 bits for page-file offset, 4 bits to select the paging file, and 3 bits that describe the page state. A page-file PTE is marked to be an invalid virtual address to the MMU. Since executable code and memory-mapped files already have a copy on disk, they do not need space in a paging file. If one of these pages is not in physical memory, the PTE structure is as follows. The most significant bit is used to specify the page protection, the next 28 bits are used to index into a system data structure that indicates a file and offset within the file for the page, and the lower 3 bits specify the page state.

Invalid virtual addresses can also be in a number of temporary states that are part of the paging algorithms. When a page is removed from a process working set it is moved to either the modified list (to be written to disk) or directly to the standby list. If written to the standby list, the page is reclaimed without reading from disk if it is needed again before it is moved to the free list. When possible, the VM manager uses idle CPU cycles to zero pages on the free list and move them to the zeroed list. Transition pages have been allocated a physical page, and are awaiting the completion of the paging I/O before the PTE is marked as valid.

Windows XP uses section objects to describe pages that are sharable between processes. Each process has its own set of virtual page tables, but the section object also contains a set of page tables containing the master (or prototype) PTEs. When a PTE in a process page table is marked valid it points at the physical page frame containing the page, as it must on IA32 processors where the hardware MMU reads the page tables directly from memory. But when a shared page is made invalid, the PTE is edited to point to the prototype PTE associated with the section object.

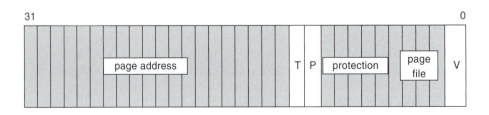

Figure 21.5   Page-file page-table entry. The valid bit is zero.

The page tables associated with a section object are virtual so far as they are created and trimmed as needed. The only prototype PTEs needed are those that describe pages for which there is a currently mapped view. This greatly improves performance and allows more efficient use of kernel virtual addresses.

The prototype PTE contains the page-frame address and the protection and state bits. Thus, the first access by a process to a shared page generates a page fault. After the first access, further accesses are performed in the normal manner. If a process writes to a copy-on-write page marked read-only in the PTE, the VM manager makes a copy of the page and marks the PTE writable, and the process effectively does not have a shared page any longer. Shared pages never appear in the page file, but are instead found in the file-system.

The VM manager keeps track of all pages of physical memory in a **page-frame database**. There is one entry for every page of physical memory in the system. The entry points to the PTE which in turn points to the page frame, so the VM manager can maintain the state of the page. Page frames not referenced by a valid PTE are linked to lists according to page type such as zeroed, modified, free, etc.

If a shared physical page is marked as valid for any process, the page cannot be removed from memory. The VM manager keeps a count of valid PTEs for each page in the page-frame database. When the count goes to zero the physical page can be reused once its contents have been written back to disk (if it was marked dirty).

When a page fault occurs, the VM manager finds a physical page to hold the data. For zero-on-demand pages the first choice is to find a page that has already been zeroed. If none is available, a page from the free list or standby list is chosen and the page is zeroed before proceeding. If the faulted page has been marked as in transition, it is either already being read in from disk, or has been unmapped or trimmed and is still available on the standby or modified list. The thread either waits for the I/O to complete or, in the latter cases, reclaims the page from the appropriate list.

Otherwise, an I/O must be issued to read the page in from the paging file or file system. The VM manager tries to allocate an available page from either the free list or the standby list. Pages in the modified list cannot be used until they have been written back to disk and transferred to the standby list. If no pages are available, the thread blocks until the working set manager trims pages from memory, or a page in physical memory is unmapped by a process.

Windows XP uses a per-process first-in, first-out (FIFO) replacement policy to take pages from processes that are using more than their minimum working-set size. Windows XP monitors the page faulting of each process that is at its minimum working-set size, and adjusts the working-set size accordingly. When a process is started, it is assigned a default minimum working-set size of 50 pages. The VM manager replaces and trims pages in the working set of a process according to their age. The age of a page is determined by counting how many trimming cycles have occurred without the PTE. Trimmed pages are moved to the standby or modified list, depending on whether the modified bit is set in the page's PTE.

The VM manager does not fault in only the page immediately needed. Research shows that the memory referencing of a thread tends to have a **locality** property; when a page is used, it is likely that adjacent pages will be referenced in the near future. (Think of iterating over an array, or fetching sequential instructions that form the executable code for a thread.) Because of locality, when the VM manager faults in a page, it also faults in a few adjacent pages. This prefetching tends to reduce the total number of page faults. Writes are also clustered to reduce the number of independent I/O operations.

In addition to managing committed memory, the VM manager manages each process's reserved memory, or virtual address space. Each process has an associated splay tree that describes the ranges of virtual addresses in use, and what the use is. This allows the VM manager to fault in page tables as needed. If the PTE for a faulting address does not exist, the VM manager searches for the address in the process's tree of **virtual address descriptors** (VADs), and uses this information to fill in the missing PTE and retrieve the page. In some cases a page-table page itself may not exist and must be transparently allocated and initialized by the VM manager.

21.3.3.3 Process Manager

The Windows XP process manager provides services for creating, deleting, and using processes, threads and jobs. It has no knowledge about parent–child relationships or process hierarchies; those refinements are left to the particular environmental subsystem that owns the process. The process manager is also not involved in the scheduling of processes, other than setting the priorities and affinities in processes and threads when they are created. Thread scheduling takes place in the kernel dispatcher.

Processes contain one or more threads. Processes themselves can be collected together into large units called **job objects** which allow limits on CPU usage, working-set size, and processor affinities which control multiple processes at once. Job objects are used to manage large datacenter machines.

An example of process creation in the Win32 environment is as follows. When a Win32 application calls `CreateProcess`, a message is sent to the Win32 subsystem to notify it that the process is being created. `CreateProcess` in the original process then calls an API in the process manager of the NT executive to actually create the process. The process manager calls the object manager to create a process object, and returns the object handle to Win32. Win32 calls the process manager again to create a thread for the process, and returns handles to the new process and thread.

The Windows XP APIs for manipulating virtual memory, and threads, and duplicating handles take a process handle so subsystems can perform operations on behalf of a new process without having directly to execute in the new process's context. Once a new process is created, the initial thread is created and an APC is delivered to the thread to prompt the start of execution at the user-mode image loader. The loader is an ntdll.dll, which is a link library automatically mapped into every newly created process. Windows XP also supports a UNIX fork() style of process creation in order to support the POSIX environmental subsystem. Although the Win32 environment calls the process manager from the client process, POSIX uses the cross-process nature of the Windows XP APIs to create the new process from within the subsystem process.

The process manager also implements the queuing and delivery of asynchronous procedure calls (APCs) to threads. APCs are used by the system to initiate thread execution, complete I/O, terminate threads and processes, and attach debuggers. User-mode code can also queue an APC to a thread for delivery of signal-like notifications. To support POSIX the process manager provides APIs that send alerts to threads to unblock them from system calls.

The debugger support in the process manager includes the capability to suspend and resume threads, and create threads that begin in a suspended mode. There are also process-manager APIs that get and set a thread's register context and access another process's virtual memory.

Threads can be created in the current process; they can also be injected into another process. Within the executive, existing threads can temporarily attach to another process. This method is used by worker threads that need to execute in the context of the process originating a work request.

The process manager also supports impersonation. A thread running in a process with a security token belonging to one user can set a thread-specific token belonging to another user. This facility is fundamental to the client–server computing model where services need to act on behalf of a variety of clients with different security ids.

21.3.3.4 Local Procedure Call Facility

The implementation of Windows XP uses a client–server model. The environmental subsystems are servers that implement particular operating-system personalities. The client–server model is used for implementing a variety of operating system services besides the environmental subsystems. Security management, printer spooling, web services, network file systems, plug-and-play, and many other features are implemented using this model. To reduce the memory footprint, multiple services are often collected together into a few processes, which then rely on the user-mode thread-pool facilities to share threads and wait for messages (see Section 21.3.3.3).

The operating system uses the local procedure call (LPC) facility to pass requests and results between client and server processes within a single machine. In particular, LPC is used to request services from the various Windows XP subsystems. LPC is similar in many respects to the RPC mechanisms that are used by many operating systems for distributed processing across networks, but LPC is optimized for use within a single system. The

Windows XP implementation of Open Software Foundation (OSF) RPC often uses LPC as a transport on the local machine.

LPC is a message-passing mechanism. The server process publishes a globally visible connection-port object. When a client wants services from a subsystem, it opens a handle to the subsystem's connection-port object, and sends a connection request to the port. The server creates a channel and returns a handle to the client. The channel consists of a pair of private communication ports: one for client-to-server messages, and the other for server-to-client messages. Communication channels support a callback mechanism, so the client and server can accept requests when they would normally be expecting a reply.

When an LPC channel is created, one of three message-passing techniques must be specified.

1. The first technique is suitable for small messages (up to a couple hundred bytes). In this case, the port's message queue is used as intermediate storage, and the messages are copied from one process to the other.

2. The second technique is for larger messages. In this case, a shared-memory section object is created for the channel. Messages sent through the port's message queue contain a pointer and size information referring to the section object. This avoids the need to copy large messages. The sender places data into the shared section, and the receiver views them directly.

3. The third technique of LPC message passing uses the APIs that read/write directly into a process's address space. The LPC provides functions and synchronization so a server can access the data in a client.

The Win32 window manager uses its own form of message passing that is independent of the executive LPC facilities. When a client asks for a connection that uses window-manager messaging, the server sets up three objects: a dedicated server thread to handle requests, a 64 KB section object, and an event-pair object. An *event-pair object* is a synchronization object that is used by the Win32 subsystem to provide notification when the client thread has copied a message to the Win32 server, or vice versa. The section object passes the messages and the event-pair object performs synchronization. Window-manager messaging has several advantages. The section object eliminates message copying, since it represents a region of shared memory. The event-pair object eliminates the overhead of using the port object to pass messages containing pointers and lengths. The dedicated server thread eliminates the overhead of determining which client thread is calling the server, since there is one server thread per client thread. Finally, the kernel gives scheduling preference to these dedicated server threads to improve performance.

21.3.3.5 I/O Manager

The **I/O manager** is responsible for file systems, device drivers, and network drivers. It keeps track of which device drivers, filter drivers and file systems are loaded, and also manages buffers for I/O requests. It works with the VM manager to provide memory-mapped file I/O, and controls the Windows XP cache manager, which handles caching for the entire I/O system. The I/O manager is fundamentally asynchronous. Synchronous I/O is provided by explicitly waiting for an I/O operation to complete. The I/O manager provides several models of asynchronous I/O completion including setting events, delivering APCs to the initiating thread, and I/O completion ports which allow a single thread to process I/O completions from many other threads.

Device drivers are arranged as a list for each device (called a driver or I/O stack because of how device drivers are added). The I/O manager converts the requests it receives into a standard form called an **I/O request packet (IRP)**. It then forwards the IRP to the first driver in the stack for processing. After each driver processes the IRP it calls the I/O manager to either forward it to the next driver in the stack, or if all processing is finished, to complete the operation on the IRP.

Completions may occur in a different context from the original I/O request. For example, if a driver is performing its part of an I/O operation and is forced to block for an extended time, it may queue the IRP to a worker thread to continue processing in the system context. In the original thread the driver returns a status indicating the I/O request is pending so the thread can continue executing in parallel with the I/O operation. IRPs may also be processed in interrupt-service routines, and completed in an arbitrary context. Because some final processing may need to happen in the context that initiated the I/O, the I/O manager uses an APC to do final I/O completion processing in the context of the originating thread.

The device stack model is very flexible. As a driver stack is built, various drivers have the opportunity to insert themselves into the stack as **filter drivers**. Filter drivers have the opportunity to examine and potentially modify each I/O operation. Mount management, partition management and disk striping/mirroring are all examples of functionality implemented using filter drivers that execute beneath the file system in the stack. File-system filter drivers execute above the file system, and have been used to implement functionality such as hierarchical storage management, single instancing of files for remote boot, and dynamic format conversion. Third parties also use file-system filter drivers to implement virus detection.

Device drivers for Windows XP are written to the Windows Driver Model specification (WDM). This model lays out all the requirements for device drivers including how to layer filter drivers, share common code for handling power and plug-and-play requests, build correct cancellation logic, etc.

Because of the richness of the WDM, it can be an excessive amount of work to write a full WDM device driver for each new hardware device. Fortunately it is unnecessary because of the port/miniport model. For similar classes of devices, such as audio drivers, SCSI devices, and Ethernet controllers, each instance of a device in a class shares a common driver for that class called a **port driver**. The port driver implements the standard operations for the class and then calls device-specific routines in the device's **mini-port driver** to implement device-specific functionality.

21.3.3.6 Cache Manager

In many operating systems, caching is done by the file system. Instead, Windows XP provides a centralized caching facility. The **cache manager** works closely with the VM manager to provide cache services for all components under the control of the I/O manager. Caching in Windows XP is based on files rather than raw blocks.

The size of the cache changes dynamically, according to how much free memory is available in the system. Recall that the upper 2 GB of a process's address space comprise the system area; it is available in the context of all processes. The VM manager allocates up to one-half of this space to the system cache. The cache manager maps files into this address space, and uses the capabilities of the VM manager to handle file I/O.

The cache is divided into blocks of 256 KB. Each cache block can hold a view (that is, a memory-mapped region) of a file. Each cache block is described by a **virtual-address control block (VACB)** that stores the virtual address and file offset for the view, as well as the number of processes using the view. The VACBs reside in a single array maintained by the cache manager.

For each open file, the cache manager maintains a separate VACB index array that describes the caching for the entire file. This array has an entry for each 256 KB chunk of the file; so, for instance, a 2 MB file would have an 8-entry VACB index array. An entry in the VACB index array points to the VACB, if that portion of the file is in the cache; it is null otherwise. When the I/O manager receives a file's user-level read request the I/O manager sends an IRP to the device-driver stack on which the file resides. The file system attempts to look up the requested data in the cache manager (unless the request specifically asks for a noncached read). The cache manager calculates which entry of that file's VACB index array corresponds to the byte offset of the request. The entry either points to the view in the cache or is invalid. If it is invalid, the cache manager allocates a cache block (and the corresponding entry in the VACB array), and maps the view into the cache block. The cache manager then attempts to copy data from the mapped file to the caller's buffer. If the copy succeeds, the operation is completed.

If the copy fails, it does so because of a page fault, which causes the VM manager to send a noncached read request to the I/O manager. The I/O manager sends another request down the driver stack, this time requesting a *paging* operation, which bypasses the cache manager and reads the data from the file directly into the page allocated for the cache manager. Upon completion

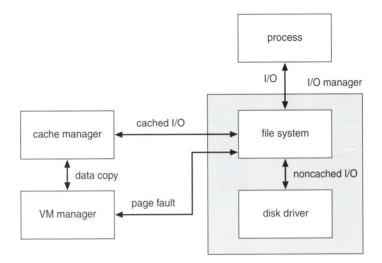

Figure 21.6   File I/O.

the VACB is set to point at the page. The data, now in the cache, is copied to the caller's buffer, and the original I/O request is completed. Figure 21.6 shows an overview of these operations.

When possible, for synchronous operations on cached files, I/O is handled by the **fast I/O mechanism**. This mechanism parallels the normal IRP-based I/O but calls into the driver stack directly rather than passing down an IRP. Because there is no IRP involved, the operation should not block for an extended period of time and cannot be queued to a worker thread. Therefore, when the operation reaches the file system and calls the cache manager, the operation fails if the information is not already in cache. The I/O manager then attempts the operation using the normal IRP path.

A kernel-level read operation is similar, except that the data can be accessed directly from the cache, rather than being copied to a buffer in user space. To use file-system metadata (data structures that describe the file system) the kernel uses the cache manager's mapping interface to read the metadata. To modify the metadata, the file system uses the cache manager's pinning interface. **Pinning** a page locks the page into a physical-memory page frame, so the VM manager cannot move or page out the page. After updating the metadata, the file system asks the cache manager to unpin the page. A modified page is marked dirty, and so the VM manager flushes the page to disk. The metadata is stored in a regular file.

To improve performance, the cache manager keeps a small history of read requests, and from this history attempts to predict future requests. If the cache manager finds a pattern in the previous three requests, such as sequential access forward or backward, it prefetches data into the cache before the next request is submitted by the application. In this way the application finds its data already cached, and does not need to wait for disk I/O. The Win32 API `OpenFile` and `CreateFile` functions can be passed the `FILE_FLAG_SEQUENTIAL_SCAN` flag, which is a hint to the cache manager to try to prefetch 192 KBs ahead of the thread's requests. Typically, Windows XP performs I/O operations in chunks of 64 KB or 16 pages; thus, this read-ahead is three times the normal amount.

The cache manager is also responsible for telling the VM manager to flush the contents of the cache. The cache manager's default behavior is write-back caching: it accumulates writes for 4 to 5 seconds, and then wakes up the cache-writer thread. When write-through caching is needed, a process can set a flag when opening the file, or the process can call an explicit cache-flush function.

A fast-writing process could potentially fill all the free cache pages before the cache-writer thread has a chance to wake up and flush the pages to disk. The cache writer prevents a process from flooding the system in the following way. When the amount of free cache memory gets low, the cache manager temporarily blocks processes attempting to write data, and wakes the cache-writer thread to flush pages to disk. If the fast-writing process is actually a network redirector for a network file system, blocking it for too long could cause network transfers to time out and be retransmitted. This retransmission would waste network bandwidth. To prevent such waste, network redirectors can instruct the cache manager to limit the backlog of writes in the cache.

Because a network file system needs to move data between a disk and the network interface, the cache manager also provides a DMA interface to move the data directly. Moving data directly avoids copying data through an intermediate buffer.

21.3.3.7 Security Reference Monitor

Centralizing management of system entities in the object manager enables the use of a uniform mechanism to perform run-time access validation and audit checks for every user-accessible entity in the system. Whenever a process opens a handle to an object, the **security reference monitor** (SRM) checks the process's security token and the object's access-control list to see whether the process has the necessary rights.

The SRM is also responsible for manipulating the privileges in security tokens. Special privileges are required for users to perform backup or restore operations on file systems, overcome certain checks as an administrator, debug processes, etc. Tokens can also be marked as being restricted in their privileges so they cannot access objects that are available to most users. Restricted tokens are primarily used to restrict the damage that can be done by execution of untrusted code.

Another responsibility of the SRM is logging security audit events. A C2 security rating requires that the system have the ability to detect and log all attempts to access system resources so that it is easier to trace attempts at unauthorized access. Because the SRM is responsible for making access checks, it generates most of the audit records in the security-event log.

21.3.3.8 Plug-and-Play and Power Managers

The operating system uses the **plug-and-play (PnP) manager** to recognize and adapt to changes in the hardware configuration. For PnP to work, both the device and driver must support the PnP standard. The PnP manager automatically recognizes installed devices and detects changes in devices as the system operates. The manager also keeps tracks of resources used by a device, as well as potential resources that could be used, and takes care of loading the appropriate drivers. This management of hardware resources—primarily interrupts and I/O memory ranges—has the goal of determining a hardware configuration in which all devices are able to operate.

For example, if device B can use interrupt 5 and device A can use 5 or 7, then the PnP manager will assign 5 to B and 7 to A. In previous versions, the user might have had to remove device A and reconfigure it to use interrupt 7, before installing device B. The user thus had to study system resources before installing new hardware, and to find out or remember which devices were using which hardware resources. The proliferation of PCMCIA cards, laptop docks, USB, IEEE 1394, Infiniband, and other hot-pluggable devices also dictates the support of dynamically configurable resources.

The PnP manager handles this dynamic reconfiguration as follows. First, it gets a list of devices from each bus driver (for example, PCI, USB). It loads the installed driver (or installs one, if necessary) and sends an `add-device` request to the appropriate driver for each device. The PnP manager figures out the optimal resource assignments and sends a `start-device` request to each driver along with the resource assignment for the device. If a device needs to be reconfigured, the PnP manager sends a `query-stop` request, which asks the driver whether the device can be temporarily disabled. If the driver can disable the device, then all pending operations are completed and new operations are prevented from starting. Next, the PnP manager sends a `stop` request; it can then reconfigure the device with another `start-device` request.

The PnP manager also supports other requests, such as `query-remove`. This request is used when the user is getting ready to eject a PCCARD device, and operates in a fashion similar to query-stop. The `surprise-remove` request is used when a device fails or, more likely, when a user removes a PCCARD device without stopping it first. The `remove` request tells the driver to stop using the device and release all resources allocated to it.

Windows XP supports sophisticated power management. Although these facilities are useful for home systems to reduce power consumption, their primary application is for ease of use (quicker access) and extending the battery life of laptops. The system and individual devices can be moved to low-power mode (called standby or sleep mode) when not in use, so the battery is primarily directed at physical memory (RAM) data retention. The system can turn itself back on when packets are received from the network, a phone line to a modem rings, or a user opens a laptop or pushes a soft power button. Windows XP can also hibernate a system by storing physical memory contents to disk and completely shutting down the machine, then restoring the system at a later point before execution continues.

Further strategies for reducing power consumption are supported. Rather than spinning in a processor loop when the CPU is idle, Windows XP moves the system to a state requiring lower power consumption. If the CPU is underutilized, Windows XP reduces the CPU clock speed, which can save significant power.

21.3.3.9 Registry

Windows XP keeps much of its configuration information in an internal database called the **registry**. A registry database is called a **hive**. There are separate hives for system information, default user preferences, software installation, and security. Because the information in the **system hive** is required in order to boot the system, the registry manager is implemented as a component of the executive.

Every time the system successfully boots it saves the system hive as *last known good*. If the user installs software, such as a device driver, that produces a system hive configuration that will not boot, the user can usually boot using the last-known-good configuration.

Damage to the system hive from installing third-party applications and drivers is so common that Windows XP has a component called **system restore** which periodically saves the hives, as well as other software states like driver executables and configuration files, so that the system can be restored to a previously working state in cases where the system boots, but no longer operates as expected.

21.3.3.10 Booting

The booting of a Windows XP PC begins when the hardware powers on and the BIOS begins executing from ROM. The BIOS identifies the **system device** to be booted, and loads and executes the bootstrap loader from the front of the disk. This loader knows enough about the file-system format to load the NTLDR program from the root directory of the system device. NTLDR is used to determine which **boot device** contains the operating system. Next the NTLDR loads in the HAL library, the kernel, and the system hive from the boot device. From the system hive it determines what device drivers are needed to boot the system (the *boot drivers*) and loads them. Finally NTLDR begins kernel execution.

The kernel initializes the system and creates two processes. The **system process** contains all the internal worker threads, and never executes in user mode. The first user-mode process created is SMSS, which is similar to the INIT (initialization) process in UNIX. SMSS does further initialization of the system, including establishing the paging files and loading device drivers, and creates the WINLOGON and CSRSS processes. CSRSS is the Win32 subsystem.

WINLOGON brings up the rest of the system, including the LSASS security subsystem and the remaining services needed to run the system.

The system optimizes the boot process by pre-loading files from disk based on previous boots of the system. Disk access patterns at boot are also used to re-layout system files on disk to reduce the number of I/O operations required. The processes required to start the system is reduced by grouping services into one process. All of these approaches contribute to a dramatic reduction in system boot time.

On the other hand, the sleep and hibernation capabilities of Windows XP allow users to power down their computer and then quickly resume where they left off, making system boot time less important than it once was.

21.4 ■ Environmental Subsystems

Environmental subsystems are user-mode processes layered over the native Windows XP executive services to enable Windows XP to run programs developed for other operating systems, including 16-bit Windows, MS-DOS, and POSIX. Each environmental subsystem provides a single application environment.

Windows XP uses the Win32 subsystem as the main operating environment, and thus it starts all processes. When an application is executed, the Win32 subsystem calls the VM manager to load the application's executable code. The memory manager returns a status to Win32 indicating the type of executable. If it is not a native Win32 executable, the Win32 environment checks whether the appropriate environmental subsystem is running; if the subsystem is not running, it is started as a user-mode process. The subsystem then takes control over the application startup.

The environmental subsystems use the LPC facility to provide operating-system services to client processes. The Windows XP subsystem architecture keeps applications from mixing API routines from different environments. For instance, a Win32 application cannot make a POSIX system call because only one environmental subsystem can be associated with each process.

Since each subsystem is run as a separate user-mode process, a crash in one has no effect on other processes. The exception is Win32 which provides all keyboard, mouse, and graphical display capabilities. If it fails, the system is effectively disabled and requires a reboot.

The Win32 environment categorizes applications as either graphical or character based, where a *character-based application* is one that thinks interactive output goes to a character-based (command) window. Win32 transforms the output of a character-based application to a graphical representation in the command window. This transformation is easy: Whenever an output routine is called, the environmental subsystem calls a Win32 routine to display the text. Since the Win32 environment performs this function for all character-based windows, it can transfer screen text between windows via the clipboard. This transformation works for MS-DOS applications, as well as for POSIX command-line applications.

21.4.1 MS-DOS Environment

The MS-DOS environment does not have the complexity of the other Windows XP environmental subsystems. It is provided by a Win32 application called the **virtual DOS machine (VDM)**. Since the VDM is a user-mode process, it is paged and dispatched like any other Windows XP application. The VDM has an **instruction-execution unit** to execute or emulate Intel 486 instructions. The VDM also provides routines to emulate the MS-DOS ROM BIOS and "int 21" software-interrupt services, and has virtual device drivers for the screen, keyboard, and communication ports. The VDM is based on the MS-DOS 5.0 source code; it allocates at least 620 KB of memory to the application.

The Windows XP command shell is a program that creates a window that looks like an MS-DOS environment. It can run both 16-bit and 32-bit executables. When an MS-DOS application is run, the command shell starts a VDM process to execute the program.

If Windows XP is running on a IA32-compatible processor, MS-DOS graphical applications run in full-screen mode, and character applications can run full screen or in a window. Not all MS-DOS applications run under the VDM. For example, some MS-DOS applications access the disk hardware directly, so they fail to run on Windows XP because disk access is restricted to protect the file system. In general, MS-DOS applications that directly access hardware will fail to operate under Windows XP.

Since MS-DOS is not a multitasking environment, some applications have been written in such a way as to hog the CPU. For instance, the use of busy loops can cause time delays or pauses in execution. The scheduler in the kernel dispatcher detects such delays and automatically throttles the CPU usage, but this may cause the offending application to operate incorrectly.

21.4.2 16-Bit Windows Environment

The Win16 execution environment is provided by a VDM that incorporates additional software called *Windows on Windows* (WOW32 for 16-bit applications) that provides the Windows 3.1 kernel routines and stub routines for window-manager and graphical-device-interface (GDI) functions. The stub routines call the appropriate Win32 subroutines, converting, or *thunking*, 16-bit addresses into 32-bit addresses. Applications that rely on the internal structure of the 16-bit window manager or GDI may not work, because the underlying Win32 implementation is, of course, different from true 16-bit Windows.

WOW32 can multitask with other processes on Windows XP, but it resembles Windows 3.1 in many ways. Only one Win16 application can run at a time, all applications are single threaded and reside in the same address space, and they all share the same input queue. These features imply that an application that stops receiving input will block all the other Win16 applications, just as in Windows 3.x, and one Win16 application can crash other Win16 applications by corrupting the address space. Multiple Win16 environments can coexist, however, by using the command *start /separate win16application* from the command line.

There are relatively few 16-bit applications that users need to continue to run on Windows XP, but some of them include common installation (setup) programs. Thus, the WOW32 environment continues to exist primarily because a number of 32-bit applications cannot be installed on Windows XP without it.

21.4.3 32-Bit Windows Environment on IA64

The native environment for Windows on IA64 uses 64-bit addresses and the native IA64 instruction set. To execute IA32 programs in this environment requires a thunking layer to translate 32-bit Win32 calls into the corresponding 64-bit calls—just as 16-bit applications require on IA32 systems. Thus 64-bit Windows supports the WOW64 environment. The implementations of 32-bit and 64-bit Windows are essentially identical, and the IA64 processor provides direct execution of IA32 instructions, so WOW64 achieves a higher level of compatibility than WOW32.

21.4.4 Win32 Environment

The main subsystem in Windows XP is the Win32. It runs Win32 applications, and manages all keyboard, mouse, and screen I/O. Since it is the controlling environment, it is designed to be extremely robust. Several features of Win32 contribute to this robustness. Unlike the Win16 environment, each Win32 process has its own input queue. The window manager dispatches all input on the system to the appropriate process's input queue, so a failed process does not block input to other processes.

The Windows XP kernel also provides preemptive multitasking, which enables the user to terminate applications that have failed or are no longer needed. Win32 also validates all objects before using them, to prevent crashes that could otherwise occur if an application tried to use an invalid or wrong handle. The Win32 subsystem verifies the type of the object to which a handle points before using the object. The reference counts kept by the object manager prevent objects from being deleted while they are still being used, and prevent their use after they have been deleted.

To achieve a high level of compatibility with Windows 95/98 systems, Windows XP allows users to specify that individual applications be run using a **shim layer** which modifies the Win32 APIs to better approximate the behavior expected by old applications. For example, some applications expect to see a particular version of the system, and fail on new versions. Frequently applications have latent bugs that become exposed due to changes in the implementation. For example, using memory after freeing it may cause corruption only if the order of memory reuse by the heap changes, or an application may make assumptions about which errors can be returned by a routine, or the number of valid bits in an address. Running an application with the Windows 95/98 shims enabled causes the system to provide behavior much closer to Windows 95/98 —though with reduced performance and limited interoperability with other applications.

21.4.5 POSIX Subsystem

The POSIX subsystem is designed to run POSIX applications written to follow the POSIX standard, which is based on the UNIX model. POSIX applications can be started by the Win32 subsystem or by another POSIX application. POSIX applications use the POSIX subsystem server PSXSS.EXE, the POSIX dynamic link library PSXDLL.DLL, and the POSIX console session manager POSIX.EXE.

Although the POSIX standard does not specify printing, POSIX applications can use printers transparently via the Windows XP redirection mechanism. POSIX applications have access to any file system on the Windows XP system; the POSIX environment enforces UNIX-like permissions on directory trees.

Due to scheduling issues, the POSIX system in Windows XP does not ship with the system, but is available separately for professional desktop systems and servers. It provides a much higher-level of compatibility with UNIX applications than previous versions of NT. Of the commonly available UNIX applications, most compile and run without change with the latest version of Interix.

21.4.6 Logon and Security Subsystems

Before a user can access objects on Windows XP, that user must be authenticated by the logon service, WINLOGON. WINLOGON is responsible for responding to the secure attention sequence (Control-Alt-Delete). The secure attention sequence is a required mechanism for keeping an application from acting as a trojan horse. Only WINLOGON can intercept this sequence in order to put up a logon screen, change passwords, and lock the workstation. To be authenticated, a user must have an account and provide the password for that account. Alternatively, a user logs on by using a smart card and personal identification number, subject to the security policies in effect for the domain.

The local security authority subsystem (LSASS) is the process that generates access tokens to represent users on the system. It calls an **authentication package** to perform authentication using information from the logon subsystem or network server. Typically, the authentication package simply looks up the account information in a local database and checks to see that the password is correct. The security subsystem then generates the access token for the user ID containing the appropriate privileges, quota limits, and group IDs. Whenever the user attempts to access an object in the system, such as by opening a handle to the object, the access token is passed to the security reference monitor, which checks privileges and quotas. The default authentication package for Windows XP domains is Kerberos. LSASS also has the responsibility for implementing security policy such as strong passwords, authenticating users, and performing encryption of data and keys.

21.5 ■ File System

Historically, MS-DOS systems have used the file-allocation table (FAT) file-system. The 16-bit FAT file system has several shortcomings, including internal fragmentation, a size limitation of 2 GB, and a lack of access protection for files. The 32-bit FAT file system has solved the size and fragmentation problems, but its performance and features are still weak by comparison with modern file systems. The NTFS file system is much better. It was designed to include many features, including data recovery, security, fault tolerance, large files and file systems, multiple data streams, UNICODE names, sparse files, encryption, journaling, volume shadow copies, and file compression.

Windows 2000XP continues to use FAT16, however, to read floppies and other removable media. And despite the advantages of NTFS, FAT32 continues to be important for interoperability of media with Windows 95/98 systems. Windows XP supports additional file-system types for the common formats used for CD and DVD media.

21.5.1 NTFS Internal Layout

The fundamental entity in NTFS is a volume. A volume is created by the Windows XP logical-disk-management utility, and is based on a logical-disk partition. A volume may occupy a portion of a disk, may occupy an entire disk, or may span across several disks.

NTFS does not deal with individual sectors of a disk, but instead uses clusters as the unit of disk allocation. A **cluster** is a number of disk sectors that is a power of 2. The cluster size is configured when an NTFS file system is formatted. The default cluster size is the sector size for volumes up to 512 MB, 1 KB for volumes up to 1 GB, 2 KB for volumes up to 2 GB, and 4 KB for larger volumes. This cluster size is much smaller than that for the 16-bit FAT file system, and the small size reduces the amount of internal fragmentation. As an example, consider a 1.6 GB disk with 16,000 files. If you use a FAT-16 file system, 400 MB may be lost to internal fragmentation because the cluster size is 32 KB. Under NTFS, only 17 MB would be lost when storing the same files.

NTFS uses **logical cluster numbers (LCNs)** as disk addresses. It assigns them by numbering clusters from the beginning of the disk to the end. Using this scheme, the system can calculate a physical disk offset (in bytes) by multiplying the LCN by the cluster size.

A file in NTFS is not a simple byte stream as it is in MS-DOS or UNIX; rather, it is a structured object consisting of typed **attributes**. Each attribute of a file is an independent byte stream that can be created, deleted, read, and written. Some attribute types are standard for all files, including the file name (or names, if the file has aliases such as an MS-DOS shortname), the creation time, and the security descriptor that specifies access control. User data is stored in *data attributes*.

Most traditional data files have an *unnamed* data attribute that contains all the file's data. However, additional data streams can be created with explicit names. For instance, Macintosh files stored on a Windows XP server put the resource fork as a named data stream. The IProp interfaces of the Common Object Model (COM) use a named data stream to store properties on ordinary files, including thumbnails of images. In general, attributes may be added as necessary and are accessed using a *file-name:attribute* syntax. NTFS returns the size of the unnamed attribute only in response to file-query operations, such as when running the `dir` command.

Every file in NTFS is described by one or more records in an array stored in a special file called the master file table (MFT). The size of a record is determined when the file system is created; it ranges from 1 to 4 KB. Small attributes are stored in the MFT record itself, and are called **resident attributes**. Large attributes, such as the unnamed bulk data, called **nonresident attributes**, are stored in one or more contiguous **extents** on the disk, and a pointer to each extent is stored in the MFT record. For a small file, even the data attribute may fit inside the MFT record. If a file has many attributes, or if it is highly fragmented and therefore many pointers are needed to point to all the fragments, one record in the MFT might not be large enough. In this case, the file is described by a record called the **base file record**, which contains pointers to overflow records that hold the additional pointers and attributes.

Each file in an NTFS volume has a unique ID called a **file reference**. The file reference is a 64-bit quantity that consists of a 48-bit file number and a 16-bit sequence number. The file number is the record number (that is, the array slot) in the MFT that describes the file. The sequence number is incremented every time that an MFT entry is reused. The sequence number enables NTFS to perform internal consistency checks, such as catching a stale reference to a deleted file after the MFT entry has been reused for a new file.

21.5.1.1 NTFS B+ Tree

As in MS-DOS and UNIX, the NTFS namespace is organized as a hierarchy of directories. Each directory uses a data structure called a **B+ tree** to store an index of the file names in that directory. A B+ tree is used because it eliminates the cost of reorganizing the tree and has the property that the length of every path from the root of the tree to a leaf is the same. The **index root** of a directory contains the top level of the B+ tree. For a large directory, this top level contains pointers to disk extents that hold the remainder of the tree. Each entry in the directory contains the name and file reference of the file, as well as a copy of the update timestamp and file size taken from the file's resident attributes in the MFT. Copies of this information are stored in the directory, so it is efficient to generate a directory listing. All the file names, sizes, and update times are available from the directory itself, so there is no need to gather these attributes from the MFT entries for each of the files.

21.5.1.2 NTFS Metadata

The NTFS volume's metadata are all stored in files. The first file is the MFT. The second file, which is used during recovery if the MFT is damaged, contains a copy of the first 16 entries of the MFT. The next few files are also special in purpose. They include the log file, volume file, attribute-definition table, root directory, bitmap file, boot file, and bad-cluster file. The **log file** records all metadata updates to the file system. The **volume file** contains the name of the volume, the version of NTFS that formatted the volume, and a bit that tells whether the volume may have been corrupted and needs to be checked for consistency. The **attribute-definition table** indicates which attribute types are used in the volume, and what operations can be performed on each of them.

The **root directory** is the top-level directory in the file-system hierarchy. The **bitmap file** indicates which clusters on a volume are allocated to files, and which are free. The **boot file** contains the startup code for Windows XP and must be located at a particular disk address so that it can be found easily by a simple ROM bootstrap loader. The boot file also contains the physical address of the MFT. Finally, the **bad-cluster file** keeps track of any bad areas on the volume; NTFS uses this record for error recovery.

21.5.2 Recovery

In many simple file systems, a power failure at the wrong time can damage the file-system data structures so severely that the entire volume is scrambled. Many versions of UNIX store redundant metadata on the disk, and they recover from crashes using the `fsck` program to check all the file-system data structures, and to restore them forcibly to a consistent state. Restoring them often involves deleting damaged files and freeing data clusters that had been written with user data but have not been properly recorded in the file-system's metadata structures. This checking can be a slow process, and can lose significant amounts of data.

21.5.2.1 NTFS Log File

NTFS takes a different approach to file-system robustness. In NTFS, all file-system data-structure updates are performed inside transactions. Before a data structure is altered, the transaction writes a log record that contains redo and undo information; after the data structure has been changed, the transaction writes a commit record to the log to signify that the transaction succeeded.

After a crash, the system can restore the file-system data structures to a consistent state by processing the log records, first redoing the operations for committed transactions, then undoing the operations for transactions that did not commit successfully before the crash. Periodically (usually every 5 seconds), a checkpoint record is written to the log. The system does not need log records prior to the checkpoint to recover from a crash. They can be discarded, so the log file does not grow without bounds. The first time after system startup that an NTFS volume is accessed, NTFS automatically performs file-system recovery.

This scheme does not guarantee that all the user-file contents are correct after a crash; it ensures only that the file-system data structures (the metadata files) are undamaged and reflect some consistent state that existed prior to the crash. It would be possible to extend the transaction scheme to cover user files and Microsoft may do so in the future.

The log is stored in the third metadata file at the beginning of the volume. It is created with a fixed maximum size when the file system is formatted. It has two sections: the **logging area**, which is a circular queue of log records, and the **restart area**, which holds context information, such as the position in the logging area where NTFS should start reading during a recovery. In fact, the restart area holds two copies of its information, so recovery is still possible if one copy is damaged during the crash.

The logging functionality is provided by the Windows XP **log-file service**. In addition to writing the log records and performing recovery actions, the log-file service keeps track of the free space in the log file. If the free space gets too low, the log-file service queues pending transactions, and NTFS halts all new I/O operations. After the in-progress operations complete, NTFS calls the cache manager to flush all data, then resets the log file and performs the queued transactions.

21.5.3 Security

The security of an NTFS volume is derived from the Windows XP object model. Each NTFS file references a security descriptor which contains the access token of the owner of the file, and an access-control list that states the access privileges granted to each user having access to the file.

In normal operation, NTFS does not enforce permissions on traversal of directories in file pathnames. However, for compatibility with POSIX these checks can be enabled. Traversal checks are inherently more expensive since modern parsing of file pathnames uses prefix matching rather than component-by-component opening of directory names.

21.5.4 Volume Management and Fault Tolerance

FtDisk is the fault-tolerant disk driver for Windows XP. When installed, it provides several ways to combine multiple disk drives into one logical volume, so as to improve performance, capacity, or reliability.

21.5.4.1 Volume Set

One way to combine multiple disks is to concatenate them logically to form a large logical volume, as shown in Figure 21.7. In Windows XP, this logical volume is called a **volume set**, which can consist of up to 32 physical partitions. A volume set that contains an NTFS volume can be extended without the data already stored in the file system being disturbed. The bitmap metadata on the NTFS volume are simply extended to cover the newly added space. NTFS continues to use the same LCN mechanism that it uses for a single physical disk, and the FtDisk driver supplies the mapping from a logical-volume offset to the offset on one particular disk.

21.5.4.2 Stripe Set

Another way to combine multiple physical partitions is to interleave their blocks in round-robin fashion to form what is called a **stripe set**, as shown in Figure 21.8. This scheme is also called RAID level 0, or **disk striping**. FtDisk uses a stripe size of 64 KB: The first 64 KB of the logical volume are stored in

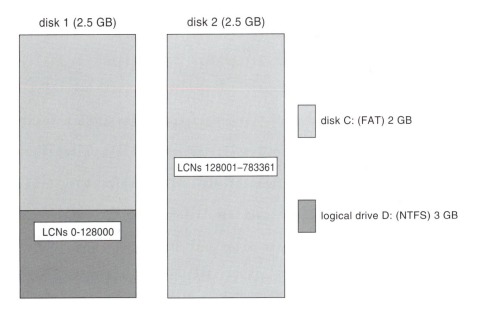

Figure 21.7   Volume set on two drives.

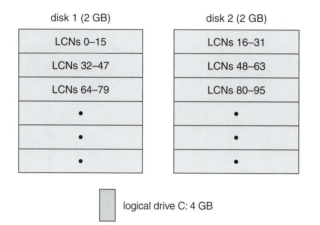

Figure 21.8   Stripe set on two drives.

the first physical partition, the second 64 KB of the logical volume are stored in the second physical partition, and so on, until each partition has contributed 64 KB of space. Then, the allocation wraps around to the first disk, allocating the second 64 KB block. A stripe set forms one large logical volume, but the physical layout can improve the I/O bandwidth, because, for a large I/O, all the disks can transfer data in parallel.

21.5.4.3 Stripe Set with Parity

A variation of this idea is the **stripe set with parity**, which is shown in Figure 21.9. This scheme is also called RAID level 5. If the stripe set has eight disks, then, for each of the seven data stripes, on seven separate disks, there is a parity stripe on the eighth disk. The parity stripe contains the byte-wise `exclusive or` of the data stripes. If any one of the eight stripes is destroyed, the system can reconstruct the data by calculating the `exclusive or` of the remaining seven. This ability to reconstruct data makes the disk array much less likely to lose data in case of a disk failure.

Notice that an update to one data stripe also requires recalculation of the parity stripe. Seven concurrent writes to seven different data stripes thus would also require seven parity stripes to be updated. If the parity stripes were all on the same disk, that disk could have seven times the I/O load of the data disks. To avoid creating this bottleneck, we spread the parity stripes over all the disks, by assigning them in round-robin style. To build a stripe set with parity, we need a minimum of three equal-sized partitions located on three separate disks.

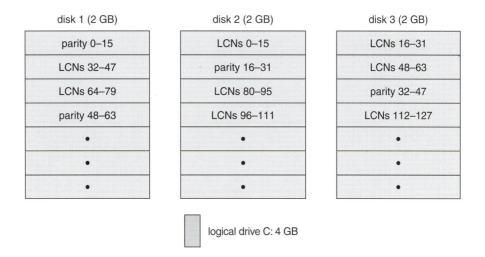

disk 1 (2 GB)   disk 2 (2 GB)   disk 3 (2 GB)

parity 0–15	LCNs 0–15	LCNs 16–31
LCNs 32–47	parity 16–31	LCNs 48–63
LCNs 64–79	LCNs 80–95	parity 32–47
parity 48–63	LCNs 96–111	LCNs 112–127

logical drive C: 4 GB

Figure 21.9   Stripe set with parity on three drives.

21.5.4.4 Disk Mirroring, Mirror Sets, RAID and Duplex Sets

An even more robust scheme is called **disk mirroring** or RAID level 1; it is depicted in Figure 21.10. A **mirror set** comprises two equal-sized partitions on two disks, such that their data contents are identical. When an application writes data to a mirror set, FtDisk writes the data to both partitions. If one partition fails, FtDisk has another copy safely stored on the mirror. Mirror sets can also improve the performance, because read requests can be split between the two mirrors, giving each mirror half of the workload. To protect against the failure of a disk controller, we can attach the two disks of a mirror set to two separate disk controllers. This arrangement is called a **duplex set**.

21.5.4.5 Sector Sparing and Cluster Remapping

To deal with disk sectors that go bad, FtDisk uses a hardware technique called sector sparing, and NTFS uses a software technique called cluster remapping. **Sector sparing** is a hardware capability provided by many disk drives. When a disk drive is formatted, it creates a map from logical block numbers to good sectors on the disk. It also leaves extra sectors unmapped, as spares. If a sector fails, FtDisk instructs the disk drive to substitute a spare. **Cluster remapping** is a software technique performed by the file system. If a disk block goes bad, NTFS substitutes a different, unallocated block by changing any affected pointers in the MFT. NTFS also makes a note that the bad block should never be allocated to any file.

When a disk block goes bad, the usual outcome is a data loss. But sector sparing or cluster remapping can be combined with fault-tolerant volumes to mask the failure of a disk block. If a read fails, the system reconstructs the

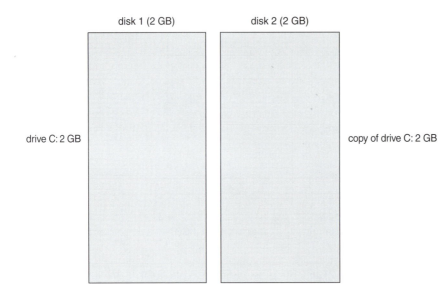

disk 1 (2 GB)   disk 2 (2 GB)

drive C: 2 GB   copy of drive C: 2 GB

Figure 21.10   Mirror set on two drives.

missing data by reading the mirror or by calculating the `exclusive or` parity in a stripe set with parity. The reconstructed data are stored into a new location that is obtained by sector sparing or cluster remapping.

21.5.5 Compression and Encryption

NTFS can perform data compression on individual files or on all data files in a directory. To compress a file, NTFS divides the file's data into **compression units**, which are blocks of 16 contiguous clusters. When each compression unit is written, a data-compression algorithm is applied. If the result fits into fewer than 16 clusters, the compressed version is stored. When reading, NTFS can determine whether data have been compressed: if they have been, the length of the stored compression unit is less than 16 clusters. To improve performance when reading contiguous compression units, NTFS prefetchs and decompresses ahead of the application requests.

For sparse files or files that contain mostly zeros, NTFS uses another technique to save space. Clusters that contain all zeros due to never having been written are not actually allocated or stored on disk. Instead, gaps are left in the sequence of virtual-cluster numbers stored in the MFT entry for the file. When reading a file, if it finds a gap in the virtual-cluster numbers, NTFS just zero-fills that portion of the caller's buffer. This technique is also used by UNIX.

NTFS supports encryption of files. Individual files, or entire directories, can be specified for encryption. The security system manages the keys used, and a key recovery service is available to retrieve lost keys.

21.5.6 Mount Points

Mount points are a form of symbolic link specific to directories on NTFS. They provide a more flexible mechanism for administrators to organize disk volumes than simply providing global names (like drive letters). Mount points are implemented as a symbolic link with associated data that contain the true volume name. Ultimately, mount points will supplant drive letters completely, but there will be a long transition due to the dependence of many applications on the drive-letter scheme.

21.5.7 Change Journal

NTFS keeps a journal describing all changes that have been made to the file system. User-mode services can receive notifications of changes to the journal, and then identify what files have changed. The content-indexing service uses this to identify files that need to be re-indexed. The file-replication service uses the change journal to identify files that need to be replicated across the network.

21.5.8 Volume Shadow Copies

Windows XP implements the capability of bringing a volume to a known state and then creating a shadow copy which can be used to back up a consistent view of the volume. Making a shadow copy of a volume is a form of copy-on-write, where blocks modified after the shadow copy is created have their original contents stashed in the copy. To achieve a consistent state for the volume requires the cooperation of applications since the system cannot know when the data used by the application is in a stable state from which the application could be safely restarted.

The server version of Windows XP uses shadow copies to efficiently maintain old versions of files stored on file servers. This allows users to see documents stored on file servers as they existed at earlier points in time. The user can use this feature to recover files that were accidentally deleted, or simply look at a previous version of the file, all without pulling out a backup tape.

21.6 ■ Networking

Windows XP supports both peer-to-peer and client–server networking. It also has facilities for network management. The networking components in Windows XP provide data transport, interprocess communication, file sharing across a network, and the ability to send print jobs to remote printers.

21.6.1 Network Interfaces

To describe networking in Windows XP, reference is made to two of the internal networking interfaces called the **network device interface specification (NDIS)** and the **transport driver interface (TDI)**. The NDIS interface was developed in 1989 by Microsoft and 3Com to separate network adapters from the transport protocols, so that either could be changed without affecting the other. NDIS resides at the interface between the data-link-control and media-access-control layers in the OSI model and enables many protocols to operate over many different network adapters. In terms of the OSI model, the TDI is the interface between the transport layer (layer 4) and the session layer (layer 5). This interface enables any session-layer component to use any available transport mechanism. (Similar reasoning led to the streams mechanism in UNIX.) The TDI supports both connection-based and connectionless transport, and has functions to send any type of data.

21.6.2 Protocols

Windows XP implements transport protocols as drivers. These drivers can be loaded and unloaded from the system dynamically, although in practice the system typically has to be rebooted after a change. Windows XP comes with several networking protocols.

21.6.2.1 Server-Message Block

The **server-message-block (SMB)** protocol was first introduced in MS-DOS 3.1. The system uses the protocol to send I/O requests over the network. The SMB protocol has four message types. The `Session control` messages are commands that start and end a redirector connection to a shared resource at the server. A redirector uses `File` messages to access files at the server. The system uses `Printer` messages to send data to a remote print queue and to receive back status information, and the `Message` message is used to communicate with another workstation. The SMB protocol was published as the **Common Internet File System** (CIFS), and is supported on a number of operating systems.

21.6.2.2 Network Basic Input/Output System

The **network basic input/output system (NetBIOS)** is a hardware-abstraction interface for networks, analogous to the BIOS hardware-abstraction interface devised for PCs running MS-DOS. NetBIOS, developed in the early 1980s, has become a standard network-programming interface. NetBIOS is used to establish logical names on the network, to establish logical connections or **sessions** between two logical names on the network, and to support reliable data transfer for a session via either NetBIOS or SMB requests.

21.6.2.3 Net BIOS Extended User Interface

The **NetBIOS extended user interface (NetBEUI)** was introduced by IBM in 1985 as a simple, efficient networking protocol for up to 254 machines. It is the default protocol for Windows 95 peer networking and for Windows for Workgroups. Windows XP uses NetBEUI when it wants to share resources with these networks. Among the limitations of NetBEUI are that it uses the actual name of a computer as the address, and that it does not support routing.

21.6.2.4 Transmission Control Protocol/Internet Protocol

The Transmission Control Protocol/Internet Protocol (TCPIP) suite that is used on the Internet has become the de facto standard networking infrastructure. Windows XP uses TCP/IP to connect to a wide variety of operating systems and hardware platforms. The Windows XP TCP/IP package includes the simple network-management protocol (SNMP), dynamic host-configuration protocol (DHCP), Windows Internet name service (WINS), and NetBIOS support.

21.6.2.5 Point-to-Point Tunneling Protocol

The **point-to-point tunneling protocol (PPTP)** is a protocol provided by Windows XP to communicate between remote-access server modules running on Windows XP Server machines and other client systems that are connected over the Internet. The remote-access servers can encrypt data sent over the connection, and they support multi-protocol **virtual private networks** (VPNs) over the Internet.

21.6.2.6 Novell NetWare Protocols

The Novell NetWare protocols (IPX datagram service on the SPX transport layer) are widely used for PC LANs. The Windows XP NWLink protocol connects the NetBIOS to NetWare networks. In combination with a redirector (such as Microsoft's Client Service for Netware or Novell's NetWare Client for Windows), this protocol enables a Windows XP client to connect to a NetWare server.

21.6.2.7 Web Distributed Authoring and Versioning Protocol

Web Distributed Authoring and Versioning (WebDAV) is a http-based protocol for collaborative authoring across the network. Windows XP builds a WebDAV redirector into the file system. By building WebDAV support directly into the file system, it can work with other features, such as encryption. Personal files can now be stored securely in a public place.

21.6.2.8 AppleTalk Protocol

The **AppleTalk protocol** was designed as a low-cost connection by Apple to allow Macintosh computers to share files. Windows XP systems can share files and printers with Macintosh computers via AppleTalk if a Windows XP server on the network is running the Windows' Services for Macintosh package.

21.6.3 Distributed-Processing Mechanisms

Although Windows XP is not a distributed operating system, it does support distributed applications. Mechanisms that support distributed processing on Windows XP include NetBIOS, named pipes and mailslots, windows sockets, RPCs, and network dynamic data exchange (NetDDE).

21.6.3.1 Net BIOS

In Windows XP, NetBIOS applications can communicate over the network using NetBEUI, NWLink, or TCP/IP.

21.6.3.2 Named Pipes

Named pipes are a connection-oriented messaging mechanism. Named pipes were originally developed as a high-level interface to NetBIOS connections over the network. A process can also use named pipes to communicate with other processes on the same machine. Since named pipes are accessed through the file-system interface, the security mechanisms used for file objects also apply to named pipes.

The name of a named pipe has a format called the **uniform naming convention (UNC)**. A UNC name looks like a typical remote file name. The format of a UNC name is \\server_name\share_name\x\y\z, where the server_name identifies a server on the network; a share_name identifies any resource that is made available to network users, such as directories, files, named pipes and printers; and the \x\y\z part is a normal file path name.

21.6.3.3 Mailslots

Mailslots are a connectionless messaging mechanism. They are unreliable when accessed across the network, in that a message sent to a mailslot may be lost before the intended recipient receives it. Mailslots are used for broadcast applications, such as finding components on the network; they are also used by the Windows Computer Browser service.

21.6.3.4 Winsock

Winsock is the Windows XP sockets API. Winsock is a session-layer interface that is largely compatible with UNIX sockets, but with some added Windows XP extensions. It provides a standardized interface to many transport protocols that may have different addressing schemes, so that any Winsock application can run on any Winsock-compliant protocol stack.

21.6.3.5 Remote Procedure Call

A remote procedure call RPC is a client–server mechanism that enables an application on one machine to make a procedure call to code on another machine. The client calls a local procedure—a **stub routine**—that packs its arguments into a message and sends them across the network to a particular server process. The client-side stub routine then blocks. Meanwhile, the server unpacks the message, calls the procedure, packs the return results into a message, and sends them back to the client stub. The client stub unblocks, receives the message, unpacks the results of the RPC, and returns them to the caller. This packing of arguments is sometimes called **marshalling**. The Windows XP RPC mechanism follows the widely used distributed-computing-environment standard for RPC messages, so programs written to use Windows XP RPCs are highly portable. The RPC standard is detailed. It hides many of the architectural differences among computers, such as the sizes of binary numbers and the order of bytes and bits in computer words, by specifying standard data formats for RPC messages.

Windows XP can send RPC messages using NetBIOS, or Winsock on TCP/IP networks, or named pipes on LAN Manager networks. The LPC facility, discussed earlier, is similar to RPC, except that in the LPC case the messages are passed between two processes running on the same computer.

21.6.3.6 Microsoft Interface Definition Language

It is tedious and error-prone to write the code to marshal and transmit arguments in the standard format, to unmarshal and execute the remote procedure, to marshal and send the return results, and to unmarshal and return them to the caller. Fortunately, however, much of this code can be generated automatically from a simple description of the arguments and return results.

Windows XP provides the **Microsoft Interface Definition Language** to describe the remote procedure names, arguments, and results. The compiler for this language generates header files that declare the stubs for the remote procedures, and the data types for the argument and return-value messages. It also generates source code for the stub routines used at the client side, and for an unmarshaller and dispatcher at the server side. When the application is linked, the stub routines are included. When the application executes the RPC stub, the generated code handles the rest.

21.6.3.7 Common Object Model

The **component object model** (COM) is a mechanism for interprocess communication that was developed for Windows. COM objects provide a well-defined interface to manipulate the data in the object. For instance, COM is the infrastructure used by Microsoft's **object linking and embedding** (OLE) technology for inserting spreadsheets into WORD documents. Windows XP has a distributed extension called **DCOM** that can be used over a network utilizing RPC to provide a transparent method of developing distributed applications.

21.6.4 Redirectors and Servers

In Windows XP, an application can use the Windows XP I/O API to access files from a remote computer as though they were local, provided that the remote computer is running a CIFS server, such as is provided by Windows XP or earlier Windows systems. A **redirector** is the client-side object that forwards I/O requests to remote files, where they are satisfied by a server. For performance and security, the redirectors and servers run in kernel mode.

In more detail, access to a remote file occurs as follows:

- The application calls the I/O manager to request that a file be opened with a file name in the standard UNC format.

- The I/O manager builds an I/O request packet, as described in Section 21.3.3.5.

- The I/O manager recognizes that the access is for a remote file, and calls a driver called a **multiple universal-naming-convention provider (MUP)**.

- The MUP sends the I/O request packet asynchronously to all registered redirectors.

- A redirector that can satisfy the request responds to the MUP. To avoid asking all the redirectors the same question in the future, the MUP uses a cache to remember which redirector can handle this file.

- The redirector sends the network request to the remote system.

- The remote-system network drivers receive the request and pass it to the server driver.

- The server driver hands the request to the proper local file-system driver.

- The proper device driver is called to access the data.

- The results are returned to the server driver, which sends the data back to the requesting redirector. The redirector then returns the data to the calling application via the I/O manager.

A similar process occurs for applications that use the Win32 network API, rather than the UNC services, except that a module called a multi-provider router is used instead of a MUP.

For portability, redirectors and servers use the TDI API for network transport. The requests themselves are expressed in a higher-level protocol, which by default is the SMB protocol mentioned in Section 21.6.2. The list of redirectors is maintained in the system registry database.

21.6.4.1 Distributed File System

The UNC names are not always convenient because multiple file servers may be available to serve the same content, and UNC names explicitly include the name of the server. Windows XP supports a **Distributed File System** (DFS) protocol that allows a network administrator to serve up files from multiple servers using a single distributed namespace.

21.6.4.2 Folder Redirection and Client-Side Caching

To improve the PC experience for business users who frequently switch among computers, Windows XP allows administrators to give users **roaming profiles** which keep the user's preferences and other settings on servers. **Folder redirection** is then used to automatically store a user's documents and other files on a server. This works well until one of the computers is no longer attached to the network, such as a laptop on an airplane. To give users off-line access to their redirected files, Windows XP uses **client-side caching** (CSC). CSC is used when on line to keep copies of the server files on the local machine for better performance. The files are pushed up to the server as they are changed. If the computer becomes disconnected, the files are still available, and the update of the server is deferred until the next time the computer is on line with a suitably performing network link.

21.6.5 Domains

Many networked environments have natural groups of users, such as students in a computer laboratory at school, or employees in one department in a business. Frequently, we want all the members of the group to be able to access shared resources on their various computers in the group. To manage the global access rights within such groups, Windows XP uses the concept of a domain. Previously, these domains had no relationship whatsoever to the domain-name system DNS that maps Internet host names to IP addresses. Now, however, they are closely related.

Specifically, a Windows XP domain is a group of Windows XP workstations and servers that share a common security policy and user database. Since Windows XP now uses the Kerberos protocol for trust and authentication, a Windows XP domain is the same thing as a Kerberos realm. Previous versions of NT used the idea of primary and backup domain controllers; now all servers in a domain are domain controllers. In addition, previous versions required the setup of one-way trusts between domains. Windows XP uses a hierarchical approach based on DNS, and allows transitive trusts that can flow up and down the hierarchy. This approach reduces the number of trusts required for n domains from $n * (n - 1)$ to $O(n)$. The workstations in the domain trust the domain controller to give correct information about the access rights of each user (via the user's access token). All users retain the ability to restrict access to their own workstations, no matter what any domain controller may say.

21.6.5.1 Domain Trees and Forests

Because a business may have many departments and a school may have many classes, it is often necessary to manage multiple domains within a single organization. A **domain tree** is a contiguous DNS naming hierarchy. For example, *bell-labs.com* might be the root of the tree, with *research.bell-labs.com* and *pez.bell-labs.com* as children—domains *research* and *pez*. A **forest** is a set of noncontiguous names. An example would be the trees *bell-labs.com* and/or *lucent.com*. A forest may be comprised of only one domain tree, however.

21.6.5.2 Trust Relationships

Trust relationships may be set up between domains in three ways, one way, transitive, and cross link. Versions of NT through Version 4.0 allowed only one-way trusts. A **one-way trust** is exactly what its name implies: domain A is told it can trust domain B. However, B would not trust A unless another relationship is configured. Under a **transitive trust**, if A trusts B and B trusts C, then A, B, and C all trust one another since transitive trusts are two-way by default. Transitive trusts are enabled by default for new domains in a tree and can be configured only among domains within a forest. The third type, a **cross-link trust**, is useful to cut down on authentication traffic. Suppose that domains A and B are leaf nodes, and that users in A often use resources in B. If a standard transitive trust is used, authentication requests must traverse up to the common ancestor of the two leaf nodes; but if A and B have a cross-linking trust established, the authentications would be sent directly to the other node.

21.6.6 Active Directory

Active Directory is the Windows XP implementation of **lightweight directory-access protocol** (LDAP) services. Active Directory stores the topology information about the domain, keeps the domain-based user and group accounts and passwords, and provides a domain-based store for technologies like **group policies** and **intellimirror**.

Administrators use group policies to establish standards for desktop preferences and software. For many corporate information-technology groups, uniformity drastically reduces the cost of computing. Intellimirror is used in conjunction with group policies to specify what software should be available to each class of user, even automatically installing it on demand from a corporate server.

21.6.7 Name Resolution in TCP/IP Networks

On an IP network, **name resolution** is the process of converting a computer name to an IP address, such as resolving *www.bell-labs.com* to 135.104.1.14. Windows XP provides several methods of name resolution, including Windows Internet Name Service (WINS), broadcast-name resolution, domain-name system (DNS), a hosts file, and an LMHOSTS file. Most of these methods are used by many operating systems, so we describe only WINS here.

Under WINS, two or more WINS servers maintain a dynamic database of name-to-IP address bindings, and client software to query the servers. At least two servers are used, so that the WINS service can survive a server failure, and so that the name-resolution workload can be spread over multiple machines.

21.6.7.1 Dynamic Host Configuration Protocol

WINS uses the dynamic host-configuration protocol (DHCP). DHCP updates address configurations automatically in the WINS database, without user or administrator intervention, as follows. When a DHCP client starts up, it broadcasts a `discover` message. Each DHCP server that receives the message replies with an `offer` message that contains an IP address and configuration information for the client. The client chooses one of the configurations and sends a `request` message to the selected DHCP server. The DHCP server responds with the IP address and configuration information it gave previously, and with a **lease** for that address. The lease gives the client the right to use the IP address for a specified period of time. When the lease time is half expired, the client attempts to renew the lease for the address. If the lease is not renewed, the client must obtain a new one.

21.7 ■ Programmer Interface

The Win32 API is the fundamental interface to the capabilities of Windows XP. This section describes five main aspects of the Win32 API: access to kernel objects, sharing of objects between processes, process management, interprocess communication, and memory management.

21.7.1 Access to Kernel Objects

The Windows XP kernel provides many services that application programs can use. Application programs obtain these services by manipulating kernel objects. A process gains access to a kernel object named XXX by calling the `CreateXXX` function to open a handle to XXX. This handle is unique to the process. Depending on which object is being opened, if the create function fails, it may return 0, or it may return a special constant named INVALID_HANDLE_VALUE. A process can close any handle by calling the Close-

Handle function, and the system may delete the object if the count of processes
using the object drops to 0.

21.7.2 Sharing Objects Between Processes

Windows XP provides three ways to share objects between processes. The first
way is for a child process to inherit a handle to the object. When the parent
calls the CreateXXX function, the parent supplies a SECURITIES_ATTRIBUTES
structure with the bInheritHandle field set to TRUE. This field creates an
inheritable handle. Next the child process is created, passing a value of TRUE
to the CreateProcess function's bInheritHandle argument. Figure 21.11
shows a code sample that creates a semaphore handle inherited by a child
process.

Assuming the child process knows which handles are shared, the parent
and child can achieve interprocess communication through the shared objects.
In the example in Figure 21.11, the child process gets the value of the handle
from the first command-line argument, and then shares the semaphore with
the parent process.

The second way to share objects is for one process to give the object a
name when the object is created, and for the second process to open the name.
This method has two drawbacks: Windows XP does not provide a way to
check whether an object with the chosen name already exists, and the object
namespace is global, without regard to the object type. For instance, two
applications may create an object named *pipe* when two distinct—and possibly
different—objects are desired.

Named objects have the advantage that unrelated processes can readily
share them. The first process calls one of the CreateXXX functions and supplies
a name in the lpszName parameter. The second process gets a handle to share

```
...
SECURITY_ATTRIBUTES sa;
sa.nlength = sizeof(sa);
sa.lpSecurityDescriptor = NULL;
sa.bInheritHandle = TRUE;
Handle a_semaphore = CreateSemaphore(&sa,1,1,NULL);
char command_line[132] ;
ostrstream ostring(command_line,sizeof(command_line));
ostring << a_semaphore << ends;
CreateProcess("another_process.exe",command_line,
              NULL,NULL,TRUE, ... );
...
```

Figure 21.11   Code for a child to share an object by inheriting a handle.

```
// process A
...
Handle a_semaphore = CreateSemaphore(NULL,1,1,"MySEM1");
...
// process B
...
Handle b_semaphore = OpenSemaphore(SEMAPHORE_ALL_ACCESS,
                        FALSE, "MySEM1");
...
```

Figure 21.12   Code for sharing an object by name lookup.

the object by calling `OpenXXX` (or `CreateXXX`) with the same name, as shown in the example of Figure 21.12.

The third way to share objects is via the `DuplicateHandle` function. This method requires some other method of interprocess communication to pass the duplicated handle. Given a handle to a process and the value of a handle within that process, a second process can get a handle to the same object, and thus share it. An example of this method is shown in Figure 21.13.

21.7.3 Process Management

In Windows XP, a **process** is an executing instance of an application, and a **thread** is a unit of code that can be scheduled by the operating system. Thus, a process contains one or more threads. A process is started when some other

```
...
// process A wants to give process B access to a semaphore
// process A
Handle a_semaphore = CreateSemaphore(NULL,1,1,NULL);
// send the value of the semaphore to process B
// using a message or shared memory
...
// process B
Handle process_a = OpenProcess(PROCESS_ALL_ACCESS,FALSE,
                        process_id_of_A);
Handle b_semaphore;
DuplicateHandle(process_a,a_semaphore,
   GetCurrentProcess(),&b_semaphore,
   0,FALSE,DUPLICATE_SAME_ACCESS);
// use b_semaphore to access the semaphore
...
```

Figure 21.13   Code for sharing an object by passing a handle.

process calls the CreateProcess routine. This routine loads any dynamic link libraries used by the process, and creates a **primary thread**. Additional threads can be created by the CreateThread function. Each thread is created with its own stack, which defaults to 1 MB unless specified otherwise in an argument to CreateThread. Because some C run-time functions maintain state in static variables, such as errno, a multithread application needs to guard against unsynchronized access. The wrapper function beginthreadex provides appropriate synchronization.

21.7.3.1 Instance Handles

Every dynamic link library or executable file loaded into the address space of a process is identified by an **instance handle**. The value of the instance handle is actually the virtual address where the file is loaded. An application can get the handle to a module in its address space by passing the name of the module to GetModuleHandle. If NULL is passed as the name, the base address of the process is returned. The lowest 64 KB of the address space are not used, so a faulty program that tries to dereference a NULL pointer gets an access violation.

Priorities in the Win32 environment are based on the Windows XP scheduling model, but not all priority values may be chosen. Win32 uses four priority classes: IDLE_PRIORITY_CLASS (priority level 4), NOR-MAL_PRIORITY_CLASS (priority level 8), HIGH_PRIORITY_CLASS (priority level 13), and REALTIME_PRIORITY_CLASS (priority level 24). Processes are typically members of the NORMAL_PRIORITY_CLASS unless the parent of the process was of the IDLE_PRIORITY_CLASS, or another class was specified when CreateProcess was called. The priority class of a process can be changed with the SetPriorityClass function, or by an argument being passed to the START command. For example, the command START /REALTIME cbserver.exe would run the cbserver program in the REALTIME_PRIORITY_CLASS. Only users with the *increase scheduling priority* privilege can move a process into the REALTIME_PRIORITY_CLASS. Administrators and power users have this privilege by default.

21.7.3.2 Scheduling Rule

When a user is running an interactive program, the system needs to provide especially good performance for the process. For this reason, Windows XP has a special scheduling rule for processes in the NORMAL_PRIORITY_CLASS. Windows XP distinguishes between the foreground process that is currently selected on the screen, and the background processes that are not currently selected. When a process moves into the foreground, Windows XP increases the scheduling quantum by some factor—typically by 3. (This factor can be changed via the performance option in the system section of the control panel.) This increase gives the foreground process three times longer to run before a time-sharing preemption occurs.

21.7.3.3 Thread Priorities

A thread starts with an initial priority determined by its class. The priority can be altered by the SetThreadPriority function. This function takes an argument that specifies a priority relative to the base priority of its class:

- THREAD_PRIORITY_LOWEST: base − 2

- THREAD_PRIORITY_BELOW_NORMAL: base − 1

- THREAD_PRIORITY_NORMAL: base + 0

- THREAD_PRIORITY_ABOVE_NORMAL: base + 1

- THREAD_PRIORITY_HIGHEST: base + 2

Two other designations are also used to adjust the priority. Recall from Section 21.3.2.1 that the kernel has two priority classes: 16–31 for the real-time class, and 0–15 for the variable-priority class. THREAD_PRIORITY_IDLE sets the priority to 16 for real-time threads, and to 1 for variable-priority threads. THREAD_PRIORITY_TIME_CRITICAL sets the priority to 31 for real-time threads, and to 15 for variable-priority threads.

As we discussed in Section 21.3.2.1, the kernel adjusts the priority of a thread dynamically depending on whether the thread is I/O bound or CPU bound. The Win32 API provides a method to disable this adjustment, via SetProcessPriorityBoost and SetThreadPriorityBoost functions.

21.7.3.4 Thread Synchronization

A thread can be created in a **suspended state**: the thread does not execute until another thread makes it eligible via the ResumeThread function. The SuspendThread function does the opposite. These functions set a counter, so if a thread is suspended twice, it must be resumed twice before it can run. To synchronize the concurrent access to shared objects by threads, the kernel provides synchronization objects, such as semaphores and mutexes.

In addition, synchronization of threads can be achieved by using the WaitForSingleObject or WaitForMultipleObjects functions. Another method of synchronization in the Win32 API is the critical section. A critical section is a synchronized region of code that can be executed by only one thread at a time. A thread establishes a critical section by calling InitializeCriticalSection. The application must call EnterCriticalSection before entering the critical section, and LeaveCriticalSection after exiting the critical section. These two routines guarantee that, if multiple threads attempt to enter the critical section concurrently, only one thread at a time is permitted to proceed, and the others wait in the EnterCriticalSection routine. The critical-section mechanism is faster than using kernel-synchronization objects because it avoids allocation of kernel objects until it first encounters contention for the critical section.

21.7.3.5 Fibers

A **fiber** is user-mode code that gets scheduled according to a user-defined scheduling algorithm. A process may have multiple fibers in it, just as it can have multiple threads. A major difference between threads and fibers is that threads can execute concurrently, but only one fiber at a time is permitted to execute, even on multiprocessor hardware. This mechanism is included in Windows XP to facilitate the porting of those legacy UNIX applications that were written for a fiber-execution model.

The system creates a fiber by calling either `ConvertThreadToFiber` or `CreateFiber`. The primary difference between these functions is that `Create-Fiber` does not begin executing the fiber that was created. To begin execution, the application must call `SwitchToFiber`. The application can terminate a fiber by calling `DeleteFiber`.

Repeated creation/deletion of threads can be expensive for applications and services that perform small amounts of work in each. The thread pool provides user-mode programs with three services: a queue to which work requests may be submitted (via the `QueueUserWorkItem` API), an API (`Reg-isterWaitForSingleObject`) which can be used to bind callbacks to waitable handles, and APIs to bind callbacks to timeouts (`CreateTimerQueue` and `CreateTimerQueueTimer`).

The thread pool's goal is to increase performance. Threads are relatively expensive, and a processor can only be executing one thing at a time no matter how many threads are used. The thread pool attempts to reduce the number of outstanding threads by slightly delaying work requests (reusing each thread for many requests), while providing enough threads to effectively utilize the machine's CPUs.

The wait and timer-callback APIs allow the thread pool to further reduce the number of threads in a process, using far fewer threads than would be necessary if a process were to devote one thread to servicing each waitable handle or timeout.

21.7.4 Interprocess Communication

One way Win32 applications handle interprocess communication is by sharing kernel objects. Another way is by passing messages, an approach that is particularly popular for Windows GUI applications. One thread can send a message to another thread or to a window by calling `PostMessage`, `PostThreadMes-sage`, `SendMessage`, `SendThreadMessage`, or `SendMessageCallback`. The difference between *posting* a message and *sending* a message is that the post routines are asynchronous: they return immediately, and the calling thread does not know when the message is actually delivered. The send routines are synchronous—they block the caller until the message has been delivered and processed.

In addition to sending a message, a thread can also send data with the message. Since processes have separate address spaces, the data must be copied. The system copies them by calling `SendMessage` to send a message of type `WM_COPYDATA` with a `COPYDATASTRUCT` data structure that contains the length and address of the data to be transferred. When the message is sent, Windows XP copies the data to a new block of memory and gives the virtual address of the new block to the receiving process.

21.7.4.1 Individual Input Queues

Unlike the 16-bit Windows environment, every Win32 thread has its own input queue from which the thread receives messages. (All input is received via messages.) This structure is more reliable than the shared input queue of 16-bit windows, because, with separate queues, one stuck application cannot block input to the other applications. If a Win32 application does not call `GetMessage` to handle events on its input queue, the queue fills up, and after about 5 seconds the system marks the application as "Not Responding".

21.7.5 Memory Management

The Win32 API provides several ways for an application to use memory: virtual memory, memory-mapped files, heaps, and thread-local storage.

21.7.5.1 Virtual Memory

An application calls `VirtualAlloc` to reserve or commit virtual memory, and `VirtualFree` to decommit or release the memory. These functions enable the application to specify the virtual address at which the memory is allocated. They operate on multiples of the memory page size, and the starting address of

```
...
// allocate 16 MB at the top of our address space
void *buf = VirtualAlloc(0,0x1000000,MEM_RESERVE | MEM_TOP_DOWN,
            PAGE_READWRITE);
// commit the upper 8 MB of the allocated space
VirtualAlloc(buf + 0x800000,0x800000,MEM_COMMIT,PAGE_READWRITE);
// do some stuff with it
// decommit
VirtualFree(buf + 0x800000,0x800000,MEM_DECOMMIT);
// release all the allocated address space
VirtualFree(buf,0,MEM_RELEASE);
...
```

Figure 21.14   Code fragments for allocating virtual memory.

an allocated region must be greater than 0x10000. Examples of these functions appear in Figure 21.14.

A process may lock some of its committed pages into physical memory by calling VirtualLock. The maximum number of pages a process can lock is 30, unless the process first calls SetProcessWorkingSetSize to increase the maximum working-set size.

21.7.5.2 Memory-Mapping Files

Another way for an application to use memory is by memory mapping a file into its address space. Memory mapping is also a convenient way for two processes to share memory: both processes map the same file into their virtual memory. Memory mapping is a multistage process, as you can see in the example of Figure 21.15.

If a process wants to map some address space just to share a memory region with another process, no file is needed. The process calls CreateFileMapping with a file handle of 0xffffffff and a particular size. The resulting file-mapping object can be shared by inheritance, by name lookup, or by duplication.

21.7.5.3 Heaps

The third way for applications to use memory is a heap. A heap in the Win32 environment is a region of reserved address space. When a Win32 process is initialized, it is created with a 1 MB **default heap**. Since many Win32 functions use the default heap, access to the heap is synchronized to protect the heap's

```
...
// open the file or create it if it does not exist
HANDLE hfile = CreateFile("somefile",GENERIC_READ | GENERIC_WRITE,
    FILE_SHARE_READ | FILE_SHARE_WRITE,NULL,OPEN_ALWAYS,
    FILE_ATTRIBUTE_NORMAL,
    NULL);
// create the file mapping 8 MB in size
HANDLE hmap = CreateFileMapping(hfile,PAGE_READWRITE,
    SEC_COMMIT,0,0x800000,"SHM_1");
// get a view to the space mapped
void *buf = MapViewOfFile(hmap,FILE_MAP_ALL_ACCESS,0,0,0 times800000);
// do some stuff with it
// unmap the file
UnmapViewOfFile(buf);
CloseHandle(hmap);
CloseHandle(hfile); ...
```

Figure 21.15   Code fragments for memory mapping of a file.

```
// reserve a slot for a variable
DWORD var_index = TlsAlloc();
// set it to some value
TlsSetValue(var_index,10);
// get the value back
int var = TlsGetValue(var_index);
// release the index
TlsFree(var_index);
```

Figure 21.16   Code for dynamic thread-local storage.

space-allocation data structures from being damaged by concurrent updates by multiple threads.

Win32 provides several heap-management functions so a process can allocate and manage a private heap. These functions are HeapCreate, HeapAlloc, HeapRealloc, HeapSize, HeapFree, and HeapDestroy. The Win32 API also provides the HeapLock and HeapUnlock functions to enable a thread to gain exclusive access to a heap. Unlike VirtualLock, these functions perform only synchronization; they do not lock pages into physical memory.

21.7.5.4 Thread-Local Storage

The fourth way for applications to use memory is a thread-local storage mechanism. Functions that rely on global or static data typically fail to work properly in a multithreaded environment. For instance, the C run-time function strtok uses a static variable to keep track of its current position while parsing a string. For two concurrent threads to execute strtok correctly, they need separate *current position* variables. The thread-local storage mechanism allocates global storage on a per-thread basis. It provides both dynamic and static methods of creating thread-local storage. The dynamic method is illustrated in Figure 21.16.

To use a thread-local static variable, the application declares the variable as follows to ensure that every thread has its own private copy:

```
__declspec(thread) DWORD cur_pos = 0;
```

21.8   ■   Summary

Microsoft designed Windows XP to be an extensible, portable operating system—one able to take advantage of new techniques and hardware. Windows XP supports multiple operating environments and symmetric multiprocessing, including both 32-bit and 64-bit processors, and NUMA computers. The use of kernel objects to provide basic services, and the support for client–server computing, enable Windows XP to support a wide variety of application environments. For instance, Windows XP can run programs compiled for MS-DOS, Win16, Windows 95, Windows XP, and/or POSIX. It provides virtual memory, integrated caching, and preemptive scheduling. Windows XP supports a security model stronger than those of previous Microsoft operating systems, and includes internationalization features. Windows XP runs on a wide variety of computers, so users can choose and upgrade hardware to match their budgets and performance requirements without needing to alter the applications they run.

■ Exercises

21.1 What type of operating system is Windows XP? Describe two of its major features.

21.2 List the design goals of Windows XP. Describe two in detail.

21.3 Describe the booting process for a Windows XP system.

21.4 Describe the three main architectural layers of Windows XP.

21.5 What is the job of the object manager?

21.6 What is a handle, and how does a process obtain a handle?

21.7 Describe the management scheme of the virtual memory manager. How does the VM manager improve performance?

21.8 What types of services does the process manager provide? What is a local procedure call?

21.9 What are the responsibilities of the I/O manager?

21.10 What manages cache in Windows XP? How is cache managed?

21.11 Does Windows XP offer any user-mode processes that enable Windows XP to run programs developed for other operating systems? Describe two of these subsystems.

21.12 What types of networking does Windows XP support? How does Windows XP implement transport protocols? Describe two networking protocols.

21.13 How is the NTFS namespace organized? Describe.

21.14 How does NTFS handle data structures? How does NTFS recover from a system crash? What is guaranteed after a recovery takes place?

21.15 What is a process, and how is it managed in Windows XP?

21.16 How does Windows XP allocate user memory?

21.17 Describe some of the ways an application can use memory via the Win32 API.

Bibliographical Notes

Solomon and Russinovich [2000] give an overview of Windows XP and considerable technical detail about the system internals and components. Tate [2000] is a good reference on using Windows XP. The Microsoft Windows XP Server Resource Kit (Microsoft [2000b]) is a six-volume set helpful for using and deploying Windows XP. The Microsoft Developer Network Library (Microsoft [2000a]) is issued quarterly. It provides a wealth of information on Windows XP and other Microsoft products.

Iseminger [2000] provides a good reference on the Windows XP Active Directory. Richter [1997] gives a detailed discussion on writing programs that use the Win32 API. Silberschatz et al. [2001] contains a good discussion of B+ trees.

Chapter 22

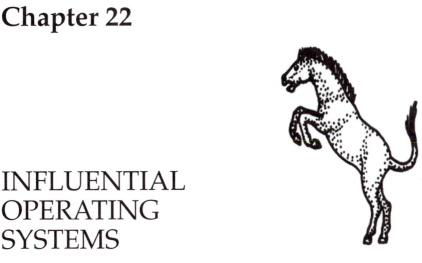

INFLUENTIAL OPERATING SYSTEMS

In Chapter 1, we presented a short historical survey of the development of operating systems. That survey lacked detail, because we had not yet presented the fundamental concepts of operating systems (CPU scheduling, memory management, processes, and so on). By now, however, you understand the basic concepts. Thus, we are in a position to examine how these concepts have been applied in several older and highly influential operating systems. Some of them (such as the XDS-940 or the THE system) were one-of-a-kind systems; others (such as OS/360) are widely used. The order of presentation highlights the similarities and differences of the systems; it is not strictly chronological or ordered by importance. The serious student of operating systems should be familiar with all these systems.

As we describe early systems, we include references to further reading. The papers, written by the designers of the systems, are important both for their technical content and for their style and flavor.

22.1 ■ Early Systems

Early computers were physically enormous machines run from a console. The programmer, who was also the operator of the computer system, would write a program, and then would operate the program directly from the operator's console. First, the program would be loaded manually into memory, from the front panel switches (one instruction at a time), from paper tape or from punched cards. Then, the appropriate buttons would be pushed to set the starting address and to start the execution of the program. As the program ran, the programmer/operator could monitor its execution by the display lights on the console. If errors were discovered, the programmer could halt the program, examine the contents of memory and registers, and debug the program directly from the console. Output was printed, or was punched onto paper tape or cards for later printing.

As time went on, additional software and hardware were developed. Card readers, line printers, and magnetic tape became commonplace. Assemblers, loaders, and linkers were designed to ease the programming task. Libraries of common functions were created. Common functions could then be copied into a new program without having to be written again, providing software reusability.

The routines that performed I/O were especially important. Each new I/O device had its own characteristics, requiring careful programming. A special subroutine—called a device driver—was written for each I/O device. A device driver knows how the buffers, flags, registers, control bits, and status bits for a particular device should be used. Each type of device has its own driver. A simple task, such as reading a character from a paper-tape reader, might involve complex sequences of device-specific operations. Rather than writing the necessary code every time, the device driver was simply used from the library.

Later, compilers for FORTRAN, COBOL, and other languages appeared, making the programming task much easier, but the operation of the computer more complex. To prepare a FORTRAN program for execution, for example, the programmer would first need to load the FORTRAN compiler into the computer. The compiler was normally kept on magnetic tape, so the proper tape would need to be mounted on a tape drive. The program would be read through the card reader and written onto another tape. The FORTRAN compiler produced assembly-language output, which then needed to be assembled. This procedure required mounting another tape with the assembler. The output of the assembler would need to be linked to supporting library routines. Finally, the binary object form of the program would be ready to execute. It could be loaded into memory and debugged from the console, as before.

A significant amount of **set-up time** could be involved in the running of a job. Each job consisted of many separate steps:

1. Loading the FORTRAN compiler tape

2. Running the compiler

3. Unloading the compiler tape

4. Loading the assembler tape

5. Running the assembler

6. Unloading the assembler tape

7. Loading the object program

8. Running the object program

If an error occurred during any step, the programmer/operator might have to start over at the beginning. Each job step might involve the loading and unloading of magnetic tapes, paper tapes, and punch cards.

The job set-up time was a real problem. While tapes were being mounted or the programmer was operating the console, the CPU sat idle. Remember that, in the early days, few computers were available, and they were expensive. A computer might have cost millions of dollars, not including the operational costs of power, cooling, programmers, and so on. Thus, computer time was extremely valuable, and owners wanted their computers to be used as much as possible. They needed high **utilization** to get as much as they could from their investments.

The solution was two-fold. First, a professional computer operator was hired. The programmer no longer operated the machine. As soon as one job was finished, the operator could start the next. Since the operator had more experience with mounting tapes than a programmer, set-up time was reduced. The programmer provided whatever cards or tapes were needed, as well as a short description of how the job was to be run. Of course, the operator could not debug an incorrect program at the console, since the operator would not understand the program. Therefore, in the case of program error, a dump of memory and registers was taken, and the programmer had to debug from the dump. Dumping the memory and registers allowed the operator to continue immediately with the next job, but left the programmer with the more difficult debugging problem.

Second, jobs with similar needs were batched together and run through the computer as a group to reduce set-up time. For instance, suppose the operator received one FORTRAN job, one COBOL job, and another FORTRAN job. If she ran them in that order, she would have to set up for FORTRAN (load the compiler tapes, and so on), then set up for COBOL, and then set up for FORTRAN again. If she ran the two FORTRAN programs as a batch, however, she could set up only once for FORTRAN, saving operator time.

But there were still problems. For example, when a job stopped, the operator would have to notice that it stopped (by observing the console), determine *why* it stopped (normal or abnormal termination), dump memory and register (if necessary), load the appropriate device with the next job, and restart the computer. During this transition from one job to the next, the CPU sat idle.

To overcome this idle time, people developed **automatic job sequencing**; with this technique, the first rudimentary operating systems were created. A small program, called a **resident monitor**, was created to transfer control automatically from one job to the next (Figure 22.1). The resident monitor is always in memory (or **resident**).

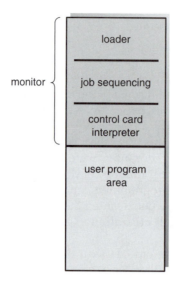

Figure 22.1   Memory layout for a resident monitor.

When the computer was turned on, the resident monitor was invoked, and it would transfer control to a program. When the program terminated, it would return control to the resident monitor, which would then go on to the next program. Thus, the resident monitor would automatically sequence from one program to another and from one job to another.

But how would the resident monitor know which program to execute? Previously, the operator had been given a short description of what programs were to be run on what data. **Control cards** were introduced to provide this information directly to the monitor. The idea is simple: In addition to the program or data for a job, the programmer included the control cards, which contained directives to the resident monitor indicating the program to run. For example, a normal user program might require one of three programs to run: the FORTRAN compiler (FTN), the assembler (ASM), or the user's program (RUN). We could use a separate control card for each of these:

> $FTN — Execute the FORTRAN compiler.
> $ASM — Execute the assembler.
> $RUN — Execute the user program.

These cards tell the resident monitor which programs to run.

We can use two additional control cards to define the boundaries of each job:

> $JOB — First card of a job.
> $END — Final card of a job.

These two cards might be useful in accounting for the machine resources used by the programmer. Parameters can be used to define the job name, account number to be charged, and so on. Other control cards can be defined for other functions, such as asking the operator to load or unload a tape.

One problem with control cards is how to distinguish them from data or program cards. The usual solution is to identify them by a special character or pattern on the card. Several systems used the dollar-sign character ($) in the first column to identify a control card. Others used a different code. IBM's Job Control Language (JCL) used slash marks (//) in the first two columns. Figure 22.2 shows a sample card-deck setup for a simple batch system.

A resident monitor thus has several identifiable parts:

- The **control-card interpreter** that is responsible for reading and carrying out the instructions on the cards at the point of execution.

- The **loader**, which is invoked by the control-card interpreter, to load systems programs and application programs into memory at intervals.

- The **device drivers**, which are used by both the control-card interpreter and the loader for the system's I/O devices to perform I/O. Often, the system and application programs are linked to these same device drivers, providing continuity in their operation, as well as saving memory space and programming time.

These batch systems work fairly well. The resident monitor provides automatic job sequencing as indicated by the control cards. When a control card indicates that a program is to be run, the monitor loads the program

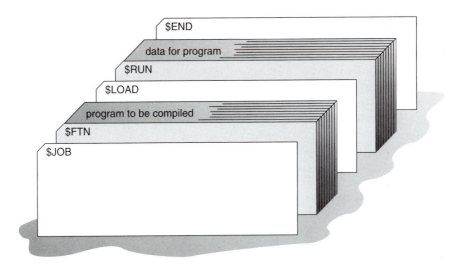

Figure 22.2   Card deck for a simple batch system.

into memory and transfers control to it. When the program completes, it transfers control back to the monitor, which reads the next control card, loads the appropriate program, and so on. This cycle is repeated until all control cards are interpreted for the job. Then, the monitor automatically continues with the next job.

The switch to batch systems with automatic job sequencing was made to improve performance. The problem, quite simply, is that humans are considerably slower than the computer. Consequently, it is desirable to replace human operation by operating-system software. Automatic job sequencing eliminates the need for human set-up time and job sequencing.

As was pointed out in Section 1.2.1, even with this arrangement, however, the CPU is often idle. The problem is the speed of the mechanical I/O devices, which are intrinsically slower than electronic devices. Even a slow CPU works in the microsecond range, with thousands of instructions executed per second. A fast card reader, on the other hand, might read 1,200 cards per minute (or 20 cards per second). Thus, the difference in speed between the CPU and its I/O devices may be three orders of magnitude or more. Over time, of course, improvements in technology resulted in faster I/O devices. Unfortunately, CPU speeds increased even faster, so that the problem was not only unresolved, but also exacerbated.

One common solution was to replace the slow card readers (input devices) and line printers (output devices) with magnetic-tape units. The majority of computer systems in the late 1950s and early 1960s were batch systems reading from card readers and writing to line printers or card punches. Rather than have the CPU read directly from cards, however, the cards were first copied onto a magnetic tape via a separate device. When the tape was sufficiently full, it was taken down and carried over to the computer. When a card was needed for input to a program, the equivalent record was read from the tape. Similarly, output was written to the tape and the contents of the tape would be printed later. The card readers and line printers were operated *off-line*, rather than by the main computer (Figure 22.3).

The main advantage of off-line operation was that the main computer was no longer constrained by the speed of the card readers and line printers, but was limited only by the speed of the much faster magnetic tape units. This technique of using magnetic tape for all I/O could be applied with any similar equipment (such as card readers, card punches, plotters, paper tape, printers).

The real gain in off-line operation comes from the possibility of using multiple reader-to-tape and tape-to-printer systems for one CPU. If the CPU can process input twice as fast as the reader can read cards, then two readers working simultaneously can produce enough tape to keep the CPU busy. On the other hand, there is now a longer delay in getting a particular job run. It must first be read onto tape. Then, it must wait until enough other jobs are read onto the tape to "fill" it. The tape must then be rewound, unloaded, hand-carried to the CPU, and mounted on a free tape drive. This process is not unreasonable for

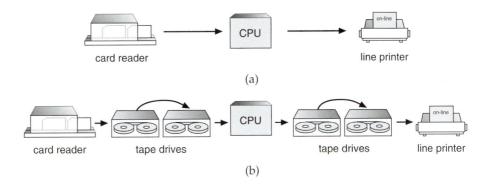

Figure 22.3   Operation of I/O devices. (a) On-line. (b) Off-line.

batch systems, of course. Many similar jobs can be batched onto a tape before it is taken to the computer.

Although off-line preparation of jobs continued for some time, it was quickly replaced in most systems. Disk systems became widely available and greatly improved on off-line operation. The problem with tape systems was that the card reader could not write onto one end of the tape while the CPU read from the other. The entire tape had to be written before it was rewound and read, because tapes are by nature **sequential-access devices**. Disk systems eliminated this problem by being **random-access devices**. Because the head is moved from one area of the disk to another, a disk can switch rapidly from the area on the disk being used by the card reader to store new cards, to the position needed by the CPU to read the "next" card.

In a disk system, cards are read directly from the card reader onto the disk. The location of card images is recorded in a table kept by the operating system. When a job is executed, the operating system satisfies its requests for card-reader input by reading from the disk. Similarly, when the job requests the printer to output a line, that line is copied into a system buffer and is written to the disk. When the job is completed, the output is actually printed. This form of processing is called **spooling** (Figure 22.4); the name is an acronym for **s**imultaneous **p**eripheral **o**peration **o**n-**l**ine. Spooling, in essence, uses the disk as a huge buffer, for reading as far ahead as possible on input devices and for storing output files until the output devices are able to accept them.

Spooling is also used for processing data at remote sites. The CPU sends the data via communications paths to a remote printer (or accepts an entire input job from a remote card reader). The remote processing is done at its own speed, with no CPU intervention. The CPU just needs to be notified when the processing is completed, so that it can spool the next batch of data.

Spooling overlaps the I/O of one job with the computation of other jobs. Even in a simple system, the spooler may be reading the input of one job while printing the output of a different job. During this time, still another job (or jobs)

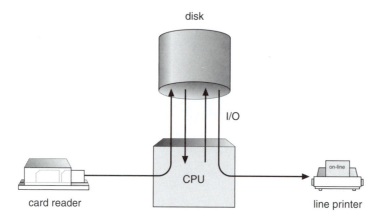

Figure 22.4   Spooling.

may be executed, reading its "cards" from disk and "printing" its output lines onto the disk.

Spooling has a direct beneficial effect on the performance of the system. For the cost of some disk space and a few tables, the computation of one job can overlap with the I/O of other jobs. Thus, spooling can keep both the CPU and the I/O devices working at much higher rates.

Spooling leads naturally to multiprogramming, which is the foundation of all modern operating systems.

22.2 ■ Atlas

The Atlas operating system (Kilburn et al. [1961], Howarth et al. [1961]) was designed at the University of Manchester in England in the late 1950s and early 1960s. Many of its basic features that were novel at the time have become standard parts of modern operating systems. Device drivers were a major part of the system. In addition, system calls were added by a set of special instructions called *extra codes*.

Atlas was a batch operating system with spooling. Spooling allowed the system to schedule jobs according to the availability of peripheral devices, such as magnetic tape units, paper tape readers, paper tape punches, line printers, card readers, or card punches.

The most remarkable feature of Atlas, however, was its memory management. **Core memory** was new and expensive at the time. Many computers, like the IBM 650, used a drum for primary memory. The Atlas system used a drum for its main memory, but it had a small amount of core memory that was used as a cache for the drum. Demand paging was used to transfer information between core memory and the drum automatically.

The Atlas system used a British computer with 48-bit words. Addresses were 24 bits, but were encoded in decimal, which allowed only 1 million words to be addressed. At that time, this was an extremely large address space. The physical memory for Atlas was a 98 KB word drum and 16 KB words of core. Memory was divided into 512-word pages, providing 32 frames in physical memory. An associative memory of 32 registers implemented the mapping from a virtual address to a physical address.

If a page fault occurred, a page-replacement algorithm was invoked. One memory frame was always kept empty, so that a drum transfer could start immediately. The page-replacement algorithm attempted to predict the future memory-accessing behavior based on past behavior. A reference bit for each frame was set whenever the frame was accessed. The reference bits were read into memory every 1,024 instructions, and the last 32 values of these bits were retained. This history was used to define the time since the most recent reference (t_1) and the interval between the last two references (t_2). Pages were chosen for replacement in the following order:

1. Any page with $t_1 > t_2 + 1$. This page is considered to be no longer in use.

2. If $t_1 \leq t_2$ for all pages, then replace that page with the largest $t_2 - t_1$.

The page-replacement algorithm assumes that programs access memory in loops. If the time between the last two references is t_2, then another reference is expected t_2 time units later. If a reference does not occur $(t_1 > t_2)$, it is assumed that the page is no longer being used, and the page is replaced. If all pages are still in use, then the page that will not be needed for the longest time is replaced. The time to the next reference is expected to be $t_2 - t_1$.

22.3 ■ XDS-940

The XDS-940 operating system (Lichtenberger and Pirtle [1965]) was designed at the University of California at Berkeley. Like the Atlas system, it used paging for memory management. Unlike the Atlas system, the XDS-940 was a time-shared system.

The paging was used only for relocation; it was not used for demand paging. The virtual memory of any user process was only 16 KB words, whereas the physical memory was 64 KB words. Pages were 2 KB words each. The page table was kept in registers. Since physical memory was larger than virtual memory, several user processes could be in memory at the same time. The number of users could be increased by sharing of pages when the pages contained read-only reentrant code. Processes were kept on a drum and were swapped in and out of memory as necessary.

The XDS-940 system was constructed from a modified XDS-930. The modifications were typical of the changes made to a basic computer to allow an operating system to be written properly. A user-monitor mode was added. Certain instructions, such as I/O and Halt, were defined to be privileged. An attempt to execute a privileged instruction in user mode would trap to the operating system.

A system-call instruction was added to the user-mode instruction set. This instruction was used to create new resources, such as files, allowing the operating system to manage the physical resources. Files, for example, were allocated in 256-word blocks on the drum. A bit map was used to manage free drum blocks. Each file had an index block with pointers to the actual data blocks. Index blocks were chained together.

The XDS-940 system also provided system calls to allow processes to create, start, suspend, and destroy subprocesses. A programmer could construct a system of processes. Separate processes could share memory for communication and synchronization. Process creation defined a tree structure, where a process is the root and its subprocesses are nodes below it in the tree. Each of the subprocesses could, in turn, create more subprocesses.

22.4 ■ THE

The THE operating system (Dijkstra [1968], McKeag and Wilson [1976]) was designed at the Technische Hogeschool at Eindhoven in the Netherlands. It was a batch system running on a Dutch computer, the EL X8, with 32 KB of 27-bit words. The system was mainly noted for its clean design, particularly its layer structure, and its use of a set of concurrent processes employing semaphores for synchronization.

Unlike the XDS-940 system, however, the set of processes in the THE system was static. The operating system itself was designed as a set of cooperating processes. In addition, five user processes were created that served as the active agents to compile, execute, and print user programs. When one job was finished, the process would return to the input queue to select another job.

A priority CPU-scheduling algorithm was used. The priorities were recomputed every 2 seconds and were inversely proportional to the amount of CPU time used recently (in the last 8 to 10 seconds). This scheme gave higher priority to I/O-bound processes and to new processes.

Memory management was limited by the lack of hardware support. However, since the system was limited and user programs could be written only in Algol, a software paging scheme was used. The Algol compiler automatically generated calls to system routines, which made sure the requested information was in memory, swapping if necessary. The backing store was a 512 KB word drum. A 512-word page was used, with an LRU page-replacement strategy.

Another major concern of the THE system was deadlock control. The banker's algorithm was used to provide deadlock avoidance.

Closely related to the THE system is the Venus system (Liskov [1972]). The Venus system was also a layer-structure design, using semaphores to synchronize processes. The lower levels of the design were implemented in microcode, however, providing a much faster system. The memory management was changed to a paged-segmented memory. The system was also designed as a time-sharing system, rather than a batch system.

22.5 ■ RC 4000

The RC 4000 system, like the THE system, was notable primarily for its design concepts. It was designed for the Danish RC 4000 computer by Regnecentralen, particularly by Brinch-Hansen (Brinch-Hansen [1970], Brinch-Hansen [1973]). The objective was not to design a batch system, or a time-sharing system, or any other specific system. Rather, the goal was to create an operating-system nucleus, or kernel, on which a complete operating system could be built. Thus, the system structure was layered, and only the lower levels—the kernel—were provided.

The kernel supported a collection of concurrent processes. A round-robin CPU scheduler supported processes. Although processes could share memory, the primary communication and synchronization mechanism was the **message system** provided by the kernel. Processes could communicate with each other by exchanging fixed-sized messages of eight words in length. All messages were stored in buffers from a common buffer pool. When a message buffer was no longer required, it was returned to the common pool.

A **message queue** was associated with each process. It contained all the messages that had been sent to that process, but had not yet been received. Messages were removed from the queue in FIFO order. The system supported four primitive operations, which were executed atomically:

- **send-message** (**in** *receiver*, **in** *message*, **out** *buffer*)

- **wait-message** (**out** *sender*, **out** *message*, **out** *buffer*)

- **send-answer** (**out** *result*, **in** *message*, **in** *buffer*)

- **wait-answer** (**out** *result*, **out** *message*, **in** *buffer*)

The last two operations allowed processes to exchange several messages at a time.

These primitives required that a process service its message queue in a FIFO order, and that it block itself while other processes were handling its messages. To remove these restrictions, the developers provided two additional communication primitives. They allowed a process to wait for the arrival of the next message or to answer and service its queue in any order:

- **wait-event** (**in** *previous-buffer*, **out** *next-buffer*, **out** *result*)

- **get-event** (**out** *buffer*)

I/O devices were also treated as processes. The device drivers were code that converted the device interrupts and registers into messages. Thus, a process would write to a terminal by sending that terminal a message. The device driver would receive the message and output the character to the terminal. An input character would interrupt the system and transfer to a device driver. The device driver would create a message from the input character and send it to a waiting process.

22.6 ■ CTSS

The Compatible Time-Sharing System (CTSS) system (Corbato et al. [1962]) was designed at MIT as an experimental time-sharing system. It was implemented on an IBM 7090 and eventually supported up to 32 interactive users. The users were provided with a set of interactive commands that allowed them to manipulate files and to compile and run programs through a terminal.

The 7090 had a 32 KB memory, made up of 36-bit words. The monitor used 5 KB words, leaving 27 KB for the users. User memory images were swapped between memory and a fast drum. CPU scheduling employed a multilevel-feedback-queue algorithm. The time quantum for level i was $2 * i$ time units. If a program did not finish its CPU burst in one time quantum, it was moved down to the next level of the queue, giving it twice as much time. The program at the highest level (with the shortest quantum) was run first. The initial level of a program was determined by its size, so that the time quantum was at least as long as the swap time.

CTSS was extremely successful and was in use as late as 1972. Although it was limited, it succeeded in demonstrating that time sharing was a convenient and practical mode of computing. One result of CTSS was increased development of time-sharing systems. Another result was the development of MULTICS.

22.7 ■ MULTICS

The MULTICS operating system (Corbato and Vyssotsky [1965], Organick [1972]) was designed at MIT as a natural extension of CTSS. CTSS and other early time-sharing systems were so successful that they created an immediate desire to proceed quickly to bigger and better systems. As larger computers became available, the designers of CTSS set out to create a time-sharing utility. Computing service would be provided like electrical power. Large computer systems would be connected by telephone wires to terminals in offices and homes throughout a city. The operating system would be a time-shared system running continuously with a vast file system of shared programs and data.

MULTICS was designed by a team from MIT, GE (which later sold its computer department to Honeywell), and Bell Laboratories (which dropped out of the project in 1969). The basic GE 635 computer was modified to a new computer system called the GE 645, mainly by the addition of paged-segmentation memory hardware.

A virtual address was composed of an 18-bit segment number and a 16-bit word offset. The segments were then paged in 1 KB word pages. The second-chance page-replacement algorithm was used.

The segmented virtual address space was merged into the file system; each segment was a file. Segments were addressed by the name of the file. The file system itself was a multilevel-tree structure, allowing users to create their own subdirectory structures.

Like CTSS, MULTICS used a multilevel-feedback queue for CPU scheduling. Protection was accomplished by an access list associated with each file and a set of protection rings for executing processes. The system, which was written almost entirely in PL/1, comprised about 300,000 lines of code. It was extended to a multiprocessor system, allowing a CPU to be taken out of service for maintenance while the system continued running.

22.8 ■ OS/360

The longest line of operating-system development is undoubtedly that of IBM computers. The early IBM computers, such as the IBM 7090 and the IBM 7094, are prime examples of the development of common I/O subroutines, followed by a resident monitor, privileged instructions, memory protection, and simple batch processing. These systems were developed separately, often by each site independently. As a result, IBM was faced with many different computers, with different languages and different system software.

The IBM/360 was designed to alter this situation. The IBM/360 was designed as a family of computers spanning the complete range from small business machines to large scientific machines. Only one set of software would be needed for these systems, which all used the same operating system: OS/360 (Mealy et al. [1966]). This arrangement was supposed to reduce the mainte-nance problems for IBM and to allow users to move programs and applications freely from one IBM system to another.

Unfortunately, OS/360 tried to be all things for all people. As a result, it did none of its tasks especially well. The file system included a type field that defined the type of each file, and different file types were defined for fixed-length and variable-length records and for blocked and unblocked files. Contiguous allocation was used, so the user had to guess the size of each output file. The Job Control Language (JCL) added parameters for every possible option, making it incomprehensible to the average user.

The memory-management routines were hampered by the architecture. Although a base-register addressing mode was used, the program could access and modify the base register, so that absolute addresses were generated by the CPU. This arrangement prevented dynamic relocation; the program was bound to physical memory at load time. Two separate versions of the operating system were produced: OS/MFT used fixed regions and OS/MVT used variable regions.

The system was written in assembly language by thousands of programmers, resulting in millions of lines of code. The operating system itself required large amounts of memory for its code and tables. Operating-system overhead often consumed one-half of the total CPU cycles. Over the years, new versions were released to add new features and to fix errors. However, fixing one error often caused another in some remote part of the system, so that the number of known errors in the system was fairly constant.

Virtual memory was added to OS/360 with the change to the IBM 370 architecture. The underlying hardware provided a segmented-paged virtual memory. New versions of OS used this hardware in different ways. OS/VS1 created one large virtual address space, and ran OS/MFT in that virtual memory. Thus, the operating system itself was paged, as well as user programs. OS/VS2 Release 1 ran OS/MVT in virtual memory. Finally, OS/VS2 Release 2, which is now called MVS, provided each user with his own virtual memory.

MVS is still basically a batch operating system. The CTSS system was run on an IBM 7094, but MIT decided that the address space of the 360, IBM's successor to the 7094, was too small for MULTICS, so they switched vendors. IBM then decided to create its own time-sharing system, TSS/360 (Lett and Konigsford [1968]). Like MULTICS, TSS/360 was supposed to be a large time-shared utility. The basic 360 architecture was modified in the model 67 to provide virtual memory. Several sites purchased the 360/67 in anticipation of TSS/360.

TSS/360 was delayed, however, so other time-sharing systems were developed as temporary systems until TSS/360 was available. A time-sharing option (TSO) was added to OS/360. IBM's Cambridge Scientific Center developed CMS as a single-user system and CP/67 to provide a virtual machine to run it on (Meyer and Seawright [1970], Parmelee et al. [1972]).

When TSS/360 was eventually delivered, it was a failure. It was too large and too slow. As a result, no site would switch from its temporary system to TSS/360. Today, time sharing on IBM systems is largely provided either by TSO under MVS or by CMS under CP/67 (renamed VM).

What went wrong with TSS/360 and MULTICS? Part of the problem was that these advanced systems were too large and too complex to be understood. Another problem was the assumption that computing power would be available from a large, remote computer by sharing time. It now appears that most computing will be done by small individual machines—personal computers—not by large, remote time-shared systems that try to be all things to all users.

22.9 ■ Mach

The Mach operating system traces its ancestry to the Accent operating system developed at Carnegie Mellon University (CMU) (Rashid and Robertson [1981]). Mach's communication system and philosophy are derived from Accent, but many other significant portions of the system (for example, the virtual memory system, task and thread management) were developed from scratch (Rashid [1986], Tevanian et al. [1989], and Accetta et al. [1986]). The Mach scheduler was described in detail by Tevanian et al. [1987a] and Black [1990]. An early version of the Mach shared memory and memory-mapping system was presented by Tevanian et al. [1987b].

The Mach operating system was designed with the following three critical goals in mind:

1. Emulate 4.3BSD UNIX so that the executable files from a UNIX system can run correctly under Mach.

2. Be a modern operating system that supports many memory models, and parallel and distributed computing.

3. Have a kernel that is simpler and easier to modify than is 4.3BSD.

Mach's development followed an evolutionary path from BSD UNIX systems. Mach code was initially developed inside the 4.2BSD kernel, with BSD kernel components being replaced by Mach components as the Mach components were completed. The BSD components were updated to 4.3BSD when that became available. By 1986, the virtual memory and communication subsystems were running on the DEC VAX computer family, including multiprocessor versions of the VAX. Versions for the IBM RT/PC and for SUN 3 workstations followed shortly. 1987 saw the completion of the Encore Multimax and Sequent Balance multiprocessor versions, including task and thread support, as well as the first official releases of the system, Release 0 and Release 1.

Through Release 2, Mach provided compatibility with the corresponding BSD systems by including much of BSD's code in the kernel. The new features and capabilities of Mach made the kernels in these releases larger than the corresponding BSD kernels. Mach 3 moved the BSD code outside of the kernel, leaving a much smaller microkernel. This system implements only basic Mach features in the kernel; all UNIX-specific code has been evicted to run in user-mode servers. Excluding UNIX-specific code from the kernel allows replacement of BSD with another operating system, or the simultaneous execution of multiple operating-system interfaces on top of the microkernel. In addition to BSD, user-mode implementations have been developed for DOS, the Macintosh operating system, and OSF/1. This approach has similarities to the virtual-machine concept, but the virtual machine is defined by software (the Mach kernel interface), rather than by hardware. As of Release 3.0, Mach became available on a wide variety of systems, including single-processor SUN, Intel, IBM, and DEC machines, and multiprocessor DEC, Sequent, and Encore systems.

Mach was propelled into the forefront of industry attention when the Open Software Foundation (OSF) announced in 1989 that it would use Mach 2.5 as the basis for its new operating system, OSF/1. The initial release of OSF/1 occurred a year later, and now competes with UNIX System V, Release 4, the operating system of choice among UNIX International (UI) members. OSF members included key technological companies such as IBM, DEC, and HP. OSF has since changed its direction and only DEC Unix is based on the Mach kernel.

Mach 2.5 is also the basis for the operating system on the NeXT workstation, the brainchild of Steve Jobs, of Apple Computer fame.

Unlike UNIX, which was developed without regard for multiprocessing, Mach incorporates multiprocessing support throughout. Its multiprocessing support is also exceedingly flexible, ranging from shared-memory systems to systems with no memory shared between processors. Mach uses lightweight processes, in the form of multiple threads of execution within one task (or address space), to support multiprocessing and parallel computation. Its extensive use of messages as the only communications method ensures that protection mechanisms are complete and efficient. By integrating messages with the virtual-memory system, Mach also ensures that messages can be handled efficiently. Finally, by having the virtual-memory system use messages to communicate with the daemons managing the backing store, Mach provides great flexibility in the design and implementation of these memory-object-managing tasks. By providing low-level, or primitive, system calls from which more complex functions may be built, Mach reduces the size of the kernel while permitting operating-system emulation at the user level, much like IBM's virtual-machine systems.

Previous editions of *Operating System Concepts* included an entire chapter on Mach. This chapter, as it appeared in the Fourth Edition, is available on the Web (http://www.bell-labs.com/topic/books/os-book/Mach.ps).

22.10 ▪ Other Systems

There are, of course, other operating systems, and most of them have interesting properties. The MCP operating system for the Burroughs computer family (McKeag and Wilson [1976]) was the first to be written in a system-programming language. It supported segmentation and multiple CPUs. The SCOPE operating system for the CDC 6600 (McKeag and Wilson [1976]) was also a multi-CPU system. The coordination and synchronization of the multiple processes were surprisingly well designed. Tenex (Bobrow et al. [1972]) was an early demand-paging system for the PDP-10 that has had a great influence on subsequent time-sharing systems, such as TOPS-20 for the DEC-20. The VMS operating system for the VAX is based on the RSX operating system for the

PDP-11. CP/M was the most common operating system for 8-bit microcomputer systems, few of which exist today; MS-DOS is the most common system for 16-bit microcomputers. **Graphical user interfaces (GUIs)** are becoming more popular to make computers easier to use. The Macintosh Operating System and Microsoft Windows are the two leaders in this area.

BIBLIOGRAPHY

[Abbot 1984] C. Abbot, "Intervention Schedules for Real-Time Programming", *IEEE Transactions on Software Engineering*, Volume SE-10, Number 3 (1984), pages 268–274.

[Accetta et al. 1986] M. Accetta, R. Baron, W. Bolosky, D. B. Golub, R. Rashid, A. Tevanian, and M. Young, "Mach: A New Kernel Foundation for Unix Development", *Proceedings of the Summer USENIX Conference* (1986), pages 93–112.

[Agrawal and Abbadi 1991] D. P. Agrawal and A. E. Abbadi, "An Efficient and Fault-Tolerant Solution of Distributed Mutual Exclusion", *ACM Transactions on Computer Systems*, Volume 9, Number 1 (1991), pages 1–20.

[Ahituv et al. 1987] N. Ahituv, Y. Lapid, and S. Neumann, "Processing Encrypted Data", *Communications of the ACM*, Volume 30, Number 9 (1987), pages 777–780.

[Ahmed 2000] I. Ahmed, "Cluster Computing: A Glance at Recent Events", *IEEE Concurrency*, Volume 8, Number 1 (2000).

[Akl 1983] S. G. Akl, "Digital Signatures: A Tutorial Survey", *Computer*, Volume 16, Number 2 (1983), pages 15–24.

[Akyurek and Salem 1993] S. Akyurek and K. Salem, "Adaptive Block Rearrangement", *Proceedings of the International Conference on Data Engineering* (1993), pages 182–189.

[Alt 1993] H. Alt, "Removable Media in Solaris", *Proceedings of the Winter USENIX Conference* (1993), pages 281–287.

[Anderson et al. 1989] T. E. Anderson, E. D. Lazowska, and H. M. Levy, "The Performance Implications of Thread Management Alternatives for Shared-Memory Multiprocessors", *IEEE Transactions on Computers*, Volume 38, Number 12 (1989), pages 1631–1644.

[Anderson et al. 1991] T. E. Anderson, B. N. Bershad, E. D. Lazowska, and H. M. Levy, "Scheduler Activations: Effective Kernel Support for the User-Level Management of Parallelism", *Proceedings of the ACM Symposium on Operating Systems Principles* (1991), pages 95–109.

[Apple 1987] *Apple Technical Introduction to the Macintosh Family*. Addison-Wesley (1987).

[Apple 1991] *Inside Macintosh, Volume VI*. Addison-Wesley (1991).

[Asthana and Finkelstein 1995] P. Asthana and B. Finkelstein, "Superdense Optical Storage", *IEEE Spectrum*, Volume 32, Number 8 (1995), pages 25–31.

[Axelsson 1999] S. Axelsson, "The Base-Rate Fallacy and Its Implications for Intrusion Detection", *Proceedings of the ACM Conference on Computer and Communications Security* (1999), pages 1–7.

[Bach 1987] M. J. Bach, *The Design of the UNIX Operating System*, Prentice Hall (1987).

[Back et al. 2000] G. Back, P. Tullman, L. Stoller, W. C. Hsieh, and J. Lepreau, "Techniques for the Design of Java Operating Systems", *2000 USENIX Annual Technical Conference* (2000).

[Baldwin 2002] J. Baldwin, "Locking in the Multithreaded FreeBSD Kernel", *USENIX BSD* (2002).

[Barrera 1991] J. S. Barrera, "A Fast Mach Network IPC Implementation", *Proceedings of the USENIX Mach Symposium* (1991), pages 1–12.

[Bayer et al. 1978] R. Bayer, R. M. Graham, and G. Seegmuller, editors, *Operating Systems-An Advanced Course*, Springer Verlag (1978).

[Beck et al. 1998] M. Beck, H. Bohme, M. Dziadzka, U. Kunitz, R. Magnus, and D. Verworner, *Linux Kernel Internals, Second Edition*, Addison-Wesley (1998).

[Belady 1966] L. A. Belady, "A Study of Replacement Algorithms for a Virtual-Storage Computer", *IBM Systems Journal*, Volume 5, Number 2 (1966), pages 78–101.

[Belady et al. 1969] L. A. Belady, R. A. Nelson, and G. S. Shedler, "An Anomaly in Space-Time Characteristics of Certain Programs Running in a Paging

Machine", *Communications of the ACM*, Volume 12, Number 6 (1969), pages 349–353.

[Ben-Ari 1990] M. Ben-Ari, *Principles of Concurrent and Distributed Programming*, Prentice Hall (1990).

[Benjamin 1990] C. D. Benjamin, "The Role of Optical Storage Technology for NASA", *Proceedings, Storage and Retrieval Systems and Applications* (1990), pages 10–17.

[Bernstein and Goodman 1980] P. A. Bernstein and N. Goodman, "Time-Stamp-Based Algorithms for Concurrency Control in Distributed Database Systems", *Proceedings of the International Conference on Very Large Databases* (1980), pages 285–300.

[Bernstein et al. 1987] A. Bernstein, V. Hadzilacos, and N. Goodman, *Concurrency Control and Recovery in Database Systems*, Addison-Wesley (1987).

[Bershad and Pinkerton 1988] B. N. Bershad and C. B. Pinkerton, "Watchdogs: Extending the Unix File System", *Proceedings of the Winter USENIX Conference* (1988).

[Bershad et al. 1990] B. N. Bershad, T. E. Anderson, E. D. Lazowska, and H. M. Levy, "Lightweight Remote Procedure Call", *ACM Transactions on Computer Systems*, Volume 8, Number 1 (1990), pages 37–55.

[Beveridge and Wiener 1997] J. Beveridge and R. Wiener, *Mutlithreading Applications in Win32*, Addison-Wesley (1997).

[Birrell and Nelson 1984] A. D. Birrell and B. J. Nelson, "Implementing Remote Procedure Calls", *ACM Transactions on Computer Systems*, Volume 2, Number 1 (1984), pages 39–59.

[Black 1990] D. L. Black, "Scheduling Support for Concurrency and Parallelism in the Mach Operating System", *Computer*, Volume 23, Number 5 (1990), pages 35–43.

[Blair et al. 1985] G. S. Blair, J. R. Malone, and J. A. Mariani, "A Critique of UNIX", *Software—Practice and Experience*, Volume 15, Number 6 (1985), pages 1125–1139.

[Bobrow et al. 1972] D. G. Bobrow, J. D. Burchfiel, D. L. Murphy, and R. S. Tomlinson, "TENEX, a Paged Time Sharing System for the PDP-10", *Communications of the ACM*, Volume 15, Number 3 (1972).

[Bourne 1978] S. R. Bourne, "The UNIX Shell", *Bell System Technical Journal*, Volume 57, Number 6 (1978), pages 1971–1990.

[Bourne 1983] S. R. Bourne, *The UNIX System*, Addison-Wesley (1983).

[Bovet and Cesati 2002] D. P. Bovet and M. Cesati, *Understanding the Linux Kernel, Second Edition*, O'Reilly & Associates (2002).

[Brain 1996] M. Brain, *Win32 System Services, Second Edition*, Prentice Hall (1996).

[Brereton 1986] O. P. Brereton, "Management of Replicated Files in a UNIX Environment", *Software—Practice and Experience*, Volume 16, (1986), pages 771–780.

[Brinch-Hansen 1970] P. Brinch-Hansen, "The Nucleus of a Multiprogramming System", *Communications of the ACM*, Volume 13, Number 4 (1970), pages 238–241 and 250.

[Brinch-Hansen 1973] P. Brinch-Hansen, *Operating System Principles*, Prentice Hall (1973).

[Brownbridge et al. 1982] D. R. Brownbridge, L. F. Marshall, and B. Randell, "The Newcastle Connection or UNIXes of the World Unite!", *Software—Practice and Experience*, Volume 12, Number 12 (1982), pages 1147–1162.

[Buhr et al. 1995] P. A. Buhr, M. Fortier, and M. H. Coffin, "Monitor Classification", *ACM Computing Survey*, Volume 27, Number 1 (1995), pages 63–107.

[Burns 1978] J. E. Burns, "Mutual Exclusion with Linear Waiting Using Binary Shared Variables", *SIGACT News*, Volume 10, Number 2 (1978), pages 42–47.

[Burns and Davies 1993] A. Burns and G. Davies, *Concurrent Programming*, Addison-Wesley (1993).

[Butenhof 1997] D. Butenhof, *Programming with POSIX Threads*, Addison-Wesley (1997).

[Buyya 1999] R. Buyya, *High Performance Cluster Computing: Architectures and Systems*, Prentice Hall (1999).

[Callaghan 2000] B. Callaghan, *NFS Illustrated*, Addison-Wesley (2000).

[Calvert and Donahoo 2001] K. Calvert and M. Donahoo, *TCP/IP Sockets in Java: Practical Guide for Programmers*, Morgan Kaufmann (2001).

[Carr and Hennessy 1981] W. R. Carr and J. L. Hennessy, "WSClock—A Simple and Effective Algorithm for Virtual Memory Management", *Proceedings of the ACM Symposium on Operating System Principles* (1981), pages 87–95.

[Carvalho and Roucairol 1983] O. S. Carvalho and G. Roucairol, "On Mutual Exclusion in Computer Networks", *Communications of the ACM*, Volume 26, Number 2 (1983), pages 146–147.

[Chang 1980] E. Chang, "N-Philosophers: An Exercise in Distributed Control", *Computer Networks*, Volume 4, Number 2 (1980), pages 71–76.

[Chang and Mergen 1988] A. Chang and M. F. Mergen, "801 Storage: Architecture and Programming", *ACM Transactions on Computer Systems*, Volume 6, Number 1 (1988), pages 28–50.

[Chen et al. 1994] P. M. Chen, E. K. Lee, G. A. Gibson, R. H. Katz, and D. A. Patterson, "RAID: High-Performance, Reliable Secondary Storage", *ACM Computing Survey*, Volume 26, Number 2 (1994), pages 145–185.

[Cheung and Loong 1995] W. H. Cheung and A. H. S. Loong, "Exploring Issues of Operating Systems Structuring: From Microkernel to Extensible Systems", *Operating Systems Review*, Volume 29, (1995), pages 4–16.

[Chi 1982] C. S. Chi, "Advances in Computer Mass Storage Technology", *Computer*, Volume 15, Number 5 (1982), pages 60–74.

[Coffman et al. 1971] E. G. Coffman, M. J. Elphick, and A. Shoshani, "System Deadlocks", *Computing Surveys*, Volume 3, Number 2 (1971), pages 67–78.

[Cohen and Jefferson 1975] E. S. Cohen and D. Jefferson, "Protection in the Hydra Operating System", *Proceedings of the ACM Symposium on Operating Systems Principles* (1975), pages 141–160.

[Comer 1999] D. Comer, *Internetworking with TCP/IP, Volume II, Third Edition*, Prentice Hall (1999).

[Comer 2000] D. Comer, *Internetworking with TCP/IP, Volume I, Fourth Edition*, Prentice Hall (2000).

[Corbato and Vyssotsky 1965] F. J. Corbato and V. A. Vyssotsky, "Introduction and Overview of the MULTICS System", *Proceedings of the AFIPS Fall Joint Computer Conference* (1965), pages 185–196.

[Corbato et al. 1962] F. J. Corbato, M. Merwin-Daggett, and R. C. Daley, "An Experimental Time-Sharing System", *Proceedings of the AFIPS Fall Joint Computer Conference* (1962), pages 335–344.

[Coulouris et al. 2001] G. Coulouris, J. Dollimore, and T. Kindberg, *Distributed Systems Concepts and Designs, Third Edition*, Addison Wesley (2001).

[Courtois et al. 1971] P. J. Courtois, F. Heymans, and D. L. Parnas, "Concurrent Control with 'Readers' and 'Writers'", *Communications of the ACM*, Volume 14, Number 10 (1971), pages 667–668.

[Custer 1994] H. Custer, *Inside the Windows NT File System*, Microsoft Press (1994).

[Davcev and Burkhard 1985] D. Davcev and W. A. Burkhard, "Consistency and Recovery Control for Replicated Files", *Proceedings of the ACM Symposium on Operating Systems Principles* (1985), pages 87–96.

[**Davies 1983**] D. W. Davies, "Applying the RSA Digital Signature to Electronic Mail", *Computer*, Volume 16, Number 2 (1983), pages 55–62.

[**deBruijn 1967**] N. G. deBruijn, "Additional Comments on a Problem in Concurrent Programming and Control", *Communications of the ACM*, Volume 10, Number 3 (1967), pages 137–138.

[**Deitel 1990**] H. M. Deitel, *An Introduction to Operating Systems, Second Edition*, Addison-Wesley (1990).

[**Denning 1968**] P. J. Denning, "The Working Set Model for Program Behavior", *Communications of the ACM*, Volume 11, Number 5 (1968), pages 323–333.

[**Denning 1980**] P. J. Denning, "Working Sets Past and Present", *IEEE Transactions on Software Engineering*, Volume SE-6, Number 1 (1980), pages 64–84.

[**Denning 1982**] D. E. Denning, *Cryptography and Data Security*, Addison-Wesley (1982).

[**Denning 1983**] D. E. Denning, "Protecting Public Keys and Signature Keys", *Computer*, Volume 16, Number 2 (1983), pages 27–35.

[**Denning 1984**] D. E. Denning, "Digital Signatures with RSA and Other Public-Key Cryptosystems", *Communications of the ACM*, Volume 27, Number 4 (1984), pages 388–392.

[**Dennis 1965**] J. B. Dennis, "Segmentation and the Design of Multiprogrammed Computer Systems", *Communications of the ACM*, Volume 8, Number 4 (1965), pages 589–602.

[**Dennis and Horn 1966**] J. B. Dennis and E. C. V. Horn, "Programming Semantics for Multiprogrammed Computations", *Communications of the ACM*, Volume 9, Number 3 (1966), pages 143–155.

[**Diffie and Hellman 1976**] W. Diffie and M. E. Hellman, "New Directions in Cryptography", *IEEE Transactions on Information Theory*, Volume 22, Number 6 (1976), pages 644–654.

[**Diffie and Hellman 1979**] W. Diffie and M. E. Hellman, "Privacy and Authentication", *Proceedings of the IEEE* (1979), pages 397–427.

[**Dijkstra 1965a**] E. W. Dijkstra, "Cooperating Sequential Processes", *Technical Report, Technological University, Eindhoven, the Netherlands* (1965), pages 43–112.

[**Dijkstra 1965b**] E. W. Dijkstra, "Solution of a Problem in Concurrent Programming Control", *Communications of the ACM*, Volume 8, Number 9 (1965), page 569.

[Dijkstra 1968] E. W. Dijkstra, "The Structure of the THE Multiprogramming System", *Communications of the ACM*, Volume 11, Number 5 (1968), pages 341–346.

[Dijkstra 1971] E. W. Dijkstra, "Hierarchical Ordering of Sequential Processes", *Acta Informatica*, Volume 1, Number 2 (1971), pages 115–138.

[DoD 1985] *Trusted Computer System Evaluation Criteria.* Department of Defense (1985).

[Dougan et al. 1999] C. Dougan, P. Mackerras, and V. Yodaiken, "Optimizing the Idle Task and Other MMU Tricks", *Proceedings of the Third Symposium on Operating System Design and Implementation* (1999).

[Eastlake 1999] D. Eastlake, "Domain Name System Security Extensions", *Network Working Group, Request for Comments: 2535* (1999).

[Eisenberg and McGuire 1972] M. A. Eisenberg and M. R. McGuire, "Further Comments on Dijkstra's Concurrent Programming Control Problem", *Communications of the ACM*, Volume 15, Number 11 (1972), page 999.

[Ekanadham and Bernstein 1979] K. Ekanadham and A. J. Bernstein, "Conditional Capabilities", *IEEE Transactions on Software Engineering*, Volume SE-5, Number 5 (1979), pages 458–464.

[Engelschall 2000] R. Engelschall, "Portable Multithreading: The Signal Stack Trick For User-Space Thread Creation", *Proceedings of the 2000 USENIX Annual Technical Conference* (2000).

[Eswaran et al. 1976] K. P. Eswaran, J. N. Gray, R. A. Lorie, and I. L. Traiger, "The Notions of Consistency and Predicate Locks in a Database System", *Communications of the ACM*, Volume 19, Number 11 (1976), pages 624–633.

[Fang et al. 2001] Z. Fang, L. Zhang, J. B. Carter, W. C. Hsieh, and S. A. McKee, "Reevaluating Online Superpage Promotion with Hardware Support", *Proceedings of the Seventh International Symposium on High-Performance Computer Architecture*, Volume 50, Number 5 (2001).

[Farley 1998] J. Farley, *Java Distributed Computing*, O'Reilly & Associates (1998).

[Farrow 1986a] R. Farrow, "Security for Superusers, or How to Break the UNIX System", *UNIX World* (May 1986), pages 65–70.

[Farrow 1986b] R. Farrow, "Security Issues and Strategies for Users", *UNIX World* (April 1986), pages 65–71.

[Feitelson and Rudolph 1990] D. Feitelson and L. Rudolph, "Mapping and Scheduling in a Shared Parallel Environment Using Distributed Hierarchical Control", *Proceedings of the International Conference on Parallel Processing* (1990).

[**Filipski and Hanko 1986**] A. Filipski and J. Hanko, "Making UNIX Secure", *Byte* (April 1986), pages 113–128.

[**Folk and Zoellick 1987**] M. J. Folk and B. Zoellick, *File Structures*, Addison-Wesley (1987).

[**Forrest et al. 1996**] S. Forrest, S. A. Hofmeyr, and T. A. Longstaff, "A Sense of Self for UNIX Processes", *Proceedings of the IEEE Symposium on Security and Privacy* (1996), pages 120–128.

[**Fortier 1989**] P. J. Fortier, *Handbook of LAN Technology*, McGraw-Hill (1989).

[**FreeBSD 1999**] FreeBSD, *FreeBSD Handbook*, The FreeBSD Documentation Project (1999).

[**Freedman 1983**] D. H. Freedman, "Searching for Denser Disks", *Infosystems* (1983), page 56.

[**Fujitani 1984**] L. Fujitani, "Laser Optical Disk: The Coming Revolution in On-Line Storage", *Communications of the ACM*, Volume 27, Number 6 (1984), pages 546–554.

[**Gait 1988**] J. Gait, "The Optical File Cabinet: A Random-Access File System for Write-On Optical Disks", *Computer*, Volume 21, Number 6 (1988).

[**Ganapathy and Schimmel 1998**] N. Ganapathy and C. Schimmel, "General Purpose Operating System Support for Multiple Page Sizes", *Proceedings of the USENIX Technical Conference* (1998).

[**Garcia-Molina 1982**] H. Garcia-Molina, "Elections in Distributed Computing Systems", *IEEE Transactions on Computers*, Volume C-31, Number 1 (1982).

[**Garfinkel and Spafford 1991**] S. Garfinkel and G. Spafford, *Practical UNIX Security*, O'Reilly & Associates (1991).

[**Gifford 1982**] D. K. Gifford, "Cryptographic Sealing for Information Secrecy and Authentication", *Communications of the ACM*, Volume 25, Number 4 (1982), pages 274–286.

[**Golden and Pechura 1986**] D. Golden and M. Pechura, "The Structure of Microcomputer File Systems", *Communications of the ACM*, Volume 29, Number 3 (1986), pages 222–230.

[**Golm et al. 2002**] M. Golm, M. Felser, C. Wawersich, and J. Kleinoder, "The JX Operating System", *2002 USENIX Annual Technical Conference* (2002).

[**Gong 2002**] L. Gong, "Peer-to-Peer Networks in Action", *IEEE Internet Computing*, Volume 6, Number 1 (2002).

[**Gong et al. 1997**] L. Gong, M. Mueller, H. Prafullchandra, and R. Schemers, "Going Beyond the Sandbox: An Overview of the New Security Architecture in the Java Development Kit 1.2", *Proceedings of the USENIX Symposium on Internet Technologies and Systems* (1997).

[**Gosling et al. 1996**] J. Gosling, B. Joy, and G. Steele, *The Java Language Specification*, Addison-Wesley (1996).

[**Grampp and Morris 1984**] F. T. Grampp and R. H. Morris, "UNIX Operating-System Security", *AT&T Bell Laboratories Technical Journal*, Volume 63, (1984), pages 1649–1672.

[**Gray 1978**] J. N. Gray, "Notes on Data Base Operating Systems", in [**Bayer et al. 1978**] (1978), pages 393–481.

[**Gray 1981**] J. N. Gray, "The Transaction Concept: Virtues and Limitations", *Proceedings of the International Conference on Very Large Databases* (1981), pages 144–154.

[**Gray 1997**] J. Gray, *Interprocess Communications in UNIX*, Prentice Hall (1997).

[**Gray et al. 1981**] J. N. Gray, P. R. McJones, and M. Blasgen, "The Recovery Manager of the System R Database Manager", *ACM Computing Survey*, Volume 13, Number 2 (1981), pages 223–242.

[**Grosshans 1986**] D. Grosshans, *File Systems Design and Implementation*, Prentice Hall (1986).

[**Grosso 2002**] W. Grosso, *Java RMI*, O'Reilly & Associates (2002).

[**Habermann 1969**] A. N. Habermann, "Prevention of System Deadlocks", *Communications of the ACM*, Volume 12, Number 7 (1969), pages 373–377, 385.

[**Halsall 1992**] F. Halsall, *Data Communications, Computer Networks and Open Systems*, Addison-Wesley (1992).

[**Han and Ghosh 1998**] K. Han and S. Ghosh, "A Comparative Analysis of Virtual Versus Physical Process-Migration Strategies for Distributed Modeling and Simulation of Mobile Computing Networks", *Wireless Networks*, Volume 4, Number 5 (1998), pages 365–378.

[**Hansen and Atkins 1993**] S. E. Hansen and E. T. Atkins, "Automated System Monitoring and Notification With Swatch", *Proceedings of the USENIX Systems Administration Conference* (1993).

[**Harchol-Balter and Downey 1997**] M. Harchol-Balter and A. B. Downey, "Exploiting Process Lifetime Distributions for Dynamic Load Balancing", *ACM Transactions on Computer Systems*, Volume 15, Number 3 (1997), pages 253–285.

[Harish and Owens 1999] V. C. Harish and B. Owens, "Dynamic Load Balancing DNS", *Linux Journal*, Volume 1999, Number 64 (1999).

[Harker et al. 1981] J. M. Harker, D. W. Brede, R. E. Pattison, G. R. Santana, and L. G. Taft, "A Quarter Century of Disk File Innovation", *IBM Journal of Research and Development*, Volume 25, Number 5 (1981), pages 677–689.

[Harold 2000] E. R. Harold, *Java Network Programming*, O'Reilly & Associates (2000).

[Harrison et al. 1976] M. A. Harrison, W. L. Ruzzo, and J. D. Ullman, "Protection in Operating Systems", *Communications of the ACM*, Volume 19, Number 8 (1976), pages 461–471.

[Havender 1968] J. W. Havender, "Avoiding Deadlock in Multitasking Systems", *IBM Systems Journal*, Volume 7, Number 2 (1968), pages 74–84.

[Hecht et al. 1988] M. S. Hecht, A. Johri, R. Aditham, and T. J. Wei, "Experience Adding C2 Security Features to UNIX", *Proceedings of the Summer USENIX Conference* (1988), pages 133–146.

[Hennessy and Patterson 2002] J. L. Hennessy and D. A. Patterson, *Computer Architecture: A Quantitative Approach, Third Edition*, Morgan Kaufmann Publishers (2002).

[Henry 1984] G. Henry, "The Fair Share Scheduler", *AT&T Bell Laboratories Technical Journal* (1984).

[Hitchens 2002] R. Hitchens, *Java NIO*, O'Reilly & Associates (2002).

[Hoagland 1985] A. S. Hoagland, "Information Storage Technology—A Look at the Future", *Computer*, Volume 18, Number 7 (1985), pages 60–68.

[Hoare 1974] C. A. R. Hoare, "Monitors: An Operating System Structuring Concept", *Communications of the ACM*, Volume 17, Number 10 (1974), pages 549–557.

[Holt 1971] R. C. Holt, "Comments on Prevention of System Deadlocks", *Communications of the ACM*, Volume 14, Number 1 (1971), pages 36–38.

[Holt 1972] R. C. Holt, "Some Deadlock Properties of Computer Systems", *Computing Surveys*, Volume 4, Number 3 (1972), pages 179–196.

[Holub 2000] A. Holub, *Taming Java Threads*, Apress (2000).

[Hong et al. 1989] J. Hong, X. Tan, and D. Towsley, "A Performance Analysis of Minimum Laxity and Earliest Deadline Scheduling in a Real-Time System", *IEEE Transactions on Computers*, Volume 38, Number 12 (1989), pages 1736–1744.

[Howard et al. 1988] J. H. Howard, M. L. Kazar, S. G. Menees, D. A. Nichols, M. Satyanarayanan, and R. N. Sidebotham, "Scale and Performance in a Distributed File System", *ACM Transactions on Computer Systems*, Volume 6, Number 1 (1988), pages 55–81.

[Howarth et al. 1961] D. J. Howarth, R. B. Payne, and F. H. Sumner, "The Manchester University Atlas Operating System, Part II: User's Description", *Computer Journal*, Volume 4, Number 3 (1961), pages 226–229.

[Hsiao et al. 1979] D. K. Hsiao, D. S. Kerr, and S. E. Madnick, *Computer Security*, Academic Press (1979).

[Hyman 1985] D. Hyman, *The Columbus Chicken Statute and More Bonehead Legislation*, S. Greene Press (1985).

[Iacobucci 1988] E. Iacobucci, *OS/2 Programmer's Guide*, Osborne McGraw-Hill (1988).

[IBM 1983] *Technical Reference*. IBM Corporation (1983).

[Iliffe and Jodeit 1962] J. K. Iliffe and J. G. Jodeit, "A Dynamic Storage Allocation System", *Computer Journal*, Volume 5, Number 3 (1962), pages 200–209.

[Intel 1985a] *iAPX 286 Programmer's Reference Manual*. Intel Corporation (1985).

[Intel 1985b] *iAPX 86/88, 186/188 User's Manual Programmer's Reference*. Intel Corporation (1985).

[Intel 1986] *iAPX 386 Programmer's Reference Manual*. Intel Corporation (1986).

[Intel 1990] *i486 Microprocessor Programmer's Reference Manual*. Intel Corporation (1990).

[Intel 1993] *Pentium Processor User's Manual, Volume 3: Architecture and Programming Manual*. Intel Corporation (1993).

[Iseminger 2000] D. Iseminger, *Active Directory Services for Microsoft Windows 2000. Technical Reference*, Microsoft Press (2000).

[Jacob and Mudge 1997] B. Jacob and T. Mudge, "Software-Managed Address Translation", *Proceedings of the Third International Symposium on High Performance Computer Architecture and Implementation* (1997).

[Jacob and Mudge 1998a] B. Jacob and T. Mudge, "Virtual Memory in Contemporary Microprocessors", *IEEE Micro Magazine*, Volume 18, (1998), pages 60–75.

[Jacob and Mudge 1998b] B. Jacob and T. Mudge, "Virtual Memory: Issues of Implementation", *IEEE Computer Magazine*, Volume 31, (1998), pages 33–43.

[Jacob and Mudge 2001] B. Jacob and T. Mudge, "Uniprocessor Virtual Memory Without TLBs", *IEEE Transactions on Computers*, Volume 50, Number 5 (2001).

[Jensen et al. 1985] E. D. Jensen, C. D. Locke, and H. Tokuda, "A Time-Driven Scheduling Model for Real-Time Operating Systems", *Proceedings of the IEEE Real-Time Systems Symposium* (1985), pages 112–122.

[Jones and Liskov 1978] A. K. Jones and B. H. Liskov, "A Language Extension for Expressing Constraints on Data Access", *Communications of the ACM*, Volume 21, Number 5 (1978), pages 358–367.

[Katz et al. 1989] R. H. Katz, G. A. Gibson, and D. A. Patterson, "Disk System Architectures for High Performance Computing", *Proceedings of the IEEE* (1989).

[Kay and Lauder 1988] J. Kay and P. Lauder, "A Fair Share Scheduler", *Communications of the ACM*, Volume 31, Number 1 (1988), pages 44–55.

[Kenville 1982] R. F. Kenville, "Optical Disk Data Storage", *Computer*, Volume 15, Number 7 (1982), pages 21–26.

[Kernighan and Pike 1984] B. W. Kernighan and R. Pike, *The UNIX Programming Environment*, Prentice Hall (1984).

[Kernighan and Ritchie 1988] B. W. Kernighan and D. M. Ritchie, *The C Programming Language, Second Edition*, Prentice Hall (1988).

[Kessels 1977] J. L. W. Kessels, "An Alternative to Event Queues for Synchronization in Monitors", *Communications of the ACM*, Volume 20, Number 7 (1977), pages 500–503.

[Khanna et al. 1992] S. Khanna, M. Sebree, and J. Zolnowsky, "Realtime Scheduling in SunOS 5.0", *Proceedings of the Winter USENIX Conference* (1992), pages 375–390.

[Kieburtz and Silberschatz 1978] R. B. Kieburtz and A. Silberschatz, "Capability Managers", *IEEE Transactions on Software Engineering*, Volume SE-4, Number 6 (1978), pages 467–477.

[Kieburtz and Silberschatz 1983] R. B. Kieburtz and A. Silberschatz, "Access Right Expressions", *ACM Transactions on Programming Languages and Systems*, Volume 5, Number 1 (1983), pages 78–96.

[Kilburn et al. 1961] T. Kilburn, D. J. Howarth, R. B. Payne, and F. H. Sumner, "The Manchester University Atlas Operating System, Part I: Internal Organization", *Computer Journal*, Volume 4, Number 3 (1961), pages 222–225.

[Kim and Spafford 1993] G. H. Kim and E. H. Spafford, "The Design and Implementation of Tripwire: A File System Integrity Checker", *Technical Report, Purdue University* (1993).

[King 1990] R. P. King, "Disk Arm Movement in Anticipation of Future Requests", *ACM Transactions on Computer Systems*, Volume 8, Number 3 (1990), pages 214–229.

[Kleinrock 1975] L. Kleinrock, *Queueing Systems, Volume II: Computer Applications*, Wiley-Interscience (1975).

[Knapp 1987] E. Knapp, "Deadlock Detection in Distributed Databases", *Computing Surveys*, Volume 19, Number 4 (1987), pages 303–328.

[Knuth 1966] D. E. Knuth, "Additional Comments on a Problem in Concurrent Programming Control", *Communications of the ACM*, Volume 9, Number 5 (1966), pages 321–322.

[Knuth 1973] D. E. Knuth, *The Art of Computer Programming, Volume 1: Fundamental Algorithms, Second Edition*, Addison-Wesley (1973).

[Koch 1987] P. D. L. Koch, "Disk File Allocation Based on the Buddy System", *ACM Transactions on Computer Systems*, Volume 5, Number 4 (1987), pages 352–370.

[Korn 1983] D. Korn, "KSH, A Shell Programming Language", *Proceedings of the Summer USENIX Conference* (1983), pages 191–202.

[Kosaraju 1973] S. Kosaraju, "Limitations of Dijkstra's Semaphore Primitives and Petri Nets", *Operating Systems Review*, Volume 7, Number 4 (1973), pages 122–126.

[Kramer 1988] S. M. Kramer, "Retaining SUID Programs in a Secure UNIX", *Proceedings of the Summer USENIX Conference* (1988), pages 107–118.

[Kurose and Ross 2001] J. Kurose and K. Ross, *Computer Networking—A Top-Down Approach Featuring the Internet*, Addison-Wesley (2001).

[Kurose and Ross 2003] J. Kurose and K. Ross, *Computer Networking—A Top-Down Approach Featuring the Internet, Second Edition*, Addison-Wesley (2003).

[Lamport 1974] L. Lamport, "A New Solution of Dijkstra's Concurrent Programming Problem", *Communications of the ACM*, Volume 17, Number 8 (1974), pages 453–455.

[Lamport 1976] L. Lamport, "Synchronization of Independent Processes", *Acta Informatica*, Volume 7, Number 1 (1976), pages 15–34.

[Lamport 1977] L. Lamport, "Concurrent Reading and Writing", *Communications of the ACM*, Volume 20, Number 11 (1977), pages 806–811.

[**Lamport 1978a**] L. Lamport, "The Implementation of Reliable Distributed Multiprocess Systems", *Computer Networks*, Volume 2, Number 2 (1978), pages 95–114.

[**Lamport 1978b**] L. Lamport, "Time, Clocks and the Ordering of Events in a Distributed System", *Communications of the ACM*, Volume 21, Number 7 (1978), pages 558–565.

[**Lamport 1981**] L. Lamport, "Password Authentication with Insecure Communications", *Communications of the ACM*, Volume 24, Number 11 (1981), pages 770–772.

[**Lamport 1986**] L. Lamport, "The Mutual Exclusion Problem", *Communications of the ACM*, Volume 33, Number 2 (1986), pages 313–348.

[**Lamport 1991**] L. Lamport, "The Mutual Exclusion Problem Has Been Solved", *Communications of the ACM*, Volume 34, Number 1 (1991), page 110.

[**Lamport et al. 1982**] L. Lamport, R. Shostak, and M. Pease, "The Byzantine Generals Problem", *ACM Transactions on Programming Languages and Systems*, Volume 4, Number 3 (1982), pages 382–401.

[**Lampson 1969**] B. W. Lampson, "Dynamic Protection Structures", *Proceedings of the AFIPS Fall Joint Computer Conference* (1969), pages 27–38.

[**Lampson 1971**] B. W. Lampson, "Protection", *Proceedings of the Fifth Annual Princeton Conference on Information Systems Science* (1971), pages 437–443.

[**Lampson 1973**] B. W. Lampson, "A Note on the Confinement Problem", *Communications of the ACM*, Volume 10, Number 16 (1973), pages 613–615.

[**Lampson and Sturgis 1976**] B. Lampson and H. Sturgis, "Crash Recovery in a Distributed Data Storage System", *Technical Report, Xerox Research Center* (1976).

[**Landwehr 1981**] C. E. Landwehr, "Formal Models of Computer Security", *Computing Surveys*, Volume 13, Number 3 (1981), pages 247–278.

[**Lann 1977**] G. L. Lann, "Distributed Systems—Toward a Formal Approach", *Proceedings of the IFIP Congress* (1977), pages 155–160.

[**Larson and Kajla 1984**] P. Larson and A. Kajla, "File Organization: Implementation of a Method Guaranteeing Retrieval in One Access", *Communications of the ACM*, Volume 27, Number 7 (1984), pages 670–677.

[**Lea 2000**] D. Lea, *Concurrent Programming in Java, Second Edition*, Addison-Wesley (2000).

[**Leffler et al. 1989**] S. J. Leffler, M. K. McKusick, M. J. Karels, and J. S. Quarterman, *The Design and Implementation of the 4.3BSD UNIX Operating System*, Addison-Wesley (1989).

[Lehmann 1987] F. Lehmann, "Computer Break-Ins", *Communications of the ACM*, Volume 30, Number 7 (1987), pages 584–585.

[Lempel 1979] A. Lempel, "Cryptology in Transition", *Computing Surveys*, Volume 11, Number 4 (1979), pages 286–303.

[Lett and Konigsford 1968] A. L. Lett and W. L. Konigsford, "TSS/360: A Time-Shared Operating System", *Proceedings of the AFIPS Fall Joint Computer Conference* (1968), pages 15–28.

[Leutenegger and Vernon 1990] S. Leutenegger and M. Vernon, "The Performance of Multiprogrammed Multiprocessor Scheduling Policies", *Proceedings of the Conference on Measurement and Modeling of Computer Systems* (1990).

[Levin et al. 1975] R. Levin, E. S. Cohen, W. M. Corwin, F. J. Pollack, and W. A. Wulf, "Policy/Mechanism Separation in Hydra", *Proceedings of the ACM Symposium on Operating Systems Principles* (1975), pages 132–140.

[Levine 2003] G. Levine, "Defining Deadlock", *Operating Systems Review*, Volume 37, Number 1 (2003).

[Lewis and Berg 1998] B. Lewis and D. Berg, *Multithreaded Programming with Pthreads*, Sun Microsystems Press (1998).

[Lewis and Berg 2000] B. Lewis and D. Berg, *Multithreaded Programming with Java Technology*, Sun Microsystems Press (2000).

[Lichtenberger and Pirtle 1965] W. W. Lichtenberger and M. W. Pirtle, "A Facility for Experimentation in Man-Machine Interaction", *Proceedings of the AFIPS Fall Joint Computer Conference* (1965), pages 589–598.

[Lindholm and Yellin 1999] T. Lindholm and F. Yellin, *The Java Virtual Machine Specification, Second Edition*, Addison-Wesley (1999).

[Ling et al. 2000] Y. Ling, T. Mullen, and X. Lin, "Analysis of Optimal Thread Pool Size", *Operating System Review*, Volume 34, Number 2 (2000).

[Lipner 1975] S. Lipner, "A Comment on the Confinement Problem", *Operating System Review*, Volume 9, Number 5 (1975), pages 192–196.

[Lipton 1974] R. Lipton, "On Synchronization Primitive Systems", *Ph.D. Thesis, Carnegie-Mellon University* (1974).

[Liskov 1972] B. H. Liskov, "The Design of the Venus Operating System", *Communications of the ACM*, Volume 15, Number 3 (1972), pages 144–149.

[Lobel 1986] J. Lobel, *Foiling the System Breakers: Computer Security and Access Control*, McGraw-Hill (1986).

[**Maekawa 1985**] M. Maekawa, "A Square Root Algorithm for Mutual Exclusion in Decentralized Systems", *ACM Transactions on Computer Systems*, Volume 3, Number 2 (1985), pages 145–159.

[**Maher et al. 1994**] C. Maher, J. S. Goldick, C. Kerby, and B. Zumach, "The Integration of Distributed File Systems and Mass Storage Systems", *Proceedings of the IEEE Symposium on Mass Storage Systems* (1994), pages 27–31.

[**Massalin and Pu 1989**] H. Massalin and C. Pu, "Threads and Input/Output in the Synthesis Kernel", *Proceedings of the ACM Symposium on Operating Systems Principles* (1989), pages 191–200.

[**Mattson et al. 1970**] R. L. Mattson, J. Gecsei, D. R. Slutz, and I. L. Traiger, "Evaluation Techniques for Storage Hierarchies", *IBM Systems Journal*, Volume 9, Number 2 (1970), pages 78–117.

[**Mauro and McDougall 2001**] J. Mauro and R. McDougall, *Solaris Internals: Core Kernel Architecture*, Prentice Hall (2001).

[**McGraw and Andrews 1979**] J. R. McGraw and G. R. Andrews, "Access Control in Parallel Programs", *IEEE Transactions on Software Engineering*, Volume SE-5, Number 1 (1979), pages 1–9.

[**McKeag and Wilson 1976**] R. M. McKeag and R. Wilson, *Studies in Operating Systems*, Academic Press (1976).

[**McKeon 1985**] B. McKeon, "An Algorithm for Disk Caching with Limited Memory", *Byte*, Volume 10, Number 9 (1985), pages 129–138.

[**McKusick et al. 1984**] M. K. McKusick, W. N. Joy, S. J. Leffler, and R. S. Fabry, "A Fast File System for UNIX", *ACM Transactions on Computer Systems*, Volume 2, Number 3 (1984), pages 181–197.

[**McKusick et al. 1996**] M. K. McKusick, K. Bostic, and M. J. Karels, *The Design and Implementation of the 4.4 BSD UNIX Operating System*, John Wiley and Sons (1996).

[**McVoy and Kleiman 1991**] L. W. McVoy and S. R. Kleiman, "Extent-like Performance from a UNIX File System", *Proceedings of the Winter USENIX Conference* (1991), pages 33–44.

[**Mealy et al. 1966**] G. H. Mealy, B. I. Witt, and W. A. Clark, "The Functional Structure of OS/360", *IBM Systems Journal*, Volume 5, Number 1 (1966).

[**Menasce and Muntz 1979**] D. Menasce and R. R. Muntz, "Locking and Deadlock Detection in Distributed Data Bases", *IEEE Transactions on Software Engineering*, Volume SE-5, Number 3 (1979), pages 195–202.

[Meyer and Seawright 1970] R. A. Meyer and L. H. Seawright, "A Virtual Machine Time-Sharing System", *IBM Systems Journal*, Volume 9, Number 3 (1970), pages 199–218.

[Microsoft 1986] *Microsoft MS-DOS User's Reference and Microsoft MS-DOS Programmer's Reference*. Microsoft Press (1986).

[Microsoft 1996] *Microsoft Windows NT Workstation Resource Kit*. Microsoft Press (1996).

[Microsoft 2000a] *Microsoft Developer Network Development Library*. Microsoft Press (2000).

[Microsoft 2000b] *Microsoft Windows 2000 Server Resource Kit*. Microsoft Press (2000).

[Milenkovic 1987] M. Milenkovic, *Operating Systems: Concepts and Design*, McGraw-Hill (1987).

[Miller and Katz 1993] E. L. Miller and R. H. Katz, "An Analysis of File Migration in a UNIX Supercomputing Environment", *Proceedings of the Winter USENIX Conference* (1993), pages 421–434.

[Milo et al. 2000] D. Milo, F. Douglis, Y. Paindaveine, R. Wheeler, and S. Zhou, "Process Migration", *ACM Computing Survey*, Volume 32, Number 3 (2000), pages 241 – 299.

[Mockapetris 1987] P. Mockapetris, "Domain Names—Concepts and Facilities", *Network Working Group, Request for Comments: 1034* (1987).

[Mohan and Lindsay 1983] C. Mohan and B. Lindsay, "Efficient Commit Protocols for the Tree of Processes Model of Distributed Transactions", *Proceedings of the ACM Symposium on Principles of Database Systems* (1983).

[Morris 1973] J. H. Morris, "Protection in Programming Languages", *Communications of the ACM*, Volume 16, Number 1 (1973), pages 15–21.

[Morris and Thompson 1979] R. Morris and K. Thompson, "Password Security: A Case History", *Communications of the ACM*, Volume 22, Number 11 (1979), pages 594–597.

[Morris et al. 1986] J. H. Morris, M. Satyanarayanan, M. H. Conner, J. H. Howard, D. S. H. Rosenthal, and F. D. Smith, "Andrew: A Distributed Personal Computing Environment", *Communications of the ACM*, Volume 29, Number 3 (1986), pages 184–201.

[Morshedian 1986] D. Morshedian, "How to Fight Password Pirates", *Computer*, Volume 19, Number 1 (1986).

[Motorola 1989] *MC68000 Family Reference, Second Edition*. Prentice Hall (1989).

[**Motorola 1993**] *PowerPC 601 RISC Microprocessor User's Manual*. Motorola Inc. (1993).

[**Murray 1998**] J. Murray, *Inside Microsoft Windows CE*, Microsoft Press (1998).

[**Navarro et al. 2002**] J. Navarro, S. Lyer, P. Druschel, and A. Cox, "Practical, Transparent Operating System Support for Superpages", *USENIX Symposium on Operating Systems Design and Implementation* (2002).

[**Needham and Walker 1977**] R. M. Needham and R. D. H. Walker, "The Cambridge CAP Computer and Its Protection System", *Proceedings of the Sixth Symposium on Operating System Principles* (1977), pages 1–10.

[**Nelson et al. 1988**] M. Nelson, B. Welch, and J. K. Ousterhout, "Caching in the Sprite Network File System", *ACM Transactions on Computer Systems*, Volume 6, Number 1 (1988), pages 134–154.

[**Nian-Min et al. 2002**] Y. Nian-Min, Z. Ming-Yang, and J. Jiu-Bin, "Pipeline: A New Architecture of High Performance Servers", *Operating Systems Review*, Volume 36, Number 4 (2002).

[**Norton and Wilton 1988**] P. Norton and R. Wilton, *The New Peter Norton Programmer's Guide to the IBM PC & PS/2*, Microsoft Press (1988).

[**Nutt 2000**] G. Nutt, *Operating Systems: A Modern Perspective, Second Edition*, Addison-Wesley (2000).

[**Oaks and Wong 1999**] S. Oaks and H. Wong, *Java Threads, Second Edition*, O'Reilly & Associates (1999).

[**Obermarck 1982**] R. Obermarck, "Distributed Deadlock Detection Algorithm", *ACM Transactions on Database Systems*, Volume 7, Number 2 (1982), pages 187–208.

[**O'Leary and Kitts 1985**] B. T. O'Leary and D. L. Kitts, "Optical Device for a Mass Storage System", *Computer*, Volume 18, Number 7 (1985).

[**Olsen and Kenley 1989**] R. P. Olsen and G. Kenley, "Virtual Optical Disks Solve the On-Line Storage Crunch", *Computer Design*, Volume 28, Number 1 (1989), pages 93–96.

[**Organick 1972**] E. I. Organick, *The Multics System: An Examination of Its Structure*, MIT Press (1972).

[**Ortix 2001**] S. Ortix, "Embedded OSs Gain the Inside Track", *Computer*, Volume 34, Number 11 (2001).

[**Ousterhout et al. 1985**] J. K. Ousterhout, H. D. Costa, D. Harrison, J. A. Kunze, M. Kupfer, and J. G. Thompson, "A Trace-Driven Analysis of the UNIX 4.2 BSD File System", *Proceedings of the ACM Symposium on Operating Systems Principles* (1985), pages 15–24.

[**Ousterhout et al. 1988**] J. K. Ousterhout, A. R. Cherenson, F. Douglis, M. N. Nelson, and B. B. Welch, "The Sprite Network-Operating System", *Computer*, Volume 21, Number 2 (1988), pages 23–36.

[**Parameswaran et al. 2001**] M. Parameswaran, A. Susarla, and A. B. Whinston, "P2P Networking: An Information-Sharing Alternative", *Computer*, Volume 34, Number 7 (2001).

[**Parmelee et al. 1972**] R. P. Parmelee, T. I. Peterson, C. C. Tillman, and D. Hatfield, "Virtual Storage and Virtual Machine Concepts", *IBM Systems Journal*, Volume 11, Number 2 (1972), pages 99–130.

[**Parnas 1975**] D. L. Parnas, "On a Solution to the Cigarette Smokers' Problem Without Conditional Statements", *Communications of the ACM*, Volume 18, Number 3 (1975), pages 181–183.

[**Patil 1971**] S. Patil, "Limitations and Capabilities of Dijkstra's Semaphore Primitives for Coordination Among Processes", *Technical Report, MIT* (1971).

[**Patterson and Hennessy 1998**] D. A. Patterson and J. L. Hennessy, *Computer Organization and Design—The Hardware/Software Interface, Second Edition*, Morgan Kaufmann Publishers (1998).

[**Patterson et al. 1988**] D. A. Patterson, G. Gibson, and R. H. Katz, "A Case for Redundant Arrays of Inexpensive Disks (RAID)", *Proceedings of the ACM SIGMOD International Conference on the Management of Data* (1988).

[**Pease et al. 1980**] M. Pease, R. Shostak, and L. Lamport, "Reaching Agreement in the Presence of Faults", *Communications of the ACM*, Volume 27, Number 2 (1980), pages 228–234.

[**Pechura and Schoeffler 1983**] M. A. Pechura and J. D. Schoeffler, "Estimating File Access Time of Floppy Disks", *Communications of the ACM*, Volume 26, Number 10 (1983), pages 754–763.

[**Peterson 1981**] G. L. Peterson, "Myths About the Mutual Exclusion Problem", *Information Processing Letters*, Volume 12, Number 3 (1981).

[**Pfleeger 1989**] C. Pfleeger, *Security in Computing*, Prentice Hall (1989).

[**Pinilla and Gill 2003**] R. Pinilla and M. Gill, "JVM: Platform Independent vs. Performance Dependent", *Operating System Review* (2003).

[**Popek 1974**] G. J. Popek, "Protection Structures", *Computer*, Volume 7, Number 6 (1974), pages 22–33.

[**Popek and Walker 1985**] G. Popek and B. Walker, editors, *The LOCUS Distributed System Architecture*, MIT Press (1985).

[Prieve and Fabry 1976] B. G. Prieve and R. S. Fabry, "VMIN—An Optimal Variable Space Page-Replacement Algorithm", *Communications of the ACM*, Volume 19, Number 5 (1976), pages 295–297.

[Psaltis and Mok 1995] D. Psaltis and F. Mok, "Holographic Memories", *Scientific American*, Volume 273, Number 5 (1995), pages 70–76.

[Purdin et al. 1987] T. D. M. Purdin, R. D. Schlichting, and G. R. Andrews, "A File Replication Facility for Berkeley UNIX", *Software—Practice and Experience*, Volume 17, (1987), pages 923–940.

[Quinlan 1991] S. Quinlan, "A Cached WORM", *Software—Practice and Experience*, Volume 21, Number 12 (1991), pages 1289–1299.

[Rago 1993] S. Rago, *UNIX System V Network Programming*, Addison-Wesley (1993).

[Rashid 1986] R. F. Rashid, "From RIG to Accent to Mach: The Evolution of a Network Operating System", *Proceedings of the ACM/IEEE Computer Society, Fall Joint Computer Conference* (1986).

[Rashid and Robertson 1981] R. Rashid and G. Robertson, "Accent: A Communication-Oriented Network Operating System Kernel", *Proceedings of the ACM Symposium on Operating System Principles* (1981).

[Raynal 1986] M. Raynal, *Algorithms for Mutual Exclusion*, MIT Press (1986).

[Raynal 1991] M. Raynal, "A Simple Taxonomy for Distributed Mutual Exclusion Algorithms", *Operating Systems Review*, Volume 25, Number 1 (1991), pages 47–50.

[Redell and Fabry 1974] D. D. Redell and R. S. Fabry, "Selective Revocation of Capabilities", *Proceedings of the IRIA International Workshop on Protection in Operating Systems* (1974), pages 197–210.

[Reed 1983] D. P. Reed, "Implementing Atomic Actions on Decentralized Data", *ACM Transactions on Computer Systems*, Volume 1, Number 1 (1983), pages 3–23.

[Reed and Kanodia 1979] D. P. Reed and R. K. Kanodia, "Synchronization with Eventcounts and Sequences", *Communications of the ACM*, Volume 22, Number 2 (1979), pages 115–123.

[Reid 1987] B. Reid, "Reflections on Some Recent Widespread Computer Break-Ins", *Communications of the ACM*, Volume 30, Number 2 (1987), pages 103–105.

[Rhodes and McKeehan 1999] N. Rhodes and J. McKeehan, *Understanding The Linux Kernel*, O'Reilly & Associates (1999).

[Ricart and Agrawala 1981] G. Ricart and A. K. Agrawala, "An Optimal Algorithm for Mutual Exclusion in Computer Networks", *Communications of the ACM*, Volume 24, Number 1 (1981), pages 9–17.

[Richards 1990] A. E. Richards, "A File System Approach for Integrating Removable Media Devices and Jukeboxes", *Optical Information Systems*, Volume 10, Number 5 (1990), pages 270–274.

[Richter 1997] J. Richter, *Advanced Windows*, Microsoft Press (1997).

[Ripeanu et al. 2002] M. Ripeanu, A. Immnitchi, and I. Foster, "Mapping the Gnutella Network", *IEEE Internet Computing*, Volume 6, Number 1 (2002).

[Ritchie 1979] D. Ritchie, "The Evolution of the UNIX Time-Sharing System", *Language Design and Programming Methodology, Lecture Notes on Computer Science, Springer-Verlag*, Volume 79, (1979).

[Ritchie and Thompson 1974] D. M. Ritchie and K. Thompson, "The UNIX Time-Sharing System", *Communications of the ACM*, Volume 17, Number 7 (1974), pages 365–375.

[Rivest et al. 1978] R. L. Rivest, A. Shamir, and L. Adleman, "On Digital Signatures and Public Key Cryptosystems", *Communications of the ACM*, Volume 21, Number 2 (1978), pages 120–126.

[Rosenkrantz et al. 1978] D. J. Rosenkrantz, R. E. Stearns, and P. M. Lewis, "System Level Concurrency Control for Distributed Database Systems", *ACM Transactions on Database Systems*, Volume 3, Number 2 (1978), pages 178–198.

[Ruemmler and Wilkes 1991] C. Ruemmler and J. Wilkes, "Disk Shuffling", *Technical Report, Hewlett-Packard Laboratories* (1991).

[Ruemmler and Wilkes 1993] C. Ruemmler and J. Wilkes, "Unix Disk Access Patterns", *Proceedings of the Winter USENIX Conference* (1993), pages 405–420.

[Ruemmler and Wilkes 1994] C. Ruemmler and J. Wilkes, "An Introduction to Disk Drive Modeling", *Computer*, Volume 27, Number 3 (1994), pages 17–29.

[Rushby 1981] J. M. Rushby, "Design and Verification of Secure Systems", *Proceedings of the ACM Symposium on Operating Systems Principles* (1981), pages 12–21.

[Rushby and Randell 1983] J. Rushby and B. Randell, "A Distributed Secure System", *Computer*, Volume 16, Number 7 (1983), pages 55–67.

[Russell and Gangemi 1991] D. Russell and G. T. Gangemi, *Computer Security Basics*, O'Reilly & Associates (1991).

[**Saltzer and Schroeder 1975**] J. H. Saltzer and M. D. Schroeder, "The Protection of Information in Computer Systems", *Proceedings of the IEEE* (1975), pages 1278–1308.

[**Sandberg 1987**] R. Sandberg, *The Sun Network File System: Design, Implementation and Experience*, Sun Microsystems (1987).

[**Sandberg et al. 1985**] R. Sandberg, D. Goldberg, S. Kleiman, D. Walsh, and B. Lyon, "Design and Implementation of the Sun Network Filesystem", *Proceedings of the Summer USENIX Conference* (1985), pages 119–130.

[**Sargent and Shoemaker 1995**] M. Sargent and R. Shoemaker, *The Personal Computer from the Inside Out, Third Edition*, Addison-Wesley (1995).

[**Sarisky 1983**] L. Sarisky, "Will Removable Hard Disks Replace the Floppy?", *Byte* (1983), pages 110–117.

[**Satyanarayanan 1990**] M. Satyanarayanan, "Scalable, Secure and Highly Available Distributed File Access", *Computer*, Volume 23, Number 5 (1990), pages 9–21.

[**Schell 1983**] R. R. Schell, "A Security Kernel for a Multiprocessor Microcomputer", *Computer* (1983), pages 47–53.

[**Schindler and Gregory 1999**] J. Schindler and G. Gregory, "Automated Disk Drive Characterization", *Technical Report, Carnegie-Mellon University* (1999).

[**Schlichting and Schneider 1982**] R. D. Schlichting and F. B. Schneider, "Understanding and Using Asynchronous Message Passing Primitives", *Proceedings of the Symposium on Principles of Distributed Computing* (1982), pages 141–147.

[**Schneider 1982**] F. B. Schneider, "Synchronization in Distributed Programs", *ACM Transactions on Programming Languages and Systems*, Volume 4, Number 2 (1982), pages 125–148.

[**Schrage 1967**] L. E. Schrage, "The Queue M/G/I with Feedback to Lower Priority Queues", *Management Science*, Volume 13, (1967), pages 466–474.

[**Schwartz and Weissman 1967**] J. I. Schwartz and C. Weissman, "The SDC Time-Sharing System Revisited", *Proceedings of the ACM National Meeting* (1967), pages 263–271.

[**Schwartz et al. 1964**] J. I. Schwartz, E. G. Coffman, and C. Weissman, "A General Purpose Time-Sharing System", *Proceedings of the AFIPS Spring Joint Computer Conference* (1964), pages 397–411.

[**Seely 1989**] D. Seely, "Password Cracking: A Game of Wits", *Communications of the ACM*, Volume 32, Number 6 (1989), pages 700–704.

[Seltzer et al. 1990] M. Seltzer, P. Chen, and J. Ousterhout, "Disk Scheduling Revisited", *Proceedings of the Winter USENIX Conference* (1990), pages 313–323.

[Shrivastava and Panzieri 1982] S. K. Shrivastava and F. Panzieri, "The Design of a Reliable Remote Procedure Call Mechanism", *IEEE Transactions on Computers*, Volume C-31, Number 7 (1982), pages 692–697.

[Silberschatz et al. 2001] A. Silberschatz, H. F. Korth, and S. Sudarshan, *Database System Concepts, Fourth Edition*, McGraw-Hill (2001).

[Silverman 1983] J. M. Silverman, "Reflections on the Verification of the Security of an Operating System Kernel", *Proceedings of the ACM Symposium on Operating Systems Principles* (1983), pages 143–154.

[Silvers 2000] C. Silvers, "UBC: An Efficient Unified I/O and Memory Caching Subsystem for NetBSD", *USENIX Annual Technical Conference—FREENIX Track* (2000).

[Simmons 1979] G. J. Simmons, "Symmetric and Asymmetric Encryption", *Computing Surveys*, Volume 11, Number 4 (1979), pages 304–330.

[Sincerbox 1994] G. T. Sincerbox, editor, *Selected Papers on Holographic Storage*, Optical Engineering Press (1994).

[Singhal 1989] M. Singhal, "Deadlock Detection in Distributed Systems", *Computer*, Volume 22, Number 11 (1989), pages 37–48.

[Smith 1982] A. J. Smith, "Cache Memories", *ACM Computing Surveys*, Volume 14, Number 3 (1982), pages 473–530.

[Smith 1985] A. J. Smith, "Disk Cache-Miss Ratio Analysis and Design Considerations", *ACM Transactions on Computer Systems*, Volume 3, Number 3 (1985), pages 161–203.

[Solomon 1998] D. A. Solomon, *Inside Windows NT, Second Edition*, Microsoft Press (1998).

[Solomon and Russinovich 2000] D. A. Solomon and M. E. Russinovich, *Inside Microsoft Windows 2000, Third Edition*, Microsoft Press (2000).

[Spafford 1989] E. H. Spafford, "The Internet Worm: Crisis and Aftermath", *Communications of the ACM*, Volume 32, Number 6 (1989), pages 678–687.

[Spector and Schwarz 1983] A. Z. Spector and P. M. Schwarz, "Transactions: A Construct for Reliable Distributed Computing", *ACM SIGOPS Operating Systems Review*, Volume 17, Number 2 (1983), pages 18–35.

[Stallings 2000a] W. Stallings, *Local and Metropolitan Area Networks*, Prentice Hall (2000).

[**Stallings 2000b**] W. Stallings, *Operating Systems, Fourth Edition*, Prentice Hall (2000).

[**Stankovic 1982**] J. S. Stankovic, "Software Communication Mechanisms: Procedure Calls Versus Messages", *Computer*, Volume 15, Number 4 (1982).

[**Staunstrup 1982**] J. Staunstrup, "Message Passing Communication Versus Procedure Call Communication", *Software—Practice and Experience*, Volume 12, Number 3 (1982), pages 223–234.

[**Stevens 1992**] R. Stevens, *Advanced Programming in the UNIX Environment*, Addison-Wesley (1992).

[**Stevens 1994**] R. Stevens, *TCP/IP Illustrated Volume 1: The Protocols*, Addison-Wesley (1994).

[**Stevens 1995**] R. Stevens, *TCP/IP Illustrated, Volume 2: The Implementation*, Addison-Wesley (1995).

[**Stevens 1997**] W. R. Stevens, *UNIX Network Programming—Volume I*, Prentice Hall (1997).

[**Stevens 1998**] W. R. Stevens, *UNIX Network Programming—Volume II*, Prentice Hall (1998).

[**Stevens 1999**] W. R. Stevens, *UNIX Network Programming Interprocess Communications—Volume 2*, Prentice Hall (1999).

[**Strachey 1959**] C. Strachey, "Time Sharing in Large Fast Computers", *Proceedings of the International Conference on Information Processing* (1959), pages 336–341.

[**Su 1982**] Z. Su, "A Distributed System for Internet Name Service", *Network Working Group, Request for Comments: 830* (1982).

[**Sun 1990**] *Network Programming Guide*. Sun Microsystems (1990).

[**Svobodova 1984**] L. Svobodova, "File Servers for Network-Based Distributed Systems", *ACM Computing Survey*, Volume 16, Number 4 (1984), pages 353–398.

[**Talluri et al. 1995**] M. Talluri, M. D. Hill, and Y. A. Khalidi, "A New Page Table for 64-bit Address Spaces", *Proceedings of the ACM Symposium on Operating Systems Principles* (1995).

[**Tanenbaum 1990**] A. S. Tanenbaum, *Structured Computer Organization, Third Edition*, Prentice Hall (1990).

[**Tanenbaum 2001**] A. S. Tanenbaum, *Modern Operating Systems*, Prentice Hall (2001).

[**Tanenbaum 2003**] A. S. Tanenbaum, *Computer Networks, Fourth Edition*, Prentice Hall (2003).

[**Tanenbaum and van Steen 2002**] A. Tanenbaum and M. van Steen, *Distributed Systems: Principles and Paradigms*, Prentice Hall (2002).

[**Tanenbaum and Woodhull 1997**] A. S. Tanenbaum and A. S. Woodhull, *Operating System Design and Implementation, Second Edition*, Prentice Hall (1997).

[**Tate 2000**] S. Tate, *Windows 2000 Essential Reference*, New Riders (2000).

[**Tay and Ananda 1990**] B. H. Tay and A. L. Ananda, "A Survey of Remote Procedure Calls", *Operating Systems Review,* Volume 24, Number 3 (1990), pages 68–79.

[**Teorey and Pinkerton 1972**] T. J. Teorey and T. B. Pinkerton, "A Comparative Analysis of Disk Scheduling Policies", *Communications of the ACM*, Volume 15, Number 3 (1972), pages 177–184.

[**Tevanian et al. 1987a**] A. Tevanian, Jr., R. F. Rashid, D. B. Golub, D. L. Black, E. Cooper, and M. W. Young, "Mach Threads and the Unix Kernel: The Battle for Control", *Proceedings of the Summer USENIX Conference* (1987).

[**Tevanian et al. 1987b**] A. Tevanian, Jr., R. F. Rashid, M. W. Young, D. B. Golub, M. R. Thompson, W. Bolosky, and R. Sanzi, "A UNIX Interface for Shared Memory and Memory Mapped Files Under Mach", *Technical Report, Carnegie-Mellon University* (1987).

[**Tevanian et al. 1989**] A. Tevanian, Jr., and B. Smith, "Mach: The Model for Future Unix", *Byte* (1989).

[**Toigo 2000**] J. Toigo, "Avoiding a Data Crunch", *Scientific American*, Volume 282, Number 5 (2000), pages 58–74.

[**Traiger et al. 1982**] I. L. Traiger, J. N. Gray, C. A. Galtieri, and B. G. Lindsay, "Transactions and Consistency in Distributed Database Management Systems", *ACM Transactions on Database Systems*, Volume 7, Number 3 (1982), pages 323–342.

[**Tucker and Gupta 1989**] A. Tucker and A. Gupta, "Process Control and Scheduling Issues for Multiprogrammed Shared-Memory Multiprocessors", *Proceedings of the ACM Symposium on Operating Systems Principles* (1989).

[**Vahalia 1996**] U. Vahalia, *Unix Internals: The New Frontiers*, Prentice Hall (1996).

[**Vee and Hsu 2000**] V. Vee and W. Hsu, ""Locality-Preserving Load-Balancing Mechanisms for Synchronous Simulations on Shared-Memory Multiprocessors", *Proceedings of the Fourteenth Workshop on Parallel and Distributed Simulation* (2000), pages 131–138.

[**Venners 1998**] B. Venners, *Inside the Java Virtual Machine*, McGraw-Hill (1998).

[**Wah 1984**] B. W. Wah, "File Placement on Distributed Computer Systems", *Computer*, Volume 17, Number 1 (1984), pages 23–32.

[**Wallach et al. 1987**] D. S. Wallach, D. Balfanz, D. Dean, and E. W. Felten, "Extensible Security Architectures for Java", *Proceedings of the ACM Symposium on Operating Systems Principles* (1987).

[**Welsh et al. 2001**] M. Welsh, D. Culler, and E. Brewer, "SEDA: An Architecture for Well-Conditioned, Scalable Internet Services", *Proceedings of the ACM Symposium on Operating Systems Principles* (2001).

[**Williams 2001**] R. Williams, *Computer Systems Architecture—A Networking Approach*, Addison-Wesley (2001).

[**Williams 2002**] N. Williams, "An Implementation of Scheduler Activations on the NetBSD Operating System", *2002 USENIX Annual Technical Conference, FREENIX Track* (2002).

[**Wood and Kochan 1985**] P. Wood and S. Kochan, *UNIX System Security*, Hayden (1985).

[**Woodside 1986**] C. Woodside, "Controllability of Computer Performance Tradeoffs Obtained Using Controlled-Share Queue Schedulers", *IEEE Transactions on Software Engineering*, Volume SE-12, Number 10 (1986), pages 1041–1048.

[**Worthington et al. 1994**] B. L. Worthington, G. R. Ganger, and Y. N. Patt, "Scheduling Algorithms for Modern Disk Drives", *Proceedings of the ACM Sigmetrics Conference on Measurement and Modeling of Computer Systems* (1994), pages 241–251.

[**Worthington et al. 1995**] B. L. Worthington, G. R. Ganger, Y. N. Patt, and J. Wilkes, "On-Line Extraction of SCSI Disk Drive Parameters", *Proceedings of the ACM Sigmetrics Conference on Measurement and Modeling of Computer Systems* (1995), pages 146–156.

[**Wulf 1969**] W. A. Wulf, "Performance Monitors for Multiprogramming Systems", *Proceedings of the ACM Symposium on Operating Systems Principles* (1969), pages 175–181.

[**Wulf et al. 1981**] W. A. Wulf, R. Levin, and S. P. Harbison, *Hydra/C.mmp: An Experimental Computer System*, McGraw-Hill (1981).

[**Yeong et al. 1995**] W. Yeong, T. Howes, and S. Kille, "Lightweight Directory Access Protocol", *Network Working Group, Request for Comments: 1777* (1995).

[**Zabatta and Young 1998**] F. Zabatta and K. Young, "A Thread Performance Comparison: Windows NT and Solaris on a Symmetric Multiprocessor", *Proceedings of the 2nd USENIX Windows NT Symposium* (1998).

[**Zahorjan and McCann 1990**] J. Zahorjan and C. McCann, "Processor Scheduling in Shared-Memory Multiprocessors", *Proceedings of the Conference on Measurement and Modeling of Computer Systems* (1990).

[**Zhao 1989**] W. Zhao, editor, *Special Issue on Real-Time Operating Systems*, Operating System Review (1989).

CREDITS

Figure 3.9: From Iaccobucci, *OS/2 Programmer's Guide*, ©1988, McGraw-Hill, Inc., New York, New York. Figure 1.7, p. 20. Reprinted with permission of the publisher.

Figure 6.8: From Khanna/Sebree/Zolnowsky, "Realtime Scheduling in SunOS 5.0," Proceedings of Winter USENIX, January 1992, San Francisco, California. Derived with permission of the authors.

Figure 6.10 adapted with permission from Sun Microsystems, Inc.

Figure 9.21: From *80386 Programmer's Reference Manual*, Figure 5-12, p. 5-12. Reprinted by permission of Intel Corporation, Copyright / Intel Corporation 1986.

Figure 10.16: From *IBM Systems Journal*, Vol. 10, No. 3, ©1971, International Business Machines Corporation. Reprinted by permission of IBM Corporation.

Figure 12.9: From Leffler/McKusick/Karels/Quarterman, *The Design and Implementation of the 4.3BSD UNIX Operating System*, ©1989 by Addison-Wesley Publishing Co., Inc., Reading, Massachusetts. Figure 7.6, p. 196. Reprinted with permission of the publisher.

Figure 13.4: From *Pentium Processor User's Manual: Architecture and Programming Manual*, Volume 3, Copyright 1993. Reprinted by permission of Intel Corporation.

Figures 15.4, 15.5, and 15.7: From Halsall, *Data Communications, Computer Networks, and Open Systems, Third Edition*, ©1992, Addison-Wesley Publishing Co., Inc., Reading, Massachusetts. Figure 1.9, p. 14, Figure 1.10, p. 15, and Figure 1.11, p. 18. Reprinted with permission of the publisher.

Index

Note: bold page numbers indicate a section reference.